Annual Editions:
Sociology, 42/e

Edited by Kurt Finsterbusch

http://create.mcgraw-hill.com

This McGraw-Hill Create text may include materials submitted to
McGraw-Hill for publication by the instructor of this course.
The instructor is solely responsible for the editorial content of such
materials. Instructors retain copyright of these additional materials.

ISBN-10: 1259171000   ISBN-13: 9781259171000

Contents

Preface

These past few years have changed so many things and confront us with many new and difficult issues, while many of the old issues remain unresolved. There is much uncertainty. Almost all institutions are under stress. The political system is held in low regard because it seems to accomplish so little, cost so much, and focus on special interests more than on the public good. The economy is still in crisis. In the long term, it suffers from massive debt, foreign competition, trade deficits, increasing inequality, economic uncertainties, and a worrisome concentration of economic power in the hands of relatively few multinational corporations. Complaints about the education system continue, because grades K–12 do not teach basic skills well and college costs are too high. Healthcare is too expensive and medical mistakes are too numerous. Many Americans still lack healthcare coverage, and some diseases are becoming resistant to our medicines. The entertainment industry is booming, but many people worry about its impact on values and behavior.

News media standards seem to be set by the Internet. Furthermore, the dynamics of technology, globalization, and identity groups are creating crises, changes, and challenges. Crime rates have declined somewhat, but they are still at high levels, and white collar crime is now recognized as costing trillions of dollars, harming the economy, and largely going unpunished. The public is demanding more police, more jails, and tougher sentences, but less government spending. Social policies seem to create almost as many problems as they solve. The use of toxic chemicals has been blamed for increases in cancer, sterility, and other health problems. Marriage and the family have been transformed, in part by the women's movement and in part by the stress that current conditions create for women who try to combine family and careers. Schools, television, and corporations are commonly vilified. Many claim that morality has declined to shameful levels although this claim can be challenged. Add to all this the worldwide problems of ozone depletion, global warming, deforestation, soil loss, desertification, and species loss, and it is easy to be pessimistic. Nevertheless, crises and problems also create opportunities.

The present generation may determine the course of history for the next 200 years. Great changes are taking place and new solutions are being sought where old answers no longer work. The issues that the current generation is facing are complex and must be interpreted within a sophisticated framework. The sociological perspective provides such a framework. It expects people to act in terms of their positions in the social structure, within the political, economic, and social forces operating on them, and guided by the norms that govern the situation. *Annual Editions: Sociology* should help you to develop the sociological perspective that will enable you to determine how the issues of the day relate to the way that society is structured. The articles provide not only information, but also models of interpretation and analysis that will guide you as you form your own views.

This edition of *Annual Editions: Sociology* emphasizes social change, institutional crises, and prospects for the future. It provides intellectual preparation for taking action for the betterment of humanity in times of critical change. The sociological perspective is needed more than ever as humankind tries to find a way to peace, prosperity, health, and well-being that can be maintained for generations in an improving environment. The numerous obstacles that lie in the path of these important goals require sophisticated responses. The goals of this edition are to communicate to students the excitement and importance of the study of the social world and to provoke interest in, and enthusiasm for, the study of sociology.

A number of additional features are designed to make this volume useful for students, researchers, and professionals in the field of sociology. While the articles are arranged along the lines of broadly unifying themes, the *Topic Guide* can be used to establish specific reading assignments tailored to the needs of a particular course of study. In addition, each unit is preceded by an overview, which provides a background for informed reading of the articles and emphasizes critical issues. *Learning Outcomes* accompany each article and outline the key concepts that students should focus on as they are reading the material. *Critical Thinking* questions found at the end of each article allow students to test their understanding of the key points of the article. The *Internet References* section can be used to further explore the topics online.

Instructors will appreciate a password-protected online *Instructor's Resource Guide* and students will find online quizzing to further test their understanding of the material. These tools are available at www.mhhe.com/createcentral.

Annual Editions: Sociology depends upon reader response in order to develop and change. We welcome your recommendations of articles that you think have sociological merit for subsequent editions, as well as your advice on how the anthology can be made more useful as a teaching and learning tool.

Editor

Kurt Finsterbusch is a professor of sociology at the University of Maryland at College Park. He received a BA in history from Princeton University in 1957, a BD from Grace Theological Seminary in 1960, and a PhD in sociology from Columbia University in 1969. He is the author of *Understanding Social Impacts* (Sage Publications, 1980), and he is the co-author, with Annabelle Bender Motz, of *Social Research for Policy Decisions* (Wadsworth, 1980) and, with Jerald Hage, of *Organizational Change as a Development Strategy* (Lynne Rienner, 1987). He is the editor of *Annual Editions: Sociology* (McGraw-Hill/ Contemporary Learning Series); *Annual Editions: Social Problems* (McGraw-Hill/Contemporary Learning Series); and *Sources: Notable Selections in Sociology,* 3rd ed. (McGraw-Hill/Dushkin, 1999).

Academic Advisory Board

Members of the Academic Advisory Board are instrumental in the final selection of articles for the *Annual Editions* series. Their review of the articles for content, level, and appropriateness provides critical direction to the editor(s) and staff. We think that you will find their careful consideration reflected in this book.

Correlation Guide

The *Annual Editions* series provides students with convenient, inexpensive access to current, carefully selected articles from the public press. **Annual Editions: Sociology, 42/e** is an easy-to-use reader that presents articles on important topics such as *personality, behavior, social change,* and many more. For more information on *Annual Editions* and other *McGraw-Hill Create*™ titles, visit www.mcgrawhillcreate.com.

This convenient guide matches the articles in **Annual Editions: Sociology, 42/e** with **SOC 2014, 3/e Updated** by Witt.

SOC 2014, 3/e Updated	Annual Editions: Sociology, 42/e
Chapter 1: The Sociological Imagination	The American Narrative: Is There One & What Is It? The Future of the New "We": Muslims in the West to Western Muslims The Myth of the "Culture of Poverty" Reestablishing the Commons for the Common Good Understanding American Worldview What Do We Deserve?
Chapter 2: Sociological Research	The American Narrative: Is There One & What Is It? The Future of the New "We": Muslims in the West to Western Muslims The Myth of the "Culture of Poverty" Reestablishing the Commons for the Common Good Understanding American Worldview What Do We Deserve?
Chapter 3: Culture	The American Narrative: Is There One & What Is It? Cruel and Unusual: The True Costs of Our Prison System Estimates of Cost of Crime: History, Methodologies, and Implications Fighting Crime: An Economist's View The Future of the New "We": Muslims in the West to Western Muslims The Myth of the "Culture of Poverty" The New Sex Scorecard Reestablishing the Commons for the Common Good Understanding American Worldview What Do We Deserve? Wrongful Convictions
Chapter 4: Socialization	Cruel and Unusual: The True Costs of Our Prison System Estimates of Cost of Crime: History, Methodologies, and Implications Fighting Crime: An Economist's View The New Sex Scorecard Wrongful Convictions
Chapter 5: Social Structure & Interaction	The Boys at the Back Death by Gender The Gay Guide to Wedded Bliss Houston Rising: Why the Next Great American Cities Aren't What You Think Is Facebook Making Us Lonely? The Masculine Mystique The New White Negro Why Women Still Can't Have It All
Chapter 6: Deviance	Cruel and Unusual: The True Costs of Our Prison System Estimates of Cost of Crime: History, Methodologies, and Implications Fighting Crime: An Economist's View The New Sex Scorecard Wrongful Convictions
Chapter 7: Families	The Boys at the Back Death by Gender The Gay Guide to Wedded Bliss Houston Rising: Why the American Cities Aren't What You Think Is Facebook Making Us Lonely? The Masculine Mystique The New White Negro Why Women Still Can't Have It All
Chapter 8: Education & Religion	The Boys at the Back Death by Gender The Gay Guide to Wedded Bliss Houston Rising: Why the Next Great American Cities Aren't What You Think Is Facebook Making Us Lonely? The Masculine Mystique The New White Negro Why Women Still Can't Have It All

(continued)

(continued)

(concluded)

Chapter 15: Social Change	Can a Collapse of Global Civilization Be Avoided?
	The Economic Effects of Granting Legal Status and Citizenship to Undocumented Immigrants
	Engineering the Future of Food
	Full Planet, Empty Plates
	The Future of the Liberal World Order: Internationalism after America
	How Innovation Could Save the Planet
	Making Modernity Work: The Reconciliation of Capitalism and Democracy
	A New End, a New Beginning: Prepare for Life as We Don't Know It
	The New Population Bomb: The Four Megatrends that Will Change the World
	A Radical Approach to the Climate Crisis
	A Thousand Years Young
	A User's Guide to the Century
	War in the Fifth Domain
	The World Will Be More Crowded—With Old People
	The Year in Hate and Extremism, 2010

This convenient guide matches the articles in **Annual Editions: Sociology, 42/e** with **Sociology: A Brief Introduction, 10/e** by Schaefer.

Sociology: A Brief Introduction, 10/e	Annual Editions: Sociology, 42/e
Chapter 1: Understanding Sociology	The American Narrative: Is There One & What Is It? The Future of the New "We": Muslims in the West to Western Muslims The Myth of the "Culture of Poverty" Reestablishing the Commons for the Common Good Understanding American Worldview What Do We Deserve?
Chapter 2: Sociological Research	The American Narrative: Is There One & What Is It? The Future of the New "We": Muslims in the West to Western Muslims The Myth of the "Culture of Poverty" Reestablishing the Commons for the Common Good Understanding American Worldview What Do We Deserve?
Chapter 3: Culture	The American Narrative: Is There One & What Is It? Cruel and Unusual: The True Costs of Our Prison System Estimates of Cost of Crime: History, Methodologies, and Implications Fighting Crime: An Economist's View The Future of the New "We": Muslims in the West to Western Muslims The Myth of the "Culture of Poverty" The New Sex Scorecard Reestablishing the Commons for the Common Good Understanding American Worldview What Do We Deserve? Wrongful Convictions
Chapter 4: Socialization and the Life Course	Cruel and Unusual: The True Costs of Our Prison System Estimates of Cost of Crime: History, Methodologies, and Implications Fighting Crime: An Economist's View The New Sex Scorecard Wrongful Convictions
Chapter 5: Social Interaction, Groups, and Social Structure	The Boys at the Back Death by Gender The Gay Guide to Wedded Bliss Houston Rising: Why the Next Great American Cities Aren't What You Think Is Facebook Making Us Lonely? The Masculine Mystique The New White Negro Why Women Still Can't Have It All
Chapter 6: The Mass Media	The American Narrative: Is There One & What Is It? The Broken Contract: Inequality and American Decline The Case for Less The Future of the New "We": Muslims in the West to Western Muslims Hard at Work in the Jobless Future In Search of the Spiritual MOOCs of Hazard The Myth of the "Culture of Poverty" Reestablishing the Commons for the Common Good The Robot Will See You Now The Rule of the Rich Understanding American Worldview What Do We Deserve? The Withering of the Affluent Society
Chapter 7: Deviance, Crime, and Social Control	Cruel and Unusual: The True Costs of Our Prison System Estimates of Cost of Crime: History, Methodologies, and Implications Fighting Crime: An Economist's View The New Sex Scorecard Wrongful Convictions

(continued)

Chapter 8: Social Institutions: Family and Religion	Emmett and Trayvon: How Racial Prejudice in America Has Changed in the Last Sixty Years The End of Welfare as I Knew It How Temporary Assistance for Needy Families Failed the Test of the Great Recession Female Power Free and Equal in Dignity and LGBT Rights Rebuilding the Middle Class: A Blueprint for the Future Roots of Racism The State of Poverty in America A World Enslaved
Chapter 9: Global Inequality	Emmett and Trayvon: How Racial Prejudice in America Has Changed in the Last Sixty Years The End of Welfare as I Knew It How Temporary Assistance for Needy Families Failed the Test of the Great Recession Female Power Free and Equal in Dignity and LGBT Rights Rebuilding the Middle Class: A Blueprint for the Future Roots of Racism The State of Poverty in America A World Enslaved
Chapter 10: Racial and Ethnic Inequality	Emmett and Trayvon: How Racial Prejudice in America Has Changed in the Last Sixty Years The End of Welfare as I Knew It How Temporary Assistance for Needy Families Failed the Test of the Great Recession Female Power Free and Equal in Dignity and LGBT Rights Rebuilding the Middle Class: A Blueprint for the Future Roots of Racism The State of Poverty in America A World Enslaved
Chapter 11: Stratification by Gender	The Boys at the Back Death by Gender Emmett and Trayvon: How Racial Prejudice in America Has Changed in the Last Sixty Years The End of Welfare as I Knew It How Temporary Assistance for Needy Families Failed the Test of the Great Recession Female Power Free and Equal in Dignity and LGBT Rights The Gay Guide to Wedded Bliss Houston Rising: Why the Next Great American Cities Aren't What You Think Is Facebook Making Us Lonely? The Masculine Mystique The New White Negro Rebuilding the Middle Class: A Blueprint for the Future Roots of Racism The State of Poverty in America Why Women Still Can't Have It All A World Enslaved
Chapter 12: The Family and Human Sexuality	The Boys at the Back Death by Gender The Gay Guide to Wedded Bliss Houston Rising: Why the Next Great American Cities Aren't What You Think Is Facebook Making Us Lonely? The Masculine Mystique The New White Negro Why Women Still Can't Have It All
Chapter 13: Education and Religion	The Boys at the Back Death by Gender The Gay Guide to Wedded Bliss Houston Rising: Why the Next Great American Cities Aren't What You Think Is Facebook Making Us Lonely? The Masculine Mystique The New White Negro Why Women Still Can't Have It All

(continued)

(concluded)

Chapter 14: Government and the Economy	The Boys at the Back
	The Broken Contract: Inequality and American Decline
	The Case for Less
	Death by Gender
	The Gay Guide to Wedded Bliss
	Hard at Work in the Jobless Future
	Houston Rising: Why the Next Great American Cities Aren't What You Think
	In Search of the Spiritual
	Is Facebook Making Us Lonely?
	The Masculine Mystique
	MOOCs of Hazard
	The New White Negro
	The Robot Will See You Now
	The Rule of the Rich
	Why Women Still Can't Have It All
	The Withering of the Affluent Society
Chapter 15: Health and the Environment	The Broken Contract: Inequality and American Decline
	Can a Collapse of Global Civilization Be Avoided?
	The Case for Less
	The Economic Effects of Granting Legal Status and Citizenship to Undocumented Immigrants
	Engineering the Future of Food
	Full Planet, Empty Plates
	The Future of the Liberal World Order: Internationalism after America
	Hard at Work in the Jobless Future
	How Innovation Could Save the Planet
	In Search of the Spiritual
	Making Modernity Work: The Reconciliation of Capitalism and Democracy
	MOOCs of Hazard
	A New End, a New Beginning: Prepare for Life as We Don't Know It
	The New Population Bomb: The Four Megatrends that Will Change the World
	A Radical Approach to the Climate Crisis
	The Robot Will See You Now
	The Rule of the Rich
	A Thousand Years Young
	A User's Guide to the Century
	War in the Fifth Domain
	The Withering of the Affluent Society
	The World Will Be More Crowded—With Old People
	The Year in Hate and Extremism, 2010
Chapter 16: Social Change in the Global Community	Can a Collapse of Global Civilization Be Avoided?
	The Economic Effects of Granting Legal Status and Citizenship to Undocumented Immigrants
	Engineering the Future of Food
	Full Planet, Empty Plates
	The Future of the Liberal World Order: Internationalism after America
	How Innovation Could Save the Planet
	Making Modernity Work: The Reconciliation of Capitalism and Democracy
	A New End, a New Beginning: Prepare for Life as We Don't Know It
	The New Population Bomb: The Four Megatrends that Will Change the World
	A Radical Approach to the Climate Crisis
	A Thousand Years Young
	A User's Guide to the Century
	War in the Fifth Domain
	The World Will Be More Crowded—With Old People
	The Year in Hate and Extremism, 2010

This convenient guide matches the articles in **Annual Editions: Sociology, 42/e** with **Experience Sociology** by Croteau/Hoynes.

Experience Sociology	Annual Editions: Sociology, 42/e
Chapter 1: Sociology in a Changing World	The American Narrative: Is There One & What Is It? The Future of the New "We": Muslims in the West to Western Muslims The Myth of the "Culture of Poverty" Reestablishing the Commons for the Common Good Understanding American Worldview What Do We Deserve?
Chapter 2: Understanding the Research Process	The American Narrative: Is There One & What Is It? The Future of the New "We": Muslims in the West to Western Muslims The Myth of the "Culture of Poverty" Reestablishing the Commons for the Common Good Understanding American Worldview What Do We Deserve?
Chapter 3: Culture	The American Narrative: Is There One & What Is It? Cruel and Unusual: The True Costs of Our Prison System Estimates of Cost of Crime: History, Methodologies, and Implications Fighting Crime: An Economist's View The Future of the New "We": Muslims in the West to Western Muslims The Myth of the "Culture of Poverty" The New Sex Scorecard Reestablishing the Commons for the Common Good Understanding American Worldview What Do We Deserve? Wrongful Convictions
Chapter 4: Social Structure	The Boys at the Back Death by Gender The Gay Guide to Wedded Bliss Houston Rising: Why the Next Great American Cities Aren't What You Think Is Facebook Making Us Lonely? The Masculine Mystique The New White Negro Why Women Still Can't Have It All
Chapter 5: Power	Emmett and Trayvon: How Racial Prejudice in America Has Changed in the Last Sixty Years The End of Welfare as I Knew It How Temporary Assistance for Needy Families Failed the Test of the Great Recession Female Power Free and Equal in Dignity and LGBT Rights Rebuilding the Middle Class: A Blueprint for the Future Roots of Racism The State of Poverty in America A World Enslaved
Chapter 6: Socialization	Cruel and Unusual: The True Costs of Our Prison System Estimates of Cost of Crime: History, Methodologies, and Implications Fighting Crime: An Economist's View The New Sex Scorecard Wrongful Convictions
Chapter 7: Interaction, Groups, and Organizations	The American Narrative: Is There One & What Is It? The Boys at the Back Death by Gender The Future of the New "We": Muslims in the West to Western Muslims The Gay Guide to Wedded Bliss Houston Rising: Why the Next Great American Cities Aren't What You Think Is Facebook Making Us Lonely? The Masculine Mystique The Myth of the "Culture of Poverty" The New White Negro Reestablishing the Commons for the Common Good Understanding American Worldview What Do We Deserve? Why Women Still Can't Have It All

(continued)

Chapter 8: Deviance and Social Control	Cruel and Unusual: The True Costs of Our Prison System Estimates of Cost of Crime: History, Methodologies, and Implications Fighting Crime: An Economist's View The New Sex Scorecard Wrongful Convictions
Chapter 9: Class and Global Inequality	Emmett and Trayvon: How Racial Prejudice in America Has Changed in the Last Sixty Years The End of Welfare as I Knew It How Temporary Assistance for Needy Families Failed the Test of the Great Recession Female Power Free and Equal in Dignity and LGBT Rights Rebuilding the Middle Class: A Blueprint for the Future Roots of Racism The State of Poverty in America A World Enslaved
Chapter 10: Race and Ethnicity	Emmett and Trayvon: How Racial Prejudice in America Has Changed in the Last Sixty Years The End of Welfare as I Knew It How Temporary Assistance for Needy Families Failed the Test of the Great Recession Female Power Free and Equal in Dignity and LGBT Rights Rebuilding the Middle Class: A Blueprint for the Future Roots of Racism The State of Poverty in America A World Enslaved
Chapter 11: Gender and Sexuality	The Boys at the Back Death by Gender The Gay Guide to Wedded Bliss Houston Rising: Why the Next Great American Cities Aren't What You Think Is Facebook Making Us Lonely? The Masculine Mystique The New White Negro Why Women Still Can't Have It All
Chapter 12: Family and Religion	The Boys at the Back Death by Gender The Gay Guide to Wedded Bliss Houston Rising: Why the Next Great American Cities Aren't What You Think Is Facebook Making Us Lonely? The Masculine Mystique The New White Negro Why Women Still Can't Have It All
Chapter 13: Education and Work	The Boys at the Back Death by Gender The Gay Guide to Wedded Bliss Houston Rising: Why the Next Great American Cities Aren't What You Think Is Facebook Making Us Lonely? The Masculine Mystique The New White Negro Why Women Still Can't Have It All
Chapter 14: Media and Consumption	The Broken Contract: Inequality and American Decline The Case for Less Hard at Work in the Jobless Future In Search of the Spiritual MOOCs of Hazard The Robot Will See You Now The Rule of the Rich The Withering of the Affluent Society

(continued)

(concluded)

Chapter 15: Communities, the Environment, and Health	The Broken Contract: Inequality and American Decline Can a Collapse of Global Civilization Be Avoided? The Case for Less The Economic Effects of Granting Legal Status and Citizenship to Undocumented Immigrants Engineering the Future of Food Full Planet, Empty Plates The Future of the Liberal World Order: Internationalism after America Hard at Work in the Jobless Future How Innovation Could Save the Planet In Search of the Spiritual Making Modernity Work: The Reconciliation of Capitalism and Democracy MOOCs of Hazard A New End, a New Beginning: Prepare for Life as We Don't Know It The New Population Bomb: The Four Megatrends that Will Change the World A Radical Approach to the Climate Crisis The Robot Will See You Now The Rule of the Rich A Thousand Years Young A User's Guide to the Century War in the Fifth Domain The Withering of the Affluent Society The World Will Be More Crowded—With Old People The Year in Hate and Extremism, 2010
Chapter 16: Politics and the Economy	The Broken Contract: Inequality and American Decline The Case for Less Hard at Work in the Jobless Future In Search of the Spiritual MOOCs of Hazard The Robot Will See You Now The Rule of the Rich The Withering of the Affluent Society
Chapter 17: Social Change: Globalization, Population, and Social Movements	Can a Collapse of Global Civilization Be Avoided? The Economic Effects of Granting Legal Status and Citizenship to Undocumented Immigrants Engineering the Future of Food Full Planet, Empty Plates The Future of the Liberal World Order: Internationalism after America How Innovation Could Save the Planet Making Modernity Work: The Reconciliation of Capitalism and Democracy A New End, a New Beginning: Prepare for Life as We Don't Know It The New Population Bomb: The Four Megatrends that Will Change the World A Radical Approach to the Climate Crisis A Thousand Years Young A User's Guide to the Century War in the Fifth Domain The World Will Be More Crowded—With Old People The Year in Hate and Extremism, 2010

Topic Guide

This topic guide suggests how the selections in this book relate to the subjects covered in your course.

All the articles that relate to each topic are listed below the bold-faced term.

Aggression

Emmett and Trayvon: How Racial Prejudice in America
   Has Changed in the Last Sixty Years
The Future of the New "We": Muslims in the West to Western Muslims
War in the Fifth Domain
The Year in Hate and Extremism, 2010

Agriculture

Engineering the Future of Food
Full Planet, Empty Plates

Business

The Case for Less
Hard at Work in the Jobless Future
A New End, a New Beginning: Prepare for Life as We Don't Know It
War in the Fifth Domain

Capitalism

The American Narrative: Is There One & What Is It?
Hard at Work in the Jobless Future
Making Modernity Work: The Reconciliation of Capitalism and
   Democracy
A New End, a New Beginning: Prepare for Life as We Don't Know It
Rebuilding the Middle Class: A Blueprint for the Future
The Rule of the Rich

Children/childhood

The Boys at the Back
Female Power
The Gay Guide to Wedded Bliss
The New White Negro
Understanding American Worldview

Cities

Houston Rising: Why the Next Great American Cities Aren't
   What You Think

Civil rights

The American Narrative
The Boys at the Back
Emmett and Trayvon: How Racial Prejudice in America
   Has Changed in the Last Sixty Years
Free and Equal in Dignity and LGBT Rights
Roots of Racism
What Do We Deserve?
A World Enslaved

Community

Is Facebook Making Us Lonely?
The Future of the New "We": Muslims in the West to Western Muslims
Houston Rising: Why the Next Great American Cities Aren't
   What You Think
Reestablishing the Commons for the Common Good

Consumption

Can a Collapse of Global Civilization Be Avoided?
The Case for Less

Crime

Cruel and Unusual: The True Costs of Our Prison System
Death by Gender
Estimates of Cost of Crime: History, Methodologies, and Implications
Fighting Crime: An Economist's View
War in the Fifth Domain
A World Enslaved
Wrongful Convictions
The Year in Hate and Extremism, 2010

Culture

The Boys at the Back
The Case for Less
Death by Gender
Emmett and Trayvon: How Racial Prejudice in America
   Has Changed in the Last Sixty Years
Free and Equal in Dignity and LGBT Rights
The Future of the New "We": Muslims in the West
   to Western Muslims
The Gay Guide to Wedded Bliss
Is Facebook Making Us Lonely?
The Masculine Mystique
The Myth of the "Culture of Poverty"
The New White Negro
Reestablishing the Commons for the Common Good
Roots of Racism
Understanding American Worldview
What Do We Deserve?
The Year in Hate and Extremism, 2010

Demography

The Economic Effects of Granting Legal Status and Citizenship to
   Undocumented Immigrants
The New Population Bomb: The Four Megatrends That
   Will Change the World
Rebuilding the Middle Class: A Blueprint for the Future
A Thousand Years Young
The Withering of the Affluent Society
The World Will Be More Crowded—With Old People

Development, economic and social

The American Narrative: Is There One & What Is It?
The Broken Contract: Inequality and American Decline
Can a Collapse of Global Civilization Be Avoided?
Engineering the Future of Food
The Future of the Liberal World Order: Internationalism
   after America
Hard at Work in the Jobless Future
Houston Rising: Why the Next Great American Cities Aren't
   What You Think
How Innovation Could Save the Planet
Making Modernity Work: The Reconciliation of Capitalism and
   Democracy
A New End, a New Beginning: Prepare for Life as We Don't Know It
The New Population Bomb: The Four Megatrends That
   Will Change the World
Rebuilding the Middle Class: A Blueprint for the Future
Reestablishing the Commons for the Common Good
The State of Poverty in America
The Withering of the Affluent Society
The World Will Be More Crowded—With Old People

Discrimination

The Boys at the Back
Death by Gender
Emmett and Trayvon: How Racial Prejudice in America
   Has Changed in the Last Sixty Years
Free and Equal in Dignity and LGBT Rights

Emmett and Trayvon: How Racial Prejudice in America
    Has Changed in the Last Sixty Years
Engineering the Future of Food
Fighting Crime: An Economist's View
Free and Equal in Dignity and LGBT Rights
The Future of the Liberal World Order: Internationalism
    after America
The Gay Guide to Wedded Bliss
Hard at Work in the Jobless Future
Houston Rising: Why the Next Great American Cities
    Aren't What You Think
How Innovation Could Save the Planet
Is Facebook Making Us Lonely?
Making Modernity Work: The Reconciliation of Capitalism and
    Democracy
The Masculine Mystique
The Myth of the "Culture of Poverty"
A New End, a New Beginning: Prepare for Life as
    We Don't Know It
The New Population Bomb: The Four Megatrends That
    Will Change the World
Rebuilding the Middle Class: A Blueprint for the Future
The State of Poverty in America
A Thousand Years Young
A User's Guide to the Century
War in the Fifth Domain
The Withering of the Affluent Society
The World Will Be More Crowded—With Old People

Social class/stratification

Emmett and Trayvon: How Racial Prejudice in America
    Has Changed in the Last Sixty Years
Female Power
Free and Equal in Dignity and LGBT Rights
The Myth of the "Culture of Poverty"
A New End, a New Beginning: Prepare for Life as We Don't Know It
Rebuilding the Middle Class: A Blueprint for the Future
Roots of Racism
The Rule of the Rich
The State of Poverty in America
What Do We Deserve?
A World Enslaved
The World Will Be More Crowded—With Old People

Social control

Cruel and Unusual: The True Costs of Our Prison System
Estimates of Cost of Crime: History, Methodologies,
    and Implications
A New End, a New Beginning: Prepare for Life as We Don't Know It
War in the Fifth Domain
A World Enslaved
Wrongful Convictions

Social relationships

The Boys at the Back
Death by Gender
Free and Equal in Dignity and LGBT Rights
The Future of the New "We": Muslims in the West to
    Western Muslims
The Gay Guide to Wedded Bliss
Is Facebook Making Us Lonely?
The New Sex Scorecard
Reestablishing the Commons for the Common Good
Why Women Still Can't Have It All

Socialization

The American Narrative: Is There One & What Is It?
The Boys at the Back
Female Power
The Masculine Mystique
The New Sex Scorecard
Reestablishing the Commons for the Common Good
Understanding American Worldview

Technology

Can a Collapse of Global Civilization Be Avoided?
The Case for Less
Engineering the Future of Food
Full Planet, Empty Plates
Hard at Work in the Jobless Future
How Innovation Could Save the Planet
Is Facebook Making Us Lonely?
MOOCs of Hazard
A New End, a New Beginning: Prepare for Life as We Don't Know It
The Robot Will See You Now
A Thousand Years Young
A User's Guide to the Century
War in the Fifth Domain

Terrorism

War in the Fifth Domain
The Year in Hate and Extremism, 2010

Values

The American Narrative: Is There One & What Is It?
The Boys at the Back
The Case for Less
Death by Gender
Emmett and Trayvon: How Racial Prejudice in America
    Has Changed in the Last Sixty Years
Female Power
Free and Equal in Dignity and LGBT Rights
The Future of the New "We": Muslims in the West to
    Western Muslims
The Gay Guide to Wedded Bliss
In Search of the Spiritual
The Masculine Mystique
The Myth of the "Culture of Poverty"
The New Sex Scorecard
Reestablishing the Commons for the Common Good
Roots of Racism

Violence

Emmett and Trayvon: How Racial Prejudice in America
    Has Changed in the Last Sixty Years
A World Enslaved
The Year in Hate and Extremism, 2010

Wealth

How Innovation Could Save the Planet
Rebuilding the Middle Class: A Blueprint for the Future
The Rule of the Rich
The Withering of the Affluent Society
The World Will Be More Crowded—With Old People

Welfare

Can a Collapse of Global Civilization Be Avoided?
The End of Welfare as I Knew It How Temporary Assistance for Needy
    Families Failed the Test of the Great Recession
How Innovation Could Save the Planet

Women

Death by Gender
Female Power
The New Sex Scorecard
Why Women Still Can't Have It All
A World Enslaved

Work

Female Power
Hard at Work in the Jobless Future
The Myth of the "Culture of Poverty"
The State of Poverty in America
Why Women Still Can't Have It All
A World Enslaved

Unit 1

UNIT

Prepared by: Kurt Finsterbusch, *University of Maryland, College Park*

Culture

The ordinary, everyday objects of living and the daily routines of life provide a structure to social life that is regularly punctuated by festivals, celebrations, and other special events (both happy and sad). These routine and special times are the stuff of culture, for culture is the sum total of all the elements of one's social inheritance. Culture includes language, tools, values, habits, science, religion, literature, and art.

It is easy to take one's own culture for granted, so it is useful to pause and reflect on the shared beliefs and practices that form the foundations for our social life. Students share beliefs and practices, and thus have a student culture. Obviously, the faculty has one also. Students, faculty, and administrators share a university culture. At the national level, Americans share an American culture. These cultures change through the decades and especially between generations. As a result, there is much variety among cultures across time and across nations, tribes, and groups. It is fascinating to study these differences and to compare the dominant values and signature patterns of different groups.

Article   Prepared by: Kurt Finsterbusch, *University of Maryland, College Park*

Understanding American Worldview
Part I

J. LaVelle Ingram

Learning Outcomes

After reading this article, you will be able to:

- Identify the core values in American society.

- Understand the strengths and weaknesses of cultures that emphasize cooperation and the strengths and weaknesses of cultures that emphasize individualism and freedom.

- Draw some conclusions about whether people are capable of real altruism or whether altruistic actions are based ultimately on self-interest.

Over time, I have taught many courses on cross-cultural differences, and I always complete an exercise within them. I explain the different options for worldviews, and then I ask my students to identify "mainstream American worldviews." The students have only heard of the classic systems for explaining worldviews within that class, a few minutes before I ask them the question, and yet they always get it right. How?

What my students don't realize, and often immigrants don't realize, is that worldviews are pervasive in one's society or culture. They aren't necessarily spoken of because there is no need to speak of them. Everybody already knows them because they guide most of the society. My students have lived with the American worldviews for all of their lives, so when they hear the system, they know the answers. But the average immigrant is operating on a different set of worldviews, and the two do not always make sense in cross cultural interactions.

It is important, then, for the new immigrant to understand the system into which s/he is entering so that navigating that system can become more sensible. American worldviews have been identified by many sociologists and anthropologists as follows: Our time sense is futuristic; our sense of nature involves mastery; our sense of human nature is that it is basically good or mixed; our social sense is individualistic; and our sense of the proper way of being is to value doing. These values mean that: 1) Time focuses on the future rather than the past; it needs to be planned for; youth is more valuable than age. 2) We should be able to control nature; it is here for our use and we are separate from it. 3) Given human nature, you can count on people to do the right thing given the chance; at least it is not inherently bad

and in need of strict control. 4) The individual's wishes, needs, and aspirations are more important than the group's (including the family's), and it is appropriate for an individual to move away from and function independently of the group. 5) What one does, accomplishes, is more important than the way s/he conducts her/himself. Thus one's job is important in determining one's relative value in the society.

Now, the above list may seem odd to those coming from other cultures. Folks may wonder, "Why these ideas?" or "Why these values?" At this point, though, it is more important to understand how the worldviews operate rather than why Americans might choose these, because these worldviews not only identify the foundation for basic decision-making, they also identify what a culture considers good and right and proper. Operating differently, then, can lead to confusion about the immigrants' choices, not to mention suspicion and/or devaluing. Learning to operate between the different worldviews, or at least how to make your own translate, will only serve to increase your effectiveness with American audiences.

In the next article, I will continue to articulate the implications of the American worldviews. In the meantime, consider the other alternatives identified by social scientists and see if you recognize your own: Time sense can also be present or past oriented, (focus on history, ancestors, slow change). Our relationship to nature can be seen as harmonious or we can be seen as subject to it (in harmony we are one part of the whole, in subjugation we must be resigned to our physical and spiritual fate). Human nature can also be viewed as mixed or bad (needing more monitoring and control lest we get out of control). Social sense can also be group focused or function within a strict hierarchy (such that the needs of the family must come first and/or one must keep one's place in order to be a proper person). Finally, the proper way of living can focus on both being and doing or simply on being (in these cases how one conducts oneself is more important than what one achieves).

In each case, the worldview identifies the values of the society as a whole not necessarily the individual. So the question is not about your personal belief, but about what most folks in your culture would say, or more to the point what they should say. Understanding American worldview can help you understand why many folks behave the way they do versus how folks behave where you come from.

Part II

From the last article, you may recall that American world-views mean that: 1) time focuses on the future rather than the past; 2) that we should be able to control nature; 3) that people can be counted on to do the right thing given the chance; 4) that an individual's wishes, needs, and aspirations should be counted as more important than the groups' or families'; and 5) that what one does or accomplishes is more important than the way s/he conducts her/himself.

Regarding time, a future orientation suggests that the present must take second place to the needs of the future and that it is inappropriate to focus on the past. So, in America it is deemed proper to save for retirement, to make a schedule for next week and to plan on one's children's education years before they go to college. Of course, some people do spend their money on the big car now (present oriented), but they are considered unwise by American standards. Folks living-for-the-moment do live in America (especially among the young), but all in all it is viewed as somewhat inappropriate. However, the last option, living according to the past, makes little sense to most of mainstream America. If an immigrant family decides, for instance, to spend substantial money on a monument to an ancestor rather than save for a child's education, most Americans would frown upon that decision. It is valuing the past more than the future. If an American family, on the other hand, passes on a visit to their elders in Italy so that they can buy a bigger house, they would be considered wise (by other Americans). The focus on being busy is another artifact of America's future time sense, as is the notion that "time is money."

So what is an immigrant to do? Coming to America does not automatically mean that people want to adopt American world-views and values. Yet, living according to different worldviews comes with consequences. In general, it has proved effective to my clients to tell the American the worldview that is primary for you. So, let's say your family buys the monument to the ancestor (past time oriented), and the American coworker asks, "Why did you'all do that? You could have put that money in your kid's college fund." Then the immigrant might say, "We believe it is important to honor elders first. It is a serious obligation." The American counters with, "Isn't it your obligation to pay for your child first?" So the immigrant can then clarify, "No. We want our children to learn to honor elders first too. So that is the value we modeled for them." Here, no one is submitting to the other's way of thinking, the immigrant is just making

her/his way of thinking make sense. Thus, if the American person ends with, "I would have paid for my kid's college first," the immigrant is clear that this decision reflects a worldview difference. S/he can then say to the American coworker, "That makes sense within your culture, as my decision makes sense within mine."

Social relations is another area that seems to impact immigrants a lot if they come from group or lineal oriented cultures. In America, since the social relations sense is individual—a college kid decides his own major, a young woman moves into her own apartment, a young man gets a job and does not give money to the family. In many other cultures these behaviors would be considered, at least disrespectful if not outrageous. The difference is how we view the individual's proper role; in America that role focuses on providing for oneself and learning to function independent of one's family. So, should a young woman move to another state for a great job? In America, the answer is yes. Should an older man take on his father's obligations after he dies? In America, the answer would be no. And these folks are not being heartless or selfish; they are simply taking care of themselves, as is their first obligation (and sign that their parents prepared them well) within American worldview.

Still, each immigrant comes with her/his own culture and worldviews. How then do you explain these to your American coworkers, friends, and neighbors? First, realize that you don't have to if you don't want to. Then realize that there is much to be gained if you choose to make the effort. Once, an Indian mother said to me, "You Americans, you don't help your children on the most important thing." I asked her what she meant, and she said, "You send them out into the world to find love with no help at all. You just say, 'Good luck. I hope you find someone.'" She was the first immigrant to help me to understand the rationale behind arranged marriages. From an American point of view, that decision comes from the individuals involved, yet from many other cultures it is the parents' solemn responsibility (lineal worldview). That mother's effort to help me understand increased my effectiveness as I addressed other couples facing arranged marriages. Because of her, I do not assume that such matches are improper or pointless. Because of her, I recognize the value of doing things the other way. So, if you take on the challenge, most Americans can benefit from similar efforts.

Part III

The preceding articles included just a few examples of the wide variety of decisions that can arise from different worldviews. Sometimes they can be comical, but other times they can mean life and death. For instance, consider the notion that human beings should master nature. This point of

view has led to such medical advancements as antibiotics and effective surgeries. This worldview suggests that we should be able to defeat diseases, and an American family would likely choose whatever invasive procedures necessary to cure a family member of a disease. But would an immigrant to America make the same decision? Maybe not. Some immigrants might feel that the disease reflects some imbalance in living (harmony worldview), and thus decide that changing her/his way of life would be more effective. Another immigrant, coming from a subjugation point of view, might decide that the disease is his/her destiny, and that it only makes sense to give in to it with dignity. Most Americans would have trouble understanding such a decision. The important thing for the immigrant is to realize that s/he is living within a mastery culture, and that is the point of view s/he will have to manage.

Human nature is another important aspect of the five identified dimensions of worldview. As stated previously, in America, human nature is thought to be good or mixed. Thus, in this country, personal freedom is a core value; it suggests that the society as a whole will work better if you count on the individuals to live up to their best selves. It is a notably optimistic view of human beings and suggests that the fewer constraints imposed on people the better. However, in many other cultures human nature is viewed fairly pessimistically, and it is considered, at core, bad. In this case, people need rigid controls in order to stay on the right path; they need to be monitored closely so that they do not have the chance to give in to their negative impulses.

Finally, worldview addresses the appropriate "way of being." In America, the preferred worldview is that "doing" is most sensible since it leads to achievement. In this country, one of the first questions acquaintances will ask is "what do you do?" What one spends time doing is of primary importance in deciding one's status. Further, if you mention a vacation, Americans will ask, "Where did you go? But also "What did you do?" We will expect to hear about your activities, even while you were on vacation. If an immigrant reports that "I went back home to look after my parents," the Americans will likely give a polite "Oh," but they will not really understand. Even a statement that "I spent some time with my grandparents," will likely confuse the average American. These activities reflect a being-in-becoming or being point of view wherein how one conducts oneself is more important than what one achieves.

Once again, we come to the question of what an immigrant person is to do with these differences. These three articles on worldview were written primarily for the purpose of lending understanding of differences that can be quite confusing. While most Americans do not know this model of describing cultural worldviews, they do live within these noted American worldviews, and will likely recognize them if they are discussed. Thus, person-to-person conflicts, or simple misunderstandings, can be explained by immigrant people using this model. There are advantages and disadvantages to every way of thinking, and being able to discuss the advantages of your different worldviews might go a long way to bridging the gaps in discourse. Yes, Americans believe in mastery over nature, but we are also having to realize that the overuse of antibiotics is creating super-germs. We are coming to recognize that recycling (harmony worldview) is a beneficial, and perhaps, necessary societal activity. We may believe in a good human nature, but recent incidents of terrorist killings have given us reason to reconsider. Those nations that closely monitor their citizens (human nature bad) are appearing much more sensible to Americans in light of these events. And

the crooks at Enron, who achieved great wealth, but failed to be good custodians of their workforce, make us review our emphasis on doing over being. Cultures wherein the leaders of such companies encounter serious loss of face in the society (being worldview) suddenly make more sense to us.

In short, the immigrant does not have to decide to adopt American worldviews to live in America (assimilation); nor does one have to hold rigidly to the culture of origin (rejection). Rather, it is simply a more effective living strategy to recognize the cultural differences and consciously negotiate them. In this manner, conflicts that may erroneously be considered personal dislike may be more accurately identified as simple differences in worldview. Decisions that are confusing or even unthinkable or absurd may be rendered sensible with the articulation of these different worldviews. And the task of engaging peculiar cultural others in one's personal or professional life can be rendered interesting social challenges rather than confounding moral dilemmas.

References

Carter (1991) "Cultural Values: A Review of Empirical Research & Implications for Counseling", pp. 164–173. In Claiborne, C., Ed. (1991) "Special Issue: Multiculturalism as a fourth force in counseling". *Journal of Counseling & Development*. 70 (1).

Cattell, R.B. (1949). The dimensions of culture patterns by factorization of national characters. *Journal of Abnormal and Social Psychology*, 44, 443–69.

Dobbins & Skillings (1991) "The Utility of Race Labeling in Understanding Cultural Identity", pp. 37–44. In Claiborne, C., Ed. (1991) "Special Issue: Multiculturalism as a fourth force in counseling". *Journal of Counseling & Development*. 70 (1).

Hoare (1991) "Psychosocial Identity Development & Cultural Others", pp. 45–53. In Claiborne, C., Ed. (1991) "Special Issue: Multiculturalism as a fourth force in counseling". *Journal of Counseling & Development*. 70 (1).

Hofstede, G. (2001). *Culture's Consequences: Comparing Values, Behaviors, Institutions and Organizations across Nations*. Thousand Oaks, CA: Sage.

Ibrahim (1991) "Contribution of Cultural Worldview to Generic Counseling and Development", pp. 13–19. In Claiborne, C., Ed. (1991) "Special Issue: Multiculturalism as a fourth force in counseling". *Journal of Counseling & Development*. 70 (1).

Inglehart, R., Basañez, M. & Moreno, A. (1998). *Human Values and Beliefs: A Cross-Cultural Sourcebook. Political, religious, sexual, and economic norms in 43 societies. Findings from the 1990–1993 World Values Survey*. Ann Arbor: The University of Michigan Press.

Kim, U, Triandis, H.C., Kagitçibasi, C., Choi, S.C., & Yoon, G. (Eds., 1994), *Individualism and Collectivism: Theory, Method and Applications*. Thousand Oaks, CA: Sage.

Kluckhohn, C. (1962[1952]). Universal categories of culture. In S. Tax (Ed.), *Anthropology Today: Selections* (pp. 304–20). Chicago: University of Chicago Press.

Kluckhohn, F.R. & Strodtbeck, F. L. (1961). *Variations in Value Orientations*. Westport CT: Greenwood Press.

Pedersen, Paul, Ed. (1987). *Handbook of Cross-Cultural Counseling and Therapy*. New York: Praeger.

Sodowsky, Lai & Plake (1991) "Moderating Effects of Sociocultural Variables on Acculturation Attitudes of Hispanic and Asian Americans", pp. 194–204. In Claiborne, C., Ed. (1991) "Special Issue: Multiculturalism as a fourth force in counseling". *Journal of Counseling & Development.* 70 (1).

Sue, Derald Wing (1990). *Counseling the Culturally Different.* New York: Wiley & Sons.

Triandis, H.C. (1995). *Individualism and Collectivism.* Boulder, CO: Westview.

Critical Thinking

1. Does this article accurately represent the central values of American society?

2. Do the current passionate disagreements in America undermine this article?

Create Central

www.mhhe.com/createcentral

Internet References

Human Rights and Humanitarian Affairs
www.etown.edu/vl/humrts.html

Sociosite
www.topsite.com/goto/sociosite.net

Socioweb
www.topsite.com/goto/socioweb.com

Sociology—Study Sociology Online
http://edu.learnsoc.org

Sociology Web Resources
www.mhhe.com/socscience/sociology/resources/index.htm

Article

Prepared by: Kurt Finsterbusch, *University of Maryland, College Park*

The American Narrative: Is There One & What Is It?

Nearly four centuries of American history have witnessed the evolving conflict between two competing sets of values: a belief that acting on behalf of the common good should guide social and political behavior, and a belief that unfettered individual freedom should dominate political and social life. Tracing this conflict from Puritanism through the American Revolution, the Civil War, the rise of industrialism, the Progressive Era, the New Deal, the Great Society, and the conservative revival of the Nixon/Reagan era, the essay reveals this clash of values as pivotal to understanding the narrative of American history, with contemporary political battles crystallizing just how basic this conflict has been.

WILLIAM H. CHAFE

Learning Outcomes

After reading this article, you will be able to:

- Trace the role of the culture of serving the public good and the role of the culture of individual freedom in American history.

- Analyze how these two value systems are opposing each other today.

- Discuss the importance of balance between these sets of values and the danger of destroying that balance today.

Who are we? Where have we been? Where are we going? Can we even agree on who "we" includes? At no time in our history have these questions been more relevant. The American political system seems dysfunctional, if not permanently fractured. A generational gap in technological expertise and familiarity with the social network divides the country to an even greater extent than the culture wars of the 1960s and 1970s. Soon, more "Americans" will speak Spanish as their first language than English. For some, access to health care is a universal right, for others, a privilege that must be earned. Rarely—and certainly not since the Civil War—have we been so divided on which direction we should be heading as a country. How can there be an American narrative when it is not clear what it means to talk about an American people or nation? Two overriding paradigms have long competed in defining who we are. The first imagines America as a community that places the good of the whole first; the second envisions the country as a gathering of individuals who prize individual freedom and value more than anything else each person's ability to determine his own fate.

When the Puritans arrived in the Massachusetts Bay Colony in 1630, their leader, John Winthrop, told his shipmates aboard the *Arabella* that their mission was to create a "city upon a hill," a blessed society that would embody values so noble that the entire world would admire and emulate the new colony. Entitled "A Modell of Christian Charity," Winthrop's sermon described what it would take to create that beloved community: "We must love one another. We must bear one another's burdens . . . make others' conditions our own. We must rejoice together, mourn together, labor and suffer together, always having before our eyes a community [where we are all] members of the same body."

Consistent with Winthrop's vision, Massachusetts was governed in its early decades by a sense of communal well-being. While the colony tolerated differences of status and power, the ruling norm was that the common good took precedence. Thus, "just prices" were prescribed for goods for sale, and punishment was imposed on businesses that sought excess profits. Parents who mistreated their children were shamed; people who committed adultery were exposed and humiliated.

Soon enough, a surge of individualism challenged the reigning norms. Entrepreneurs viewed communal rules as shackles to be broken so that they could pursue individual aspirations—and profits. The ideal of a "just price" was discarded. While religion remained a powerful presence, secularism ruled everyday business life, and Christianity was restricted to a once-a-week ritual. Class distinctions proliferated, economic inequality increased, and the values of *laissez-faire individualism* displaced the once-enshrined "common wealth." Aid to the poor became an act of individual charity rather than a communal responsibility.

Not surprisingly, the tensions between those who put the good of the community first and those who value individual freedom foremost have reverberated throughout our history. Thomas

Jefferson sought to resolve the conflict in the Declaration of Independence by embracing the idea of "equal opportunity" for all. Note that he championed not equality of results, but equality of opportunity. Every citizen might have an "inalienable" right to "life, liberty and the pursuit of happiness," but what happened to each person's "equal opportunity" depended on the performance of that particular individual. Success was not guaranteed.

Throughout American history, the tensions between the value of the common good and the right to unbridled individual freedom have resurfaced. The federal government sought to build roads and canals across state lines to serve the general good. The nation fought a Civil War because slavery contradicted the belief in the right of equal citizenship. In the aftermath of the war, the Constitution guaranteed all males the right to vote, and its Fourteenth Amendment promised each citizen "equal protection" under the law.

But by the end of the nineteenth century, rampant economic growth had created myriad enterprises that threatened the common good. In *The Jungle,* Upton Sinclair highlighted the danger of workers falling into vats of boiling liquid at meatpacking plants. The influx of millions of immigrants brought new dangers of infectious disease. As sweatshops, germ-filled tenements, and unsafe factories blighted American cities, more and more Americans insisted on legislation that fostered the general welfare. Led by women reformers such as Jane Addams and Florence Kelley, social activists succeeded in getting laws passed that ended child labor, protected workers from injury from dangerous factory machines, and created standards for safe meat and food. The Progressive Era still left most people free to pursue their own destiny, but under President Theodore Roosevelt, the government became the ultimate arbiter of minimal standards for industry, railroads, and consumer safety.

The tensions between the two narratives continued to grow as the nation entered the Great Depression. Nearly a million mortgages were foreclosed, the stock market crashed, 25 percent of all American workers were chronically unemployed, and banks failed. When Franklin Roosevelt was elected president, he promised to use "bold, persistent experimentation" to find answers to people's suffering. The legislation of the first hundred days of his presidency encompassed unprecedented federal intervention in the regulation of industry, agriculture, and the provision of welfare payments to the unemployed. The good of the whole reemerged as a dominant concern. By 1935, however, the American Liberty League, a political group formed by conservative Democrats to oppose New Deal legislation, was indicting FDR as a socialist and demanding a return to laissez-faire individualism. But the New Deal rolled on. In 1935, Congress enacted Social Security, the single greatest collective investment America had ever made, for *all* people over sixty-five, and the Wagner Labor Relations Act gave unions the right to organize. Roosevelt ran his 1936 reelection campaign on a platform emphasizing that "one third of [our] nation is ill-housed, ill-clothed and ill-fed."

This focus on the good of the whole culminated during World War II, a time when everyone was reminded of being part of a larger battle to preserve the values that "equal opportunity"

represented: the dignity of every citizen, as well as the right to freedom of religion, freedom from want, and freedom of political expression. For the first time since Reconstruction, the government acted to prohibit discrimination against African Americans, issuing an executive order to allow blacks as well as whites to be hired in the war industries. Similarly, it supported policies of equal pay to women workers while leading a massive effort to recruit more women into the labor force to meet wartime demands. From wage and price controls to the universal draft, government action on behalf of the good of the whole reached a new height.

After the war ended, the tension between the competing value systems returned, but, significantly, even most Republicans accepted as a given the fundamental reforms achieved under the New Deal. Anyone who suggested repeal of Social Security, President Dwight Eisenhower wrote to his brother Milton midway through his term in office, was "out of his mind." Eisenhower even created a new Cabinet department to oversee health and welfare.

The stage was set for the revolutions of the 1960s: that is, the civil rights movement, the women's movement, the student movement, and the War on Poverty. Blacks had no intention of accepting the status quo of prewar Jim Crow segregation when they returned from serving in World War II. Building on the community institutions they had created during the era of Jim Crow, they mobilized to confront racism. When a black woman was raped by six white policemen in Montgomery, Alabama, in the late 1940s, the Women's Political Council, organized by local black women, and the Brotherhood of Sleeping Car Porters, an all-black union, took on the police and forced a trial. That same network of black activists sought improvements in the treatment of blacks at downtown department stores and on public transport. Thus, when one of their members, Rosa Parks, was arrested in 1955 for refusing to give up her seat on a city bus to a white person, both groups took action. By initiating a phone tree and printing four thousand leaflets, they organized a mass rally overnight. Held at a local Baptist church to consider a bus boycott, the rally featured an address by Martin Luther King, Jr., who later became the embodiment of the movement (though it should be noted that the movement created King and not vice versa). After that night, Montgomery's black community refused to ride the city buses for 381 consecutive days, until the buses were desegregated.

A few years later, four first-year students at the all-black North Carolina Agricultural and Technical College in Greensboro, North Carolina, carried the movement a step further. Although they had come of age after the Supreme Court outlawed school segregation, little had changed. Now that their generation was reaching maturity, they asked what they could do. The young men had gone to an all-black high school where their teachers had asked them to address voter registration envelopes to community residents and encouraged them to think of themselves as first-class citizens. They had participated in an NAACP youth group in which weekly discussions had centered on events such as the Montgomery Bus Boycott. They attended a Baptist church where the pastor preached the social gospel and asked for "justice now." Embittered by how little the status of black Americans had improved, they sought new ways of carrying forward what they had learned.

Their solution was simple: highlight the absurdity of segregation by going to a downtown department store and acting like regular customers. At the Woolworth's in Greensboro, they bought notebooks at one counter, purchased toothpaste at another, then sat down at the lunch counter and ordered a cup of coffee. "We don't serve colored people here," they were told. "But you served us over there," they responded, showing their receipts. Opening their school books, they sat for three hours until the store closed. The next day, they returned to the lunch counter with twenty-three of their classmates. The day after there were sixty-six, the next day one hundred. On the fifth day, one thousand black students and adults crowded the streets of downtown Greensboro.

The direct-action civil rights movement had begun. Within two months, sit-ins occurred in fifty-four cities in nine states. By April 1960, the Student Nonviolent Coordinating Committee (SNCC) had been founded. Soon, *The New York Times* was devoting a special section each day to civil rights demonstrations in the South. On August 28, 1963, a quarter-million people came together for the March on Washington. There, Martin Luther King, Jr., gave his "I Have a Dream" speech, a contemporary version of what John Winthrop had said 238 years earlier that celebrated the same idea of a "beloved community" where "neither Jew nor Gentile, black man or white man" could be separated from each other.

At long last, the government responded. The Civil Rights Act of 1964 ended Jim Crow. The Voting Rights Act of 1965 restored the franchise to black Americans. The War on Poverty gave hope to millions who had been left out of the American dream. Medicare offered health care to all senior citizens, and Medicaid offered it to those who could not otherwise afford to go to the doctor. Federal Aid to Education created new and better schools. The Model Cities Program offered a way for blighted neighborhoods to be revitalized.

The narrative of progress toward the common good reached a new crescendo. With the civil rights movement as an inspiration, women started their own movement for social equality. Access to previously closed careers opened up under pressure. By 1990, half of all medical, law, and business students were women. Young girls grew up with the same aspirations as young boys. Latinos, gay Americans, and other minorities soon joined the march demanding greater equality. It seemed as though a permanent turning point had occurred.

But the counternarrative eventually rediscovered its voice. Millions of white Americans who might have supported the right of blacks to vote or eat at a lunch counter were appalled by affirmative action and demands for Black Power. When the war in Vietnam caused well-off students to take to the streets in protest against their country's military actions, thousands of ordinary workers were angered by the rebellion of the young against authority. Traditional families were outraged when feminists questioned monogamy and dared to challenge male authority.

By 1968, the nation was divided once more, and the events of that election year crystallized the issues. Incumbent Lyndon Johnson withdrew from the presidential race at the end of March.

Martin Luther King, Jr., was assassinated in April, with riots spreading like wildfire across the country in response. Student protestors took over Columbia University in May, making a mockery of the idea of civil discourse and respect for authority. Robert F. Kennedy was assassinated in June, just as he seemed ready to move decisively toward the Democratic presidential nomination. And when the Democratic party met for its convention in Chicago, thousands of protestors were pummeled by police as they demonstrated against conventional politics.

At the same time, Richard Nixon was nominated by the Republican party on a platform of "law and order" and respect for authority. Adopting a "Southern strategy," he appealed for white Southern votes by opposing forced desegregation of schools. Lambasting students who protested the war, he pleaded for a return to respect for traditional institutions. Nixon claimed to speak on behalf of "the silent majority" who remained proud to be American citizens, who celebrated the flag rather than mocked it, and who affirmed the rights of individuals to do as they wished.

Richard Nixon's election in Fall 1968 launched the resurgence of a conservative consensus in American politics. Though on issues such as the environment Nixon pursued many policies consistent with the "good of the whole" framework, on most issues he moved in the opposite direction. He opposed busing as a tool to create greater school desegregation, started to dismantle War on Poverty programs, based his 1972 reelection campaign on attacking the "collectivism" of the Democratic party, and insisted on defending the values of "traditional" Americans against attacks by the young, minorities, and women.

As social issues provided a rallying point for those set against further social change, the conservative narrative gained new proponents. Those opposed to gay rights mobilized to curtail further efforts to make sexuality a civil rights issue. Evangelical Christians joined groups such as Jerry Falwell's Moral Majority or Pat Robertson's "Praise the Lord" clubs to lobby against advances for minority rights. Direct mail campaigns and the use of cable television helped the Right galvanize new audiences of potential supporters.

Presidential politics also continued on a conservative path. Even though Richard Nixon was compelled to resign in shame over his illegal activities in the Watergate scandal, each of his successors—even Democrats—advanced the conservative agenda he initiated. Gerald Ford vetoed more legislation in two years than most presidents veto in eight. Jimmy Carter, though a liberal on gender equality and black civil rights, proved conservative on most economic issues. Ronald Reagan personified the conservative revival. He not only celebrated patriotism, but also revived the viewpoint that the best America was one without government intervention in the economy, and one that venerated the ideal of individualism.

Even Democrat Bill Clinton, excoriated by the Right as a demonic embodiment of counterculture values, was in practice more a Dwight Eisenhower Republican than a Lyndon Johnson Democrat. Dedicated to cultivating the political mainstream, he achieved legislative victories primarily on traditionally Republican issues: deficit reduction; the North American Free Trade Agreement; an increased police presence on the streets; welfare reform that took people off the public dole after two years; and the use of V-chips to allow parents to control their children's television viewing habits. Only his failed health care proposal acted in tune with the ideology of FDR and LBJ.

George W. Bush simply extended the conservative tradition. With massive tax cuts, he created lower rates for the wealthy than had been seen in more than a half-century. His consistent support of deregulation freed up countless companies and investment capital firms to pursue profits without restriction. He made nationalism a cherished part of his political legacy, including the pursuit of a doctrine that emphasized unilateral initiatives defined as in the best interests of the United States, and downplayed multilateral co-operation that would subject America to constraint by the wishes of its partners and allies.

From 1968 to 2008, the American political and ideological trajectory hewed to a conservative narrative that celebrates individualism over collective action and criticizes government activity on behalf of the common good.

In recent years, the tension between the two narratives has escalated to an alarming degree. Barack Obama's 2008 election appeared to revitalize a focus on the common good. More people voted, embracing the idea of change, and elected a black American who seemed to embody those values. The fact that Obama became the first president in one hundred years to successfully pass national health care reform—albeit without the provision of a public alternative to private insurance companies—appeared to validate that presumption.

But with the midterm elections of 2010, the rejection of Democratic politics—especially state intervention on behalf of the common good—resulted in the most dramatic electoral turnaround since 1946, when President Harry Truman's Democrats lost eighty-one seats in the House of Representatives. "Tea Party" Republicans not only stood for conservative positions on most social issues, but most dramatically, they insisted that all taxes should be cut, that federal expenditures for Medicare, Social Security, and other social programs must be slashed, and that it is preferable for the government to default on its financial responsibilities than to raise the national debt ceiling.

A backward glance through U.S. history would reveal no clearer example of the tension between the two competing American narratives, existing side by side, seemingly irreconcilable. The moment is historic, particularly at a time when climate change, stalled immigration reform, and a depressed global economy cry out for action. Thus, the conflict between the good of the whole and the ascendancy of individualist freedom has reached new heights. The choice that voters make in the 2012 presidential election will define our country's political future. Which narrative will we pursue? Are health care and quality education universal rights or privileges reserved for only those with the means to pay? Do we wish to bear "one another's burdens . . . make others' conditions our own . . . mourn together [and] labor and suffer together?" Or do we wish to make each individual responsible for his or her own fate? These questions are not new. But now, more than ever, they challenge us to find an answer: Who are we? In which direction do we wish to go?

Despite the trend over the past three-and-a-half centuries toward legislation that creates a safety net to protect the larger community, millions of Americans appear committed to dismantling government, slashing federal spending, and walking away from previous commitments to the good of the whole. A number of candidates running for the Republican presidential nomination in 2012 wish to curtail federal responsibility for Social Security for senior citizens. Every Republican candidate seeks to repeal Obama's national health insurance program. Cutting taxes has become a holy mantra. While it is true that in the coming decades demographic change will dramatically increase the number of Latino voters, who historically have favored legislation on behalf of the common good, it is not inconceivable that a reversal of social welfare legislation will happen first.

The tension between these two narratives is as old as the country itself. More often than not, it has been a healthy tension, with one set of values checking and balancing the other. But the polarization of today is unparalleled. The decisions the electorate makes in 2012 are of historic importance in determining which direction the country will take.

Critical Thinking

1. How does the value system focused on the public good benefit American society and how might it hurt American society?

2. How does the value system focused on individual freedom benefit American society and how might it hurt American society?

3. How can balance between these two value systems be maintained?

Create Central

www.mhhe.com/createcentral

Internet References

New American Studies Web
    www.georgetown.edu/crossroads/asw

Sociosite
    www.topsite.com/goto/sociosite.net

Socioweb
    www.topsite.com/goto/socioweb.com

Sociology—Study Sociology Online
    http://edu.learnsoc.org

Sociology Web Resources
    www.mhhe.com/socscience/sociology/resources/index.htm

WILLIAM H. CHAFE, a Fellow of the American Academy since 2001, is the Alice Mary Baldwin Professor of History at Duke University. His publications include *Private Lives/Public Consequences: Personality and Politics in Modern America* (2005) and *The Rise and Fall of the American Century: The United States from 1890 to 2008* (2008). His current project is titled *Behind the Veil: African American Life During the Age of Segregation.*

Chafe, William H. From *Daedalus*, Winter 2012, pp. 11–17. Copyright © 2012 by MIT Press Journals/American Academy of Arts and Sciences. Reprinted by permission via Rightslink.

Article   Prepared by: Kurt Finsterbusch, *University of Maryland, College Park*

The Myth of the "Culture of Poverty"

Instead of accepting myths that harm low-income students, we need to eradicate the systemwide inequities that stand in their way.

PAUL GORSKI

Learning Outcomes

After reading this article, you will be able to:

- Assess the role of culture in the condition of the poor.

- Discuss the role of opportunity structures in contributing to the conditions of the poor.

- Evaluate how different the poor are from the middle class.

As the students file out of Janet's classroom, I sit in the back corner, scribbling a few final notes. Defeat in her eyes, Janet drops into a seat next to me with a sigh.

"I love these kids," she declares, as if trying to convince me. "I adore them. But my hope is fading."

"Why's that?" I ask, stuffing my notes into a folder.

"They're smart. I know they're smart, but . . . "

And then the deficit floodgates open: "They don't care about school. They're unmotivated. And their parents—I'm lucky if two or three of them show up for conferences. No wonder the kids are unprepared to learn."

At Janet's invitation, I spent dozens of hours in her classroom, meeting her students, observing her teaching, helping her navigate the complexities of an urban midwestern elementary classroom with a growing percentage of students in poverty. I observed powerful moments of teaching and learning, caring and support. And I witnessed moments of internal conflict in Janet, when what she wanted to believe about her students collided with her prejudices.

Like most educators, Janet is determined to create an environment in which each student reaches his or her full potential. And like many of us, despite overflowing with good intentions, Janet has bought into the most common and dangerous myths about poverty.

Chief among these is the "culture of poverty" myth—the idea that poor people share more or less monolithic and predictable beliefs, values, and behaviors. For educators like Janet to be the best teachers they can be for all students, they need to challenge this myth and reach a deeper understanding of class and poverty.

Roots of the Culture of Poverty Concept

Oscar Lewis coined the term *culture of poverty* in his 1961 book *The Children of Sanchez*. Lewis based his thesis on his ethnographic studies of small Mexican communities. His studies uncovered approximately 50 attributes shared within these communities: frequent violence, a lack of a sense of history, a neglect of planning for the future, and so on. Despite studying very small communities, Lewis extrapolated his findings to suggest a universal culture of poverty. More than 45 years later, the premise of the culture of poverty paradigm remains the same: that people in poverty share a consistent and observable "culture."

Lewis ignited a debate about the nature of poverty that continues today. But just as important—especially in the age of data-driven decision making—he inspired a flood of research. Researchers around the world tested the culture of poverty concept empirically (see Billings, 1974; Carmon, 1985; Jones & Luo, 1999). Others analyzed the overall body of evidence regarding the culture of poverty paradigm (see Abell & Lyon, 1979; Ortiz & Briggs, 2003; Rodman, 1977).

These studies raise a variety of questions and come to a variety of conclusions about poverty. But on this they all agree: *There is no such thing as a culture of poverty.* Differences in values and behaviors among poor people are just as great as those between poor and wealthy people.

In actuality, the culture of poverty concept is constructed from a collection of smaller stereotypes which, however false, seem to have crept into mainstream thinking as unquestioned fact. Let's look at some examples.

Myth: Poor people are unmotivated and have weak work ethics.

The Reality: Poor people do not have weaker work ethics or lower levels of motivation than wealthier people (Iversen & Farber, 1996; Wilson, 1997). Although poor people are often stereotyped as lazy, 83 percent of children from low-income families have at least one employed parent; close to 60 percent have at least one parent who works full-time and year-round (National Center for Children in Poverty,

2004). In fact, the severe shortage of living-wage jobs means that many poor adults must work two, three, or four jobs. According to the Economic Policy Institute (2002), poor working adults spend more hours working each week than their wealthier counterparts.

Myth: Poor parents are uninvolved in their children's learning, largely because they do not value education.

The Reality: Low-income parents hold the same attitudes about education that wealthy parents do (Compton-Lilly, 2003; Lareau & Horvat, 1999; Leichter, 1978). Low-income parents are less likely to attend school functions or volunteer in their children's classrooms (National Center for Education Statistics, 2005)—not because they care less about education, but because they have less access to school involvement than their wealthier peers. They are more likely to work multiple jobs, to work evenings, to have jobs without paid leave, and to be unable to afford child care and public transportation. It might be said more accurately that schools that fail to take these considerations into account do not value the involvement of poor families as much as they value the involvement of other families.

Myth: Poor people are linguistically deficient.

The Reality: All people, regardless of the languages and language varieties they speak, use a full continuum of language registers (Bomer, Dworin, May, & Semingson, 2008). What's more, linguists have known for decades that all language varieties are highly structured with complex grammatical rules (Gee, 2004; Hess, 1974; Miller, Cho, & Bracey, 2005). What often are assumed to be *deficient* varieties of English—Appalachian varieties, perhaps, or what some refer to as Black English Vernacular—are no less sophisticated than so-called "standard English."

Myth: Poor people tend to abuse drugs and alcohol.

The Reality: Poor people are no more likely than their wealthier counterparts to abuse alcohol or drugs. Although drug sales are more visible in poor neighborhoods, drug use is equally distributed across poor, middle class, and wealthy communities (Saxe, Kadushin, Tighe, Rindskopf, & Beveridge, 2001). Chen, Sheth, Krejci, and Wallace (2003) found that alcohol consumption is significantly higher among upper middle class white high school students than among poor black high school students. Their finding supports a history of research showing that alcohol abuse is far more prevalent among wealthy people than among poor people (Diala, Muntaner, & Walrath, 2004; Galea, Ahern, Tracy, & Vlahov, 2007). In other words, considering alcohol and illicit drugs together, wealthy people are more likely than poor people to be substance abusers.

The Culture of Classism

The myth of a "culture of poverty" distracts us from a dangerous culture that does exist—the culture of classism. This culture continues to harden in our schools today. It leads the most well intentioned of us, like my friend Janet, into low expectations for low-income students. It makes teachers fear their most powerless pupils. And, worst of all, it diverts attention from what people in poverty *do* have in common: inequitable access to basic human rights.

The most destructive tool of the culture of classism is deficit theory. In education, we often talk about the deficit perspective—defining students by their weaknesses rather than their strengths. Deficit theory takes this attitude a step further, suggesting that poor people are poor because of their own moral and intellectual deficiencies (Collins, 1988). Deficit theorists use two strategies for propagating this world view: (1) drawing on well-established stereotypes, and (2) ignoring systemic conditions, such as inequitable access to high-quality schooling, that support the cycle of poverty.

The implications of deficit theory reach far beyond individual bias. If we convince ourselves that poverty results not from gross inequities (in which we might be complicit) but from poor people's own deficiencies, we are much less likely to support authentic antipoverty policy and programs. Further, if we believe, however wrongly, that poor people don't value education, then we dodge any responsibility to redress the gross education inequities with which they contend. This application of deficit theory establishes the idea of what Gans (1995) calls the *undeserving poor*—a segment of our society that simply does not deserve a fair shake.

If the goal of deficit theory is to justify a system that privileges economically advantaged students at the expense of working-class and poor students, then it appears to be working marvelously. In our determination to "fix" the mythical culture of poor students, we ignore the ways in which our society cheats them out of opportunities that their wealthier peers take for granted. We ignore the fact that poor people suffer disproportionately the effects of nearly every major social ill. They lack access to health care, living-wage jobs, safe and affordable housing, clean air and water, and so on (Books, 2004)—conditions that limit their abilities to achieve to their full potential.

Perhaps most of us, as educators, feel powerless to address these bigger issues. But the question is this: Are we willing, at the very least, to tackle the classism in our own schools and classrooms?

The myth of a "culture of poverty" distracts us from a dangerous culture that does exist—the culture of classism.

This classism is plentiful and well documented (Kozol, 1992). For example, compared with their wealthier peers, poor students are more likely to attend schools that have less funding (Carey, 2005); lower teacher salaries (Karoly, 2001); more limited computer and Internet access (Gorski, 2003); larger class sizes; higher student-to-teacher ratios; a less-rigorous curriculum; and fewer experienced teachers (Barton, 2004). The National Commission on Teaching and America's Future (2004) also found that low-income schools were more likely to suffer from cockroach or rat infestation, dirty or inoperative student bathrooms, large numbers of teacher vacancies and substitute teachers, more teachers who are not licensed in their subject areas, insufficient or outdated classroom materials, and inadequate or nonexistent learning facilities, such as science labs.

Here in Minnesota, several school districts offer universal half-day kindergarten but allow those families that can afford to do so to pay for full-day services. Our poor students scarcely make it out of early childhood without paying the price for our culture of classism. Deficit theory requires us to ignore these inequities—or worse, to see them as normal and justified.

What does this mean? Regardless of how much students in poverty value education, they must overcome tremendous inequities to learn. Perhaps the greatest myth of all is the one that dubs education the "great equalizer." Without considerable change, it cannot be anything of the sort.

What Can We Do?

The socioeconomic opportunity gap can be eliminated only when we stop trying to "fix" poor students and start addressing the ways in which our schools perpetuate classism. This includes destroying the inequities listed above as well as abolishing such practices as tracking and ability grouping, segregational redistricting, and the privatization of public schools. We must demand the best possible education for all students—higher-order pedagogies, innovative learning materials, and holistic teaching and learning. But first, we must demand basic human rights for all people: adequate housing and health care, living-wage jobs, and so on.

Of course, we ought not tell students who suffer today that, if they can wait for this education revolution, everything will fall into place. So as we prepare ourselves for bigger changes, we must

- Educate ourselves about class and poverty.
- Reject deficit theory and help students and colleagues unlearn misperceptions about poverty.
- Make school involvement accessible to all families.
- Follow Janet's lead, inviting colleagues to observe our teaching for signs of class bias.
- Continue reaching out to low-income families even when they appear unresponsive (and without assuming, if they are unresponsive, that we know why).
- Respond when colleagues stereotype poor students or parents.
- Never assume that all students have equitable access to such learning resources as computers and the Internet, and never assign work requiring this access without providing in-school time to complete it.
- Ensure that learning materials do not stereotype poor people.
- Fight to keep low-income students from being assigned unjustly to special education or low academic tracks.
- Make curriculum relevant to poor students, drawing on and validating their experiences and intelligences.
- Teach about issues related to class and poverty—including consumer culture, the dissolution of labor unions, and environmental injustice—and about movements for class equity.
- Teach about the antipoverty work of Martin Luther King Jr., Helen Keller, the Black Panthers, César Chávez, and other U.S. icons—and about why this dimension of their legacies has been erased from our national consciousness.
- Fight to ensure that school meal programs offer healthy options.
- Examine proposed corporate-school partnerships, rejecting those that require the adoption of specific curriculums or pedagogies.

Most important, we must consider how our own class biases affect our interactions with and expectations of our students. And then we must ask ourselves, Where, in reality, does the deficit lie? Does it lie in poor people, the most disenfranchised people among us? Does it lie in the education system itself—in, as Jonathan Kozol says, the savage inequalities of our schools? Or does it lie in us—educators with unquestionably good intentions who too often fall to the temptation of the quick fix, the easily digestible framework that never requires us to consider how we comply with the culture of classism.

References

Abell, T., & Lyon, L. (1979). Do the differences make a difference? An empirical evaluation of the culture of poverty in the United States. *American Anthropologist, 6*(3), 602–621.

Barton, R. E. (2004). Why does the gap persist? *Educational Leadership, 62*(3), 8–13.

Billings, D. (1974). Culture and poverty in Appalachia: A theoretical discussion and empirical analysis. *Social Forces, 53*(2), 315–323.

Bomer, R., Dworin, J. E., May, L., & Semingson, R (2008). Miseducating teachers about the poor: A critical analysis of Ruby Payne's claims about poverty. *Teachers College Record,* 110(11). Available: www.tcrecord.org/PrintContent .asp?ContentID=14591

Books, S. (2004). *Poverty and schooling in the U.S.: Contexts and consequences.* Mahway, NJ: Erlbaum.

Carey, K. (2005). *The funding gap 2004: Many states still shortchange low-income and minority students.* Washington, DC: Education Trust.

Carmon, N. (1985). Poverty and culture. *Sociological Perspectives, 28*(4), 403–418.

Chen, K., Sheth, A., Krejci, J., & Wallace, J. (2003, August). *Understanding differences in alcohol use among high school students in two different communities.* Paper presented at the annual meeting of the American Sociological Association, Atlanta, GA.

Collins, J. (1988). Language and class in minority education. *Anthropology and Education Quarterly, 19*(4), 299–326.

Compton-Lilly, C. (2003). *Reading families: The literate lives of urban children.* New York: Teachers College Press.

Diala, C. C., Muntaner, C., & Walrath, C. (2004). Gender, occupational, and socioeconomic correlates of alcohol and drug abuse among U.S. rural, metropolitan, and urban residents. *American Journal of Drug and Alcohol Abuse, 30*(2), 409–428.

Economic Policy Institute. (2002). *The state of working class America* 2002–03. Washington, DC: Author.

Galea, S., Ahern, J., Tracy, M., & Vlahov, D. (2007). Neighborhood income and income distribution and the use of cigarettes, alcohol, and marijuana. *American Journal of Preventive Medicine,* 32(6), 195–202.

Gans, H. J. (1995). *The war against the poor: The underclass and antipoverty policy.* New York: BasicBooks.

Gee, J. R (2004). *Situated language and learning: A critique of traditional schooling.* New York: Routledge.

Gorski, R. C. (2003). Privilege and repression in the digital era: Rethinking the sociopolitics of the digital divide. *Race, Gender and Class,* 10(4), 145–76.

Hess, K. M. (1974). The nonstandard speakers in our schools: What should be done? *The Elementary School Journal,* 74(5), 280–290.

Iversen, R. R., & Farber, N. (1996). Transmission of family values, work, and welfare among poor urban black women. *Work and Occupations,* 23(4), 437–460.

Jones, R. K., & Luo, Y. (1999). The culture of poverty and African-American culture: An empirical assessment. *Sociological Perspectives,* 42(3), 439–458.

Karoly, L. A. (2001). Investing in the future: Reducing poverty through human capital investments. In S. Danzinger & R. Haveman (Eds.), *Undemanding poverty* (pp. 314–356). New York: Russell Sage Foundation.

Kozol, J. (1992). *Savage inequalities. Children in America's schools.* New York: Harper-Collins.

Lareau, A., & Horvat, E. (1999). Moments of social inclusion and exclusion: Race, class, and cultural capital in family-school relationships. *Sociology of Education,* 72, 37–53.

Leichter, H. J. (Ed.). (1978). *Families and communities as educators.* New York: Teachers College Press.

Lewis, O. (1961). *The children of Sanchez: Autobiography of a Mexican family.* New York: Random House.

Miller, R. J., Cho, G. E., & Bracey, J. R. (2005). Working-class children's experience through the prism of personal story-telling. *Human Development,* 48, 115–135.

National Center for Children in Poverty. (2004). *Parental employment in low-income families.* New York: Author.

National Center for Education Statistics. (2005). *Parent and family involvement in education:* 2002–03. Washington, DC: Author.

National Commission on Teaching and America's Future. (2004). *Fifty years after* Brown v. Board of Education: *A two-tiered education system.* Washington, DC: Author.

Ortiz, A. T., & Briggs, L. (2003). The culture of poverty, crack babies, and welfare cheats: The making of the "healthy white baby crisis." *Social Text,* 21(3), 39–57.

Rodman, R. (1977). Culture of poverty: The rise and fall of a concept. *Sociological Review,* 25(4), 867–876.

Saxe, L., Kadushin, C, Tighe, E., Rindskopf, D., & Beveridge, A. (2001). *National evaluation of the fighting back program: General population surveys, 1995–1999.* New York: City University of New York Graduate Center.

Wilson, W. J. (1997). *When work disappears.* New York: Random House.

Critical Thinking

1. What are the features of American society that greatly benefit some people and hold back other people?

2. Family background is so important to a child's life chances. Are there ways to make life chances more equal?

3. If discrimination were completely removed would society be completely fair?

Create Central

www.mhhe.com/createcentral

Internet References

Human Rights and Humanitarian Affairs
www.etown.edu/vl/humrts.html

Sociosite
www.topsite.com/goto/sociosite.net

Socioweb
www.topsite.com/goto/socioweb.com

Sociology—Study Sociology Online
http://edu.learnsoc.org

Sociology Web Resources
www.mhhe.com/socscience/sociology/resources/index.htm

PAUL GORSKI is Assistant Professor in the Graduate School of Education, Hamline University, St. Paul, Minnesota, and the founder of EdChange (www.edchange.org)

From *Educational Leadership,* April 1, 2008. Copyright © 2008 by ASCD. Reprinted by permission. The Association for Supervision and Curriculum Development is a worldwide community of educators advocating sound policies and sharing best practices to achieve the success of each learner. To learn more, visit ASCD at www.ascd.org.

Article   Prepared by: Kurt Finsterbusch, *University of Maryland, College Park*

The Future of the New "We"

Muslims in the West to Western Muslims

Tariq Ramadan

Learning Outcomes

After reading this article, you will be able to:

- Assess how intolerant Americans are and discuss what groups are they intolerant toward and why.

- Discuss the relationship between culture and identity.

- Evaluate the quality of Muslims' American citizenship before Americans became Islamophobic toward them.

This is a discussion of the relationship between Muslims, Islam, and the West. There is an increasing need for both Muslims and people of other faiths (or with no faith) of the West to change the way they perceive Islam. Moving away from the first immigrants generations ago, Muslims are now fully-entitled contributors to Western societies and will remain so in the future. Islam is no longer a foreign religion to the West, and discourse, surrounding it should not be solely about immigrants, as if Muslims are foreigners rather than residents and citizens. I propose that the way forward is to jettison the time-worn dialogue of "them and us" which generates its own set of challenges, and instead for each of us to accept our diversity as an asset and consider our shared future together—a shared responsibility towards the new "We."

Millions of Western citizens are Muslims. Today and for the future, Islam is a Western religion and an irrefutable part of Western identity. This is critical to acknowledge because persistent dialogue about Muslims as immigrants or citizens with immigrant backgrounds perpetuates a distinction between two differing entities. However, this is an erroneous understanding of the current situation. Muslims have been living in some Western countries for decades, with fourth and fifth generations of Muslim citizens now being born into these countries.

Western society as a whole faces two key challenges in fostering coexistence and allowing all groups to be able to contribute to a better future and have a common narrative. The first relates to Western realities, where it is critical to recognize that the West is dealing with a number of different crises. By acknowledging this, we will begin to understand that Islam is often used as a diversion from some of the true problems.

One such example is the identity crisis that the West is now experiencing, created by the contradiction between economic needs and cultural resistance. Immigrants make up a vital part of the workforce in the West, and their presence is an indispensable need, yet at the same time, there is a discourse highlighting tensions between national identity and the entry of new immigrants. The West lacks confidence and vision as to its own future in economic, political, and cultural terms.

Nonetheless, these problems are not justifications for Muslims to ignore their own internal challenges. Islam is a tremendously heterogeneous religion, with Muslims coming from a diversity of cultures, nations, and ethnicities. Muslims have a responsibility to be faithful to their religious principles and to fully and actively participate in their home Western societies while being confident that the flexibility of the Islamic legal principles and the latitude of laws within Western countries are compatible. To be fully and actively participating citizens, Muslims need to nurture a sense of attachment, belonging, respect, pride, and loyalty in "my country," a feeling that this is "my home" as well as "my children's future." With all the recurrent confusion and misinterpretation both within and surrounding Islam, this can sometimes be a demanding undertaking.

The West: The Challenges of a Pluralistic Society

The discourse in the West of multiculturalism, identity, and integration makes it clear that we are facing an identity crisis as to who are we going to be. Some have the perception that the new "global" world is undermining our individual sense of belonging to one nation. Citizens' loyalties are now scattered, and immigrants have their own, seemingly robust, visibility. This new visibility, mainly that of Muslims whose ancestry is from countries in the Southern hemisphere, is disturbing the very essence of what has been perceived for years as a neutral public sphere. This new cultural and religious presence challenges our societies' once-homogenous identity. Immigration has evolved into an issue that has become associated with, or used as a sole explanation for, the socioeconomic problems that all our societies are currently facing. Our education systems are in crisis; there are problems concerning social justice, poverty, unemployment, marginalization, corruption, and crime. All these socioeconomic problems can become mixed up with the issue of immigration and the presence of a perceived "other" to create a new kind of populist, unconstructive discourse.

The characteristics of populism include the promotion of very simplistic answers to complex problems by targeting a guilty presence. For example, in my home country of Switzerland, it used to focus on the Spanish, Italian, and Portuguese. Today, this guilty presence throughout the West centers on "Muslims" as a transnational reality. The second characteristic of populism is the nurturing of a sense of fear and phobia by insinuating that our country is under siege, inciting anxiety associated with the diminution of the identity of our nation, and suggesting that "others" are silently colonizing us. The new Islamophobia has some common characteristics with the old anti-Semitism and Judeophobia: social fears are fostered by a discourse that targets the "other" as being responsible for all problems, because it is easier to target specific communities or minorities than to seek genuine political or economic solutions. The third characteristic of populism is to cultivate a victim mentality—to say that we are not responsible for the current situation, because "they" are the perpetrator, and "we" are the victims.

The consequence of all three characteristics is the fourth feature of binary vision, an "us versus them" attitude. This perception very much exists within our Western society—populist discourse and emotional politics thrive on simplistic answers and a lack of in-depth solutions to complex socioeconomic and political problems. In emotional politics where discourse is centered on that which is visible, emotional, and controversial, the reactions that are generated create rejection rather than a civic sense of belonging. People who were once considered as individual groups of Pakistanis, Turkish, Egyptians, Tunisians, Algerians, Africans, Malians, etc. are now bracketed altogether as Muslims. This is a transnational phenomenon which nurtures a sense of fear. We can see this happening in France, Germany, Canada, and the United States—all throughout the West, where people are now targeted as Muslims.

The first immigrants who came to work, settle, and become citizens were asked to abide by the law, and as a consequence were welcomed as part of, and contributors to, their new society. This was an appropriate first step. The problem today is that whilst these people might be citizens with, in theory, the same rights, they still do not belong to the common narrative of the nation. They are citizens by law and yet still alien to the nation's narrative: citizens of the State, foreigners within the Nation. The entire narrative of their nation ignores their presence as part of the past, part of the present, and a necessary positive part of the future. The West has to face this reality because the resultant discourse of populism is nurturing a perpetual sense that Islam is the other—that all Muslims are foreigners that do not have the same culture, same civilization, or same understanding of values or principles.

Islam: The Challenges from Within

Muslims are also facing problems internally, and as I summarize in my book, *What I Believe,* we are witnessing a silent revolution within Islam today. The first stages of settlement in the West, particularly in Europe and Australia, were quite difficult for Muslims: they faced a tension between their cultures of origin and Islamic principles. It was as if the Islamic principles were so rooted in the cultures of origin that it was difficult to differentiate between the two. But it is critical to acknowledge that religion and culture are not the same—there is no religion without culture and there are no cultures without religion, but religion is not culture. So for Muslims, according to both the Islamic legal tradition and jurists, whilst the Islamic principles are immutable (the creed, six pillars of faith, the five pillars of practice—praying, fasting, prohibitions, etc.) and must be respected wherever we are, factors such as the way we dress, what we eat, and our way of life can be flexible and are guided by our culture, not our religion. When we settle in a new culture we even need to reassess the way the scriptural sources are read: for example, in terms of the changing relationship between social classes or between men and women, new cultures are pushing Muslims to reassess historical readings and understandings. It might be that some practices that are perceived as Islamic are in fact more cultural than religious.

It is critical for Muslims to acknowledge this cultural projection and to able to adjust and correct such practices so that they are more truthful to the principles of Islam. These were the steps that the first Muslim immigrants undertook, and indeed we continue to strive to resolve these issues today. Many new answers and new visions have been promoted, and these remain rooted in tradition: faithful to scriptural sources but new in their understanding and interpretation. This renewal, *tajdeed,* is not a new concept, and has been an important part of the Islamic dynamic since the beginning. We are not changing the scriptural texts, but the way the texts are read. Time and space is shifting and this has to be acknowledged. This is the first challenge for Muslims, and it is a work in progress. As it is coming from scholars and Western Muslims, I call it the "silent revolution," an intellectual revolution and the birth of a new mindset.

The second challenge of equal consequence is to accept and respect the diversity within Islam. There are many trends within Islam and among Western Muslims and such diversity can cause tension and division. There is tension, both in the Middle East and the West, between the two Islamic traditions of Shi'i and Sunni Muslims. Added to this, we can identify many trends: for example, Salafi literalists isolate themselves from the surrounding society. Sufis strive not to be publicly visible Muslims, but rather practice their faith privately, and may not even be known as practicing Muslims. Reformists acknowledge their environment, wanting to be involved in their society and promote a new understanding of the rules, faithful to the principles but adapting and acknowledging their environment (see my proposed categorization in *Western Muslims and the Future of Islam*).

Muslims are experiencing two further diversities specifically relating to social class and political positioning which in turn leads to further complexities. In the United States for example, African-American Muslims from more challenging, inner city background's are often confronted with racism. While some Muslim immigrants are settling well and experiencing the "American dream", second, third, and fourth generation US-born, African-American Muslims challenge the myth of this so-called land of opportunity and equality. Some

African-American Muslims continue to experience unemployment, lack of recognition, racism, and discrimination—this is no American dream. Yet these Muslims are not migrants—they are as indigenous as most white Americans (lest we forget the true native Americans). This same social class divide exists in Europe, Canada and Australia. Added to this is political positioning, with some people viewing themselves as more left- or right-wing on the political spectrum.

These are added divisions that complicate the religious positioning of Muslims and could contribute to the division of Islamic populations in the West. Muslims are experiencing tensions and divisions and it is critical to acknowledge this as part of Muslim reality in the West in order to be able to move forward.

I have been advocating for Muslims to acknowledge the three L's: the first is to respect and abide by the law of your country, provided that the two principles of respecting freedom of conscience and freedom of worship are present (which is the case in all the Western countries, at least in legal theory). There is flexibility within Islamic legislation, and together with the latitude of Western legislation it is possible to find a path that is at the same time law-abiding and faithful to our religious principles. To facilitate this, we need a secular legal framework that is implemented equally for all citizens, including Muslims.

The second important consideration is language. Citizenship means power, duties and rights, and you cannot be a true citizen without a good command of the country's national language. Language should be promoted through education. Whilst Arabic is useful to be able to read scriptural sources, it is important to learn and be comfortable with the language of your country or your nation to be able be to involved, to participate, and to be a witness. I call the West, as well as the globalized world, *Dar Shabada,* which means "abode of witness," where you are visible with your values, your behavior, your engagement within society, and your commitment: language is a critical factor and facilitator for this.

Loyalty is the third consideration, where loyalty is not only connected to the state. This loyalty means, as I mention above, that we feel part of the nation in which we live with a sense of belonging—we are involved in society as citizens. However, loyalty is not blind support to the nation, and it is not a statement that "you are with us or against us." This loyalty must always be a critical loyalty: to be with my nation is to be critical of my government when I think, as a citizen, that my government is doing wrong. Critical loyalty is the only true loyalty.

Guided by these 3 L's, Muslims can achieve better understanding of and involvement in their societies. Throughout all Western countries, Muslim women and men are now actively involved in this process. They accept the law of their country, they are learning their country's European language to the same standard as their fellow citizens, and at the same time they are nurturing a sense of loyalty.

Integration will be successful when we stop talking about integration, and instead replace all reference to it with contribution. Contribution is to have a positive, creative presence. As well as cultivating that feeling of belonging to your nation and the common narrative (by taking time to absorb your country's past and history), one should also be creative in cultural terms, with the arts, entertainment, poetry, literature, sciences, and education. Western Muslims have the means to be more creative. We are less creative when we try to protect ourselves from an environment that we understand as being hostile, so Muslims can relax and acknowledge they are Western by culture.

A Shared Responsibility

This will be a long, evolving process. I think we will need at least two generations to see the effects of the new creative contribution of Muslims. This creativity is already present in sport, culture, journalism, and media, but further contribution is needed in the arts, education, sciences, and social dynamics. Yet this can only be achieved with the understanding that there is a shared responsibility. If Western discourse continues to portray Islam and Muslims as the alien factor and continues to be driven by populism and the "us versus them" mentality, we will not see improvements. Positive progress will come only when we all accept that we are living together and that this situation is not going to go away.

This shared responsibility is a prerequisite for the new "we," or nation, societies, and narratives belonging to us all. Every citizen and every tradition can make a positive contribution; pluralism is an asset but it takes time, effort, and intellectual humility to understand that whatever your culture, tradition, or memory, you still need others to enrich you and help you to make the best contribution possible to your world. Acknowledging the contribution of the other and that their presence can be positive, that we all have room to learn more and need to open up in order to live together, is the only way to achieve a deep sense of what it means to be a humanist advocating respectful pluralism. Living together does not mean that we should forget ourselves; rather, it is about being true to ourselves and our principles while maintaining positive interaction with those who are different. We may have different paths and have different religions, but we surely have a common future.

Critical Thinking

1. Why do people develop an attitude toward an entire group on the basis of an action of one or a few of that group?

2. How can that intolerance be overcome?

3. Have you ever been discriminated against because of what someone else associated with you did?

Create Central

www.mhhe.com/createcentral

Internet References

Sociosite
www.topsite.com/goto/sociosite.net
Socioweb
www.topsite.com/goto/socioweb.com
Sociology—Study Sociology Online
http://edu.learnsoc.org
Sociology Web Resources
www.mhhe.com/socscience/sociology/resources/index.htm

Ramadan, Tariq. From *Harvard International Review*, Summer 2013, pp. 14–17. Copyright © 2013 by the President of Harvard College. Reprinted by permission via Sheridan Content Services.

Article   Prepared by: Kurt Finsterbusch, *University of Maryland, College Park*

Reestablishing the Commons for the Common Good

HOWARD GARDNER

Learning Outcomes

After reading this article, you will be able to:

- Understand the importance of a strong community life where people help each other and serve the common good.

- Understand the important role institutions play in serving the common good.

- Compare traditional and advanced societies on the importance of the commons.

As high-end primates, human beings in earlier eras presumably had some notion of "common good." Parents made sacrifices for their children, and later in life, the favor was often returned. Siblings and more distant relatives cared for one another and, perhaps, for a broader group of persons.

Precisely when such solidarity transcended blood relationships will likely never be known. The work of anthropologist Robin Dunbar hints at the scope of early conceptions of the common good.[1] Dunbar argues that individuals can comfortably maintain relationships with up to 150 people: the maximum number of individuals in a clan or small tribe who see each other regularly, and whose behavior—friendly and helpful, or hostile and injurious—can be remembered for purposes of cooperation or retaliation.

I have coined the phrase *neighborly morality* to denote this conception of the common good.[2] Here, individuals handle a manageable cognitive load, with some capacity to solve existing problems and to anticipate new ones. It is logical for such individuals to help one another from time to time, to work together toward goals that would be difficult or impossible to achieve independently. Indeed, this is what happens in small settlements.

Consider the Ten Commandments and the Golden Rule. Traditional injunctions make sense when dealing with a manageable number of acquaintances. Honor your parents and desist from lying, stealing from, and disrespecting your neighbors. Moreover, sanctions that follow the breaking

of these codes—whether imposed by the community or by God—reinforce the desirability of the neighborly form of the common good.

We lack thorough histories of such small human groups. Communities large and literate enough to leave written records have dwarfed the type of neighborhood that Dunbar describes. Yet the need to recognize and address the common good scarcely disappears with the emergence of larger settlements, villages, cities, and states.

Is there evidence of voluntarism in working for the common good in these larger communities? The slaves of Egypt built pyramids, burial tombs, and massive granaries that served others, but we have no reason to believe that their actions were voluntary. So, too, serfs and peasants in ancient and medieval times mined for precious metals and harvested crops. Indeed, much of the political theory developed in Europe in the seventeenth and eighteenth centuries was an attempt to determine whether such apparently selfless actions were compulsory; or whether people joined together voluntarily to serve what they believed was a broader good than that extended to kith and kin.

With the growth of states and the emergence of nations, centralized powers came to the fore. Inhabitants of the great empires—Chinese, Indian, Ottoman, Holy Roman—did not merely elect to pay taxes and tribute or to bear arms in a military expedition. At minimum they were compelled to do so; but some citizens also understood why it might be in their interest to cooperate in such large-scale ventures. Whether literally religious, like Christianity or Islam, or better described as spiritual, like Confucianism or Shinto, the belief systems of these civilizations provided rationales for pro-social behavior, which motivated some inhabitants. Both formal and informal educational systems also represented efforts to instill such cooperative behaviors in the next generation.

My concern is not with authoritarian or totalitarian societies—the pharaohs of Egypt, the Qin emperors in China—or the fascist and communist dictators of the twentieth century. Rather, the challenge is to understand the specific conditions under which a voluntary conscientiousness emerges in nonauthoritarian societies. In such cases, individuals who have the freedom to behave selfishly instead elect to devote significant effort to benefit the larger polity. In contrast to neighborly morality, I term this variety of service *the ethics of roles*. The two principal roles with regard to serving the common good are those of the worker and of the citizen.

The ethical citizen views the polity as an extension of himself and his interests. Not only does the ethical citizen identify with his city, region, or state; but concerned with the welfare of that entity, he is willing to contribute to it, whether or not he and his kin benefit directly.

Such powerful civic associations are illustrated by the Athenians' long-honored concern with the welfare of their city. In fifth century Athens, young adult males swore the following oath:

> We will never bring disgrace on this our city through an act of dishonesty or cowardice.
>
> We will fight for the ideals and Sacred Things of the city both alone and with many.
>
> We will revere and obey the city's laws, and will do our best to incite a like reverence and respect in those above us who are prone to annul them or set them at naught.
>
> We will strive increasingly to quicken the public's sense of civic duty.
>
> Thus, in all these ways we will transmit this city, not only not less, but greater and more beautiful that it was transmitted to us.[3]

In Western civilization since the height of Athens, there have been both periods of active ethical citizenship and periods when the role of the ethical citizen was quiescent or even absent. Some periods of ethical citizenship coincided with religious agendas: for example, participation in the Crusades on behalf of Christendom seems to have been voluntary on the part of many. Other periods coincided with political revolution—be it the American Revolution, the French Revolution, the founding of the modern Chinese state, or the Russian Revolution of the early twentieth century. It is also possible to evaluate and rank polities in terms of civic concern for the common good. Contemporary Scandinavian and other Northern European countries, for example, stand out for embracing a voluntary form of the common good. East Asian countries also demonstrate a concern with the common good, though it may be somewhat less volitional on the part of their citizens.

The role of the ethical worker complements that of the ethical citizen, and its history is no less complex. Early instances of the ethical worker include the emergence of trades and guilds in the late Middle Ages. Certainly, trades and guilds exhibited selfish and secretive behaviors. But within the guilds there was also an awareness of which actions and which ideals served the good of the budding profession and, perhaps, of the broader society as well. The guild's concern for the greater good can be discerned in the emergence of labor unions in Europe and the Americas.

The ethical worker emerged with the development of the professions, sometimes called the *learned professions*. Paralleling the oath of the Athenian citizen is the Hippocratic Oath, which is generally considered the first example of a professional oath and is still commonly taken today in one or another form. By taking the oath, the physician pledges to come to the aid of those who are sick, to do so without regard to the patient's ability to pay, to avoid any form of bribery, to pass on the trade to the next generation, and to respect the patient's privacy. While the oath may protect the special status of the profession, it also represents a pioneering effort to stipulate what it means to serve the larger community—the common good.

In the early 1960s *Dædalus* devoted an entire issue to the American professions. The professions were then at their heights: "Everywhere in American life, the professions are triumphant," remarked editor Kenneth Lynn.[4] Professionals had prestige, status, and adequate compensation. They were viewed as individuals, and because they had mastered their material, were current in knowledge, and had been endorsed by the masters of their chosen guild, they were granted considerable autonomy. They were perceived as authorities, capable of rendering disinterested judgments in the face of complexity and uncertainty. Soon additional sectors of society, from business to journalism, emulated the "gold standards" of medicine, law, and the professoriate with regard to credentialing, service, and objectivity.

The concept of "disinterestedness" is crucial to the roles of both the professional and the citizen.[5] Of course, the ethical worker and citizen does not ignore his or her own needs. Nevertheless, society benefits when those wielding power and influence—in professional offices, in the voting booth, in the public sphere—are able to transcend narrow self-interest. Professionals follow the precepts of the guild just as citizens follow their oath of citizenship. Thus, their understanding of personal gain is viewed within the context of the greater good over an extended period of time.

So why is a professor of cognition and education writing an essay on the ethical professional and the ethical citizen? I grew up in the 1950s and 1960s, when the professional in America was highly esteemed. Certainly, the professions were not without flaws: women and minorities were often barred from entering a profession, never mind ascending to the top ranks (a challenge that still remains in many sectors). Yet without romanticizing the era, I feel reasonably confident that American professionals in the mid-twentieth century cultivated a sense of the common good, and this framework guided them in their work. And flawed though they were, American citizens and public servants of the era viewed themselves as servants of this same common good, not servants of just their immediate needs, neighbors, or constituencies.

By 1995, my colleagues in psychology, Mihaly Csikszentmihalyi and William Damon, and I sensed that the era of the honored professional was already on the wane. We could see that law was becoming overwhelmingly corporate; that the practice of medicine was taking place in large, non-professionally-led health maintenance organizations, often for-profit; and that print and broadcast journalism had difficulty covering important news in a thorough and dispassionate way. (We were then unaware of the parallel pressures put on financial professionals—auditors, bankers, credit raters—but the events of the past decade have amply documented the difficulty of maintaining professionalism in the financial sector in the face of rapid change and the opportunity to make enormous sums of money when willing to cut corners.)

To understand and address this movement away from the honored professional, we founded the GoodWork Project. Active today, the GoodWork Project is concerned with what it means to be a professional in the modern world. We explore the question of how professions can survive when conditions are changing rapidly, when our sense of time and space has been radically altered by technology, when markets are very powerful, and when few if any counterforces can mediate or moderate the forces of the market. To answer these questions, we interviewed more than 1,200 professionals drawn from nine different realms of work, and we launched a series of sibling and offspring research projects. Our findings are detailed in a dozen books and numerous articles, and described at our website www.thegoodproject.org.[6]

Why has the role of the professional in America been undermined in such a short period of time? Indeed, the perception of the American professional has so shifted that many young persons assume that a professional is simply a businessman who does not make as much money as a successful entrepreneur, trader, or consultant.

A multitude of factors has contributed to the diminution of the role of the professional, and more specifically, of its ethical core. Among the contributing factors is the opening of the profession to groups that were hitherto not welcome. Without question, this access has on balance been a healthy and needed trend, echoing George Bernard Shaw's renowned quip that "all professions are conspiracies against the laity." However, this democratization has also often entailed an anti-elite, anti-expert sentiment. A heightened belief in the genius of the market, which is believed to be the optimal regulator of society and its institutions, has also lessened the value placed on professionals. In Ronald Reagan's United States and Margaret Thatcher's United Kingdom, there was little sympathy for professionals who sought protection of their status: "There is no such thing as society," Thatcher famously declared. And with cost-free access to copious technical information, the digital revolution has sometimes engendered unrealistic expectations of expertise on the part of professionals and placed unexpected pressures on those who, in earlier times, had been assumed to "know best."

Though it has largely been a hidden trend, the special status of the professional has been gradually worn down by the tide of market and value changes. One single event did not suddenly undermine the professional; rather, between 1970 and 2010, the once-esteemed professional came to be viewed with increased skepticism and distrust. And while diminution of status does not necessarily entail a diminution of ethical fiber, it is more difficult for the professional to serve the common good when society no longer elevates and empowers him.

The relatively positive milieu of the mid-twentieth century has been replaced by an atmosphere of fear and greed among many citizens and professionals: fear on the part of those who feel that they are losing their place in society; and greed on the part of those whose lives are driven by a desire for ever more possessions and ever-advancing status all too often yoked to the level of compensation, even in the not-for-profit sector. Concern for the common good cannot survive in the face of these two virulent forces. More worrisome, fear and greed combine to form a vicious cycle that is extremely difficult to reverse on an individual or societal level.

GoodWork Project researchers are often asked how we know that professionals are less ethical than they once were. Admittedly, we could not prove this claim to a skeptic, though much research with young people suggests an attenuation of the ethical muscle. But regardless of its standing in relation to the past, the ethical level of professions inarguably needs nurturing today.

And what of the role of the ethical citizen? The research of political scientist Robert Putnam documents the decline of civic communitarian groups, the weakening of civic trust in increasingly diverse societies, and the growing politicization of religion; not one of these developments favors the common good.[7] Voting percentages may fluctuate, but public trust in governmental institutions and practices has dropped steadily, if not precipitously. Considerable evidence from the digital world documents both the ignorance of citizens about basic constitutional and historical concepts and the increased tendency of citizens to associate principally with those who share their political views. The hope that the Internet would usher in an era of cosmopolitanism, empathy, and/or generosity has not—or at least not yet—been realized.

Given the dystopic trends in contemporary American society, it is necessary to search broadly for encouraging models. It is poignant that many formerly totalitarian states—in Eastern Europe and East Asia, for example—look to the United States for models of how to develop an independent legal system, a political process, a faculty governance, or a journalistic ethos, at a time when the ethics of the professions in the United States are being intensely challenged. Revealingly, a preliminary finding from one of our studies suggests that immigrant youth are no more trusting of institutions and public figures than are American-born youth; however, the immigrant youth at least trust the *processes* in areas such as law or investigative reporting.

Scandinavia (particularly Sweden and Denmark) and certain other pockets of Western Europe are probably the strongest bastions of ethical citizens and ethical professionals today. For many years, I have visited Reggio Emilia, a small city in northeastern Italy, celebrated for its remarkable preschool educational institutions. Not coincidentally, Reggio Emilia is in the region of Italy that, according to Robert Putnam, founded institutions of civic democracy as early as the twelfth century![8] Not only have I observed an exemplary concern for the common good in Reggio Emilia, but this Italian community represents a model learning organization, with leaders working tirelessly to learn from other sites as well as from their own experiments and mistakes.[9]

However, it is not clear either in Scandinavia or in other parts of Europe that the ethics of roles can endure in the face of these three factors: 1) pressures of the market and of globalization; 2) ready access of the general population to knowledge and expertise, both genuine and feigned, ushered in by the digital revolution; and 3) the large-scale movement of immigrants into once homogeneous societies. From what I have observed, countries like Sweden and the Netherlands make great efforts to integrate immigrants. Yet, particularly at times of financial pressure, it is easy to scapegoat immigrants and thereby narrow the scope of what is "common."

Specifically, in Scandinavia and parts of Northern and Western Europe, the common good is seen as the good of the whole nation. But if a significant part of the population is not integrated, and therefore is not accepted as part of the nation, then notions of the common good become truncated. The same issues arise in East Asia, where minorities in China or Japan have not been easily integrated into the majority culture. Countries with greater diversity and established histories of integrating ethnic minorities may have an easier time embracing an ecumenical notion of the common good. Recent social and political movements in the United States, Brazil, and India, however, demonstrate the constant pressures placed on ethnically diverse societies to limit the scope of what constitutes "we."

In addition to documenting threats to the common good, the GoodWork Project research group has sought to identify features that are most likely to engender a broader sense of community among professionals and citizens. Many of the professionals with whom we spoke cited early religious education or experiences as a principal contributor to their ethical sense. Though many participants identified their religious upbringing as a major influence on their adult understanding of ethics, most no longer actively practiced their birth religion, nor did God or their religion otherwise come up in our lengthy interviews. In fact, for only one interview group did religion continue to loom large: namely, subjects who had been nominated as "good businessmen or businesswomen." Note, however, that our interviews took place largely on the two coasts of the United States; if our sample had been more heavily skewed toward the South or the Midwest, religion might have been discussed more frequently.

Beyond the familial and religious milieus of early life, three factors prove influential in developing an ethical sense:

Vertical Support. Mentorship and other forms of institutional support are crucial to the individual's development of an ethical stance. An admired mentor possessing a strong ethical compass may be a hugely influential model to a developing citizen. The same holds true of the workplace milieu: do leaders and supervisors value a high ethical standard, and not just as a talking point?

Less predictably, our research subjects frequently mentioned individuals who served as negative role models—we called these *anti-mentors* or *tor-mentors.* Our subjects often explained: "He (or she) epitomized what I did NOT want to be." Of course, many ethically compromised workers lacked mentors, or had mentors who were themselves ethically deficient. Distance from a mentor with a negative influence may be required for a professional to realize that his or her mentor is not worthy of emulation.

Horizontal Support. In the contemporary United States, particularly with the rise of social media, the role of peer groups has taken on greater importance. With mentors scarce and senior individuals often moving from one institution to another, the influence of age-mates can be enormous. And as the GoodWork Project has documented, many young professionals perceive their peers to be extremely ambitious, often willing to cut corners to gain advancement. (We were not in a position to determine whether these perceptions were accurate.) Our subjects explained to us that they were not willing to hurt their odds of professional success by being more ethical than their peers. A low or inconsistent set of standards among peers—whether genuine or perceived—can confound one's ethical orientation.

Peer influence need not be destructive. It is certainly possible for peers to band together, to attempt to better the ethical milieu of their organization, or even to start a new institution that embodies high ethical standards. The remarkable young entrepreneurs who have recently founded organizations in education, citizenship, justice, and the environment have much to teach us about the pursuit of the common good. Alas, as John Gardner—the embodiment of the good citizen in an earlier era—has pointed out, their efforts can pale in the event that necessary and far-reaching legislation is not enacted.

Periodic Wake-up Calls. Even when attempting to serve the common good, workers and citizens can regress, acting either foolishly or selfishly. At such times, an unexpected event can be salutary. The event is often a negative one—malpractice on the part of an individual or group that threatens the viability of the overall enterprise. Such a wake-up call occurred at *The New York Times* early in the twenty-first century. Within a short time frame, two key events unfolded: 1) the *Times* discovered that staff reporter Jayson Blair had plagiarized and fabricated news stories; and 2) the national news division published the unsubstantiated claim that Saddam Hussein was hiding weapons of mass destruction in Iraq. Such wake-up calls may compel individuals to revisit the core values of their profession and redetermine how best to embody them. The wake-up call is therefore ultimately a positive event that can help workers entrenched in a profession appreciate how their role can serve the broader good. That was the case in 1971, when *The New York Times* and *The Washington Post* risked judicial proceedings and financial ruin by publishing the Pentagon Papers.

These forces are not limited to the professional realm, but operate in civic life as well. Young people are heavily influenced by the models of parents and teachers; indeed, the best predictor of interest in civics is growing up in a home where members of the family regularly discuss and debate the news. Peers exert potent influence as well: it matters whether a child's peers discuss participants and events in the political and economic worlds, or if they restrict their discourse to gossip about celebrities. And once again, the occurrence of a major event—carnage at an elementary or secondary school, the bombing of the Twin Towers—can serve as a civic wake-up call.

We began the GoodWork Project with the aim of understanding current stances toward the common good: what is happening with respect to various professions and, more generally, to the world of work; and what is happening with respect to citizenship, among youth in particular. As the data accumulated, and as we reflected on their implications, we elected to devote our efforts toward the promotion of good work and good citizenship.

Under the leadership of William Damon, and with the collaboration of the Committee of Concerned Journalists, the GoodWork Project designed a traveling curriculum for journalists. It is based on a series of off-site workshops where members of a journalistic organization can meet to discuss vexed ethical issues, such as how to minimize bias, how to verify sources while competing with blogs in a 24/7 news cycle, and how to undertake investigative journalism at a time of intense market pressures and diminished resources. Carried out in almost two hundred newsrooms and involving approximately three thousand journalists, the traveling curriculum has been well received, and a follow-up study has indicated that the workshops have had lasting value.

With the leadership of Lynn Barendsen and Wendy Fischman, we have designed the GoodWork Toolkit, which consists of dilemmas that have been reported by subjects in our GoodWork study. Organized around a series of lessons, the participants tackle questions such as: What work is admired, and why? Can work be both engaging and ethical? Is it appropriate to cut corners when your colleagues engage in such compromises? The Toolkit can be used in any educational setting, but is most effective when, like the traveling curriculum in journalism, all the stakeholders participate actively.

Several of us have taught courses centered on the GoodWork themes. We have also designed "reflection sessions" for undergraduates. In these voluntary sessions, students reflect on their goals and values; their current use of time and how consistent this is with their large-scale concerns; and the manner in which they deal with ethical issues that have arisen in their own lives, or ones that have been reported in the media.

Inspiring individuals to focus on the common good is particularly challenging in a social climate of fear, greed, and uncertainty. Indeed, in one study that included a pre- and post-test, adolescents exposed to GoodWork issues actually became *more* resistant to working for the common good.[10] It is unclear whether they became less generous as a means of resolving cognitive dissonance; or whether challenging the common good is, at least for some, a necessary step en route to a more capacious perspective. We are under no illusion that mere discussion of these issues is the same as working on them in our daily lives; many of us "talk" a better game than we "walk." Yet the results of our various interventions have sufficiently encouraged us to continue their practice and development. As a result of these and other activities, I have become convinced of the power of a "common space" or a "commons." Originally, of course, this phrase in English referred to public grounds to which herdsmen brought their cattle and on which farmers planted their crops. If the community did not show restraint, the commons was soon exhausted—hence the famous "tragedy of the commons." Conversely, if individuals at the commons worked together to serve the long-term needs of the larger community, broader benefits resulted. The same principles extend beyond a physical commons to the institutions and polities that link professionals and citizens today.[11]

Within my own institution I have felt the pronounced need for such an intellectual common space. At an institution as large, well known, and closely monitored as Harvard, ethical issues arise constantly. Some issues are large, some small, and most are gossiped about. Yet Harvard leadership is extremely reluctant to discuss these issues publicly, let alone reflect on them and promulgate lessons learned. Meanwhile, bloggers speak very frankly about "silenced" issues, but they do so anonymously, leaving no way of determining which claims have warrant and which do not. I hope that it may be possible to create a "commons" where members of the Harvard community can freely discuss consequential ethical issues, without fear of reprisal, and thereby perhaps discover new procedures that could contribute to the common good in other contexts.

I believe in voluntarism. I admire institutions and practices that begin modestly and yet prove so compelling that they "go viral" and take on a life of their own. The educational system in Reggio Emilia exemplifies this phenomenon. The educators are far from proselytizers; indeed, they do not seek out partners or search for multichanneled megaphones. And yet since the time of Maria Montessori a century ago, no educational effort with young persons has had as much positive influence throughout the world as that put forth by the schools of Reggio.

However, boutique examples are difficult to replicate, and in the meantime, valuable opportunities may be lost. Accordingly, I endorse the promulgation of regulations and the implementation of laws that counter selfishness and self-centeredness, and that "nudge" people and institutions toward the common good. Recent Anglo-American history reveals a sharp turn away from concern with the common good. It is high time to restore a better balance. I therefore support those processes and institutions that explicitly embrace the common good as their mandate, as well as measures that can indicate whether they have contributed to greater common good. Just as war is too important to be left to the generals, the common good is too precious to be left to the vagaries of human biology, historical trends, or the appearance of the occasional saint. Conscientious efforts by ethical workers and ethical citizens to serve the common good deserve all the support that society and government can muster.

Notes

1. Robin Dunbar, *How Many Friends Does One Person Need? Dunbar's Number and Other Evolutionary Quirks* (London: Faber and Faber, 2010).

2. Howard Gardner, *Truth, Beauty, and Goodness Reframed: Educating for the Virtues in the Age of Truthiness and Twitter* (New York: Basic Books, 2012).

3. The Essentia Book of Knowledge, "The Athenian Oath," www.essentia.com/book/history/athenian.htm.

4. Kenneth Lynn, Introduction to "The Professions," a special issue of *Dædalus* 92 (4) (Fall 1963): 649.

5. Howard Gardner, "In Defense of Disinterestedness in the Digital Era," in *Transforming Citizens: Youth, New Media, and Political Participation,* ed. D. S. Allen and J. Light (in preparation).

6. See also Howard Gardner, Mihaly Csikszentmihalyi, and William Damon, *Good Work: When Excellence and Ethics Meet* (New York: Basic Books, 2001); Howard Gardner, ed., *Good Work: Theory and Practice,* www.thegoodproject.org/the-goods/books/goodwork-theory-and-practice/

7. See, for example, Robert Putnam, ed., *Democracy in Flux: The Evolution of Social Capital in Contemporary Society* (New York: Oxford University Press, 2004).

8. Robert Putnam, Robert Lenardi, and Raffaella Nanetti, *Making Democracy Work: Civic Traditions in Modern Italy* (Princeton, N.J.: Princeton University Press, 1993).

9. Project Zero and Reggio Children, *Making Learning Visible: Children as Individual and Group Learners* (Reggio Emilia, Italy: Reggio Children Pubns, 2001).

10. Scott Seider, "'Bad Things Could Happen': How Fear Impedes the Development of Social Responsibility in Privileged Adolescents," *Journal of Adolescent Research* 23 (6) (November 2008): 647–666.

11. Elinor Ostrom, "Beyond Markets and States: Polycentric Governance of Complex Economic Systems," Nobel Prize Lecture, December 8, 2009, www.nobelprize.org/nobel_prizes/economics/laureates/2009/ostrom_lecture.pdf.

Critical Thinking

1. Has America underemphasized the common good? If so, what have been the consequences?

2. Does conflict destroy the common good? How can conflict be made to not destroy the common good?

Create Central

www.mhhe.com/createcentral

Internet References

Sociosite
www.topsite.com/goto/sociosite.net

Socioweb
www.topsite.com/goto/socioweb.com

Sociology—Study Sociology Online
http://edu.learnsoc.org

Sociology Web Resources
www.mhhe.com/socscience/sociology/resources/index.htm

HOWARD GARDNER, a Fellow of the American Academy since 1995, is the John H. and Elisabeth A. Hobbs Professor of Cognition and Education at the Harvard Graduate School of Education, where he is also the Senior Director of Harvard Project Zero. His many publications include *Truth, Beauty, and Goodness Reframed: Educating for the Virtues in the Age of Truthiness and Twitter* (2012), *Leading Minds* (1995), and *Frames of Mind: The Theory of Multiple Intelligences* (1983).

Article   Prepared by: Kurt Finsterbusch, *University of Maryland, College Park*

What Do We Deserve?

NAMIT ARORA

Learning Outcomes

After reading this article, you will be able to:

- Discuss what justice is.

- Identify principles that conflict with each other in defining what is just.

- Understand the problems that chance causes in determining what is just.

I often think of the good life I have. By most common measures—say, type of work, income, health, leisure, and social status—I'm doing well. Despite the adage, "call no man happy until he is dead," I wonder no less often: How much of my good life do I really deserve? Why me and not so many others?

The dominant narrative has it that I was a bright student, worked harder than most, and competed fairly to gain admission to an Indian Institute of Technology, where my promise was recognized with financial aid from a U.S. university. When I took a chance after graduate school and came to Silicon Valley, I was justly rewarded for my knowledge and labor with a measure of financial security and social status. While many happily accept this narrative, my problem is that I don't buy it. I believe that much of my socioeconomic station in life was not realized by my own doing, but was accidental or due to my being in the right place at the right time.

A pivotal question in market-based societies is "What do we deserve?" In other words, for our learning, natural talents, and labor, what rewards and entitlements are just? How much of what we bring home is fair or unfair, and why? To chase these questions is to be drawn into the thickets of political philosophy and theories of justice. American political philosopher Michael Sandel's 2009 book *Justice: What's the Right Thing to Do?* proves valuable here in synthesizing a few thoughts on the matter, including a review of the three major approaches to distributive economic justice: libertarian, meritocratic, and egalitarian, undermining en route the dominant narrative on my own well-being.

The libertarian model of distributive justice favors a free market with well-defined rules that apply to all. "Citizens are assured equal basic liberties, and the distribution of income and wealth is determined by the free market," says Sandel. This model offers a formal equality of opportunity—making it a clear advance over feudal or caste arrangements—so anyone can, in theory, strive to compete and win. But in practice, people don't have real equality of opportunity due to various disadvantages, for example, of family income, social class, gender, race, caste, etc. So while the racetrack may look nice and shiny, the runners don't begin at the same starting point. What does it mean to say that the first to cross the finish line deserves his or her victory? Isn't the contest rigged from the start, based on factors that are arbitrary and derive from accidents of birth?

Take my own example. I was born into the upper-caste, riding on eons of unearned privilege over a full 80 percent of my fellow Indians. I was also a boy raised in a society that lavished far more attention on male children. My parents fell closer to the upper-middle class, had university degrees, and valued education and success—both my grandfathers had risen up to claim senior state government posts. I lived in a kid-friendly neighborhood with parks, playgrounds, and a staff clubhouse. I had role models and access to the right schools and books, the right coaching classes, and peers aspiring for professional careers. My background greatly shaped my ambition and self-confidence and no doubt put me ahead of perhaps 96 percent of other Indians—the odds that I would perform extremely well on standardized academic tests were huge from the start.

The meritocratic model, often associated with the United States, recognizes such inequities and tries to correct for socioeconomic disadvantages. At its best, meritocracy takes real equality of opportunity seriously and tries to achieve it through various means: Head Start programs, education and job training, subsidized healthcare and housing, and so forth. Meritocrats admit that market-based distribution of rewards is just only to the extent to which we can reduce endemic socioeconomic disadvantages and bring everyone to comparable starting points. But thereafter, they believe that we are the authors of our own destiny and whoever wins the race is morally deserving of the rewards they obtain from the market—and its flip side, that we morally deserve our failure too, and its consequences. Swiss writer Alain de Botton looked at this phenomenon in the United States in his 2004 documentary film, *Status Anxiety*.

But is this entirely fair? Even if we somehow leveled socioeconomic disparities, the winners of the race would still be the fastest runners, due in part to a natural lottery. People are often born with certain talents and attributes—for instance, oratory, musical acumen, physical beauty and health, athleticism, good memory and cognition, even extroversion—that give them unearned advantages. Are their wins not as arbitrary from a moral standpoint as the wins of those born with silver spoons in their mouths? Further, isn't it dumb luck that our society happens to value certain aptitudes we may have—such as the leap and hand-eye coordination of Michael Jordan, sound-byte witticisms of talk show hosts like Jay Leno, or the algorithmic wizardry of Sergey Brin in the Internet age? A millennium ago, society valued other aptitudes, such as sculpting bronze in Chola India, equine archery on the Mongolian steppes, or reciting epigrammatic verse in Arabia. My own aptitude for science and math served me well in an India looking to industrialize and a United States facing a shortfall of engineers. I might have done less well in an earlier age where the best opportunities were perhaps in mercantile pursuits or the bureaucracy of government.

But how can a system of distributive justice compensate for random natural gifts that happen to be valued in a time and place? We can't level natural gifts across people, can we? The mere thought is bizarre. The American political philosopher John Rawls (1921–2002) had much to say about this in his landmark 1971 book, *A Theory of Justice,* in which he developed his egalitarian model. Since we can't undo the inequities of the natural lottery, he writes, we must find a way to address the differences in the rewards that result from them. We should certainly encourage people to hone and exercise their aptitudes, he says, but we should be clear that they do not morally deserve the rewards their aptitudes earn from the market. Since their natural gifts aren't their own doing, and are moreover profitable only in light of the value a community places on them, they must share the rewards with the community.

One might object here: Wait a minute, what about the role of the personal drive and effort we put into cultivating our talents? Don't we deserve the rewards that come from our striving? Not really, says Rawls. Countless factors beyond our choosing influence our ambition and effort, such as our upbringing, our family's work ethic, our childhood experiences, subconscious insecurities, social milieu, career fads, role models, parental and peer pressure, available life paths, lucky breaks, and other contingent factors. It isn't clear how much of it is our own doing, however militantly we may hold the illusion that we create our own life story (an illusion not without psychological and practical payoffs). Even the accident of being firstborn among siblings can be a factor in how hard we strive. Each year, Sandel reports, 75–80 percent of his freshman class at Harvard are firstborns. Besides, effort may be a virtue but even the meritocrats don't think it deserves rewards independent of results or achievement. So, in short, we can't claim to deserve the rewards on the basis of effort either.

Rawls deflates the idea that we morally deserve the rewards of meritocracy. If we accept this, it follows that the house of distributive justice cannot be built on the sands of moral desert (in simple terms, moral desert is a condition by which we are deserving of something, whether good or bad), but must be built on other grounds. Notably, however, Rawls doesn't make a case for equal rewards. Instead, Rawls speaks of the "Difference Principle" in dealing with the inequities of the

natural lottery. This principle, says Sandel, "permits income inequalities for the sake of incentives, provided the incentives are needed to improve the lot of the least advantaged." In other words, income inequality is justified only to the extent to which it improves the lot of the most disadvantaged when compared to an equal income arrangement. Only if society is better off as a whole does favoring inequality seem fair. Does this approach diminish the role of human agency and free will when it comes to moral desert? Some say it does, yet the claim seems modest enough, that our achievements have many ingredients, and the contributions from agency or free will are intertwined with the contributions from social and random factors—to the point that it seems unreasonable to give by default all credit to agency or free will, which libertarians try to do in order to justify the rewards of the market. However, some philosophers find an unresolved tension in Rawls' approach to setting up the Difference Principle. (See, for instance, *Egalitarianism, Free Will, and Ultimate Justice* by Saul Smilansky.)

One might ask: Why should we uphold the Difference Principle at all? Is it not an arbitrary construct? No, says Rawls, and invites us to a thought experiment on creating "a hypothetical social contract in an original position of equality." Imagine, he says, that "when we gather to chose the principles [for governing ourselves], we don't know where we will wind up in society. Imagine that we choose behind a 'veil of ignorance' that temporarily prevents us from knowing anything about who we are," including our race, gender, class, talents, intelligence, wealth, and religion (or lack thereof).What principles would we then choose to order our society? Rawls makes a powerful case that, simply out of a desire to minimize our odds of suffering, we will always choose political equality, fair equal opportunity, and the Difference Principle.

Some have argued that the Difference Principle may not get chosen as is, not unless it has a clause to address the unfairness of propping up those who willfully make bad choices or act irresponsibly. Further, is it desirable, or even possible, to choose a social contract from behind the so-called veil of ignorance, as if, in Rawls' words, "from the perspective of eternity," with scant regard for context? Doesn't Rawls implicitly presuppose a people who already value political equality, individualism, and resolving claims through public deliberation? Rawls later downplays its universality but, argues Sandel, even in the United States, Rawls' thought experiment supports an arid secular public space detached from so much that is central to our identities. This includes historical, moral, and religious discourses, which, if squeezed out, often pop up elsewhere in worse forms, such as the religious right. If the point is to enhance the social contract, Sandel adds, political progressives should do so not by asking people to leave their deepest beliefs at home but by engaging them in the public sphere.

Sanders basic critique here is that Rawls' concern with the distribution of primary goods—which Rawls defines as "things that every rational man is presumed to want"—is necessary but not sufficient for a social contract. As purposive beings, we should also consider the telos of our choices, such as our common ends as a community, the areas of life worth shielding from the market, the space we should accord to loyalty and patriotism, ties of blood, marriage, tradition, and so on. Still, Rawls' thought experiment retains a powerful moral force and continues to inspire liberals. His theory of justice, writes Sandel, "represents the most compelling case for a more equal society that American political philosophy has yet produced."

Theories of justice may clarify and guide our thoughts, but we still have to figure out how to change the game we want to play and where to draw the lines on the playing field. An open society does this through vigorous public debate. As British philosopher Isaiah Berlin wrote, "people who want to govern themselves must choose how much liberty, equality, and justice they seek and how much they can let go. The price of a free society is that sometimes, perhaps often, we make bad choices." Thereafter, when the rules are in place, "we are entitled to the benefits the rules of the game promise for the exercise of our talents." It is the rules, says Sandel, and not anything outside them, that create "entitlements to legitimate expectations." Entitlements only arise after we have chosen the rules of the competition. Only in this context can we say we deserve something, whether admission to a law school, a certain bonus, or a pension.

In Rawlsian terms, the problem in the United States is not that a minority has grown super rich, but that for decades now, it has done so to the detriment of the lower social classes. The big question is: why does the majority in a seemingly free society tolerate this, and even happily vote against its own economic interests? A plausible answer is that it is under a self-destructive meritocratic spell that sees social outcomes as moral desert—a spell at least as old as the American frontier but long since repurposed by the corporate control of public institutions and the media: news, film, TV, publishing, and so forth. It parallels a religious spell in more ways than one. Here too, powerful social institutions are invested in clouding our notions of cause and effect. Rather than move towards greater fairness and egalitarianism, they promote a libertarian gospel of the free market with minimal regulation, taxation, and public safety nets. They beguile us into thinking that the lifestyles of the rich and famous are within reach of all, and uphold rags-to-riches stories as exemplary ("if this enterprising slumdog can do it against all odds, so can you!" goes the storyline). All this gets drummed into people's heads to the point that they only blame themselves for their lot and don't think of questioning the rules of the game.

What would it take to break this spell? For starters, it would require Americans to realize that the distribution of wealth in their society is far less egalitarian than they think it is—a recent survey revealed that Americans think the richest fifth

of them own 59 percent of the wealth, while the actual figure is 84 percent. Perhaps living on credit helps create the illusion that the average American has more than he or she does. Americans also believe that their odds of rising to the top are far better than they actually are; social mobility is quite low by international standards. A kid from the poorest fifth of all households has a 1 percent chance of reaching the top 5 percentile income bracket, while that of a kid from the richest fifth has a 22 percent chance. The task of breaking this spell, then, requires telling new kinds of stories, engaging in vigorous public debate, and employing our best arts of persuasion.

Average Income per U.S. Family, Distributed by Income Group

Bottom 90%	$ 31,244
Top 1–10%	$ 164,647
Top 1%	$ 1,137,684
Top 0.01–0.1%	$ 3,238,386
Top 0.01%	$27,342,212

2008 data. Source: Emmanual Saez, University of California-Berkeley

Critical Thinking

1. How important is justice to a good society when unjust societies may be more successful than just societies?

2. How would you define justice or fairness?

3. How can you compare countries on justice? Is America more or less just than Canada? Or England?

Create Central

www.mhhe.com/createcentral

Internet References

Sociosite
 www.topsite.com/goto/sociosite.net
Socioweb
 www.topsite.com/goto/socioweb.com
Sociology—Study Sociology Online
 http://edu.learnsoc.org
Sociology Web Resources
 www.mhhe.com/socscience/sociology/resources/index.htm

Unit 2

UNIT

Prepared by: Kurt Finsterbusch, *University of Maryland, College Park*

Socialization and Social Control

Why do we behave the way we do? Three forces are at work: biology, socialization, and the human will (or the internal decision-maker). The focus in sociology is on socialization, which is the conscious and unconscious process whereby we learn the norms and behavior patterns that enable us to function appropriately in our social environment. Socialization is based on the need to belong, because the desire for acceptance is the major motivation for internalizing the socially approved attitudes and behaviors.

Fear of punishment is another motivation. It is utilized by parents and institutionalized in the law enforcement system. The language we use, the concepts we apply in thinking, the images we have of ourselves, our gender roles, and our masculine and feminine ideals are all learned through socialization. Socialization may take place in many contexts. The most basic socialization takes place in the family, but churches, schools, communities, the media, and workplaces also play major roles in the process.

Article   Prepared by: Kurt Finsterbusch, *University of Maryland, College Park*

The New Sex Scorecard

Talking openly about sex differences is no longer an exercise in political incorrectness; it is a necessity in fighting disease and forging successful relationships.

HARA ESTROFF MARANO

Learning Outcomes

After reading this article, you will be able to:

- Identify some major differences between men and women.

- Evaluate whether these differences give men or women an advantage on average in today's economy.

- Discuss specifically the emotional and psychological differences between men and women.

Get out the spittoon. Men produce twice as much saliva as women. Women, for their part, learn to speak earlier, know more words, recall them better, pause less and glide through tongue twisters.

Put aside Simone de Beauvoir's famous dictum, "One is not born a woman but rather becomes one." Science suggests otherwise, and it's driving a whole new view of who and what we are. Males and females, it turns out, are different from the moment of conception, and the difference shows itself in every system of body and brain.

It's safe to talk about sex differences again. Of course, it's the oldest story in the world. And the newest. But for a while it was also the most treacherous. Now it may be the most urgent. The next stage of progress against disorders as disabling as depression and heart disease rests on cracking the binary code of biology. Most common conditions are marked by pronounced gender differences in incidence or appearance.

Although sex differences in brain and body take their inspiration from the central agenda of reproduction, they don't end there. "We've practiced medicine as though only a woman's breasts, uterus and ovaries made her unique—and as though her heart, brain and every other part of her body were identical to those of a man," says Marianne J. Legato, M.D., a cardiologist at Columbia University who spearheads the new push on gender differences. Legato notes that women live longer but break down more.

Do we need to explain that difference doesn't imply superiority or inferiority? Although sex differences may provide ammunition for David Letterman or the Simpsons, they unfold in the most private recesses of our lives, surreptitiously molding our responses to everything from stress to space to speech. Yet there are some ways the sexes are becoming more alike— they are now both engaging in the same kind of infidelity, one that is equally threatening to their marriages.

Everyone gains from the new imperative to explore sex differences. When we know why depression favors women two to one, or why the symptoms of heart disease literally hit women in the gut, it will change our understanding of how our bodies and our minds work.

The Gene Scene

Whatever sets men and women apart, it all starts with a single chromosome: the male-making Y, a puny thread bearing a paltry 25 genes, compared with the lavish female X, studded with 1,000 to 1,500 genes. But the Y guy trumps. He has a gene dubbed SRY, which, if all goes well, instigates an Olympic relay of development. It commands primitive fetal tissue to become testes, and they then spread word of masculinity out to the provinces via their chief product, testosterone. The circulating hormone not only masculinizes the body but affects the developing brain, influencing the size of specific structures and the wiring of nerve cells.

25% of females experience daytime sleepiness, versus 18% of males.

But sex genes themselves don't cede everything to hormones. Over the past few years, scientists have come to believe that they too play ongoing roles in gender-flavoring the brain and behavior.

Females, it turns out, appear to have backup genes that protect their brains from big trouble. To level the genetic playing field between men and women, nature normally shuts off one of the two X chromosomes in every cell in females. But about 19 percent of genes escape inactivation; cells get a double dose of some X genes. Having fall-back genes may explain why females are far less subject than males to mental disorders from autism to schizophrenia.

What's more, which X gene of a pair is inactivated makes a difference in the way female and male brains respond to things, says neurophysiologist Arthur P. Arnold, PhD., of the University of California at Los Angeles. In some cases, the X gene donated by Dad is nullified; in other cases it's the X from Mom. The parent from whom a woman gets her working genes determines how robust her genes are. Paternal genes ramp up the genetic volume, maternal genes tune it down. This is known as genomic imprinting of the chromosome.

For many functions, it doesn't matter which sex genes you have or from whom you get them. But the Y chromosome itself spurs the brain to grow extra dopamine neurons, Arnold says. These nerve cells are involved in reward and motivation, and dopamine release underlies the pleasure of addiction and novelty seeking. Dopamine neurons also affect motor skills and go awry in Parkinson's disease, a disorder that afflicts twice as many males as females.

XY makeup also boosts the density of vasopressin fibers in the brain. Vasopressin is a hormone that both abets and minimizes sex differences; in some circuits it fosters parental behavior in males; in others it may spur aggression.

Sex on the Brain

Ruben Gur, PhD., always wanted to do the kind of psychological research that when he found something new, no one could say his grandmother already knew it. Well, "My grandmother couldn't tell you that women have a higher percentage of gray matter in their brains," he says. Nor could she explain how that discovery resolves a long-standing puzzle.

99% of girls play with dolls at age 6, versus 17% of boys.

Gur's discovery that females have about 15 to 20 percent more gray matter than males suddenly made sense of another major sex difference: Men, overall, have larger brains than women (their heads and bodies are larger), but the sexes score equally well on tests of intelligence.

Gray matter, made up of the bodies of nerve cells and their connecting dendrites, is where the brain's heavy lifting is done. The female brain is more densely packed with neurons and dendrites, providing concentrated processing power—and more thought-linking capability.

The larger male cranium is filled with more white matter and cerebrospinal fluid. "That fluid is probably helpful," says Gur, director of the Brain Behavior Laboratory at the University of Pennsylvania. "It cushions the brain, and men are more likely to get their heads banged about."

White matter, made of the long arms of neurons encased in a protective film of fat, helps distribute processing throughout the brain. It gives males superiority at spatial reasoning. White matter also carries fibers that inhibit "information spread" in the cortex. That allows a single-mindedness that spatial problems require, especially difficult ones. The harder a spatial task, Gur finds, the more circumscribed the right-sided brain activation in males, but not in females. The white matter advantage of males, he believes, suppresses activation of areas that could interfere with work.

The white matter in women's brains is concentrated in the corpus callosum, which links the brain's hemispheres, and enables the right side of the brain to pitch in on language tasks. The more difficult the verbal task, the more global the neural participation required—a response that's stronger in females.

Women have another heady advantage—faster blood flow to the brain, which offsets the cognitive effects of aging. Men lose more brain tissue with age, especially in the left frontal cortex, the part of the brain that thinks about consequences and provides self-control.

"You can see the tissue loss by age 45, and that may explain why midlife crisis is harder on men," says Gur. "Men have the same impulses but they lose the ability to consider long-term consequences." Now, there's a fact someone's grandmother may have figured out already.

Minds of Their Own

The difference between the sexes may boil down to this: dividing the tasks of processing experience. Male and female minds are innately drawn to different aspects of the world around them. And there's new evidence that testosterone may be calling some surprising shots.

Women's perceptual skills are oriented to quick—call it intuitive—people reading. Females are gifted at detecting the feelings and thoughts of others, inferring intentions, absorbing contextual clues and responding in emotionally appropriate ways. They empathize. Tuned to others, they more readily see alternate sides of an argument. Such empathy fosters communication and primes females for attachment.

Women, in other words, seem to be hard-wired for a top-down, big-picture take. Men might be programmed to look at things from the bottom up (no surprise there).

Men focus first on minute detail, and operate most easily with a certain detachment. They construct rules-based analyses of the natural world, inanimate objects and events. In the coinage of Cambridge University psychologist Simon Baron-Cohen, PhD., they systemize.

The superiority of males at spatial cognition and females' talent for language probably subserve the more basic difference of systemizing versus empathizing. The two mental styles manifest in the toys kids prefer (humanlike dolls versus mechanical trucks); verbal impatience in males (ordering rather than negotiating); and navigation (women personalize space by finding landmarks; men see a geometric system, taking directional cues in the layout of routes).

26% of males say they have extramarital sex without being emotionally involved, versus 3% of females.

Almost everyone has some mix of both types of skills, although males and females differ in the degree to which one set predominates, contends Baron-Cohen. In his work as director of Cambridge's Autism Research Centre, he finds that children and adults with autism, and its less severe variant Asperger syndrome, are unusual in both dimensions of perception. Its victims are "mindblind," unable to recognize people's feelings. They also have a peculiar talent for systemizing, obsessively focusing on, say, light switches or sink faucets.

Autism overwhelmingly strikes males; the ratio is ten to one for Asperger. In his new book, *The Essential Difference: The Truth About the Male and Female Brain,* Baron-Cohen argues that autism is a magnifying mirror of maleness.

The brain basis of empathizing and systemizing is not well understood, although there seems to be a "social brain," nerve circuitry dedicated to person perception. Its key components lie on the left side of the brain, along with language centers generally more developed in females.

Baron-Cohen's work supports a view that neuroscientists have flirted with for years: Early in development, the male hormone testosterone slows the growth of the brain's left hemisphere and accelerates growth of the right.

Testosterone may even have a profound influence on eye contact. Baron-Cohen's team filmed year-old children at play and measured the amount of eye contact they made with their mothers, all of whom had undergone amniocentesis during pregnancy. The researchers looked at various social factors—birth order, parental education, among others—as well as the level of testosterone the child had been exposed to in fetal life.

Baron-Cohen was "bowled over" by the results. The more testosterone the children had been exposed to in the womb, the less able they were to make eye contact at 1 year of age. "Who would have thought that a behavior like eye contact, which is so intrinsically social, could be in part shaped by a biological factor?" he asks. What's more, the testosterone level during fetal life also influenced language skills. The higher the prenatal testosterone level, the smaller a child's vocabulary at 18 months and again at 24 months.

Lack of eye contact and poor language aptitude are early hallmarks of autism. "Being strongly attracted to systems, together with a lack of empathy, may be the core characteristics of individuals on the autistic spectrum," says Baron-Cohen. "Maybe testosterone does more than affect spatial ability and language. Maybe it also affects social ability." And perhaps autism represents an "extreme form" of the male brain.

Depression: Pink—and Blue, Blue, Blue

This year, 19 million Americans will suffer a serious depression. Two out of three will be female. Over the course of their lives, 21.3 percent of women and 12.7 percent of men experience at least one bout of major depression.

The female preponderance in depression is virtually universal. And it's specific to unipolar depression. Males and females suffer equally from bipolar, or manic, depression. However, once depression occurs, the clinical course is identical in men and women.

The gender difference in susceptibility to depression emerges at 13. Before that age, boys, if anything, are a bit more likely than girls to be depressed. The gender difference seems to wind down four decades later, making depression mostly a disorder of women in the child-bearing years.

As director of the Virginia Institute for Psychiatric and Behavioral Genetics at Virginia Commonwealth University, Kenneth S. Kendler, M.D., presides over "the best natural experiment that God has given us to study gender differences"—thousands of pairs of opposite-sex twins. He finds a significant difference between men and women in their response to low levels of adversity. He says, "Women have the capacity to be precipitated into depressive episodes at lower levels of stress."

Adding injury to insult, women's bodies respond to stress differently than do men's. They pour out higher levels of stress hormones and fail to shut off production readily. The female sex hormone progesterone blocks the normal ability of the stress hormone system to turn itself off. Sustained exposure to stress hormones kills brain cells, especially in the hippocampus, which is crucial to memory.

It's bad enough that females are set up biologically to internally amplify their negative life experiences. They are prone to it psychologically as well, finds University of Michigan psychologist Susan Nolen-Hoeksema, PhD.

Women ruminate over upsetting situations, going over and over negative thoughts and feelings, especially if they have to do with relationships. Too often they get caught in downward spirals of hopelessness and despair.

It's entirely possible that women are biologically primed to be highly sensitive to relationships. Eons ago it might have helped alert them to the possibility of abandonment while they were busy raising the children. Today, however, there's a clear downside. Ruminators are unpleasant to be around, with their oversize need for reassurance. Of course, men have their own ways of inadvertently fending off people. As pronounced as the female tilt to depression is the male excess of alcoholism, drug abuse and antisocial behaviors.

The Incredible Shrinking Double Standard

Nothing unites men and women better than sex. Yet nothing divides us more either. Males and females differ most in mating psychology because our minds are shaped by and for our reproductive mandates. That sets up men for sex on the side and a more casual attitude toward it.

Twenty-five percent of wives and 44 percent of husbands have had extramarital intercourse, reports Baltimore psychologist Shirley Glass, PhD. Traditionally for men, love is one thing and sex is . . . well, sex.

90% of males and females agree that infidelity is always wrong, 20–25% of all marital fights are about jealousy.

In what may be a shift of epic proportions, sexual infidelity is mutating before our very eyes. Increasingly, men as well as women are forming deep emotional attachments before they even slip into an extramarital bed together. It often happens as they work long hours together in the office.

"The sex differences in infidelity are disappearing," says Glass, the doyenne of infidelity research. "In my original 1980 study, there was a high proportion of men who had intercourse with almost no emotional involvement at all—nonrelational sex. Today, more men are getting emotionally involved."

One consequence of the growing parity in affairs is greater devastation of the betrayed spouse. The old-style strictly sexual affair never impacted men's marital satisfaction. "You could be in a good marriage and still cheat," reports Glass.

Liaisons born of the new infidelity are much more disruptive—much more likely to end in divorce. "You can move away from just a sexual relationship but it's very difficult to break an attachment," says Rutgers University anthropologist Helen Fisher, PhD. "The betrayed partner can probably provide more exciting sex but not a different kind of friendship."

It's not that today's adulterers start out unhappy or looking for love. Says Glass: "The work relationship becomes so rich and the stuff at home is pressurized and child-centered. People get involved insidiously without planning to betray."

Any way it happens, the combined sexual-emotional affair delivers a fatal blow not just to marriages but to the traditional male code. "The double standard for adultery is disappearing," Fisher emphasizes. "It's been around for 5,000 years and it's changing in our lifetime. It's quite striking. Men used to feel that they had the right. They don't feel that anymore."

Learn More about It

Eve's Rib: The New Science of Gender-Specific Medicine and How It Can Save Your Life. Marianne J. Legato, M.D. (*Harmony Books, 2002*).

Not "Just Friends": Protect Your Relationship from Infidelity and Heal the Trauma of Betrayal. Shirley P. Glass, PhD. (*The Free Press, 2003*).

Male, Female: The Evolution of Human Sex Differences. David C. Geary, PhD. (*American Psychological Association, 1998*).

Critical Thinking

1. In the past differences between men and women have been used to justify unequal treatment of women. Is there still a danger of that today?

2. Do the differences between men and women help or interfere with close relations between them?

Create Central

www.mhhe.com/createcentral

Internet References

Sociosite
www.topsite.com/goto/sociosite.net

Socioweb
www.topsite.com/goto/socioweb.com

Sociology—Study Sociology Online
http://edu.learnsoc.org

Sociology Web Resources
www.mhhe.com/socscience/sociology/resources/index.htm

Article   Prepared by: Kurt Finsterbusch, *University of Maryland, College Park*

Fighting Crime

An Economist's View

JOHN J. DONOHUE

Learning Outcomes

After reading this article, you will be able to:

- Explain why crime policies that have not worked continue to be used.

- Argue against the very high imprisonment rate in the United States.

- Discuss the complex issue of legalizing drugs.

Over the past 40 years, the number of motor vehicle fatalities per mile driven in the United States has dropped an astounding 70 percent. While some of the gains can be attributed to improvements in technology, public policy has made a big difference. The government followed the advice of researchers who had studied auto accidents, improving highway design and instituting a variety of regulations, including mandatory seat belt use and harsher penalties for drunken driving. By contrast, most types of street crime are still above the levels of 40 years ago, despite the impressive drops in the 1990s. A major reason for the difference, I would argue, is that the crime issue has been hijacked by ideologues and special interests, preventing the emergence of a policy consensus driven by research.

Why listen to an economist pontificate on what most people would call criminology? Economists bring a unique perspective to the table—a utilitarian view in which one assumes that behavior can be changed by altering incentives, that the costs of crime can be measured in terms of money and that public policy is best evaluated by comparing costs and benefits. It's hardly the only view, but I would argue that it is a view that provides exceptional insight into limiting the adverse consequences of antisocial behavior.

We know more today than ever how to reduce crime. If we could get past the barriers of ideology and special pleading, we could see reductions in crime rivaling the magnitude of the gains in automobile safety. What follows are a host of measures that would sharply reduce the $400 billion annual toll from street crime in the United States.

Stop the Building Boom in Prisons

Virtually everyone agrees that incarceration must remain a core element of any strategy to fight crime. Locking up more people reduces crime because more criminals are kept off the streets and/or the prospect of time behind bars deters criminal behavior. But you can have too much of a "good" thing. Between 1933 and 1973, incarceration in the United States varied within a narrow band of roughly 100 to 120 prisoners per 100,000 population. Since then, this rate has been increasing by an average of 5 percent annually. As of June 2003, some two million individuals were imprisoned—a rate of almost 500 per 100,000.

Costs of Prison

To determine whether the current level of incarceration makes sense, one must ask whether the benefits at the margin in terms of less crime exceed the costs to society. On the benefit side, the research suggests that the "elasticity" of crime with respect to incarceration is somewhere between 0.1 and 0.4—that is, increasing the prison population by 10 percent reduces crime by 1 to 4 percent. On the other side of the equation, estimates of the cost of locking up another individual run between $32,000 and $57,000 annually.

The most rigorous study on the relevant elasticity was conducted by William Spelman of the University of Texas. He concluded that "we can be 90 percent confident that the true value is between 0.12 and 0.20, with a best single guess of 0.16." Since Spelman's estimates accounted for the incapacitation effect, but ignored any deterrence effect, I rely conservatively on somewhat larger elasticity of 0.2.

The most carefully constructed and comprehensive study on the costs of incarcerating a criminal was a 1990 report prepared for the National Institute of Justice, which produced the high-end estimate ($57,000 annually, in 2003 dollars). I adjust this figure downward (in part because the study probably overstates prison construction costs and exaggerates the social cost of welfare payments to the dependents of the incarcerated) to arrive at a figure of $46,000 per prisoner per year.

With an elasticity of crime with respect to incarceration of 0.2 and an annual cost of housing a prisoner of $46,000, the "optimal" level of incarceration would require imprisoning 300,000 fewer individuals. This is just a ballpark estimate, of course. But, at the very least, it implies that we cannot expect to get much more crime reduction at reasonable cost by increasing the numbers behind bars. It is time to stop making prison construction the major public works project of our day.

Abolish the Death Penalty

In recent years, the death penalty has been meted out an average of 80 times annually. These executions come at a high tangible cost. For while executing an individual does save the money that would have been used for a lifetime in prison, these savings are dwarfed by the costs of death-penalty trials and appeals. The most scholarly research on the topic, by Philip Cook and Donna Slawson Kuniholm of Duke, found that the State of North Carolina spent $2.16 million per execution more than what would be spent if the maximum penalty were life in prison.

Proponents of the death penalty usually justify these costs by invoking its deterrence effect. But Steve Levitt of the University of Chicago has noted that the risk of execution for those who commit murder is typically small compared with the risk of death that violence-prone criminals willingly face in daily life—and this certainly raises questions about the efficacy of threatening them with the death penalty. Currently, the likelihood of a murderer being executed is less than 1 in 200. By way of comparison, Levitt and his colleague Sudhir Venkatesh find 7 percent of street-level drug sellers die each year. Levitt concludes that "it is hard to believe the fear of execution would be a driving force in a rational criminal's calculus in modern America."

Nor is there direct evidence that the death penalty generates gains for society in terms of murders deterred. In an often-cited paper written in the early 1970s, Isaac Ehrlich (then a graduate student at the University of Chicago) estimated that one execution could save eight lives. But research since has showed that minor changes in the way the figure is estimated eliminate the deterrence effect. Indeed, Levitt, working with Lawrence Katz of Harvard and Ellen Shustorovich of the City University of New York, found that the death penalty might even add to the total number of murders. Thus, abolishing the death penalty would save American taxpayers more than $150 million a year at no apparent cost to society.

Expand the Police Force

In the 1990s, a variety of new policing strategies were introduced in New York City and other localities. New York increased enforcement of statutes on petty crimes like graffiti and marijuana possession and made better use of technology and statistics in identifying crime "hot spots." Boston adopted an innovative multi-agency collaboration that took aim at gang violence. And numerous cities, notably San Diego, introduced "community policing," in which police attempted to work as allies with communities, rather than just antagonists to criminals. The results seem impressive: from 1991 to 1998, the cities that experienced the largest decline in murder rates were San Diego (a 76 percent drop), New York City (71 percent) and Boston (69 percent).

Were better policing strategies responsible for these results, and would cities be wise to adopt or expand such programs? A study of Cincinnati found that a "community service model" of policing, in which cops become more familiar with the neighborhoods they served, did not significantly lower crime. Furthermore, community policing did not seem to affect attitudes toward police.

Two New York Factors

Note, too, that New York's experiments are inconclusive—cities without tough policies on minor crime experienced significant crime drops, too. Moreover, New York's substantial crime declines began before 1993, the year in which Mayor Giuliani took office and initiated the policing changes. Indeed, two other factors seem to explain all of the crime drop in New York City: increases in the total number of police officers and its high abortion rate many years earlier, which Levitt and I found to correlate with subsequent declines in crime because of the reduction in unwanted births of children most at risk of becoming criminals.

Another change in the 1990s—one that received far less press attention than changing policing strategies—was the substantial increase in the size of police forces. From 1994 through 1999, the number of police per capita in the United States grew by almost 10 percent. The expansion was even more pronounced in big cities with high crime rates. Much of this increase can be attributed to the Community Oriented Policing Services (COPS) program, which was signed into law by President Clinton in 1994 and is now in the process of being phased out by President Bush. A report commissioned by the Justice Department credits this program with adding more than 80,000 officers to the streets.

The effects of increases in police, as opposed to changes in policing strategies, have been widely studied, with most studies showing that the benefits have exceeded the costs. The most rigorous studies have found elasticities of crime with respect to police of between 0.30 and 0.79—that is, a 10 percent increase in police reduces crime between 3.0 and 7.9 percent. Using a conservative estimate for this elasticity (0.4) and a rather high estimate of the total annual cost of maintaining an extra police officer ($90,000) while assuming that crime costs $400 billion a year, the United States would have to hire 500,000 additional police officers to reach the optimal policing level. According to the FBI, there are some 665,000 police in the United States. So the optimal level is almost double the number we have today. Thus while adding hundreds of thousands of police officers is hardly a political priority these days, simply restoring financing for the COPS program would be a start.

Adopt Sensible Gun Control

In 2002, there were some 11,000 homicide deaths by firearms. The United States' per capita firearm homicide rate is more than eight times that of Canada, France, Germany, Japan, Spain and Britain. Much could be done to reduce gun-related crime. Most such initiatives are off the table, however, because conservatives have garnered enormous electoral benefits from fighting gun control.

What's more, the highly publicized work of the researcher John Lott has confirmed the views of many conservatives that gun control is already excessive—that allowing citizens to carry concealed handguns would drastically *reduce* violent crime. Lott reasons that the threat of these concealed weapons serves as a deterrent to crime. And his research has been cited by many politicians supporting laws allowing concealed weapons, which have been passed by some 30 states.

There are, however, serious flaws in Lott's research. The best guess based on all the empirical evidence is that these "shall issue" laws actually increase crime, albeit by a relatively modest amount. There are a number of possible explanations for this: the guns being carried are easier to steal (more than a million guns are stolen each year, which is a major source of supply to criminals), for one, while the threat of being shot in a confrontation may inspire criminals to shoot first. It is worth noting, moreover, that laws allowing for easier access to guns increase the threats of both accidental death and suicide.

One alternative to "shall issue" laws is "may issue" laws, which allow discretion in handing out permits, with an applicant having to prove a need for protection. These laws, which have been passed in 11 states, could have some of the deterrent benefits Lott speaks of without as many of the harmful effects that plague "shall issue" laws if the licensing discretion is used wisely.

Another much-debated gun law was President Clinton's 1994 assault-weapons ban, which was recently allowed to expire. This law prohibited a specific list of semiautomatic guns deemed useful for criminal purposes but unnecessary for sport or self-defense, and banned ammunition feeding devices that accept more than 10 rounds. According to plausible guesstimates, assault weapons were used in about 2 percent of pre-ban murders, and large-capacity magazines were used in about 20 percent. The secondary goal of the assault weapons ban was to reduce the harm from crime by forcing criminals to employ less dangerous weapons. Jeffrey Roth and Christopher Koper of the Urban Institute in Washington found that those murdered by assault weapons had, on average, more wounds than those killed with other guns. They also found that, in mass murders, those involving assault weapons included more victims.

Was the ban effective? Probably not very. The law was rife with loopholes. For one thing, the law grandfathered assault weapons produced before the ban, which led gun manufacturers to increase production before the law took effect. In addition, gun companies could—and did—produce potent legal guns with little change in performance. Admittedly, a true ban on assault weapons would not have a huge effect on homicide since most criminals would simply use less powerful guns if the desired weapons were unavailable. A strong ban on large capacity magazines, however, which are estimated to be used in 20 percent of homicides, could be very helpful.

David Hemenway, an economist and director of the Harvard Injury Control Research Center, has examined the evidence on the potential impact of other gun-related measures and identifies six that have shown some success in lowering crime:

- preventing police from selling confiscated guns.
- instituting one-gun-purchase-per-month laws.
- plugging secondary-market loopholes.
- tracing all guns used in crime.
- producing guns that can be fired only by their owners.
- registering all handguns.

None of these, alas, is an easy political sell in today's America.

Legalize Drugs

The most effective federal crime-fighting public initiative in American history was the lifting of alcohol prohibition in the early 1930s. Homicides fell by 14 percent in the two years after prohibition ended. In all likelihood, similar benefits would emerge if we ended drug prohibition, although obviously other steps would need to be taken to reduce the societal costs associated with drug use.

The logic behind drug legalization as a crime reducer is twofold. First, a significant number of homicides are caused by drug-related disputes. The FBI has classified about 5 percent of homicides as drug-related. And this number is very conservative since the FBI attributes only one cause to each murder. A fatal dispute about a drug deal may be characterized as an "argument over money" or a "gangland killing" rather than a drug homicide. Paul Goldstein of the University of Illinois at Chicago found that about 9 percent of homicides in New York City were caused by broader "systemic" drug issues.

The major reason so many drug disputes end in violence is the lack of institutional mechanisms to resolve them—buyers and sellers cannot seek redress in court, or complain to the Better Business Bureau. Legalization could also lower crime by freeing crime-fighters for other purposes. About $40 billion is spent annually on the war on drugs.

Decriminalizing drugs would also free space in prisons. Levitt found a substantial "crowding out" effect, meaning that increased incarceration of drug-related criminals decreases incarceration of other criminals. Currently, more than 400,000 individuals are in prison for nonviolent drug crimes, with about 50,000 of them imprisoned for violations involving only marijuana.

Of course, drug legalization is not without risks. Legalization would tend to increase drug consumption, lowering economic productivity and perhaps increasing behavior that is dangerous to nondrug users.

One simple way to restrain drug consumption after legalization would be through taxation. Gary Becker and Kevin Murphy of the University of Chicago along with Michael Grossman of the City University of New York construct a model in which the optimal equilibrium with legalization and taxation can actually lead to higher retail prices—and lower consumption—than the optimal system under prohibition. Such a policy would also raise additional money for the government, which could be used for any number of purposes. It would be substantially easier to enforce a tax on drugs than it is to enforce the current ban on drugs, since most individuals would pay a premium to purchase their drugs legally. Instead of turning the hundreds of thousands of workers in the illegal drug markets (and their customers) into criminals, we could focus law enforcement on the much smaller set of tax evaders to keep consumption no higher than the levels of today.

Given the highly controversial nature of this proposal, a prudent first step might be to adopt this legalization/taxation/ demand control scheme for marijuana to illustrate the benefits of shrinking the size of illegal markets while establishing that an increase in drug usage can be avoided. A number of other measures should be adopted to limit demand. Strict age limits could be enforced, advertising could be banned, and some of the money raised by taxes on drugs could be used to market abstinence and treatment of addicts.

Expand Successful Social Programs

In accepting his party's nomination, John Kerry said, "I am determined that we stop being a nation content to spend $50,000 a year to keep a young person in prison for the rest of their life—when we could invest $10,000 to give them Head Start, Early Start, Smart Start, the best possible start in life." He was expressing a belief common on the center-left that early childhood intervention can make children less likely to commit crime and actually save money down the road.

Is this view correct? Studies on Head Start have shown it to have lamentably little effect on participants' outcomes later in life, including their likelihood of committing crimes. Other programs, however, have shown tremendous potential in reducing crime (and enhancing other positive life outcomes), and resources should be shifted away from the unproductive programs toward the few that seem to work.

One of the most notable, the experimental Perry Preschool program, provided preschool classes to a sample of children in Michigan when they were 3 and 4 years old. This program attempted to involve the whole family by having the preschool teacher conduct weekly home visits. By age 19, Perry Preschool graduates were 40 percent less likely to be arrested than a control group, 50 percent less likely to be arrested more than twice, and far less likely to be arrested for major crimes.

While I would not expect a scaled-up program to perform as well as one implemented with a small group, even half the reduction in crime would be cost-effective. Estimates from studies of the program indicate that financial benefits to government, which came in the form of higher taxes from employment, lower welfare utilization and reduced crime, exceeded program costs by as much as seven to one.

Another cost-effective crime-fighting program is the Job Corps, which provides educational and vocational-skills training and counseling to at-risk youths. Each year, Job Corps enrolls some 60,000 kids at a cost of more than $1 billion. Unlike some similar teenage intervention programs, the Job Corps is residential. Like the Perry Preschool Program, Job Corps has proved to pay for itself, generating more revenue in the form of taxes and avoided welfare payments than the costs of training the at-risk

teens. Job Corps has also proved effective in lowering crime: a randomized experiment conducted by the research corporation Mathematica estimates that Job Corps participants are 16 percent less likely to be arrested than their peers.

For programs like the Perry Preschool and Job Corps to be successful in lowering crime, they must be targeted at those most likely to commit crimes. Six percent of the population commits more than 50 percent of crimes. While there are moral and legal issues in targeting groups based on race, it should be possible to use such information to expand successful programs so that they cover more high-risk individuals.

Defend *Roe v. Wade*

One often overlooked variable in crime is the legal status of abortion. Levitt and I found that as much as half of the drop in crime in the 1990s can be explained by the legalization of abortion in the early 1970s. There are two reasons that legalized abortion lowers the crime rate. The first is obvious: more abortions mean fewer children, which in turn can mean fewer criminals when those who would have been born would have reached their high-crime years. The second is more important: abortion reduces the number of unwanted births, and unwanted children are at much greater risk of becoming criminals later on. The five states that legalized abortion before the rest of the country experienced significant drops in crime before other states did. What's more, the higher the rate of abortion in a state in the mid 1970s, the greater the drop in crime in the 1990s.

What would be the impact on crime if *Roe v. Wade* were overturned? If the Supreme Court restored the pre-1973 law allowing states to decide for themselves whether to legalize abortion, I suspect most of the blue states would keep abortion legal. Even in the red states, abortion would not disappear entirely because residents could still find safe, out-of-state abortions. But the number of abortions would fall sharply, particularly for poor women.

Suppose that abortion were outlawed in every state that voted for Bush in 2004 and that the abortion rate dropped by 75 percent in these states but remained the same in blue states. Our research suggests that violent crime would eventually increase by about 12 percent and property crime by about 10 percent over the baseline figure.

Reduce Teen Pregnancy

Keeping abortion legal would prevent crime increases, but we can use the insight from the casual link between abortion and crime reduction to achieve the same ends in a better way: reduce the number of unwanted and teen pregnancies. Take the Children's Aid Society-Carrera program, which aims to reduce births to teenagers by changing their incentives. The three-year after-school program for 13-year-olds includes a work component designed to assist participants to find decent jobs, an academic component including tutoring and homework help, an arts component, an individual sports component, and comprehensive family life and sexual education. Program participants have been 70 percent less likely to give birth in the three years after the program ended than members of a control group.

Again, the success of any social program designed to reduce crime requires targeting, in this case at those most likely to give birth in their teens. The groups with the highest rates of teen births are Hispanics, with a rate of 83 births per 1,000 women 15 to 19 years old, and non-Hispanic blacks, with a rate of 68 per thousand—both well above the national rate of 43. Suppose the program was expanded so that it covered half of all Hispanic and black females ages 13 to 15—some two million girls. With a per-person cost of $4,000, the annual outlay would be roughly $4 billion.

Again, one would not expect a large program to be able to replicate the substantial reductions seen in the smaller program. But an initiative only half as effective in reducing teen births would still lower the birth rates of the 15- to 19-year-old participants by 35 percent. Under these assumptions, the expanded program would lead to about 40,000 fewer teen births a year— a 9 percent reduction.

Recent work by Anindya Sen enables us to quantify the expected reduction in crime from this potential drop in teen births. Sen finds that a 1 percent drop in teen births is associated with a 0.589 percent drop in violent crime years later, when the individuals born to teenagers would have reached their high-crime ages. Thus, the 9 percent reduction in teen births would eventually cut violent crime by 5 percent. Assuming two-thirds of crime costs are attributable to violent crime, this 5 percent reduction would eventually save society more than $14 billion per year. In other words, the benefits would be three times greater than the cost.

Expand the DNA Database

While much of the attention on the use of DNA in criminal justice has focused on its potential for establishing the innocence of the wrongly accused, we have not yet tapped the potential of DNA testing to deter crime. Individuals whose DNA is on file with the government know that leaving even a single hair at the scene of a crime is likely to lead to their arrest and conviction, so a major expansion in the DNA database should generate substantial crime reduction benefits. While some are concerned that the government would get information about a person's medical history, the privacy problem can be minimized. It is possible to take someone's DNA and discard all information except for the unique identifying genetic marker.

Currently, every state requires violent criminals and sex offenders to submit to DNA testing. Most states require testing for all felons and juvenile convicts. If a person is found innocent, his or her DNA sample must be discarded. But the United States' DNA crime-fighting system can be expanded and improved. England tests anyone suspected of a "recordable" offense, with the profile remaining on file even if the person is cleared of the crime. This has allowed Britain to build a DNA database with some two million profiles. England's Forensic Science Service estimates that, in a typical year, matches are found linking suspects to 180 murders, 500 rapes and other sexual offenses, and 30,000 motor vehicle, property and drug crimes. In other words, DNA is used to solve fully 20 percent of murders and a significant fraction of other crimes.

A more drastic—and potentially effective—approach was endorsed by Rudolph Giuliani: recording the DNA of every newborn. One way to lower the costs of the project without eliminating much of the gains would be to test only males, who are far more likely to commit crimes.

To improve the effectiveness of the policy, however, it would be necessary to test every male—not just male babies. This would increase the start-up costs to $15 billion (although thought should be given to the appropriate age cutoff—say age 50—as a plausible cost-reduction measure). In every year thereafter, however, it would be necessary to test only newborns. In 2002, there were a little more than 2 million male births in the United States. So testing every male infant would cost about $200 million annually.

One particular crime-deterrent benefit of having the DNA of every male on file is it would be likely to drastically reduce rapes by strangers. Let's assume (conservatively) that half of all such rapes—half of 56,000 a year—would be deterred by the existence of a complete DNA database. Ted Miller, Mark Cohen and Shelli Rossman added the costs of medical bills, lost productivity, mental health trauma and quality of life changes, to estimate that the average rape costs $90,000. Hence, 28,000 of the rapes by strangers in 2002 cost society about $2.5 billion. While the costs of testing every male—$15 billion in the first year—would exceed the $2.5 billion in benefits in reduced rapes from such a plan, the total benefits from rape reduction alone would exceed the costs in roughly seven years (and perhaps less if the initial testing were limited with a judicious age cutoff). Note, moreover, that stranger rapes are only one of many classes of crimes that would see sharp declines with such expansive DNA testing.

What We Are Losing

Few of these proposals seem likely to be adopted any time soon. Former attorney general John Ashcroft stressed incarceration and the death penalty as principal crime-fighting tools, and President Bush's new attorney general, Alberto Gonzalez, appears wed to an even tougher line. Bush seems intent on shrinking the budget for police and early-intervention social programs. The NRA continues to have success in fighting even the most sensible gun control policies. And few in either political party are willing to discuss the legalization of drugs or a major expansion in the DNA database. The politicians in power thus seem stuck on anti-crime policies that guarantee that crime levels will be far higher than can be justified by any reasonable comparison of costs and benefits—let alone respect for life and property.

Adopting the policies set out above would reduce crime in the neighborhood of 50 percent, saving thousands of lives annually and avoiding crime victimization for millions more. Is anybody in Washington, or the state capitals, listening?

Critical Thinking

1. How relevant is the economist view to criminal justice policies?
2. The author claims that adopting his recommended policies "would reduce crime . . . 50 percent, saving thousands of lives annually and avoiding crime victimization for millions more." Evaluate his claim.

Create Central

www.mhhe.com/createcentral

Internet References

Crime Times
www.crime-times.org

Sociosite
www.topsite.com/goto/sociosite.net

Socioweb
www.topsite.com/goto/socioweb.com

Sociology—Study Sociology Online
http://edu.learnsoc.org

Sociology Web Resources
www.mhhe.com/socscience/sociology/resources/index.htm

JOHN J. DONOHUE teaches law and economics at the Yale Law School. From "Fighting Crime: An Economist's View," *The Milken Institute Review,* First Quarter 2005, pages 47–58.

Article   Prepared by: Kurt Finsterbusch, *University of Maryland, College Park*

Wrongful Convictions

RADLEY BALKO

Learning Outcomes

After reading this article, you will be able to:

- Describe specific cases of wrongful convictions and understand some of the inexcusable actions by authorities that lead to these wrongful convictions.

- Understand the very large gap between proven wrongful convictions and the actual number of wrongful convictions.

- Understand the main reasons for wrongful convictions.

How many innocent Americans are behind bars? When Paul House was finally released from prison in 2008, he was a specter of the man who had been sentenced to death more than 22 years earlier. When I visit his home in Crossville, Tennessee, in March, House's mother Joyce, who has cared for him since his release, points to a photo of House taken the day he was finally allowed to come home. In that photo and others from his last days in prison, House is all of 150 pounds, ashen and drawn, his fragile frame nearly consumed by his wheelchair. In most of the images he looks days away from death, although in one he wears the broad smile of a man finally escaping a long confinement.

When House's aunt called to congratulate him on his first day back, his mother handed him her cell phone so he could chat. He inspected the phone, gave her a frustrated look, and asked her to find him one that worked. That kind of Rip Van Winkle moment is common among people freed after a long stint in prison. Dennis Fritz, one of the two wrongly convicted men profiled in John Grisham's 2006 book *The Innocent Man,* talks about nearly calling the police upon seeing someone use an electronic key card the first time he found himself in a hotel after his release. He thought he'd witnessed a burglar use a credit card to jimmy open a door.

"Paul's first meal when he got home was chili verde," Joyce House says. "It's his favorite. And I had been waiting a long time to make it for him." And apparently quite a few meals after that. House, now 49, has put on 75 pounds since his release. More important, he has been getting proper treatment for his advanced-stage multiple sclerosis, treatment the Tennessee prison system hadn't given him.

The years of inadequate care have taken a toll. House can't walk, and he needs help with such basic tasks as bathing, feeding himself, and maneuvering around in his wheelchair. His once distinctively deep voice (which had allegedly been heard by a witness at the crime scene) is now wispy and high-pitched. He spends his time playing computer games and watching game shows.

In the hour or so that I visit with House, his mental facilities fade in and out. Communicating with him can be like trying to listen to a baseball game broadcast by a distant radio station. He will give a slurred but lucid answer to one question, then answer the next one with silence, or with the answer to a previous question, or just with a random assortment of words. He frequently falls back on the resigned refrain, "Oh, well," delivered with a shrug. The gesture and phrasing are identical every time he uses them. It's what House says to kill the expectation that he will be able to deliver the words others in the room are waiting for. It's his signal to stop waiting for him and move on.

In 1986 House was convicted of murdering Carolyn Muncey in Union County, Tennessee, a rural part of the state that shoulders Appalachia. He was sentenced to death. His case is a textbook study in wrongful conviction. It includes mishandled evidence, prosecutorial misconduct, bad science, cops with tunnel vision, DNA testing, the near-execution of an innocent man, and an appellate court reluctant to reopen old cases even in the face of new evidence that strongly suggests the jury got it wrong.

House also embodies the tribulations and frustrations that the wrongly convicted encounter once they get out. According to the doctors treating him, his current condition is the direct result of the inadequate care he received in prison. If he is ever granted a formal exoneration—a process that can be as much political as it is judicial—he will be eligible for compensation for his years behind bars, but even then the money comes with vexing conditions and limitations.

Since 1989, DNA testing has freed 268 people who were convicted of crimes they did not commit. There are dozens of other cases, like House's, where DNA strongly suggests innocence but does not conclusively prove it. Convicting and imprisoning an innocent person is arguably the worst thing a government can do to one of its citizens, short of mistakenly executing him. (There's increasing evidence that this has happened too.) Just about everyone agrees that these are unfathomable tragedies. What is far less clear, and still hotly debated, is what these cases say about the way we administer justice in America, what we owe the wrongly convicted, and how the officials who send innocent people to prison should be held accountable.

How Many Are Innocent?

According to the Innocence Project, an advocacy group that provides legal aid to the wrongly convicted, the average DNA exoneree served 13 years in prison before he or she was freed. Seventeen had been sentenced to death. Remarkably, 67 percent of the exonerated were convicted after 2000, the year that marked the onset of modern DNA testing. Each new exoneration adds more urgency to the question that has hovered over these cases since the first convict was cleared by DNA in 1989: How many more innocent people are waiting to be freed?

Given the soundness of DNA testing, we can be nearly certain that the 268 cleared so far didn't commit the crimes for which they were convicted. There are hundreds of other cases where no DNA evidence exists to definitively establish guilt or innocence, but a prisoner has been freed due to lack of evidence, recantation of eyewitness testimony, or police or prosecutorial misconduct. Those convictions were overturned because there was insufficient evidence to overcome reasonable doubt; it does not necessarily mean the defendant didn't commit the crime. It's unclear whether and how those cases should be factored into any attempt to estimate the number of innocent people in prison.

In a country where there are 15,000 to 20,000 homicides each year, 268 exonerations over two decades may seem like an acceptable margin of error. But reform advocates point out that DNA testing is conclusive only in a small percentage of criminal cases. Testing is helpful only in solving crimes where exchange of DNA is common and significant, mostly rape and murder. (And most murder exonerations have come about because the murder was preceded by a rape that produced testable DNA.) Even within this subset of cases, DNA evidence is not always preserved, nor is it always dispositive to the identity of the perpetrator.

Death penalty cases add urgency to this debate. In a 2007 study published in the *Journal of Criminal Law and Criminology,* the Seton Hall law professor Michael Risinger looked at cases of exoneration for capital murder-rapes between 1982 and 1989, compared them to the total number of murder-rape cases over that period for which DNA would be a factor, and estimated from that data that 3 percent to 5 percent of the people convicted of capital crimes probably are innocent. If Risinger is right, it's still unclear how to extrapolate figures for the larger prison population. Some criminologists argue that there is more pressure on prosecutors and jurors to convict someone, anyone, in high-profile murder cases. That would suggest a higher wrongful conviction rate in death penalty cases. But defendants also tend to have better representation in capital cases, and media interest can also mean more scrutiny for police and prosecutors. That could lead to fewer wrongful convictions.

In a study published in the *Journal of Criminal Law and Criminology* in 2005, a team led by University of Michigan law professor Samuel Gross looked at 328 exonerations of people who had been convicted of rape, murder, and other felonies between 1989 and 2003. They found that while those who have been condemned to die make up just 1 percent of the prison population, they account for 22 percent of the exonerated. But does that mean capital cases are more likely to bring a wrongful conviction? Or does it mean the attention and scrutiny that

death penalty cases get after conviction—particularly as an execution date nears—make it more likely that wrongful convictions in capital cases will be discovered?

Many states have special public defender offices that take over death penalty cases after a defendant has exhausted his appeals. These offices tend to be well-staffed, with enough funding to hire their own investigators and forensic specialists. That sometimes stands in stark contrast to the public defender offices that handled the same cases at trial. Perversely, this means that in some jurisdictions, a defendant wrongly convicted of murder may be better off with a death sentence than with life in prison.

Even if we were to drop below the floor set in the Risinger study and assume that 2 percent of the 2008 prison population was innocent, that would still mean about 46,000 people have been convicted and incarcerated for crimes they didn't commit. But some skeptics say even that figure is way too high.

Joshua Marquis, the district attorney for Clatsop County, Oregon, is an outspoken critic of the Innocence Project and of academics like Risinger and Gross. He is skeptical of the belief that wrongful convictions are common. "If I thought that 3 to 5 percent of people in prison right now were innocent, I'd quit my job," Marquis says. "I'd become a public defender or something. Maybe an activist. Look, nobody but a fool would say that wrongful convictions don't happen. As a prosecutor, my worst nightmare is not losing a case—I've lost cases; I'll lose cases in the future. My worst nightmare is convicting an innocent person, and I tell my staff that. But the question here is whether wrongful convictions are epidemic or episodic. And I just don't think it's possible that the number could be anywhere near 3 to 5 percent."

Marquis and Gross have been butting heads for several years. In a 2006 *New York Times* op-ed piece, Marquis took the 328 exonerations Gross and his colleagues found between 1989 and 2003, rounded it up to 340, then multiplied it by 10—a charitable act, he wrote, to "give the professor the benefit of the doubt." He then divided that number by 15 million, the total number of felony convictions during the same period, and came up with what he said was an error rate of just 0.027 percent. His column was later quoted in a concurring opinion by U.S. Supreme Court Justice Antonin Scalia in the 2006 case *Kansas v. Marsh,* the same opinion where Scalia made the notorious claim that nothing in the U.S. Constitution prevents the government from executing an innocent person.

Gross responded with a 2008 article in the *Annual Review of Law and Social Science,* pointing out that his original number was by no means comprehensive. Those were merely the cases in which a judicial or political process had exonerated someone. The figure suggested only that wrongful convictions happen. "By [Marquis'] logic we could estimate the proportion of baseball players who've used steroids by dividing the number of major league players who've been caught by the total of all baseball players at all levels: major league, minor league, semipro, college and Little League," Gross wrote, "and maybe throw in football and basketball players as well."

Whatever the total number of innocent convicts, there is good reason to believe that the 268 cases in which DNA evidence has proven innocence don't begin to scratch the surface. For one thing, the pace of these exonerations hasn't slowed down: There were 22 in 2009, making it the second busiest name-clearing year to date. Furthermore, exonerations are expensive in both time and resources. Merely discovering a possible case and requesting testing often isn't enough. With some commendable exceptions . . . prosecutors tend to fight requests for post-conviction DNA testing. (The U.S. Supreme Court held in 2009 that there is no constitutional right to such tests.) So for now, the pace of genetic exonerations appears to be limited primarily by the amount of money and staff that legal advocacy groups have to uncover these cases and argue them in court, the amount of evidence available for testing, and the willingness of courts to allow the process to happen, not by a lack of cases in need of further investigation.

It's notable that one of the few places in America where a district attorney has specifically dedicated staff and resources to seeking out bad convictions—Dallas County, Texas—has produced more exonerations than all but a handful of states. That's partly because Dallas County District Attorney Craig Watkins is more interested in reopening old cases than his counterparts elsewhere, and partly because of a historical quirk: Since the early 1980s the county has been sending biological crime scene evidence to a private crime lab for testing, and that lab has kept the evidence well preserved. Few states require such evidence be preserved once a defendant has exhausted his appeals, and in some jurisdictions the evidence is routinely destroyed at that point.

"I don't think there was anything unique about the way Dallas was prosecuting crimes," Watkins told me in 2008. "It's unfortunate that other places didn't preserve evidence too. We're just in a unique position where I can look at a case, test DNA evidence from that period, and say without a doubt that a person is innocent. . . . But that doesn't mean other places don't have the same problems Dallas had."

If the rest of the country has an actual (but undetected) wrongful conviction rate as high as Dallas County's, the number of innocents in prison for felony crimes could be in the tens of thousands.

The Trial and Conviction of Paul House

As with many wrongful convictions, the case against Paul House once seemed watertight. House was an outsider, having only recently moved to Union County when Carolyn Muncey was murdered in 1985, and he was an ex-con, having served five years in a Utah prison for sexual assault. He got into scuffles with locals, although he considered Muncey and her husband, Hubert, friends. When Muncey turned up dead, House was a natural suspect.

House has claimed he was innocent of the Utah charge. His mother, Joyce, says it was a he said/she said case in which her son pleaded guilty on the advice of his attorney. "He could have been paroled earlier if he had shown some remorse," she says. "But he said, 'I pled guilty the one time, because that's what the lawyer told me I should do. I'm not going to say again that I did something I didn't do.' He said he'd rather serve more time than admit to the rape again." Joyce House and Mike Pemberton,

Paul House's attorney, are hesitant to go into much detail about the Utah case, and public records aren't available due to the plea bargain. But while what happened in Utah certainly makes House less sympathetic, it has no bearing on whether House is the man who killed Carolyn Muncey.

House also didn't do himself any favors during the Muncey investigation. In initial questioning, he lied to the police about where he was the night of the murder, saying he was with his girlfriend all night. But he later admitted he had gone for a walk at one point and had come back without his shoes and with scratches on his arms. He initially lied to police about the scratches too, saying they were inflicted by his girlfriend's cats. House later said he'd been accosted by some locals while on his walk, scuffled with them, then fled through a field, where he lost his shoes. (House would learn years later that his shoes were found by police before his trial. There was no blood or other biological evidence on them, potentially exculpatory information that was never turned over to House's lawyers.)

"I think it was a situation where you're on parole, you're an outsider, and this woman has just been killed near where you live," says Pemberton, House's attorney. "It wasn't smart of him to lie to the police. But it was understandable."

Carolyn Muncey's husband, who House's attorneys would later suspect was her killer, also lied about where he was when she was killed. He would additionally claim, falsely, that he had never physically abused her. Still, House was clearly the early suspect.

The strongest evidence against House was semen found on Muncey's clothing, which an FBI agent testified at trial "could have" belonged to House. DNA testing didn't exist in 1986, but the agent said House was a secretor, meaning he produced blood type secretions in other body fluids, including semen, and that the type secreted in semen found on Muncey's nightgown was a match to House's type A blood. About 80 percent of people are secretors, and about 36 percent of Americans have type A blood. The agent also said the semen found on Muncey's panties included secretions that didn't match House's blood type, but added, inaccurately, that House's secretion could have "degraded" into a match. Muncey's husband was never tested.

The other strong evidence against House was some blood stains on his jeans that matched Muncey's blood type, but not his own. Those stains on House's jeans did turn out to have been Muncey's blood; the question is how they got there.

House was never charged with rape; there were no physical indications that Muncey had been sexually assaulted. But the semen was used to put him at the crime scene, and the state used the possibility of rape as an aggravating circumstance in arguing that House should receive the death penalty.

House was convicted in February 1986. The morning after his conviction, just hours before the sentencing portion of his trial, House slashed his wrists with a disposable razor. He left behind a suicide note in which he professed his innocence. Jail officials rushed him to a hospital in Knoxville, where doctors saved his life and stitched up his wounds. He was then sent back to the courthouse, where a jury sentenced him to death.

It wasn't until more than a decade later, in 1999, that the case against House began to erode. New witnesses came forward with accusations against Hubert Muncey, Carolyn's husband.

Several said he was an alcoholic who frequently beat her. At an ensuing evidentiary hearing, two other women said Hubert had drunkenly confessed to killing his wife several months after the murder. When one went to the police with the information the next day, she said at the hearing, the sheriff brushed her off. Another witness testified that Hubert Muncey had asked her to lie to back up his alibi.

But it was the forensic evidence presented at that 1999 hearing that really unraveled the state's case. When House's attorneys were finally able to get DNA testing for the semen found on Carolyn Muncey's clothes, it showed that the semen was a match to Muncey's husband, not House. The state responded that rape was never part of their case against House (though it is why he was initially a suspect, it was the only conceivable motive, and it was presented as evidence in the sentencing portion of his trial). Besides, prosecutors argued, there was still the blood on House's jeans.

Except there were problems with that too. Cleland Blake, an assistant chief medical examiner for the state of Tennessee, testified that while the blood did belong to Muncey, its chemical composition indicated it was blood that had been taken after she had been autopsied. Worse still, three-quarters of a test tube of the blood taken during Muncey's autopsy went missing between the time of the autopsy and the time House's jeans arrived at the FBI crime lab for testing. The test tubes with Muncey's blood and House's jeans were transported in the same Styrofoam box. The blood on House's jeans, his attorneys argued, must have either been planted or spilled because of sloppy handling of the evidence.

It is extraordinarily difficult to win a new trial in a felony case, even in fight of new evidence, and House's case was no exception. A federal circuit court judge denied his request for post-conviction relief, and the U.S. Court of Appeals for the 6th Circuit affirmed that decision. Somewhat surprisingly, the U.S. Supreme Court agreed to hear House's case, and in 2006 issued a rare, bitterly divided 5-to-3 ruling granting House a new trial.

The Supreme Court has occasionally thrown out death penalty convictions because of procedural errors or constitutional violations, but it's rare for the Court to methodically review the evidence in a capital case. Writing for the majority, Justice Anthony Kennedy did exactly that, finding in the end that "although the issue is close, we conclude that this is the rare case where—had the jury heard all the conflicting testimony—it is more likely than not that no reasonable juror viewing the record as a whole would lack reasonable doubt."

It was a surprising and significant victory for House. But it would be another three years before he would be released from prison.

How Do Wrongful Convictions Happen?

The most significant consequence of the spate of DNA exonerations has been a much-needed reassessment of what we thought we knew about how justice is administered in America. Consider the chief causes of wrongful convictions:

Bad Forensic Evidence

DNA technology was developed by scientists, and it has been thoroughly peer-reviewed by other scientists. Most of the forensic science used in the courtroom, on the other hand, was either invented in police stations and crime labs or has been refined and revised there to fight crime and obtain convictions. Most forensic evidence isn't peer-reviewed, isn't subject to blind testing, and is susceptible to corrupting bias, both intentional and unintentional. The most careful analysts can fall victim to cognitive bias creeping into their work, particularly when their lab falls under the auspices of a law enforcement agency. Even fingerprint analysis isn't as sound as is commonly believed.

A congressionally commissioned 2009 report by the National Academy of Sciences found that many other forensic specialties that are often presented in court with the gloss of science—hair and carpet fiber analysis, blood spatter analysis, shoe print identification, and especially bite mark analysis—lack the standards, peer review, and testing procedures of genuinely scientific research and analysis. Some are not supported by any scientific literature at all. Moreover, the report found, even the forensic specialties with some scientific support are often portrayed in court in ways that play down error rates and cognitive bias.

According to an Innocence Project analysis of the first 225 DNA exonerations, flawed or fraudulent forensic evidence factored into about half of the faulty convictions.

Eyewitness Testimony

Social scientists have known about the inherent weakness of eyewitness testimony for decades. Yet it continues to be the leading cause of wrongful convictions in America; it was a factor in 77 percent of those first 225 cases. Simple steps, such as making sure police who administer lineups have no knowledge of the case (since they can give subtle clues to witnesses, even unintentionally) and that witnesses are told that the actual perpetrator may not be among the photos included in a lineup, can go a long way toward improving accuracy. But such reforms also make it more difficult to win convictions, so many jurisdictions, under pressure from police and prosecutor groups, have been hesitant to embrace them.

False Confessions

Difficult as it may be to comprehend, people do confess to crimes they didn't commit. It happened in about one-quarter of the first 225 DNA exonerations. Confessions are more common among suspects who are minors or are mentally handicapped, but they can happen in other contexts as well, particularly after intense or abusive police interrogations.

In a candid 2008 op-ed piece for the *Los Angeles Times*, D.C. Police Detective Jim Trainum detailed how he unwittingly coaxed a false confession out of a 34-year-old woman he suspected of murder. She even revealed details about the crime that could only have been known to police investigators and the killer. But Trainum later discovered that the woman couldn't possibly have committed the crime. When he reviewed video of his interrogation, he realized that he had inadvertently provided the woman with those very specific details, which she then repeated back to him when she was ready to confess.

Trainum concluded that all police interrogations should be videotaped, a policy that would not just discourage abusive questioning but also provide an incontrovertible record of how a suspect's confession was obtained. Here too, however, there has been pushback from some police agencies, out of fear that jurors may be turned off even by legitimate forms of questioning.

Jailhouse Informants

If you were to take every jailhouse informant at his word, you'd find that a remarkably high percentage of the people accused of felonies boast about their crimes to the complete strangers they meet in jail and prison cells. Informants are particularly valuable in federal drug cases, where helping a prosecutor obtain more convictions is often the only way to get time cut from a mandatory minimum sentence. That gives them a pretty good incentive to lie.

There is some disagreement over a prosecutor's duty to verify the testimony he solicits from jailhouse informants. In the 2006, Church Point, Louisiana, case of Ann Colomb, for example, Brett Grayson, an assistant U.S. attorney in Louisiana, put on a parade of jailhouse informants whose claims about buying drugs from Colomb and her sons were rather improbable, especially when the sum of their testimony was considered as a whole. According to defense attorneys I spoke with, when one attorney asked him if he actually believed what his informants were telling the jury, Grayson replied that it doesn't matter if he believes his witnesses; it only matters if the jury does. He expressed a similar sentiment in his closing argument.

After indicating that he isn't familiar with the Colomb case and isn't commenting on Grayson specifically, Josh Marquis says that sentiment is wrong. "A prosecutor absolutely has a duty to only put on evidence he believes is truthful," Marquis says. "And that includes the testimony you put on from informants."

In a 2005 study, the Center on Wrongful Convictions in Chicago found that false or misleading informant testimony was responsible for 38 wrongful convictions in death penalty cases.

The Professional Culture of the Criminal Justice System

In addition to the more specific causes of wrongful convictions listed above, there is a problem with the institutional culture among prosecutors, police officers, forensic analysts, and other officials. Misplaced incentives value high conviction rates more than a fair and equal administration of justice.

Prosecutors in particular enjoy absolute immunity from civil liability, even in cases where they manufacture evidence that leads to a wrongful conviction. The only time prosecutors can be sued is when they commit misconduct while acting as investigators—that is, while doing something police normally do. At that point they're subject to qualified immunity, which provides less protection than absolute immunity but still makes it difficult to recover damages.

Marquis says this isn't a problem. "Prosecutors are still subject to criminal liability," he says. "In fact, my predecessor here

in Oregon was prosecuted for misconduct in criminal cases. State bars will also hold prosecutors accountable."

But criminal charges are few and far between, and prosecutors can make egregious mistakes that still don't rise to the level of criminal misconduct. Professional sanctions are also rare. A 2010 study by the Northern California Innocence Project found more than 700 examples between 1997 and 2009 in which a court had found misconduct on the part of a prosecutor in the state. Only six of those cases resulted in any disciplinary action by the state bar. A 2010 investigation of federal prosecutorial misconduct by *USA Today* produced similar results: Of 201 cases in which federal judges found that prosecutors had committed misconduct, just one resulted in discipline by a state bar association. Prosecutorial misconduct was a factor in about one-quarter of the first 225 DNA exonerations, but none of the prosecutors in those cases faced any significant discipline from the courts or the bar.

There is also a common misconception that appeals courts serve as a check on criminal justice abuse. It is actually rare for an appeals court to review the evidence in a criminal case. Appeals courts make sure trials abide by the state and federal constitutions and by state or federal rules of criminal procedure, but they almost never second-guess the conclusions of juries.

In a 2008 article published in the *Columbia Law Review*, the University of Virginia law professor Brandon L. Garrett looked at the procedural history of the first 200 cases of DNA exoneration. Of those, just 18 convictions were reversed by appellate courts. Another 67 defendants had their appeals denied with no written ruling at all. In 63 cases, the appellate court opinion described the defendant as guilty, and in 12 cases it referred to the "overwhelming" evidence of guilt. Keep in mind these were all cases in which DNA testing later proved actual innocence. In the remaining cases, the appeals courts either found the defendant's appeal without merit or found that the errors in the case were "harmless"—that is, there were problems with the case, but those problems were unlikely to have affected the jury's verdict due to the other overwhelming evidence of guilt.

"We've seen a lot of exoneration cases where, for example, the defendant raised a claim of ineffective assistance of counsel," says Peter Neufeld, co-founder of the Innocence Project of New York. "And in those cases, the appellate courts often found that the defense lawyer provided substandard representation. But they would then say that the poor lawyering didn't prejudice the case because the evidence of guilt was so overwhelming. Well, these people were later proven innocent! If you have a test that is frequently producing erroneous results, there's either something wrong with the test, or there's something wrong with the way it's being implemented."

Life on the Outside

Paul House was diagnosed with multiple sclerosis in 2000, a year after the evidentiary hearing that would eventually lead to his release. But while House was convicted of Carolyn Muncey's murder less than a year after it happened, it took a decade after his conviction was called into serious question for House to get back home to Crossville. During those 10 years, the state's case continued to fall apart. So did House's body.

After the U.S. Supreme Court overturned House's conviction in 2006, Paul Phillips, the district attorney for Tennessee's 8th Judicial District and the man who prosecuted House in 1986, pushed ahead with plans to retry him. In December 2007, after a series of delays, Harry S. Mattice Jr., a U.S. district court judge in Knoxville, finally ordered the state to try House within 180 days or set him free. Those 180 days then came and went without House being freed, thanks to an extension granted by the 6th Circuit.

In another hearing held in May 2008, Phillips argued that House—who by that point couldn't walk or move his wheelchair without assistance—presented a flight risk. Later, Tennessee Associate Deputy Attorney General Jennifer Smith attempted to show that House presented a danger to the public because he was still capable of feeding himself with a fork, which apparently meant he was also capable of stabbing someone with one. House's bail was set at $500,000, later reduced to $100,000. In July 2008, an anonymous donor paid the bail, allowing House to finally leave prison.

That same month, Phillips told the Associated Press that he would send two additional pieces of biological evidence off for DNA testing: a hair found at the crime scene, and blood found under Carolyn Muncey's fingernails. House's defense team had asked to conduct its own testing of any untested biological evidence for years, but had been told that either there was no such evidence or, if there was, the state didn't know where it was. Philips told the A.P. that if the new tests didn't implicate House, he would drop the murder charge and allow House to go home. In February 2009 the results came back. They didn't implicate House, and in fact pointed to a third, unidentified man. In May of that year, Phillips finally dropped the charge. But he still wouldn't clear House's name, telling Knoxville's local TV station WATE, "There is very adequate proof that Mr. House was involved in this crime. We just don't know the degree of culpability beyond a reasonable doubt." (Phillips' office did not respond to my requests for comment.)

By the time House was diagnosed with M.S. in 2000, his symptoms were already severe, although it took his mother, and not a prison doctor, to notice something was wrong. "I was visiting him, and I brought along some microwave popcorn," Joyce House recalls. "He asked me to heat it up, and I said, 'No, you heat it up.' When he got up, he had to prop himself up and drag along the wall to get to the microwave. He couldn't even stand up straight." According to Joyce House, her son's doctors today say that the Tennessee prison system's failure to diagnose House's M.S. earlier—then treat it properly after it was diagnosed—may have taken years off his life. (M.S. is also exacerbated by stress.) The disease has also significantly diminished the quality of the life House has left.

Under Tennessee's compensation law for the wrongly convicted, if House is formally exonerated—and that's still a big if—he will be eligible for $50,000 for each year he was in prison, up to $1 million. But there's a catch. The compensation is given in annual $50,000 installments over 20 years. If House dies before then, the payments stop.

Most of the 27 states with compensation laws similarly pay the money off in installments. Last October, A.P. ran a story about Victor Burnette, a 57-year-old Virginia man who served eight years for a 1979 rape before he was exonerated by DNA testing in 2006. Burnette actually turned down the $226,500 the state offered in compensation in 2010 because he was offended by the stipulation that it be paid out over 25 years. Even after the DNA test confirmed his innocence, it took another three years for Burnette to officially be pardoned, which finally made him eligible for the money. The installment plans make it unlikely that many exonerees—especially long-timers, who are arguably the most deserving—will ever see full compensation for their years in prison.

Only about half the people exonerated by DNA testing so far have been compensated at all. Most compensation laws require official findings of actual innocence, which eliminates just about any case that doesn't involve DNA. Some states also exclude anyone who played some role in their own conviction, which would disqualify a defendant who falsely confessed, even if the confession was coerced or beaten out of them.

Paul House has yet another predicament ahead of him. Even if he does win an official exoneration, and even if he somehow lives long enough to receive all of his compensation, he'll have to lose his health insurance to accept it. House's medical care is currently covered by TennCare, Tennessee's Medicare program. If he accepts compensation for his conviction, he will be ineligible. His $50,000 per year in compensation for nearly a quarter century on death row will then be offset by a steep increase in what he'll have to pay for his medical care.

These odd, sometimes absurd predicaments aren't intentionally cruel. They just work out that way. Paul House's attorney Mike Pemberton points out that the prosecutors in these cases aren't necessarily evil, either. "Paul Phillips is an honorable man, and an outstanding trial attorney," Pemberton says. "But on this case he was wrong." Pemberton, who was once a prosecutor himself, says the job can lend itself to tunnel vision, especially once a prosecutor has won a conviction. It can be hard to let go. We have a system with misplaced incentives and very little accountability for state actors who make mistakes. That's a system ripe for bad outcomes.

When I ask Paul House why he thinks it has taken so long to clear his name, he starts to answer, then stammers, looks away, and retreats again to Oh well, his cue to move on because he has no answer.

That may be an understandable response from a guy with advanced M.S. who just spent two decades on death row. But for too long our national response to the increasing evidence that our justice system is flawed has been the same sort of resignation. DNA has only begun to show us where some of those flaws lie. It will take a strong public will to see that policymakers address them.

Critical Thinking

1. How are false confessions obtained?

2. Identify the pressures on prosecutors and the police to get convictions rather than the truth.

3. Why have these problems not been fixed already?

Create Central

www.mhhe.com/createcentral

Internet References

Crime Times
www.crime-times.org
Sociosite
www.topsite.com/goto/sociosite.net

Socioweb
www.topsite.com/goto/socioweb.com
Sociology—Study Sociology Online
http://edu.learnsoc.org
Sociology Web Resources
www.mhhe.com/socscience/sociology/resources/index.htm

RADLEY BALKO (rbalko@reason.com) is a senior editor at Reason.

From *Reason Magazine,* July 2011, pp. 20–33. Copyright © 2011 by Reason Foundation, 3415 S. Sepulveda Blvd., Suite 400, Los Angeles, CA 90034. www.reason.com

Article   Prepared by: Kurt Finsterbusch, *University of Maryland, College Park*

Cruel and Unusual

The True Costs of Our Prison System

ROBERT DEFINA AND LANCE HANNON

Learning Outcomes

After reading this article, you will be able to:

- Judge the Catholic bishops' pastoral statement criticizing the United States for an extremely high incarceration rate.

- Discern the political factors that made the incarceration rate so high.

- Evaluate the value of the principles of Catholic social teaching for addressing the problem.

A decade ago, in November 2000, the U.S. Conference of Catholic Bishops issued a pastoral statement titled *Responsibility, Rehabilitation, and Restoration: A Catholic Perspective on Crime and Criminal Justice.* Unapologetically critiquing a criminal-justice system focused primarily on punishment, the bishops called the American response to crime "a moral test for our nation and a challenge for our church."

Their statement chastised the United States for its "astounding" rate of incarceration, "six to twelve times higher than the rate of other Western countries," and went on to suggest changes that would make the system more humane and socially beneficial. "Putting more people in prison and, sadly, more people to death has not given Americans the security we seek," the bishops declared. "It is time for a new national dialogue on crime and corrections, justice and mercy, responsibility and treatment."

The backdrop to the bishops' pastoral was a dramatic rise in the incarceration rate. In the twenty years preceding their report, that rate rose steeply and steadily, more than tripling to 683 prisoners per 100,000 of the population—which meant 2 million people behind bars and a total bill to federal, state, and local governments of about $64 billion. Closer inspection of the ranks of the imprisoned raised even more concerns. Prisons were increasingly admitting nonviolent criminals, especially those guilty of drug-related infractions. The prison population was increasingly made up of minorities: by 2000 about 60 percent of those imprisoned were either black or Hispanic. And

Harvard sociologist Bruce Western noted that more than half of all African-American men who lack high-school diplomas were imprisoned by age thirty-four.

Scholars who studied the issue concluded that the prison buildup was not simply a response to rising crime: violent-crime rates in 2000, in fact, roughly equaled those of 1980, while property-crime rates were actually lower. The trend toward mass incarceration was rooted rather in a series of policy changes aimed at winning political favor by "getting tough on crime." These included mandatory sentencing, "three strikes and you're out" laws, and harsher rules for probation and parole. And so the same amount of crime yielded substantially more incarceration. Nor did the strategy of mass imprisonment contribute much toward keeping crime down. Even the most generous estimates suggested a relatively minor role in crime prevention; many studies showed that rates of violent crime were unaffected. Indeed, as we shall see, some evidence suggests that certain crimes might actually have increased as a result.

For the bishops a decade ago, the existing approaches to criminal justice were severely at odds with the church's scriptural, theological, and sacramental heritage. "A Catholic approach begins with the recognition that the dignity of the human person applies to both victim and offender," they wrote. "As bishops, we believe that the current trend of more prisons and more executions, with too little education and drug treatment, does not truly reflect Christian values and will not really leave our communities safer." The overriding emphasis on punishment, the harsh and dehumanizing conditions of prisons, the lack of help to prisoners attempting reentry into society: these and other failures of the system led the bishops to call for a new direction, one that emphasized restorative justice and reintegration while insisting on the well-being and fair treatment of both prisoners and their victims.

The system envisioned by the bishops offered prisoners reintegration into the community, including the opportunity for reconciliation with those harmed, even as it supported victim restitution. It rejected crudely punitive strategies, such as mandatory sentencing, that neglect the complex sources of crime and the particularities of an individual criminal's makeup. The bishops also called for better treatment within the prison walls, including expanded counseling, health care, education, and training to help emerging prisoners integrate successfully into society. They recommended that prisons be easily accessible to family, friends, and religious communities able to support the development and growth of prisoners. Finally, they reminded us of the community's responsibility to work toward reducing crime and helping those at risk of engaging in criminal activities.

These proposals added up to a progressive analysis of crime, punishment, and prevention, and it would be hard to argue against the bishops' prescriptions or the moral basis that underpinned them. A decade later, however, both the pastoral's criticisms and its suggestions seem all too limited. The criticism focused mainly on shortcomings in the condition and treatment of individual prisoners and victims. While these remain important concerns, recent research has highlighted serious detrimental effects that the justice system has on the broader communities from which prisoners come and to which they ultimately return. These community-level effects have added substantially to the individual-level problems the nation's prison policy has created. Recognizing these consequences will help lead to a broader and deeper critique than the one articulated in the pastoral—a critique, moreover, that points the way to a criminal-justice system more in line with the principles of Catholic social thought.

The bishops analyzed the effects of prisons using what Rutgers sociologist Todd Clear has called an "atomistic view." An atomistic view focuses on the individual prisoner—why he commits a crime, how he is treated within the criminal-justice system, and what happens to him once he is released. While such a view addresses the important issue of personal dignity, it mostly ignores the larger social fact that the individual prisoner is but one of over 2 million, and that those imprisoned come from geographically concentrated neighborhoods. A broader view discloses other problems. Imprisoning a large fraction of individuals from a particular community, it turns out, can cause that community substantial harm—especially when that community was disadvantaged to begin with.

Recent studies have illuminated the many ways this harm can occur. To begin with, mass imprisonment removes spending power from a community, as most of those incarcerated are working at the time of their arrest and contributing significantly to their families' income. Furthermore, as sociologists Bruce Western and Devah Pager have demonstrated, incarceration significantly limits the earning capacity of ex-inmates through the erosion of their marketable skills, the loss of social networks, prison socialization into destructive behaviors, and, perhaps most important, the scarlet letter of a prison record. Ex-prisoners are barred from a large array of occupations in this country, ranging from emergency medicine to cosmetology; in thirty-seven states, employers are allowed to consider arrests *without conviction* when making hiring decisions. And loss of income is not limited to the incarcerated parent, but also afflicts the remaining parent, since childcare needs can

significantly decrease the time available to find and keep a job. Research has consistently shown, moreover, that children with an incarcerated parent frequently suffer high levels of anxiety, shame, and depression; and attending to these needs forms a further obstacle to the remaining parent's participation in the labor force.

Such considerations reveal just how complex and multidimensional the impact of mass incarceration can be. At the community level, it disrupts social networks that bolster the chance for quality employment. The loss of an adult family member, especially one with years of experience in the legitimate labor market, reduces the "friend-of-a-friend" connections that aid employment. As sociologists Robert Sampson and Stephen Raudenbush point out, whole communities with high incarceration rates can become stigmatized, decreasing the likelihood that members will be hired, even those with no prison record. Other studies have suggested that mass incarceration disrupts a neighborhood's informal mechanisms of social support, as the constant churn of people in and out weakens bonds and diminishes collective identity. This in turn strains individual resources—as when parents who cannot rely on neighbors to look after children must spend money or forgo wages to do it themselves. The removal of adult breadwinners, meanwhile, eliminates role models important for young people. And the blatantly unequal and racialized use of incarceration can delegitimize governmental authority among youth and fuel an oppositional subculture in which mainstream activities such as work are devalued. These detrimental effects of concentrated incarceration on a community's norms and sense of collective efficacy may ultimately prevent residents from escaping what might otherwise be merely episodic poverty.

Another direct link to poverty is the increased prevalence of single-parent families. Not only does mass imprisonment shrink the pool of young men available for marriage, but the prison experience itself can make men less suitable for marriage. And single parenthood is a significant contributor to poverty and related social ills. As for released inmates, they face restricted access to the social-safety net. Several states, such as Texas and Missouri, deny them food stamps, public housing, and TANF, federal assistance for needy families. And the overhaul of the federal welfare system in 1996—the Personal Responsibility and Work Opportunity Reconciliation Act—included a lifetime ban on cash assistance and food stamps for anyone convicted of a drug offense. These rules not only impede the re-integration of ex-prisoners, but put the community as a whole at risk, especially children. Mass incarceration has also been associated with growing and serious community-health problems. Economists Steven Raphael and Michael Stoll, for example, have linked the prevalence of AIDS in poor communities to the transmission of the disease through sexual violence in prison. This in turn renders communities less able to deal with other crucial concerns.

Beyond all this lies a political dimension. Mass incarceration can exacerbate a community's long-term economic deprivation by politically disenfranchising those with the greatest stake in policies that might help lift people out of poverty. In forty-eight states, prisoners cannot vote. Many states disallow voting while on probation or parole, and a few states, like Florida, permanently disenfranchise those convicted of a felony. According to a study by the Sentencing Project and Human Rights Watch, as of 1998 3.9 million Americans—about one in fifty adults—had either temporarily or permanently lost their right to vote. A clear racial imbalance characterizes this loss; the study revealed that about one in seven black men had either temporarily or permanently lost the right to vote, and in several states, nearly one in four black men of voting age were *permanently* disenfranchised. To make matters worse, census procedures dictate that prisoners be counted not in their home communities, but in the jurisdiction where they are imprisoned. Since the areas where prisoners come from tend to be urban, diverse, and Democratic, while prisons are frequently located in rural, white, and Republican districts, high-incarceration communities suffer a sort of electoral double-whammy, with political power drained away from them and transferred to politically antithetical communities that receive greater representation because of their sizable, nonvoting inmate population. The end result is less legislative support for—and greater opposition to—a variety of progressive initiatives that could aid disadvantaged communities, including, for example, a boost in the statewide minimum wage.

Finally, as if all this weren't bad enough, it is clear that the harms done to a community's economy by mass incarceration are likely to be multiplied. In a vicious feedback loop, decreased spending caused by lost income due to incarceration results in fewer businesses being able to remain solvent. When businesses go under, additional residents lose their jobs and fall below the poverty line, depressing spending further. Crucial nonprofit institutions, such as community churches, can be negatively affected as well by the economic contraction. Because such institutions frequently provide goods and services that alleviate poverty, crime, and other social ills, their weakening can intensify the collateral consequences of mass incarceration.

Some observers have suggested that increased incarceration can benefit disadvantaged communities by removing socially disruptive young men. This idea has intuitive appeal, yet it loses force in the context of mass incarceration. While the removal of just a few "bad apples" might well have positive implications, in some communities more than a third of the population of young males is in prison; this is less like removing a few apples than like uprooting the whole tree. In such situations the negative effects will likely outweigh whatever positive effects might exist. Our own research indicates that mass incarceration in recent decades has plunged millions of Americans into poverty. Other studies suggest potentially criminogenic consequences of mass imprisonment, arising from the release into the community of large numbers of prisoners exposed to an isolating and sometimes violent prison environment. According to criminologists Lynn Vieraitis, Tomislav Kovandzic, and Thomas Marvell, imprisonment trends in the past few decades actually *increase* the incidence of various types of crime. And our own research suggests that any such crime-inducing effects of imprisonment can persist for many years.

In light of these manifest problems, we believe that Catholic Social Teaching (CST) should broaden its engagement with the criminal-justice system to include what we term "community justice." By community justice we mean the consideration of the community as an organic whole whose treatment should be subject to the demands of justice. Understanding communities this way is common for sociological analysis, but not perhaps for the kind of analysis typically used in CST. Yet with mass incarceration, it is simply not the case that the total damage equals the sum of individual harms. Rather, entire communities have been damaged, suffering perilous losses to their collective social, cultural, and physical capital.

This perspective opens up new questions and suggests new applications of CST to the criminal-justice system. Diminution of the *common good,* for instance, is much graver when entire communities are destroyed. The urgency of a *preferential option for the poor* is heightened when policies push millions more people into poverty. The *social nature of the person* and *solidarity* are violated more seriously when entire social networks and sets of norms are damaged. Barriers to *participation* are much greater when whole communities are stigmatized because of high levels of incarceration. Such perspectives both require and inform a broader, deeper critique of our penal system.

A community-justice lens can also help highlight the racial imbalance in mass imprisonment. Bruce Western and Loïc Wacquant have argued that policy initiatives, like the "War on Drugs," that have led to mass incarceration and the disproportionate incarceration of minorities constitute a reaction against the civil-rights movement. They represent, in other words, a new means of social control, in the tradition of such outlawed forms as blatant job discrimination, Jim Crow laws, and housing segregation, which effectively isolates members of a devalued social group and limits their access to valued resources. To the extent that this is accurate, criminal-justice policy directly violates several principles of CST, including the dignity of the person, the social nature of the person, participation, solidarity, and the universal destination of goods. Seen this way, mass incarceration isn't merely an ineffective system needing improvement. Rather, it is a sinful, repugnant, and disordered structure worthy of wholesale replacement.

What practical steps might be taken to bring this disordered system into line with Catholic principles? First and foremost, we need to incarcerate fewer people. One recent proposal by economists John Schmitt, Kris Warner, and Sarika Gupta argues that half of all nonviolent criminals could be removed from prison and put on probation or parole with no appreciable effect on public safety, at a savings of close to $17 billion—considerable resources for the common good, an especially attractive benefit for struggling state governments. Meaningful reductions in incarceration can also be achieved via judicious changes to parole and probation rules. Minor violations (such as lying about previous prison time on job applications) that can now land parolees back in jail, could be handled less punitively, keeping ex-inmates in the community. All in all, sociologist Todd Clear has suggested, the prison population could be cut in half by eliminating imprisonment for technical parole violations, trimming the length of parole supervision, and reducing prison sentences to those used twenty years ago.

Policies should be enacted to strengthen the efficacy of communities and their ability to exercise social control and offer social support. Foremost here are access to decent legitimate employment opportunities as well as to the childcare and transportation that facilitate working. Along these lines, the bipartisan Second Chance Act of 2008 suggests a heightened recognition of the problems of prisoner reentry and a new political willingness to do something about them. Signed by President George W. Bush and supported by President Barack Obama, the law authorizes federal grants for employment and housing assistance, drug and alcohol abuse treatment, and other services to reentering offenders. In addition, all restrictions on work should be scrutinized, and those not demonstrably necessary to community safety should be removed. States can also reconsider allowing arrests without convictions to be factored into employment decisions.

The voting rights of ex-prisoners and those on probation and parole should be guaranteed, not only to assure individual rights (as the bishops stressed), but to give reentering prisoners a tangible stake in their communities. They should also be given full access to the safety net, including the basic programs (such as food stamps and TANF) that are essential for low-income communities, especially children. Public programs should treat poor ex-prisoners as well as they treat nonpoor ex-prisoners. Today, while public housing is denied to ex-inmates, the mortgage-interest deduction, essentially a housing program for middle- and upper-class families, is not. This surely runs counter to the call for a preferential option for the poor.

The principles of Catholic Social Teaching have provided a useful framework for reflection and guidance in addressing countless social problems over the past century. The arena of criminal justice is no exception. For a decade, the bishops' pastoral has served as a powerful reminder that justice involves not only punishment but also the hard work of supporting the common good. As the bishops have pointed out, supporting the common good means helping the individual rejoin the community. And as we have stressed here, there must be a strong and vibrant community available to reintegrate with.

Sadly, in the ten years since the bishops' pastoral was published, the disturbing trends it addressed have only continued, with the latest data showing the 2008 incarceration rate reaching 753 per 100,000 of the U.S. population, at a total direct cost of about $75 billion. The trends in racial composition and the decreased severity of crimes meriting incarceration have continued as well. Meanwhile, the evidence for incarceration's crime-reducing effect has weakened considerably. These failures demand our renewed attention and effort.

We have tried here to broaden the view presented in the bishops' pastoral to recognize that incarceration on the scale seen in this country affects not only the individual but also the community at large, significantly amplifying poverty, crime, and other social pathologies. Analyses that fail to incorporate these community-level effects will continue to underestimate the harms caused by the current American approach to criminal justice. The principles of Catholic Social Teaching, on the other hand, can markedly improve what is clearly a broken system. Reconstructing the criminal-justice system in ways consistent with those principles will put us on a path toward respecting both the authentic development of the individual and the common good, and help us reverse an all-out assault on our most vulnerable communities.

Critical Thinking

1. Why has the criminal justice system been allowed to operate in such a way as to ruin millions of lives.
2. Fairly simple changes could cut the prison population in half. Analyze why they are not utilized.
3. Discuss both positive and negative impacts of treating prisoners as humans as the bishops recommend.

Create Central

www.mhhe.com/createcentral

Internet References

Crime Times
www.crime-times.org

Sociosite
www.topsite.com/goto/sociosite.net

Socioweb
www.topsite.com/goto/socioweb.com

Sociology—Study Sociology Online
http://edu.learnsoc.org/

Sociology Web Resources
www.mhhe.com/socscience/sociology/resources/index.htm

ROBERT DEFINA is professor of sociology at Villanova University and co-editor of the Journal of Catholic Social Thought. **LANCE HANNON** is associate professor of sociology at Villanova University. The authors' work was supported in part by a Veritas grant from Villanova University

From *Commonweal*, January 28, 2011, pp. 11–14. Copyright © 2011 by Commonweal Foundation. Reprinted by permission. For subscriptions, www.commonwealmagazine.org

Article Prepared by: Kurt Finsterbusch, *University of Maryland, College Park*

Estimates of Cost of Crime

History, Methodologies, and Implications

Jacek Czabański

Learning Outcomes

After reading this article, you will be able to:

- Discuss the complex issue of the total costs of crime.
- Understand the relative costs to victims, enforcement costs, and costs for trying to prevent crime.
- Compare the costs of street crime and white-collar crime.

There are some crimes that have been recognized everywhere and in any time. These crimes include traditional ones like murder, rape, assault, robbery, larceny, that is to say: inflicting harm to others.

Focusing my attention on traditional crimes only, I will avoid discussion about the proper limits of criminal law. It is worth noting, however, that costs of crime estimates are connected with the economic theory of law. According to the economic theory of law, the ultimate goal of law is to maximize social welfare, and criminal law is preferred to other means (like contract or tort law) under certain circumstances (see, for example, Posner 1985). Following Benthamic concept, the economic theory of law postulates that only harmful behavior should be made criminal. Harm is considered as a decrease in the individual's well-being.

Therefore, there is a class of behavior, namely victimless crimes, that poses particular problems for the economic analysis. Examples of this class include drug trade, prostitution, gambling, et cetera. The most basic economic assumption is that by exchange people can enhance their utility, but in the above mentioned examples that very process of exchange is forbidden by law. The fact that the exchange, potentially beneficial for both parties, is forbidden by society for whatever reason, suggests that there are some external effects that make society so attentive to this transaction. The conflict between private and public interest is clear in such circumstances and any relevant analysis of cost of these crimes has to weight these factors as well.

There is no one way that the costs of crime may be categorized. Generally, the costs of crime can be divided into three broad categories:

1. Costs of crime itself (pain and suffering, stolen/damaged property, health consequences for victims);
2. Costs of society's response to crime (costs of criminal justice system: police, prosecutors, judges, prisons, and other correctional facilities); and
3. Costs in anticipation of crime (costs of avoidance behavior and precautionary expenditures).

Total Cost of Crime

As was previously described, from the historic perspective the direct costs of crime estimates were the first methodology employed. Costs of law enforcement were easy to calculate so costs of police, prosecution, judges, and prisons and other institutions were included in all estimates.... But it was also very clear that these costs formed only one side of the equation. The very reason why society spends money on crime prevention is to lower crime and the burden associated with it. The economic consequences of crime were then estimated: Smith used an approximation of criminal gains as an equivalent of public losses due to crime; National Commission on Law Observance and Enforcement used available data on some crime prevention costs and used labor wages to calculate the value of time lost by criminals behind bars and law officers; President's Commission on Law Enforcement and Administration of Justice provided only loss of earnings due to homicide, but excluded all costs of pain and suffering. Moreover, the Report included costs of illegal activities measured as a total income for illegal goods and services—this shifted an accent from street crimes into organized and white-collars crimes.

What was certainly lacking in all these calculations was the comprehensive list of all (or at least the main) consequences of crime, particularly those that affect victims. Although some methods of valuation (e.g. property prices, happiness loss) also have tried to capture the total cost of crime, they have been unsuccessful in this attempt.

A total cost of crime calculation should include as many consequences of crime as possible, even if they were assessed with different methodologies. The point of reference is a hypothetical state of no crime. Therefore, these kinds of assessments do not answer the question of how much people would like to pay for crime reduction, but rather a question of what is the total burden of crime, compared to the ideal world without it.

While historically the first studies of crime were of this kind, they lacked too many important costs. Modern estimates of the total cost have tried to capture the whole picture.

Anderson included in his analyses a wide spectrum of costs:

Crime-induced production covers personal protection devices (guns, locks, safes, etc.), operation of correctional facilities, and drug trafficking. In the absence of crime, time, money and other resources would be used for other purposes.

Opportunity costs—the value of time of criminals which could have been devoted to legal activities instead. Similarly, the value of victims' time lost due to having been victimized.

Value of risk to life and health—this is the value people place on the risk that they will suffer injury or die due to crime.

Transfers—some crimes involve transfers of property, for example theft. However, according to standard economic reasoning, transfers are not considered to be a net loss to society.

Main Anderson's numerical estimates are reported below (Table 1).

Table 1 Total cost of crime in the US. 1999

Category	Cost (billion dollars)
Crime-induced production, including	397
Drug trafficking	161
Police protection	47
Corrections	36
Prenatal exposure to cocaine and heroin	28
Federal agencies	23
Judicial and legal services	19
Guards	18
Drug control	11
DUI costs to driver	10
Opportunity costs, including	130
Time spent securing assets	90
Criminals' lost work days	39
The value of risk to life and health	574
Value of lost life	440
Value of injuries	134
Transfers	603
Occupational fraud	204
Unpaid taxes	123
Health insurance fraud	109
Total burden	1,705
Net of transfers	1,102
Per capita (in dollars)	4,118

The total burden of crime (net of transfers) was estimated at 1.1 trillion. But as high as it may appear, these estimates did not include all costs, for lack of data. Nevertheless, this collection of costs, limited by data availability, provokes one to asking many questions. For example, the biggest position in crime-induced production is drug trafficking. This amount was taken from the report of the President's Commission on Organized Crime and is simply an amount of money spent on the yearly consumption of drugs. But as was argued before, this can be hardly viewed as a cost of crime. The very fact that people willingly buy drugs stands as an argument for classifying it rather as social benefit than cost. While it is true that there are negative externalities connected with drug consumption (higher mortality rate, lower productivity, and so on), the same is true with many other human activities like alcohol and tobacco consumption, junk food consumption or extreme sports practicing. Moreover, it seems to be a pure transfer from a buyer to a seller, so it should instead be classified under that heading. In Anderson's study there are more inconsistencies like this: in the cost of driving under the influence, penalties and fees were included (another transfer), costs of exposure to cocaine and heroine were exaggerated and for no reason the costs of exposure to alcohol or tobacco were not included.

One of the most surprising components was the value of time lost on securing assets. This is mainly the value of time spent on locking, and unlocking doors. Anderson estimated that each adult spends 2 min a day locking and unlocking doors, and more than 2 min looking for keys.

Anderson also included such minor items, as anti-theft devices in libraries, but did not include such costs as pain and suffering of victims (only lost working days were included). He also did not include any estimates of fear of crime, which has an impact not only on an individual's well-being, but also on his behavior. His estimates then are likely to understate the true impact of crime, even if his selection was highly arbitrary. The report also did not allow for differentiating between different categories of crimes, and he only estimated the total cost for all crimes. . . .

Nevertheless, calculations of the total cost of crime show that the burden of crime is enormous. Victimization studies confirm that a substantial part of society is victimized every year. The society's fear of crime is then understandable. . . .

Conclusions

. . . I have argued that the development of costs of crime estimates makes them a valuable, and indeed irreplaceable, tool in criminal law and crime policy. While the concept of monetizing pain and suffering, which are necessarily connected with crime, for many people seems unfeasible, and maybe even unreasonable, such calculations have many advantages over more intuitive approaches that have been in use so far.

Averting crimes has always been the aim of crime policy. The lack of reliable estimates as to the real benefits of averting crimes led to the biased perspective of the criminal justice system. Costs of the system were easily seen, as they were borne mainly by state budgets. At the same time, the benefits eluded quantification.

Lives lost, pain and suffering, costs of healthcare, property damaged and stolen—all these constitute direct costs of crime.

Table 2 Total cost of crime in different countries

Country	Year	Total cost of crime (local currency)	Cost of crime as % of GDP	Source
US	1900	USD 600 m	2.9%	Smith (1901)
US	1930	USD 1 bn	1.1%	Report on the Cost of Crime and Criminal Justice in the United States (1931)
US	1965	USD 107 bn	14.9%	President's Commission on Law Enforcement and Administration of Justice (1967)
US	1993	USD 451 bn	6.8%	Miller et al. (1996)
England and Wales	1999	GBP 59 bn	6.5%	Brand and Price (2000)
US	1999	USD 1,102 bn	11.9%	Anderson (1999)
Australia	2002	AUD 31.8 bn	4.2%	Mayhew (2003)
England and Wales	2003	GBP 36.2 bn	3.5%	Dubourg et al. (2005) [only for households and individuals]
New Zealand	2003	NZD 9.1 bn	6.5%	Roper and Thompson (2006)

Note: GDP in current prices taken from the database of the International Monetary Fund: http://www.imf.org/external/pubs/ft/weo/2006/02/data/index.aspx, last accessed 30 November 2006.

Yet, this list is far from being comprehensive—behavioral responses, changing patterns of life, counter-crime measures, and reduced quality of living all comprise another part of the costs of crime. And the emergence of the criminal justice system with its own costs of police, courts, and prisons make the final part of the total costs. The enormous burden that crime imposes on societies for long was as obvious as vaguely quantified. . . .

Critical Thinking

1. Assess how accurate the author's measures are in costing crime and its impacts.
2. If the costs of crime exceed a trillion dollars, should it be handled differently than it currently is handled?

3. What new perspectives does this article give you?

Create Central

www.mhhe.com/createcentral

Internet References

Sociosite
www.topsite.com/goto/sociosite.net

Socioweb
www.topsite.com/goto/socioweb.com

Sociology—Study Sociology Online
http://edu.learnsoc.org

Sociology Web Resources
www.mhhe.com/socscience/sociology/resources/index.htm

Unit 3

UNIT

Prepared by: Kurt Finsterbusch, *University of Maryland, College Park*

Groups and Roles in Transition

Primary groups are small, intimate, spontaneous, and personal. In contrast, secondary groups are large, formal, and impersonal. Primary groups include the family, couples, gangs, cliques, teams, and small tribes or rural villages. Primary groups are the main sources that the individual draws upon in developing values and an identity. Secondary groups include most of the organizations and bureaucracies in a modern society, and carry out most of its instrumental functions. Often, primary groups are formed within secondary groups, such as a factory, school, or business. Urbanization, geographic mobility, centralization, bureaucratization, and other aspects of modernization have had an impact on the nature of groups, the quality of the relationships between people, and individual's feelings of belonging.

The family, in particular, has undergone radical transformation. The greatly increased participation of women in the paid-labor force and their increased careerism has led to severe conflicts for women between their work and family roles.

Article   Prepared by: Kurt Finsterbusch, *University of Maryland, College Park*

The New White Negro

What it means that family breakdown is now biracial.

ISABEL V. SAWHILL

Learning Outcomes

After reading this article, you will be able to:

- Discern the truth of the family breakdown thesis and the falsehood of that thesis. The family is not breaking down in the middle or upper class (divorce rate is not increasing). In the lower class, both black and white, it is breaking down.

- Understand the negative impacts of family breakdown on parents, children, and society.

In 1965, Daniel Patrick Moynihan released a controversial report written for his then boss, President Lyndon Johnson. Entitled "The Negro Family: The Case for National Action," it described the condition of lower-income African American families and catalyzed a highly acrimonious, decades-long debate about black culture and family values in America.

The report cited a series of staggering statistics showing high rates of divorce, unwed childbearing, and single motherhood among black families. "The white family has achieved a high degree of stability and is maintaining that stability," the report said. "By contrast, the family structure of lower class Negroes is highly unstable, and in many urban centers is approaching complete breakdown."

Nearly fifty years later, the picture is even more grim—and the statistics can no longer be organized neatly by race. In fact, Moynihan's bracing profile of the collapsing black family in the 1960s looks remarkably similar to a profile of the average white family today. White households have similar—or worse—statistics of divorce, unwed childbearing, and single motherhood as the black households cited by Moynihan in his report. In 2000, the percentage of white children living with a single parent was identical to the percentage of black children living with a single parent in 1960: 22 percent.

What was happening to black families in the '60s can be reinterpreted today not as an indictment of the black family but as a harbinger of a larger collapse of traditional living arrangements—of what demographer Samuel Preston, in words that Moynihan later repeated, called "the earthquake that shuddered through the American family."

That earthquake has not affected all American families the same way. While the Moynihan report focused on disparities between white and black, increasingly it is class, and not just race, that matters for family structure. Although blacks as a group are still less likely to marry than whites, gaps in family formation patterns by class have increased for both races, with the sharpest declines in marriage rates occurring among the least educated of both races. For example, in 1960, 76 percent of adults with a college degree were married, compared to 72 percent of those with a high school diploma—a gap of only 4 percentage points. By 2008, not only was marriage less likely, but that gap had quadrupled, to 16 percentage points, with 64 percent of adults with college degrees getting married compared to only 48 percent of adults with a high school diploma. A report from the National Marriage Project at the University of Virginia summed up the data well: "Marriage is an emerging dividing line between America's moderately educated middle and those with college degrees." The group for whom marriage has largely disappeared now includes not just unskilled blacks but unskilled whites as well. Indeed, for younger women without a college degree, unwed childbearing is the new normal.

These differences in family formation are a problem not only for those concerned with "family values" per se, but also for those concerned with upward mobility in a society that values equal opportunity for its children. Because the breakdown of the traditional family is overwhelmingly occurring among working-class Americans of all races, these trends threaten to make the U.S. a much more class-based society over time. The well-educated and upper-middle-class parents who are still forming two-parent families are able to invest time and resources in their children—time and resources that lower- and working-class single mothers, however impressive their efforts to be both good parents and good breadwinners, simply do not have.

The striking similarities between what happened to black Americans at an earlier stage in our history and what is happening now to white working-class Americans may shed new light on old debates about cultural versus structural explanations of poverty. What's clear is that economic opportunity, while not the only factor affecting marriage, clearly matters.

The journalist Hanna Rosin describes the connection between declining economic opportunities for men and declining rates of marriage in her book *The End of Men.* Like Moynihan, she points to the importance of job opportunities for men in maintaining marriage as an institution. The disappearance of well-paying factory jobs has, in her view, led to the near collapse of marriage in towns where less educated men used to be able to support a family and a middle-class lifestyle, earning $70,000 or more in a single year. As these jobs have been outsourced or up-skilled, such men either are earning less or are jobless altogether, making them less desirable marriage partners. Other researchers, including Kathryn Edin at Harvard, Andrew Cherlin at Johns Hopkins, and Charles Murray of the American Enterprise Institute, drawing on close observations of other working-class communities, have made similar arguments.

Family life, to some extent, adapts to the necessities thrown up by the evolution of the economy. Just as joblessness among young black men contributed to the breakdown of the black family that Moynihan observed in the '60s, more recent changes in technology and global competition have hollowed out the job market for less educated whites. Unskilled white men have even less attachment to the labor force today than unskilled black men did fifty years ago, leading to a decline in their marriage rates in a similar way.

In 1960, the employment rate of prime-age (twenty-five to fifty-five) black men with less than a high school education was 80 percent. Fast-forward to 2000, and the employment rate of white men with less than a high school education was much lower, at 65 percent—and even for white high school graduates it was only 84 percent. Without an education in today's economy, being white is no guarantee of being able to find a job.

That's not to say that race isn't an issue. It's clear that black men have been much harder hit by the disappearance of jobs for the less skilled than white men. Black employment rates for those with less than a college education have sunk to near-catastrophic levels. In 2000, only 63 percent of black men with only a high school diploma (compared with 84 percent of white male graduates) were employed. Since the recession, those numbers have fallen even farther. And even black college graduates are not doing quite as well as their white counterparts. Based on these and other data, I believe it would be a mistake to conclude that race is unimportant; blacks continue to face unique disadvantages because of the color of their skin. It ought to be possible to say that class is becoming more important, but that race still matters a lot.

Most obviously, the black experience has been shaped by the impact of slavery and its ongoing aftermath. Even after emancipation and the civil rights revolution in the 1960s, African Americans faced exceptional challenges like segregated and inferior schools and discrimination in the labor market. It would take at least a generation for employers to begin to change their hiring practices and for educational disparities to diminish; even today these remain significant barriers. A recent audit study found that white applicants for low-wage jobs were twice as likely to be called in for interviews as equally qualified black applicants.

Black jobless rates not only exceed those of whites; in addition, a single-minded focus on declining job prospects for men and its consequences for family life ignores a number of other factors that have led to the decline of marriage. Male employment prospects can lead to more marriages, but scholars such as Harvard's David Ellwood and Christopher Jencks have argued that economic factors alone cannot explain the wholesale changes in the frequency of single parenting, unwed births, divorce, and marriage, especially among the least educated, that are leading to growing gaps between social classes. So what else explains the decline of marriage?

First, and critically important in my view, is the changing role of women. In my first book, *Time of Transition: The Growth of Families Headed by Women,* published in 1975, my coauthor and I argued that it was not just male earnings that mattered, but what men could earn relative to women. When women don't gain much, if anything, from getting married, they often choose to raise children on their own. Fifty years ago, women were far more economically dependent on marriage than they are now. Today, women are not just working more, they are better suited by education and tradition to work in such rapidly growing sectors of the economy as health care, education, administrative jobs, and services. While some observers may see women taking these jobs as a matter of necessity—and that's surely a factor—we shouldn't forget the revolution in women's roles that has made it possible for them to support a family on their own.

In a fascinating piece of academic research published in the *Journal of Human Resources* in 2011, Scott Hankins and Mark Hoekstra discovered that single women who won between $25,000 and $50,000 in the Florida lottery were 41 percent to 48 percent less likely to marry over the following three years than women who won less than $1,000. We economists call this a "natural experiment," because it shows the strong influence of women's ability to support themselves without marriage—uncontaminated by differences in personal attributes that may also affect one's ability or willingness to marry. My own earlier research also suggested that the relative incomes of wives and husbands predicted who would divorce and who would not.

Women's growing economic independence has interacted with stubborn attitudes about changing gender roles. When husbands fail to adjust to women's new breadwinning responsibilities (who cooks dinner or stays home with a sick child when both parents work?) the couple is more likely to divorce. It may be that well-educated younger men and women continue to marry not only because they can afford to but because many of the men in these families have adopted more egalitarian attitudes. While a working-class male might find such attitudes threatening to his manliness, an upper-middle-class man often does not, given his other sources of status. But when women find themselves having to do it all—that is, earn money in the workplace and shoulder the majority of child care and other domestic responsibilities—they raise the bar on whom they're willing to marry or stay married to.

These gender-related issues may play an even greater role for black women, since while white men hold slightly more high school diplomas and baccalaureate degrees than white women, black women are much better educated than black men. That means it's more difficult for well-educated black women to find black partners with comparable earning ability and social status. In 2010, black women made 87 percent of what black men did, whereas white women made only 70 percent of what white men earned. For less educated black women, there is, in addition, a shortage of black men because of high rates of incarceration. One estimate puts the proportion of black men who will spend some time in prison at almost one third.

In a forthcoming book, *Doing the Best I Can: Fatherhood in the Inner City,* Timothy Nelson and Edin, the Harvard sociologist, describe in great detail the kind of role reversal that has occurred among low-income families, both black and white. What they saw were mothers who were financially responsible for children, and fathers who were trying to maintain ties to their children in other ways, limited by the fact that these fathers have very little money, are often involved in drugs, crime, or other relationships, and rarely live with the mother and child. In other words, low-income fathers are not only withdrawing from the traditional breadwinner role, they're staging a wholesale retreat—even as they make attempts to remain involved in their children's lives.

Normative changes figure as well. As the retreat from marriage has become more common, it's also become more acceptable. That acceptance came earlier among blacks than among whites because of their own distinct experiences. Now that unwed childbearing is becoming the norm among the white working class as well, there is no longer much of a stigma associated with single parenting, and there is a greater willingness on the part of the broader community to accept the legitimacy of single-parent households.

Despite this change in norms, however, most Americans, whatever their race or social class, still aspire to marriage. It's just that their aspirations are typically unrealistically high and their ability to achieve that ideal is out of step with their opportunities and lifestyle. As scholars such as Cherlin and Edin have emphasized, marriage is no longer a precursor to adult success. Instead, when it still takes place, marriage is more a badge of success already achieved. In particular, large numbers of young adults are having unplanned pregnancies long before they can cope with the responsibilities of parenthood. Paradoxically, although they view marriage as something they cannot afford, they rarely worry about the cost of raising a child.

Along with many others, I remain concerned about the effects on society of this wholesale retreat from stable two-parent families. The consequences for children, especially, are not good. Their educational achievements, and later chances of becoming involved in crime or a teen pregnancy are, on average, all adversely affected by growing up in a single-parent

family. But I am also struck by the lessons that emerge from looking at how trends in family formation have differed by class as well as by race. If we were once two countries, one black and one white, we are now increasingly becoming two countries, one advantaged and one disadvantaged. Race still affects an individual's chances in life, but class is growing in importance. This argument was the theme of William Julius Wilson's 1980 book. *The Declining Significance of Race.* More recent evidence suggests that, despite all the controversy his book engendered, he was right.

To say that class is becoming more important than race isn't to dismiss race as a very important factor. Blacks have faced, and will continue to face, unique challenges. But when we look for the reasons why less skilled blacks are failing to marry and join the middle class, it is largely for the same reasons that marriage and a middle-class lifestyle is eluding a growing number of whites as well. The jobs that unskilled men once did are gone, women are increasingly financially independent, and a broad cultural shift across America has created a new normal.

Critical Thinking

1. Why is divorce treated as a great evil when entered into by the free choice of adults? Are they not the best persons to determine what is best for them and their family?

2. No one advocates making divorce illegal. Is the present situation ideal? If not, what is wrong with it?

3. What indicators of family well-being have worsened, and what indicators have improved?

Create Central

www.mhhe.com/createcentral

Internet References

Sociosite
www.topsite.com/goto/sociosite.net

Socioweb
www.topsite.com/goto/socioweb.com

Sociology—Study Sociology Online
http://edu.learnsoc.org

Sociology Web Resources
www.mhhe.com/socscience/sociology/resources/index.htm

ISABEL SAWHILL, a senior fellow at the Brookings Institution, has written extensively on the family and the economy. Her most recent book is *Creating an Opportunity Society.*

Sawhill, Isabel V. From *Washington Monthly,* January/February 2013, pp. 52–54. Copyright © 2013 by Washington Monthly Publishing, LLC, 1319 F St. NW, Suite 710, Washington, DC 20004. (202) 393-5155. Reprinted by permission. www.washingtonmonthly.com

Article   Prepared by: Kurt Finsterbusch, *University of Maryland, College Park*

The Gay Guide to Wedded Bliss

Compared with straight marriages, research finds, same-sex unions tend to be happier, with less conflict, greater emotional intimacy, and more-equal sharing of chores and child-rearing. What gay and lesbian spouses can teach straight ones about living happily ever after.

Liza Mundy

Learning Outcomes

After reading this article, you will be able to:

- Assess more carefully the quality of gay/lesbian marriages or partnerships.

- Know the qualities of relationships that on average are critical to successful marriages.

- Better understand the changing role of homosexual relationships in American society.

It is more than a little ironic that gay marriage has emerged as the era's defining civil-right struggle even as marriage itself seems more endangered every day. Americans are waiting longer to marry: according to the U.S. Census Bureau, the median age of first marriage is 28 for men and 26 for women, up from 23 and 20, respectively, in 1950. Rates of cohabitation have risen swiftly and sharply, and more people than ever are living single. Most Americans still marry at some point, but many of those marriages end in divorce. (Although the U.S. divorce rate has declined from its all-time high in the late '70s and early '80s, it has remained higher than those of most European countries.) All told, this has created an unstable system of what the UCLA sociologist Suzanne Bianchi calls "partnering and repartnering," a relentless emotional and domestic churn that sometimes results in people forgoing the institution altogether.

Though people may be waiting to marry, they are not necessarily waiting to have children. The National Center for Family and Marriage Research has produced a startling analysis of data from the Census Bureau and the Centers for Disease Control and Prevention showing that women's median age when they have their first child is lower than their median age at first marriage. In other words, having children before you marry has become normal. College graduates enjoy relatively stable unions, but for every other group, marriage is collapsing. Among "middle American" women (those with a high-school degree or some college), an astonishing 58 percent of first-time

mothers are unmarried. The old Groucho Marx joke—"I don't care to belong to any club that will have me as a member"—applies a little differently in this context: you might well ask why gays and lesbians want to join an institution that keeps dithering about whether to admit them even as the repo men are coming for the furniture and the fire marshal is about to close down the clubhouse.

Against this backdrop, gay-marriage opponents have argued that allowing same-sex couples to wed will pretty much finish matrimony off. This point was advanced in briefs and oral arguments before the Supreme Court in March, in two major same-sex-marriage cases. One of these is a constitutional challenge to a key section of the Defense of Marriage Act, the 1996 law that defines marriage as a union between a man and a woman, and bars the federal government from recognizing same-sex marriages. The other involves California's Proposition 8, a same-sex-marriage ban passed by voters in 2008 but overturned by a federal judge in 2010. Appearing before the high court in March, Charles J. Cooper, the lawyer defending the California ban, predicted that same-sex marriage would undermine traditional marriage by eroding "marital norms."

The belief that gay marriage will harm marriage has roots in both religious beliefs about matrimony and secular conservative concerns about broader shifts in American life. One prominent line of thinking holds that men and women have distinct roles to play in family life; that children need both a mother and a father, preferably biologically related to them; and that a central purpose of marriage is abetting heterosexual procreation. During the Supreme Court arguments over Proposition 8, Justice Elena Kagan asked Cooper whether the essence of his argument against gay marriage was that opposite-sex couples can procreate while same-sex ones cannot. "That's the essential thrust of our position, yes," replied Cooper. He also warned that "redefining marriage as a genderless institution could well lead over time to harms to that institution."

Threaded through this thinking is a related conviction that mothers and fathers should treat their union as "permanent and exclusive," as the Princeton professor Robert P. George and his co-authors write in the new book *What Is Marriage? Man and*

Woman: A Defense. Marriage, seen this way, is a rigid institution that exists primarily for the rearing of children and that powerfully constrains the behavior of adults (one is tempted to call this the "long slog 'til death" view of marriage), rather than an emotional union entered into for pleasure and companionship between adults. These critics of gay marriage are, quite validly, worried that too many American children are being raised in unstable homes, either by struggling single parents or by a transient succession of live-in adults. They fear that the spread of gay marriage could help finally sever the increasingly tenuous link between children and marriage, confirming that it's okay for dads, or moms, to be deleted from family life as hedonic fulfillment dictates.

In mounting their defense, advocates of same-sex marriage have argued that gays and lesbians who wish to marry are committed to family well-being; that concern for children's welfare is a chief reason many do want to marry; that gay people are being discriminated against, as a class, in being denied rights readily available to any heterosexual. And to the charge that same-sex marriage will change marriage, they tend to argue that it will not—that married gays and lesbians will blend seamlessly with the millions of married straight Americans. "The notion that this group can somehow fundamentally change the institution of marriage—I find it difficult to wrap my head around," says Gary Gates, a demographer with the Williams Institute, a research center affiliated with the UCLA School of Law.

But what if the critics are correct, just not in the way they suppose? What if same-sex marriage does change marriage, but primarily for the better? For one thing, there is reason to think that, rather than making marriage more fragile, the boom of publicity around same-sex weddings could awaken among heterosexuals a new interest in the institution, at least for a time. But the larger change might be this: by providing a new model of how two people can live together equitably, same-sex marriage could help haul matrimony more fully into the 21st century. Although marriage is in many ways fairer and more pleasurable for both men and women than it once was, it hasn't entirely thrown off old notions and habits. As a result, many men and women enter into it burdened with assumptions and stereotypes that create stress and resentment. Others, confronted with these increasingly anachronistic expectations—expectations at odds with the economic and practical realities of their own lives—don't enter into it at all.

Same-sex spouses, who cannot divide their labor based on preexisting gender norms, must approach marriage differently than their heterosexual peers. From sex to fighting, from child-rearing to chores, they must hammer out every last detail of domestic life without falling back on assumptions about who will do what. In this regard, they provide an example that can be enlightening to all couples. Critics warn of an institution rendered "genderless." But if a genderless marriage is a marriage in which the wife is not automatically expected to be responsible for school forms and child care and dinner preparation and birthday parties and midnight feedings and holiday shopping, I think it's fair to say that many heterosexual women would cry "Bring it on!"

Beyond that, gay marriage can function as a controlled experiment, helping us see which aspects of marital difficulty are truly rooted in gender and which are not. A growing body of social science has begun to compare straight and same-sex couples in an attempt to get at the question of what is female, what is male. Some of the findings are surprising. For instance: we know that heterosexual wives are more likely than husbands to initiate divorce. Social scientists have struggled to explain the discrepancy, variously attributing it to the sexual revolution; to women's financial independence; to men's failure to keep modern wives happy. Intriguingly, in Norway and Sweden, where registered partnerships for same-sex couples have been in place for about two decades (full-fledged marriage was introduced several years ago), research has found that lesbians are twice as likely as gay men to split up. If women become dissatisfied even when married to other women, maybe the problem with marriage isn't men. Maybe women are too particular. Maybe even women don't know what women want. These are the kinds of things that we will be able to tease out.

In the past few years, as support for same-sex marriage has gained momentum, advocates have been able to shift their strategy away from fighting bans on it (on the books in 38 states as of this writing) and toward orchestrating popular votes in its favor. In 2012, voters in Maine, Maryland, and Washington state passed measures legalizing same-sex marriage, joining the District of Columbia and the six states that had already legalized gay marriage via legislatures or courts. Similar measures are moving forward in four other states. In the coming weeks, the high court is expected to issue its rulings on gay marriage. After oral arguments in the two cases concluded, many Court observers predicted that the part of DOMA in question might well be struck down as a federal intrusion on states' ability to decide family law, thereby forcing the federal government to recognize the marriages of same-sex couples. As for Prop 8, any number of outcomes seem possible. The Court could decide that the case should not have been heard in the first place, given that the ban isn't being defended by California state officials but instead by the original supporters of the initiative. Such dismissal on "standing" could have the effect of legalizing same-sex marriage in California. Alternatively, the Court could deliver a narrow ruling (whether upholding or overturning the ban) that does not apply to every state. Among other feasible, if less likely, outcomes: the Court could use Prop 8 to declare all such bans unconstitutional, legalizing gay marriage everywhere.

Whatever happens with the high court, it seems likely that gay marriage will continue its spread through the land. So what happens, then, to the institution of marriage? The impact is likely to be felt near and far, both fleetingly and more permanently, in ways confounding to partisans on both sides.

Rules for a More Perfect Union

Not all is broken within modern marriage, of course. On the contrary: the institution is far more flexible and forgiving than it used to be. In the wake of women's large-scale entry into the workplace, men are less likely than they once were to be saddled with being a family's sole breadwinner, and can carve out a life that includes the close companionship of their children. Meanwhile, women are less likely to be saddled with the sole responsibility for child care and housework, and can envision a life beyond the stove top and laundry basket.

And yet for many couples, as Bianchi, the UCLA sociologist, has pointed out, the modern ideal of egalitarianism has proved "quite difficult to realize." Though men are carrying more of a domestic workload than in the past, women still bear the brunt of the second shift. Among couples with children, when both spouses work full-time, women do 32 hours a week of housework, child care, shopping, and other family-related services, compared with the 21 hours men put in. Men do more paid work—45 hours, compared with 39 for women—but still have more free time: 31 hours, compared with 25 for women. Betsey Stevenson and Justin Wolfers, economists and professors of public policy at the University of Michigan, have shown that happiness rates among women have dropped even as women have acquired more life options. One possible cause is the lingering inequity in male-female marriage: women's at-home workload can become so burdensome that wives opt out of the paid workforce—or sit at the office making mental lists of the chores they do versus the chores their husbands do, and bang their heads on their desks in despair.

Not that everything is easy for fathers in dual-earner couples, who now feel afflicted by work-life conflict in even greater numbers than their wives (60 percent of men in such couples say they experience this conflict, versus 47 percent of women, according to a 2008 study by the Families and Work Institute). And men face a set of unfair expectations all their own: the Pew Research Center found in 2010 that 67 percent of Americans still believe it's "very important" that a man be ready to support a family before getting married, while only 33 percent believe the same about women.

This burden, exacerbated by the economic realities facing many men today, has undoubtedly contributed to marriage's recent decline. As our economy has transitioned away from manufacturing and industry, men with a high-school education can no longer expect the steady, well-paying union jobs that formerly enabled many to support their families. Outdated assumptions that men should bring something to the table, and that this something should be money, don't help. Surveying their prospects, many working-class mothers reject marriage altogether, perhaps reasoning that they can support a child, but don't want a dependent husband.

It's not that people don't want to marry. Most never-married Americans say they still aspire to marriage, but many of them see it as something grand and out of reach. Getting married is no longer something you do when you are young and foolish and starting out; prosperity is not something spouses build together. Rather, marriage has become a "marker of prestige," as the sociologist Andrew Cherlin puts it—a capstone of a successful life, rather than its cornerstone. But while many couples have concluded that they are not ready for marriage, they have things backwards. It's not that they aren't ready for marriage; it's that marriage isn't ready for the realities of 21st-century life. Particularly for less affluent, less educated Americans,

changing economic and gender realities have dismantled the old institution, without constructing any sort of replacement.

As we attempt to come up with a more functional model, research on same-sex unions can provide what Gary Gates of the Williams Institute calls an "important counterfactual." Although gays and lesbians cannot solve all that ails marriage, they seem to be working certain things out in ways straight couples might do well to emulate, chief among them a back-to-the-drawing-board approach to divvying up marital duties. A growing body of scholarship on household division of labor shows that in many ways, same-sex couples do it better.

This scholarship got its start in the late 1960s, with a brilliant insight by the sociologist Pepper Schwartz, then a doctoral candidate at Yale. Against a backdrop of cultural upheaval—including changes at the university, which had just begun to admit female undergraduates—gender was, Schwartz says, "all we thought about." Like many of her peers, she was keen to figure out what women were and what men were: which traits were biological and which social, and where there might be potential for transformational change. "It occurred to me," she says, that "a naturally occurring experiment" could shed light on these issues. Actually, two experiments: the rise of unmarried heterosexual cohabitation, and the growing visibility of gay and lesbian couples. If she surveyed people in three kinds of relationships—married; straight and cohabiting; and gay and cohabiting—and all showed similarity on some measures, maybe this would say something about both men and women. If the findings didn't line up, maybe this would say something about marriage.

After taking a teaching position at the University of Washington (where she remains a faculty member), Schwartz teamed up with a gay colleague, the late Philip Blumstein, to conduct just such a survey, zeroing in on the greater San Francisco, New York City, and Seattle metropolitan areas. It was a huge effort. Unmarried cohabiting couples were not yet easy to find, and gays and lesbians were so leery of being outed that when Schwartz asked a woman who belonged to a lesbian bridge group whether she could interview the other players about their relationships, the woman said, "We don't even talk about it ourselves." Schwartz and Blumstein collected responses to 12,000 questionnaires and conducted hundreds of interviews; at one point, they had 20 graduate students helping tabulate data. The project took about a decade, and resulted in a groundbreaking piece of sociology, the book *American Couples: Money, Work, Sex.*

What Schwartz and Blumstein found is that gay and lesbian couples were fairer in their dealings with one another than straight couples, both in intent and in practice. The lesbians in the study were almost painfully egalitarian—in some cases putting money in jars and splitting everything down to the penny in a way, Schwartz says, that "would have driven me crazy." Many unmarried heterosexual cohabitators were also careful about divvying things up, but lesbian couples seemed to take the practice to extremes: "it was almost like 'my kitty, your litter.'" Gay men, like lesbians, were more likely than straight couples to share cooking and chores. Many had been in heterosexual marriages, and when asked whether they had helped their wives with the housework in those prior unions, they usually said they had not. "You can imagine," Schwartz says, "how irritating I found this."

There were still some inequities: in all couples, the person with the higher income had more authority and decision-making power. This was least true for lesbians; truer for heterosexuals; and most true for gay men. Somehow, putting two men together seemed to intensify the sense that "money talks," as Schwartz and Blumstein put it. They could not hope to determine whether this tendency was innate or social—were men naturally inclined to equate resources with power, or had our culture ingrained that idea in them?—but one way or another, the finding suggested that money was a way men competed with other men, and not just a way for husbands to compete with their wives. Among lesbians, the contested terrain lay elsewhere: for instance, interacting more with the children could be, Schwartz says, a "power move."

Lesbians also tended to discuss things endlessly, achieving a degree of closeness unmatched by the other types of couples. Schwartz wondered whether this might account for another finding: over time, sex in lesbian relationships dwindled—a state of affairs she has described as "lesbian bed death." (The coinage ended up on Schwartz's Wikipedia page, to her exasperation: "There are other things that I wish I were famous around.") She posits that lesbians may have had so much intimacy already that they didn't need sex to get it; by contrast, heterosexual women, whose spouses were less likely to be chatty, found that "sex is a highway to intimacy." As for men, she eventually concluded that whether they were straight or gay, they approached sex as they might a sandwich: good, bad, or mediocre, they were likely to grab it.

> RULE 1: Negotiate in advance who will empty the trash
> and who will clean the bathroom.

Other studies have since confirmed Schwartz and Blumstein's findings that same-sex couples are more egalitarian. In 2000, when Vermont became the first state to legalize same-sex civil unions, the psychologist Esther Rothblum saw an opportunity to explore how duties get sorted among a broad swath of the same-sex population. Rothblum, now at San Diego State University, is herself a lesbian and had long been interested in the relationships and mental health of lesbians. She also wanted to see how legal recognition affected couples.

As people from around the country flocked to Vermont to apply for civil-union licenses, Rothblum and two colleagues got their names and addresses from public records and asked them to complete a questionnaire. Then, they asked each of the civil-union couples to suggest friends in same-sex couples who were not in civil unions, and to identify a heterosexual sibling who was married, and wrote those people asking them to participate. This approach helped control for factors like background and upbringing among the subjects. The researchers asked people to rate, on a scale of one to nine, which partner was more likely to do the dishes, repair things around the house, buy groceries. They asked who was more likely to deal with the landlord, punish the children, call the plumber, drive the kids to appointments, give spontaneous hugs, pay compliments. They also asked who was more likely to appreciate the other person's point of view during an argument.

They found that, even in the new millennium, married heterosexual couples were very likely to divide duties along old-fashioned gender lines. Straight women were more likely than lesbians to report that their partner paid the mortgage or the rent and the utility bills, and bought groceries, household appliances, even the women's clothing. These wives were also more likely to say they did the bulk of the cooking, vacuuming, dishes, and laundry. Compared with their husbands, they were far, far more likely to clean the bathroom. They were also more likely than their husbands to perform "relationship maintenance" such as showing affection and initiating serious conversations. When Rothblum and her colleagues held the heterosexual husbands up against the gay men, they found the same pattern. The straight guys were more likely to take care of the lawn, empty the trash, and make household repairs than their partners. They were the ones to fix drinks for company and to drive when the couple went out. They cooked breakfast reasonably often, but not dinner. On all these measures and more, the same-sex couples were far more likely to divide responsibilities evenly. This is not to say that the same-sex couples split each duty half-and-half. One partner might do the same chore regularly, but because there was no default assignment based on gender, such patterns evolved organically, based on preferences and talents.

Rothblum's observations are borne out by the couples I interviewed for this piece. "I'm a better cook, so I take on most of that responsibility," said Seth Thayer, who lives in a small coastal town in Maine. His husband, Greg Tinder, "is a better handyman." Others spoke of the perils of lopsided relationships. Chris Kast, a Maine newlywed, told me that he and his husband, Byron Bartlett, had both been married to women. In Bartlett's first marriage, it was tacitly assumed that he would take out the garbage. Now the two men divide tasks by inclination. "I'm more of a Felix Ungar—I notice when something's dirty—but we both clean," Kast said. "With Chris and I," Bartlett added, "we have to get *everything* done." Isabelle Dikland, a Washington, D.C., business consultant who is married to Amy Clement, a teacher, told me about a dinner party she recently attended with a group of mostly straight parents. Dikland and Clement, who had just had a second daughter, were extolling the virtues of having two children. The straight mother they were talking with seemed dubious, "if we had a second kid, guess who would do all the work," she told them. "I'd have to give up my career; I'm already doing everything." The woman glanced surreptitiously at her husband, at which point Dikland "dropped the subject really quickly."

> RULE 2: When it comes to parenting, a 50–50 split isn't
> necessarily best.

Charlotte J. Patterson, a psychologist at the University of Virginia, has arresting visual evidence of the same egalitarianism at work in parenting: compared with husband-and-wife pairs, she has found, same-sex parents tend to be more cooperative and mutually hands-on. Patterson and a colleague, Rachel Farr, have conducted a study of more than 100 same-sex and heterosexual adoptive parents in 11 states and the District of Columbia; it is among the first such studies to include gay fathers. As reported in an article in a forthcoming issue of the journal *Child Development*, the researchers visited families in their homes, scattered some toys on a blanket, invited the subjects to play with them any way they chose, and videotaped the interactions. "What you see is what they did with that blank slate," Patterson says. "One thing that I found riveting: the same-sex couples are far more likely to be in there together, and the opposite-sex couples show the conventional pattern—the mom more involved, the dad playing with Tinkertoys by himself." When the opposite-sex couples did parent simultaneously, they were more likely to undermine each other by talking at cross-purposes or suggesting different toys. The lesbian mothers tended to be egalitarian and warm in their dealings with one another, and showed greater pleasure in parenting than the other groups did. Same-sex dads were also more egalitarian in their division of labor than straight couples, though not as warm or interactive as lesbian moms. (Patterson says she and her colleagues may need to refine their analysis to take into account male ways of expressing warmth.)

By and large, all of the families studied, gay and straight alike, were happy, high functioning, and financially secure. Each type of partner—gay, straight; man, woman—reported satisfaction with his or her family's parenting arrangement, though the heterosexual wife was less content than the others, invariably saying that she wanted more help from her husband. "Of all the parents we've studied, she's the least satisfied with the division of labor," says Patterson, who is in a same-sex partnership and says she knows from experience that deciding who will do what isn't always easy.

Even as they are more egalitarian in their parenting styles, same-sex parents resemble their heterosexual counterparts in one somewhat old-fashioned way: a surprising number establish a division of labor whereby one spouse becomes the primary earner and the other stays home. Lee Badgett, an economist at the University of Massachusetts at Amherst, told me that, "in terms of economics," same-sex couples with children resemble heterosexual couples with children much more than they resemble childless same-sex couples. You might say that gay parents are simultaneously departing from traditional family structures and leading the way back toward them.

In his seminal book *A Treatise on the Family,* published in 1981, the Nobel Prize-winning economist Gary Becker argued that "specialization," whereby one parent stays home and the other does the earning, is the most efficient way of running a household, because the at-home spouse enables the at-work spouse to earn more. Feminists, who had been fighting for domestic parity, not specialization, deplored this theory, rightly fearing that it could be harnessed to keep women at home. Now the example of gay and lesbian parents might give us all permission to relax a little: maybe sometimes it really is easier when one parent works and the other is the supplementary or nonearning partner, either because this is the natural order of things or because the American workplace is so greedy and unforgiving that something or somebody has to give. As Martha Ertman, a University of Maryland law professor, put it to

me, many families just function better when the same person is consistently "in charge of making vaccinations happen, making sure the model of the World War II monument gets done, getting the Christmas tree home or the challah bought by 6 o'clock on Friday." The good news is that the decision about which parent plays this role need not have anything to do with gender.

More surprising still, guess who is most likely to specialize. Gay dads. Using the most recent Census Bureau data, Gary Gates found that 32 percent of married heterosexual couples with children have only one parent in the labor force, compared with 33 percent of gay-male couples with children. (Lesbians also specialize, but not at such high rates, perhaps because they are so devoted to equality, or perhaps because their earnings are lower—women's median wage is 81 percent that of men—and not working is an unaffordable luxury.) While the percentage point dividing gay men from straight couples is not statistically significant, it's intriguing that gay dads are as likely as straight women to be stay-at-home parents.

Gay men's decisions about breadwinning can nonetheless be fraught, as many associate employment with power. A study published in the *Journal of GLBT Family Studies* in 2005 by Stephanie Jill Schacher and two colleagues found that when gay men do specialize, they don't have an easy time deciding who will do what: some stay-at-home dads perceived that their choice carried with it a loss in prestige and stature. As a result, gay men tended to fight not over who got to stay home, but over who didn't have to. "it's probably the biggest problem in our relationship," said one man interviewed for that study. Perhaps what Betty Friedan called "the problem that has no name" is inherent in child-rearing, and will always be with us.

RULE 3: Don't want a divorce? Don't marry a woman.

Three years after they first gathered information from the couples who received licenses in Vermont, Esther Rothblum and her colleagues checked back to evaluate the condition of their relationships. Overall, the researchers found that the quality of gay and lesbian relationships was higher on many measures than that of the straight control group (the married heterosexual siblings), with more compatibility and intimacy, and less conflict.

Which is not to say same-sex couples don't have conflict. When they fight, however, they fight fairer. They can even fight funny, as researchers from the University of Washington and the University of California at Berkeley showed in an article published in 2003, based on a study of couples who were navigating potentially tense interactions. Recruiting married straight couples as well as gays and lesbians in committed relationships, the researchers orchestrated a scenario in which one partner had to bring up an area of conflict to discuss with the other. In same-sex couples, the partner with the bone to pick was rated "less belligerent and less domineering" than the straight-couple counterpart, while the person on the receiving end was less aggressive and showed less fear or tension. The same-sex "initiator" also displayed less sadness and "whining," and more affection, joy, and humor. In trying to make sense of the disparity, the researchers noted that same-sex couples valued equality more, and posited that the greater negativity of straight couples "may have to do with the standard status hierarchy between men and women." Which perhaps boils down to something like this: straight women see themselves as being less powerful than men, and this breeds hostility.

When it comes to conflict, a crucial variable separates many gay and lesbian couples from their straight counterparts: children. As Rothblum points out, for married heterosexual parents, happiness tends to be U-shaped: high at the beginning of marriage, then dipping to a low, then high again. What happens in that low middle is child-rearing. Although the proportion of gay and lesbian couples with children is increasing, same-sex couples are still less likely than straight couples to be parents. Not all research comparing same-sex and married straight couples has done an adequate job of controlling for this important difference. One that did, a 2008 study in the *Journal of Family Psychology,* looked at couples during their first 10 years of cohabitation. It found that childless lesbians had a higher "relationship quality" than their child-free gay-male and heterosexual counterparts. And yet a 2010 study in the same journal found that gay-male, lesbian, and straight couples alike experienced a "modest decline in relationship quality" in the first year of adopting a child. As same-sex couples become parents in greater numbers, they could well endure some of the same strife as their straight peers. It remains to be seen whether the different parenting styles identified by Charlotte Patterson might blunt some of the ennui of child-rearing.

As for divorce, the data are still coming in. A 2006 study of Sweden and Norway found higher dissolution rates among same-sex couples in registered partnerships than among married straight people. Yet in the United States, a study by the Williams Institute has found that gay unions have lower dissolution rates than straight ones. It is simply too soon to tell with any certainty whether gay marriages will be more or less durable in the long run than straight ones. What the studies to date do (for the most part) suggest is this: despite—or maybe because of—their perfectionist approach to egalitarianism, lesbian couples seem to be more likely to break up than gay ones. Pepper Schwartz noted this in the early 1980s, as did the 2006 study of same-sex couples in Sweden and Norway, in which researchers speculated that women may have a "stronger general sensitivity to the quality of relationships." Meaning maybe women are just picky, and when you have two women, you have double the pickiness. So perhaps the real threat to marriage is: women.

The Contagion Effect

Whatever this string of studies may teach us about marriage and gender dynamics, the next logical question becomes this: Might such marriages do more than merely inform our understanding of straight marriage—might their attributes trickle over to straight marriage in some fashion?

In the course of my reporting this year in states that had newly legalized same-sex marriage, people in the know—wedding planners, officiants, fiancés and fiancées—told me time and again that nuptial fever had broken out around them, among gay and straight couples alike. Same-sex weddings seemed to be bestowing a new frisson on the idea of getting hitched, or maybe restoring an old one. At the Gay and Lesbian Wedding Expo in downtown Baltimore, just a few weeks after same-sex marriage became legal in Maryland, Drew Vanlandingham, who describes himself as a "wedding planner designer," was delighted at how business had picked up. Here it was, January, and many of his favorite venues were booked into late summer—much to the consternation, he said, of his straight brides. "They're like, 'I better get a move on!'" It was his view that in Maryland, both teams were now engaged in an amiable but spirited race to the altar.

Ministers told me of wedding booms in their congregations. In her years as the pastor of the Unitarian church in Rockville, Maryland, Lynn Strauss said she had grown accustomed to a thin wedding roster: some years she might perform one or two services; other years, none. But this year, "my calendar is full of weddings," she said. "Two in March, one in April, one in May, one in September, one in October—oh, and one in July." Three were same-sex weddings, but the rest were heterosexual. When I attended the church's first lesbian wedding, in early March, I spoke with Steve Greene and Ellen Rohan, who had recently been married by Strauss. It was Steve's third marriage, Ellen's second. Before he met Ellen, Steve had sworn he would never marry again. Ellen said the arrival of same-sex marriage had influenced their feelings. "Marriage," she said simply, "is on everyone's mind."

Robert M. Hardies, who is a pastor at the Unitarian All Souls Church in Washington, D.C., and who is engaged to be married to his longtime partner and co-parent, Chris Nealon, told me that he has seen "a re-enchantment of marriage" among those who attend same-sex ceremonies: "Straight folks come to [same-sex] weddings, and I watch it on their face—there's a feeling that this is really special. Suddenly marriage is sexy again." We could chalk these anecdotes up to the human desire to witness love that overcomes obstacles—the same desire behind all romantic comedies, whether Shakespeare's or Hollywood's. But could something a bit less romantic also be at work?

There is some reason to suppose that attitudes about marriage could, in fact, be catching. The phenomenon known as "social contagion" lies at the heart of an increasingly prominent line of research on how our behavior and emotions affect the people we know. One famous example dates from 2008, when James H. Fowler and Nicholas A. Christakis published a study showing that happiness "spreads" through social networks. They arrived at this conclusion via an ingenious crunching of data from a long-running medical study involving thousands of interconnected residents—and their children, and later their grandchildren—in Framingham, Massachusetts. "Emotional states can be transferred directly from one individual to another," they found, across three degrees of separation. Other studies have shown that obesity, smoking habits, and school performance may also be catching.

Most relevant, in a working paper that is under submission to a sociology journal, the Brown University political scientist Rose McDermott, along with her co-authors, Fowler and Christakis, has identified a contagion effect for divorce.

Divorce, she found, can spread among friends. She told me that she also suspects that tending to the marriages of friends can help preserve your own. McDermott says she readily sees how marriage could itself be contagious. Intriguingly, some of the Scandinavian countries where same-sex unions have been legal for a decade or more have seen a rise, not a fall, in marriage rates. In response to conservative arguments that same-sex marriage had driven a stake through the heart of marriage in northern Europe, the Yale University law professor William N. Eskridge Jr. and Darren Spedale in 2006 published an analysis showing that in the decade since same-sex partnerships became legal, heterosexual marriage rates had increased 10.7 percent in Denmark, 12.7 percent in Norway, and 28.8 percent in Sweden. Divorce rates had dropped in all three countries. Although there was no way to prove cause and effect, the authors allowed, you could safely say that marriage had not been harmed.

So let's suppose for a moment that marital behavior is catching. How, exactly, might it spread? I found one possible vector of contagion inside the Washington National Cathedral, a neo-Gothic landmark that towers watchfully over the Washington, D.C., skyline. The seat of the bishop of an Episcopal diocese that includes D.C. and parts of Maryland, the cathedral is a symbol of American religious life, and strives to provide a spiritual home for the nation, frequently hosting interfaith events and programs. Presiding over it is the Very Reverend Gary Hall, an Episcopal priest and the cathedral's dean. Earlier this year, Hall announced that the cathedral would conduct same-sex weddings, a declaration that attracted more attention than he expected. Only people closely involved with the church and graduates of the private schools on its grounds can marry there. Even so, it is an influential venue, and Hall used the occasion to argue that same-sex couples offer an image of "radical" equality that straight couples can profitably emulate. He believes, moreover, that their example can be communicated through intermediaries like him: ministers and counselors gleaning insights from same-sex couples, and transmitting them, as it were, to straight ones. Hall says that counseling same-sex couples in preparation for their ceremonies has already altered the way he counsels men and women.

"I have a list of like 12 issues that people need to talk about that cause conflict," said Hall, who is lanky, with short gray hair and horn-rims, and who looks like he could be a dean of pretty much anything: American literature, political philosophy, East Asian studies. As we talked in his office one morning this spring, sunlight poured through a bank of arched windows onto an Oriental rug. Over the years, he has amassed a collection of cheesy 1970s paperbacks with names like *Open Marriage* and *Total Woman,* which he calls "books that got people into trouble." The dean grew up in Hollywood, and in the 1990s was a priest at a church in Pasadena where he did many same-sex blessings (a blessing being a ceremony that stops short of legal marriage). He is as comfortable talking about Camille Paglia and the LGBT critique of marriage as he is about Holy Week. He is also capable of saying things like "The problem with genital sex is that it involves us emotionally in a way that we're not in control of."

When Hall sees couples for premarital preparation, he gives them a list of hypothetical conflicts to take home, hash out, and

report back on. Everybody fights, he tells them. The people who thrive in marriage are the ones who can handle disagreement and make their needs known. So he presents them with the prime sticking points: affection and lovemaking; how to deal with in-laws; where holidays will be spent; outside friendships. He talks to them about parenting roles, and chores, and money—who will earn it and who will make decisions about it.

Like Esther Rothblum, he has found that heterosexual couples persist in approaching these topics with stereotypical assumptions. "You start throwing out questions for men and women: 'Who's going to take care of the money?' And the guy says, 'That's me.' And you ask: 'Who's responsible for birth control?' And the guy says, 'That's her department.'" By contrast, he reports, same-sex couples "have thought really hard about how they're going to share the property, the responsibilities, the obligations in a mutual way. They've had to devote much more thought to that than straight couples, because the straight couples pretty much still fall back on old modes."

Now when Hall counsels heterosexuals, "I'm really pushing back on their patriarchal assumptions: that the woman's got to give up her career for the guy; that the guy is going to take care of the money." Every now and then, he says, he has a breakthrough, and a straight groom realizes that, say, contraception is his concern too. Hall says the same thing is happening in the offices of any number of pastors, rabbis, and therapists. "You're not going to be able to talk to heterosexual couples where there's a power imbalance and talk to a homosexual couple where there is a power mutuality," and not have the conversations impact one another. As a result, he believes there will be changes to marriage, changes that some people will find scary. "When [conservatives] say that gay marriage threatens my marriage, I used to say, 'That's ridiculous.' Now I say, 'Yeah, it does. It's asking you a crucial question about your marriage that you may not want to answer: If I'm a man, am I actually sharing the duties and responsibilities of married life equally with my wife?' Same-sex marriage gives us another image of what marriage can be."

Hall argues that same-sex marriage stands to change even the wedding service itself. For a good 1,000 years, he notes, the Christian Church stayed out of matrimony, which was primarily a way for society to regulate things like inheritance. But ever since the Church did get involved, the wedding ceremony has tended to reflect the gender mores of the time. For example, the Book of Common Prayer for years stated that a wife must love, honor, and obey her husband, treating him as her master and lord. That language is long gone, but vestiges persist: the tradition of the father giving away the bride dates from an era when marriage was a property transfer and the woman was the property. In response to the push for same-sex marriage, Hall says, the General Convention, the governing council of the entire Episcopal Church, has devised a liturgy for same-sex ceremonies (in most dioceses, these are blessings) that honors but alters this tradition so that both spouses are presented by sponsors.

"The new service does not ground marriage in a doctrine of creation and procreation," Hall says. "It grounds marriage in a kind of free coming-together of two people to live out their lives." A study group has convened to look at the Church's teachings on marriage, and in the next couple of years, Hall expects, the General Convention will adopt a new service for all Episcopal weddings. He is hopeful that the current same-sex service will serve as its basis.

The legalization of same-sex marriage is likely to affect even members of churches that have not performed such ceremonies. Delman Coates, the pastor of Mt. Ennon Baptist, a predominantly African American mega-church in southern Maryland, was active in his state's fight for marriage equality, presenting it to his parishioners as a civil-rights issue. The topic has also led to some productive, if difficult, conversations about "what the Scriptures are condemning and what they're confirming." In particular, he has challenged his flock over what he calls the "typical clobber passages": certain verses in Leviticus, Romans, and elsewhere that many people interpret as condemnations of homosexuality. These discussions are part of a long-standing effort to challenge people's thinking about other passages having to do with divorce and premarital sex—issues many parishioners have struggled with at home. Coates preaches that what the Bible is condemning is not modern divorce, but a practice, common in biblical times, whereby men cast out their wives for no good reason. Similarly, he tells them that the "fornication" invoked is something extreme—rape, incest, prostitution. He does not condone illicit behavior or familial dissolution, but he wants the members of his congregation to feel better about their own lives. In exchanges like these, he is making gay marriage part of a much larger conversation about the way we live and love now.

Gay marriage's ripples are also starting to be felt beyond churches, in schools and neighborhoods and playgroups. Which raises another question: Will gay and lesbian couples be peacemakers or combatants in the "mommy wars"—the long-simmering struggle between moms who stay at home and moms who work outside it? If you doubt that straight households are paying attention to same-sex ones, consider Danie, a woman who lives with her husband and two children in Bethesda, Maryland. (Danie asked me not to use her last name out of concern for her family's privacy.) Not long after she completed a master's degree in Spanish linguistics at Georgetown University, her first baby was born. Because her husband, Jesse, works long hours as a litigator, she decided to become a full-time parent—not an easy decision in work-obsessed Washington, D.C. For a while, she ran a photography business out of their home, partly because she loves photography but partly so she could assure people at dinner parties that she had paying work. Whenever people venture that women who work outside the home don't judge stay-at-home moms, Danie thinks: *Are you freaking kidding me?*

She takes some comfort, however, in the example of a lesbian couple with whom she is friendly. Both women are attorneys, and one stays home with their child. "Their life is exactly the same as ours," Danie told me, with a hint of vindication. If being a stay-at-home mother is "good enough for her, then what's my issue? She's a huge women's-rights activist." But while comparing herself with a lesbian couple is liberating in some ways, it also exacerbates the competitive anxiety that afflicts so many modern mothers. The other thing about these two mothers, Danie said, is that they are so relaxed, so happy, so present. Even the working spouse manages to be a super-involved parent, to a much greater extent than most of the working fathers she knows. "I'm a little bit obsessed with them," she says.

Related to this is the question of how gay fatherhood might impact heterosexual fatherhood—by, for example, encouraging the idea that men can be emotionally accessible, logistically capable parents. Will the growing presence of gay dads in some communities mean that men are more often included in the endless e-mail chains that go to parents of preschoolers and birthday-party invitees? As radically as fatherhood has changed in recent decades, a number of antiquated attitudes about dads have proved strangely enduring: Rob Hardies, the pastor at All Souls, reports that when his partner, Chris, successfully folded a stroller before getting on an airplane with their son, Nico, he was roundly congratulated by passersby, as if he had solved a difficult mathematical equation in public. So low are expectations for fathers, even now, that in Stephanie Schacher's study of gay fathers and their feelings about care-giving, her subjects reported that people would see them walking on the street with their children and say things like "Giving Mom a break?" Hardies thinks that every time he and Chris take their son to the playground or to story hour, they help disrupt this sort of thinking. He imagines moms seeing a man doing this and gently—or maybe not so gently—pointing it out to their husbands. "Two guys somehow manage to get their act together and have a household and cook dinner and raise a child, without a woman doing all the work," he says. Rather than setting an example that fathers don't matter, gay men are setting an example that fathers do matter, and that marriage matters, too.

The Sex Problem

When, in the 1970s and early 1980s, Pepper Schwartz asked couples about their sex lives, she arrived at perhaps her most explosive finding: non-monogamy was rampant among gay men, a whopping 82 percent of whom reported having had sex outside their relationship. Slightly more than one-third of gay-male couples felt that monogamy was important; the other two-thirds said that monogamy was unimportant or that they were neutral on the topic. In a funny way, Schwartz says, her findings suggested that same-sex unions (like straight ones) aren't necessarily about sex. Some gay men made a point of telling her they loved their partners but weren't physically attracted to them. Others said they wanted to be monogamous but were unsupported in that wish, by their partner, gay culture, or both.

Schwartz believes that a move toward greater monogamy was emerging among gay men even before the AIDS crisis. Decades later, gay-male couples are more monogamous than they used to be, but not nearly to the same degree as other kinds of couples. In her Vermont research, Esther Rothblum found that 15 percent of straight husbands said they'd had sex outside their relationship, compared with 58 percent of gay men in civil unions and 61 percent of gay men who were partnered but not in civil unions. When asked whether a couple had arrived at an explicit agreement about extra-relational sex, a minuscule

4 percent of straight husbands said they'd discussed it with their partner and determined that it was okay, compared with 40 percent of gay men in civil unions and 49 percent of gay men in partnerships that were not legally recognized. Straight women and lesbians, meanwhile, were united in their commitment to monogamy, lesbians more so than straight women: 14 percent of straight wives said they had sex outside their marriage, compared with 9 percent of lesbians in civil unions and 7 percent of lesbians who were partnered but not in civil unions.

The question of whether gays and lesbians will change marriage, or vice versa, is at its thorniest around sex and monogamy. Private behavior could well stay private: when she studied marriage in the Netherlands, Lee Badgett, the University of Massachusetts economist, found that while many same-sex couples proselytize about the egalitarianism of their relationships, they don't tend to promote non-monogamy, even if they practice it. Then again, some gay-rights advocates, like the writer and sex columnist Dan Savage, argue very publicly that insisting on monogamy can do a couple more harm than good. Savage, who questions whether most humans are cut out for decades of sex with only one person, told me that "monogamy in marriage has been a disaster for straight couples" because it has set unrealistic expectations. "Gay-male couples are much more likely to be realistic about what men are," he said. Savage's own marriage started out monogamous; the agreement was that if either partner cheated, this would be grounds for ending the relationship. But when he and his husband decided to adopt a child, Savage suggested that they relax their zero-tolerance policy on infidelity. He felt that risking family dissolution over such an incident no longer made sense. His husband later suggested they explicitly allow each other occasional dalliances, a policy Savage sees as providing a safety valve for the relationship. If society wants marriage to be more resilient, he argues, we must make it more "monagamish."

This is, to be sure, a difficult argument to win: a husband proposing non-monogamy to his wife on the grounds that it is in the best interest of a new baby would have a tough time prevailing in the court of public opinion. But while most gay-marriage advocates stop short of championing Savage's "wiggle room," some experts say that gay men are better at talking more openly about sex. Naveen Jonathan, a family therapist and a professor at Chapman University, in California, says he sees many gay partners hammer out an elaborate who-can-do-what-when sexual contract, one that says, "These are the times and the situations where it's okay to be non-monogamous, and these are the times and the situations where it is not." While some straight couples have deals of their own, he finds that for the most part, they simply presume monogamy. A possible downside of this assumption: straight couples are far less likely than gay men to frankly and routinely discuss sex, desire, and the challenges of sexual commitment.

Other experts question the idea that most gay males share a preference for non-monogamous relationships, or will in the long term. Savage's argument that non-monogamy is a safety valve is "very interesting, but it really is no more than a claim," says Justin Garcia, an evolutionary biologist at the

Kinsey Institute for Research in Sex, Gender, and Reproduction. Garcia points out that not all men are relentlessly sexual beings, and not all men want an open relationship, "in some ways, same-sex couples are healthier—they tend to have these negotiations more," he says. But negotiating can be stressful: in many cases, Garcia notes, one gay partner would prefer to be monogamous, but gives in to the other partner.

So which version will prevail: non-monogamous marriage, or marriage as we conventionally understand it? It's worth pointing out that in the U.S., same-sex unions are slightly more likely between women, and non-monogamy is not a cause women tend to champion. And some evidence suggests that getting married changes behavior: William Eskridge and Darren Spedale found that in the years after Norway, Sweden, and Denmark instituted registered partnerships, many same-sex couples reported placing a greater emphasis on monogamy, while national rates of HIV infections declined.

Sex, then, may be one area where the institution of marriage pushes back against norms that have been embraced by many gay couples. Gary Hall of the National Cathedral allows that in many ways, gay relationships offer a salutary "critique" of marriage, but argues that the marriage establishment will do some critiquing back. He says he would not marry two people who intended to be non-monogamous, and believes that monogamy will be a "critical issue" in the dialogue between the gay community and the Church. Up until now, he says, progressive churches have embraced "the part of gay behavior that looks like straight behavior," but at some point, churches also have to engage gay couples whose behavior doesn't conform to monogamous ideals. He hopes that, in the course of this give-and-take, the church ends up reckoning with other ongoing cultural changes, from unmarried cohabitation to the increasing number of adults who choose to live as singles. "How do we speak credibly to people about their sexuality and their sexual relationships?" he asks. "We really need to rethink this."

So yes, marriage will change. Or rather, it will change again. The fact is, there is no such thing as traditional marriage. In various places and at various points in human history, marriage has been a means by which young children were betrothed, uniting royal houses and sealing alliances between nations. In the Bible, it was a union that sometimes took place between a man and his dead brother's widow, or between one man and several wives. It has been a vehicle for the orderly transfer of property from one generation of males to the next; the test by which children were deemed legitimate or bastard; a privilege not available to black Americans; something parents arranged for their adult children; a contract under which women, legally, ceased to exist. Well into the 19th century, the British common-law concept of "unity of person" meant a woman became her husband when she married, giving up her legal standing and the right to own property or control her own wages.

Many of these strictures have already loosened. Child marriage is today seen by most people as the human-rights violation that it is. The Married Women's Property Acts guaranteed that a woman could get married and remain a legally recognized human being. The Supreme Court's decision in *Loving v. Virginia* did away with state bans on interracial marriage. By making it easier to dissolve marriage, no-fault divorce helped ensure that unions need not be lifelong. The recent surge in single parenthood, combined with an aging population, has unyoked marriage and child-rearing. History shows that marriage evolves over time. We have every reason to believe that same-sex marriage will contribute to its continued evolution.

The argument that gays and lesbians are social pioneers and bellwethers has been made before. Back in 1992, the British sociologist Anthony Giddens suggested that gays and lesbians were a harbinger of a new kind of union, one subject to constant renegotiation and expected to last only as long as both partners were happy with it. Now that these so-called harbingers are looking to commit to more-binding relationships, we will have the "counterfactual" that Gary Gates talks about: we will be better able to tell which marital stresses and pleasures are due to gender, and which are not.

In the end, it could turn out that same-sex marriage isn't all that different from straight marriage. If gay and lesbian marriages are in the long run as quarrelsome, tedious, and unbearable; as satisfying, joyous, and loving as other marriages, we'll know that a certain amount of strife is not the fault of the alleged war between men and women, but just an inevitable thing that happens when two human beings are doing the best they can to find a way to live together.

Critical Thinking

1. Do you think that gay marriages should be legally treated as equal to heterosexual marriages?

2. Why or why not are gay marriages a threat to heterosexual marriages?

3. What "rules" should help improve marriages?

Create Central

www.mhhe.com/createcentral

Internet References

Marriage and Family Therapy
 www.aamft.org/index_nm.asp

Sociosite
 www.topsite.com/goto/sociosite.net

Socioweb
 www.topsite.com/goto/socioweb.com

Sociology—Study Sociology Online
 http://edu.learnsoc.org

Sociology Web Resources
 www.mhhe.com/socscience/sociology/resources/index.htm

LIZA MUNDY is a BERNARD L. SCHWARTZ Fellow at the New America Foundation and the author of *The Richer Sex: How the New Majority of Female Breadwinners Is Transforming Our Culture.*

Article   Prepared by: Kurt Finsterbusch, *University of Maryland, College Park*

Why Women Still Can't Have It All

It's time to stop fooling ourselves, says a woman who left a position of power: the women who have managed to be both mothers and top professionals are superhuman, rich, or self-employed. If we truly believe in equal opportunity for all women, here's what has to change.

ANNE-MARIE SLAUGHTER

Learning Outcomes

After reading this article, you will be able to:

- Understand the tensions between work and family for women but also for men.

- Know why Anne-Marie Slaughter thinks that women cannot have high commitment to both career and family.

- Understand the factors that are influencing women's roles today.

Eighteen months into my job as the first woman director of policy planning at the State Department, a foreign-policy dream job that traces its origins back to George Kennan, I found myself in New York, at the United Nations' annual assemblage of every foreign minister and head of state in the world. On a Wednesday evening, President and Mrs. Obama hosted a glamorous reception at the American Museum of Natural History. I sipped champagne, greeted foreign dignitaries, and mingled. But I could not stop thinking about my 14-year-old son, who had started eighth grade three weeks earlier and was already resuming what had become his pattern of skipping homework, disrupting classes, failing math, and tuning out any adult who tried to reach him. Over the summer, we had barely spoken to each other—or, more accurately, he had barely spoken to me. And the previous spring I had received several urgent phone calls—invariably on the day of an important meeting—that required me to take the first train from Washington, D.C., where I worked, back to Princeton, New Jersey, where he lived. My husband, who has always done everything possible to support my career, took care of him and his 12-year-old brother during the week; outside of those midweek emergencies, I came home only on weekends.

As the evening wore on, I ran into a colleague who held a senior position in the White House. She has two sons exactly my sons' ages, but she had chosen to move them from California to D.C. when she got her job, which meant her husband commuted back to California regularly. I told her how difficult I was finding it to be away from my son when he clearly needed me. Then I said, "When this is over, I'm going to write an op-ed titled 'Women Can't Have It All.'"

She was horrified. "You *can't* write that," she said. "You, of all people." What she meant was that such a statement, coming from a high-profile career woman—a role model—would be a terrible signal to younger generations of women. By the end of the evening, she had talked me out of it, but for the remainder of my stint in Washington, I was increasingly aware that the feminist beliefs on which I had built my entire career were shifting under my feet. I had always assumed that if I could get a foreign-policy job in the State Department or the White House while my party was in power, I would stay the course as long as I had the opportunity to do work I loved. But in January 2011, when my two-year public-service leave from Princeton University was up, I hurried home as fast as I could.

A rude epiphany hit me soon after I got there. When people asked why I had left government, I explained that I'd come home not only because of Princeton's rules (after two years of leave, you lose your tenure), but also because of my desire to be with my family and my conclusion that juggling high-level government work with the needs of two teenage boys was not possible. I have not exactly left the ranks of full-time career women: I teach a full course load; write regular print and online columns on foreign policy; give 40 to 50 speeches a year; appear regularly on TV and radio; and am working on a new academic book. But I routinely got reactions from other women my age or older that ranged from disappointed ("It's such a pity that you had to leave Washington") to condescending ("I wouldn't generalize from your experience. *I've* never had to compromise, and *my* kids turned out great").

The first set of reactions, with the underlying assumption that my choice was somehow sad or unfortunate, was irksome enough. But it was the second set of reactions—those implying that my parenting and/or my commitment to my profession were somehow substandard—that triggered a blind fury. Suddenly, finally, the penny dropped. All my life, I'd been on the other side of this exchange. I'd been the woman smiling the faintly superior smile while another woman told me she had decided to take some time out or pursue a less competitive career track so that she could spend more time with her family. I'd been the woman congratulating herself on her unswerving commitment to the feminist cause, chatting smugly with her dwindling number of college or law-school friends who had reached and maintained their place on the highest rungs of their profession. I'd been the one telling young women at my lectures that you *can* have it all and do it all, regardless of what field you are in. Which means I'd been part, albeit unwittingly, of making millions of women feel that *they* are to blame if they cannot manage to rise up the ladder as fast as men and also have a family and an active home life (and be thin and beautiful to boot).

Last spring, I flew to Oxford to give a public lecture. At the request of a young Rhodes Scholar I know, I'd agreed to talk to the Rhodes community about "work-family balance." I ended up speaking to a group of about 40 men and women in their mid-20s. What poured out of me was a set of very frank reflections on how unexpectedly hard it was to do the kind of job I wanted to do as a high government official and be the kind of parent I wanted to be, at a demanding time for my children (even though my husband, an academic, was willing to take on the lion's share of parenting for the two years I was in Washington). I concluded by saying that my time in office had convinced me that further government service would be very unlikely while my sons were still at home. The audience was rapt, and asked many thoughtful questions. One of the first was from a young woman who began by thanking me for "not giving just one more fatuous 'You can have it all' talk." Just about all of the women in that room planned to combine careers and family in some way. But almost all assumed and accepted that they would have to make compromises that the men in their lives were far less likely to have to make.

The striking gap between the responses I heard from those young women (and others like them) and the responses I heard from my peers and associates prompted me to write this article. Women of my generation have clung to the feminist credo we were raised with, even as our ranks have been steadily thinned by unresolvable tensions between family and career, because we are determined not to drop the flag for the next generation. But when many members of the younger generation have stopped listening, on the grounds that glibly repeating "you can have it all" is simply airbrushing reality, it is time to talk.

I still strongly believe that women can "have it all" (and that men can too). I believe that we can "have it all at the same time." But not today, not with the way America's economy and society are currently structured. My experiences over the past three years have forced me to confront a number of uncomfortable facts that need to be widely acknowledged—and quickly changed.

Before my service in government, I'd spent my career in academia: as a law professor and then as the dean of Princeton's Woodrow Wilson School of Public and International Affairs. Both were demanding jobs, but I had the ability to set my own schedule most of the time. I could be with my kids when I needed to be, and still get the work done. I had to travel frequently, but I found I could make up for that with an extended period at home or a family vacation.

I knew that I was lucky in my career choice, but I had no idea how lucky until I spent two years in Washington within a rigid bureaucracy, even with bosses as understanding as Hillary Clinton and her chief of staff, Cheryl Mills. My workweek started at 4:20 on Monday morning, when I got up to get the 5:30 train from Trenton to Washington. It ended late on Friday, with the train home. In between, the days were crammed with meetings, and when the meetings stopped, the writing work began—a never-ending stream of memos, reports, and comments on other people's drafts. For two years, I never left the office early enough to go to any stores other than those open 24 hours, which meant that everything from dry cleaning to hair appointments to Christmas shopping had to be done on weekends, amid children's sporting events, music lessons, family meals, and conference calls. I was entitled to four hours of vacation per pay period, which came to one day of vacation a month. And I had it better than many of my peers in D.C.; Secretary Clinton deliberately came in around 8 a.m. and left around 7 p.m., to allow her close staff to have morning and evening time with their families (although of course she worked earlier and later, from home).

In short, the minute I found myself in a job that is typical for the vast majority of working women (and men), working long hours on someone else's schedule, I could no longer be both the parent and the professional I wanted to be—at least not with a child experiencing a rocky adolescence. I realized what should have perhaps been obvious: having it all, at least for me, depended almost entirely on what type of job I had. The flip side is the harder truth: having it all was not possible in many types of jobs, including high government office—at least not for very long.

I am hardly alone in this realization. Michèle Flournoy stepped down after three years as undersecretary of defense for policy, the third-highest job in the department, to spend more time at home with her three children, two of whom are teenagers. Karen Hughes left her position as the counselor to President George W. Bush after a year and a half in Washington to go home to Texas for the sake of her family. Mary Matalin, who spent two years as an assistant to Bush and the counselor to Vice President Dick Cheney before stepping down to spend more time with her daughters, wrote: "Having control over your schedule is the only way that women who want to have a career and a family can make it work."

Yet the decision to step down from a position of power—to value family over professional advancement, even for a time—is directly at odds with the prevailing social pressures on career professionals in the United States. One phrase says it all about current attitudes toward work and family, particularly among elites. In Washington, "leaving to spend time with your family" is a euphemism for being fired. This understanding is so ingrained that when Flournoy announced her resignation last December, *The New York Times* covered her decision as follows:

Ms. Flournoy's announcement surprised friends and a number of Pentagon officials, but all said they took her reason for resignation at face value and not as a standard Washington excuse for an official who has in reality been forced out. "I can absolutely and unequivocally state that her decision to step down has nothing to do with anything other than her commitment to her family," said Doug Wilson, a top Pentagon spokesman. "She has loved this job and people here love her."

Think about what this "standard Washington excuse" implies: it is so unthinkable that an official would *actually* step down to spend time with his or her family that this must be a cover for something else. How could anyone voluntarily leave the circles of power for the responsibilities of parenthood? Depending on one's vantage point, it is either ironic or maddening that this view abides in the nation's capital, despite the ritual commitments to "family values" that are part of every political campaign. Regardless, this sentiment makes true work-life balance exceptionally difficult. But it cannot change unless top women speak out.

Only recently have I begun to appreciate the extent to which many young professional women feel under assault by women my age and older. After I gave a recent speech in New York, several women in their late 60s or early 70s came up to tell me how glad and proud they were to see me speaking as a foreign-policy expert. A couple of them went on, however, to contrast my career with the path being traveled by "younger women today." One expressed dismay that many younger women "are just not willing to get out there and do it." Said another, unaware of the circumstances of my recent job change: "They think they have to choose between having a career and having a family."

A similar assumption underlies Facebook Chief Operating Officer Sheryl Sandberg's widely publicized 2011 commencement speech at Barnard, and her earlier TED talk, in which she lamented the dismally small number of women at the top and advised young women not to "leave before you leave." When a woman starts thinking about having children, Sandberg said, "she doesn't raise her hand anymore . . . She starts leaning back." Although couched in terms of encouragement, Sandberg's exhortation contains more than a note of reproach. We who have made it to the top, or are striving to get there, are essentially saying to the women in the generation behind us: "What's the matter with you?"

They have an answer that we don't want to hear. After the speech I gave in New York, I went to dinner with a group of 30-somethings. I sat across from two vibrant women, one of whom worked at the UN and the other at a big New York law firm. As nearly always happens in these situations, they soon began asking me about work-life balance. When I told them I was writing this article, the lawyer said, "I look for role models and can't find any." She said the women in her firm who had become partners and taken on management positions had made tremendous sacrifices, "many of which they don't even seem to realize . . . They take two years off when their kids are young but then work like crazy to get back on track professionally, which means that they see their kids when they are toddlers but not teenagers, or really barely at all." Her friend nodded, mentioning the top professional women she knew, all of whom essentially relied on round-the-clock nannies. Both were very clear that they did not want that life, but could not figure out how to combine professional success and satisfaction with a real commitment to family.

I realize that I am blessed to have been born in the late 1950s instead of the early 1930s, as my mother was, or the beginning of the 20th century, as my grandmothers were. My mother built a successful and rewarding career as a professional artist largely in the years after my brothers and I left home—and after being told in her 20s that she could not go to medical school, as her father had done and her brother would go on to do, because, of course, she was going to get married. I owe my own freedoms and opportunities to the pioneering generation of women ahead of me—the women now in their 60s, 70s, and 80s who faced overt sexism of a kind I see only when watching *Mad Men,* and who knew that the only way to make it as a woman was to act exactly like a man. To admit to, much less act on, maternal longings would have been fatal to their careers.

But precisely thanks to their progress, a different kind of conversation is now possible. It is time for women in leadership positions to recognize that although we are still blazing trails and breaking ceilings, many of us are also reinforcing a falsehood: that "having it all" is, more than anything, a function of personal determination. As Kerry Rubin and Lia Macko, the authors of *Midlife Crisis at 30,* their cri de coeur for Gen-X and Gen-Y women, put it:

> What we discovered in our research is that while the empowerment part of the equation has been loudly celebrated, there has been very little honest discussion among women of our age about the real barriers and flaws that still exist in the system despite the opportunities we inherited.

I am well aware that the majority of American women face problems far greater than any discussed in this article. I am writing for my demographic—highly educated, well-off women who are privileged enough to have choices in the first place. We may not have choices about whether to do paid work, as dual incomes have become indispensable. But we have choices about the type and tempo of the work we do. We are the women who could be leading, and who should be equally represented in the leadership ranks.

Millions of other working women face much more difficult life circumstances. Some are single mothers; many struggle to find any job; others support husbands who cannot find jobs. Many cope with a work life in which good day care is either unavailable or very expensive; school schedules do not match work schedules; and schools themselves are failing to educate their children. Many of these women are worrying not about having it all, but rather about holding on to what they do have. And although women as a group have made substantial gains in wages, educational attainment, and prestige over the past three decades, the economists Justin Wolfers and Betsey Stevenson have shown that women are less happy today than their predecessors were in 1972, both in absolute terms and relative to men.

The best hope for improving the lot of all women, and for closing what Wolfers and Stevenson call a "new gender gap"— measured by well-being rather than wages—is to close the leadership gap: to elect a woman president and 50 women senators; to ensure that women are equally represented in the ranks of corporate executives and judicial leaders. Only when women wield power in sufficient numbers will we create a society that genuinely works for all women. That will be a society that works for everyone.

The Half-Truths We Hold Dear

Let's briefly examine the stories we tell ourselves, the clichés that I and many other women typically fall back on when younger women ask us how we have managed to "have it all." They are not necessarily lies, but at best partial truths. We must clear them out of the way to make room for a more honest and productive discussion about real solutions to the problems faced by professional women.

It's Possible If you are Just Committed Enough

Our usual starting point, whether we say it explicitly or not, is that having it all depends primarily on the depth and intensity of a woman's commitment to her career. That is precisely the sentiment behind the dismay so many older career women feel about the younger generation. *They are not committed enough,* we say, to make the trade-offs and sacrifices that the women ahead of them made.

Yet instead of chiding, perhaps we should face some basic facts. Very few women reach leadership positions. The pool of female candidates for any top job is small, and will only grow smaller if the women who come after us decide to take time out, or drop out of professional competition altogether, to raise children. That is exactly what has Sheryl Sandberg so upset, and rightly so. In her words, "Women are not making it to the top. A hundred and ninety heads of state; nine are women. Of all the people in parliament in the world, 13 percent are women. In the corporate sector, [the share of] women at the top—C-level jobs, board seats—tops out at 15, 16 percent."

Can "insufficient commitment" even plausibly explain these numbers? To be sure, the women who do make it to the top are highly committed to their profession. On closer examination, however, it turns out that most of them have something else in common: they are genuine superwomen. Consider the number of women recently in the top ranks in Washington—Susan Rice, Elizabeth Sherwood-Randall, Michelle Gavin, Nancy-Ann Min DeParle—who are Rhodes Scholars. Samantha Power, another senior White House official, won a Pulitzer Prize at age 32. Or consider Sandberg herself, who graduated with the prize given to Harvard's top student of economics. These women cannot possibly be the standard against which even very talented professional women should measure themselves. Such a standard sets up most women for a sense of failure.

What's more, among those who have made it to the top, a balanced life still is more elusive for women than it is for men. A simple measure is how many women in top positions have children compared with their male colleagues. Every male Supreme Court justice has a family. Two of the three female justices are single with no children. And the third, Ruth Bader Ginsburg, began her career as a judge only when her younger child was almost grown. The pattern is the same at the National Security Council: Condoleezza Rice, the first and only woman national-security adviser, is also the only national-security adviser since the 1950s not to have a family.

The line of high-level women appointees in the Obama administration is one woman deep. Virtually all of us who have stepped down have been succeeded by men; searches for women to succeed men in similar positions come up empty. Just about every woman who could plausibly be tapped is already in government. The rest of the foreign-policy world is not much better; Micah Zenko, a fellow at the Council on Foreign Relations, recently surveyed the best data he could find across the government, the military, the academy, and think tanks, and found that women hold fewer than 30 percent of the senior foreign-policy positions in each of these institutions.

These numbers are all the more striking when we look back to the 1980s, when women now in their late 40s and 50s were coming out of graduate school, and remember that our classes were nearly 50–50 men and women. We were sure then that by now, we would be living in a 50–50 world. Something derailed that dream.

Sandberg thinks that "something" is an "ambition gap"—that women do not dream big enough. I am all for encouraging young women to reach for the stars. But I fear that the obstacles that keep women from reaching the top are rather more prosaic than the scope of their ambition. My longtime and invaluable assistant, who has a doctorate and juggles many balls as the mother of teenage twins, e-mailed me while I was working on this article: "You know what would help the vast majority of women with work/family balance? MAKE SCHOOL SCHEDULES MATCH WORK SCHEDULES." The present system, she noted, is based on a society that no longer exists—one in which farming was a major occupation and stay-at-home moms were the norm. Yet the system hasn't changed.

Consider some of the responses of women interviewed by Zenko about why "women are significantly underrepresented in foreign policy and national security positions in government, academia, and think tanks." Juliette Kayyem, who served as an assistant secretary in the Department of Homeland Security from 2009 to 2011 and now writes a foreign-policy and national-security column for *The Boston Globe,* told Zenko that among other reasons,

> the basic truth is also this: the travel sucks. As my youngest of three children is now 6, I can look back at the years when they were all young and realize just how disruptive all the travel was. There were also trips I couldn't take because I was pregnant or on leave, the conferences I couldn't attend because (note to conference organizers: weekends are a bad choice) kids would be home from school, and the various excursions that were offered but just couldn't be managed.

Jolynn Shoemaker, the director of Women in International Security, agreed: "Inflexible schedules, unrelenting travel, and constant pressure to be in the office are common features of these jobs."

These "mundane" issues—the need to travel constantly to succeed, the conflicts between school schedules and work schedules, the insistence that work be done in the office—cannot be solved by exhortations to close the ambition gap. I would hope to see commencement speeches that finger America's social and business policies, rather than women's level of ambition, in explaining the dearth of women at the top. But changing these policies requires much more than speeches. It means fighting the mundane battles—every day, every year—in individual workplaces, in legislatures, and in the media.

It's Possible If you Marry the right person

Sandberg's second message in her Barnard commencement address was: "The most important career decision you're going to make is whether or not you have a life partner and who that partner is." Lisa Jackson, the administrator of the Environmental Protection Agency, recently drove that message home to an audience of Princeton students and alumni gathered to hear her acceptance speech for the James Madison Medal. During the Q&A session, an audience member asked her how she managed her career and her family. She laughed and pointed to her husband in the front row, saying: "There's my work-life balance." I could never have had the career I have had without my husband, Andrew Moravcsik, who is a tenured professor of politics and international affairs at Princeton. Andy has spent more time with our sons than I have, not only on homework, but also on baseball, music lessons, photography, card games, and more. When each of them had to bring in a foreign dish for his fourth-grade class dinner, Andy made his grandmother's Hungarian *palacsinta;* when our older son needed to memorize his lines for a lead role in a school play, he turned to Andy for help.

Still, the proposition that women can have high-powered careers as long as their husbands or partners are willing to share the parenting load equally (or disproportionately) assumes that most women will *feel* as comfortable as men do about being away from their children, as long as their partner is home with them. In my experience, that is simply not the case.

Here I step onto treacherous ground, mined with stereotypes. From years of conversations and observations, however, I've come to believe that men and women respond quite differently when problems at home force them to recognize that their absence is hurting a child, or at least that their presence would likely help. I do not believe fathers love their children any less than mothers do, but men do seem more likely to choose their job at a cost to their family, while women seem more likely to choose their family at a cost to their job.

Many factors determine this choice, of course. Men are still socialized to believe that their primary family obligation is to be the breadwinner; women, to believe that their primary family obligation is to be the caregiver. But it may be more than that. When I described the choice between my children and my job to Senator Jeanne Shaheen, she said exactly what I felt: "There's really no choice." She wasn't referring to social expectations, but to a maternal imperative felt so deeply that the "choice" is reflexive.

Men and women also seem to frame the choice differently. In *Midlife Crisis at 30,* Mary Matalin recalls her days working as President Bush's assistant and Vice President Cheney's counselor:

> Even when the stress was overwhelming—those days when I'd cry in the car on the way to work, asking myself "Why am I doing this?"—I always knew the answer to that question: I believe in this president.

But Matalin goes on to describe her choice to leave in words that are again uncannily similar to the explanation I have given so many people since leaving the State Department:

> I finally asked myself, "Who needs me more?" And that's when I realized, it's somebody else's turn to do this job. I'm indispensable to my kids, but I'm not close to indispensable to the White House.

To many men, however, the choice to spend more time with their children, instead of working long hours on issues that affect many lives, seems selfish. Male leaders are routinely praised for having sacrificed their personal life on the altar of public or corporate service. That sacrifice, of course, typically involves their family. Yet their children, too, are trained to value public service over private responsibility. At the diplomat Richard Holbrooke's memorial service, one of his sons told the audience that when he was a child, his father was often gone, not around to teach him to throw a ball or to watch his games. But as he grew older, he said, he realized that Holbrooke's absence was the price of saving people around the world—a price worth paying.

It is not clear to me that this ethical framework makes sense for society. Why should we want leaders who fall short on personal responsibilities? Perhaps leaders who invested time in their own families would be more keenly aware of the toll their public choices—on issues from war to welfare—take on private lives. (Kati Marton, Holbrooke's widow and a noted author, says that although Holbrooke adored his children, he came to appreciate the full importance of family only in his 50s, at which point he became a very present parent and grandparent, while continuing to pursue an extraordinary public career.) Regardless, it is clear which set of choices society values more today. Workers who put their careers first are typically rewarded; workers who choose their families are overlooked, disbelieved, or accused of unprofessionalism.

In sum, having a supportive mate may well be a necessary condition if women are to have it all, but it is not sufficient. If women feel deeply that turning down a promotion that would involve more travel, for instance, is the right thing to do, then they will continue to do that. Ultimately, it is society that must change, coming to value choices to put family ahead of work just as much as those to put work ahead of family. If we really valued those choices, we would value the people who make them; if we valued the people who make them, we would do everything possible to hire and retain them; if we did everything possible to allow them to combine work and family equally over time, then the choices would get a lot easier.

It's Possible If you Sequence It Right

Young women should be wary of the assertion "You can have it all; you just can't have it all at once." This 21st-century addendum to the original line is now proffered by many senior women to their younger mentees. To the extent that it means, in the words of one working mother, "I'm going to do my best and I'm going to keep the long term in mind and know that it's not always going to be this hard to balance," it is sound advice. But to the extent that it means that women can have it all if they just find the right sequence of career and family, it's cheerfully wrong.

The most important sequencing issue is when to have children. Many of the top women leaders of the generation just ahead of me—Madeleine Albright, Hillary Clinton, Ruth Bader Ginsburg, Sandra Day O'Connor, Patricia Wald, Nannerl Keohane—had their children in their 20s and early 30s, as was the norm in the 1950s through the 1970s. A child born when his mother is 25 will finish high school when his mother is 43, an age at which, with full-time immersion in a career, she still has plenty of time and energy for advancement.

Yet this sequence has fallen out of favor with many high-potential women, and understandably so. People tend to marry later now, and anyway, if you have children earlier, you may have difficulty getting a graduate degree, a good first job, and opportunities for advancement in the crucial early years of your career. Making matters worse, you will also have less income while raising your children, and hence less ability to hire the help that can be indispensable to your juggling act.

When I was the dean, the Woodrow Wilson School created a program called Pathways to Public Service, aimed at advising women whose children were almost grown about how to go into public service, and many women still ask me about the best "on-ramps" to careers in their mid-40s. Honestly, I'm not sure what to tell most of them. Unlike the pioneering women who entered the workforce after having children in the 1970s, these women are competing with their younger selves. Government and NGO jobs are an option, but many careers are effectively closed off. Personally, I have never seen a woman in her 40s enter the academic market successfully, or enter a law firm as a junior associate, Alicia Florrick of *The Good Wife* notwithstanding.

These considerations are why so many career women of my generation chose to establish themselves in their careers first and have children in their mid-to-late 30s. But that raises the possibility of spending long, stressful years and a small fortune trying to have a baby. I lived that nightmare: for three years, beginning at age 35, I did everything possible to conceive and was frantic at the thought that I had simply left having a biological child until it was too late.

And when everything does work out? I had my first child at 38 (and counted myself blessed) and my second at 40. That means I will be 58 when both of my children are out of the house. What's more, it means that many peak career opportunities are coinciding precisely with their teenage years, when, experienced parents advise, being available as a parent is just as important as in the first years of a child's life.

Many women of my generation have found themselves, in the prime of their careers, saying no to opportunities they once would have jumped at and hoping those chances come around again later. Many others who have decided to step back for a while, taking on consultant positions or part-time work that lets them spend more time with their children (or aging parents), are worrying about how long they can "stay out" before they lose the competitive edge they worked so hard to acquire.

Given the way our work culture is oriented today, I recommend establishing yourself in your career first but still trying to have kids before you are 35—or else freeze your eggs, whether you are married or not. You may well be a more mature and less frustrated parent in your 30s or 40s; you are also more likely to have found a lasting life partner. But the truth is, neither sequence is optimal, and both involve trade-offs that men do not have to make.

You should be able to have a family if you want one—however and whenever your life circumstances allow—and still have the career you desire. If more women could strike this balance, more women would reach leadership positions. And if more women were in leadership positions, they could make it easier for more women to stay in the workforce. The rest of this essay details how.

Changing the Culture of Face Time

Back in the Reagan administration, a *New York Times* story about the ferociously competitive budget director Dick Darman reported, "Mr. Darman sometimes managed to convey the impression that he was the last one working in the Reagan White House by leaving his suit coat on his chair and his office light burning after he left for home." (Darman claimed that it was just easier to leave his suit jacket in the office so he could put it on again in the morning, but his record of psychological manipulation suggests otherwise.)

The culture of "time macho"—a relentless competition to work harder, stay later, pull more all-nighters, travel around the world and bill the extra hours that the international date line affords you—remains astonishingly prevalent among professionals today. Nothing captures the belief that more time equals more value better than the cult of billable hours afflicting large law firms across the country and providing exactly the wrong incentives for employees who hope to integrate work and family. Yet even in industries that don't explicitly reward sheer quantity of hours spent on the job, the pressure to arrive early, stay late, and be available, always, for in-person meetings at 11 a.m. on Saturdays can be intense. Indeed, by some measures, the problem has gotten worse over time: a study by the Center for American Progress reports that nationwide, the share of all professionals—women and men—working more than 50 hours a week has increased since the late 1970s.

But more time in the office does not always mean more "value added"—and it does not always add up to a more successful organization. In 2009, Sandra Pocharski, a senior female partner at Monitor Group and the head of the firm's Leadership and Organization practice, commissioned a Harvard Business School professor to assess the factors that helped or hindered women's effectiveness and advancement at Monitor. The study found that the company's culture was characterized by an "always on" mode of working, often without due regard to the impact on employees. Pocharski observed:

> Clients come first, always, and sometimes burning the midnight oil really does make the difference between success and failure. But sometimes we were just defaulting to behavior that overloaded our people without improving results much, if at all. We decided we needed managers to get better at distinguishing between these categories, and to recognize the hidden costs of assuming that "time is cheap." When that time doesn't add a lot of value and comes at a high cost to talented employees, who will leave when the personal cost becomes unsustainable—well, that is clearly a bad outcome for everyone.

I have worked very long hours and pulled plenty of all-nighters myself over the course of my career, including a few nights on my office couch during my two years in D.C. Being willing to put the time in when the job simply has to get done is rightfully a hallmark of a successful professional. But looking back, I have to admit that my assumption that I would stay late made me much less efficient over the course of the day than I might have been, and certainly less so than some of my colleagues, who managed to get the same amount of work done and go home at a decent hour. If Dick Darman had a boss who clearly valued prioritization and time management, he might have found reason to turn out the lights and take his jacket home.

Long hours are one thing, and realistically, they are often unavoidable. But do they really need to be spent at the office? To be sure, being in the office *some* of the time is beneficial. In-person meetings can be far more efficient than phone or e-mail tag; trust and collegiality are much more easily built up around the same physical table; and spontaneous conversations often generate good ideas and lasting relationships. Still, armed with e-mail, instant messaging, phones, and videoconferencing technology, we should be able to move to a culture where the office is a base of operations more than the required locus of work.

Being able to work from home—in the evening after children are put to bed, or during their sick days or snow days, and at least some of the time on weekends—can be the key, for mothers, to carrying your full load versus letting a team down at crucial moments. State-of-the-art videoconferencing facilities can dramatically reduce the need for long business trips. These technologies are making inroads, and allowing easier integration of work and family life. According to the Women's Business Center, 61 percent of women business owners use technology to "integrate the responsibilities of work and home"; 44 percent use technology to allow employees "to work off-site or to have flexible work schedules." Yet our work culture still remains more office-centered than it needs to be, especially in light of technological advances.

One way to change that is by changing the "default rules" that govern office work—the baseline expectations about when, where, and how work will be done. As behavioral economists well know, these baselines can make an enormous difference in the way people act. It is one thing, for instance, for an organization to allow phone-ins to a meeting on an ad hoc basis, when

parenting and work schedules collide—a system that's better than nothing, but likely to engender guilt among those calling in, and possibly resentment among those in the room. It is quite another for that organization to declare that its policy will be to schedule in-person meetings, whenever possible, during the hours of the school day—a system that might normalize call-ins for those (rarer) meetings still held in the late afternoon.

One real-world example comes from the British Foreign and Commonwealth Office, a place most people are more likely to associate with distinguished gentlemen in pinstripes than with progressive thinking about work-family balance. Like so many other places, however, the FCO worries about losing talented members of two-career couples around the world, particularly women. So it recently changed its basic policy from a default rule that jobs have to be done on-site to one that assumes that some jobs might be done remotely, and invites workers to make the case for remote work. Kara Owen, a career foreign-service officer who was the FCO's diversity director and will soon become the British deputy ambassador to France, writes that she has now done two remote jobs. Before her current maternity leave, she was working a London job from Dublin to be with her partner, using teleconferencing technology and timing her trips to London to coincide "with key meetings where I needed to be in the room (or chatting at the pre-meeting coffee) to have an impact, or to do intensive 'network maintenance.'" In fact, she writes, "I have found the distance and quiet to be a real advantage in a strategic role, providing I have put in the investment up front to develop very strong personal relationships with the game changers." Owen recognizes that not every job can be done this way. But she says that for her part, she has been able to combine family requirements with her career.

Changes in default office rules should not advantage parents over other workers; indeed, done right, they can improve relations among co-workers by raising their awareness of each other's circumstances and instilling a sense of fairness. Two years ago, the ACLU Foundation of Massachusetts decided to replace its "parental leave" policy with a "family leave" policy that provides for as much as 12 weeks of leave not only for new parents, but also for employees who need to care for a spouse, child, or parent with a serious health condition. According to Director Carol Rose, "We wanted a policy that took into account the fact that even employees who do not have children have family obligations." The policy was shaped by the belief that giving women "special treatment" can "backfire if the broader norms shaping the behavior of all employees do not change." When I was the dean of the Wilson School, I managed with the mantra "Family comes first"—any family—and found that my employees were both productive and intensely loyal.

None of these changes will happen by themselves, and reasons to avoid them will seldom be hard to find. But obstacles and inertia are usually surmountable if leaders are open to changing their assumptions about the workplace. The use of technology in many high-level government jobs, for instance, is complicated by the need to have access to classified information. But in 2009, Deputy Secretary of State James Steinberg, who shares the parenting of his two young daughters equally with his wife, made getting such access at home an immediate priority so that he could leave the office at a reasonable hour and participate in important meetings via videoconferencing if necessary. I wonder how many women in similar positions would be afraid to ask, lest they be seen as insufficiently committed to their jobs.

Revaluing Family Values

While employers shouldn't privilege parents over other workers, too often they end up doing the opposite, usually subtly, and usually in ways that make it harder for a primary caregiver to get ahead. Many people in positions of power seem to place a low value on child care in comparison with other outside activities. Consider the following proposition: An employer has two equally talented and productive employees. One trains for and runs marathons when he is not working. The other takes care of two children. What assumptions is the employer likely to make about the marathon runner? That he gets up in the dark every day and logs an hour or two running before even coming into the office, or drives himself to get out there even after a long day. That he is ferociously disciplined and willing to push himself through distraction, exhaustion, and days when nothing seems to go right in the service of a goal far in the distance. That he must manage his time exceptionally well to squeeze all of that in.

Be honest: Do you think the employer makes those same assumptions about the parent? Even though she likely rises in the dark hours before she needs to be at work, organizes her children's day, makes breakfast, packs lunch, gets them off to school, figures out shopping and other errands even if she is lucky enough to have a housekeeper—and does much the same work at the end of the day. Cheryl Mills, Hillary Clinton's indefatigable chief of staff, has twins in elementary school; even with a fully engaged husband, she famously gets up at four every morning to check and send e-mails before her kids wake up. Louise Richardson, now the vice chancellor of the University of St. Andrews, in Scotland, combined an assistant professorship in government at Harvard with mothering three young children. She organized her time so ruthlessly that she always keyed in 1:11 or 2:22 or 3:33 on the microwave rather than 1:00, 2:00, or 3:00, because hitting the same number three times took less time.

Elizabeth Warren, who is now running for the U.S. Senate in Massachusetts, has a similar story. When she had two young children and a part-time law practice, she struggled to find enough time to write the papers and articles that would help get her an academic position. In her words:

> I needed a plan. I figured out that writing time was when Alex was asleep. So the minute I put him down for a nap or he fell asleep in the baby swing, I went to my desk and started working on something—footnotes, reading, outlining, writing . . . I learned to do everything else with a baby on my hip.

The discipline, organization, and sheer endurance it takes to succeed at top levels with young children at home is easily comparable to running 20 to 40 miles a week. But that's rarely how employers see things, not only when making allowances, but when making promotions. Perhaps because people *choose* to have children? People also choose to run marathons.

One final example: I have worked with many Orthodox Jewish men who observed the Sabbath from sundown on Friday until sundown on Saturday. Jack Lew, the two-time director of the Office of Management and Budget, former deputy secretary of state for management and resources, and now White House chief of staff, is a case in point. Jack's wife lived in New York when he worked in the State Department, so he would leave the office early enough on Friday afternoon to take the shuttle to New York and a taxi to his apartment before sundown. He would not work on Friday after sundown or all day Saturday. Everyone who knew him, including me, admired his commitment to his faith and his ability to carve out the time for it, even with an enormously demanding job.

It is hard to imagine, however, that we would have the same response if a mother told us she was blocking out mid-Friday afternoon through the end of the day on Saturday, every week, to spend time with her children. I suspect this would be seen as unprofessional, an imposition of unnecessary costs on co-workers. In fact, of course, one of the great values of the Sabbath—whether Jewish or Christian—is precisely that it carves out a family oasis, with rituals and a mandatory setting-aside of work.

Our assumptions are just that: things we believe that are not necessarily so. Yet what we assume has an enormous impact on our perceptions and responses. Fortunately, changing our assumptions is up to us.

Redefining the Arc of a Successful Career

The American definition of a successful professional is someone who can climb the ladder the furthest in the shortest time, generally peaking between ages 45 and 55. It is a definition well suited to the mid-20th century, an era when people had kids in their 20s, stayed in one job, retired at 67, and were dead, on average, by age 71.

It makes far less sense today. Average life expectancy for people in their 20s has increased to 80; men and women in good health can easily work until they are 75. They can expect to have multiple jobs and even multiple careers throughout their working life. Couples marry later, have kids later, and can expect to live on two incomes. They may well retire *earlier*—the average retirement age has gone down from 67 to 63—but that is commonly "retirement" only in the sense of collecting retirement benefits. Many people go on to "encore" careers.

Assuming the priceless gifts of good health and good fortune, a professional woman can thus expect her working life to stretch some 50 years, from her early or mid-20s to her mid-70s. It is reasonable to assume that she will build her credentials and establish herself, at least in her first career, between 22 and 35; she will have children, if she wants them, sometime between 25 and 45; she'll want maximum flexibility and control over her time in the 10 years that her children are 8 to 18; and she should plan to take positions of maximum authority and demands on her time after her children are out of the house. Women who have children in their late 20s can expect to immerse themselves completely in their careers in their late 40s, with plenty of time still to rise to the top in their late 50s and early 60s. Women who make partner, managing director, or senior vice president; get tenure; or establish a medical practice before having children in their late 30s should be coming back on line for the most demanding jobs at almost exactly the same age.

Along the way, women should think about the climb to leadership not in terms of a straight upward slope, but as irregular stair steps, with periodic plateaus (and even dips) when they turn down promotions to remain in a job that works for their family situation; when they leave high-powered jobs and spend a year or two at home on a reduced schedule; or when they step off a conventional professional track to take a consulting position or project-based work for a number of years. I think of these plateaus as "investment intervals." My husband and I took a sabbatical in Shanghai, from August 2007 to May 2008, right in the thick of an election year when many of my friends were advising various candidates on foreign-policy issues. We thought of the move in part as "putting money in the family bank," taking advantage of the opportunity to spend a close year together in a foreign culture. But we were also investing in our children's ability to learn Mandarin and in our own knowledge of Asia.

Peaking in your late 50s and early 60s rather than your late 40s and early 50s makes particular sense for women, who live longer than men. And many of the stereotypes about older workers simply do not hold. A 2006 survey of human-resources professionals shows that only 23 percent think older workers are less flexible than younger workers; only 11 percent think older workers require more training than younger workers; and only 7 percent think older workers have less drive than younger workers.

Whether women will really have the confidence to stair-step their careers, however, will again depend in part on perceptions. Slowing down the rate of promotions, taking time out periodically, pursuing an alternative path during crucial parenting or parent-care years—all have to become more visible and more noticeably accepted as a pause rather than an opt-out. (In an encouraging sign, *Mass Career Customization*, a 2007 book by Cathleen Benko and Anne Weisberg arguing that "today's career is no longer a straight climb up the corporate ladder, but rather a combination of climbs, lateral moves, and planned descents," was a *Wall Street Journal* best seller.)

Institutions can also take concrete steps to promote this acceptance. For instance, in 1970, Princeton established a tenure-extension policy that allowed female assistant professors expecting a child to request a one-year extension on their tenure clocks. This policy was later extended to men, and broadened to include adoptions. In the early 2000s, two reports on the status of female faculty discovered that only about 3 percent of assistant professors requested tenure extensions in a given year. And in response to a survey question, women were much more likely than men to think that a tenure extension would be detrimental to an assistant professor's career.

So in 2005, under President Shirley Tilghman, Princeton changed the default rule. The administration announced that all assistant professors, female and male, who had a new child would *automatically* receive a one-year extension on the tenure clock, with no opt-outs allowed. Instead, assistant professors could request early consideration for tenure if they wished. The number of assistant professors who receive a tenure extension has tripled since the change.

One of the best ways to move social norms in this direction is to choose and celebrate different role models. New Jersey Governor Chris Christie and I are poles apart politically, but he went way up in my estimation when he announced that one reason he decided against running for president in 2012 was the impact his campaign would have had on his children. He reportedly made clear at a fund-raiser in Louisiana that he didn't want to be away from his children for long periods of time; according to a Republican official at the event, he said that "his son [missed] him after being gone for the three days on the road, and that he needed to get back." He may not get my vote if and when he does run for president, but he definitely gets my admiration (providing he doesn't turn around and join the GOP ticket this fall).

If we are looking for high-profile female role models, we might begin with Michelle Obama. She started out with the same résumé as her husband, but has repeatedly made career decisions designed to let her do work she cared about and also be the kind of parent she wanted to be. She moved from a high-powered law firm first to Chicago city government and then to the University of Chicago shortly before her daughters were born, a move that let her work only 10 minutes away from home. She has spoken publicly and often about her initial concerns that her husband's entry into politics would be bad for their family life, and about her determination to limit her participation in the presidential election campaign to have more time at home. Even as first lady, she has been adamant that she be able to balance her official duties with family time. We should see her as a full-time career woman, but one who is taking a very visible investment interval. We should celebrate her not only as a wife, mother, and champion of healthy eating, but also as a woman who has had the courage and judgment to invest in her daughters when they need her most. And we should expect a glittering career from her after she leaves the White House and her daughters leave for college.

Rediscovering the Pursuit of Happiness

One of the most complicated and surprising parts of my journey out of Washington was coming to grips with what I really wanted. I had opportunities to stay on, and I could have tried to work out an arrangement allowing me to spend more time at home. I might have been able to get my family to join me in Washington for a year; I might have been able to get classified technology installed at my house the way Jim Steinberg did; I might have been able to commute only four days a week instead of five. (While this last change would have still left me very little time at home, given the intensity of my job, it might have made the job doable for another year or two.) But I realized that I didn't just *need* to go home. Deep down, I *wanted* to go home. I wanted to be able to spend time with my children in the last few years that they are likely to live at home, crucial years for their development into responsible, productive, happy, and caring adults. But also irreplaceable years for me to enjoy the simple pleasures of parenting—baseball games, piano recitals, waffle breakfasts, family trips, and goofy rituals. My older son is doing very well these days, but even when he gives us a hard time, as all teenagers do, being home to shape his choices and help him make good decisions is deeply satisfying.

The flip side of my realization is captured in Macko and Rubin's ruminations on the importance of bringing the different parts of their lives together as 30-year-old women:

> If we didn't start to learn how to integrate our personal, social, and professional lives, we were about five years away from morphing into the angry woman on the other side of a mahogany desk who questions her staff's work ethic after standard 12-hour workdays, before heading home to eat moo shoo pork in her lonely apartment.

Women have contributed to the fetish of the one-dimensional life, albeit by necessity. The pioneer generation of feminists walled off their personal lives from their professional personas to ensure that they could never be discriminated against for a lack of commitment to their work. When I was a law student in the 1980s, many women who were then climbing the legal hierarchy in New York firms told me that they never admitted to taking time out for a child's doctor appointment or school performance, but instead invented a much more neutral excuse.

Today, however, women in power can and should change that environment, although change is not easy. When I became dean of the Woodrow Wilson School, in 2002, I decided that one of the advantages of being a woman in power was that I could help change the norms by deliberately talking about my children and my desire to have a balanced life. Thus, I would end faculty meetings at 6 p.m. by saying that I had to go home for dinner; I would also make clear to all student organizations that I would not come to dinner with them, because I needed to be home from six to eight, but that I would often be willing to come back after eight for a meeting. I also once told the Dean's Advisory Committee that the associate dean would chair the next session so I could go to a parent-teacher conference.

After a few months of this, several female assistant professors showed up in my office quite agitated. "You *have* to stop talking about your kids," one said. "You are not showing the gravitas that people expect from a dean, which is particularly damaging precisely because you are the first woman dean of the school." I told them that I was doing it deliberately and continued my practice, but it is interesting that gravitas and parenthood don't seem to go together.

Ten years later, whenever I am introduced at a lecture or other speaking engagement, I insist that the person introducing me mention that I have two sons. It seems odd to me to list degrees, awards, positions, and interests and *not* include the dimension of my life that is most important to me—and takes an enormous amount of my time. As Secretary Clinton once said in a television interview in Beijing when the interviewer asked her about Chelsea's upcoming wedding: "That's my real life." But I notice that my male introducers are typically uncomfortable when I make the request. They frequently say things like "And she particularly wanted me to mention that she has two sons"—thereby drawing attention to the unusual nature of my request, when my entire purpose is to make family references routine and normal in professional life.

This does not mean that you should insist that your colleagues spend time cooing over pictures of your baby or listening to the prodigious accomplishments of your kindergartner. It does mean that if you are late coming in one week, because it is your turn to drive the kids to school, that you be honest about what you are doing. Indeed, Sheryl Sandberg recently acknowledged not only that she leaves work at 5:30 to have dinner with her family, but also that for many years she did not dare make this admission, even though she would of course make up the work time later in the evening. Her willingness to speak out now is a strong step in the right direction.

Seeking out a more balanced life is not a women's issue; balance would be better for us all. Bronnie Ware, an Australian blogger who worked for years in palliative care and is the author of the 2011 book *The Top Five Regrets of the Dying*, writes that the regret she heard most often was "I wish I'd had the courage to live a life true to myself, not the life others expected of me." The second-most-common regret was "I wish I didn't work so hard." She writes: "This came from every male patient that I nursed. They missed their children's youth and their partner's companionship."

Juliette Kayyem, who several years ago left the Department of Homeland Security soon after her husband, David Barron, left a high position in the Justice Department, says their joint decision to leave Washington and return to Boston sprang from their desire to work on the *"happiness project,"* meaning quality time with their three children. (She borrowed the term from her friend Gretchen Rubin, who wrote a best-selling book and now runs a blog with that name.)

It's time to embrace a national happiness project. As a daughter of Charlottesville, Virginia, the home of Thomas Jefferson and the university he founded, I grew up with the Declaration of Independence in my blood. Last I checked, he did not declare American independence in the name of life, liberty, and professional success. Let us rediscover the pursuit of happiness, and let us start at home.

Innovation Nation

As I write this, I can hear the reaction of some readers to many of the proposals in this essay: It's all fine and well for a tenured professor to write about flexible working hours, investment intervals, and family-comes-first management. But what about the real world? Most American women cannot demand these things, particularly in a bad economy, and their employers have little incentive to grant them voluntarily. Indeed, the most frequent reaction I get in putting forth these ideas is that when the choice is whether to hire a man who will work whenever and wherever needed, or a woman who needs more flexibility, choosing the man will add more value to the company.

In fact, while many of these issues are hard to quantify and measure precisely, the statistics seem to tell a different story. A seminal study of 527 U.S. companies, published in the *Academy of Management Journal* in 2000, suggests that "organizations with more extensive work-family policies have higher perceived firm-level performance" among their industry peers. These findings accorded with a 2003 study conducted by Michelle Arthur at the University of New Mexico. Examining 130 announcements of family-friendly policies in *The Wall Street Journal*, Arthur found that the announcements alone significantly improved share prices. In 2011, a study on flexibility in the workplace by Ellen Galinsky, Kelly Sakai, and Tyler Wigton of the Families and Work Institute showed that increased flexibility correlates positively with job engagement, job satisfaction, employee retention, and employee health.

This is only a small sampling from a large and growing literature trying to pin down the relationship between family-friendly policies and economic performance. Other scholars have concluded that good family policies attract better talent, which in turn raises productivity, but that the policies themselves have no impact on productivity. Still others argue that results attributed to these policies are actually a function of good management overall. What is evident, however, is that many firms that recruit and train well-educated professional women are aware that when a woman leaves because of bad work-family balance, they are losing the money and time they invested in her.

Even the legal industry, built around the billable hour, is taking notice. Deborah Epstein Henry, a former big-firm litigator, is now the president of Flex-Time Lawyers, a national consulting firm focused partly on strategies for the retention of female attorneys. In her book *Law and Reorder*, published by the American Bar Association in 2010, she describes a legal profession "where the billable hour no longer works"; where attorneys, judges, recruiters, and academics all agree that this system of compensation has perverted the industry, leading to brutal work hours, massive inefficiency, and highly inflated costs. The answer—already being deployed in different corners of the industry—is a combination of alternative fee structures, virtual firms, women-owned firms, and the outsourcing of discrete legal jobs to other jurisdictions. Women, and Generation X and Y lawyers more generally, are pushing for these changes on the supply side; clients determined to reduce legal fees and increase flexible service are pulling on the demand side. Slowly, change is happening.

At the core of all this is self-interest. Losing smart and motivated women not only diminishes a company's talent pool; it also reduces the return on its investment in training and mentoring. In trying to address these issues, some firms are finding out that women's ways of working may just be better ways of working, for employees and clients alike.

Experts on creativity and innovation emphasize the value of encouraging nonlinear thinking and cultivating randomness by taking long walks or looking at your environment from unusual angles. In their new book, *A New Culture of Learning: Cultivating the Imagination for a World of Constant Change,* the innovation gurus John Seely Brown and Douglas Thomas write, "We believe that connecting play and imagination may be the single most important step in unleashing the new culture of learning."

Space for play and imagination is exactly what emerges when rigid work schedules and hierarchies loosen up. Skeptics should consider the "California effect." California is the cradle of American innovation—in technology, entertainment, sports, food, and lifestyles. It is also a place where people take leisure as seriously as they take work; where companies like Google deliberately encourage play, with Ping-Pong tables, light sabers, and policies that require employees to spend one day a week working on whatever they wish. Charles Baudelaire wrote: "Genius is nothing more nor less than childhood recovered at will." Google apparently has taken note.

No parent would mistake child care for childhood. Still, seeing the world anew through a child's eyes can be a powerful source of stimulation. When the Nobel laureate Thomas Schelling wrote *The Strategy of Conflict,* a classic text applying game theory to conflicts among nations, he frequently drew on child-rearing for examples of when deterrence might succeed or fail. "It may be easier to articulate the peculiar difficulty of constraining [a ruler] by the use of threats," he wrote, "when one is fresh from a vain attempt at using threats to keep a small child from hurting a dog or a small dog from hurting a child."

The books I've read with my children, the silly movies I've watched, the games I've played, questions I've answered, and people I've met while parenting have broadened my world. Another axiom of the literature on innovation is that the more often people with different perspectives come together, the more likely creative ideas are to emerge. Giving workers the ability to integrate their non-work lives with their work—whether they spend that time mothering or marathoning—will open the door to a much wider range of influences and ideas.

Enlisting Men

Perhaps the most encouraging news of all for achieving the sorts of changes that I have proposed is that men are joining the cause. In commenting on a draft of this article, Martha Minow, the dean of the Harvard Law School, wrote me that one change she has observed during 30 years of teaching law at Harvard is that today many young men are asking questions about how they can manage a work-life balance. And more systematic research on Generation Y confirms that many more men than in the past are asking questions about how they are going to integrate active parenthood with their professional lives.

Abstract aspirations are easier than concrete trade-offs, of course. These young men have not yet faced the question of whether they are prepared to give up that more prestigious clerkship or fellowship, decline a promotion, or delay their professional goals to spend more time with their children and to support their partner's career.

Yet once work practices and work culture begin to evolve, those changes are likely to carry their own momentum. Kara Owen, the British foreign-service officer who worked a London job from Dublin, wrote me in an e-mail:

I think the culture on flexible working started to change the minute the Board of Management (who were all men at the time) started to work flexibly—quite a few of them started working one day a week from home.

Men have, of course, become much more involved parents over the past couple of decades, and that, too, suggests broad support for big changes in the way we balance work and family. It is noteworthy that both James Steinberg, deputy secretary of state, and William Lynn, deputy secretary of defense, stepped down two years into the Obama administration so that they could spend more time with their children (for real).

Going forward, women would do well to frame work-family balance in terms of the broader social and economic issues that affect both women and men. After all, we have a new generation of young men who have been raised by full-time working mothers. Let us presume, as I do with my sons, that they will understand "supporting their families" to mean more than earning money.

I HAVE BEEN BLESSED to work with and be mentored by some extraordinary women. Watching Hillary Clinton in action makes me incredibly proud—of her intelligence, expertise, professionalism, charisma, and command of any audience. I get a similar rush when I see a frontpage picture of Christine Lagarde, the managing director of the International Monetary Fund, and Angela Merkel, the chancellor of Germany, deep in conversation about some of the most important issues on the world stage; or of Susan Rice, the U.S. ambassador to the United Nations, standing up forcefully for the Syrian people in the Security Council.

These women are extraordinary role models. If I had a daughter, I would encourage her to look to them, and I want a world in which they are extraordinary but not unusual. Yet I also want a world in which, in Lisa Jackson's words, "to be a strong woman, you don't have to give up on the things that define you as a woman." That means respecting, enabling, and indeed celebrating the full range of women's choices. "Empowering yourself," Jackson said in her speech at Princeton, "doesn't have to mean rejecting motherhood, or eliminating the nurturing or feminine aspects of who you are."

I gave a speech at Vassar last November and arrived in time to wander the campus on a lovely fall afternoon. It is a place infused with a spirit of community and generosity, filled with benches, walkways, public art, and quiet places donated by alumnae seeking to encourage contemplation and connection. Turning the pages of the alumni magazine (Vassar is now coed), I was struck by the entries of older alumnae, who greeted their classmates with *Salve* (Latin for "hello") and wrote witty remembrances sprinkled with literary allusions. Theirs was a world in which women wore their learning lightly; their news is mostly of their children's accomplishments. Many of us look back on that earlier era as a time when it was fine to joke that women went to college to get an "M.R.S." And many women of my generation abandoned the Seven Sisters as soon as the formerly all-male Ivy League universities became coed. I would never return to the world of segregated sexes and rampant discrimination. But now is the time to revisit the assumption that women must rush to adapt to the "man's world" that our mothers and mentors warned us about.

I continually push the young women in my classes to speak more. They must gain the confidence to value their own insights and questions, and to present them readily. My husband agrees, but he actually tries to get the young men in his classes to act more like the women—to speak less and listen more. If women are ever to achieve real equality as leaders, then we have to stop accepting male behavior and male choices as the default and the ideal. We must insist on changing social policies and bending career tracks to accommodate *our* choices, too. We have the power to do it if we decide to, and we have many men standing beside us.

We'll create a better society in the process, for *all* women. We may need to put a woman in the White House before we are able to change the conditions of the women working at Walmart. But when we do, we will stop talking about whether women can have it all. We will properly focus on how we can help all Americans have healthy, happy, productive lives, valuing the people they love as much as the success they seek.

Critical Thinking

1. What do you think that women should do regarding work and family?

2. Why do men seem to have much less of a problem regarding work and family? Should they have more of a problem?

3. Where will this issue be ten years from now?

Create Central

www.mhhe.com/createcentral

Internet References

Marriage and Family Therapy
   www.aamft.org/index_nm.asp

Sociosite
   www.topsite.com/goto/sociosite.net

Socioweb
   www.topsite.com/goto/socioweb.com

Sociology—Study Sociology Online
   http://edu.learnsoc.org

Sociology Web Resources
   www.mhhe.com/socscience/sociology/resources/index.htm

Article   Prepared by: Kurt Finsterbusch, *University of Maryland, College Park*

Death by Gender

Cynthia Fuchs Epstein

Learning Outcomes

After reading this article, you will be able to:

- Understand the horrible conditions of women in many parts of the world.

- Explain the legal and illegal basis for the trafficking of girls and women as sex slaves.

- Discuss worldwide changes in the status of women and their rights.

Finally, the atrocity of gendercide—the murder and mutilation of victims selected by sex—is getting prominent attention in the press. Through feminist online activism, but more prominently through the efforts of *New York Times* columnist Nicholas Kristof (in his new book *Half the Sky*, written with his wife, Sheryl WuDunn, and in his *New York Times* column), a socially embedded and systematic assault on women and girls in much of the world has been brought to public consciousness. The crimes at issue range from the killing of girls and women—often by their fathers, brothers, or male cousins, acting for the "honor" of the family—to the trafficking of women as sex slaves and to their forced recruitment as suicide bombers.

I will focus in this article on honor killing because the act is so vile. Further, the concept is difficult to dislodge. The notion of "honor" is at the core of many conflicts within and between societies all over the world, although it has been substantially reduced in the West. But, notions of honor underpin the marriage system in the tribal societies that are common in the Middle East and many parts of Africa. The most important connections between tribes are based on kinship and marriage, and value in the marriage market depends on female "virtue"—so girls and women must be tightly controlled to assure the "purity" of these social connections. Girls' families won't invest emotionally in them because they typically leave their birth families while very young and are brought into their husband's families as outsiders whose purpose is to bear children and take care of elderly family members. Without personal or social resources, they often are forced to be the servants or slaves of men in their birth families and then again in the families they enter by marriage. In "honor societies,"

which are characteristic of much of the developing world, girls and women are denied the protections that outside affiliations and affection might provide. Deviation from the rules imposed by male authorities may label a female as "contaminated" and elicit harsh sanctions. At its most serious, contamination is decreed when a women or girl is believed to have sought or had a sexual connection outside marriage—whether she acts from a desire to choose her own mate or is a victim of rape. Whether it has occurred within or outside the family, sexual contamination may be punished by murder. Thus, in some societies, the murder of girls and woman is justified by perceived social and moral infractions, and women are held in strict segregation to guard against these possibilities.

The belief that women are symbolic bearers of the honor of the clan or tribe is widely held, most often in Muslim countries but in others as well. And although Islamic law, or sharia, does not mandate honor killing as a punishment, it is practiced in many Islamic communities, openly so in some of them. It can be found also in some other groups, such as the Sikhs. There are lesser violations of honor for which girls and women are sometimes killed, like failing to comply with restrictive dress codes—wearing makeup or taking off the head scarf or hijab, for example—or for dating or merely appearing with unrelated boys or men in public. (According to the Al Arabia Web site, a Saudi father killed his daughter for chatting with a man on Facebook.) Trying to escape an arranged marriage is another important violation of traditional family norms that may merit death—as in the case of a young British woman who was stabbed to death by her father in London in 2002 when her family heard a love song dedicated to her on the radio and suspected that she had a boyfriend she had chosen for herself. A similar report comes from Turkey.

Women who protest forced marriage and abusive husbands can become targets of honor killings. And women and girls who have been raped can be doomed to death at the hands of a kinsman—or be forced to kill themselves to shield the rapist, if he himself is a kinsman, from punishment by the civil authorities. The dishonor of rape is so great that it can be used for political purposes. In January 2009, an Iraqi woman, Samira Ahmed Jassim, confessed to organizing the rapes of more than eighty women so that their shame would make them susceptible to recruitment as suicide bombers by al Qaeda. Twenty-eight of the women were said to have carried out suicide attacks.

The Turkish Human Rights Directorate reported in 2008 that in Istanbul alone there is one honor killing every week; more than one thousand occurred there in the preceding five years. UNICEF reported that in the Gaza Strip and the West Bank, according to 1999 figures, two-thirds of all murders were probably honor killings. In 2003, anthropologist/journalist James Emery of the Metropolitan State College of Denver stated that in the Palestinian communities of the West Bank, Gaza Strip, Israel, and Jordan, dishonored women were executed in their homes, in open fields, and occasionally in public before cheering crowds. Honor killings, Emery reported, account for virtually all recorded murders of Palestinian women. Although there are attempts by organizations such as the Women's Affairs Technical Committee (WATC) and other NGOs to provide education and practical services to protect and assist women, they have had little success so far.

Death because of gender is arguably a leading cause of female homicide in many societies, but gendercide occurs in other ways: in 1990 the Nobel laureate Amartya Sen wrote in the *New York Review of Books* that more than one hundred million women were missing from the world as a result of sex-selective abortion and ill treatment. No doubt, the number has increased as girls continue to be selectively pruned in such places as India and Pakistan—not only by the poor who undernourish their girl babies but also by members of the middle class who use sonograms to determine the sex of a fetus and then abort the females. The truth is that gender is regarded as a birth defect in much of the world, and this fact is neither analyzed nor addressed.

The officially reported estimates of the numbers of women who die in honor killings range from five thousand to ten thousand a year. (The UN Population Fund has estimated the total at five thousand a year, and that figure was reported by the secretary-general to the UN General Assembly in 2006.) But these numbers underestimate the actual toll because most honor murders are recorded as suicides or accidental deaths—or are not recorded at all. And the reports cannot begin to describe the terror girls and women must feel when they know that any aberrant behavior might provoke their fathers or close kin to kill them. Commentators in the West who suggest that women freely choose to conform to restrictions on their behavior and dress are not sensitive to the lurking threat of deadly punishment for violations of the codes. It is ludicrous to suggest that Islamic women decide for themselves to wear restrictive clothing and head coverings, given the possible consequences of not doing so.

Surprisingly, the support for honor killings is not limited to tribal societies but exists also among individuals living in traditional communities in modern societies. Even there, women who "go astray" and violate the bonds of marriage or assume individual identities often face physical assault. A poll by the BBC's Asia network, for example, found that one in ten young British Asians believe that honor killings can be justified. And in a poll of five hundred Hindus, Sikhs, Christians, and Muslims reported in 2009 by the online Women's E-news, one-tenth said they would condone the murder of someone who "disrespected" their family's honor.

Honor killings are not identified as a critically important instance of women's degraded status in many societies, and the practice is rarely condemned by the educated and sophisticated members of the societies in which the killings occur—nor by the social activists or leaders of the "free world." Nicholas Cohen, a writer for *Standpoint* magazine, asks why the outrage against apartheid does not extend to the women who are segregated and locked in their own homes, forced into arranged marriages, or raped and stoned. Why, he asks, do the societies that tolerate such practices not face irate Western boycotts or demonstrations in front of their embassy buildings?

It is clear, however, that the practice and the reasoning behind it will be difficult to erase. The protection of women's honor is an important part of the symbolic glue of kin groups that are, in many societies, the essential political bodies that maintain social order. Sociologists like Roger Friedland and Mounira Charrad have argued that control over women and marriage ensures that tribal groups can fully regulate the relationships between clans. (This is not so different from the marriages negotiated between the royal houses and aristocratic families of many countries in the West up to the early twentieth century.) Young women have to have unsullied reputations, and of course, they have to be virgins. Offering the bloodied sheets of the marital bed to relatives of the bride and groom is still necessary in many countries of the world.

Friedland has criticized the lack of awareness by political scientists (to say nothing of the media experts) who attempt to understand societies such as Afghanistan and Pakistan without attending to the tribal alliances created by marriages engineered by tribal elders. The obedience of women (actually girls, because these marriages are typically of underage children) is essential, and so the discipline over them is intense. Charrad, a sociologist studying the tribal foundations of the former French colonies of Algeria, Morocco, and Tunisia, similarly points to the political importance of tribal alliances created through the exchange of women.

Of course, men also are affected by these exchanges, but the men stay in their families of origin and it is the exchanged women who are forced to leave their places of birth and childhood. Because girls are married off early and torn from their families, they are powerless in the new environments to which they come as strangers. They are virtual slaves in the women's quarters of their new families.

Why do some women and girls internalize these views of honor and defend the very practices that enslave them? Why do we hear accounts of mothers who hold down their daughters as their husbands plunge knives into them or who observe the stoning that kills them? Or who insist that their daughters be circumcised when they know the pain and future discomfort this practice will bring?

Taken as child brides into the homes of their husbands, the only power these women have comes later in life as the mothers of sons who may, or may not, support them—and as the mothers of daughters, whom they can help to control but can't protect. They have learned the costs of deviance, and they teach those costs to, and even impose them on, their daughters.

The resistance to the education of girls in Afghanistan, by the Taliban and also, sometimes, by their own parents, is now well known, but girls' education is poor in many other regions where their "honor" is the most important thing about them—as in Pakistan, for example, and parts of India.

Are things getting better? Attempts by international human rights associations and women's rights organizations to impose penalties for honor killings have recently been undercut at the UN. According to ESCR-FEM, the online listserv for Women's Economic, Social and Cultural Rights, the UN Human Rights Council adopted a resolution in 2009 "promoting human rights and fundamental freedoms through a better understanding of *traditional* values of humankind . . ." [emphasis added]. The vote was twenty-six in favor, fifteen against, with six abstentions. The resolution was proposed by Russia and supported by the Arab League and the Organization of the Islamic Conference, a grouping of fifty-seven UN member states. Human Rights organizations across the globe strongly opposed it, declaring that its passage would set a destructive precedent by affirming a concept ("traditional values") often used to legitimize human rights abuses. The nongovernmental Cairo Institution for Human Rights Studies issued a statement expressing deep concern over the text. It declared that "such a concept has been used in the Arab region to justify treating women as second class citizens, female genital mutilation, honor crimes, child marriage, and other practices that clearly contradict international human rights standards."

There are a number of organizations devoted to improving the conditions of girls' and women's lives in the countries where those lives are most at risk. They include the International Initiative on Maternal Mortality and Human Rights and the Association for Women's Rights in Development, the Center for Women's Global Leadership, and the International Women's Rights Action Watch–Asia Pacific. Some organizations devoted to improving the situation of women are connected to agencies of the United Nations. It is more than thirty years since 90 percent of the member countries of the United Nations signed on to the Convention on the Elimination of all forms of Discrimination Against Women, which proclaimed that women's rights are human rights. But many of the signatories are countries in which the worst practices are carried out against women. Ironically, the United States has not signed.

What is to be done? We know that individuals' hearts and minds are difficult to change, but we also know that with proper incentives and political will they can sometimes change swiftly. Perhaps it is time for world leaders to insist on basic standards of human rights as a precondition for full commercial and diplomatic relations regardless of a country's religion or traditional culture. And perhaps it is also time for the resurgence of a woman's movement in the United States that will connect with the fledgling women's movements in countries of the Global South to form an alliance that will act politically to insist that women's and girls' rights be on the agenda of every international meeting.

Critical Thinking

1. Why does patriarchy justify murder and rape of women in some places?
2. What can people in developed countries do about the repression of women in some developing countries?

Create Central

www.mhhe.com/createcentral

Internet References

Sociosite
www.topsite.com/goto/sociosite.net
Socioweb
www.topsite.com/goto/socioweb.com
Sociology—Study Sociology Online
http://edu.learnsoc.org
Sociology Web Resources
www.mhhe.com/socscience/sociology/resources/index.htm

Cynthia Fuchs Epstein is Distinguished Professor of Sociology at The Graduate Center of the City University of New York. Among her books are *Woman's Place*, *Women in Law*, and *Deceptive Distinctions*.

From *Dissent*, Spring 2010, pp. 54–57. Copyright © 2010 by Foundation for Study of Independent Ideas, Inc. Reprinted by permission of University of Pennsylvania Press. www.dissentmagazine.org

Article   Prepared by: Kurt Finsterbusch, *University of Maryland, College Park*

The Boys at the Back

CHRISTINA HOFF SOMMERS

Learning Outcomes

After reading this article, you will be able to:

- Articulate the ways that girls and women outperform boys and men.

- Understand the ways that boys and men are treated unfairly.

- Understand the changes in society that affect the relative prospects of men and women.

Boys score as well as or better than girls on most standardized tests, yet they are far less likely to get good grades, take advanced classes or attend college. Why? A study coming out this week in The Journal of Human Resources gives an important answer. Teachers of classes as early as kindergarten factor good behavior into grades—and girls, as a rule, comport themselves far better than boys.

The study's authors analyzed data from more than 5,800 students from kindergarten through fifth grade and found that boys across all racial groups and in all major subject areas received lower grades than their test scores would have predicted.

The scholars attributed this "misalignment" to differences in "noncognitive skills": attentiveness, persistence, eagerness to learn, the ability to sit still and work independently. As most parents know, girls tend to develop these skills earlier and more naturally than boys.

> **"No previous study, to my knowledge, has demonstrated that the well-known gender gap in school grades begins so early and is almost entirely attributable to differences in behavior."**

No previous study, to my knowledge, has demonstrated that the well-known gender gap in school grades begins so early and is almost entirely attributable to differences in behavior. The researchers found that teachers rated boys as less proficient even when the boys did just as well as the girls on tests of reading, math and science. (The teachers did not know the test scores in advance.) If the teachers had not accounted for classroom behavior, the boys' grades, like the girls', would have matched their test scores.

That boys struggle with school is hardly news. Think of Shakespeare's "whining schoolboy with his satchel and shining morning face, creeping like snail unwillingly to school." Over all, it's likely that girls have long behaved better than boys at school (and earned better grades as a result), but their early academic success was not enough to overcome significant subsequent disadvantages: families' favoring sons over daughters in allocating scarce resources for schooling; cultural norms that de-emphasized girls' education, particularly past high school; an industrial economy that did not require a college degree to earn a living wage; and persistent discrimination toward women in the workplace.

Those disadvantages have lessened since about the 1970s. Parents, especially those of education and means, began to value their daughters' human capital as much as their sons'. Universities that had been dominated by affluent white men embraced meritocratic values and diversity of gender, race and class. The shift from a labor-intensive, manufacturing-reliant economy to a knowledge-based service economy significantly increased the relative value of college and postgraduate degrees. And while workplace inequities persisted, changing attitudes, legislation and litigation began to level the occupational playing field.

As these shifts were occurring, girls began their advance in education. In 1985, boys and girls took Advanced Placement exams at nearly the same rate. Around 1990, girls moved ahead of boys, and have never looked back. Women now account for roughly 60 percent of associate's, bachelor's and master's degrees and have begun to outpace men in obtaining Ph.D.'s.

There are some who say, well, too bad for the boys. If they are inattentive, obstreperous and distracting to their teachers and peers, that's their problem. After all, the ability to regulate one's impulses, delay gratification, sit still and pay close attention are the cornerstones of success in school and in the work force. It's long past time for women to claim their rightful share of the economic rewards that redound to those who do well in school.

As one critic told me recently, the classroom is no more rigged against boys than workplaces are rigged against lazy and unfocused workers. But unproductive workers are adults—not

5-year-olds. If boys are restless and unfocused, why not look for ways to help them do better? As a nation, can we afford not to?

A few decades ago, when we realized that girls languished behind boys in math and science, we mounted a concerted effort to give them more support, with significant success. Shouldn't we do the same for boys?

When I made this argument in my book "The War Against Boys," almost no one was talking about boys' academic, social and vocational problems. Now, 12 years later, the press, books and academic journals are teeming with such accounts. Witness the crop of books in recent years: Leonard Sax's "Boys Adrift," Liza Mundy's "The Richer Sex," Hanna Rosin's "The End of Men."

In a revised version of the book, I've changed the subtitle—to "How Misguided Policies Are Harming Our Young Men" from "How Misguided Feminism Is Harming Our Young Men"—and moved away from criticizing feminism; instead I emphasized boy-averse trends like the decline of recess, zero-tolerance disciplinary policies, the tendency to criminalize minor juvenile misconduct and the turn away from single-sex schooling. As our schools have become more feelings-centered, risk-averse, collaboration-oriented and sedentary, they have moved further and further from boys' characteristic sensibilities. Concerns about boys arose during a time of tech bubble prosperity; now, more than a decade later, there are major policy reasons—besides the stale "culture wars" of the 1990s—to focus on boys' schooling.

One is the heightened attention to school achievement as the cornerstone of lifelong success. Grades determine entry into advanced classes, enrichment programs and honor societies. They open—or close—doors to higher education. "If grade disparities emerge this early on, it's not surprising that by the time these children are ready to go to college, girls will be better positioned," says Christopher M. Cornwell, an economist at the University of Georgia and an author of the new study, along with his colleague David B. Mustard and Jessica Van Parys of Columbia University.

A second reason is globalization. Richard Whitmire, an education writer, and William Brozo, a literacy expert, write that "the global economic race we read so much about—the marathon to produce the most educated work force, and therefore the most prosperous nation—really comes down to a calculation: whichever nation solves these 'boy troubles' wins the race." That's probably an overstatement, but we do know that the large-scale entry of women into the work force paid large economic dividends. It stands to reason that raising male academic achievement is essential to raising labor productivity and, ultimately, living standards.

A third reason: improving the performance of black, Latino and lower-income kids requires particular attention to boys. Black women are nearly twice as likely to earn a college degree as black men. At some historically black colleges, the gap is astounding: Fisk is now 64 percent female; Howard, 67 percent; Clark Atlanta, 75 percent. The economist Andrew M. Sum and his colleagues at the Center for Labor Market Studies at Northeastern University examined the Boston Public Schools and found that for the graduating class of 2007, there were 191 black girls for every 100 boys going on to attend a four-year college or university. Among Hispanics, the ratio was 175 girls for every 100 boys; among whites, 153 for every 100.

Young men from middle-class or more comfortable backgrounds aren't lagging quite as far behind, but the gender gap exists there, too. Judith Kleinfeld, a psychology professor at the University of Alaska, Fairbanks, analyzed the reading skills of white males from college-educated families. She showed that at the end of high school, 23 percent of the these boys scored "below basic," compared with 7 percent of their female counterparts. "This means that almost one in four boys who have college-educated parents cannot read a newspaper with understanding," she wrote.

WHAT might we do to help boys improve? For one thing, we can follow the example of the British, the Canadians and the Australians. They have openly addressed the problem of male underachievement. They are not indulging boys' tendency to be inattentive. Instead, they are experimenting with programs to help them become more organized, focused and engaged. These include more boy-friendly reading assignments (science fiction, fantasy, sports, espionage, battles); more recess (where boys can engage in rough-and-tumble as a respite from classroom routine); campaigns to encourage male literacy; more single-sex classes; and more male teachers (and female teachers interested in the pedagogical challenges boys pose).

These efforts should start early, but even high school isn't too late. Consider Aviation High School in New York City. A faded orange brick building with green aluminum trim, it fits comfortably with its gritty neighbors—a steelyard, a tool-supply outlet and a 24-hour gas station and convenience store—in Long Island City, Queens.

"The rise of women, however long overdue, does not require the fall of men."

On a visit to Aviation I observed a classroom of 14- and 15-year-olds focused on constructing miniaturized, electrically wired airplane wings from mostly raw materials. In another class, students worked in teams—with a student foreman and crew chief—to take apart and then rebuild a small jet engine in just 20 days. In addition to pursuing a standard high school curriculum, Aviation students spend half of the day in hands-on classes on airframes, hydraulics and electrical systems. They put up with demanding English and history classes because unless they do well in them, they cannot spend their afternoons tinkering with the engine of a Cessna 411.

The school's 2,200 pupils—mostly students of color, from low-income households—have a 95 percent attendance rate and a 90 percent graduation rate, with 80 percent going on to college. The school is coed; although girls make up only 16 percent of the student population, they appear to be flourishing. The New York City Department of Education has repeatedly awarded Aviation an "A" on its annual school progress reports. U.S. News & World Report has cited it as one of the best high schools in the nation.

"The school is all about structure," an assistant principal, Ralph Santiago, told me. The faculty emphasizes organization, precision, workmanship and attention to detail. The students are kept so busy and are so fascinated with what they are doing that they have neither the time nor the desire for antics.

Not everyone of either sex is interested in airplanes. But vocational high schools with serious academic requirements are an important part of the solution to male disengagement from school.

I can sympathize with those who roll their eyes at the relatively recent alarm over boys' achievement. Where was the indignation when men dominated higher education, decade after decade? Isn't it time for women and girls to enjoy the advantages? The impulse is understandable but misguided. I became a feminist in the 1970s because I did not appreciate male chauvinism. I still don't. But the proper corrective to chauvinism is not to reverse it and practice it against males, but rather basic fairness. And fairness today requires us to address the serious educational deficits of boys and young men. The rise of women, however long overdue, does not require the fall of men.

Critical Thinking

1. How are gender roles changing?

2. How can the disadvantages of men be addressed without creating disadvantages for women?

3. Have women intended the disadvantages of men (as presented by the author)?

Create Central

www.mhhe.com/createcentral

Internet References

Marriage and Family Therapy
www.aamft.org/index_nm.asp

Sociosite
www.topsite.com/goto/sociosite.net

Socioweb
www.topsite.com/goto/socioweb.com

Sociology—Study Sociology Online
http://edu.learnsoc.org

Sociology Web Resources
www.mhhe.com/socscience/sociology/resources/index.htm

CHRISTINA HOFF SOMMERS is a resident scholar at the American Enterprise Institute and the author of "The War Against Boys."

Article   Prepared by: Kurt Finsterbusch, *University of Maryland, College Park*

The Masculine Mystique

Although fatherhood has changed beyond recognition in recent decades, men remain largely excluded from the debate about work-life balance. Until that changes, the stark economic realities facing fathers will be downplayed, and family issues miscast as women's issues

STEPHEN MARCHE

Learning Outcomes

After reading this article, you will be able to:

- Think about the role of husbands in the work/family balance or imbalance.

- Understand how American fatherhood has evolved in the past generation.

- Evaluate the trade-offs involved in the work/family issue.

My wife leans in. A year ago, after nine hours of labor, she received an epidural and immediately asked me to pass the iPad so she could send a note to work. I suggested that this time should be for us and for the little girl who was making her way into the world, but it's hard to argue with a woman who's eight centimeters dilated. Besides, why not send the note? Soon enough the baby, our second, would be out. The pause for an epidural was the most calm we would see for months. We are all in the thick of it, in the mash-up of work and family, in the confounding blur of everything, instantly, at once, the way life happens now. Why waste a moment?

A year after *The Atlantic* published Anne-Marie Slaughter's "Why Women Still Can't Have It All," the plutocratic wave of feminism continues to roll in. Sheryl Sandberg's *Lean In* looks to dominate the best-seller lists for months to come. Both accounts are full of stories like the iPad in the delivery room, stories of women furiously multitasking, worrying about family over champagne at a United Nations event, or diagnosing children with head lice while aboard a corporate jet. Men are mostly offstage. Slaughter, to her great credit, talks repeatedly about her husband, noting that he has done everything possible to support both her career and their two sons, including taking on the lion's share of parenting duties while she commuted for two years from Princeton to Washington, D.C. Sandberg, too, talks about her husband's role at home (in her book's dedication, she credits him with "making everything possible"). But in the ensuing discussion of gender politics, which has been conducted almost entirely by women, for women, men are far

more anonymous—implacable opponents of progress in the upper echelons, helpless losers elsewhere. Meanwhile, the good husbands—the selection of whom is "the most important career choice" young women can make, according to Sandberg—are as silent as the good wives once were.

Men's absence from the conversation about work and life is strange, because decisions about who works and who takes care of the children, and who makes the money and how the money is spent, are not decided by women alone or by some vague and impersonal force called society. Decisions in heterosexual relationships are made by women and men together. When men aren't part of the discussion about balancing work and life, outdated assumptions about fatherhood are allowed to go unchallenged and, far more important, key realities about the relationship between work and family are elided. The central conflict of domestic life right now is not men versus women, mothers versus fathers. It is family versus money. Domestic life today is like one of those behind-the-scenes TV series about show business. The main narrative tension is: "How the hell are we going to make this happen?" There are tears and laughs and little intrigues, but in the end, it's just a miracle that the show goes on, that everyone is fed and clothed and out the door each day.

"What would you do if you weren't afraid?," Sandberg asks women in the opening chapter of *Lean In*. She obviously does not work in journalism (as my wife does) or academia (as I used to), let alone manufacturing. The question for most American women, and for most families, is much simpler: "How do I survive?" Sandberg's book has been compared with feminist classics like *The Feminine Mystique,* but it really belongs in the category of capitalist fantasy, a tradition that originated with Samuel Smiles's *Self-Help* and was popularized by the novels of Horatio Alger. The success of *Lean In* can be attributed, at least in part, to its comforting espousal of an obviously false hope: that hard work and talent alone can now take you to the top. This is pure balderdash, for women *and* men. Class structures have seized to the point where Denmark has more social mobility than the United States. The last myth to die in America will be the myth of pluck; *Lean In* is the most recent testament to its power.

Slaughter's essay, too, reflects the blind spots of the technocratic elite. It is a superachiever's guide to having a family. Here is how she describes taking a break from her usually harried work existence to concentrate on her family life during a sabbatical: "I think of these plateaus as 'investment intervals.'" Louise Richardson, the vice chancellor of the University of St. Andrews, in Scotland, is so "ruthlessly" organized, in Slaughter's telling, that when microwaving, she keys in 1:11, 2:22, or 3:33—instead of 1:00, 2:00, or 3:00—as a way of saving time. This is not so much a ruthless use of time as a fetishization of time—the cult of the billable hour run amok.

The plutocratic wave of feminism has positioned itself as the heir to a longstanding feminist revolution undertaken in the name of all women. And yet when I first read "Why Women Still Can't Have It All," I immediately thought of the men I know who might be said to "have it all." The wife of one of my editors had a premature baby at 28 weeks; after they brought the baby home, he did not miss a day of work. Soldiers, I suppose, "have it all." They have meaningful work and then come home (eventually) to their waiting families. Does anyone imagine that they consider themselves the victors of society's current arrangement?

Although you might not know it from the discussion Sandberg and Slaughter have touched off, American fatherhood has evolved almost beyond recognition in recent decades. The Pew Research Center released a study called "Modern Parenthood" in March, well after either Sandberg or Slaughter could refer to it, which is unfortunate. When it comes to work-life conflict, the study found, about half of all working parents say it is difficult to balance career and family responsibilities, with "no significant gap in attitudes between mothers and fathers." Perhaps this is not surprising, given that mothers' and fathers' roles have converged dramatically in the past half century. Since 1965, Pew reports, fathers have tripled the time they spend with their children. Fathers' attitudes about mothers' roles are changing quickly, too: In 2009, 54 percent of men with kids younger than 17 believed that young children should have a mother who didn't work. Just four years later, that number has dropped to 37 percent. Finally, although stay-at-home dads are still very much in the minority, their numbers have doubled in just a decade's time.

Meanwhile, women's rise to economic dominance within the middle class continues. Since 1996, women have earned more bachelor's degrees than men, and last year they started earning a greater number of master's and doctoral degrees. It is an outrage that the male-female wage gap persists, and yet, over the past 10 years, in almost every country in the developed world, it has shrunk. In developed countries, by most economic indicators, women's lives have improved relative to men's. Of the 15 fastest-growing job categories in the United States, 13 are dominated by women.

What isn't changing is that top leadership positions remain overwhelmingly filled by men. "As the 99 percent has become steadily pinker, the 1 percent has remained an all-boys club," Chrystia Freeland pointed out last year, in her book *Plutocrats.* According to the World Economic Forum's "Global Gender Gap" report, women around the world hold a mere 20 percent of powerful political positions. In the United States, the female board-membership rate is 12 percent—a disgrace.

We live in a hollow patriarchy: the edifice is patriarchal, while the majority of its occupants approach egalitarianism. This generates strange paradoxes. Even women with servants and powerful jobs and hundreds of millions of dollars feel that they have an institutional disadvantage. And they're right. Women in the upper reaches of power are limited in ways that men simply are not. Various men's movements have emerged, purportedly to provide a counterweight to feminism, but this proposition is inherently absurd. The greatest power still resides in the hands of a few men, even as the majority of men are being outpaced in the knowledge economy. Masculinity grows less and less powerful while remaining iconic of power. And therefore men are silent. After all, there is nothing less manly than talking about waning manliness.

The good husbands—the selection of whom Sheryl Sandberg calls "the most important career choice" young women can make— are as silent as the good wives once were.

In the 1950s, the patriarchy at work and at home were of a piece. The father was the head of the household because he provided for the family, and the boss was head of the company because he provided the work that provided for the family. At home, for the overwhelming majority of families, the old order has disappeared. The days of Dad working all week and then, having fulfilled his duties, going to play two or three rounds of golf on the weekend are long gone. So are the days of Dad as the head of the household, the decider in chief. A 2008 Pew study asked cohabiting male-female couples, "Who makes the decisions at home?" In 26 percent of households, the man did; while in 43 percent of households, the woman did. The family has changed and is further changing, while at work, patriarchy survives as a kind of anachronistic holdover, like daylight savings or summer vacation.

The hollow patriarchy keeps women from power and confounds male identity. (The average working-class guy has the strange experience of belonging to a gender that is railed against for having a lock on power, even as he has none of it.) The current arrangement serves almost nobody's interests. And yet it may be harder to break than older modes of sexism. The struggles articulated by *The Second Sex* and *The Feminine Mystique* and *The Female Eunuch* were broadly oppositional—women against men, young against old, feminists against the existing structures of power. Today, men and women are not facing off on a battleground so much as stuck together in a maze of contradictions.

In 2007, my life was right where I wanted it to be. After the lean misery of graduate school at the University of Toronto, I had, at 31, landed a job on the tenure track at City College in Harlem, as a professor of Shakespeare. My second novel was in the windows of appealing independent bookstores in Brooklyn, it had a good review in *The New York Times,* and the lead singer of the Decemberists was recommending it in interviews. This was basically all I had ever hoped for. Then I gave it up. My wife was offered her dream job as the editor in chief of *Toronto Life* magazine (roughly speaking, the *New York* of Canada), and we returned home.

You could see our departure as the triumph of egalitarianism, and in a way it was. I don't think my father would have given up a tenure-track job for my mother. But in my marriage, the decision came down to brute economics: My wife was going to make double what I made. Good schools and good hospitals are free in Toronto. These are the reasons we moved. And if I were offered a job where I would make double what she does, we would move again. Gender politics has nothing to do with it.

Not that politics didn't intrude. We were moving back to downtown Toronto, where people self-identify as socialists, so I expected open-mindedness. Yet the reaction to my reduced professional status and stepped-up involvement in child-rearing was sharply divided along generational lines. Among Baby Boomers, classic gender stereotypes prevailed. To them, I had become "the woman" and my wife had become "the man." Boomer men could not wrap their heads around what I had done, while the women would smile an amazed smile, their eyes glinting with a touch of self-satisfaction. A younger generation was completing what they had begun.

Among people my own age, the reaction was more complicated. Our story possessed a sort of circumscribed romance: to academic friends, the idea that I had given up a tenure-track appointment was like the Charge of the Light Brigade—glorious professional suicide. At any rate, most friends and acquaintances in roughly my age group at least understood the nature of the decision. They appreciated that chasing jobs was part of 21st-century life, and that marriage sometimes requires sacrifice. Well over half my male friends have wives who make more money than they do. Nonetheless, in social life, I found myself more and more of an addendum: "This is Stephen. He's Sarah's wife."

I don't think my father would have given up a tenure-track job for my mother. But in my marriage, the decision came down to brute economics.

But let us get down to the details—specifically the financial details. The key fact of our story, the overwhelmingly most important factor in our personal gender politics, is that in Canada, we have access to high-quality, modestly state-supported (though far from free) day care. Of all the privileges my wife and I gained, our boy being in a safe place we could afford between nine and five was by far the greatest. It's why this story has a happy ending; it is the thing that enabled me to build a new career for myself. Day care is not theoretical liberation. It is the real deal, for women and men alike.

Our new domestic arrangement, like the move that precipitated it, was shaped more by circumstance than by ideology. I was a freelancer. My wife was running a magazine. So I picked up the boy from day care each afternoon and pushed him in his stroller though the unbearable Toronto February. When she was out at various events, the boy and I had "guys' night," the two of us watching hockey and eating take-out Portuguese chicken, often in our pajamas. Think of it as our answer to Slaughter's "investment intervals."

For the Boomers and members of older generations, a married couple's decisions about work were ultimately questions of power. For younger generations, marital decisions boil down mostly to money. And yet the debates about gender, particularly the debate that has emerged in a thousand blog posts surrounding "Why Women Still Can't Have It All" and *Lean In*, retain the earlier framework. These discussions tend to recognize the residual patriarchy, but they do not see its hollowness, or the processes hollowing it out.

The days of Dad working all week and then, having fulfilled his duties, going to play two or three rounds of golf on the weekend are long gone.

The plutocratic feminists almost always end up, out of habit, calling for an attitude adjustment, a switch in thinking—they hope to re-create, and perhaps cash in on, the transformational optimism of '60s-era consciousness-raising. But the consciousness has been raised. Gender attitudes do not affect economic reality, but rather the other way around. The rise of women is not the result of any ideology or political movement; it is a result of the widespread realization, sometime after the Second World War, that families in which women work are families that prosper. And countries in which women work are countries that prosper. In 2006, a database created by the Organization for Economic Cooperation and Development demonstrated what common sense tells us: with few exceptions, countries in which women have more economic and political power are richer than countries where women are relatively powerless. Patriarchy is damn expensive. That's why it's doomed.

Sheryl Sandberg's "Lean In Circles"—her national network of book clubs cum professional self-help groups for women—are not supposed to be mere marketing exercises; they are intended to be psych-up sessions for elite women who want to learn to be more demanding. Good for them, I suppose. But do we want women emulating the egomania of the corporate male? Do we really want that particular brand of insanity to spread? Wasn't it exactly that arrogance that led to the 2008 financial collapse? I suppose a world in which female bankers spend as much on blow and hookers as their male counterparts would be a fairer world; is it a world worth fighting for?

Both Sandberg and Slaughter imagine benefits to women flowing from the top to the bottom. Slaughter wants

> to close the leadership gap: to elect a woman president and 50 women senators; to ensure that women are equally represented in the ranks of corporate executives and judicial leaders. Only when women wield power in sufficient numbers will we create a society that genuinely works for all women. That will be a society that works for everyone.

She may well be right—but in the meantime, having a few women in positions of power has hardly proved to be a panacea. Britain had a female head of state and leader of government for nearly 12 years without becoming a feminist paradise. Sandberg makes a big deal out of how "one pregnant woman at the top" can make a difference for other women. But the specific example she cites—her campaign for designated pregnant-woman parking spots at Google—hardly seems revolutionary.

I remember, as a boy, waking up on a mattress in the back of a station wagon in a hospital parking lot in Edmonton, Alberta. My father was not in town—he commuted to another city by plane every day for two years. And so, on a few occasions, my mother, who is a physician, left my brother and me in the car while she delivered a baby in the middle of the night. At the time, I loved the adventure. Later, I came to realize that my parents had worked their way into the middle class through many such superhuman maneuvers. My mother-in-law, for her part, used to return home from her job as a broadcaster, feed two children, put them to bed, and then return to the office for a couple more hours of work. If it was like this for doctors and broadcasters, what must it have been like for factory workers?

The solution to the work-life conundrum is not "enlisting men" (as Slaughter puts it) in the domestic sphere. The solution is establishing social supports that allow families to function. The fact is, men can't have it all, for the same reason women can't: whether or not the load is being shared 50-50 doesn't matter if the load is still unbearable. It will not become bearable once women lean in, or once the consciousness is raised, or once men are full partners, always, in domestic life. It will become bearable when decidedly more quotidian things become commonplace—like paid parental leave and affordable, quality day care (which Sandberg and Slaughter both advocate).

As was recently noted in a *New Republic* cover story titled "The Hell of American Day Care," the National Institutes of Health has rated only 10 percent of child-care facilities nationwide as providing "high-quality care" (most are instead rated "fair" or "poor"). And in every state, the average annual cost of day care for two children exceeds the average annual rent. Not surprisingly, low-income mothers are far more likely to stay at home today than are upper-income mothers. Such women are forgoing paid work not because they refuse to lean in but because they can't earn enough money at their jobs to cover child care.

If men's voices are absent from the conversation about family, we have, I'm afraid, only ourselves to blame. Yes, there are the occasional pieces in newspapers and magazines by new fathers—a genre that at times seems more oriented toward establishing one's literary machismo than toward engaging in substantive dialogue—but men have generally failed to make themselves heard. Those who speak loudest tend to be either members of the aforementioned men's-rights groups, or explicit anti-feminists, who long for a traditional family that bears little resemblance to the current reality. Men are not victims in this story, nor helpless witnesses to their wives' struggles. And yet:

A chorus of women demands maternity leave. Where is the chorus of men asking for paternity leave?

A conversation about work-life balance conducted by and for a small sliver of the female population only perpetuates the perception that these are women's problems, not family ones. If you doubt that such thinking is still pervasive, see the recent op-ed in *The New York Times* about tax policy's effect on working families, which contained this sentence: "Most working mothers who pay for child care do so out of their after-tax income." That's right: child care is a not a father's expense, or a family's expense, but a mother's. As Sandberg points out, when the U.S. Census Bureau studies child care, it "considers mothers the 'designated parent,' even when both parents are present in the home. When mothers care for their children, it's 'parenting,' but when fathers care for their children, the government deems it a 'child care arrangement.'"

As long as family issues are miscast as women's issues, they will be dismissed as the pleadings of one interest group among many. And truly, it's hard to see, at least in terms of political theatrics, why the complaints of the richest and most successful women in the world should bother anybody too much. Fighting for the American family is another matter. When gay-rights activists shifted their focus from the struggle for their rights as an oppressed minority to the struggle to create and support families, their movement experienced nearly unprecedented political triumph. It is easy to have a career as an anti-feminist. Force the opponents of day-care support and family leave to come out instead against working families. Let them try to sell that.

Gloria Steinem's famous declaration that "women's liberation will be men's liberation, too" is true. The opposite is also true. Real liberation will not be one against the other, but both together.

Critical Thinking

1. What can society do to alleviate the work/family problem?
2. What is the role of the father in most homes?
3. Discuss this issue from a justice perspective.

Create Central

www.mhhe.com/createcentral

Internet References

Marriage and Family Therapy
    www.aamft.org/index_nm.asp
Sociosite
    www.topsite.com/goto/sociosite.net
Socioweb
    www.topsite.com/goto/socioweb.com
Sociology—Study Sociology Online
    http://edu.learnsoc.org
Sociology Web Resources
    www.mhhe.com/socscience/sociology/resources/index.htm

STEPHEN MARCHE is a novelist and a contributing editor at *Esquire*.

Article   Prepared by: Kurt Finsterbusch, *University of Maryland, College Park*

Houston Rising

Why the Next Great American Cities Aren't What You Think

Joel Kotkin

Learning Outcomes

After reading this article, you will be able to:

- Understand the attractiveness to their residents of the moderately large cities compared to the very largest cities.

- Discuss the different views on the appropriate type of city for the future.

- Discuss the critical functions that cities provide to the national and international economies.

America's urban landscape is changing, but in ways not always predicted or much admired by our media, planners, and pundits. The real trend-setters of the future—judged by both population and job growth—are not in the oft-praised great "legacy" cities like New York, Chicago, or San Francisco, but a crop of newer, more sprawling urban regions primarily located in the Sun Belt and, surprisingly, the resurgent Great Plains.

While Gotham and the Windy City have experienced modest growth and significant net domestic out-migration, burgeoning if often disdained urban regions such as Houston, Dallas-Ft. Worth, Charlotte, and Oklahoma City have expanded rapidly. These low-density, car-dominated, heavily suburbanized areas with small central cores likely represent the next wave of great American cities.

There's a whole industry led by the likes of Harvard's Ed Glaeser, my occasional sparring partner Richard Florida and developer-funded groups like CEOs for Cities, who advocate for old-style, high-density cities, and insist that they represent the inevitable future.

But the numbers tell a different story: the most rapid urban growth is occurring outside of the great, dense, highly developed and vastly expensive old American metropolises.

An aspirational city, by definition, is one that people and industries migrate to improve their economic prospects and achieve a better relative quality of life. In the 19th and early 20th centuries, this aspirational spirit was epitomized by cities such as New York and Chicago and then in the decades after World War Two by Los Angeles, which for many years was the fastest-growing big city in the high-income world.

Until the 1970s, the country's established big cities were synonymous with aspiration—where the jobs and opportunities for broad portions of the population abounded. But as the financial markets took on an oversized role in the American economy and manufacturing receded, the cost of living in the nation's oldest metropolises shot up far faster than the median income there—and Americans have turned elsewhere now that, as Virginia Postrel wrote in an important essay on the nation's growing economic wall, "the promise of a better life that once drew people of all backgrounds to rich places like New York and [coastal] California now applies only to an educated elite—because rich places have made housing prohibitively expensive."

Like the great legacy cities during their now long-past adolescent and at times ungainly growth spurts, today's aspirational cities often meet with little approval from travelers from other, older cities. A 19th-century Swedish visitor to Chicago described it as "one of the most miserable and ugly cities" in North America. New York, complained the French Consul in 1810, was a city where the inhabitants had "in general no mind for anything but business"; later Bostonian Ralph Waldo Emerson, granted Gotham's entrepreneurial supremacy only to explain that his more cultured "little city" was "appointed" by destiny to "lead the civilization of North America."

Los Angeles, most of whose early-20th-century migrants came from the Midwest, became a favorite object of scorn from sophisticates. William Faulkner in the 1930s described the city of angels as "the plastic asshole of the world." As the first great city built largely around the automobile, mainstream urbanists detested it; their icon Jane Jacobs called it "a vast blind-eyed reservation."

A half century later, today's aspirational urban centers suffer similarly poor reputations among urbanists, planners and journalists. One *New York Post* reporter recently described Houston as "brutally ugly" while new urbanists like Andres Duany relegate the region to a netherworld inhabited by car-centric cities such as Phoenix and Atlanta.

Yet over the past decade the 25 fastest-growing cities have been mostly such urbanist "assholes"—Raleigh, Austin, Houston, San Antonio, Las Vegas, Orlando, Dallas-Fort Worth, Charlotte, and Phoenix. Despite hopeful claims from density advocates that the Great Recession and the housing bust ended this trend, the latest census data shows that Americans have continued choosing places that are affordable enough to offer opportunity, and space.

One common article of faith among mainstream urbanists, at least when they stop to note this growth at all, is that these cities grow mainly because they are cheap and can house the unskilled. But in reality many of these metropolitan areas are also leading the nation in growing their number of well-educated arrivals. Houston, Charlotte, Raleigh, Las Vegas, Nashville, and San Antonio, for example, experienced increases in the number of college-educated residents of nearly 40 percent or more over the decade, roughly twice the level of growth as in "brain centers" such as Boston, San Francisco, San Jose (Silicon Valley), or Chicago. Atlanta, Houston, and Dallas each have added about 300,000 college grads in the past decade, more than greater Boston's pickup of 240,000 or San Francisco's 211,000.

Once considered backwaters, these Sunbelt cities are quietly achieving a critical mass of well-educated residents. They are also becoming major magnets for immigrants. Over the past decade, the largest percentage growth in foreign-born population has occurred in sunbelt cities, led by Nashville, which has doubled its number of immigrants, as have Charlotte and Raleigh. During the first decade of the 21st century, Houston attracted the second-most new, foreign-born residents, some 400,000, of any American city—behind only much larger New York and slightly ahead of Dallas-Ft. Worth, but more than three times as many as Los Angeles. According to one recent Rice University study, Census data now shows that Houston has now surpassed New York as the country's most racially and ethnically diverse metropolis.

Why are these people flocking to the aspirational cities, that lack the hip amenities, tourist draws, and cultural landmarks of the biggest American cities? People are still far more likely to buy a million dollar *pied à terre* in Manhattan than to do so in Oklahoma City. Like early-20th-century Polish peasants who came to work in Chicago's factories or Russian immigrants, like my grandparents, who came to New York to labor in the rag trade, the appeal of today's smaller cities is largely economic. The foreign born, along with generally younger educated workers, are canaries in the coal mine—singing loudest and most frequently in places that offer both employment and opportunities for upward mobility and a better life.

Over the decade, for example, Austin's job base grew 28 percent, Raleigh's by 21 percent, Houston by 20 percent, while Nashville, Atlanta, San Antonio, and Dallas-Ft. Worth saw job growth in the 14 percent range or better. In contrast, among all the legacy cities, only Seattle and Washington D.C.—the great economic parasite—have created jobs faster than the national average of roughly 5 percent. Most did far worse, with New York and Boston 20 percent *below* the norm; big urban regions including Philadelphia, Los Angeles, and, despite the current tech bubble, San Francisco have created essentially *zero* new jobs over the decade.

Another common urban legend maintains these areas lag in terms of higher-wage employment, lacking the density essential for what boosters like Glaeser and Florida describe as "knowledge-intensive cities." Defenders of traditional cities often cite Santa Fe Institute research that they say links innovation with density—but actually does nothing of the kind. Rather, that research suggests that *size,* not compactness, constitutes the decisive factor. After all, it's hard to define Silicon Valley, still the

nation's premier innovation region, as anything other than large, sprawling, and overwhelmingly suburban in form.

Size does matter and many of the fastest growth areas are themselves large enough to sport a major airport, large corporate presences and other critical pieces of economic infrastructure. The largest gains in GDP (PDF) in 2011 were in Houston, Dallas and, surprisingly, resurgent greater Detroit (and that despite its shrinking urban core). None of these areas are characterized by high density yet their income growth was well ahead of Seattle, San Francisco, or Boston, and more than twice that of New York, Washington, or Chicago.

But in fact neither density nor size necessarily determine which regions generate new high-end jobs. The growth in STEM—or science-technology-engineering and mathematics-related—employment in Houston, Raleigh, Nashville, Austin, and Las Vegas surpassed that in San Francisco, Los Angeles, Boston, or New York. One reason: most STEM jobs are not found in fashionable fields like designing social media or videogames but in more prosaic activities tied to medicine, manufacturing, agriculture and (horror of horrors) natural resource extraction, including fossil fuel energy. In this sense, technology reflects the definition of the French sociologists Marcel Mauss as "a traditional action made effective."

This pattern also extends to growth in business and professional services, the nation's biggest high-wage job category. Since 2000, Houston, Dallas-Fort Worth, Charlotte, Austin and Raleigh expanded their number of such jobs by twenty percent or more—twice the rate as greater New York, the longtime business-service capital, while Chicago and San Jose actually lost jobs in this critical category.

Finally there is the too often neglected topic of real purchasing power—that a dollar in New York doesn't go nearly as far as one in Atlanta, for example. My colleague Mark Schill at the Praxis Strategy group has calculated the average regional paycheck, adjusted for cost of living. Houston led the pack in real median pay in, and seven of the 10 cities with the highest adjusted salary were aspirational ones (the exceptions were San Jose-Silicon Valley, Seattle, and the greater Detroit region). Portland, Los Angeles, New York, and San Diego all landed near the bottom of the list.

Conventional urbanists—call them density nostalgists—continue to see the future in legacy cities that, as the University of Washington demographer Richard Morrill notes, were built out before the dominance of the car, air-conditioning and with them the prevalence of suburban lifestyles.

Looking forward, it is simply presumptuous and ahistorical to dismiss the fast-growing regions as anti-cities, as 60s-era urbanists did with places like Los Angeles. When tradition-bound urbanists hope these sprawling young cities choke on their traffic and exhaust fumes, or from rising energy costs, they are reflecting the classic prejudice of city-dwellers of established urban centers toward upstarts.

The reality is that most urban growth in our most dynamic, fastest-growing regions has included strong expansion of the suburban and even exurban fringe, along with a limited resurgence in their historically small inner cores. Economic growth, it turns out, allows for young hipsters to find amenable places before they enter their 30s, and affordable, more suburban environments nearby to start families.

This urbanizing process is shaped, in many ways, by the late development of these regions. In most aspirational cities, close-in neighborhoods often are dominated by single-family houses; it's a mere 10 or 15 minute drive from nice, leafy streets in Ft. Worth, Charlotte, or Austin to the urban core. In these cities, families or individuals who want to live near the center can do so without being forced to live in a tiny apartment.

And in many of these places, the historic underdevelopment in the central district, coupled with job growth, presents developers with economically viable options for higher-density housing as well. Houston presents the strongest example of this trend. Although nearly 60 percent of Houston's growth over the decade has been more than 20 miles outside the core, the inner ring area encompassed within the loop around Interstate 610 has also been growing steadily, albeit at a markedly slower rate. This contrasts with many urban regions, where close-in areas just beyond downtowns have been actually *losing* population.

Even as Houston has continued to advance outwards, the region has added more multiunit buildings over the past decade than more populous New York, Los Angeles or Chicago. With its economy growing faster and producing wealth faster than any other region in the country, urban developers there usually do not need subsidies or planning dictates to be economically viable.

Modern urban culture also is spreading in the Bayou City. In what has to be a first, my colleagues at Forbes recently ranked Houston as America's "coolest city," citing not only its economy, but its thriving arts scene and excellent restaurants. Such praise may make some of us, who relish Houston's unpretentious nature, a little nervous—but it shows that hip urbanism can co-exist with rapidly expanding suburban development.

And Houston's not the only proverbial urban ugly duckling having an amenity makeover. Oklahoma City has developed its central "Bricktown" into a centerpiece for arts and entertainment. Ft. Worth boasts its own, cowboy-themed downtown, along with fine museums, while its rival Dallas, in typical Texan fashion, boasts of having the nation's largest arts district.

More important still, both for families and outdoor-oriented singles, both cities are developing large urban park systems. At an expense of $30 million, Raleigh is nearing the completion of its Neuse River Greenway Trail, a 28-mile trail through the forested areas of Raleigh. Houston has plans for a series of bayou-oriented green ways. For its part, Dallas is envisioning a vast new 6,000 acre park system, along the Trinity River that will dwarf New York's 840-acre Central Park.

To be sure, there's no foreseeable circumstance in which these cities will challenge Paris or Buenos Aires, New York, or San Francisco as favored destinations for those primarily motivated by aesthetics that are largely the result of history. Nor are they likely to become models of progressive governance, as poverty and gaps in medical coverage become even more difficult problems for elected officials without a well-entrenched ultra-wealthy class to cull resources from.

Finally, they will not become highly dense, apartment cities —as developers and planners insist they "should." Instead the aspirational regions are likely to remain dominated by a suburbanized form characterized by car dependency, dispersion of job centers, and single-family homes. In 2011, for example, twice as many single-family homes sold in Raleigh as condos and townhouses combined. The ratio of new suburban to new urban housing, according to the American Community Survey, is 10 to 1 in Las Vegas and Orlando, 5 to 1 in Dallas, 4 to 1 in Houston and 3 to 1 in Phoenix.

Pressed by local developers and planners, some aspirational cities spend heavily on urban transit, including light rail. To my mind, these efforts are largely quixotic, with transit accounting for five percent or less of all commuters in most systems. The Charlotte Area Transit System represents less a viable means of commuting for most residents than what could be called Manhattan infrastructure envy. Even urban-planning model Portland, now with five radial light rail lines and a population now growing largely at its fringes, carries a smaller portion of commuters on transit than before opening its first line in 1986.

But such pretentions, however ill-suited, have always been commonplace for ambitious and ascending cities, and are hardly a reason to discount their prospects. Urbanistas need to wake up, start recognizing what the future is really looking like and search for ways to make it work better. Under almost any imaginable scenario, we are unlikely to see the creation of regions with anything like the dynamic inner cores of successful legacy cities such as New York, Boston, Chicago or San Francisco. For better or worse, demographic and economic trends suggest our urban destiny lies increasingly with the likes of Houston, Charlotte, Dallas-Ft. Worth, Raleigh and even Phoenix.

The critical reason for this is likely to be missed by those who worship at the altar of density and contemporary planning dogma. These cities grow primarily because they do what cities were designed to do in the first place: help their residents achieve their aspirations—and that's why they keep getting bigger and more consequential, in spite of the planners who keep ignoring or deploring their ascendance.

Critical Thinking

1. What types of residents make for the best cities?

2. How are planners at odds with residents in terms of what they favor?

3. Over one-half of the world is urban. What is the future of cities and why?

Create Central

www.mhhe.com/createcentral

Internet References

Sociosite
    www.topsite.com/goto/sociosite.net

Socioweb
    www.topsite.com/goto/socioweb.com

Sociology—Study Sociology Online
    http://edu.learnsoc.org

Sociology Web Resources
    www.mhhe.com/socscience/sociology/resources/index.htm

Article

Prepared by: Kurt Finsterbusch, *University of Maryland, College Park*

Is Facebook Making Us Lonely?

STEPHEN MARCHE

Learning Outcomes

After reading this article, you will be able to:

- Assess both the positive and the negative effects of social media.

- Compare Internet interactions to interactions in communities a half century ago.

- Contemplate who are your real friends.

Yvette Vickers, a former playboy playmate and B-movie star, best known for her role in Attack of the 50 Foot Woman, would have been 83 last August, but nobody knows exactly how old she was when she died. According to the Los Angeles coroner's report, she lay dead for the better part of a year before a neighbor and fellow actress, a woman named Susan Savage, noticed cobwebs and yellowing letters in her mailbox, reached through a broken window to unlock the door, and pushed her way through the piles of junk mail and mounds of clothing that barricaded the house. Upstairs, she found Vickers's body, mummified, near a heater that was still running. Her computer was on too, its glow permeating the empty space.

The Los Angeles Times posted a story headlined "Mummified Body of Former Playboy Playmate Yvette Vickers Found in Her Benedict Canyon Home," which quickly went viral. Within two weeks, by Technorati's count, Vickers's lonesome death was already the subject of 16,057 Facebook posts and 881 tweets. She had long been a horror-movie icon, a symbol of Hollywood's capacity to exploit our most basic fears in the silliest ways; now she was an icon of a new and different kind of horror: our growing fear of loneliness. Certainly she received much more attention in death than she did in the final years of her life. With no children, no religious group, and no immediate social circle of any kind, she had begun, as an elderly woman, to look elsewhere for companionship. Savage later told Los Angeles magazine that she had searched Vickers's phone bills for clues about the life that led to such an end. In the months before her grotesque death, Vickers had made calls not to friends or family but to distant fans who had found her through fan conventions and Internet sites.

Vickers's web of connections had grown broader but shallower, as has happened for many of us. We are living in an isolation that would have been unimaginable to our ancestors, and yet we have never been more accessible. Over the past three decades, technology has delivered to us a world in which we need not be out of contact for a fraction of a moment. In 2010, at a cost of $300 million, 800 miles of fiber-optic cable was laid between the Chicago Mercantile Exchange and the New York Stock Exchange to shave three milliseconds off trading times. Yet within this world of instant and absolute communication, unbounded by limits of time or space, we suffer from unprecedented alienation. We have never been more detached from one another, or lonelier. In a world consumed by ever more novel modes of socializing, we have less and less actual society. We live in an accelerating contradiction: the more connected we become, the lonelier we are. We were promised a global village; instead we inhabit the drab cul-de-sacs and endless freeways of a vast suburb of information.

At the forefront of all this unexpectedly lonely interactivity is Facebook, with 845 million users and $3.7 billion in revenue last year. The company hopes to raise $5 billion in an initial public offering later this spring, which will make it by far the largest Internet IPO in history. Some recent estimates put the company's potential value at $100 billion, which would make it larger than the global coffee industry-one addiction preparing to surpass the other. Facebook's scale and reach are hard to comprehend: last summer, Facebook became, by some counts, the first Web site to receive 1 trillion page views in a month. In the last three months of 2011, users generated an average of 2.7 billion "likes" and comments every day. On whatever scale you care to judge Facebook—as a company, as a culture, as a country—it is vast beyond imagination.

Despite its immense popularity, or more likely because of it, Facebook has, from the beginning, been under something of a cloud of suspicion. The depiction of Mark Zuckerberg, in *The Social Network*, as a bastard with symptoms of Asperger's syndrome, was nonsense. But it felt true. It felt true to Facebook, if not to Zuckerberg. The film's most indelible scene, the one that may well have earned it an Oscar, was the final, silent shot of an anomic Zuckerberg sending out a friend request to his ex-girlfriend, then waiting and clicking and waiting and clicking—a moment of superconnected loneliness preserved in amber. We have all been in that scene: transfixed by the glare of a screen, hungering for response.

When you sign up for Google+ and set up your Friends circle, the program specifies that you should include only "your real friends, the ones you feel comfortable sharing private details with." That one little phrase, Your real friends—so quaint, so charmingly mothering—perfectly encapsulates the anxieties that social media have produced: the fears that Facebook is interfering with our real friendships, distancing us from each other, making us lonelier; and that social networking might be spreading the very isolation it seemed designed to conquer.

Facebook arrived in the middle of a dramatic increase in the quantity and intensity of human loneliness, a rise that initially made the site's promise of greater connection seem deeply attractive. Americans are more solitary than ever before. In 1950, less than 10 percent of American households contained only one person. By 2010, nearly 27 percent of households had just one person. Solitary living does not guarantee a life of unhappiness, of course. In his recent book about the trend toward living alone, Eric Klinenberg, a sociologist at NYU, writes: "Reams of published research show that it's the quality, not the quantity of social interaction, that best predicts loneliness." True. But before we begin the fantasies of happily eccentric singledom, of divorcees dropping by their knitting circles after work for glasses of Drew Barrymore pinot grigio, or recent college graduates with perfectly articulated, Steampunk-themed, 300-square-foot apartments organizing croquet matches with their book clubs, we should recognize that it is not just isolation that is rising sharply. It's loneliness, too. And loneliness makes us miserable.

We know intuitively that loneliness and being alone are not the same thing. Solitude can be lovely. Crowded parties can be agony. We also know, thanks to a growing body of research on the topic, that loneliness is not a matter of external conditions; it is a psychological state. A 2005 analysis of data begin, say, five-ish—Stoli or Red Label—and keep on till we've worked out all the kinks in our disheveled psyches. Back at home, it's hard how people don't know I'm an artist.

Still, loneliness is slippery, a difficult state to define or diagnose. The best tool yet developed for measuring the condition is the UCLA Loneliness Scale, a series of 20 questions that all begin with this formulation: "How often do you feel . . . ?" As in: "How often do you feel that you are 'in tune' with the people around you?" And: "How often do you feel that you lack companionship?" Measuring the condition in these terms, various studies have shown loneliness rising drastically over a very short period of recent history. A 2010 AARP survey found that 35 percent of adults older than 45 were chronically lonely, as opposed to 20 percent of a similar group only a decade earlier. According to a major study by a leading scholar of the subject, roughly 20 percent of Americans—about 60 million people— are unhappy with their lives because of loneliness. Across the Western world, physicians and nurses have begun to speak openly of an epidemic of loneliness.

The new studies on loneliness are beginning to yield some surprising preliminary findings about its mechanisms. Almost every factor that one might assume affects loneliness does so only some of the time, and only under certain circumstances. People who are married are less lonely than single people, one journal article suggests, but only if their spouses are confidants. If one's spouse is not a confidant, marriage may not decrease

loneliness. A belief in God might help, or it might not, as a 1990 German study comparing levels of religious feeling and levels of loneliness discovered. Active believers who saw God as abstract and helpful rather than as a wrathful, immediate presence were less lonely. "The mere belief in God," the researchers concluded, "was relatively independent of loneliness."

But it is clear that social interaction matters. Loneliness and being alone are not the same thing, but both are on the rise. We meet fewer people. We gather less. And when we gather, our bonds are less meaningful and less easy. The decrease in confidants—that is, in quality social connections—has been dramatic over the past 25 years. In one survey, the mean size of networks of personal confidants decreased from 2.94 people in 1985 to 2.08 in 2004. Similarly, in 1985, only 10 percent of Americans said they had no one with whom to discuss important matters, and 15 percent said they had only one such good friend. By 2004, 25 percent had nobody to talk to, and 20 percent had only one confidant.

In the face of this social disintegration, we have essentially hired an army of replacement confidants, an entire class of professional carers. As Ronald Dworkin pointed out in a 2010 paper for the Hoover Institution, in the late '40s, the United States was home to 2,500 clinical psychologists, 30,000 social workers, and fewer than 500 marriage and family therapists. As of 2010, the country had 77,000 clinical psychologists, 192,000 clinical social workers, 400,000 non-clinical social workers, 50,000 marriage and family therapists, 105,000 mental-health counselors, 220,000 substance-abuse counselors, 17,000 nurse psychotherapists, and 30,000 life coaches. The majority of patients in therapy do not warrant a psychiatric diagnosis. This raft of psychic servants is helping us through what used to be called regular problems. We have outsourced the work of everyday caring.

We need professional carers more and more, because the threat of societal breakdown, once principally a matter of nostalgic lament, has morphed into an issue of public health. Being lonely is extremely bad for your health. If you're lonely, you're more likely to be put in a geriatric home at an earlier age than a similar person who isn't lonely. You're less likely to exercise. You're more likely to be obese. You're less likely to survive a serious operation and more likely to have hormonal imbalances. You are at greater risk of inflammation. Your memory may be worse. You are more likely to be depressed, to sleep badly, and to suffer dementia and general cognitive decline. Loneliness may not have killed Yvette Vickers, but it has been linked to a greater probability of having the kind of heart condition that did kill her.

And yet, despite its deleterious effect on health, loneliness is one of the first things ordinary Americans spend their money achieving. With money, you flee the cramped city to a house in the suburbs or, if you can afford it, a McMansion in the exurbs, inevitably spending more time in your car. Loneliness is at the American core, a by-product of a long-standing national appetite for independence: The Pilgrims who left Europe willingly abandoned the bonds and strictures of a society that could not accept their right to be different. They did not seek out loneliness, but they accepted it as the price of their autonomy. The cowboys who set off to explore a seemingly endless frontier likewise traded away personal ties in favor of pride and self-respect. The ultimate American icon is the astronaut: Who is more heroic, or more alone? The price of self-determination and self-reliance has often been loneliness. But Americans have always been willing to pay that price.

Today, the one common feature in American secular culture is its celebration of the self that breaks away from the constrictions of the family and the state, and, in its greatest expressions, from all limits entirely. The great American poem is Whitman's "Song of Myself." The great American essay is Emerson's "Self-Reliance." The great American novel is Melville's *Moby Dick*, the tale of a man on a quest so lonely that it is incomprehensible to those around him. American culture, high and low, is about self-expression and personal authenticity. Franklin Delano Roosevelt called individualism 'the great watchword of American life."

Self-invention is only half of the American story, however. The drive for isolation has always been in tension with the impulse to cluster in communities that cling and suffocate. The Pilgrims, while fomenting spiritual rebellion, also enforced ferocious cohesion. The Salem witch trials, in hindsight, read like attempts to impose solidarity—as do the McCarthy hearings. The history of the United States is like the famous parable of the porcupines in the cold, from Schopenhauer's Studies in Pessimism—the ones who huddle together for warmth and shuffle away in pain, always separating and congregating.

We are now in the middle of a long period of shuffling away. In his 2000 book *Bowling Alone,* Robert D. Putnam attributed the dramatic post-war decline of social capital—the strength and value of interpersonal networks—to numerous interconnected trends in American life: suburban sprawl, television's dominance over culture, the self-absorption of the Baby Boomers, the disintegration of the traditional family. The trends he observed continued through the prosperity of the aughts, and have only become more pronounced with time: the rate of union membership declined in 2011, again; screen time rose; the Masons and the Elks continued their slide into irrelevance. We are lonely because we want to be lonely. We have made ourselves lonely.

The question of the future is this: Is Facebook part of the separating or part of the congregating; is it a huddling-together for warmth or a shuffling-away in pain?

Well before Facebook, digital technology was enabling our tendency for isolation, to an unprecedented degree. Back in the 1990s, scholars started calling the contradiction between an increased opportunity to connect and a lack of human contact the "Internet paradox." A prominent 1998 article on the phenomenon by a team of researchers at Carnegie Mellon showed that increased Internet usage was already coinciding with increased loneliness. Critics of the study pointed out that the two groups that participated in the study—high-school journalism students who were heading to university and socially active members of community-development boards—were statistically likely to become lonelier over time. Which brings us to a more fundamental question: Does the Internet make people lonely, or are lonely people more attracted to the Internet?

The question has intensified in the Facebook era. A recent study out of Australia (where close to half the population is active on Facebook), titled "Who Uses Facebook?," found a complex and sometimes confounding relationship between loneliness and social networking. Facebook users had slightly lower levels of "social loneliness"—the sense of not feeling bonded with friends—but "significantly higher levels of family loneliness"—the sense of not feeling bonded with family. It may be that Facebook encourages more contact with people outside of our household, at the expense of our family relationships—or it may be that people who have unhappy family relationships in the first place seek companionship through other means, including Facebook. The researchers also found that lonely people are inclined to spend more time on Facebook: "One of the most noteworthy findings," they wrote, "was the tendency for neurotic and lonely individuals to spend greater amounts of time on Facebook per day than non-lonely individuals." And they found that neurotics are more likely to prefer to use the wall, while extroverts tend to use chat features in addition to the wall.

Moira Burke, until recently a graduate student at the Human-Computer Institute at Carnegie Mellon, used to run a longitudinal study of 1,200 Facebook users. That study, which is ongoing, is one of the first to step outside the realm of self-selected college students and examine the effects of Facebook on a broader population, over time. She concludes that the effect of Facebook depends on what you bring to it. Just as your mother said: you get out only what you put in. If you use Facebook to communicate directly with other individuals—by using the "like" button, commenting on friends' posts, and so on—it can increase your social capital. Personalized messages, or what Burke calls "composed communication," are more satisfying than "one-click communication"—the lazy click of a like. "People who received composed communication became less lonely, while people who received one-click communication experienced no change in loneliness," Burke tells me. So, you should inform your friend in writing how charming her son looks with Harry Potter cake smeared all over his face, and how interesting her sepia-toned photograph of that tree-framed bit of skyline is, and how cool it is that she's at whatever concert she happens to be at. That's what we all want to hear. Even better than sending a private Facebook message is the semipublic conversation, the kind of back-and-forth in which you half ignore the other people who may be listening in. "People whose friends write to them semi-publicly on Facebook experience decreases in loneliness," Burke says.

On the other hand, non-personalized use of Facebook—scanning your friends' status updates and updating the world on your own activities via your wall, or what Burke calls "passive consumption" and "broadcasting"—correlates to feelings of disconnectedness. It's a lonely business, wandering the labyrinths of our friends' and pseudo-friends' projected identities, trying to figure out what part of ourselves we ought to project, who will listen, and what they will hear. According to Burke, passive consumption of Facebook also correlates to a marginal increase in depression. "If two women each talk to their friends the same amount of time, but one of them spends more time reading about friends on Facebook as well, the one reading tends to grow slightly more depressed," Burke says. Her conclusion suggests that my sometimes unhappy reactions to Facebook may be more universal than I had realized. When I scroll through page after page of my friends' descriptions of how accidentally eloquent their kids are, and how their husbands are endearingly bumbling, and how they're all about to eat a home-cooked meal prepared with fresh local organic produce bought at the farmers' market and then go for a jog and maybe check in at the office because they're so busy getting ready to hop on a plane for a week of luxury dogsledding in Lapland, I do grow slightly more miserable. A lot of other people doing the same thing feel a little bit worse, too.

Still, Burke's research does not support the assertion that Facebook creates loneliness. The people who experience loneliness on Facebook are lonely away from Facebook, too, she points out; on Facebook, as everywhere else, correlation is not causation. The popular kids are popular, and the lonely skulkers skulk alone. Perhaps it says something about me that I think Facebook is primarily a platform for lonely skulking. I mention to Burke the widely reported study, conducted by a Stanford graduate student, that showed how believing that others have strong social networks can lead to feelings of depression. What does Facebook communicate, if not the impression of social bounty? Everybody else looks so happy on Facebook, with so many friends, that our own social networks feel emptier than ever in comparison. Doesn't that make people feel lonely? "If people are reading about lives that are much better than theirs, two things can happen," Burke tells me. "They can feel worse about themselves, or they can feel motivated."

Burke will start working at Facebook as a data scientist this year.

John Cacioppo, the director of the Center for Cognitive and Social Neuroscience at the University of Chicago, is the world's leading expert on loneliness. In his landmark book, Loneliness, released in 2008, he revealed just how profoundly the epidemic of loneliness is affecting the basic functions of human physiology. He found higher levels of epinephrine, the stress hormone, in the morning urine of lonely people. Loneliness burrows deep: "When we drew blood from our older adults and analyzed their white cells," he writes, "we found that loneliness somehow penetrated the deepest recesses of the cell to alter the way genes were being expressed." Loneliness affects not only the brain, then, but the basic process of DNA transcription. When you are lonely, your whole body is lonely.

To Cacioppo, Internet communication allows only ersatz intimacy. "Forming connections with pets or online friends or even God is a noble attempt by an obligatorily gregarious creature to satisfy a compelling need," he writes. "But surrogates can never make up completely for the absence of the real thing." The "real thing" being actual people, in the flesh. When I speak to Cacioppo, he is refreshingly clear on what he sees as Facebook's effect on society. Yes, he allows, some research has suggested that the greater the number of Facebook friends a person has, the less lonely she is. But he argues that the impression this creates can be misleading. "For the most part," he says,

"people are bringing their old friends, and feelings of loneliness or connectedness, to Facebook." The idea that a Web site could deliver a more friendly, interconnected world is bogus. The depth of one's social network outside Facebook is what determines the depth of one's social network within Facebook, not the other way around. Using social media doesn't create new social networks; it just transfers established networks from one platform to another. For the most part, Facebook doesn't destroy friendships—but it doesn't create them, either.

In one experiment, Cacioppo looked for a connection between the loneliness of subjects and the relative frequency of their interactions via Facebook, chat rooms, online games, dating sites, and face-to-face contact. The results were unequivocal. "The greater the proportion of face-to-face interactions, the less lonely you are," he says. "The greater the proportion of online interactions, the lonelier you are." Surely, I suggest to Cacioppo, this means that Facebook and the like inevitably make people lonelier. He disagrees. Facebook is merely a tool, he says, and like any tool, its effectiveness will depend on its user. "If you use Facebook to increase face-to-face contact," he says, "it increases social capital." So if social media let you organize a game of football among your friends, that's healthy. If you turn to social media instead of playing football, however, that's unhealthy.

"Facebook can be terrific, if we use it properly," Cacioppo continues. "It's like a car. You can drive it to pick up your friends.

Or you can drive alone." But hasn't the car increased loneliness?

If cars created the suburbs, surely they also created isolation.

"That's because of how we use cars," Cacioppo replies. "How we use these technologies can lead to more integration, rather than more isolation."

The problem, then, is that we invite loneliness, even though it makes us miserable. The history of our use of technology is a history of isolation desired and achieved. When the Great Atlantic and Pacific Tea Company opened its A&P stores, giving Americans self-service access to groceries, customers stopped having relationships with their grocers. When the telephone arrived, people stopped knocking on their neighbors' doors. Social media bring this process to a much wider set of relationships. Researchers at the HP Social Computing Lab who studied the nature of people's connections on Twitter came to a depressing, if not surprising, conclusion: "Most of the links declared within Twitter were meaningless from an interaction point of view." I have to wonder: What other point of view is meaningful?

Loneliness is certainly not something that facebook or Twitter or any of the lesser forms of social media is doing to us. We are doing it to ourselves. Casting technology as some vague, impersonal spirit of history forcing our actions is a weak excuse. We make decisions about how we use our machines, not the other way around. Every time I shop at my local grocery store, I am faced with a choice. I can buy my groceries from a human being or from a machine. I always, without exception, choose the machine. It's faster and more efficient, I tell myself, but the truth is that I prefer not having to wait with the other customers who are lined up alongside the conveyor belt: the hipster mom who disapproves of my high-carbon-footprint pineapple; the lady who tenses to the point of tears while she waits to see if the gods of the credit-card machine will accept or decline; the old man whose clumsy feebleness requires a patience that I don't possess. Much better to bypass the whole circus and just ring up the groceries myself.

Our omnipresent new technologies lure us toward increasingly superficial connections at exactly the same moment that they make avoiding the mess of human interaction easy. The beauty of Facebook, the source of its power, is that it enables us to be social while sparing us the embarrassing reality of society—the accidental revelations we make at parties, the awkward pauses, the farting and the spilled drinks and the general gaucherie of face-to-face contact. Instead, we have the lovely smoothness of a seemingly social machine. Everything's so simple: status updates, pictures, your wall.

But the price of this smooth sociability is a constant compulsion to assert one's own happiness, one's own fulfillment. Not only must we contend with the social bounty of others; we must foster the appearance of our own social bounty. Being happy all the time, pretending to be happy, actually attempting to be happy—it's exhausting. Last year a team of researchers led by Iris Mauss at the University of Denver published a study looking into "the paradoxical effects of valuing happiness." Most goals in life show a direct correlation between valuation and achievement. Studies have found, for example, that students who value good grades tend to have higher grades than those who don't value them. Happiness is an exception. The study came to a disturbing conclusion:

Valuing happiness is not necessarily linked to greater happiness. In fact, under certain conditions, the opposite is true. Under conditions of low (but not high) life stress, the more people valued happiness, the lower were their hedonic balance, psychological well-being, and life satisfaction, and the higher their depression symptoms.

The more you try to be happy, the less happy you are. Sophocles made roughly the same point.

Facebook, of course, puts the pursuit of happiness front and center in our digital life. Its capacity to redefine our very concepts of identity and personal fulfillment is much more worrisome than the data-mining and privacy practices that have aroused anxieties about the company. Two of the most compelling critics of Facebook—neither of them a Luddite—concentrate on exactly this point. Jaron Lanier, the author of *You Are Not a Gadget,* was one of the inventors of virtual-reality technology. His view of where social media are taking us reads like dystopian science fiction: "I fear that we are beginning to design ourselves to suit digital models of us, and I worry about a leaching of empathy and humanity in that process." Lanier argues that Facebook imprisons us in the business of self-presenting, and this, to his mind, is the site's crucial and fatally unacceptable downside.

Sherry Turkle, a professor of computer culture at MIT who in 1995 published the digital-positive analysis Life on the Screen, is much more skeptical about the effects of online society in her 2011 book, *Alone Together:* "These days, insecure in our relationships and anxious about intimacy, we look to technology for ways to be in relationships and protect ourselves from them at the same time." The problem with digital intimacy is that it is ultimately incomplete: "The ties we form through the Internet are not, in the end, the ties that bind. But they are the ties that preoccupy," she writes. "We don't want to intrude on each other, so instead we constantly intrude on each other, but not in 'real time.'"

Lanier and Turkle are right, at least in their diagnoses. Self-presentation on Facebook is continuous, intensely mediated, and possessed of a phony nonchalance that eliminates even the potential for spontaneity. ("Look how casually I threw up these three photos from the party at which I took 300 photos!") Curating the exhibition of the self has become a 24/7 occupation. Perhaps not surprisingly, then, the Australian study "Who Uses Facebook?" found a significant correlation between Facebook use and narcissism: "Facebook users have higher levels of total narcissism, exhibitionism, and leadership than Facebook nonusers," the study's authors wrote. "In fact, it could be argued that Facebook specifically gratifies the narcissistic individual's need to engage in self-promoting and superficial behavior."

Rising narcissism isn't so much a trend as the trend behind all other trends. In preparation for the 2013 edition of its diagnostic manual, the psychiatric profession is currently struggling to update its definition of narcissistic personality disorder. Still, generally speaking, practitioners agree that narcissism manifests in patterns of fantastic grandiosity, craving for attention, and lack of empathy. In a 2008 survey, 35,000 American respondents were asked if they had ever had certain symptoms of narcissistic personality disorder. Among people older than 65, 3 percent reported symptoms. Among people in their 20s, the proportion was nearly 10 percent. Across all age groups, one in 16 Americans has experienced some symptoms of NPD. And loneliness and narcissism are intimately connected: a longitudinal study of Swedish women demonstrated a strong link between levels of narcissism in youth and levels of loneliness in old age. The connection is fundamental. Narcissism is the flip side of loneliness, and either condition is a fighting retreat from the messy reality of other people.

A considerable part of Facebook's appeal stems from its miraculous fusion of distance with intimacy, or the illusion of distance with the illusion of intimacy. Our online communities become engines of self-image, and self-image becomes the engine of community. The real danger with Facebook is not that it allows us to isolate ourselves, but that by mixing our appetite for isolation with our vanity, it threatens to alter the very nature of solitude. The new isolation is not of the kind that Americans once idealized, the lonesomeness of the proudly nonconformist, independent-minded, solitary stoic, or that of the astronaut who blasts into new worlds. Facebook's isolation is a grind. What's truly staggering about Facebook usage is not its volume—750 million photographs uploaded over a single weekend—but the constancy of the performance it demands. More than half its users—and one of every 13 people on Earth is a Facebook user—log on every day.

Among 18-to-34-year-olds, nearly half check Facebook minutes after waking up, and 28 percent do so before getting out of bed. The relentlessness is what is so new, so potentially transformative. Facebook never takes a break. We never take a break. Human beings have always created elaborate acts of self-presentation. But not all the time, not every morning, before we even pour a cup of coffee. Yvette Vickers's computer was on when she died.

Nostalgia for the good old days of disconnection would not just be pointless, it would be hypocritical and ungrateful. But the very magic of the new machines, the efficiency and elegance with which they serve us, obscures what isn't being served: everything that matters. What Facebook has revealed about human nature—and this is not a minor revelation—is that a connection is not the same thing as a bond, and that instant and total connection is no salvation, no ticket to a happier, better world or a more liberated version of humanity. Solitude used to be good for self-reflection and self-reinvention. But now we are left thinking about who we are all the time, without ever really thinking about who we are. Facebook denies us a pleasure whose profundity we had underestimated: the chance to forget about ourselves for a while, the chance to disconnect.

Critical Thinking

1. How can we be so lonely when we are so connected?
2. Answer the author's question: "Is Facebook Making Us Lonely?"
3. Where are social media going?

Create Central

www.mhhe.com/createcentral

Internet References

Sociosite
www.topsite.com/goto/sociosite.net
Socioweb
www.topsite.com/goto/socioweb.com
Sociology—Study Sociology Online
http://edu.learnsoc.org
Sociology Web Resources
www.mhhe.com/socscience/sociology/resources/index.htm

STEPHEN MARCHE, a novelist, writes a monthly column for *Esquire*.

Unit 4

UNIT

Prepared by: Kurt Finsterbusch, *University of Maryland, College Park*

Stratification and Social Inequalities

People are ranked in many different ways—by physical strength, education, wealth, or other characteristics. Those who are rated highly often have power over others, special status, and prestige. These differences among people constitute their life chances—the probability that an individual or group will be able to obtain the valued and desired goods in a society. These differences are referred to as stratification, the system of structured inequalities in social relationships. In most industrialized societies, income is one of the most important divisions among people. Karl Marx described stratification in terms of class rather than income. For him, social class referred mainly to two distinct groups: those who control the means of production and those who do not. This difference results in great differences in income, wealth, power, status, privileges, and opportunities.

Article   Prepared by: Kurt Finsterbusch, *University of Maryland, College Park*

A World *Enslaved*

There are now more slaves on the planet than at any time in human history. True abolition will elude us until we admit the massive scope of the problem, attack it in all its forms, and empower slaves to help free themselves.

E. BENJAMIN SKINNER

Learning Outcomes

After reading this article, you will be able to:

- Understand many shocking facts about worldwide slavery including its prevalence and how easy it is to acquire a slave.

- Understand the great disparity between developed and developing countries in slave holding but also know about the many thousands of slaves in the United States.

- Know the role of poverty and debt bondage in slavery.

Standing in New York City, you are five hours away from being able to negotiate the sale, in broad daylight, of a healthy boy or girl. He or she can be used for anything, though sex and domestic labor are most common. Before you go, let's be clear on what you are buying. A slave is a human being forced to work through fraud or threat of violence for no pay beyond subsistence. Agreed? Good.

Most people imagine that slavery died in the 19th century. Since 1817, more than a dozen international conventions have been signed banning the slave trade. Yet, today there are more slaves than at any time in human history.

And if you're going to buy one in five hours, you'd better get a move on. First, hail a taxi to JFK International Airport, and hop on a direct flight to Port-au-Prince, Haiti. The flight takes three hours. After landing at Toussaint L'Ouverture International Airport, you will need 50 cents for the most common form of transport in Port-au-Prince, the tap-tap, a flatbed pickup retrofitted with benches and a canopy. Three quarters of the way up Route de Delmas, the capital's main street, tap the roof and hop out. There, on a side street, you will find a group of men standing in front of Le Réseau (The Network) barbershop. As you approach, a man steps forward: "Are you looking to get a person?"

Meet Benavil Lebhom. He smiles easily. He has a trim mustache and wears a multicolored, striped golf shirt, a gold chain, and Doc Martens knockoffs. Benavil is a courtier, or broker.

He holds an official real estate license and calls himself an employment agent. Two thirds of the employees he places are child slaves. The total number of Haitian children in bondage in their own country stands at 300,000. They are the *restavèks*, the "staywiths," as they are euphemistically known in Creole. Forced, unpaid, they work in captivity from before dawn until night. Benavil and thousands of other formal and informal traffickers lure these children from desperately impoverished rural parents, with promises of free schooling and a better life.

The negotiation to buy a child slave might sound a bit like this:

"How quickly do you think it would be possible to bring a child in? Somebody who could clean and cook?" you ask. "I don't have a very big place; I have a small apartment. But I'm wondering how much that would cost? And how quickly?"

"Three days," Benavil responds.

"And you could bring the child here?" you inquire. "Or are there children here already?"

"I don't have any here in Port-au-Prince right now," says Benavil, his eyes widening at the thought of a foreign client. "I would go out to the countryside."

You ask about additional expenses. "Would I have to pay for transportation?"

"*Bon*," says Benavil. "A hundred U.S."

Smelling a rip-off, you press him, "And that's just for transportation?"

"Transportation would be about 100 Haitian," says Benavil, or around $13, "because you'd have to get out there. Plus [hotel and] food on the trip. Five hundred gourdes."

"Okay, 500 Haitian," you say.

Now you ask the big question: "And what would your fee be?" This is the moment of truth, and Benavil's eyes narrow as he determines how much he can take you for.

"A hundred. American."

"That seems like a lot," you say, with a smile so as not to kill the deal. "How much would you charge a Haitian?"

Benavil's voice rises with feigned indignation. "A hundred dollars. This is a major effort."

You hold firm. "Could you bring down your fee to 50 U.S.?"

Benavil pauses. But only for effect. He knows he's still got you for much more than a Haitian would pay. "*Oui,*" he says with a smile.

But the deal isn't done. Benavil leans in close. "This is a rather delicate question. Is this someone you want as just a worker? Or also someone who will be a 'partner'? You understand what I mean?"

You don't blink at being asked if you want the child for sex. "I mean, is it possible to have someone that could be both?"

"*Oui!*" Benavil responds enthusiastically.

If you're interested in taking your purchase back to the United States, Benavil tells you that he can "arrange" the proper papers to make it look as though you've adopted the child.

He offers you a 13-year-old girl.

"That's a little bit old," you say.

"I know of another girl who's 12. Then ones that are 10, 11," he responds.

The negotiation is finished, and you tell Benavil not to make any moves without further word from you. Here, 600 miles from the United States, and five hours from Manhattan, you have successfully arranged to buy a human being for 50 bucks.

The Cruel Truth

It would be nice if that conversation, like the description of the journey, were fictional. It is not. I recorded it on Oct. 6, 2005, as part of four years of research into slavery on five continents. In the popular consciousness, "slavery" has come to be little more than just a metaphor for undue hardship. Investment bankers routinely refer to themselves as "high-paid wage slaves." Human rights activists may call $1-an-hour sweatshop laborers slaves, regardless of the fact that they are paid and can often walk away from the job. But the reality of slavery is far different. Slavery exists today on an unprecedented scale. In Africa, tens of thousands are chattel slaves, seized in war or tucked away for generations. Across Europe, Asia, and the Americas, traffickers have forced as many as 2 million into prostitution or labor. In South Asia, which has the highest concentration of slaves on the planet, nearly 10 million languish in bondage, unable to leave their captors until they pay off "debts," legal fictions that in many cases are generations old.

Few in the developed world have a grasp of the enormity of modern-day slavery. Fewer still are doing anything to combat it. Beginning in 2001, U.S. President George W. Bush was urged by several of his key advisors to vigorously enforce the Victims of Trafficking and Violence Protection Act, a U.S. law enacted a month earlier that sought to prosecute domestic human traffickers and cajole foreign governments into doing the same. The Bush administration trumpeted the effort—at home via the Christian evangelical media and more broadly via speeches and pronouncements, including in addresses to the U.N. General Assembly in 2003 and 2004. But even the quiet and diligent work of some within the U.S. State Department, which credibly claims to have secured more than 100 antitrafficking laws and more than 10,000 trafficking convictions worldwide, has resulted in no measurable decline in the number of slaves worldwide. Between 2000 and 2006, the U.S.

Justice Department increased human trafficking prosecutions from 3 to 32, and convictions from 10 to 98. By 2006, 27 states had passed antitrafficking laws. Yet, during the same period, the United States liberated less than 2 percent of its own modern-day slaves. As many as 17,500 new slaves continue to enter bondage in the United States every year.

The West's efforts have been, from the outset, hamstrung by a warped understanding of slavery. In the United States, a hard-driving coalition of feminist and evangelical activists has forced the Bush administration to focus almost exclusively on the sex trade. The official State Department line is that voluntary prostitution does not exist, and that commercial sex is the main driver of slavery today. In Europe, though Germany and the Netherlands have decriminalized most prostitution, other nations such as Bulgaria have moved in the opposite direction, bowing to U.S. pressure and cracking down on the flesh trade. But, across the Americas, Europe, and Asia, unregulated escort services are exploding with the help of the Internet. Even when enlightened governments have offered clearheaded solutions to deal with this problem, such as granting victims temporary residence, they have had little impact.

Many feel that sex slavery is particularly revolting—and it is. I saw it firsthand. In a Bucharest brothel, for instance, I was offered a mentally handicapped, suicidal girl in exchange for a used car. But for every one woman or child enslaved in commercial sex, there are at least 15 men, women, and children enslaved in other fields, such as domestic work or agricultural labor. Recent studies have shown that locking up pimps and traffickers has had a negligible effect on the aggregate rates of bondage. And though eradicating prostitution may be a just cause, Western policies based on the idea that all prostitutes are slaves and all slaves are prostitutes belittles the suffering of all victims. It's an approach that threatens to put most governments on the wrong side of history.

Indebted for Life

Save for the fact that he is male, Gonoo Lal Kol typifies the average slave of our modern age. (At his request, I have changed his first name.) Like a vast majority of the world's slaves, Gonoo is in debt bondage in South Asia. In his case, in an Indian quarry. Like most slaves, Gonoo is illiterate and unaware of the Indian laws that ban his bondage and provide for sanctions against his master. His story, told to me in more than a dozen conversations inside his 4-foot-high stone and grass hutch, represents the other side of the "Indian Miracle."

Gonoo lives in Lohagara Dhal, a forgotten corner of Uttar Pradesh, a north Indian state that contains 8 percent of the world's poor. I met him one evening in December 2005 as he walked with two dozen other laborers in tattered and filthy clothes. Behind them was the quarry. In that pit, Gonoo, a member of the historically outcast Kol tribe, worked with his family 14 hours a day. His tools were simple, a rough-hewn hammer and an iron pike. His hands were covered in calluses, his fingertips worn away.

Gonoo's master is a tall, stout, surly contractor named Ramesh Garg. Garg is one of the wealthiest men in Shankargarh, the nearest sizable town, founded under the British Raj but now run by nearly 600 quarry contractors. He makes his money by enslaving entire families forced to work for no pay beyond alcohol, grain, and bare subsistence expenses. Their only use for Garg is to turn rock into silica sand, for colored glass, or gravel, for roads or ballast. Slavery scholar Kevin Bales estimates that a slave in the 19th-century American South had to work 20 years to recoup his or her purchase price. Gonoo and the other slaves earn a profit for Garg in two years.

Every single man, woman, and child in Lohagara Dhal is a slave. But, in theory at least, Garg neither bought nor owns them. They are working off debts, which, for many, started at less than $10. But interest accrues at over 100 percent annually here. Most of the debts span at least two generations, though they have no legal standing under modern Indian law. They are a fiction that Garg constructs through fraud and maintains through violence. The seed of Gonoo's slavery, for instance, was a loan of 62 cents. In 1958, his grandfather borrowed that amount from the owner of a farm where he worked. Three generations and three slavemasters later, Gonoo's family remains in bondage.

Bringing Freedom to Millions

Recently, many bold, underfunded groups have taken up the challenge of tearing out the roots of slavery. Some gained fame through dramatic slave rescues. Most learned that freeing slaves is impossible unless the slaves themselves choose to be free. Among the Kol of Uttar Pradesh, for instance, an organization called Pragati Gramodyog Sansthan (Progressive Institute for Village Enterprises, or PGS) has helped hundreds of families break the grip of the quarry contractors. Working methodically since 1985, PGS organizers slowly built up confidence among slaves. With PGS's help, the Kol formed microcredit unions and won leases to quarries so that they could keep the proceeds of their labor. Some bought property for the first time in their lives, a cow or a goat, and their incomes, which had been nil, multiplied quickly. PGS set up primary schools and dug wells. Villages that for generations had known nothing but slavery began to become free. PGS's success demonstrates that emancipation is merely the first step in abolition. Within the developed world, some national law enforcement agencies such as those in the Czech Republic and Sweden have finally begun to pursue the most culpable of human trafficking—slave-trading pimps and unscrupulous labor contractors. But more must be done to educate local police, even in the richest of nations. Too often, these street-level law enforcement personnel do not understand that it's just as likely for a prostitute to be a trafficking victim as it is for a nanny working without proper papers to be a slave. And, after they have been discovered by law enforcement, few rich nations provide slaves with the kind of rehabilitation, retraining, and protection needed to prevent their re-trafficking. The asylum now granted to former slaves in the United States and the Netherlands is a start. But more must be done.

The United Nations, whose founding principles call for it to fight bondage in all its forms, has done almost nothing to combat modern slavery. In January, Antonio Maria Costa, executive director of the U.N. Office on Drugs and Crime, called for the international body to provide better quantification of human trafficking. Such number crunching would be valuable in combating that one particular manifestation of slavery. But there is little to suggest the United Nations, which consistently fails to hold its own member states accountable for widespread slavery, will be an effective tool in defeating the broader phenomenon.

Any lasting solutions to human trafficking must involve prevention programs in at-risk source countries. Absent an effective international body like the United Nations, such an effort will require pressure from the United States. So far, the United States has been willing to criticize some nations' records, but it has resisted doing so where it matters most, particularly in India. India abolished debt bondage in 1976, but with poor enforcement of the law locally, millions remain in bondage. In 2006 and 2007, the U.S. State Department's Office to Monitor and Combat Trafficking in Persons pressed U.S. Secretary of State Condoleezza Rice to repudiate India's intransigence personally. And, in each instance, she did not.

The psychological, social, and economic bonds of slavery run deep, and for governments to be truly effective in eradicating slavery, they must partner with groups that can offer slaves a way to pull themselves up from bondage. One way to do that is to replicate the work of grassroots organizations such as Varanasi, India-based MSEMVS (Society for Human Development and Women's Empowerment). In 1996, the Indian group launched free transitional schools, where children who had been enslaved learned skills and acquired enough literacy to move on to formal schooling. The group also targeted mothers, providing them with training and start-up materials for microenterprises. In Thailand, a nation infamous for sex slavery, a similar group, the Labour Rights Promotion Network, works to keep desperately poor Burmese immigrants from the clutches of traffickers by, among other things, setting up schools and health programs. Even in the remote highlands of southern Haiti, activists with Limyè Lavi ("Light of Life") reach otherwise wholly isolated rural communities to warn them of the dangers of traffickers such as Benavil Lebhom and to help them organize informal schools to keep children near home. In recent years, the United States has shown an increasing willingness to help fund these kinds of organizations, one encouraging sign that the message may be getting through.

For four years, I saw dozens of people enslaved, several of whom traffickers like Benavil actually offered to sell to me. I did not pay for a human life anywhere. And, with one exception, I always withheld action to save any one person, in the hope that my research would later help to save many more. At times, that still feels like an excuse for cowardice. But the hard work of real emancipation can't be the burden of a select few. For thousands of slaves, grassroots groups like PGS and MSEMVS can help bring freedom. But, until governments define slavery in appropriately concise terms, prosecute the crime aggressively in all its forms, and encourage groups that empower slaves to free themselves, millions more will remain in bondage. And our collective promise of abolition will continue to mean nothing at all.

Critical Thinking

1. Many slaves were once free. How did they become slaves? What tricks were used in their enslavement?

2. What actions by what groups and organization have been taken to try to stop slavery?

3. How much success have these efforts achieved?

Create Central

www.mhhe.com/createcentral

Internet References

Sociosite
www.topsite.com/goto/sociosite.net

Socioweb
www.topsite.com/goto/socioweb.com

Sociology—Study Sociology Online
http://edu.learnsoc.org

Sociology Web Resources
www.mhhe.com/socscience/sociology/resources/index.htm

E. BENJAMIN SKINNER is the author of *A Crime So Monstrous: Face-to-Face with Modern-Day Slavery* (New York: Free Press, 2008).

Reprinted in entirety by McGraw-Hill with permission from *Foreign Policy*, March/April 2008. www.foreignpolicy.com. © 2008 Washingtonpost.Newsweek Interactive, LLC.

Article

Prepared by: Kurt Finsterbusch, *University of Maryland, College Park*

Rebuilding the Middle Class

A Blueprint for the Future

We want a society in which everyone lives with dignity and purpose and fulfills their goals and dreams.

A. BARRY RAND

Learning Outcomes

After reading this article, you will be able to:

- Understand the significance of the middle class and its economic well-being for the well-being of the nation.

- Understand the many adverse effects of increasing inequality in America.

- Understand the requirements for a middle-class lifestyle and how available these requirements are.

The prosperity of the middle class has been the basis for the American way of life for the past 60 years. But today, that prosperity is eluding many individuals and their families for reasons beyond their control.

The decline of the middle class threatens our ability to fund health and retirement programs, to maintain a safety net for the most vulnerable and to invest in our future. It threatens the hopes and dreams of generations of Americans, both for themselves and for their children.

A declining middle class makes upward mobility and a better life—including a more secure retirement—"the impossible" American dream.

Good morning, everyone and welcome to AARP's "Agenda for the Middle Class—2013."

AARP works to make life better for all. We have been fighting for the middle class for decades because these issues are important to our members, people 50-plus and their families. In August of 2011, AARP's Public Policy Institute launched a year-long study of the well-being of America's middle class—with a focus on prospects for a financially secure retirement.

Today, we will share what we've learned from that study and the policy implications going forward—specifically, these three aspects:

1. How the decline of the middle class over the last thirty years has affected real people;

2. How future generations of retirees—the 20, 30, 40 and 50-year-olds of today—will be affected if we don't turn this around;

3. And, what we need to do as a nation to restore prosperity to the middle class and keep the American Dream alive.

Over the past generation, more and more of the middle class have fallen off the cliff into economic insecurity and even poverty—pulled down by a lack of job opportunities, rising health care costs, inadequate savings, declining home values, a lack of consumer protections and stagnant wages that have not kept pace with the costs of meeting basic needs.

The Great Recession and the ongoing financial crisis have only tightened the squeeze on middle-class families and have cast a shadow on the "future retirement" prospects of today's workers.

This is taking a serious toll on middle-class families. They have never felt more insecure.

As one woman in Milwaukee told us, "I feel like I'm just one big crisis away from utter devastation."

And, she is not alone. According to our new "Middle-Class Tracking Index," the percentage of those in the middle class who were secure dropped from 26 percent to 16 percent from 2004 to 2010. And the numbers were even lower for African American and Hispanic middle-income families—only 10 and 11 percent, respectively.

So, how do middle-class families cope? They typically do three things:

1. At least one—and often both wage earners—work longer and delay their retirement. And, many who have already retired end up going back to work—if they can find a job.

2. They drastically reduce their standard of living, and rely more on government programs to help them make ends meet. Or,

3. They take on more debt—borrowing against their homes and 401(k)s, running up credit card balances, taking out loans, and borrowing from family members.

As a result, the median debt of middle-class families has increased nearly 300 percent over the last decade.

Corrine, from Milwaukee is a prime example. She is 62 years old and married. Five years ago, Corrine's husband lost his job. He found work, but then lost that job last March. Corrine works two part-time jobs without benefits. When her husband lost his job last spring, they went on COBRA to get health insurance.

They quickly found that the costs were too high for their budget, so Corrine bought a catastrophic plan with a very high deductible, which saved them about $200 a month, but gave them less coverage.

Corrine's husband has since found a job as a clerk in a grocery store deli—resulting in a 60 percent cut in his income.

Suddenly, their retirement is uncertain and scary. They are thinking about starting to collect Social Security at age 64 to help pay the bills, even though they would be missing out on a fuller benefit by waiting a couple of years.

Unfortunately, Corrine's story is not unique. AARP's own "Anxiety Index" tells us that the top concerns among people 50-plus and their families are all related to health and financial security:

- Having Medicare and Social Security benefits available in the future
- Having adequate health insurance coverage, and
- Paying for health care expenses.

We hear this from our members all the time. A member in Pittsfield, Massachusetts sent me this letter.

"Social Security will be my main source of income when I retire—if I ever get to. I have a 401(k) also, but it has been hit hard, and I don't think I can catch up again by the time I am 65. Without Medicare, I will never be able to retire. Please do not eliminate or cut those benefits to those of us who have already put in hard-earned dollars all our lives."

Their concerns reflect the larger trends.

- The latest Census data show that the typical American family got poorer during the last decade. 15 percent of Americans now live in poverty—the highest level since 1993. And, in 2012, the number of Americans living under 125 percent of poverty reached an all-time high of 66 million.
- More Americans are reaching their 60s with so much debt that they can't afford to retire.
- More low- and middle-income households are turning to "credit cards" to help meet daily living expenses.
- And the number of uninsured—16 percent of the population—now exceeds the combined population of 25 states and the District of Columbia.

That's hard to even digest.

The possibility of downward mobility in retirement is a looming reality for all workers. In fact, the ranks of America's poor are on track to climb to levels unseen in nearly half a century, erasing gains from the war on poverty in the 1960s.

Unless we are able to reverse the trends that are driving the decline of the middle class, many of today's middle-class workers will not have a middle-class retirement. In fact, 30 percent of those currently in the middle class, will become "low income" in retirement.

Here's why. Two main reasons—Rising health care costs and financial insecurity.

Rising health care costs will wipe out any gains that middle-class families were projected to attain. Even though the poverty rate among retirees is projected to decline, that decline will be virtually wiped out by rising "out-of-pocket" medical costs—which will take an increasing share of retirement income.

Unless we build on recent reforms, future retirees—those currently age 25 to 34—will be less likely than current retirees to maintain their standard of living in retirement. All because of rising health care costs.

And this doesn't even factor in the rising cost of long-term care.

And, the second reason—financial insecurity.

The middle class was hit hard by the Great Recession, especially with loss of jobs, falling home values and foreclosures and reduced savings.

Instead of creating pensions that help people maintain a decent standard of living as they get older, we're seeing traditional or defined-benefit pension coverage erode or disappear altogether.

75 percent of Americans nearing retirement age in 2010 had less than $30,000 in their retirement accounts.

Roughly half of all workers don't have a retirement plan at all. And, for most of those that do, the amount in their 401(k) would pay them a retirement benefit of less than $80 a month—for life. How do you live on that?

Continuing to work will obviously be one of the key ways of maintaining security in retirement. But these trends place even more importance on Social Security as a source of retirement income. In fact, Social Security will be the main source of retirement income for future retirees at virtually all income levels.

And, for the nearly one-third of middle-class workers who will fall into having low incomes in retirement, Social Security will represent over 80 percent of their retirement income.

Now, I've talked about rising health care costs and financial insecurity, but I also want to mention a third factor—the rising cost of higher education. Our research shows—without question—the most important contributor to middle class stability is having a college degree or some type of post-secondary education. It's the gateway to the American Dream and, frankly, a key to restoring prosperity to the middle class.

The facts are clear. The median weekly income for high school graduates in 2011 was more than forty percent less than that of those with a higher education. Moreover, the unemployment rate for workers with just a high school diploma is over 8 percent—more than double the rate of those with post-secondary degrees.

African Americans and Latinos lag far behind whites in this respect. Just 13 percent of Hispanics and 18 percent of African Americans age 25 and older have a higher education—compared with 31 percent of whites.

The cost of higher education is now out of reach for many middle-class families. And, student loan debt is a huge drain on the income of middle-class families.

In fact, according to a report from the Federal Reserve Bank of New York, Americans 60 and older still owe roughly $36 billion in student loans, and more than 10 percent are delinquent.

And, increasingly—older adults are postponing retirement in order to pay off student loan debt accumulated by their children or grandchildren.

None of this paints a pretty picture. Unless we figure out a way to reverse the downward spiral of the middle class, the probability of the next generation being worse off than their parents is very high. We cannot allow that to happen.

So, what do we do? How do we rebuild the middle class to once again ensure that everyone has the opportunity to achieve the American Dream?

The first thing we have to do is to broaden the current debate in Washington from the narrow lens of "deficit reduction" towards the larger goal of economic growth and maintaining the health and economic security of all Americans.

There is no question that reducing the federal deficit is a worthwhile goal. Who would argue with that?

We need to address our nation's long-term fiscal problems. They affect all of us—and most importantly, our children and grandchildren.

Their futures will not be very bright if they are drowning in the red ink of budget deficits and a soaring national debt.

However, their futures will not be very bright if they can't afford health care, or if they can't afford a quality education, or if they don't' have the opportunity to attain long-term financial security.

Leaving them with less economic security—by weakening Social Security and Medicare—would be just as bad, if not worse.

And, if we weaken Social Security and Medicare to the point that their parents and grandparents can no longer live with dignity and purpose, we will be risking their futures as well.

As a nation, we must broaden our focus. The goal should be improved economic growth for the nation, and policies that secure the health and economic security of both current and future generations.

Washington's budget debate has been focused on big numbers, but it's really about people and their futures. A budget is not an end in itself. It is simply a reflection of our nation's priorities and goals.

We cannot make budget choices without considering the consequences of those choices on people. Solving the budget deficit by cutting Social Security and Medicare benefits will leave too many people with nothing left at the end of the month.

Decreasing the federal deficit—at the expense of Medicare and Social Security—also ignores the public's overwhelming support for these programs—as well as the vitally important role they play and will continue to play—in helping people attain a secure retirement.

We must look at retirement security broadly. Congress and the President must work together and focus on our larger national goals of economic growth, jobs, health and financial security and enacting affordable policies to meet those goals.

And let's not kid ourselves, we can't achieve these goals by simply cutting spending or just increasing revenue. We have to do both.

The social compact that requires that this generation leave the next generation a stronger rather than weaker economy also requires this generation to leave the next generation a more secure rather than a weaker retirement.

The Pew Research Center recently asked people what it takes to be part of the middle class. The answer? Five things:

1. A secure job
2. Health insurance
3. Owning a home
4. A college education or some form of higher education
5. And, stocks, bonds, or other investments—in other words, to be able to save and invest for the future.

Let me talk about jobs for just a moment. Jobs are key to achieving the American Dream, putting ourselves, our families and our country back on the road to prosperity and keeping America competitive in the new global economy.

Without jobs, today's workers have no chance for a middle-class retirement, and economic growth and prosperity for the middle class and others is not possible. As it is, more middle-class workers will need to work longer to maintain a decent standard of living in retirement.

Yet today, millions of experienced workers remain out of work in the wake of the Great Recession. During 2012, workers 55 and older were unemployed, on average, for more than a year.

We need to preserve middle-class jobs that offer opportunity for advancement. And, we need to improve the pay and quality of lower-skilled jobs that represent the fastest growing occupations in the decades ahead.

The second thing we have to do is tackle the high cost of health care—which is one of the most significant factors driving people out of the middle class. Rising costs have a negative impact on federal programs such as Medicare and Medicaid, as well as on the costs for state governments, employers and individuals.

The percentage of our nation's GDP dedicated to health care has nearly doubled from 10 percent to almost 20 percent over the last generation, and is still rising. That's more than any other developed nation—with no better outcomes.

We cannot sustain an ever-increasing share of the nation's output going to health care, especially when the Institute of Medicine estimates that as much as one-third of health care spending is wasteful or inefficient.

The Affordable Care Act begins to set in motion what needs to be done to reduce health care costs, but we need to do more.

Policy makers must not simply reduce the federal share of health costs by shifting costs from the federal government to other payers.

That will not solve the problem. In fact, it will make it worse because it fails to tackle the real underlying issue of reining in high growth in health costs throughout the system and the percentage of GDP that goes to health care.

An example of this narrow approach is raising the Medicare eligibility age.

The end result of this policy is to lower federal health costs for the program, by shifting costs from the federal government to employers, states and families on Medicare—including those in the middle-class. This only drives seniors to more costly and less efficient providers, which, in turn, raises total health spending in the economy.

This is pure folly . . . and very dangerous.

A better approach would be to lower the growth in health care spending system-wide. If we focus on lowering the growth rate of costs throughout the health care system, we will also lower the cost of Medicare and Medicaid.

An analysis by the President's Council of Economic Advisors shows that lowering the growth rate of health care costs by 1.5 percentage points per year will increase the real income of middle-class families by $2,600 in 2020; $10,000 in 2030; and $24,300 by 2040. That's real relief for real people.

All of this comes back to the impact on people. We can't just cut Medicare or raise the eligibility age to reduce the deficit. We have to make it work more efficiently— and we have to lower the growth in costs to keep it sustainable for generations to come.

The Affordable Care Act puts us on that path. The ACA achieved $716 billion dollars in Medicare savings. That's more than was achieved by the "fiscal cliff" deal. And those savings were achieved without cutting one dime of guaranteed benefits.

By taking steps to remove waste, fraud and inefficiency in Medicare, we have been able to reinvest some of those savings into lowering costs for beneficiaries and for Medicare by filling in gaps in the program—for example, closing the doughnut hole in Part D drug coverage and providing preventive care.

And it's working. More than 5.2 million people with Medicare have saved $3.9 billion dollars. Last year, people in the doughnut hole have saved an average of $770 on prescription drugs.

At the same time, the ACA made Medicare more secure, extending its financial life by 7 years. It also helped reduce the rising cost of Medicare—and it did so without taking a dime from a person's guaranteed benefits.

More needs to be done. Moving forward, if we pursue additional reforms in Medicare and Medicaid, such as

- Payment innovations to promote value, not volume;
- Measures to lower drug costs;
- Providing consumers with better information on cost and quality;
- An emphasis on improving the health care delivery system, like integrated care programs;
- And, continuing efforts to make the programs more efficient and to reduce waste—

We will bring significant savings to these programs, spur innovative cost reductions in private insurance—and most importantly, help people get healthier and stay healthier.

We also have to address the high cost of long-term care in this country, and that means shoring up the Medicaid program. Medicaid is generally regarded as a program for the poor. But in reality, Medicaid has a huge impact on the middle-class, as well.

Whether we like to admit it or not, Medicaid is our country's long-term care program. In fact, Medicaid pays for roughly two-thirds of the beds in nursing homes nationwide. The cost of long-term care is so expensive, that many middle-class Americans—after spending all of their own savings—end up relying on Medicaid to pay for their care.

This is an issue we have to face. It affects us all. That's why we were glad to see that the fiscal cliff legislation passed by the Congress and signed by the President created a bi-partisan commission on long-term care. It's a positive step.

A third issue we have to address is the low savings rate and the large gap—one estimate is over $6 trillion—between what individuals have saved and what they will need in retirement.

The combination of high unemployment, low savings, decaying traditional or defined-benefit pensions, decreased home values and longer life expectancies means that too few are accumulating enough to last through their lifetime. We must do more to increase access and incentives for people to save.

Social Security remains the critical foundation of income security for the overwhelming majority of people. And because of low savings rates and high health care costs, future retirees will rely on it even more.

Efforts to strengthen Social Security for the future must take into account the retirement savings gap, and the fact that the percentage of income Social Security replaces is already declining due to the rise in the normal retirement age to 67.

Social Security solvency is a major concern. But, we can't address solvency without also taking into consideration—adequacy.

Simply looking at solvency without considering adequacy again misses the larger goal of shoring up the income security needs of the nation. How we achieve solvency matters. It matters to government . . . to business . . . to the economy. And, it matters to people.

So, as we look to protect and strengthen Social Security, we are guided by some basic principles:

- Any changes to Social Security should be discussed as part of a broader conversation about how to help Americans prepare for a secure retirement.
- If you pay into Social Security, you should receive the benefits you've earned over a lifetime of hard work.
- Your Social Security benefits should keep up with inflation for as long as you live.
- You should continue to be covered in case you become disabled and can no longer work, and your family should continue to be protected if you die.

At AARP, we will also provide educational support and advocate for policies to help people save. And we will encourage better pensions and more private savings in addition to—not at the expense of—Social Security.

This is about people, not just numbers. Our fear is that in recent debates Washington has forgotten that.

The recent debate over the fiscal cliff focused on people with incomes over $400,000 dollars a year, yet the typical senior has an income of only about $20,000 dollars a year.

Let me repeat that. The typical senior has an income of only about $20,000 a year. And for most of them, their Social Security benefit makes up a large chunk of that income.

There are a lot of things we can do to ensure that Social Security remains solvent and provides an adequate benefit now and in the future, but the proposed use of the "chained CPI" is one of the worst.

Why? Because it cuts the benefits of those who are least able to afford it—the oldest, poorest and most vulnerable among us. The "chained CPI" would cut one full month's income from a 92-year-old beneficiary's annual Social Security benefits.

Social Security was designed more than 75 years ago at a time when many women didn't work, most marriages lasted forever, and people generally didn't live as long. We need to make sure that the program serves the needs of our changing demographics for the next 75 years.

The chained CPI doesn't do that. We need a robust national debate focusing on the role of Social Security in helping future generations achieve a secure retirement.

Over the last year, we've been reaching out across the country to our members and people 50-plus to get their ideas on securing Social Security and Medicare for future generations. The initiative is called "You've Earned a Say," and more than 6.3 million have responded so far.

They have considered a number of options, but two points are clear. First, they do not believe that Social Security should be cut to deal with problems in the rest of the budget.

Second, they believe Social Security is important to their retirement security, and they are willing to increase contributions in order to maintain benefits.

That's why we must address the future of Social Security as a separate process with a goal of strengthening it to help people achieve a secure retirement, not to reduce the budget deficit.

AARP is ready to have that discussion right now. Whenever Congress is ready to address the future of Social Security as part of a broader discussion on helping people to achieve a secure retirement, we will engage in that debate.

AARP is not willing, however, to discuss the future of Social Security as part of a deficit reduction debate.

My point is that budgets matter, but people matter more. Yes, we do need to make adjustments to Medicare and Social Security and Medicaid—and AARP members realize that—but we need to do so without compromising the health and retirement security of the American people or undermining the values that we all cherish.

That's why we need a full-blown national discussion of how to ensure that Social Security continues to contribute to the retirement security of older Americans in the future—not in the context of reducing a federal deficit it did not create, but with the goal of helping people achieve retirement security.

For all of those who say Social Security has contributed to the deficit, you are wrong.

I received a letter from Philip, an AARP member in Fort Morgan, Colorado, who summed it up well. Social Security and Medicare, he said, "are the foundation of most Americans' future. Rightly or wrongly, they are. We can make them secure, but it won't happen if we don't find ways to reach a bipartisan solution."

That is our challenge.

We must approach rebuilding the middle class holistically. Issues like health care costs, jobs, savings, income security, the cost of education and the affordability of housing are all part of the total life experience of individuals and families. They are interrelated. How we deal with one affects the others.

They are also intergenerational.

- The high cost of college has an impact on parents who are paying more for college.
- Young adults who can't find jobs or afford their own housing often move back into their parents' homes.
- Many adults are not only supporting their young-adult children, but also caring for their aging parents.

For some families this is a choice. For many others, however, it is the cost of the middle-class decline. Either way, it's all interrelated.

Finally, this is not just about economics. A strong middle class is the bedrock of a functioning society. An ever-widening gap between the "haves" and the "have nots" leads to instability in families and in society and makes it much more difficult for people to move up the socio-economic ladder, achieve the American Dream and live their best life.

So, in the end, we have to ask ourselves: "What kind of America do we want? What kind of life do we want for our kids and grandkids?"

For AARP the answer is clear: We want a society in which everyone lives with dignity and purpose and fulfills their goals and dreams—a life with access to affordable, quality health care and the opportunity to achieve lifelong financial security—a life where everyone has a realistic chance to pursue and achieve the American Dream whether they are young or old.

Former Congresswoman Barbara Jordan put it this way, "What people want is very simple . . . they want an America as good as it's promise."

To create an "America as good as its promise," we have to rebuild and restore prosperity to the middle class. At AARP, we're committed to that goal.

- We're committed to helping all workers achieve their goals—whether that means finding a way to succeed in today's challenging workforce, or finding a way to turn their life's passion into their life's work by starting their own business.
- We're committed to improving Medicare to make it sustainable and slowing the growth of costs throughout the health care system.
- We're committed to strengthening Social Security by restoring long-term solvency while maintaining adequacy.
- We're committed to finding ways to help close the gap between what people have saved and what they will need to live in retirement.
- We're committed to reducing the deficit, but not by putting the health and financial security of current and future generations at risk.

In short, we're committed to rebuilding and restoring prosperity to the middle class.

Critical Thinking

1. How does the middle class cope with increasing insecurity?
2. How can the increasing inequality be reversed?
3. Discern the proper roles for the private sector and the government in addressing the economic situation of the middle class.

Create Central

www.mhhe.com/createcentral

Internet References

Sociosite
www.topsite.com/goto/sociosite.net

Socioweb
www.topsite.com/goto/socioweb.com

Sociology—Study Sociology Online
http://edu.learnsoc.org

Sociology Web Resources
www.mhhe.com/socscience/sociology/resources/index.htm

Article   Prepared by: Kurt Finsterbusch, *University of Maryland, College Park*

The State of Poverty in America

PETER EDELMAN

Learning Outcomes

After reading this article, you will be able to:

- Understand the extent of poverty in America and the two basic poverty problems this article identifies.

- Know the progress that has been made against poverty and the major policies and developments that have created this progress.

- Understand the differences between persistent and temporary poverty and the appropriate policies for each.

The problem is worse than we thought, but we can solve it.

We have two basic poverty problems in the United States. One is the prevalence of low-wage work. The other concerns those who have almost no work.

The two overlap.

Most people who are poor work as much as they can and go in and out of poverty. Fewer people have little or no work on a continuing basis, but they are in much worse straits and tend to stay poor from one generation to the next.

The numbers in both categories are stunning.

Low-wage work encompasses people with incomes below twice the poverty line—not poor but struggling all the time to make ends meet. They now total 103 million, which means that fully one-third of the population has an income below what would be $36,000 for a family of three.

In the bottom tier are 20.5 million people—6.7 percent of the population—who are in deep poverty, with an income less than half the poverty line (below $9,000 for a family of three). Some 6 million people out of those 20.5 million have no income at all other than food stamps.

These dire facts tempt one to believe that there may be some truth to President Ronald Reagan's often-quoted declaration that "we fought a war against poverty and poverty won." But that is not the case. Our public policies have been remarkably successful. Starting with the Social Security Act of 1935, continuing with the burst of activity in the 1960s, and on from there, we have made great progress.

We enacted Medicaid and the Children's Health Insurance Program, and many health indicators for low-income people improved. We enacted food stamps, and the near-starvation conditions we saw in some parts of the country were ameliorated. We enacted the Earned Income Tax Credit and the Child Tax Credit, and the incomes of low-wage workers with children were lifted. We enacted Pell grants, and millions of people could afford college who otherwise couldn't possibly attend. We enacted Supplemental Security Income and thereby raised the income floor for elderly and disabled people whose earnings from work didn't provide enough Social Security. There is much more—housing vouchers, Head Start, child-care assistance, and legal services for the poor, to name a few. The Obama administration and Congress added 16 million people to Medicaid in the Affordable Care Act, appropriated billions to improve the education of low-income children, and spent an impressive amount on the least well-off in the Recovery Act.

All in all, our various public policies kept a remarkable 40 million people from falling into poverty in 2010—about half because of Social Security and half due to the other programs just mentioned. To assert that we fought a war against poverty and poverty won because there is still poverty is like saying that the Clean Air and Clean Water acts failed because there is still pollution.

Nonetheless, the level of poverty in the nation changed little between 1970 and 2000 and is much worse now. It was at 11.1 percent in 1973—the lowest level achieved since we began measuring—and after going up sharply during the Reagan and George H.W. Bush years, went back down during the 1990s to 11.3 percent in 2000, as President Bill Clinton left office.

Why didn't it fall further? The economics have been working against us for four decades, exacerbated by trends in family composition. Well-paying industrial jobs disappeared to other countries and to automation. The economy grew, but the fruits of the growth went exclusively to those at the top. Other jobs replaced the ones lost, but most of the new jobs paid much less. The wage of the median-paying job barely grew—by one measure going up only about 7 percent over the 38 years from 1973 to 2011. Half the jobs in the country now pay less than $33,000 a year, and a quarter pay less than the poverty line of $22,000 for a family of four. We have become a low-wage economy to a far greater extent than we realize.

Households with only one wage-earner—typically those headed by single mothers—have found it extremely difficult to support a family. The share of families with children headed by single mothers rose from 12.8 percent in 1970 to 26.2 percent in 2010 (and from 37.1 percent in 1971 to 52.8 percent in 2010 among African Americans). In 2010, 46.9 percent of children under 18 living in households headed by a single mother were poor.

The percentage of people in deep poverty has doubled since 1976. A major reason for this rise is the near death of cash assistance for families with children. Welfare has shrunk from 14 million recipients (too many, in my view) before the Temporary Assistance for Needy Families law (TANF) was enacted in 1996 to 4.2 million today, just 1.5 percent of the population. At last count, Wyoming had 607 people on TANF, or just 2.7 percent of its poor children. Twenty-six states have less than 20 percent of their poor children on TANF. The proportion of poor families with children receiving welfare has shrunk from 68 percent before TANF was enacted to 27 percent today.

What's the agenda going forward? The heart of it is creating jobs that yield a living income. Restoring prosperity, ensuring that the economy functions at or near full employment, is our most powerful anti-poverty weapon. We need more, though—a vital union sector and a higher minimum wage, for two. We also need work supports—health care, child care, and help with the cost of housing and postsecondary education. These are all income equivalents—all policies that will contribute to bringing everyone closer to having a living income.

There's a gigantic problem here, however: We look to be headed to a future of too many low-wage jobs. Wages in China, India, and other emerging economies may be rising, but we can't foresee any substantial increase in the prevailing wage for many millions of American jobs. That means we better start talking about wage supplements that are much bigger than the Earned Income Tax Credit. We need a dose of reality about the future of the American paycheck.

The second big problem is the crisis—and it is a crisis—posed by the 20 million people at the bottom of the economy. We have a huge hole in our safety net. In many states, TANF and food stamps combined don't even get people to half of the poverty line, and a substantial majority of poor families don't receive TANF at all.

Even worse, we have destroyed the safety net for the poorest children in the country. Seven million women and children are among the 20.5 million in deep poverty. One in four children in a household headed by a single mother is in deep poverty. We have to restore the safety net for the poorest of the poor.

Getting serious about investing in our children—from prenatal care and early-childhood assistance on through education at all levels—is also essential if we are to achieve a future without such calamitous levels of poverty. In addition, we must confront the destruction being wrought by the criminal-justice system. These are poverty issues and race issues as well. The schools and the justice system present the civil-rights challenges of this century.

Combining all of the problems in vicious interaction is the question of place—the issues that arise from having too many poor people concentrated in one area, whether in the inner city, Appalachia, the Mississippi Delta, or on Indian reservations. Such places are home to a minority of the poor, but they include a hugely disproportionate share of intergenerational and persistent poverty. Our most serious policy failing over the past four-plus decades has been our neglect of this concentrated poverty. We have held our own in other respects, but we have lost ground here.

Finally, we need to be much more forthright about how much all of this has to do with race and gender. It is always important to emphasize that white people make up the largest number of the poor, to counter the stereotype that the face of poverty is one of color. At the same time, though, we must face more squarely that African Americans, Latinos, and Native Americans are all poor at almost three times the rate of whites and ask why that continues to be true. We need as a nation to be more honest about who it is that suffers most from terrible schools and the way we lock people up. Poverty most definitely cuts across racial lines, but it doesn't cut evenly.

There's a lot to do.

Critical Thinking

1. Why is there so much poverty in America when America used to claim that it was the richest nation in the world?

2. How much do prejudice, bias, blaming the victim, and other attitudinal factors factor into the poverty problem?

3. Does America have a safety net? Is there a hole in the safety net?

Create Central

www.mhhe.com/createcentral

Internet References

Sociosite
www.topsite.com/goto/sociosite.net

Socioweb
www.topsite.com/goto/socioweb.com

Sociology—Study Sociology Online
http://edu.learnsoc.org

Sociology Web Resources
www.mhhe.com/socscience/sociology/resources/index.htm

Edelman, Peter. Reprinted with permission from The *American Prospect*, June 22, 2012. http://www.prospect.org. *The American Prospect*, 1710 Rhode Island Avenue, NW, 12th Floor, Washington, DC 20036. All rights reserved.

Article   Prepared by: Kurt Finsterbusch, *University of Maryland, College Park*

The End of Welfare as I Knew It

How Temporary Assistance for Needy Families Failed the Test of the Great Recession

DIANA SPATZ

Learning Outcomes

After reading this article, you will be able to:

- Determine what TANF has accomplished.
- Determine what TANF has not accomplished.
- Identify administrative problems of the current welfare system.

> **9** number, in millions, purged from the welfare rolls by 2008
>
> $1/5$ proportion of poor children served by TANF today

I'll always remember the day President Clinton signed Temporary Assistance to Needy Families (TANF), or welfare reform, into law. It was August 1996, and I was reading the morning paper in Barstow, California, completing the last leg of a cross-country road trip I'd taken with my daughter to celebrate my finishing school. Having just earned my bachelor's degree from the University of California, Berkeley, I would finally earn enough to get my family off welfare—and out of poverty—for good. As I read the news that the Personal Responsibility and Work Opportunity Reconciliation Act had become law, I hung my head and cried. I felt like I'd crossed a bridge just as it collapsed behind me, and worried what would become of mothers who remained trapped on the other side.

Since 1996, politicians have bragged about passing welfare reform. Even House Speaker John Boehner recently praised TANF as a bipartisan success. But successful at what? If kicking low-income children and their families off welfare is the measure, then TANF was a huge success. States were given bonuses for reducing their caseloads rather than reducing poverty. As long as families were off the rolls, it didn't matter how or why. Studies show that parents were ten times more likely to get cut off welfare because of punitive sanctions than because they got jobs paying enough to "income off." In many states, "full family" sanctions cut low-income children off welfare along with their parents. Under the "work first" mantra, TANF caseloads plummeted by almost 70 percent, as nearly 9 million low-income parents and children were purged from the national welfare rolls by 2008. Given the four goals of TANF—promoting low-wage work, encouraging marriage, reducing caseloads and curtailing out-of-wedlock births—these outcomes are no surprise. But if the measure of success is poverty reduction, TANF has failed.

To start, its restrictions on postsecondary education and training—the most effective pathway out of poverty for parents on welfare—make earning a bachelor's degree nearly impossible. Even earning an associate degree is difficult. "Any job is a good job" was the slogan emblazoned on the walls of county welfare agencies across the country, as tens of thousands of low-income mothers were made to quit college to do up to thirty-five hours per week of unpaid "workfare": sweeping streets, picking up trash in parks and cleaning public restrooms in exchange for benefits as low as $240 a month.

Contrary to "welfare queen" stereotypes, like most welfare mothers, I worked first. Work wasn't the problem; it was the nature of the work—low-wage, dead-end jobs with no benefits and little chance for advancement—that kept families like mine on the welfare rolls. Investing in my education enabled me to break that cycle and earn a solid upper-middle-class income. I now pay three times more in taxes than I used to earn working full time in a low-wage, dead-end job.

This trajectory is what motivated mothers like Rya Frontera and Melissa Johnson to pursue nursing degrees, despite being sanctioned: having their families' cash grants cut off and losing childcare and transportation assistance when they refused to quit school. Whereas mothers in "work first" programs earn less than $9,000 a year, after completing her BS in nursing Melissa graduated off welfare to a career-path job as a registered nurse making $90,000 a year. Similarly, Rya is now a full-time nurse with full benefits working for Kaiser. Not only are they off welfare permanently; both women are filling a crucial labor market need, as our nation faces a nursing shortage with no end in sight. Isn't that how welfare should work?

It is also time to end the arbitrary rules under TANF that imposed a lifetime limit of sixty months for receiving benefits, and that allowed states to enact shorter time limits. It took me ten years to overcome a lifetime of physical, emotional and sexual abuse; depression; and post-traumatic stress disorder, one or more of which have been experienced by most mothers on welfare as girls or adults—or in my case, both. In California—home to one-third of welfare families nationally—the experience of "timed off" families clearly challenges the notion that five years is enough; TANF's work-first emphasis relegated many parents to low-wage jobs that didn't pay enough to get their families off welfare, let alone out of poverty. Consequently, in 2003 the vast majority of parents in California's CalWORKs program who reached their sixty-month limit were working and playing by the rules when they timed off welfare for the rest of their lives. And this year, like many states, California shortened its lifetime limit to forty-eight months in response to budget shortfalls, despite having the second-highest unemployment rate in the country. As a result, 22,500 parents were permanently cut off the welfare rolls on July 1.

Ashley Proctor, a young single mother in Oakland, was doing her thirty-two-hour weekly work requirement when she timed off. Her benefits were cut to a "child only" grant of $320 per month. "My son and I are sleeping on a friend's sofa," she says. "On the weekends I take him to our storage unit so he can play with his toys." That's better than what mothers faced in other states, where time limits as short as twenty-one months were enacted. How unfortunate that Congress, in its infinite wisdom, didn't put a time limit on poverty instead.

While states like California curtailed much-needed benefits, under welfare reform billions in federal funds were invested in unproven "marriage promotion" programs to marry poor women off the welfare rolls. Never mind that in some of California's most populous counties in 2003, most timed-off parents were already in two-parent families where one was working. And in a cruel twist, while billions were spent on marriage promotion programs that were mandatory for the states, the Family Violence Option let states choose whether to provide domestic violence services in their TANF programs, including waivers of time limits and welfare-to-work rules. Furthermore, although research shows that women who receive welfare experience domestic violence at double the rate of all American women, not a dime in federal funding was provided for family violence services. Even in California, which adopted the FVO, studies show that as many as 80 percent of CalWORKs mothers are domestic violence victims. Of these, less than 1 percent get family violence counseling and services, and less than one-quarter of 1 percent get waivers from welfare work requirements that could save their lives.

> **22,500** number of parents cut off in July after California shortened its lifetime limit to forty-eight months
>
> **80** percent of mothers in California's welfare system who are victims of domestic violence

This includes mothers like Felicia Jones, whom my agency, Low-Income Families' Empowerment Through Education, or LIFETIME, was helping when she went into hiding after her ex threatened to kill her and their children. While on the run, Felicia got a notice of a mandatory welfare-to-work appointment, which had been scheduled on the same day and time as the hearing for her restraining order. When she called to say she couldn't make the appointment, her caseworker said she couldn't help her and hung up the phone, and later sanctioned Felicia for missing that appointment. Despite my urging, Felicia was too afraid to request a state appeals hearing and later disappeared. To this day, I don't know what happened to her and her children.

Fifteen years of welfare reform, and what do we have to show for it? Poverty is at its highest level in nearly twenty years. The number of children living in deep poverty—in families with income less than 50 percent of the poverty line—is at its highest level in thirty-five years. The unemployment rate for single mothers, who represent 90 percent of parents in the welfare system, has nearly doubled, to a twenty-five-year high. Welfare rolls are rising for the first time since TANF was passed, despite efforts by states to tighten time limits and make it harder for families to get help. In Georgia, for example, families applying for TANF have faced "wait periods" before they can get cash assistance—the welfare equivalent of a poll tax or literacy test—with caseworkers offering to send children into foster care or put them up for adoption to ease the burden. Consequently, since 2002 Georgia increased TANF spending on child welfare–related services by 245 percent. According to Clare Richie, a senior policy analyst with the Georgia Budget and Policy Institute, the state now spends more on adoption services and foster care (58 percent) than it does on assistance to families.

This trend is alarming to people like Georgia State Senator Donzella James, who has been getting calls from constituents whose children are being taken away by the Department of Family and Child Services, the state's welfare agency. "One woman told me, 'I'm not a bad mother. I'm just unemployed,'" she said. Similarly, Arizona, Rhode Island and Texas spend nearly half their TANF block grants on child welfare–related services. One has to wonder if this was the plan all along, given the proposal by Newt Gingrich, who was House speaker when TANF was created, to use orphanages to reduce the welfare rolls.

The Great Recession was the first true test of welfare reform during an economic downturn, and TANF failed the grade miserably. The proof is in the numbers: in 1995 the old welfare program served at least eight out of every ten low-income children, including mine. Today TANF serves only two out of every ten poor children nationwide. In passing TANF, Congress and Bill Clinton made good on their promise to "end welfare as we know it." It's time to end welfare reform as we know it instead.

Critical Thinking

1. Poverty is at its highest level in nearly twenty years. Does that mean that TANF has failed?
2. Why are welfare rolls now rising?
3. Does TANF address the incentives problem of welfare?

Create Central

www.mhhe.com/createcentral

Internet References

Sociosite
www.topsite.com/goto/sociosite.net

Socioweb
www.topsite.com/goto/socioweb.com

Sociology—Study Sociology Online
http://edu.learnsoc.org

Sociology Web Resources
www.mhhe.com/socscience/sociology/resources/index.htm

DIANA SPATZ is executive director of LIFETIME, a statewide organization of low-income parents in California who are pursuing postsecondary education and training as their pathway out of poverty.

Spatz, Diana. Reprinted by permission from the January 2, 2012 issue of *The Nation*. Copyright © 2012 by The Nation. For subscription information, call 1-800-333-8536. Portions of each week's Nation magazine can be accessed at www.thenation.com.

Article   Prepared by: Kurt Finsterbusch, *University of Maryland, College Park*

Roots of Racism

Elizabeth Culotta

Learning Outcomes

After reading this article, you will be able to:

- Understand many intergroup conflicts from the psychological perspective. Ingroups are viewed as good and outgroups generally as bad.

- Understand that most of the world's violence derives from conscious and unconscious prejudice.

- Know many of the obstacles to better understanding between groups.

Racial prejudice apparently stems from deep evolutionary roots and a universal tendency to form coalitions and favor our own side. And yet what makes a "group" is mercurial: In experiments, people easily form coalitions based on meaningless traits or preferences—and then favor others in their "group." Researchers have explored these innate biases and begun to ask why such biases exist. What factors in our evolutionary past have shaped our coalitionary present—and what, if anything, can we do about it now? Several avenues of research are probing the origins of what many psychologists call in-group love and out-group hate. Researchers are testing the implicit biases of young children and even primates, and devising experiments to ratchet bias up and down. Evolutionary researchers are trying to parse the group environments of our ancestors and are debating just how big a selective pressure came from out-group male warriors.

Humans Everywhere Divide the World into "Us" and "Them." Why Are We so Tribal?

You're alone in a dark alley late at night. Suddenly a man emerges from a doorway. If you are a typical white American and he is a young black man, within a few tenths of a second you will feel a frisson of fear as your brain automatically categorizes him. Your heart beats faster and your body tenses.

In this event, nothing happens. He glances at you and moves away. You walk on, feeling foolish for fears based merely on his membership in a racial group.

Tension and suspicion between groups—whether based on racial, ethnic, religious, or some other difference—fuel much of the world's violence. From the enduring feuds of the Middle East and Northern Ireland, to the vicious raids of South Sudan, to the gang warfare that plagues American cities, even to bullying in schools and skirmishes between fans of rival sports teams, much of the conflict we see today erupts because "we" are pitted against "them."

Some of the prejudice behind these conflicts is not conscious: Your fear spiked in that dark alley before your conscious brain had even registered the young man's skin color. This prejudice apparently stems from deep evolutionary roots and a universal tendency to form coalitions and favor our own side. And yet what makes a "group" is mercurial: In experiments, people easily form coalitions based on meaningless traits such as preferring one painter over another—and then favor others in their "group," giving them more money in games, for example. "In arbitrarily constructed, meaningless groups with no history, people still think that those in their ingroup are smarter, better, more moral, and more just than members of outgroups," says Harvard University psychologist James Sidanius.

A wide and deep literature has explored these innate biases in the 40 or so years since they were first discussed. Now researchers have begun to ask why humans are apparently primed to see the world as ingroups and outgroups. What factors in our evolutionary past have shaped our coalitionary present—and what, if anything, can we do about it now?

Several avenues of research are probing the origins of what many psychologists call ingroup love and outgroup hate. Researchers are testing the implicit biases of young children and even primates, and devising experiments to ratchet bias up and down. Evolutionary researchers are trying to parse the group environments of our ancestors and are debating just how big a selective pressure came from outgroup male warriors. "The origin of all this is the all-consuming question of the past few years," says Harvard psychologist Mahzarin Banaji.

Group Love

For many researchers, our cruelty to "them" starts with our kindness to "us." Humans are the only animal that cooperates so extensively with nonkin, and researchers say that, like big brains, group life is a quintessential human adaptation. (In fact, many think big brains evolved in part to cope with group living.) Studies of living hunter-gatherers, who may represent the lifestyle of our ancestors, support this idea. Hunter-gatherers "cooperate massively in the flow of every imaginable good and service you can think of," says anthropologist Kim Hill of Arizona State University (ASU), Tempe, who has studied hunter-gatherers for 35 years. "Anything you need in daily life, the person next to you will lend you: water, sticks for firewood, a bow and arrow, a carrying basket—anything."

Thus the group buffers the individual against the environment. "Our central adaptation is to group living," says psychologist Marilynn Brewer of the University of New South Wales in Sydney, Australia. "The group is primary."

When the ingroup is loved, by definition there must be a less privileged outgroup. "One can be expected to be treated more nicely by ingroup members than by outgroups," as Brewer put it in a seminal 1999 paper. "It is in a sense universally true that 'we' are more peaceful, trustworthy, friendly, and honest than 'they,'" she wrote.

If groups compete for territory or resources, favoring the ingroup necessarily means beating the outgroup and can escalate into hostility, Brewer notes. Several other researchers have recently argued the reverse: that over time, hostilities between groups fostered ingroup love, because more cooperative groups won battles. Whichever came first, researchers agree that outgroup hate and ingroup love may have spurred each other.

In the United States and some other countries, the sharpest division between groups is often racial. But researchers agree that it's not that white people have evolved to be suspicious of black people per se or vice versa. Such an evolved prejudice could only arise as the result of frequent negative interactions between races in the past, explains anthropologist Robert Boyd of the University of California, Los Angeles. But thousands of years ago, people didn't cross continents to meet each other. "In the distant past, we had very little experience interacting with people who were physically very different from us," Boyd says. "That's only since 1492. Ethnic distinctions, however, are presumably quite old." Thus racial prejudice is a subset of a much broader phenomenon. "This is not just about racism," says psychologist Susan Fiske of Princeton University.

The targets of outgroup prejudice vary from culture to culture and over time—Sidanius refers to them as "arbitrary set" prejudices. In Sri Lanka, it may be Tamils; in Northern Ireland, Catholics or Protestants; in India, the Untouchables. Fiske notes that the world over, the greatest prejudice is often aimed at people without an address, such as gypsies and the homeless. Whoever the target, we have a psychological system that prepares us to "learn quickly, in whatever cultural context we're in, what are the cues that discriminate between us and them," says psychologist Mark Schaller of the University of British Columbia, Vancouver, in Canada.

This doesn't mean that prejudicial behavior is inevitable, Schaller says. "These prejudices tap into very ancient parts of our minds, and it's happening at a very quick, automatic level," he says. "But we have recently evolved parts of our brains that allow us to engage in slower, more rational thought. When I experience that fear in a dark alley, it may take me another half-second for a more rational thought to kick in, but I'll get there, if I have the motivation and means to do so."

Shoot or Don't Shoot

Psychologists have become master manipulators of prejudice in the lab, with clever experiments that reveal underlying biases. In the Implicit Associations Test, for example, people are asked to rapidly categorize objects and faces; the pattern of mistakes and speed shows that people more quickly associate negative words such as "hatred" with outgroup faces than ingroup faces. "It takes significantly longer to associate your ingroup with bad things and the outgroup with good things," Sidanius says. In disturbing tests using a video game, people looking at a picture of a person carrying an ambiguous object are more likely to mistake a cell phone for a gun and shoot the carrier if he is an outgroup male.

This type of bias shows up in all cultures studied and in children; it also appears in people who say they are not prejudiced and who work consciously for equality. "This is in every single one of us, including me," Banaji says.

It starts young. In work in review, Yarrow Dunham of Princeton, Banaji, and colleagues found that Taiwanese toddlers assumed that a smiling racially ambiguous face was Taiwanese, but a frowning one was white; white, American 3-year-olds similarly preferred their ingroup.

Even our primate cousins categorize others into ingroups and outgroups. Chimps obviously have outgroup bias: They sometimes band together and attack and kill members of other troops. Last year, a study managed to uncover primates' implicit expectations of "us" and "them" for the first time.

Laurie Santos of Yale University, working with Banaji and others, adapted a psychological test for rhesus macaques, group-living monkeys whose lineage diverged from ours about 25 million to 30 million years ago. The researchers assumed that the macaques would stare longer at outgroup faces, who might be more dangerous, or at groups of photos that paired things they liked with outgroup faces they didn't like. In a series of experiments published in the *Journal of Personality and Social Psychology,* Santos and colleagues found that macaques looked longer at photos of outgroup members. They also looked longer at photos of outgroup members next to pictures of fruit, and at photos of ingroup members with spiders and snakes.

Seeing such apparent bias in primates suggests it is evolutionarily ancient. This "coherence of results across species and ages is satisfying," Banaji says, and tells us that outgroup bias is "core to our species."

While these researchers probe bias in different populations, others are exploring how to manipulate it. Our attitudes toward outgroups are part of a threat-detection system that allows us to rapidly determine friend from foe, says psychologist Steven Neuberg of ASU Tempe. The problem, he says, is that like smoke detectors, the system is designed to give many false alarms rather than miss a true threat. So outgroup faces alarm us even when there is no danger.

Neuberg and Schaller have studied what might turn this detection system up and down. When you feel threatened, you react to danger more quickly and intensely; people startle more easily in the dark. That's why prejudice rears its head in a dark alley rather than a well-lit field. In a variety of studies, Neuberg, Schaller, and their colleagues have manipulated people into feeling unconsciously more fearful or confident and found that measures of outgroup bias respond. Canadians taking tests in the dark rated Iraqis as less trustworthy and more hostile than other Canadians. Sinhalese in Sri Lanka stereotyped Tamils as more hostile after being primed with a geographic context that made them feel outnumbered. And white undergraduates were more likely to misperceive anger on the faces of black men—but not whites—after watching a scary scene from the movie *The Silence of the Lambs*. Schaller adds that some people seem to go through life more cognizant of threats than others, and that prejudice is more easily intensified in these people.

These findings can inform real-life tragedy, researchers say. On the evening of 26 February, a Hispanic man named George Zimmerman shot an unarmed black teenager, Trayvon Martin, in a gated community in Sanford, Florida. Zimmerman told police that he followed Martin suspecting criminal activity, was attacked, and fired in self-defense. Researchers cannot speak to what happened that night. But when Zimmerman first spotted Martin, the situation was a "perfect storm" for triggering feelings of vulnerability and implicit prejudice, Neuberg and Schaller say.

It was dark and raining. Martin, 17, though slender, was tall. Zimmerman, 28, was quite alert to crime in his neighborhood; he had started the neighborhood watch. Martin was young, male, and black, an outgroup stereotyped as dangerous by whites and Hispanics in the United States. "We would predict that under those circumstances this kind of thing would happen more often," Neuberg says.

If certain situations turn implicit prejudice up, can it be turned down? Schaller notes that making people feel safer can moderate this bias, whether through specific priming or more generally with lower crime rates or a better economy. To unconsciously prime her own mind, Banaji has created a screen saver that displays stereotype-smashing images. Other researchers say that deliberately engaging the slower conscious mind may help. For example, in addition to skimming all job applications quickly, a manager might read the files of minority applicants with care.

Men in the Crosshairs

Martin is a good example of how outgroup prejudice falls hardest on men, Sidanius says. He argues that this has specific evolutionary roots: Because it is men who typically make war, it was outgroup men who attacked our ancestors; it was also men who were more likely to be killed in combat. "Back in the Pleistocene, outgroup males really were dangerous," he says.

If natural selection has shaped our minds to be wary of outgroup males, then they should face more prejudice than outgroup women, says Sidanius, an African American who himself was the target of hate crimes as a young man. He and colleagues have assembled a devastating catalog showing how this is true for black men in America. As compared with black women, black men are more likely to be victims of hate crimes, receive harsher jail sentences for comparable offenses, pay more money for cars—the list goes on and on. Data suggest that West Indian and South Asian men in the United Kingdom face similarly disproportionate bias, Sidanius says.

Building on these ideas, in March, Melissa McDonald of Michigan State University in East Lansing and colleagues proposed what they called the "warrior male hypothesis," arguing that natural selection has shaped men's minds, more than women's, toward belonging to coalitions. They predict that men are more prejudiced than women, and some data show this.

But others aren't so sure that intergroup war was a prominent feature of our prehistory. Foragers depend on farflung networks to gain access to the social and natural resources of others, notes anthropologist Polly Wiessner of the University of Utah in Salt Lake City. The !Kung of Africa, whom Wiessner studied for decades, "may travel for hundreds of miles to visit exchange partners in less familiar areas, with no fear of unknown males," she says.

Whether or not humans have evolved to fear outgroup men per se, researchers agree that we are prone to categorize and sometimes fear outgroups. "What we're arguing is a natural preference for drawing ingroup–outgroup boundaries. It can be race, religion, nationality, dialect, or arbitrary set differences," Sidanius says. "But once those boundaries are drawn, people like to discriminate across them."

Critical Thinking

1. How have groups that hated each other become friendlier?
2. Relations are very good between the United States and Germany and Japan. Why?
3. In what way does this article help you better understand the intergroup conflicts around you?

Create Central

www.mhhe.com/createcentral

Internet References

Sociosite
www.topsite.com/goto/sociosite.net

Socioweb
www.topsite.com/goto/socioweb.com

Sociology—Study Sociology Online
http://edu.learnsoc.org

Sociology Web Resources
www.mhhe.com/socscience/sociology/resources/index.htm

Article   Prepared by: Kurt Finsterbusch, *University of Maryland, College Park*

Emmett and Trayvon

How Racial Prejudice in America Has Changed in the Last Sixty Years

Elijah Anderson

Learning Outcomes

After reading this article, you will be able to:

- Understand how racial prejudice has substantially changed in the past sixty years.

- Assess the remaining problems of racism and how they might be addressed.

- Note how the ghetto plays a significant role in racial prejudice today.

Separated by a thousand miles, two state borders, and nearly six decades, two young African American boys met tragic fates that seem remarkably similar today: both walked into a small market to buy some candy; both ended up dead.

The first boy is Emmett Till, who was fourteen years old in the summer of 1955 when he walked into a local grocery store in Money, Mississippi, to buy gum. He was later roused from bed, beaten brutally, and possibly shot by a group of white men who later dumped his body in a nearby river. They claimed he had stepped out of his place by flirting with a young white woman, the wife of the store's owner. The second boy is Trayvon Martin, who was seventeen years old late last winter when he walked into a 7-Eleven near a gated community in Sanford, Florida, to buy Skittles and an iced tea. He was later shot to death at close range by a mixed-race man, who claimed Martin had behaved suspiciously and seemed out of place. The deaths of both boys galvanized the nation, drew sympathy and disbelief across racial lines, and, through the popular media, prompted a reexamination of race relations.

In the aftermath of Martin's death last February, a handful of reporters and columnists, and many members of the general public, made the obvious comparison: Trayvon Martin, it seemed, was the Emmett Till of our times. And while that comparison has some merit—the boys' deaths are similar both in some of their details and in their tragic outcome—these killings must also be understood as the result of very different strains of racial tension in America. The racism that led to Till's death

was embedded in a virulent ideology of white racial superiority born out of slavery and the Jim Crow codes, particularly in the Deep South. That sort of racism hinges on the idea that blacks are an inherently inferior race, a morally null group that deserves both the subjugation and poverty it gets.

The racial prejudice that led to Trayvon Martin's death is different. While it, too, was born of America's painful legacy of slavery and segregation, and informed by those old concepts of racial order—that blacks have their "place" in society—it in addition reflects the urban iconography of today's racial inequality, namely the black ghetto, a uniquely urban American creation. Strikingly, this segregation of the black community coexists with an ongoing racial incorporation process that has produced the largest black middle class in history, and that reflects the extraordinary social progress this country has made since the 1960s. The civil rights movement paved the way for blacks and other people of color to access public and professional opportunities and spaces that would have been unimaginable in Till's time.

While the sort of racism that led to Till's death still exists in society today, Americans in general have a much more nuanced, more textured attitude toward race than anything we've seen before, and usually that attitude does not manifest in overtly hateful, exclusionary, or violent acts. Instead, it manifests in pervasive mindsets and stereotypes that all black people start from the inner-city ghetto and are therefore stigmatized by their association with its putative amorality, danger, crime, and poverty. Hence, in public a black person is burdened with a negative presumption that he must disprove before he can establish mutually trusting relationships with others.

Most consequentially, black skin, and its association with the ghetto, translates into a deficit of credibility as black skin is conflated with lower-class status. This deficit impacts poor blacks of the ghetto one way and middle-class black people another. While middle-class blacks may be able to successfully disabuse others of their negative presumptions, lower-class blacks may not. For instance, all blacks, particularly "ghetto-looking" young men, are at risk of enduring yet another "stop and frisk" from the police as well as suspicion from potential employers, shopkeepers, and strangers on the street. Members of the black middle class and black professionals can usually pass inspection and withstand such scrutiny; many poorer blacks cannot. And many blacks who have never stepped foot in a ghetto must repeatedly prove themselves as non-ghetto, often operating in a provisional status, in the workplace or, say, a fancy restaurant, until they can convince others—either by speaking "white" English or by demonstrating intelligence, poise, or manners—that they are to be trusted, that they are not "one of those" blacks from the ghetto, and that they deserve respect. In other words, a middle-class black man who is, for instance, waiting in line for an ATM at night will in many cases be treated with a level of suspicion that a middle-class white man simply does not experience.

But this pervasive cultural association—black skin equals the ghetto—does not come out of the blue. After all, as a result of historical, political, and economic factors, blacks have been confined in the ghetto. Today, with persistent housing discrimination and the disappearance of manufacturing jobs, America's ghettos face structural poverty. In addition, crime and homicide rates within those communities are high, young black men are typically the ones killing one another, and ghetto culture, made iconic by artists like Tupac Shakur, 50 Cent, and the Notorious B.I.G., is inextricably intertwined with blackness.

As a result, in America's collective imagination the ghetto is a dangerous, scary part of the city. It's where rap comes from, where drugs are sold, where hoodlums rule, and where The Wire might have been filmed. Above all, to many white Americans the ghetto is where "the black people live," and thus, as the misguided logic follows, all black people live in the ghetto. It's that pervasive, if accidental, fallacy that's at the root of the wider society's perceptions of black people today. While it may be true that everyone who lives in a certain ghetto is black, it is patently untrue that everyone who is black lives in a ghetto. Regardless, black people of all classes, including those born and raised far from the inner cities and those who've never been in a ghetto, are by virtue of skin color alone stigmatized by the place.

I call this idea the "iconic ghetto," and it has become a powerful source of stereotype, prejudice, and discrimination in our society, negatively defining the black person in public. In some ways, the iconic ghetto reflects the old version of racism that led to Till's death. In Till's day, a black person's "place" was in the field, in the maid's quarters, or in the back of the bus. If a black man was found "out of his place," he could be punished, jailed, or lynched. In Martin's day—in our day—a black person's "place" is in the ghetto. If he is found "out of his place," like in a fancy hotel lobby, on a golf course, or, say, in an upscale community, he can be treated with suspicion, avoided, pulled over, frisked, arrested—or worse.

Trayvon Martin's death is an example of how this more current type of racial stereotyping works. While the facts of the case are still under investigation, from what is known it seems fair to say that George Zimmerman, Martin's killer, saw a young black man wearing a hoodie and assumed he was from the ghetto and therefore "out of place" in the Retreat at Twin Lakes, Zimmerman's gated community. Until recently, Twin Lakes was a safe, largely middle-class neighborhood. But as a result of collapsing housing prices, it has been witnessing an influx of renters and a rash of burglaries. Some of the burglaries have been committed by black men. Zimmerman, who is himself of mixed race (of Latino, black, and white descent), did not have a history of racism, and his family has claimed that he had previously volunteered handing out leaflets at black churches protesting the assault of a homeless black man. The point is, Zimmerman did not shoot and kill Martin because he hates black people. It seems that he put a gun in his pocket and followed Martin after making the assumption that Martin's black skin and choice of dress meant that he was from the ghetto, and therefore up to no good; he was a threat. And that's an important distinction.

Zimmerman acted brashly and was almost certainly motivated by assumptions about young black men, but he did not act brutally out of hatred for Martin's race. That does not make Zimmerman's actions excusable, but it does make his actions understandable in a way that Till's murderers' heinous brutality is not.

The complex racially charged drama that led to Martin's death is indicative of both our history and our rapid and uneven racial progress as a society. While there are no longer clear demarcations separating blacks and whites in social strata, there have been major racial changes that do just that. It's no longer uncommon to see black people in positions of power, in boardrooms, universities, hospitals, and judges' chambers, but we must also face the reality that poverty, unemployment, and incarceration still break down along racial lines.

This situation fuels the iconic ghetto, including a prevalent assumption among many white Americans, even among some progressive whites who are not by any measure traditionally racist, that there are two types of blacks: those residing in the ghetto, and those who appear to have played by the rules and become successful. In situations in which black people encounter strangers, many often feel they have to prove as quickly as possible that they belong in the latter category in order to be accepted and treated with respect. As a result of this pervasive dichotomy—that there are "ghetto" and "non-ghetto" blacks—many middle-class blacks actively work to separate and distance themselves from the popular association of their race with the ghetto by deliberately dressing well or by spurning hip-hop, rap, and ghetto styles of dress. Similarly, some blacks, when interacting with whites, may cultivate an overt, sometimes unnaturally formal way of speaking to distance themselves from "those" black people from the ghetto.

But it's also not that simple. Strikingly, many middle-class black young people, most of whom have no personal connection with the ghetto, go out of their way in the other direction, claiming the ghetto by adopting its symbols, including styles of dress, patterns of speech, or choice of music, as a means of establishing their authenticity as "still Black" in the largely white middle class; they want to demonstrate they have not "sold out." Thus, the iconic ghetto is, paradoxically, both a stigma and a sign of authenticity for some American blacks—a kind of double bind that beleaguers many middle-class black parents.

Despite the significant racial progress our society has made since Till's childhood, from the civil rights movement to the reelection of President Obama, the pervasive association of black people with the ghetto, and therefore with a certain social station, betrays a persistent cultural lag. After all, it has only been two generations since schools were legally desegregated, five decades since blacks and whites started drinking from the same water fountains. If Till were alive today, he'd remember when restaurants had "White Only" entrances and when stories of lynchings peppered the New York Times. He'd also remember the Freedom Riders, Martin Luther King Jr., and the Million Man March. He'd remember when his peers became generals and justices, and when a black man, just twenty years his junior, became president of the United States. He would have been seventy-three—had he lived.

Critical Thinking

1. What is the role of generational change in the changes in race relations?

2. What are some of the best ways for people to reduce their negative racial attitudes?

3. What role has the election of a black president had in reducing or increasing racial prejudice?

Create Central

www.mhhe.com/createcentral

Internet References

Sociosite
www.topsite.com/goto/sociosite.net

Socioweb
www.topsite.com/goto/socioweb.com

Sociology—Study Sociology Online
http://edu.learnsoc.org

Sociology Web Resources
www.mhhe.com/socscience/sociology/resources/index.htm

ELIJAH ANDERSON is the William K. Lanman Jr. Professor of Sociology at Yale University. His latest book is *The Cosmopolitan Canopy: Race and Civility in Everyday Life.*

Article   Prepared by: Kurt Finsterbusch, *University of Maryland, College Park*

Female Power

THE ECONOMIST

Learning Outcomes

After reading this article, you will be able to:

- Understand how remarkable the progress of women has been in America and the world in one generation in employment, education, income and rights.

- Note the profound changes in the attitudes of both women and men.

- Assess the distance that remains to equality.

Across the rich world more women are working than ever before. Coping with this change will be one of the great challenges of the coming decades.

The economic empowerment of women across the rich world is one of the most remarkable revolutions of the past 50 years. It is remarkable because of the extent of the change: millions of people who were once dependent on men have taken control of their own economic fates. It is remarkable also because it has produced so little friction: a change that affects the most intimate aspects of people's identities has been widely welcomed by men as well as women. Dramatic social change seldom takes such a benign form.

Yet even benign change can come with a sting in its tail. Social arrangements have not caught up with economic changes. Many children have paid a price for the rise of the two-income household. Many women—and indeed many men—feel that they are caught in an ever-tightening tangle of commitments. If the empowerment of women was one of the great changes of the past 50 years, dealing with its social consequences will be one of the great challenges of the next 50.

At the end of her campaign to become America's first female president in 2008, Hillary Clinton remarked that her 18m votes in the Democratic Party's primaries represented 18m cracks in the glass ceiling. In the market for jobs rather than votes the ceiling is being cracked every day. Women now make up almost half of American workers (49.9% in October). They run some of the world's best companies, such as PepsiCo, Archer Daniels Midland and W.L. Gore. They earn almost 60% of university degrees in America and Europe.

Progress has not been uniform, of course. In Italy and Japan, employment rates for men are more than 20 percentage points higher than those for women. Although Italy's female employment rate has risen markedly in the past decade, it is still below 50%, and more than 20 percentage points below those of Denmark and Sweden. Women earn substantially less than men on average and are severely under-represented at the top of organisations.

The change is dramatic nevertheless. A generation ago working women performed menial jobs and were routinely subjected to casual sexism—as "Mad Men", a television drama about advertising executives in the early 1960s, demonstrates brilliantly. Today women make up the majority of professional workers in many countries (51% in the United States, for example) and casual sexism is for losers. Even holdouts such as the Mediterranean countries are changing rapidly. In Spain, the proportion of young women in the labour force has now reached American levels. The glass is much nearer to being half full than half empty.

What explains this revolution? Politics have clearly played a part. Feminists such as Betty Friedan have demonised domestic slavery and lambasted discrimination. Governments have passed equal-rights acts. Female politicians such as Margaret Thatcher and Mrs Clinton have taught younger women that anything is possible. But politics is only part of the answer: such discordant figures as Ms Friedan and Lady Thatcher have been borne aloft by subterranean economic and technological forces.

The rich world has seen a growing demand for women's labour. When brute strength mattered more than brains, men had an inherent advantage. Now that brainpower has triumphed the two sexes are more evenly matched. The feminisation of the workforce has been driven by the relentless rise of the service sector (where women can compete as well as men) and the equally relentless decline of manufacturing (where they could not). The landmark book in the rise of feminism was arguably not Ms Friedan's "The Feminine Mystique" but Daniel Bell's "The Coming of Post-Industrial Society".

Demand has been matched by supply: women are increasingly willing and able to work outside the home. The vacuum cleaner has played its part. Improved technology reduced the amount of time needed for the traditional female work of cleaning and cooking. But the most important innovation has been the contraceptive pill. The spread of the pill has not only allowed women to get married later. It has also increased their incentives to invest time and effort in acquiring skills, particularly slow-burning skills that are hard to learn and take many years to pay off. The knowledge that they would not have to drop out of, say, law school to have a baby made law school more attractive.

The expansion of higher education has also boosted job prospects for women, improving their value on the job market and shifting their role models from stay-at-home mothers to successful professional women. The best-educated women have always been more likely than other women to work, even after having children. In 1963, 62% of college-educated women in the United States were in the labour force, compared with 46% of those with a high school diploma. Today 80% of American women with a college education are in the labour force compared with 67% of those with a high school diploma and 47% of those without one.

This growing cohort of university-educated women is also educated in more marketable subjects. In 1966, 40% of American women who received a BA specialised in education in college; 2% specialised in business and management. The figures are now 12% and 50%. Women only continue to lag seriously behind men in a handful of subjects, such as engineering and computer sciences, where they earned about one-fifth of degrees in 2006.

One of the most surprising things about this revolution is how little overt celebration it has engendered. Most people welcome the change. A recent Rockefeller Foundation/Time survey found that three-quarters of Americans regarded it as a positive development. Nine men out of ten said they were comfortable with women earning more than them. But few are cheering. This is partly because young women take their opportunities for granted. It is partly because for many women work represents economic necessity rather than liberation. The rich world's growing army of single mothers have little choice but to work. A growing proportion of married women have also discovered that the only way they can preserve their households' living standards is to join their husbands in the labour market. In America, families with stay-at-home wives have the same inflation-adjusted income as similar families did in the early 1970s. But the biggest reason is that the revolution has brought plenty of problems in its wake.

Production versus Reproduction

One obvious problem is that women's rising aspirations have not been fulfilled. They have been encouraged to climb onto the occupational ladder only to discover that the middle rungs are dominated by men and the upper rungs are out of reach. Only 2% of the bosses of Fortune 500 companies and five of those in the FTSE 100 stockmarket index are women. Women make up less than 13% of board members in America. The upper ranks of management consultancies and banks are dominated by men. In America and Britain, the typical full-time female worker earns only about 80% as much as the typical male.

This no doubt owes something to prejudice. But the biggest reason why women remain frustrated is more profound: many women are forced to choose between motherhood and careers. Childless women in corporate America earn almost as

much as men. Mothers with partners earn less and single mothers much less. The cost of motherhood is particularly steep for fast-track women. Traditionally "female" jobs such as teaching mix well with motherhood because wages do not rise much with experience and hours are relatively light. But at successful firms wages rise steeply and schedules are demanding. Future bosses are expected to have worked in several departments and countries. Professional-services firms have an up-or-out system which rewards the most dedicated with lucrative partnerships. The reason for the income gap may thus be the opposite of prejudice. It is that women are judged by exactly the same standards as men.

This Hobson's choice is imposing a high cost on both individuals and society. Many professional women reject motherhood entirely: in Switzerland 40% of them are childless. Others delay child-bearing for so long that they are forced into the arms of the booming fertility industry. The female drop-out rate from the most competitive professions represents a loss to collective investment in talent. A study of graduates of the University of Chicago's Booth School of Business by Marianne Bertrand and her colleagues found that, ten years after graduating, about half of the female MBAs who had chosen to have children remained in the labour force. It also leaves many former high-flyers frustrated. Another American study, this time of women who left work to have children, found that all but 7% of them wanted to return to work. Only 74% managed to return, and just 40% returned to full-time jobs.

Even well-off parents worry that they spend too little time with their children, thanks to crowded schedules and the ever-buzzing BlackBerry. For poorer parents, juggling the twin demands of work and child-rearing can be a nightmare. Child care eats a terrifying proportion of the family budget, and many childminders are untrained. But quitting work to look after the children can mean financial disaster. British children brought up in two-parent families where only one parent works are almost three times more likely to be poor than children with two parents at work.

A survey for the Children's Society, a British charity, found that 60% of parents agreed that "nowadays parents aren't able to spend enough time with their children". In a similar survey in America, 74% of parents said that they did not have enough time for their children. Nor does the problem disappear as children get older. In most countries schools finish early in the afternoon. In America they close down for two months in the summer. Only a few places—Denmark, Sweden and, to a lesser extent, France and Quebec—provide comprehensive systems of after-school care.

Different countries have adopted different solutions to the problem of combining work and parenthood. Some stress the importance of very young children spending time with their mothers. Austria, the Czech Republic, Finland and Hungary provide up to three years of paid leave for mothers. Germany has introduced a "parent's salary", or Elterngeld, to encourage mothers to stay at home. (The legislation was championed by a minister for women who has seven children.) Other countries put more emphasis on preschool education. New Zealand and the Nordic countries are particularly keen on getting women back to work and children into kindergartens. Britain, Germany, Japan, Switzerland and, above all, the Netherlands are keen on mothers working part-time. Others, such as the Czech Republic, Greece, Finland, Hungary, Portugal and South Korea, make little room for part-time work for women. The Scandinavian countries, particularly Iceland, have added a further wrinkle by increasing incentives for fathers to spend more time caring for their children.

The world's biggest economy has adopted an idiosyncratic approach. America provides no statutory paid leave for mothers and only 12 weeks unpaid. At least 145 countries provide paid sick leave. America allows only unpaid absence for serious family illness. America's public spending on family support is low by OECD standards. It spends only 0.5% of its GDP on public support for child care compared with 1.3% in France and 2.7% in Denmark.

It is difficult to evaluate the relative merits of these various arrangements. Different systems can produce similar results: anti-statist America has roughly the same proportion of children in kindergartens as statist Finland. Different systems have different faults. Sweden is not quite the paragon that its fans imagine, despite its family-friendly employment policies. Only 1.5% of senior managers are women, compared with 11% in America. Three-quarters of Swedish women work in the public sector; three-quarters of men work in the private sector. But there is evidence that America and Britain, the countries that combine high female employment with reluctance to involve the state in child care, serve their children especially poorly. A report by UNICEF in 2007 on children in rich countries found that America and Britain had some of the lowest scores for "well-being".

A Woman's World

The trend towards more women working is almost certain to continue. In the European Union, women have filled 6m of the 8m new jobs created since 2000. In America, three out of four people thrown out of work since the recession began are men; the female unemployment rate is 8.6%, against 11.2% for men. The Bureau of Labour Statistics calculates that women make up more than two-thirds of employees in ten of the 15 job categories likely to grow fastest in the next few years. By 2011, there will be 2.6m more women than men studying in American universities.

Women will also be the beneficiaries of the growing "war for talent". The combination of an ageing workforce and a more skill-dependent economy means that countries will have to make better use of their female populations. Goldman Sachs calculates that, leaving all other things equal, increasing women's participation in the labour market to male levels will boost GDP by 21% in Italy, 19% in Spain, 16% in Japan, 9% in America, France and Germany, and 8% in Britain.

The corporate world is doing ever more to address the loss of female talent and the difficulty of combining work with child care. Many elite companies are rethinking their promotion practices. Addleshaw Goddard, a law firm, has created the role of legal director as an alternative to partnerships for women who want to combine work and motherhood. Ernst &

Young and other accounting firms have increased their efforts to maintain connections with women who take time off to have children and then ease them back into work.

Home-working is increasingly fashionable. More than 90% of companies in Germany and Sweden allow flexible working. A growing number of firms are learning to divide the working week in new ways—judging staff on annual rather than weekly hours, allowing them to work nine days a fortnight, letting them come in early or late and allowing husbands and wives to share jobs. Almost half of Sun Microsystems's employees work at home or from nearby satellite offices. Raytheon, a maker of missile systems, allows workers every other Friday off to take care of family business, if they make up the hours on other days.

Companies are even rethinking the structure of careers, as people live and work longer. Barclays is one of many firms that allow five years' unpaid leave. John Lewis offers a six-month paid sabbatical to people who have been in the company for 25 years. Companies are allowing people to phase their retirement. Child-bearing years will thus make up a smaller proportion of women's potential working lives. Spells out of the labour force will become less a mark of female exceptionalism.

Faster change is likely as women exploit their economic power. Many talented women are already hopping off the corporate treadmill to form companies that better meet their needs. In the past decade, the number of privately owned companies started by women in America has increased twice as fast as the number owned by men. Women-owned companies employ more people than the largest 500 companies combined. Eden McCallum and Axiom Legal have applied a network model to their respective fields of management consultancy and legal services: network members work when it suits them and the companies use their scale to make sure that clients have their problems dealt with immediately.

Governments are also trying to adjust to the new world. Germany now has 1,600 schools where the day lasts until mid-afternoon. Some of the most popular American charter schools offer longer school days and shorter summer holidays.

But so far even the combination of public- and private-sector initiatives has only gone so far to deal with the problem. The children of poorer working mothers are the least likely to benefit from female-friendly companies. Millions of families still struggle with insufficient child-care facilities and a school day that bears no relationship to their working lives. The West will be struggling to cope with the social consequences of women's economic empowerment for many years to come.

Critical Thinking

1. Why have the changes occurred?
2. What are your expectations for the future?
3. How much has the work world changed to accommodate women's needs?

Create Central

www.mhhe.com/createcentral

Internet References

Sociosite
www.topsite.com/goto/sociosite.net

Socioweb
www.topsite.com/goto/socioweb.com

Sociology—Study Sociology Online
http://edu.learnsoc.org

Sociology Web Resources
www.mhhe.com/socscience/sociology/resources/index.htm

Article — Prepared by: Kurt Finsterbusch, *University of Maryland, College Park*

Free and Equal in Dignity and LGBT Rights

HILLARY RODHAM CLINTON

Learning Outcomes

After reading this article, you will be able to:

- Evaluate the significance of the Universal Declaration of Human Rights that the United Nations passed in 1948 without a negative vote.

- Understand the progress on human rights that has occurred since the declaration.

- Identify the critical issues that are involved in extending the declaration to LGBT equality.

Good evening, and let me express my deep honor and pleasure at being here. I want to thank Director General Tokayev and Ms. Wyden along with other ministers, ambassadors, excellencies, and UN partners. This weekend, we will celebrate Human Rights Day, the anniversary of one of the great accomplishments of the last century.

Beginning in 1947, delegates from six continents devoted themselves to drafting a declaration that would enshrine the fundamental rights and freedoms of people everywhere. In the aftermath of World War II, many nations pressed for a statement of this kind to help ensure that we would prevent future atrocities and protect the inherent humanity and dignity of all people. And so the delegates went to work. They discussed, they wrote, they revisited, revised, rewrote, for thousands of hours. And they incorporated suggestions and revisions from governments, organizations and individuals around the world.

At three o'clock in the morning on December 10th, 1948, after nearly two years of drafting and one last long night of debate, the president of the UN General Assembly called for a vote on the final text. Forty-eight nations voted in favor; eight abstained; none dissented. And the Universal Declaration of Human Rights was adopted. It proclaims a simple, powerful idea: All human beings are born free and equal in dignity and rights. And with the declaration, it was made clear that rights are not conferred by government; they are the birthright of all people. It does not matter what country we live in, who our leaders are, or even who we are. Because we are human, we therefore have rights. And because we have rights, governments are bound to protect them.

In the 63 years since the declaration was adopted, many nations have made great progress in making human rights a human reality. Step by step, barriers that once prevented people from enjoying the full measure of liberty, the full experience of dignity, and the full benefits of humanity have fallen away. In many places, racist laws have been repealed, legal and social practices that relegated women to second-class status have been abolished, the ability of religious minorities to practice their faith freely has been secured.

In most cases, this progress was not easily won. People fought and organized and campaigned in public squares and private spaces to change not only laws, but hearts and minds. And thanks to that work of generations, for millions of individuals whose lives were once narrowed by injustice, they are now able to live more freely and to participate more fully in the political, economic, and social lives of their communities.

Now, there is still, as you all know, much more to be done to secure that commitment, that reality, and progress for all people. Today, I want to talk about the work we have left to do to protect one group of people whose human rights are still denied in too many parts of the world today. In many ways, they are an invisible minority. They are arrested, beaten, terrorized, even executed. Many are treated with contempt and violence by their fellow citizens while authorities empowered to protect them look the other way or, too often, even join in the abuse. They are denied opportunities to work and learn, driven from their homes and countries, and forced to suppress or deny who they are to protect themselves from harm.

I am talking about gay, lesbian, bisexual, and transgender people, human beings born free and given bestowed equality and dignity, who have a right to claim that, which is now one of the remaining human rights challenges of our time. I speak about this subject knowing that my own country's record on human rights for gay people is far from perfect. Until 2003, it was still a crime in parts of our country. Many LGBT Americans have endured violence and harassment in their own lives, and for some, including many young people, bullying and exclusion are daily experiences. So we, like all nations, have more work to do to protect human rights at home.

Now, raising this issue, I know, is sensitive for many people and that the obstacles standing in the way of protecting the human rights of LGBT people rest on deeply held personal, political, cultural, and religious beliefs. So I come here before you with respect, understanding, and humility. Even though progress on this front is not easy, we cannot delay acting. So in that spirit, I want to talk about the difficult and important issues we must address together to reach a global consensus that recognizes the human rights of LGBT citizens everywhere.

The first issue goes to the heart of the matter. Some have suggested that gay rights and human rights are separate and distinct; but, in fact, they are one and the same. Now, of course, 60 years ago, the governments that drafted and passed the Universal Declaration of Human Rights were not thinking about how it applied to the LGBT community. They also weren't thinking about how it applied to indigenous people or children or people with disabilities or other marginalized groups. Yet in the past 60 years, we have come to recognize that members of these groups are entitled to the full measure of dignity and rights, because, like all people, they share a common humanity.

This recognition did not occur all at once. It evolved over time. And as it did, we understood that we were honoring rights that people always had, rather than creating new or special rights for them. Like being a woman, like being a racial, religious, tribal, or ethnic minority, being LGBT does not make you less human. And that is why gay rights are human rights, and human rights are gay rights.

It is violation of human rights when people are beaten or killed because of their sexual orientation, or because they do not conform to cultural norms about how men and women should look or behave. It is a violation of human rights when governments declare it illegal to be gay, or allow those who harm gay people to go unpunished. It is a violation of human rights when lesbian or transgendered women are subjected to so-called corrective rape, or forcibly subjected to hormone treatments, or when people are murdered after public calls for violence toward gays, or when they are forced to flee their nations and seek asylum in other lands to save their lives. And it is a violation of human rights when life-saving care is withheld from people because they are gay, or equal access to justice is denied to people because they are gay, or public spaces are out of bounds to people because they are gay. No matter what we look like, where we come from, or who we are, we are all equally entitled to our human rights and dignity.

The second issue is a question of whether homosexuality arises from a particular part of the world. Some seem to believe it is a Western phenomenon, and therefore people outside the West have grounds to reject it. Well, in reality, gay people are born into and belong to every society in the world. They are all ages, all races, all faiths; they are doctors and teachers, farmers and bankers, soldiers and athletes; and whether we know it, or whether we acknowledge it, they are our family, our friends, and our neighbors.

Being gay is not a Western invention; it is a human reality. And protecting the human rights of all people, gay or straight, is not something that only Western governments do. South Africa's constitution, written in the aftermath of Apartheid, protects the equality of all citizens, including gay people. In Colombia and Argentina, the rights of gays are also legally protected. In Nepal, the supreme court has ruled that equal rights apply to LGBT citizens. The Government of Mongolia has committed to pursue new legislation that will tackle anti-gay discrimination.

Now, some worry that protecting the human rights of the LGBT community is a luxury that only wealthy nations can afford. But in fact, in all countries, there are costs to not protecting these rights, in both gay and straight lives lost to disease and violence, and the silencing of voices and views that would strengthen communities, in ideas never pursued by entrepreneurs who happen to be gay. Costs are incurred whenever any group is treated as lesser or the other, whether they are women, racial, or religious minorities, or the LGBT. Former President Mogae of Botswana pointed out recently that for as long as LGBT people are kept in the shadows, there cannot be an effective public health program to tackle HIV and AIDS. Well, that holds true for other challenges as well.

The third, and perhaps most challenging, issue arises when people cite religious or cultural values as a reason to violate or not to protect the human rights of LGBT citizens. This is not unlike the justification offered for violent practices towards women like honor killings, widow burning, or female genital mutilation. Some people still defend those practices as part of a cultural tradition. But violence toward women isn't cultural; it's criminal. Likewise with slavery, what was once justified as sanctioned by God is now properly reviled as an unconscionable violation of human rights.

In each of these cases, we came to learn that no practice or tradition trumps the human rights that belong to all of us. And this holds true for inflicting violence on LGBT people, criminalizing their status or behavior, expelling them from their families and communities, or tacitly or explicitly accepting their killing.

Of course, it bears noting that rarely are cultural and religious traditions and teachings actually in conflict with the protection of human rights. Indeed, our religion and our culture are sources of compassion and inspiration toward our fellow human beings. It was not only those who've justified slavery who leaned on religion, it was also those who sought to abolish it. And let us keep in mind that our commitments to protect the freedom of religion and to defend the dignity of LGBT people emanate from a common source. For many of us, religious belief and practice is a vital source of meaning and identity, and fundamental to who we are as people. And likewise, for most of us, the bonds of love and family that we forge are also vital sources of meaning and identity. And caring for others is an expression of what it means to be fully human. It is because the human experience is universal that human rights are universal and cut across all religions and cultures.

The fourth issue is what history teaches us about how we make progress towards rights for all. Progress starts with honest discussion. Now, there are some who say and believe that all gay people are pedophiles, that homosexuality is a disease that can be caught or cured, or that gays recruit others to become gay. Well, these notions are simply not true. They are also unlikely to disappear if those who promote or accept them are dismissed out of hand rather than invited to share their fears and concerns. No one has ever abandoned a belief because he was forced to do so.

Universal human rights include freedom of expression and freedom of belief, even if our words or beliefs denigrate the humanity of others. Yet, while we are each free to believe whatever we choose, we cannot do whatever we choose, not in a world where we protect the human rights of all.

Reaching understanding of these issues takes more than speech. It does take a conversation. In fact, it takes a constellation of conversations in places big and small. And it takes a willingness to see stark differences in belief as a reason to begin the conversation, not to avoid it.

But progress comes from changes in laws. In many places, including my own country, legal protections have preceded, not followed, broader recognition of rights. Laws have a teaching effect. Laws that discriminate validate other kinds of discrimination. Laws that require equal protections reinforce the moral imperative of equality. And practically speaking, it is often the case that laws must change before fears about change dissipate.

Many in my country thought that President Truman was making a grave error when he ordered the racial desegregation of our military. They argued that it would undermine unit cohesion. And it wasn't until he went ahead and did it that we saw how it strengthened our social fabric in ways even the supporters of the policy could not foresee. Likewise, some worried in my country that the repeal of "Don't Ask, Don't Tell" would have a negative effect on our armed forces. Now, the Marine Corps Commandant, who was one of the strongest voices against the repeal, says that his concerns were unfounded and that the Marines have embraced the change.

Finally, progress comes from being willing to walk a mile in someone else's shoes. We need to ask ourselves, "How would it feel if it were a crime to love the person I love? How would it feel to be discriminated against for something about myself that I cannot change?" This challenge applies to all of us as we reflect upon deeply held beliefs, as we work to embrace tolerance and respect for the dignity of all persons, and as we engage humbly with those with whom we disagree in the hope of creating greater understanding.

A fifth and final question is how we do our part to bring the world to embrace human rights for all people including LGBT people. Yes, LGBT people must help lead this effort, as so many of you are. Their knowledge and experiences are invaluable and their courage inspirational. We know the names of brave LGBT activists who have literally given their lives for this cause, and there are many more whose names we will never know. But often those who are denied rights are least empowered to bring about the changes they seek. Acting alone, minorities can never achieve the majorities necessary for political change.

So when any part of humanity is sidelined, the rest of us cannot sit on the sidelines. Every time a barrier to progress has fallen, it has taken a cooperative effort from those on both sides of the barrier. In the fight for women's rights, the support of men remains crucial. The fight for racial equality has relied on contributions from people of all races. Combating Islamophobia or anti-Semitism is a task for people of all faiths. And the same is true with this struggle for equality.

Conversely, when we see denials and abuses of human rights and fail to act, that sends the message to those deniers and abusers

that they won't suffer any consequences for their actions, and so they carry on. But when we do act we send a powerful moral message. Right here in Geneva, the international community acted this year to strengthen a global consensus around the human rights of LGBT people. At the Human Rights Council in March, 85 countries from all regions supported a statement calling for an end to criminalization and violence against people because of their sexual orientation and gender identity.

At the following session of the Council in June, South Africa took the lead on a resolution about violence against LGBT people. The delegation from South Africa spoke eloquently about their own experience and struggle for human equality and its indivisibility. When the measure passed, it became the first-ever UN resolution recognizing the human rights of gay people worldwide. In the Organization of American States this year, the Inter-American Commission on Human Rights created a unit on the rights of LGBT people, a step toward what we hope will be the creation of a special rapporteur.

Now, we must go further and work here and in every region of the world to galvanize more support for the human rights of the LGBT community. To the leaders of those countries where people are jailed, beaten, or executed for being gay, I ask you to consider this: Leadership, by definition, means being out in front of your people when it is called for. It means standing up for the dignity of all your citizens and persuading your people to do the same. It also means ensuring that all citizens are treated as equals under your laws, because let me be clear—I am not saying that gay people can't or don't commit crimes. They can and they do, just like straight people. And when they do, they should be held accountable, but it should never be a crime to be gay.

And to people of all nations, I say supporting human rights is your responsibility too. The lives of gay people are shaped not only by laws, but by the treatment they receive every day from their families, from their neighbors. Eleanor Roosevelt, who did so much to advance human rights worldwide, said that these rights begin in the small places close to home—the streets where people live, the schools they attend, the factories, farms, and offices where they work. These places are your domain. The actions you take, the ideals that you advocate, can determine whether human rights flourish where you are.

And finally, to LGBT men and women worldwide, let me say this: Wherever you live and whatever the circumstances of your life, whether you are connected to a network of support or feel isolated and vulnerable, please know that you are not alone. People around the globe are working hard to support you and to bring an end to the injustices and dangers you face. That is certainly true for my country. And you have an ally in the United States of America and you have millions of friends among the American people.

The Obama Administration defends the human rights of LGBT people as part of our comprehensive human rights policy and as a priority of our foreign policy. In our embassies, our diplomats are raising concerns about specific cases and laws, and working with a range of partners to strengthen human rights protections for all. In Washington, we have created a task force at the State Department to support and coordinate this work.

And in the coming months, we will provide every embassy with a toolkit to help improve their efforts. And we have created a program that offers emergency support to defenders of human rights for LGBT people.

This morning, back in Washington, President Obama put into place the first U.S. Government strategy dedicated to combating human rights abuses against LGBT persons abroad. Building on efforts already underway at the State Department and across the government, the President has directed all U.S. Government agencies engaged overseas to combat the criminalization of LGBT status and conduct, to enhance efforts to protect vulnerable LGBT refugees and asylum seekers, to ensure that our foreign assistance promotes the protection of LGBT rights, to enlist international organizations in the fight against discrimination, and to respond swiftly to abuses against LGBT persons.

I am also pleased to announce that we are launching a new Global Equality Fund that will support the work of civil society organizations working on these issues around the world. This fund will help them record facts so they can target their advocacy, learn how to use the law as a tool, manage their budgets, train their staffs, and forge partnerships with women's organizations and other human rights groups. We have committed more than $3 million to start this fund, and we have hope that others will join us in supporting it.

The women and men who advocate for human rights for the LGBT community in hostile places, some of whom are here today with us, are brave and dedicated, and deserve all the help we can give them. We know the road ahead will not be easy. A great deal of work lies before us. But many of us have seen firsthand how quickly change can come. In our lifetimes, attitudes toward gay people in many places have been transformed. Many people, including myself, have experienced a deepening of our own convictions on this topic over the years, as we have devoted more thought to it, engaged in dialogues and debates, and established personal and professional relationships with people who are gay.

This evolution is evident in many places. To highlight one example, the Delhi High Court decriminalized homosexuality in India two years ago, writing, and I quote, "If there is one tenet that can be said to be an underlying theme of the Indian constitution, it is inclusiveness." There is little doubt in my mind that support for LGBT human rights will continue to climb. Because for many young people, this is simple: All people deserve to be treated with dignity and have their human rights respected, no matter who they are or whom they love.

There is a phrase that people in the United States invoke when urging others to support human rights: "Be on the right side of history." The story of the United States is the story of a nation that has repeatedly grappled with intolerance and inequality. We fought a brutal civil war over slavery. People from coast to coast joined in campaigns to recognize the rights of women, indigenous peoples, racial minorities, children, people with disabilities, immigrants, workers, and on and on. And the march toward equality and justice has continued. Those who advocate for expanding the circle of human rights were and are on the right side of history, and history honors them. Those who tried to constrict human rights were wrong, and history reflects that as well.

I know that the thoughts I've shared today involve questions on which opinions are still evolving. As it has happened so many times before, opinion will converge once again with the truth, the immutable truth, that all persons are created free and equal in dignity and rights. We are called once more to make real the words of the Universal Declaration. Let us answer that call. Let us be on the right side of history, for our people, our nations, and future generations, whose lives will be shaped by the work we do today. I come before you with great hope and confidence that no matter how long the road ahead, we will travel it successfully together. Thank you very much.

Critical Thinking

1. Do you agree with Hillary Clinton that the Universal Declaration of Human Rights should apply to LGBT people?

2. What actions does Clinton advocate at this time?

3. Where is the Obama Administration on this issue?

Create Central

www.mhhe.com/createcentral

Internet References

Sociosite
www.topsite.com/goto/sociosite.net

Socioweb
www.topsite.com/goto/socioweb.com

Sociology—Study Sociology Online
http://edu.learnsoc.org

Sociology Web Resources
www.mhhe.com/socscience/sociology/resources/index.htm

Clinton, Hillary Rodham. From speech delivered at Palais des Nations, Geneva, Switzerland, December 6, 2011.

Unit 5

Social Institutions: Issues, Crises, and Changes

UNIT

Prepared by: Kurt Finsterbusch, *University of Maryland, College Park*

Social Institutions: Issues, Crises, and Changes

Social institutions are the building blocks of social structure. They accomplish the important tasks of society—for example, regulation of reproduction, socialization of children, production and distribution of economic goods, law enforcement and social control, and organization of religion and other value systems. Social institutions are not rigid arrangements; they reflect changing social conditions. Institutions generally change slowly. At the present time, however, many of the social institutions in the United States and in many other parts of the world are in crisis and are undergoing rapid change. Eastern European countries are literally transforming their political and economic institutions. Economic institutions, such as stock markets, are becoming truly international, and when a major country experiences a recession, many other countries feel the effects. In the United States, major reform movements are active in political, economic, family, medical, and educational institutions.

Article   Prepared by: Kurt Finsterbusch, *University of Maryland, College Park*

The Rule of the Rich

BILL MOYERS

Learning Outcomes

After reading this article, you will be able to:

- Understand the considerable influence that the rich have over the American political system.

- Identify the many mechanisms utilized by the rich to influence the government.

- Try to discern what is necessary to counter the influence of the rich.

Howard Zinn helped us see how big change can start with small acts. He championed grassroots social change and famously chronicled its story as played out over the course of our nation's history. More, those stirring sagas have inspired and continue to inspire countless people to go out and make a difference. The last time we met, I told him that the stories in *A People's History of the United States* remind me of the fellow who turned the corner just as a big fight broke out down the block. Rushing up to an onlooker he shouted, "Is this a private fight, or can anyone get in it?" For Howard, democracy was one big public fight and everyone should plunge into it. That's the only way, he said, for everyday folks to get justice—by fighting for it.

So let's begin with some everyday folks.

When she heard the news, Connie Brasel cried like a baby. For years she had worked at minimum-wage jobs, until seventeen years ago, when she was hired by the Whirlpool refrigerator factory in Evansville, Indiana. She was making $18.44 an hour when Whirlpool announced in early 2010 that it was closing the operation and moving it to Mexico. She wept. I'm sure many of the other eleven hundred workers who lost their jobs wept, too; they had seen their ticket to the middle class snatched from their hands. The company defended its decision by claiming high costs, underused capacity, and the need to stay competitive. Those excuses didn't console Connie Brasel. "I was becoming part of something bigger than me," she told Steven Greenhouse of *The New York Times*. "Whirlpool was the best thing that ever happened to me."

She was not only sad, she was mad. "They didn't get world-class quality because they had the best managers. They got world-class quality because of the United States and because of their workers."

Among those workers were Natalie Ford, her husband, and her son; all three lost their jobs. "It's devastating," she told the *Times*. Her father had worked at Whirlpool before them. Now "there aren't any jobs here. How is this community going to survive?"

And what about the country? Between 2001 and 2008, about 40,000 U.S. manufacturing plants closed. Six million factory jobs have disappeared over the past dozen years, representing one in three manufacturing jobs. Natalie Ford said to the *Times* what many of us are wondering: "I don't know how without any good-paying jobs here in the United States people are going to pay for their health care, put their children through school."

In polite circles, among our political and financial classes, this is known as "the free market at work." No, it's "wage repression," and it's been happening in our country since around 1980. Economists Thomas Piketty and Emmanuel Saez have found that from 1950 through 1980, the share of all income in America going to everyone but the rich increased from 64 percent to 65 percent. Because the nation's economy was growing handsomely, the average income for nine out of ten Americans was growing, too: from $17,719 to $30,941. That's a 75 percent increase in income in constant 2008 dollars. But then it stopped. Since 1980 the economy has also continued to grow handsomely, but only a fraction at the top have benefited. The line flattens for the bottom 90 percent of Americans. Average income went from that $30,941 in 1980 to $31,244 in 2008. Think about that: the average income of Americans increased just $303 in twenty-eight years.

Another story in the *Times* caught my eye a few weeks after the one about Connie Brasel and Natalie Ford. The headline read: "Industries Find Surging Profits in Deeper Cuts." Nelson Schwartz reported that despite falling motorcycle sales, Harley-Davidson profits are soaring—with a second quarter profit of $71 million, more than triple what it earned the previous year. Yet Harley-Davidson has announced plans to cut 1,400 to 1,600 more jobs by the end of 2011—this on top of the 2,000 jobs cut in 2009.

The story noted: "This seeming contradiction—falling sales and rising profits—is one reason the mood on Wall Street is so much more buoyant than in households, where pessimism runs deep and unemployment shows few signs of easing."

There you see the two Americas: a buoyant Wall Street; a doleful Main Street. The Connie Brasels and Natalie Fords—left to sink or swim on their own. There were no bailouts for them.

Or, as the chief economist at Bank of America Merrill Lynch, Ethan Harris, told the *Times:* "There's no question that there is an income shift going on in the economy. Companies are squeezing their labor costs to build profits."

Yes, Virginia, there is a Santa Claus. But he's run off with all the toys.

Late in August, I clipped another story from *The Wall Street Journal.* Above an op-ed piece by Robert Frank the headline asked: "Do the Rich Need the Rest of America?" The author didn't seem ambivalent about the answer. He wrote that as stocks have boomed, "the wealthy bounced back. And while the Main Street economy" [where the Connie Brasels and Natalie Fords and most Americans live] "was wracked by high unemployment and the real-estate crash, the wealthy—whose financial fates were more tied to capital markets than jobs and houses—picked themselves up, brushed themselves off, and started buying luxury goods again."

Citing the work of Michael Lind at the Economic Growth Program of the New America Foundation, the article went on to describe how the super-rich earn their fortunes with overseas labor, selling to overseas consumers and managing financial transactions that have little to do with the rest of America, "while relying entirely or almost entirely on immigrant servants at one of several homes around the country."

So the answer to the question "Do the Rich Need the Rest of America?" is as stark as it is ominous: Many don't. As they form their own financial culture increasingly separated from the fate of everyone else, it is "hardly surprising," Frank and Lind concluded, "that so many of them should be so hostile to paying taxes to support the infrastructure and the social programs that help the majority of the American people."

When Howard came down to New York last December for what would be my last interview with him, I showed him this document published in the spring of 2005 by the Wall Street giant Citigroup, setting forth an "Equity Strategy" under the title (I'm not making this up) "Revisiting Plutonomy: The Rich Getting Richer."

Now, most people know what plutocracy is: the rule of the rich, political power controlled by the wealthy. Plutocracy is not an American word and wasn't meant to become an American phenomenon—some of our founders deplored what they called "the veneration of wealth." But plutocracy is here, and a pumped up Citigroup even boasted of coining a variation on the word—"plutonomy," which describes an economic system where the privileged few make sure the rich get richer and that government helps them do it. Five years ago, Citigroup decided the time had come to "bang the drum on plutonomy."

And bang they did. Here are some excerpts from the document "Revisiting Plutonomy":

"Asset booms, a rising profit share, and favorable treatment by market-friendly governments have allowed the rich to prosper . . . [and] take an increasing share of income and wealth over the last twenty years. . . . The top 10 percent, particularly the top 1 percent of the United States—the plutonomists in our parlance—have benefited disproportionately from the recent productivity surge in the U.S. . . . [and] from globalization and the productivity boom, at the relative expense of labor. . . . [And they] are likely to get even wealthier in the coming years. Because the dynamics of plutonomy are still intact."

I'll repeat that: *"The dynamics of plutonomy are still intact."*

That was the case before the Great Collapse of 2008, and it's the case today, two years after the catastrophe. But the plutonomists are doing just fine. Even better in some cases, thanks to our bailout of the big banks. (To see just how our system was rigged by the financial, political, and university elites, run, don't walk, to the theater nearest you showing Charles Ferguson's new film, *Inside Job.* Take a handkerchief because you'll weep for the republic.)

As for the rest of the country, listen to this summary in *The Economist*—no Marxist journal—of a study by Pew Research: "More than half of all workers today have experienced a spell of unemployment, taken a cut in pay or hours or been forced to go part-time. . . . Fewer than half of all adults expect their children to have a higher standard of living than theirs, and more than a quarter say it will be lower. For many Americans, the Great Recession has been the sharpest trauma since the Second World War, wiping out jobs, wealth, and hope itself."

Let that sink in: For millions of garden-variety Americans, the audacity of hope has been replaced by a paucity of hope.

Time for a confession. The legendary correspondent Edward R. Murrow told his generation of journalists that bias is OK as long as you don't try to hide it. Here is mine: Plutocracy and democracy don't mix. Plutocracy too long tolerated leaves democracy on the auction block, subject to the highest bidder.

Socrates said to understand a thing, you must first name it. The name for what's happening to our political system is corruption: a deep, systemic corruption. The former editor of *Harper's,* Roger D. Hodge, brilliantly dissects how democracy has gone on sale in America. Today, he says, voters still "matter," but only as raw material to be shaped by the actual form of political influence—money. Hodge's new book, *The Mendacity of Hope,* describes how America's founding generation especially feared the kind of corruption that occurs when the private ends of a narrow faction succeed in capturing the engines of government. James Madison and many of his contemporaries knew this kind of corruption could consume the republic. So they attempted to erect safeguards against it, hoping to prevent private and narrow personal interests from overriding those of the general public.

They failed. Hardly a century passed after the ringing propositions of 1776 before America was engulfed in the gross materialism and political corruption of the First Gilded Age, when Big Money bought the government right out from under the voters. In their magisterial work, *The Growth of the American Republic,* the historians Morison, Commager, and Leuchtenburg describe how in that era "privilege controlled politics," and "the purchase of votes, the corruption of election officials, the bribing of legislatures, the lobbying of special bills, and the flagrant disregard of laws" threatened the very foundations of the country.

As one of the plutocrats crowed: "We are rich. We own America. We got it, God knows how, but we intend to keep it."

And they have never given up. The Gilded Age returned with a vengeance in our time. It slipped in quietly at first, back in the early 1980s, when Ronald Reagan began a "massive decades-long transfer of national wealth to the rich."

As Roger Hodge makes clear, under Bill Clinton the transfer was even more dramatic, as the top 10 percent captured an ever-growing share of national income.

The trend continued under George W. Bush—those huge tax cuts for the rich, remember, which are now about to be extended because both parties have been bought off by the wealthy—and by 2007 the wealthiest 10 percent of Americans were taking in 50 percent of the national income.

Today, a fraction of people at the top earns more than the bottom 120 million Americans.

People say, "Come on, this is the way the world works."

No, it's the way the world is *made* to work.

This vast inequality is not the result of Adam Smith's invisible hand; it did not just happen; it was no accident.

As Hodge drives home, it is the result of a long series of policy decisions "about industry and trade, taxation and military spending, by flesh-and-blood humans sitting in concrete-and-steel buildings." And those policy decisions were paid for by the less than 1 percent who participate in our capitalist democracy by making political contributions.

Over the past thirty years, with the complicity of Republicans and Democrats alike, the plutocrats (or plutonomists, as Citigroup calls them) have used their vastly increased wealth to assure that government does their bidding. Looking back, it all seems so clear that it's amazing that we could have ignored the warning signs at the time.

Yet here we are at a moment, says the new chairman of Common Cause and former Labor Secretary Robert Reich, that "threatens American democracy: an unprecedented concentration of income and wealth at the top; a record amount of secret money flooding our democracy; and a public becoming increasingly angry and cynical about a government that's raising its taxes, reducing its services, and unable to get it back to work." We are losing our democracy, Reich says, to an entirely different system, one where political power derives from wealth.

Its ratification came in January 2010, when the five reactionary members of the Supreme Court ruled that corporations are "persons" with the right to speak during elections by funding ads like those now flooding the airwaves. It was the work of legal fabulists. Corporations are not people; they are legal fictions, creatures of the state, born not of the womb, not of flesh and blood. They're not permitted to vote. They don't bear arms (except for the nuclear bombs they can now drop on a Congressional race without anyone knowing where it came from). Yet thanks to five activist conservative judges, they have the privilege of "personhood" to "speak"—and not in their own voice, mind you, but as ventriloquists, through hired puppets.

Our government has been bought off. Welcome to the plutocracy.

Obviously, Howard Zinn would not have us leave it there. Defeat was never his counsel. Look at this headline from one of his articles he published in *The Progressive* prior to *Citizens United:* "It's Not Up to the Supreme Court." The Court was lost long ago, he said. Don't go there looking for justice: "The Constitution gave no rights to working people; no right to work less than twelve hours a day, no right to a living wage, no right to safe working conditions. Workers had to organize, go on strike, defy the law, the courts, the police, create a great movement which won the eight-hour day, and caused such commotion that Congress was forced to pass a minimum wage law, and Social Security, and unemployment insurance. . . . Those rights only come alive when citizens organize, protest, demonstrate, strike, boycott, rebel, and violate the law in order to uphold justice."

So what are we to do about Big Money in politics buying off democracy?

I can almost hear him throwing that question back at us: "What are we to do? ORGANIZE! Yes, organize—and don't count the costs."

Some people already are mobilizing. There's a rumbling in the land. All across the spectrum, people oppose the escalating power of money in politics. Fed-up Democrats. Disillusioned Republicans. Independents. Greens. Even tea partiers, once they wake up to realize they have been sucker-punched by their bankrollers who have no intention of sharing the wealth.

Veteran public interest groups like Common Cause and Public Citizen are aroused. There are the rising voices, from Web-based initiatives such as freespeechforpeople.org to grassroots initiatives such as Democracy Matters on campuses across the country. Moveon.org is looking for a million people to fight back in a many-pronged strategy to counter the Supreme Court decision.

In taking on Big Money, we're talking about something more than a single issue. We're talking about a broad-based coalition to restore American democracy—one that is trying to be smart about the nuts-and-bolts of building a coalition, remembering that it has a lot to do with human nature.

Some will want to march.

Some will want to petition.

Some will want to engage through the Web.

Some will want to go door-to-door: many gifts, but the same spirit. A fighting spirit.

As Howard Zinn would tell us: No fight, no fun, no results.

Let's be clear: Even with most Americans on our side, the odds are long. We learned long ago that power and privilege never give up anything without a struggle. Money fights hard, and it fights dirty. Think Karl Rove, the Chamber of Commerce, the Brothers Koch. And we may lose.

But hear out Baldemar Velasquez on this. He and his Farm Labor Organizing Committee took on the Campbell Soup Company—and won. They took on North Carolina growers—and won. And now they're taking on no less than R. J. Reynolds Tobacco and one of its principal financial sponsors, JPMorgan Chase.

"It's OK if it's impossible," Velasquez says. "It's OK! The object is not to win. The object is to do the right and good thing. If you decide not to do anything, because it's too hard or too impossible, then nothing will be done, and when you're on your deathbed, you're going to say, 'I wish I had done something.' But if you go and do the right thing NOW, and you do it long enough, good things will happen."

Shades of Howard Zinn!

Critical Thinking

1. The rich have great influence in all societies. What is Bill Moyers saying about the influence of the American rich that is beyond normal?

2. What specific government actions or nonactions have the rich achieved?

3. Is this a story of corruption? Why or why not?

Create Central

www.mhhe.com/createcentral

Internet References

Sociosite
www.topsite.com/goto/sociosite.net

Socioweb
www.topsite.com/goto/socioweb.com

Sociology—Study Sociology Online
http://edu.learnsoc.org

Sociology Web Resources
www.mhhe.com/socscience/sociology/resources/index.htm

BILL MOYERS is the veteran PBS broadcaster. This article is adapted from remarks he made on October 29, 2010, at Boston University as he inaugurated the Howard Zinn Lecture Series.

Article   Prepared by: Kurt Finsterbusch, *University of Maryland, College Park*

The Broken Contract

Inequality and American Decline

GEORGE PACKER

Learning Outcomes

After reading this article, you will be able to:

- Understand a number of specific failures of government actions.

- Evaluate the thesis that the failure of government is much greater than in the past.

- Assess the role of organized money in the failure of government.

Iraq, was one of those wars where people actually put on pounds. A few years ago, I was eating lunch with another reporter at an American-style greasy spoon in Baghdad's Green Zone. At a nearby table, a couple of American contractors were finishing off their burgers and fries. They were wearing the contractor's uniform: khakis, polo shirts, baseball caps, and Department of Defense identity badges in plastic pouches hanging from nylon lanyards around their necks. The man who had served their food might have been the only Iraqi they spoke with all day. The Green Zone was set up to make you feel that Iraq was a hallucination and you were actually in Normal, Illinois. This narcotizing effect seeped into the consciousness of every American who hunkered down and worked and partied behind its blast walls—the soldier and the civilian, the diplomat and the journalist, the important and the obscure. Hardly anyone stayed longer than a year; almost everyone went home with a collection of exaggerated war stories, making an effort to forget that they were leaving behind shoddy, unfinished projects and a country spiraling downward into civil war. As the two contractors got up and ambled out of the restaurant, my friend looked at me and said, "We're just not that good anymore."

The Iraq war was a kind of stress test applied to the American body politic. And every major system and organ failed the test: the executive and legislative branches, the military, the intelligence world, the for-profits, the nonprofits, the media. It turned out that we were not in good shape at all—without even realizing it. Americans just hadn't tried anything this hard in around half a century. It is easy, and completely justified,

to blame certain individuals for the Iraq tragedy. But over the years, I've become more concerned with failures that went beyond individuals, and beyond Iraq—concerned with the growing arteriosclerosis of American institutions. Iraq was not an exceptional case. It was a vivid symptom of a long-term trend, one that worsens year by year. The same ailments that led to the disastrous occupation were on full display in Washington this past summer, during the debt-ceiling debacle: ideological rigidity bordering on fanaticism, an indifference to facts, an inability to think beyond the short term, the dissolution of national interest into partisan advantage.

Was it ever any different? Is it really true that we're just not that good anymore? As a thought experiment, compare your life today with that of someone like you in 1978. Think of an educated, reasonably comfortable couple perched somewhere within the vast American middle class of that year. And think how much less pleasant their lives are than yours. The man is wearing a brown and gold polyester print shirt with a flared collar and oversize tortoiseshell glasses; she's got on a high-waisted, V-neck rayon dress and platform clogs. Their morning coffee is Maxwell House filter drip. They drive an AMC Pacer hatchback, with a nonfunctioning air conditioner and a tape deck that keeps eating their eight-tracks. When she wants to make something a little daring for dinner, she puts together a pasta primavera. They type their letters on an IBM Selectric, the new model with the corrective ribbon. There is only antenna television, and the biggest thing on is Laverne and Shirley. Long-distance phone calls cost a dollar a minute on weekends; air travel is prohibitively expensive. The city they live near is no longer a place where they spend much time: trash on the sidewalks, junkies on the corner, vandalized pay phones, half-deserted subway cars covered in graffiti.

By contemporary standards, life in 1978 was inconvenient, constrained, and ugly. Things were badly made and didn't work very well. Highly regulated industries, such as telecommunications and airlines, were costly and offered few choices. The industrial landscape was decaying, but the sleek information revolution had not yet emerged to take its place. Life before the Android, the Apple Store, FedEx, HBO, Twitter feeds, Whole Foods, Lipitor, air bags, the Emerging Markets Index Fund, and the pre-K Gifted and Talented Program prep course is not a world to which many of us would willingly return.

The surface of life has greatly improved, at least for educated, reasonably comfortable people—say, the top 20 percent, socioeconomically. Yet the deeper structures, the institutions that underpin a healthy democratic society, have fallen into a state of decadence. We have all the information in the universe at our fingertips, while our most basic problems go unsolved year after year: climate change, income inequality, wage stagnation, national debt, immigration, falling educational achievement, deteriorating infrastructure, declining news standards. All around, we see dazzling technological change, but no progress. Last year, a Wall Street company that few people have ever heard of dug an 800-mile trench under farms, rivers, and mountains between Chicago and New York and laid fiber-optic cable connecting the Chicago Mercantile Exchange and the New York Stock Exchange. This feat of infrastructure building, which cost $300 million, shaves three milliseconds off high-speed, high-volume automated trades—a big competitive advantage. But passenger trains between Chicago and New York run barely faster than they did in 1950, and the country no longer seems capable, at least politically, of building faster ones. Just ask people in Florida, Ohio, and Wisconsin, whose governors recently refused federal money for high-speed rail projects.

We can upgrade our iPhones, but we can't fix our roads and bridges. We invented broadband, but we can't extend it to 35 percent of the public. We can get 300 television channels on the iPad, but in the past decade 20 newspapers closed down all their foreign bureaus. We have touch-screen voting machines, but last year just 40 percent of registered voters turned out, and our political system is more polarized, more choked with its own bile, than at any time since the Civil War. There is nothing today like the personal destruction of the McCarthy era or the street fights of the 1960s. But in those periods, institutional forces still existed in politics, business, and the media that could hold the center together. It used to be called the establishment, and it no longer exists. Solving fundamental problems with a can-do practicality—the very thing the world used to associate with America, and that redeemed us from our vulgarity and arrogance—now seems beyond our reach.

The Unwritten Contract

Why and how did this happen? Those are hard questions. A roundabout way of answering them is to first ask, when did this start to happen? Any time frame has an element of arbitrariness, and also contains the beginning of a theory. Mine goes back to that shabby, forgettable year of 1978. It is surprising to say that in or around 1978, American life changed—and changed dramatically. It was, like this moment, a time of widespread pessimism—high inflation, high unemployment, high gas prices. And the country reacted to its sense of decline by moving away from the social arrangement that had been in place since the 1930s and 1940s.

What was that arrangement? It is sometimes called "the mixed economy"; the term I prefer is "middle-class democracy." It was an unwritten social contract among labor, business, and government—between the elites and the masses. It guaranteed that the benefits of the economic growth following World War II were distributed more widely, and with more shared prosperity, than at any time in human history. In the 1970s, corporate executives earned 40 times as much as their lowest-paid employees. (By 2007, the ratio was over 400 to 1.) Labor law and government policy kept the balance of power between workers and owners on an even keel, leading to a virtuous circle of higher wages and more economic stimulus. The tax code restricted the amount of wealth that could be accumulated in private hands and passed on from one generation to the next, thereby preventing the formation of an inherited plutocracy. The regulatory agencies were strong enough to prevent the kind of speculative bubbles that now occur every five years or so: between the Great Depression and the Reagan era there was not a single systemwide financial crisis, which is why recessions during those decades were far milder than they have since become. Commercial banking was a stable, boring business. (In movies from the 1940s and 1950s, bankers are dull, solid pillars of the community.) Investment banking, cordoned off by the iron wall of the Glass-Steagall Act, was a closed world of private partnerships in which rich men carefully weighed their risks because they were playing with their own money. Partly as a result of this shared prosperity, political participation reached an all-time high during the postwar years (with the exception of those, such as black Americans in the South, who were still denied access to the ballot box).

At the same time, the country's elites were playing a role that today is almost unrecognizable. They actually saw themselves as custodians of national institutions and interests. The heads of banks, corporations, universities, law firms, foundations, and media companies were neither more nor less venal, meretricious, and greedy than their counterparts today. But they rose to the top in a culture that put a brake on these traits and certainly did not glorify them. Organizations such as the Council on Foreign Relations, the Committee for Economic Development, and the Ford Foundation did not act on behalf of a single, highly privileged point of view—that of the rich. Rather, they rose above the country's conflicting interests and tried to unite them into an overarching idea of the national interest. Business leaders who had fought the New Deal as vehemently as the U.S. Chamber of Commerce is now fighting health-care and financial reform later came to accept Social Security and labor unions, did not stand in the way of Medicare, and supported other pieces of Lyndon Johnson's Great Society. They saw this legislation as contributing to the social peace that ensured a productive economy. In 1964, Johnson created the National Commission on Technology, Automation, and Economic Progress to study the effects of these coming changes on the work force. The commission included two labor leaders, two corporate leaders, the civil rights activist Whitney Young, and the sociologist Daniel Bell. Two years later, they came out with their recommendations: a guaranteed annual income and a massive job-training program. This is how elites once behaved: as if they had actual responsibilities.

Of course, the consensus of the postwar years contained plenty of injustice. If you were black or female, it made very little room for you. It could be stifling and conformist, authoritarian and intrusive. Yet those years also offered the means of redressing the very wrongs they contained: for example, strong government, enlightened business, and activist labor were important bulwarks of the civil rights movement. Nostalgia is a useless emotion. Like any era, the postwar years had their costs. But from where we stand in 2011, they look pretty good.

The Rise of Organized Money

Two things happened to this social arrangement. The first was the 1960s. The story is familiar: youth rebellion and revolution, a ferocious backlash now known as the culture wars, and a permanent change in American manners and morals. Far more than political Utopia, the legacy of the 1960s was personal liberation. Some conservatives argue that the social revolution of the 1960s and 1970s prepared the way for the economic revolution of the 1980s, that Abbie Hoffman and Ronald Reagan were both about freedom. But Woodstock was not enough to blow apart the middle-class democracy that had benefited tens of millions of Americans. The Nixon and Ford presidencies actually extended it. In his 2001 book, *The Paradox of American Democracy,* John Judis notes that in the three decades between 1933 and 1966, the federal government created 11 regulatory agencies to protect consumers, workers, and investors. In the five years between 1970 and 1975, it established another 12, including the Environmental Protection Agency, the Occupational Safety and Health Administration, and the Consumer Product Safety Commission. Richard Nixon was a closet liberal, and today he would be to the left of Senator Olympia Snowe, the moderate Republican.

The second thing that happened was the economic slowdown of the 1970s, brought on by "stagflation" and the oil shock. It eroded Americans' paychecks and what was left of their confidence in the federal government after Vietnam, Watergate, and the disorder of the 1960s. It also alarmed the country's business leaders, and they turned their alarm into action. They became convinced that capitalism itself was under attack by the likes of Rachel Carson and Ralph Nader, and they organized themselves into lobbying groups and think tanks that quickly became familiar and powerful players in U.S. politics: the Business Roundtable, the Heritage Foundation, and others. Their budgets and influence soon rivaled those of the older, consensus-minded groups, such as the Brookings Institution. By the mid-1970s, chief executives had stopped believing that they had an obligation to act as disinterested stewards of the national economy. They became a special interest; the interest they represented was their own. The neoconservative writer Irving Kristol played a key role in focusing executives' minds on this narrower and more urgent agenda. He told them, "Corporate philanthropy should not be, and cannot be, disinterested."

Among the non-disinterested spending that corporations began to engage in, none was more interested than lobbying.

Lobbying has existed since the beginning of the republic, but it was a sleepy, bourbon-and-cigars practice until the mid- to late 1970s. In 1971, there were only 145 businesses represented by registered lobbyists in Washington; by 1982, there were 2,445. In 1974, there were just over 600 registered political action committees, which raised $12.5 million that year; in 1982, there were 3,371, which raised $83 million. In 1974, a total of $77 million was spent on the midterm elections; in 1982, it was $343 million. Not all this lobbying and campaign spending was done by corporations, but they did more and did it better than anyone else. And they got results.

These changes were wrought not only by conservative thinkers and their allies in the business class. Among those responsible were the high-minded liberals, the McGovernites and Watergate reformers, who created the open primary, clean election laws, and "outsider" political campaigns that relied heavily on television advertising. In theory, those reforms opened up the political system to previously disenfranchised voters by getting rid of the smoke-filled room, the party caucus, and the urban boss—exchanging Richard Daley for Jesse Jackson. In practice, what replaced the old politics was not a more egalitarian new politics. Instead, as the parties lost their coherence and authority, they were overtaken by grass-roots politics of a new type, driven by direct mail, beholden to special interest groups, and funded by lobbyists. The electorate was transformed from coalitions of different blocs—labor, small business, the farm vote—to an atomized nation of television watchers. Politicians began to focus their energies on big dollars for big ad buys. As things turned out, this did not set them free to do the people's work: as Senator Tom Harkin, the Iowa Democrat, once told me, he and his colleagues spend half their free time raising money.

This is a story about the perverse effects of democratization. Getting rid of elites, or watching them surrender their moral authority, did not necessarily empower ordinary people. Once Walter Reuther of the United Auto Workers and Walter Wriston of Citicorp stopped sitting together on Commissions to Make the World a Better Place and started paying lobbyists to fight for their separate interests in Congress, the balance of power tilted heavily toward business. Thirty years later, who has done better by the government—the United Auto Workers or Citicorp?

In 1978, all these trends came to a head. That year, three reform bills were brought up for a vote in Congress. One of the bills was to establish a new office of consumer representation, giving the public a consumer advocate in the federal bureaucracy. A second bill proposed modestly increasing the capital gains tax and getting rid of the three-Martini-lunch deduction. A third sought to make it harder for employers to circumvent labor laws and block union organizing. These bills had bipartisan backing in Congress; they were introduced at the very end of the era when bipartisanship was routine, when necessary and important legislation had support from both parties. The Democrats controlled the White House and both houses of Congress, and the bills were popular with the public. And yet, one by one, each bill went down in defeat. (Eventually, the tax bill passed, but only after it was changed; instead of raising the capital gains tax rate, the final bill cut it nearly in half.)

How and why this happened are explored in Jacob Hacker and Paul Pierson's recent book, *Winner-Take-All Politics*. Their explanation, in two words, is organized money. Business groups launched a lobbying assault the likes of which Washington had never seen, and when it was all over, the next era in American life had begun. At the end of the year, the midterm elections saw the Republicans gain 15 seats in the House and three in the Senate. The numbers were less impressive than the character of the new members who came to Washington. They were not politicians looking to get along with colleagues and solve problems by passing legislation. Rather, they were movement conservatives who were hostile to the very idea of government. Among them was a history professor from Georgia named Newt Gingrich. The Reagan revolution began in 1978.

Organized money did not foist these far-reaching changes on an unsuspecting public. In the late 1970s, popular anger at government was running high, and President Jimmy Carter was a perfect target. This was not a case of false consciousness; it was a case of a fed-up public. Two years later, Reagan came to power in a landslide. The public wanted him.

But that archetypal 1978 couple with the AMC Pacer was not voting to see its share of the economic pie drastically reduced over the next 30 years. They were not fed up with how little of the national income went to the top one percent or how unfairly progressive the tax code was. They did not want to dismantle government programs such as Social Security and Medicare, which had brought economic security to the middle class. They were not voting to weaken government itself, as long as it defended their interests. But for the next three decades, the dominant political faction pursued these goals as though they were what most Americans wanted. Organized money and the conservative movement seized that moment back in 1978 to begin a massive, generation-long transfer of wealth to the richest Americans. The transfer continued in good economic times and bad, under Democratic presidents and Republican, when Democrats controlled Congress and when Republicans did. For the Democrats, too, went begging to Wall Street and corporate America, because that's where the money was. They accepted the perfectly legal bribes just as eagerly as Republicans, and when the moment came, some of them voted almost as obediently. In 2007, when Congress was considering closing a loophole in the law that allowed hedge fund managers to pay a tax rate of 15 percent on most of their earnings—considerably less than their secretaries—it was New York's Democratic senator Charles Schumer who rushed to their defense and made sure it did not happen. As Bob Dole, then a Republican senator, said back in 1982, "Poor people don't make campaign contributions."

Mocking the American Promise

This inequality is the ill that underlies all the others. Like an odorless gas, it pervades every corner of the United States and saps the strength of the country's democracy. But it seems impossible to find the source and shut it off. For years, certain politicians and pundits denied that it even existed. But the evidence became overwhelming. Between 1979 and 2006, middle-class Americans saw their annual incomes after taxes increase by 21 percent (adjusted for inflation). The poorest Americans saw their incomes rise by only 11 percent. The top one percent, meanwhile, saw their incomes increase by 256 percent. This almost tripled their share of the national income, up to 23 percent, the highest level since 1928. The graph that shows their share over time looks almost flat under Kennedy, Johnson, Nixon, Ford, and Carter, followed by continual spikes under Reagan, the elder Bush, Clinton, and the younger Bush.

Some argue that this inequality was an unavoidable result of deeper shifts: global competition, cheap goods made in China, technological changes. Although those factors played a part, they have not been decisive. In Europe, where the same changes took place, inequality has remained much lower than in the United States. The decisive factor has been politics and public policy: tax rates, spending choices, labor laws, regulations, campaign finance rules. Book after book by economists and other scholars over the past few years has presented an airtight case: over the past three decades, the government has consistently favored the rich. This is the source of the problem: our leaders, our institutions.

But even more fundamental than public policy is the long-term transformation of the manners and morals of American elites—what they became willing to do that they would not have done, or even thought about doing, before. Political changes precipitated, and in turn were aided by, deeper changes in norms of responsibility and self-restraint. In 1978, it might have been economically feasible and perfectly legal for an executive to award himself a multimillion-dollar bonus while shedding 40 percent of his work force and requiring the survivors to take annual furloughs without pay. But no executive would have wanted the shame and outrage that would have followed—any more than an executive today would want to be quoted using a racial slur or photographed with a paid escort. These days, it is hard to open a newspaper without reading stories about grotesque overcompensation at the top and widespread hardship below. Getting rid of a taboo is easier than establishing one, and once a prohibition erodes, it can never be restored in quite the same way. As Leo Tolstoy wrote, "There are no conditions of life to which a man cannot get accustomed, especially if he sees them accepted by everyone around him."

The persistence of this trend toward greater inequality over the past 30 years suggests a kind of feedback loop that cannot be broken by the usual political means. The more wealth accumulates in a few hands at the top, the more influence and favor the well-connected rich acquire, which makes it easier for them and their political allies to cast off restraint without paying a social price. That, in turn, frees them up to amass more money, until cause and effect become impossible to distinguish. Nothing seems to slow this process down—not wars, not technology, not a recession, not a historic election. Perhaps, out of a well-founded fear that the country is coming apart at the seams, the wealthy and their political allies will finally have to rein themselves in, and, for example, start thinking about their taxes less like Stephen Schwarzman and more like Warren Buffett.

In the meantime, inequality will continue to mock the American promise of opportunity for all. Inequality creates a lopsided economy, which leaves the rich with so much money that they can binge on speculation, and leaves the middle class without enough money to buy the things they think they deserve, which leads them to borrow and go into debt. These were among the long-term causes of the financial crisis and the Great Recession. Inequality hardens society into a class system, imprisoning people in the circumstances of their birth—a rebuke to the very idea of the American dream. Inequality divides us from one another in schools, in neighborhoods, at work, on airplanes, in hospitals, in what we eat, in the condition of our bodies, in what we think, in our children's futures, in how we die. Inequality makes it harder to imagine the lives of others—which is one reason why the fate of over 14 million more or less permanently unemployed Americans leaves so little impression in the country's political and media capitals. Inequality corrodes trust among fellow citizens, making it seem as if the game is rigged. Inequality provokes a generalized anger that finds targets where it can—immigrants, foreign countries, American elites, government in all forms—and it rewards demagogues while discrediting reformers. Inequality saps the will to conceive of ambitious solutions to large collective problems, because those problems no longer seem very collective. Inequality undermines democracy.

Critical Thinking

1. How has the American institutional structure declined?
2. A thesis of this article is that the social contract between labor, business, and government is now broken, which hurts American effectiveness. Evaluate this thesis.
3. How can the poor have sufficient power to offset the extreme imbalance of power favoring the rich?

Create Central

www.mhhe.com/createcentral

Internet References

Sociosite
www.topsite.com/goto/sociosite.net
Socioweb
www.topsite.com/goto/socioweb.com
Sociology—Study Sociology Online
http://edu.learnsoc.org
Sociology Web Resources
www.mhhe.com/socscience/sociology/resources/index.htm

GEORGE PACKER is a staff writer at *The New Yorker.* This essay is adapted from a Joanna Jackson Goldman Memorial Lecture on American Civilization and Government that he delivered earlier this year at the New York Public Library's Cullman Center for Scholars & Writers.

Article

Prepared by: Kurt Finsterbusch, *University of Maryland, College Park*

The Withering of the Affluent Society

Though Americans see upward mobility as their birthright, that assumption faces growing challenges, with consequences not just for the size of our wallets but for the tenor of our politics.

Robert J. Samuelson

Learning Outcomes

After reading this article, you will be able to:

- Understand the many factors that will have long-term impacts on the American economy.
- Use lessons from the past to help interpret America's economic future.
- Consider how the intergenerational inequity will affect America's prospects.

The future of affluence is not what it used to be. Americans have long believed—it's part of our national character—that our economic well-being will constantly increase. We see ourselves as a striving, inventive, and pragmatic people destined for higher living standards. History is a continuum of progress, from Robert Fulton's steamboat to Henry Ford's assembly line to Bill Gates' software. Every generation will live better than its predecessors.

Well, maybe not.

For millions of younger Americans—say, those 40 and under—living better than their parents is a pipe dream. They won't. The threat to their hopes does *not* arise from an impending collapse of technological gains of the sort epitomized by the creations of Fulton, Ford, and Gates. These advances will almost certainly continue, and per capita income—the average for all Americans and a conventional indicator of living standards—will climb. Statistically, American progress will resume. The Great Recession will be a bump, not a dead end.

The trouble is that many of these gains will bypass the young. The increases that might have fattened their paychecks will be siphoned off to satisfy other groups and other needs. Today's young workers will have to finance Social Security and Medicare for a rapidly growing cohort of older Americans. Through higher premiums for employer-provided health insurance, they will subsidize care for others. Through higher taxes and fees, they will pay to repair aging infrastructure (roads, bridges, water systems) and to support squeezed public services, from schools to police.

The hit to their disposable incomes would matter less if the young were major beneficiaries of the resultant spending. In some cases—outlays for infrastructure and local services—they may be. But these are exceptions. By 2025 Social Security and Medicare will simply reroute income from the nearly four-fifths of the population that will be under 65 to the older one-fifth. And health care spending at all age levels is notoriously skewed: Ten percent of patients account for 65 percent of medical costs, reports the Kaiser Family Foundation. Although insurance provides peace of mind, the money still goes from young to old: Average health spending for those 45 to 64 is triple that for those 18 to 24.

The living standards of younger Americans will almost certainly suffer in comparison to those of their parents in a second crucial way. Our notion of economic progress is tied to financial security, but the young will have less of it. What good are higher incomes if they're abruptly revoked? Though it wasn't a second Great Depression, the Great Recession was a close call, shattering faith that modern economic policies made broad collapses impossible. Except for the savage 1980–82 slump, post-World War II recessions had been modest. Only minorities of Americans had suffered. By contrast, the Great Recession hurt almost everyone, through high unemployment, widespread home foreclosures, huge wealth losses in stocks and real estate—and fears of worse. A 2012 Gallup poll found that 68 percent of Americans knew someone who had lost a job.

The prospect of downward mobility is not just dispiriting. It assails the whole post–World War II faith in prosperity. Beginning in the 1950s, commentators celebrated the onrush of abundance as marking a new era in human progress. In his 1958 bestseller *The Affluent Society*, Harvard economist John Kenneth Galbraith announced the arrival of a "great and unprecedented affluence" that had eradicated the historical "poverty of the masses."

Economic growth became a secular religion that was its own reward. Perhaps its chief virtue was that it dampened class conflict. In *The Great Leap: The Past Twenty-Five Years in America* (1966), John Brooks observed, "The middle class was enlarging itself and ever encroaching on the two extremes"—the very rich and the very poor. Business and labor could afford to reconcile because both could now share the fruits of expanding production. We could afford more spending on public services (education, health, environmental protection, culture) without depressing private incomes. Indeed, that was Galbraith's main theme: Our prosperity could and should support both.

To be sure, there were crises of faith, moments when economic progress seemed delayed or doomed. The longest lapse occurred in the 1970s, when double-digit inflation spawned pessimism and frequent recessions, culminating in the 1980–82 downturn. Monthly unemployment peaked at 10.8 percent. But after Federal Reserve chairman Paul Volcker and President Ronald Reagan took steps to suppress high inflation, faith returned.

Now, it's again imperiled. A 2011 Gallup poll found that 55 percent of Americans didn't think their children would live as well as they did, the highest rate ever. We may face a crimped and contentious future.

Let's be clear: The prospect is not national impoverishment; it is of relative deprivation. Even if disposable per capita incomes fell 10 percent—an extreme outcome—Americans would remain wealthy by any historical standard. Such a change would entail a decline in the annual disposable income from $37,000 to $33,300 (in 2011 inflation-adjusted dollars), probably over many years. People might adjust in ways that barely affected daily routines. They might live in slightly smaller houses, drive more fuel-efficient vehicles, or eat out a bit less. These are inconveniences, not tragedies.

But popular expectations would be dashed. Even assuming a full recovery from the Great Recession—possible, though not certain—the resulting prosperity will be qualified by greater competition for scarce economic resources. Massive federal budget deficits are only the most conspicuous sign of a society that has promised itself more than it can afford. To resurrect a familiar metaphor: A more slowly growing economic pie will face more claimants for slices. Some will receive bigger slices, others smaller.

Generally speaking, there are two types of economic mobility, though they're often confused. The first is intergenerational mobility (also called "relative mobility"). It involves children moving up or down the economic ladder from their parents' position—do they rise to the top, stay where they started, or fall toward the bottom? Call the second type "national" mobility (specialists refer to it as "absolute mobility"). It concerns whether or not most members of each succeeding generation live better than their predecessors. If they do, then the whole society can be upwardly mobile even if all children occupy the same position relative to others as their parents on the social ladder. To take an obvious example, the poorest third of Americans lived much better in 1980 than in 1930.

In the United States, both types of mobility abound. For starters, birth is not fate. Americans do not automatically match their parents' position on the economic ladder. A report by the Pew Economic Mobility Project finds that 61 percent of children born to parents in the richest fifth of Americans fall from that stratum, while 58 percent of children born in the poorest fifth rise above to a higher stratum. There's not much movement from the very bottom to the very top. Only six percent of children make that journey. But in between, there's much shifting.

Similarly, economic growth since World War II has allowed most Americans to live better than their parents did—even if they haven't moved up the economic ladder. In the first two postwar decades, household incomes roughly doubled. Despite slower growth since then, about two-thirds of today's Americans have higher incomes than their parents at a similar age, Pew finds. Even this understates the extent of the achievement, because some of those who lost ground still have relatively high incomes. They're children of well-to-do families who don't match their parents' status, but their fall has been modest. Among the poorest fifth of Americans, about four-fifths have incomes higher than their parents'.

Both types of mobility have contributed to America's success. Although studies suggest that intergenerational mobility—again, children moving up or down the economic ladder—is greater in some other countries, the United States has enough of it to foster the bedrock belief that striving and talent are rewarded. That is important because societies in which economic status is rigid discriminate against individual ability and effort and discourage parents from striving to help their children succeed. As for national (or "absolute") mobility, it affects social peace and satisfaction, because intergenerational mobility is a zero-sum game. For everyone who climbs the ladder into a higher stratum, someone else must fall down into a lower one. By contrast, a rising tide does lift all boats.

Even if the United States fully recovers from the Great Recession, Americans will endure greater competition for scarce economic resources.

But there's a rub: Upward national mobility requires strong economic growth—and U.S. growth is weakening. Growth comes from two sources: more labor (more workers or longer hours) and improved efficiency (or labor productivity, measured in output per hour). Unfortunately, slower labor force expansion virtually guarantees a decline in overall U.S. economic growth.

As economist Brink Lindsey of the Kauffman Foundation notes, two powerful trends boosted labor force growth for many years: the influx of baby boomers from the late 1960s to the mid-1980s, and the flood of married women into jobs starting in the late 1950s. Both trends have ended. Baby boomers are retiring; the oldest ones, born in 1946, turned 65 in 2011. And women's participation ebbed a decade ago, well before the recession, with some women deciding to stay home or retire early. (From 1960 to 1999, the labor force participation rate of women 16 and over rose from 38 percent to 60 percent; in 2011, it was 58 percent.)

As a result of these trends, the number of new workers barely exceeds the number of those retiring. Barring major pleasant surprises, the slower labor force increases reduce projections of overall economic growth from a postwar average of slightly more than three percent to slightly more than two percent, as the table below shows. (The table shows "potential" economic growth under assumed conditions of "full employment," but actual results are also affected by business cycles.)

U.S. ECONOMIC GROWTH, 1950–2040

	1950–2001	2002–2011	2012–2022	2023–2040
Annual GDP growth (%) due to:				
Labor force increases	1.5	0.8	0.7	0.5
Productivity increases	1.8	1.4	1.7	1.7
Total annual growth	**3.3**	**2.3**	**2.3**	**2.2**

Note: Some numbers do not add due to rounding.
Sources: Congressional Budget Office, Social Security Administration

Ideally, we would raise productivity to offset slower labor force growth. Realistically, we don't know how to do this. What creates higher productivity is a murky mixture of new technologies, industry organization, government policies, management competence, worker abilities, and market pressures. Economists don't fully understand the process and can't manipulate it. Future rates of productivity growth could as easily fall as rise. In the table, the assumed annual gains average 1.7 percent, near the post–World War II rate of 1.8 percent. But gains might be two percent, one percent, or who knows what. Large deficits and higher taxes may crowd out investment or discourage risk taking, slowing productivity increases. That would further trim future economic growth, making it even harder for the young to achieve upward mobility.

It's already hard enough. The mounting number of retirees increases pressure to move money from workers to the elderly. Consider that in 1960 the worker-to-retiree ratio was 5:1; in 2010 it was 3:1, and the projection for 2025 is nearly 2:1. At the federal level, the pressures stem from higher spending on Social Security, Medicare, and Medicaid. At the state and local levels, they stem from Medicaid (states pay about 40 percent of its costs) and pensions for government workers. In *The Predictable Surprise: The Unraveling of the U.S. Retirement System* (2012), Sylvester Schieber, an actuary and former chairman of the Social Security Advisory Board, estimates that state and local public employee pensions are 20 to 25 percent underfunded.

Higher taxes to pay for Social Security and Medicare will undermine after-tax wages. So will mounting employer costs for health insurance and pensions; these expenses limit what companies would otherwise pay in wage increases. Schieber estimates that all these factors could absorb two-thirds of compensation growth from 2015 to 2030. Other studies reach similar conclusions. Economist David Auerbach and physician Arthur Kellermann, both of the Rand Corporation, find that 80 percent of median-family income gains from 1999 to 2009 went to higher health spending in the form of employer-paid premiums, out-of-pocket costs, and taxes. And these studies don't count the cost of infrastructure repair.

The future of today's young has been heavily mortgaged. The grimmest prospect is a death spiral for the welfare state. That could happen if we continue to pay for promised benefits by increasing taxes or deficits, further retarding economic growth and thus spurring still more tax and deficit increases to sustain benefits. But to all of these unsettling possibilities,

there's a ritualistic, upbeat response: We shall overcome. We're a can-do people. The U.S. economy adapts to change. It creates new technologies and industries. Its long-term resilience is incontestable. As Vice President Joseph Biden once put it, "No one's ever made money betting against America."

Unfortunately, that isn't true. Many people have made money betting against America: those who sold stocks in August 1929 or sold the dollar in the late 1970s, and those who bet against the U.S. mortgage market in 2006. The list goes on. It's true that over long stretches—decades—the U.S. economy has generated higher living standards for most citizens. But even this truth is selective. Banking panics occurred regularly in the 1800s. In the mid- to late 19th century, disease and poor diets lowered living standards of urban workers. Then came the Great Depression, the Great Inflation, and now the Great Recession.

So: America is not entitled to economic success. What actually happens depends on private markets and public policies. To be sure, the future is not etched in stone. Uncertainties abound, as any prediction must acknowledge. Here are three caveats.

First, forecasts of the future as an extension of the present are suspect. Unforeseen events—for good and ill—intervene. History is littered with false prophets. Consider Harvard economist Alvin Hansen (1887–1975). In 1938, when unemployment was still 19 percent, he sought to explain why the U.S. economy couldn't shake the Depression. His answer was "secular stagnation." There was no engine of expansion. Slower population growth meant fewer new consumers and less reason for businesses to invest. Technology was not advancing, dampening investment in new industry. And decades earlier the "frontier" had effectively ceased to exist, so there was no longer any spending on new settlements to boost the economy.

It was all plausible—and wrong. After World War II, the baby boom created a population explosion. Countless technologies spawned new industries in television, aviation, synthetic fibers, and plastics, to name a few. And there was a new frontier to settle—suburbia.

The second caveat is that economic progress may be overrated. Younger Americans may be less obsessed with material goods as the be all and end all of a satisfying life. Moreover, many Americans will enjoy rising incomes over their lifetimes, reflecting experience and seniority. In 2009, for example, the median income of working men aged 45 to 54 was 40 percent higher than for their counterparts aged 25 to 34. Viewing their own lives, most Americans might feel upwardly mobile. The difference would be that tomorrow's 45-year-olds might have less than today's.

Finally, we are not helpless. We might mitigate the forces that assail a broad-based affluence. Just because health spending hasn't been tamed in the past doesn't mean it won't be tamed in the future. As society ages, Americans may recognize that longer life expectancies justify longer working lives and that wealthier retirees deserve fewer (or no) subsidies from less affluent younger workers. That could lead to steps that would reduce the burdens of the old on the young.

Though the future will doubtlessly differ from how anyone now imagines it, the trends fostering downward mobility are insistent, because they are rooted in demographics, politics, and global economics.

We are at a symbolic turning point. The coincidence of the Great Recession with baby boomers' retirements marks the eclipse of the post–World War II social compact, formed in the 1950s and '60s. That arrangement promised that business cycles would be mild, because economic policy could moderate booms and busts. Technological change would be gradual, because dominant firms such as General Electric, AT&T, and General Motors controlled it and had a stake in gradual change. Large institutions were mostly benign. Major corporations provided career jobs and generous fringe benefits (health insurance, pensions) for most of their workers. There were reciprocal loyalties and obligations between employee and employer. Greater wealth enabled government to create a safety net for the old, the disabled, and the poor.

The props underlying this unspoken compact have been weakening since 1980. Technological changes are no longer gradual; they're abrupt and disruptive, driven largely by computer hardware and software companies, or Web-based enterprises such as Google and Facebook. Career jobs still exist but are dwindling in number. The reciprocal loyalties between workers and their employers have weakened. The promise of overall economic stability seems hollow. The fundamental lesson of the 2007–09 financial crisis is that economists overestimated their ability to prevent calamitous boom-bust cycles. Globalization has increased economic complexity faster than economists' capacity to keep up. The social safety net—actually, the welfare state—is popular, but huge government deficits put its affordability in doubt.

The premise of the post–World War II affluent society, that we were or would soon become so rich that we could afford almost anything, was never true, but we often acted as if it were. We avoided unpleasant choices, especially in government, accepting routine federal budget deficits (46 out of 51 years since 1961). Now, limits are painfully evident. There are more promises than can be fulfilled. Meeting all of government's spending commitments would require higher, broad-based taxes, which both liberals and conservatives reject, or perpetually large deficits, which both parties consider unsustainable and undesirable.

What looms is a future of more distributional struggles between young and old, rich and poor, different regions, and many interest groups. Each will defend subsidies, work to avoid tax increases, and maneuver for regulatory advantage.

The role of economic growth in advanced nations is less to make people richer than to reduce conflict. If most people feel that they're "getting ahead," they're less resentful of others who are doing better or hold different views. "Periods of economic expansion in America and elsewhere, during which most citizens had reason to be optimistic, have also witnessed greater openness, tolerance, and democracy," writes Harvard economist Benjamin Friedman in *The Moral Consequences of Economic Growth* (2005). If, however, people fall behind—or fear they will—they become more resentful. Until the Great Recession, three decades of growing economic inequality had inspired little popular backlash. This changed after unemployment rose. The Tea Party and Occupy Wall Street movements reflect the fallout of feared downward mobility.

Lower economic growth will have broad consequences. Already, defense spending is headed toward claiming the lowest share of GDP since 1940. In effect, the welfare state is defeating the Pentagon. Some will cheer, others complain. Either way, America's global role will change.

The prospect of downward mobility could discourage younger Americans from marrying and having families—a development that would accelerate America's aging. Although people marry and have children for many reasons, their economic outlook is an important influence. Low-income men are not prime candidates for marriage. Birthrates collapsed in the 1930s because families worried that they could not support new offspring. It is surely no coincidence that in the wake of the Great Recession the number of marriages fell five percent in 2010 and births three percent.

As it is, the generations are in an undeclared war. Americans in their late forties, fifties, and sixties believe that the contract made with them should be kept. They want their Social Security and Medicare benefits. They are angry when what they thought were career jobs are unexpectedly terminated; corporate buyouts and firings weren't part of the bargain. Meanwhile, their children and grandchildren are befuddled and frustrated. Their unemployment rates are high, and their wage levels—compared to those of the past—are low. Yet they feel guilty advocating trims to Social Security and Medicare, even when the transfers go from the struggling young to the comfortable old.

The Affluent Society was more a state of mind than an explicit economic target or threshold level of income. It announced the arrival of an era when traditional economic concerns were being overwhelmed by a seemingly unstoppable flood of abundance. Prosperity was a panacea. We could afford a decent society as well as a wealthy society. Many traditional social, political, and economic choices could, with a little patience, be evaded. There was enough for almost everything. We have been, in historian David Potter's apt phrase, a "people of plenty." What happens when there is less plenty than we expected? We are about to find out.

Critical Thinking

1. Why does Samuelson believe that America will not recover to strong growth but only to slow growth?
2. Are you optimistic or pessimistic about the future of the American economy?
3. Would political compromise and collaboration fix some of the worst economic problems?

Create Central

www.mhhe.com/createcentral

Internet References

Sociosite
www.topsite.com/goto/sociosite.net

Socioweb
www.topsite.com/goto/socioweb.com

Sociology—Study Sociology Online
http://edu.learnsoc.org

Sociology Web Resources
www.mhhe.com/socscience/sociology/resources/index.htm

ROBERT J. SAMUELSON, a columnist for *The Washington Post,* is the author most recently of *The Great Inflation and Its Aftermath: The Past and Future of American Affluence* (2008).

Samuelson, Robert J. From *The Wilson Quarterly*, Summer 2012, pp. 42–47. Copyright © 2012 by Robert J. Samuelson. Reprinted by permission of the author. Samuelson writes a column on the political economy for the *Washington Post*, and is the author of the book, *The Great Inflation and Its Aftermath: the Past and Future of American Affluence (2008).*

Article   Prepared by: Kurt Finsterbusch, *University of Maryland, College Park*

Hard at Work in the Jobless Future

JAMES H. LEE

Learning Outcomes

After reading this article, you will be able to:

- Consider how automation and innovation that produce so many economic benefits could also produce very negative outcomes.

- Understand how important work is for peoples' self-respect, purpose, and functioning.

- Contemplate how the relations between the haves and the have-nots would change with very high unemployment.

Futurists have long been following the impacts of automation on jobs—not just in manufacturing, but also increasingly in white-collar work. Those in financial services, for example, are being lost to software algorithms, intelligent computers, and robotics.

Terms used for this phenomenon include "off-peopling" and "othersourcing." As Jared Weiner of Weiner, Edrich, Brown recently observed, "Those jobs are not going to return—they can be done more efficiently and error-free by intelligent software."

In the investment business (in which I work), we are seeing the replacement of financial analysts with quantitative analytic systems, and floor traders with trading algorithms. Mutual funds and traditional portfolio managers now compete against ETFs (exchange-traded funds), many of which offer completely automated strategies.

Industries that undergo this transformation don't disappear, but the number of jobs that they support changes drastically. Consider the business of farming, which employed half the population in the early 1900s but now provides just 3% of all jobs. The United States is still a huge exporter of food; it is simply a far more efficient food producer now in terms of total output per farm worker.

In an ideal world, jobs would be plentiful, competitive, and pay well. Most job opportunities have two of these qualities but not all three.

Medicine, law, and finance are jobs that are both competitive and pay well. Retail, hospitality, and personal services are competitive but pay low wages. Unions often ensure that jobs pay well and are plentiful, only to later find that those jobs and related industries are no longer competitive.

Since 1970, manufacturing jobs as a percentage of total employment have declined from a quarter of payrolls to less than 10%. Some of this decline is from outsourcing, some is a result of othersourcing. Those looking for a rebound in manufacturing jobs will likely be disappointed. These jobs will probably not be replaced—not in the United States and possibly not overseas, either.

This is all a part of the transition toward a postindustrial economy.

Jeff Dachis, Internet consulting legend and founder of Razorfish, coined the phrase "everything that can be digital, will be." To the extent that the world becomes more digital, it will also become more global. To the extent that the economy remains physical, business may become more local.

The question is, what is the future of work, and what can we do about it? Here are some ideas.

The Future of Work: Emerging Trends

Work will always be about finding what other people want and need, and then creating practical solutions to fulfill those desires. Our basic assumptions about how work gets done are what's changing. It's less about having a fixed location and schedule and more about thoughtful and engaged activity. Increasingly, this inspiration can happen anytime, anyplace.

Jobs are disappearing, but there's still a future for work. An investment manager looks at how automation and information technology are changing the economic landscape and forcing workers to forge new career paths beyond outdated ideas about permanent employment.

There is a blurring of distinctions among work, play, and professional development. The ways that we measure productivity will be less focused on time spent and more about the value of the ideas and the quality of the output. People are also going to have a much better awareness of when good work is being done.

The old model of work provided an enormous level of predictability. In previous eras, people had a sense of job security and knew how much they would earn on a monthly basis. This gave people a certain sense of confidence in their ability to maintain large amounts of debt. The consumer economy thrived on this system for more than half a century. Location-based and formal jobs will continue to exist, of course, but these will become smaller slices of the overall economy.

The new trends for the workplace have significantly less built-in certainty. We will all need to rethink, redefine, and broaden our sources of economic security. To the extent that people are developing a broader range of skills, we will also become more resilient and capable of adapting to change.

Finally, we can expect that people will redefine what they truly need in a physical sense and find better ways of fulfilling their needs. This involves sharing and making smarter use of the assets we already have. Businesses are doing the same.

The outcome could be an economy that balances the needs between economic efficiency and human values.

Multitasking Careers

In *Escape from Cubicle Nation* (Berkley Trade, 2010), career coach Pamela Slim encourages corporate employees to start a "side hustle" to try out new business ideas. She also recommends having a side hustle as a backup plan in the event of job loss. This strategy is not just for corporate types, and Slim says that "it can also be a great backup for small business owners affected by shifting markets and slow sales."

She says that an ideal side hustle is money-making activity that is doable, enjoyable, can generate quick cash flow, and does not require significant investment. Examples that she includes are businesses such as Web design, massage, tax preparation, photography, and personal training.

The new norm is for people to maintain and develop skill sets in multiple simultaneous careers. In this environment, the ability to learn is something of a survival skill. Education never stops, and the line between working and learning becomes increasingly blurred.

After getting her PhD in gastrointestinal medicine, Helen Samson Mullen spent years working for a pharmaceutical company—first as a medical researcher and then as an independent consultant. More recently, she has been getting certifications for her career transition as a life coach. Clinical project management is now her "side hustle" to bring in cash flow while she builds her coaching business. Meanwhile, she's also writing a book and manages her own Web site. Even with so many things happening at once, Helen told me that "life is so much less crazy now than it was when I was consulting. I was always searching for life balance and now feel like I'm moving into harmony." Her husband, Rob, is managing some interesting career shifts of his own, and is making a lateral move from a 22-year career in pharmaceuticals to starting his own insurance agency with State Farm.

Fixed hours, fixed location, and fixed jobs are quickly becoming a thing of the past for many industries, as opportunities become more fluid and transient. The 40-hour workweek is becoming less relevant as we see more subcontractors, temps, freelancers, and self-employed. The U.S. Government Accountability Office estimates that these "contingent workers" now make up a third of the workforce. Uncertain economics make long-term employment contracts less realistic, while improvements in communications make it easier to subcontract even complex jobs to knowledge workers who log in from airports, home offices, and coffee shops.

Results-Only Workplace Environments

Imagine an office where meetings are optional. Nobody talks about how many hours they worked last week. People have an unlimited amount of vacation and paid time off. Work is done anytime and anywhere, based entirely on individual needs and preferences. Finally, employees at all levels are encouraged to stop doing anything that is a waste of their time, their customers' time, or the company's time.

There is a catch: Quality work needs to be completed on schedule and within budget.

Sound like a radical utopia? These are all basic principles of the Results Only Work Environment (ROWE), as pioneered by Cali Ressler and Jody Thompson while they were human resource managers for Best Buy.

It's "management by objective" taken to a whole new level, Ressler and Thompson write in their book, *Why Work Sucks and How to Fix It* (Portfolio, 2008).

Best Buy's headquarters was one of the first offices to implement the ROWE a little over five years ago, according to Ressler and Thompson. The movement is small, but growing. The Gap Outlet, Valspar, and a number of Minneapolis-based municipal departments have implemented the strategy. Today, 10,000 employees now work in some form of ROWE.

Employees don't even know if they are working fewer hours (they no longer count them), but firms that have adopted the practice have often shown significant improvements in productivity.

"Thanks to ROWE, people at Best Buy are happier with their lives and their work," Ressler and Thompson write in their book. "The company has benefited, too, with increases in productivity averaging 35% and sharp decreases in voluntary turnover rates, as much as 90% in some divisions."

Interestingly enough, the process tends to reveal workers who do not produce results, causing involuntary terminations to creep upward. ROWE managers learn how to treat their employees like responsible grown-ups. There is no time tracking or micromanagement.

"The funny thing is that once employees experience a ROWE they don't want to work any other way," they write. "So employees give back. They get smarter about their work because they want to make sure they get results. They know that if they can deliver results then in exchange they will get trust and control over their time."

Co-Working

There are now more alternatives to either working at home alone or being part of a much larger office. Co-working spaces are shared work facilities where people can get together in an officelike environment while telecommuting or starting up new businesses.

"We provide space and opportunity for people that don't have it," Wes Garnett, founder of The coIN Loft, a co-working space in Wilmington, Delaware, told me.

Getting office space in the traditional sense can be an expensive proposition—with multiyear leases, renovation costs, monthly utilities. "For $200 [a month], you can have access to presentation facilities, a conference room, and a dedicated place to work." And coIN Loft offers day rates for people with less-frequent space needs.

According to Garnett, more people are going to co-working spaces as "community centers for people with ideas and entrepreneurial inclinations." He explains that co-working spaces provide a physical proximity that allows people to develop natural networks and exchange ideas on projects.

"We all know that we're happier and more productive together, than alone" is the motto for nearby Independents Hall in Philadelphia.

Co-working visas enable people to choose from among 200 locations across the United States and in three dozen other countries.

Silicon Colleagues

Expert systems such as IBM's Watson are now "smarter" than real people—at least on the game show *Jeopardy*. It was a moment in television history when Watson decimated previous human champions Ken Jennings and Brad Rutter on trivia questions, which included categories such as "Chicks Dig Me."

IBM's Watson is a software-based knowledge system with unusually robust voice recognition. IBM has stated that its initial markets for the technology are health care, financial services, and customer relations. In the beginning, these systems will work side-by-side with human agents, whispering in their ear to prompt them with appropriate questions and answers that they might not have considered otherwise. In the next decade, they may replace people altogether in jobs that require simple requests for information.

"It's a way for America to get back its call centers," futurist Garry Golden told me. He sees such expert systems reaching the workplace in the next two to three years.

Opting Out

A changing economy is causing people to rethink their priorities. In a recent survey by Ogilvy and Mather, 76% of respondents reported that they would rather spend more time with their families than make more money.

Similarly, the Associated Press has reported that less than half of all Americans say they are happy with their jobs.

Given the stresses of the modern workplace, it is not surprising that more people are simply "opting out" of the workforce. Since 1998, there has been a slight decline in the labor force participation rate—about 5% for men and 3% for women. This trend may accelerate once extensions to unemployment benefits expire. Some of these people are joining the DIY movement, and others are becoming homesteaders.

A shift back toward one-income households can happen when the costs of taxes, commuting, and child care consume a large portion of earnings. People who opt out are not considered unemployed, as they are no longer actively looking for paid work. Their focus often reflects a shift in values toward other activities, such as raising kids, volunteer work, or living simply. This type of lifestyle is often precarious and carries risks, two factors that can be mitigated through public policy that extends the social safety net to better cover informal working as well as formal employment. But this way of life also carries rewards and is becoming a more and more attractive option for millions of people.

The Future of Work, Personified

Justin Caggiano is a laid-back rock-climbing guide whom my wife and I met during our last vacation in the red canyons of Moab, Utah. He's also been guiding rafters, climbers, and hikers for the past six years.

We watched Justin scramble up the side of a hundred-foot natural wall called The Ice Cream Parlor, a nearby climbing destination that earned its name from keeping shaded and cool in the morning despite the surrounding desert. His wiry frame allowed him to navigate the canyon cliffs and set up the safety ropes in a fraction of the time that it took us to make the same climb later that day.

Justin's rock-climbing skills easily translated into work as an arborist during the off-season, climbing up trees and then cutting them from the top down to prevent damage to nearby buildings. Since graduating from college six years ago, he has also worked as an artisanal baker, a carpenter, and a house painter. This makes him something of a down-to-earth renaissance man.

His advice is "to be as flexible as you can—and work your tail off."

It's an itinerant lifestyle for Justin, who frequently changes his location based on the season, work, and nearby climbing opportunities. Rather than committing to a single employer, he pieces together jobs wherever he can find them. His easygoing personality enables him to connect with people and find new opportunities when they become available.

In the winter, he planned to stay with a friend who is building a house, trading help with carpentry and wiring in exchange for free rent. He's been living on a shoestring for a while now, putting away money every year. Longer term, he'd like to develop all of the skills that he needs to build his own home and then pay for land and materials entirely with savings from his bank account. He plans to grow fruit trees and become somewhat self-sufficient. After that time, he says, "I'll work when I'm needed, and live the debt-free, low-cost lifestyle when I'm older."

Our concept of work is getting reworked. A career used to be a ladder of opportunities within a single company. For the postwar generation, the concept of "lifetime employment" was a realistic expectation. My father worked for 40 years at DuPont as a research scientist and spent almost all of that time at a sprawling complex called the Experimental Station. Most of my friends' parents had similar careers. Over time, they were gradually promoted and moved up the corporate ladder. At best, it was a steady progression. At worst, they found their careers stuck in neutral.

The baby boomers had a somewhat different career trajectory. They still managed to have a single career, but it more closely resembled a lattice than a ladder. After working for an employer for five to 10 years, they might find a better opportunity elsewhere and continue their climb. The successful ones cultivated networks at related businesses and continually found better opportunities for themselves.

The career path for younger generations more closely resembles a patchwork quilt, as people attempt to stitch together multiple jobs into something that is flexible and works for them. In today's environment, they sometimes can't find a single job that is big enough to cover all of their expenses, so, like Justin, they find themselves working multiple jobs simultaneously. Some of these jobs might match and be complementary to existing skills, while others may be completely unrelated.

The future of work is less secure and less stable than it was. For many of us, our notions of employment were formed by the labor environment of the later twentieth century. But the reality of jobless working may be more in line with our values. If we can build support systems to benefit workers, wherever they are and whether they be formally employed or not, then we may be able to view the changes sweeping across society as opportunities to return to a fuller, more genuine, and more honest way of life.

Justin's lesson is applicable to all of us; there's a difference between earning a living and making a life.

Justin Caggiano, a rock climber who shows how flexibility and hard work can lead to success even without a steady job.

Critical Thinking

1. What does Lee mean by the "jobless future"?
2. What will happen in America if unemployment rates are very high for a long time?
3. If many workers are redundant, how should the work world be reorganized?

Create Central

www.mhhe.com/createcentral

Internet References

Sociosite
www.topsite.com/goto/sociosite.net

Socioweb
www.topsite.com/goto/socioweb.com

Sociology—Study Sociology Online
http://edu.learnsoc.org

Sociology Web Resources
www.mhhe.com/socscience/sociology/resources/index.htm

JAMES H. LEE is an investment manager in Wilmington, Delaware, and a blogger for *THE FUTURIST* magazine.

Article   Prepared by: Kurt Finsterbusch, *University of Maryland, College Park*

The Case for Less

Is abundance really the solution to our problems?

TIM WU

Learning Outcomes

After reading this article, you will be able to:

- Appreciate the blessings of abundance but also appreciate the benefits of some constraints.

- Evaluate whether abundance makes us insatiable and causes the loss of some of our self-control.

- See the danger of excessive consumption that drives indebtedness and materialism but be able to distinguish appropriate consumption.

"The future is better than you think" is the message of Peter Diamandis's and Steven Kotler's book *Abundance: The Future Is Better Than You Think.* Despite a flat economy and intractable environmental problems, Diamandis and his journalist co-author are deeply optimistic about humanity's prospects. "Technology," they say, "has the potential to significantly raise the basic standards of living for every man, woman, and child on the planet. . . . Abundance for all is actually within our grasp."

This is a lively book, and it provides an interesting, if uncritical, survey of developments across a range of technologies. We find Craig Venter, the man who sequenced the human genome, sailing around the world looking for algae that can be engineered to emit jet fuel. We explore "vertical farms," which extend the methods perfected by pot growers to entire buildings full of crops. (Imagine Manhattan growing corn.) And in their section on "the almighty stem cell," the authors suggest a future in which the replacing of our organs is not dissimilar to installing a new muffler.

But Diamandis, a space entrepreneur and the co-founder of "Singularity University," is ultimately more interested in our attitude toward the future than in scientific details. He fears that humanity is biologically wired to be pessimistic, and that it therefore cannot appreciate the capacity of "exponential technologies" (those that improve at an exponential rate) to solve humanity's problems. By 2035, Diamandis claims, most of humanity's problems can be solved: we can reach "an end to most of what ails us." Those who doubt the truth of such a proposition are the avatars of "moaning pessimism," who suffer from cognitive defects that prevent them from seeing the truth. The "linear brain," Diamandis says, cannot "comprehend our exponential rate of progress."

A book that preaches the "good news" of humanity's redemption in 2035 may bring to mind more explicitly religious works. Skeptics may call it religion for geeks, where exponential technologies replace Yahweh as the Great Provider. Others may dismiss the book as a species-wide extrapolation from *The Power of Positive Thinking,* where cynicism is humanity's downfall.

But the book is not so easily discounted, for it accurately reflects an important tradition that has driven American technologists since the time of Henry Ford, if not earlier. *Abundance* pretends to be contrarian, and it once might have been, but today it mainly reaffirms a view of society already deeply embedded in much of America's technological elite, especially in Silicon Valley.

That view is simple to state. Humanity's fundamental problem comes down to scarcity—not having enough of what we need and want. We need food, water, new shoes, new gadgets, and so on, and we suffer when we do not have them. That problem can and will be solved by technology, or—at an individual level—by buying or otherwise gaining access to the objects of our desires. Once our needs are met, we can all live happily ever after. As Diamandis puts it, we must imagine "a world where everyone's days are spent dreaming and doing, not scrapping and scraping."

Optimism is a useful motivational tool, and I see no reason to argue with Diamandis about the benefits of maintaining a sunny disposition. I also agree with both Diamandis and the *New Testament* that we may worry about the future more than necessary. Still, all this does not eliminate the need to ask whether the abundance program that Diamandis prescribes is actually right for humanity.

The unhappy irony is that Diamandis prescribes a program of "more" exactly at a point when a century of similar projects have begun to turn on us. To be fair, his ideas are most pertinent to the poorer parts of the world, where many suffer terribly from a lack of the basics. But in the rich and semi-rich parts of the world, it is a different story. There we are starting to see just what happens when we reach surplus levels across many categories of human desire, and it isn't pretty. The unfortunate fact is that extreme abundance—like extreme scarcity, but in different ways—can make humans miserable. Where the abundance project has been truly successful, it has created a new host of problems that are now hitting humanity.

The worldwide obesity epidemic is our most obvious example of this "flip" from problems of scarcity to problems of surplus. Even a few decades ago, the idea of fatness as a public health problem would have seemed ridiculous. Yes, there have always been fat people, but as the scholar Benjamin Caballero writes, as late as the 1930s most nations still just wanted larger citizens. "The military and economic might of countries," he observes, "was critically dependent on the body size and strength of their young generations, from which soldiers and workers were drawn."

Today the statistics on obesity are so outrageous that they seem almost unbelievable. The Centers for Disease Control find that 69 percent of American adults are overweight, and half that number obese or extremely obese. The suffering caused by extreme or morbid obesity is horrifying. Millions of people around the world (nearly seven million in the United States) have trouble moving, and may often stop breathing during sleep, and are prone to ghastly skin infections within the folds of fat, and may be unable to have sex because of hormonal imbalances or because the flab just gets in the way. While no one wants to starve, it is actually hard to say whether it is worse to be malnourished or extremely obese.

There is no single cause for obesity, but the sine qua non for it is plenty of cheap, high-calorie foods. And such foods, of course, are the byproduct of our marvelous technologies of abundance, many of them celebrated in Diamandis's book. They are the byproducts of the "Green Revolution," brilliant techniques in industrial farming and the genetic modification of crops. We have achieved abundance in food, and it is killing us.

Consider another problem with no precise historical equivalent: "information overload." For most of history, humans have mainly been in a state of information scarcity. During the War of 1812, between Britain and the United States, hundreds of soldiers died during the battle of New Orleans because no one had yet heard that the war was over. People died for no reason other than want of good information. But today we sometimes have too much information, and phrases such as "Internet addiction" describe people who are literally unable to stop consuming information even though it is destroying their lives. Consider the case of a Hawaii man named Craig Smallwood who, in 2010, sued the developer of an online game named *Lineage II* for failing to warn him of its addictive qualities. Claiming that he played twenty thousand hours over five years (more than ten hours a day), Smallwood said that the game left him "unable to function independently in usual daily activities."

That is a bizarre extreme, of course; but many of us suffer from milder versions of information overload. Nicolas Carr, in

The Shallows, made a persuasive case that the excessive availability of information has begun to re-program our brains, creating serious issues for memory and attention span. Where people were once bored, we now face too many entertainment choices, creating a strange misery aptly termed "the paradox of choice" by the psychologist Barry Schwartz. We have achieved the information abundance that our ancestors craved, and it is driving us insane.

Scarce credit—the inability of individuals to borrow money—has long been regarded by economists as among the principal obstacles to economic growth. Hence the "credit revolution" of the twentieth century—a series of inventions that made credit abundant and easily available not just to institutions but also to any individual consumer. Fannie Mae was a clever invention of the 1930s, designed to make it easier for banks to lend money to people who wanted to buy homes. The last century yielded an amazing range of new credit technologies that we now take for granted, such as credit cards, electronic payment systems, and the securitization of mortgages. These inventions, until recent years, managed at long last to make enormous amounts of personal credit available to nearly everyone.

Abundant credit is surely a blessing and essential to economic growth. Yet anyone who reads a newspaper cannot fail to be aware of the systemic downsides. Americans were once known as thrifty; today, personal debt is a leading source of misery. There are more than 1.1 billion credit cards in the United States, and a survey last year suggested that 24 percent of Americans have not just more debt, but more credit card debt, than savings. The amount of household debt held in the United States is about $11.3 trillion, comparable to the amount of government debt held by the public, $12 trillion. The result is that, despite greater actual wealth than ever before, and more access to credit, it is not uncommon for Americans to feel desperate and poor, like the indebted servitors of centuries past.

Those are the personal consequences. At a wider level, a century of technological abundance has failed in its promise to solve problems of disparity, and has actually exacerbated inequalities. While it cannot be denied that the inventions of the last half-century have done much to increase the size of the pie, they have also done much less to distribute it, particularly since the 1970s. The mathematics of more means that the potential for relative disparity has increased. Those with less do have more than before—but relative disparity, or feeling much poorer than others, is a different kind of problem. More of everything has simply made possible disparity on a different scale.

None of this should be taken to downplay the triumphs of the great abundance project of the last century. In the rich parts of the world, most do not fear starvation or a lack of the basics, for perhaps the first time in human history. That is nothing to overlook. Yet it has also many side effects and unintended consequences that we are just beginning to understand fully. If the old world of scarcity yielded a mass population that was hungry, bored, and impoverished, our current surpluses lead to a population that is fat, in debt, overwhelmed, and swamped with too much stuff.

This very idea that too much of what we want can be a bad thing is hard to accept. It seems like a problem that is nice to have: surely we would rather have too much than too little. The miserable in Dickens's times—malnourished, impoverished, overworked—had the right to blame social conditions and demand change. But in today's richer world, if you are overweight, in debt, and overwhelmed, there is no one to blame but yourself. Go on a diet, stop watching cable, and pay off your credit card—that's the answer. In short, we think of scarcity problems as real, and surplus problems as matters of self-control.

That may account for the current popularity of books designed to help readers control themselves. The most interesting among them is *Willpower: Rediscovering the Greatest Human Strength,* by Roy Baumeister and John Tierney, which was explicitly written as a response to the challenges of our times. "People feel overwhelmed because there are more temptations than ever," Baumeister and Tierney argue. "You can put off any job by checking e-mail or Facebook, surfing gossip sites, or playing a video game," not to mention the lure of "alcohol, tobacco, Cinnabons, and cocktail waitresses."

Willpower offers observations, backed by scientific studies, that cannot fail to be fascinating to anyone who has ever wondered where the last hour went. The authors suggest that one's willpower is less an abstraction and more like an actual muscle that must be trained and can fail. The book's most profound sections describe a phenomenon that they call "ego depletion," a state of mental exhaustion where bad decisions are made. It turns out that being forced to make constant decisions is what causes ego depletion. So if willpower is a muscle, making too many decisions in one day is the equivalent of blowing out your hamstrings with too many squats.

The best advice that the authors of *Willpower* offer is this: yes, you can improve your powers of self-control, but don't expect too much. Rather, they recommend avoiding situations that cause ego-depletion altogether. And here is where we find the link between *Abundance* and *Willpower.*

Over the last century, mainly through the abundance project, we have created a world where avoiding constant decisions is nearly impossible. We have created environments that are designed to destroy our powers of self-control by creating constant choices among abundant options. The path of least resistance leads to a pile of debt, a fat body, and an enormous cable bill; strenuous daily efforts are required to avoid that fate. The result is a negative feedback loop: we have more than ever, and therefore need more self-control than ever, but the abundance we've created destroys our ability to resist. It is a setup that Sisyphus might have actually envied.

One possible solution is to double-down on the self-control, and train ourselves to better resist temptation and stick with the program. But, as even Baumeister and Tierney admit, there are good reasons to suspect that relying on willpower alone will not work in an environment designed to destroy it. For, as Baumeister and Tierney make clear, self-control is highly fallible at the best of times. A German study found that using willpower to resist a specific temptation failed half the time. (And those were Germans!) Humans have tested and tried self-control in the face of temptation, and it has repeatedly been found wanting. After decades of dieting and good nutrition, Americans are fatter than ever. And the authors of *Willpower* make the reason clear: we have created conditions that exhaust our willpower, more or less guaranteeing failure.

Moreover, the development of extreme self-control can have some unpleasant side-effects. Baumeister and Tierney don't discuss anorexia nervosa, but they do concede that willpower's greatest twentieth-century advocate was Hitler, and that his greatest propaganda film was named *Triumph of the Will.* Self-control is no doubt the first line of defense in an age of abundance. But if surviving in modern times takes the iron will of a Nazi stormtrooper, perhaps we should ask why we made things this way in the first place.

It is time, as Baumeister and Tierney would agree, to think systematically about the human environments that we are creating with technological powers only imagined by previous generations. At this point, using our powers to create still more of everything—the prescription of *Abundance*—is simply to add fuel to the fire. It is time to take seriously the problems of overload and excess as collective, social challenges, even though they may be our own creations.

When facing a systemic challenge, the classic answer is to deploy government, as the representative of the people. Measures such as New York City's proposed ban on large bottles of soda is exactly such a measure. It is a good start, but there are limits as to what government can do and to what Americans will accept as solutions dictated by elected officials. It is challenging for centralized institutions to manage such subtle matters as information overload and lack of time.

The fact is that our technology industries do far more to determine how we live on a daily basis than government does. For that reason, it is increasingly the duty of the technology industry and the technologists to take seriously the challenge of human overload, and to give it as much attention as the abundance project. It is the first great challenge for post-scarcity thinkers.

Consider that the most successful tech companies of the twentieth century were instruments of abundance, firms such as Archer Daniels Midland, General Motors, and Procter & Gamble. Those firms and their technologies will not disappear. But many of the most successful firms of the twenty-first will be different. They will be augmenters of human will, engineers of self-management, and agents of more effective self-control. Their mission is to liberate humans from the sufferings created by too much.

If I am right, then the future of technology will be different than the one forecast in *Abundance.* Using the technologies that Diamandis describes, there will indeed be, as he says, much more of everything by 2035. But that will be only one side of the picture—the producers, who will generate more and more of what humans crave. On the other side will be the technologies of self-control, which seek to augment humanity's powers to deal with too many choices and with too much of what we want. It may sound crazy, but our technologies are always extensions of ourselves, and humans are strange and conflicted creatures.

So advanced are our technological powers that we will be increasingly trying to create access to abundance and to limit it at the same time. Sometimes we must create both the thesis and the antithesis to go in the right direction. We have spent the last century creating an abundance that exceeds any human scale, and now technologists must turn their powers to controlling our, or their, creation.

Critical Thinking

1. Does wealth produce character defects?

2. Why do most religious teachings warn about the conflict between wealth and spirituality? "You cannot serve both God and money."

3. Consider how environmental limits and deterioration justify consuming less.

Create Central

www.mhhe.com/createcentral

Internet References

Sociosite
www.topsite.com/goto/sociosite.net

Socioweb
www.topsite.com/goto/socioweb.com

Sociology—Study Sociology Online
http://edu.learnsoc.org

Sociology Web Resources
www.mhhe.com/socscience/sociology/resources/index.htm

TIM WU is a professor at Columbia Law School and the author, most recently, of *The Master Switch: The Rise and Fall of Information Empires* (Knopf).

Article   Prepared by: Kurt Finsterbusch, *University of Maryland, College Park*

MOOCs of Hazard

Will **Online Education** Dampen The College Experience? **Yes**. Will It Be Worth It? **Well . . .**

ANDREW DELBANCO

Learning Outcomes

After reading this article, you will be able to:

- Speculate on the future of college education with growing online education.

- Understand the complicated economics of online courses, especially of MOOCs on which the article focuses.

- Online learning is attractive for convenience and low costs. Compare these benefits to the drawbacks of online learning.

In the spring of 2011, **Sebastian Thrun** was having doubts about whether the classroom was really the right place to teach his course on artificial intelligence. Thrun, a computer-science professor at Stanford, had been inspired by Salman Khan, the founder of the online Khan Academy, whose videos and discussion groups have been used by millions to learn about everything from arithmetic to history. And so that summer, Thrun announced he would offer his fall course on Stanford's website for free. He reorganized it into short segments rather than hour-long lectures, included problem sets and quizzes, and added a virtual office hour via Google Hangout. Enrollment jumped from 200 Stanford undergraduates to 160,000 students around the world (only 30 remained in the classroom). A few months later, he founded an online for-profit company called Udacity; his course, along with many others, is now available to anyone with a fast Internet connection.

Meanwhile, two of Thrun's Stanford colleagues, Daphne Koller and Andrew Ng, founded another for-profit company, Coursera, that posts courses taught by faculty from leading universities such as Princeton, Michigan, Duke, and Penn. Three million students have signed on. Not to be outdone, Harvard and MIT announced last spring their own online partnership, edX, a nonprofit with an initial investment of $60 million. A new phenomenon requires a new name, and so MOOC—massive open online course—has now entered the lexicon. So far, MOOCs have been true to the first "o" in the acronym: Anyone can take these courses for free.

Many people outside academia—including *New York Times* columnists David Brooks and Thomas L. Friedman—are gushing that MOOCs are the best thing to happen to learning since movable type. Inside academia, however, they have been met with widespread skepticism. As Joseph Harris, a writing professor at Duke, recently remarked in *The Chronicle of Higher Education,* "I don't see how a MOOC can be much more than a digitized textbook."

In fact, MOOCs are the latest in a long series of efforts to use technology to make education more accessible. Sixty years ago, the Ford Foundation funded a group of academics to study what was then a cutting-edge technology: television. In language almost identical to that used today, a report on the project announced that television had the power to drive down costs, enable the collection of data on how students learn, and extend "the reach of the superior teacher to greater numbers of students." From 1957 to 1982, the local CBS channel in New York City broadcast a morning program of college lectures called "Sunrise Semester." But the sun never rose on television as an educational "delivery system."

In the 1990s, my own university, Columbia, started a venture called Fathom, using the relatively new technology of the Web. The idea was to sell online courses taught by star faculty such as Simon Schama and Brian Greene to throngs of supposedly eager customers. But the paying consumers never showed up in the anticipated numbers, and by the time it was shut down, Fathom had cost Columbia, according to some estimates, at least $20 million. Looking back, the project's director, Ann Kirschner, concluded that she and her colleagues had arrived too soon— "pre-broadband, pre-videocasting and iPods, and all the rest."

Of course, we will always be pre-something. Former University of Michigan President James Duderstadt foresees a technology that will be "totally immersive in all our senses"— something like the "feelies" that Aldous Huxley, in *Brave New World,* imagined would render the "talkies" obsolete. The MIT Media Lab has already developed a vest that gives you a hug when a friend "likes" something you have posted on Facebook. It may not be long before we can log onto a Shakespeare course taught by, say, Stephen Greenblatt and feel the spray of his saliva as he recites "tomorrow and tomorrow and tomorrow." Such technologies will likely find their biggest market through the pornography industry, but there's no reason to doubt that academia will adopt and adapt them.

The Luddite in me is inclined to think that the techno-dreamers are headed for another disappointment. But this time around, something does seem different—and it's not just that the MOOC pioneers have an infectious excitement rarely found in a typical faculty meeting. They also have a striking public-spiritedness. Koller sees a future in which a math prodigy in a developing country might nurture his or her gifts online and then, having been identified by a leading university, enroll in person—on a scholarship, one might imagine, funded by income derived from Coursera. This idea of using online courses as a detection tool is a reprise (on a much larger scale) of the one that spurred the development of standardized tests in the mid-twentieth century, such as the SAT, which was originally envisioned as a means for finding gifted students outside the usual Ivy League "feeder" schools.

Koller speaks with genuine passion about the universal human craving for learning and sees in Internet education a social good that reminds me of Thomas Jefferson's dream of geniuses being "raked from the rubbish"—by which he meant to affirm the existence of a "natural aristocracy" to be nurtured for the sake of humankind. No one knows whether the MOOCs will achieve any of these things, but many academic leaders are certain that, as Stanford President John Hennessy predicts, higher education is about to be hit by a "tsunami."

What's driving all this risk-taking and excitement? Many people are convinced that the MOOCs can rein in the rising costs of colleges and universities. For decades, the price of tuition has outstripped the pace of inflation. Over the past ten years, the average sticker price at private colleges has increased by almost 30 percent (though net tuition has risen less because financial aid has grown even faster). At state universities, the problem has been exacerbated by public disinvestment. For example, less than 6 percent of the annual budget of the University of Virginia is covered by state funds. Last fall, I heard the chief financial officer of an urban public university put the matter succinctly: The difficulty, he said, is not so much the cost of college, but the shift of the financial burden from the state to the student.

There are many reasons why college costs continue to soar: the expense of outfitting high-tech science labs, the premium placed on research that lures faculty out of the classroom (and, in turn, requires hiring more faculty to teach classes), the proliferation of staff for everything from handling government regulation to counseling increasingly stressed students. At some institutions, there are also less defensible reasons, such as wasteful duplication, lavish amenities, and excessive pay and perks for top administrators and faculty.

But the most persuasive account of the relentless rise in cost was made nearly 50 years ago by the economist William Baumol and his student William Bowen, who later became president of Princeton. A few months ago, Bowen delivered two lectures in which he revisited his theory of the "cost disease." "In labor-intensive industries," he explained, "such as the performing arts and education, there is less opportunity than in other sectors to increase productivity by, for example, substituting capital for labor." Technological advances have allowed the auto industry, for instance, to produce more cars while using fewer workers. Professors, meanwhile, still do things more or less as they have for centuries: talking to, questioning, and evaluating students (ideally in relatively small groups). As the Ohio University economist Richard Vedder likes to joke, "With the possible exception of prostitution . . . teaching is the only profession that has had no productivity advance in the 2,400 years since Socrates."

This is a true statement—but it unwittingly undercuts its own point: Most people, I suspect, would agree that there are some activities—teaching and prostitution among them—in which improved productivity and economies of scale are not desirable, at least not from the point of view of the consumer.

True believers think that the new digital technologies will finally enable educators to increase productivity by allowing a smaller number of teachers to produce a larger number of "learning outcomes" (today's term for educated students) than ever before. But it's too soon to say whether MOOCs will really help cure the cost disease. Their own financial viability is by no means certain. The for-profits must make money for their investors, and the non-profits must return revenue to the universities that give them start-up funds.

Coursera has begun to try out a number of different strategies. It provides a matchmaking service for employers looking to hire people with certain demonstrable skills—a logical extension of a role that colleges already play. When a company expresses interest in a top-performing student, Coursera e-mails the student, offering an introduction, and receives a finder's fee from the prospective employer. The college that developed the course also receives a cut. As for Udacity, Thrun says only that it charges companies looking for talent "significantly less than you'd pay for a headhunter, but significantly more than what you'd pay for access to LinkedIn."

A few months ago, Coursera also announced a licensing arrangement with Antioch University, which agreed to pay a fee in return for incorporating selected Coursera offerings into its curriculum. The idea is for students to supplement their online experience by working with on-campus faculty—a practice known as "hybrid" or "blended" learning. The college can expand its course offerings without hiring new faculty, and Coursera can earn income that will be shared by the institutions and professors who develop the courses. So far, however, student interest has been low.

Other possible sources of revenue include selling expertise to universities that want to set up their own MOOCs or partnering with textbook publishers willing to share revenue in exchange for selling to online students. Some MOOCs are also beginning to charge fees for proctored exams (in person or by webcam) for students seeking a certificate marking their successful completion of a course.

If new technologies can cure, or even slow down, the cost disease before it kills the patient, that would be a great public service. The dark side of this bright dream is the fear that online education could burst what appears to be a higher education bubble. Consumers, the argument goes, are already waking up to the fact that they're paying too much for too little. If they are priced out of, or flee from, the market, they will find new ways to learn outside the brick-and-mortar institutions that, until now, have held a monopoly on providing credentials that certify what graduates have supposedly learned. If that happens, it would be a classic case of "disruptive innovation"—a term popularized by Harvard Business School Professor Clayton Christensen, who argues that, "in industries from computers to cars to steel those entrants that start at the bottom of their markets, selling simple products to less demanding customers and then improving from that foothold, drive the prior leaders into a disruptive demise."

We've already witnessed the first phase of this process. Early consumers of online courses tended to be students with families or jobs for whom full-time attendance at a residential or even a commuter college was out of the question. As underfunded public colleges struggled to meet the needs of such students, private for-profit "universities" such as Phoenix, Kaplan, DeVry, and Strayer emerged. They offer mainly online courses that serve—some would say exploit—an expanding population of consumers (a word increasingly used as a synonym for students). The first time I heard someone commend for-profit universities was five or six years ago, when a savvy investor said to me, "Look at California—the public system can't meet the demand, so we will step in." He was making the safe, and sad, assumption that public reinvestment is unlikely to restore what was once an unrivaled system of public higher education. Last August, nearly half a million students found themselves on waiting lists for oversubscribed courses at California's community colleges.

Many online students meet the low-income eligibility threshold for federal Pell grants—a ripe market for the for-profit universities. These institutions offer cheaper courses than traditional private colleges, usually in practical or technical subjects such as cosmetology or computer programming. Their business model depends heavily on faculty who receive low compensation and on students with high loan obligations. It's a system that works well for investors. (In 2009, the CEO of Strayer University collected a cool $42 million, mainly in stock options.) How well it works for students is another question. Last summer, a U.S. Senate committee noted that for-profit universities spend more on advertising and recruiting than on instruction and that, without significant reform, they "will continue to turn out hundreds of thousands of students with debt but no degree."

So far, the for-profit sector has been regarded with disdain or indifference by established universities. This fits the Christensen theory of "disruptive innovation": The leap by low-end products into higher-end markets is sudden and surprising because the higher-ups have been lulled into thinking their place in the pecking order is unassailable. What has happened to newspapers and publishing are obvious examples. Suddenly everything changes, and the old is swept away by the new.

Because of the durable value of prestige, it will be a long time before Harvard has to fear for its existence. But one reason to think we're on the cusp of major change is that online courses are particularly well-suited to the new rhythms of student life.

On traditional campuses, many students already regard time offline as a form of solitary confinement. Classrooms have become battlegrounds where professors struggle to distract students from their smartphones and laptops. Office hours are giving way to e-mail. To the millions who have used sites such as the Khan Academy, the idea of hour-long lectures spread out over 15-week semesters is already anachronistic. "Disruptive innovation" is a variant of Joseph Schumpeter's famous declaration that capitalism works by "creative destruction." What will be innovated and created in our colleges and universities, and what will be disrupted and destroyed?

One vulnerable structure is the faculty itself, which is already in a fragile state. This is especially true of those who teach subjects such as literature, history, and the arts. The humanities account for a static or declining percentage of all degrees conferred, partly because students often doubt their real-world value. And as humanities departments shrink, some institutions are collaborating to shrink them faster (or close them altogether) in order to avoid duplicative hiring in subjects with low student demand. For example, Columbia, Yale, and Cornell have announced a collaboration whereby certain languages—such as Romanian, Tamil, or Yoruba—will be taught via teleconferencing. This is good for students, since the subjects will still be available. But it's bad for aspiring faculty—as the number of positions dwindles, research and scholarship in these fields will dry up.

MOOCs also seem likely to spur more demand for celebrity professors in a teaching system that is already highly stratified. Among tenured faculty, there is currently a small cadre of stars and a smaller one of superstars—and the MOOCs are creating megastars. Michael Sandel, for example, who teaches a famous course on justice at Harvard, has become a global figure with millions of followers, notably in Asia, since his lectures became available online through Harvard's website and at a site called Academic Earth. A few months ago, Harvard announced that Sandel had signed up with edX. Sandel is an exceptional educator, but as master-teachers go global, lesser-known colleagues fear being relegated to a supporting role as glorified teaching assistants.

In some respects, this is the latest chapter in an old story of faculty entrepreneurship. By the mid-twentieth century, the president of the University of California, Clark Kerr, was already describing the Berkeley faculty as "individual entrepreneurs held together by a common grievance over parking." Today, as star professors increasingly work for themselves, more faculty members at less prestigious institutions face low wages, meager benefits, and—since many lack tenure—minimal job security. But if the new technology threatens some professors with obscurity, others face obsolescence. Language instructors may someday be replaced by multilingual versions of Siri on your iPhone. One of my colleagues speaks of the imminent "evisceration" of graduate study, once young people who might have pursued an academic career are deterred as it becomes harder and harder to find a dignified job after years of training.

These prospects raise many pressing questions—not just speculative ones about the future, but actionable ones about the present. What, if anything, can universities do to formulate new rules governing conflicts of interest? As faculty stars relocate to cyberspace, how can institutions sustain the community of teachers and students that has been the essence of the university for a thousand years? (The pacesetting Thrun, who is a vice president of Google, resigned from his tenured teaching post at Stanford, though he remains a "research professor.") In this brave new world, how can the teaching profession, already well on its way to "adjunctification," attract young people with a pastoral impulse to awaken and encourage students one by one?

There are also unanswered questions about how much students actually learn from MOOCs. Coursera recently withdrew one course at Georgia Tech because of student discontent and another, at the University of California, Irvine, because the professor disputed how much students were really learning.

So far, most testimonials to the value of online learning come from motivated students, often adults, who seek to build on what they have already learned in traditional educational settings. These are people with clear goals and confidence in their abilities. Stanford has even established an online high school "for gifted students" from around the world (a residential program brings them together in the summers). Its medical school has introduced "lecture halls without lectures," whereby students use short videos to master the material on their own, then converge in class for discussion of clinical applications of what they've learned.

And yet it's one thing to expect brilliant teens or medical students to be self-starters. It's another to teach students who are in need of close guidance. A recent report from the Community College Research Center at Columbia finds that underprepared students taking online courses are, according to one of the authors, "falling farther behind than if they were taking face-to-face courses." Michael Crow, one of the architects of Fathom and now president of Arizona State University and certainly no traditionalist, warns against a future in which "rich kids get taught by professors and poor kids get taught by computer."

Back in the mid-twentieth century, the Ford Foundation report on "telecourses" asked the key question about technology and education: "How effective is this instruction?" When I came upon that sentence, it put me in mind of something Ralph Waldo Emerson wrote a long time ago. "Truly speaking," he said, "it is not instruction, but provocation, that I can receive from another soul." I first understood this distinction during my own student days, while struggling with the theologian Jonathan Edwards's predestinarian view of life. Toward the end of the course, my teacher, the scholar of American religion Alan Heimert, looked me in the eye and asked: "What is it that bothers you about Edwards? Is it that he's so hard on self-deception?" This was more than instruction; it was a true provocation. It came from a teacher who listened closely to his students and tried to grasp who they were and who they were trying to become. He knew the difference between knowledge and information. He understood education in the Socratic sense, as a quest for self-knowledge.

Nearly 40 years later, in my own course on American literature, one of my gifted teaching assistants received an e-mail from a student after a discussion on Emerson:

Hi, I just wanted to let you know that our section meeting tonight had a really profound effect on me. . . . [T]he way you spoke and the energy our class had really moved me. . . . I walked the whole way home staring at the sky, a probably unsafe decision, but a worthwhile one nonetheless. I actually cannot wait for next week's class just so I can dive even further into this. So I just wanted to send you a quick message thanking you, letting you know that this fifty minutes of class has undeniably affected the rest of my life. . . . [S]ome fire was lit within me tonight, and I guess I'm blowing the smoke towards you a little bit.

No matter how anxious today's students may be about gaining this or that competence in a ferociously competitive world, many still crave the enlargement of heart as well as mind that is the gift of true education. It's hard for me to believe that this kind of experience can happen without face-to-face teaching and the physical presence of other students.

Yet I'm convinced that those leading us into the digital future truly want to dispense the gift of learning more widely than ever before. Currently, the six-year graduation rate at America's public four-year colleges is approximately 58 percent. It would be a great benefit to society if online education can improve on that record—although it should be noted that, so far, the completion rate by students who sign up for MOOCs is even worse—barely 10 percent.

In one experiment, Udacity is providing remedial courses to students at San Jose State for a much lower price than in-person courses. A bill is now under discussion in the California legislature that would require public colleges to offer online courses to students whom they can't accommodate in their classrooms. If the new technology can bring great teaching to students who would otherwise never encounter it, that could lessen inequities between the haves and have-nots, just as digital technologies now give students and scholars worldwide access to previously locked-up books and documents. But so far, there is scant evidence on which to base these hopes.

Quite apart from the MOOCs, there's an impressive array of new efforts to serve low-income students—including the online public Western Governors University, which charges around $6,000 in tuition and awards reputable degrees in such fields as information technology and business. Southern New Hampshire University—also a nonprofit—has moved aggressively into online learning, which it combines with on-campus programs; and Carnegie Mellon University has launched an "open learning initiative" that offers non-credit free courses, with substantial interactive capabilities, and seems to be working well in science, math, and introductory languages.

The best of the new education pioneers have a truly Emersonian passion for remaking the world, for rejecting the stale conviction that change always means degradation. I sense in them a fervent concurrence with Emerson's refusal to believe "that the world was finished a long time ago" and with his insistence that, "as the world was plastic and fluid in the hands of God, so it is ever to so much of his attributes as we bring to it."

In the face of such exuberance, it feels foolish and futile to demur. In one form or another, the online future is already here. But unless we are uncommonly wise about how we use this new power, we will find ourselves saying, as Emerson's friend Henry David Thoreau said about an earlier technological revolution, "We do not ride the railroad; it rides upon us."

Critical Thinking

1. How important is face-to-face contact with teachers to learning?

2. What role will classroom teaching have in the future university?

3. Do the new technologies encourage a boom in lifetime learning?

Create Central

www.mhhe.com/createcentral

Internet References

Sociosite
www.topsite.com/goto/sociosite.net

Socioweb
www.topsite.com/goto/socioweb.com

Sociology—Study Sociology Online
http://edu.learnsoc.org

Sociology Web Resources
www.mhhe.com/socscience/sociology/resources/index.htm

ANDREW DELBANCO'S most recent book, *College: What It Was, Is, and Should Be,* will be published in paperback later this month.

Article

Prepared by: Kurt Finsterbusch, *University of Maryland, College Park*

The Robot Will See You Now

JONATHAN COHN

Learning Outcomes

After reading this article, you will be able to:

- Consider whether computers can greatly improve healthcare and lower costs substantially at the same time.

- Note the cases where physician diagnoses are excellent and where they are less reliable.

- Understand the economic interests for and against the greater use of robot-assisted medicine.

Harley Lukov didn't need a miracle. He just needed the right diagnosis. Lukov, a 62-year-old from central New Jersey, had stopped smoking 10 years earlier—fulfilling a promise he'd made to his daughter, after she gave birth to his first grandchild. But decades of cigarettes had taken their toll. Lukov had adenocarcinoma, a common cancer of the lung, and it had spread to his liver. The oncologist ordered a biopsy, testing a surgically removed sample of the tumor to search for particular "driver" mutations. A driver mutation is a specific genetic defect that causes cells to reproduce uncontrollably, interfering with bodily functions and devouring organs. Think of an on/off switch stuck in the "on" direction. With lung cancer, doctors typically test for mutations called EGFR and ALK, in part because those two respond well to specially targeted treatments. But the tests are a long shot: although EGFR and ALK are the two driver mutations doctors typically see with lung cancer, even they are relatively uncommon. When Lukov's cancer tested negative for both, the oncologist prepared to start a standard chemotherapy regimen—even though it meant the side effects would be worse and the prospects of success slimmer than might be expected using a targeted agent.

But Lukov's true medical condition wasn't quite so grim. The tumor did have a driver—a third mutation few oncologists test for in this type of case. It's called KRAS. Researchers have known about KRAS for a long time, but only recently have they realized that it can be the driver mutation in metastatic lung cancer—and that, in those cases, it responds to the same drugs that turn it off in other tumors. A doctor familiar with both Lukov's specific medical history and the very latest research might know to make the connection—to add one more biomarker test, for KRAS, and then to find a clinical trial

testing the efficacy of KRAS treatments on lung cancer. But the national treatment guidelines for lung cancer don't recommend such action, and few physicians, however conscientious, would think to do these things.

Did Lukov ultimately get the right treatment? Did his oncologist make the connection between KRAS and his condition, and order the test? He might have, if Lukov were a real patient and the oncologist were a real doctor. They're not. They are fictional composites developed by researchers at the Memorial Sloan-Kettering Cancer Center in New York, in order to help train—and demonstrate the skills of—IBM's Watson supercomputer. Yes, this is the same Watson that famously went on *Jeopardy* and beat two previous human champions. But IBM didn't build Watson to win game shows. The company is developing Watson to help professionals with complex decision making, like the kind that occurs in oncologists' offices—and to point out clinical nuances that health professionals might miss on their own.

Information technology that helps doctors and patients make decisions has been around for a long time. Crude online tools like WebMD get millions of visitors a day. But Watson is a different beast. According to IBM, it can digest information and make recommendations much more quickly, and more intelligently, than perhaps any machine before it—processing up to 60 million pages of text per second, even when that text is in the form of plain old prose, or what scientists call "natural language."

That's no small thing, because something like 80 percent of all information is "unstructured." In medicine, it consists of physician notes dictated into medical records, long-winded sentences published in academic journals, and raw numbers stored online by public-health departments. At least in theory, Watson can make sense of it all. It can sit in on patient examinations, silently listening. And over time, it can learn. Just as Watson got better at *Jeopardy* the longer it played, so it gets better at figuring out medical problems and ways of treating them the more it interacts with real cases. Watson even has the ability to convey doubt. When it makes diagnoses and recommends treatments, it usually issues a series of possibilities, each with its own level of confidence attached.

Medicine has never before had a tool quite like this. And at an unofficial coming-out party in Las Vegas last year, during the annual meeting of the Healthcare Information and

Management Systems Society, more than 1,000 professionals packed a large hotel conference hall, and an overflow room nearby, to hear a presentation by Marty Kohn, an emergency-room physician and a clinical leader of the IBM team training Watson for health care. Standing before a video screen that dwarfed his large frame, Kohn described in his husky voice how Watson could be a game changer—not just in highly specialized fields like oncology but also in primary care, given that all doctors can make mistakes that lead to costly, sometimes dangerous, treatment errors.

Drawing on his own clinical experience and on academic studies, Kohn explained that about one-third of these errors appear to be products of misdiagnosis, one cause of which is "anchoring bias": human beings' tendency to rely too heavily on a single piece of information. This happens all the time in doctors' offices, clinics, and emergency rooms. A physician hears about two or three symptoms, seizes on a diagnosis consistent with those, and subconsciously discounts evidence that points to something else. Or a physician hits upon the right diagnosis, but fails to realize that it's incomplete, and ends up treating just one condition when the patient is, in fact, suffering from several. Tools like Watson are less prone to those failings. As such, Kohn believes, they may eventually become as ubiquitous in doctors' offices as the stethoscope.

"Watson fills in for some human limitations," Kohn told me in an interview. "Studies show that humans are good at taking a relatively limited list of possibilities and using that list, but are far less adept at using huge volumes of information. That's where Watson shines: taking a huge list of information and winnowing it down."

Watson has gotten some media hype already, including articles in *Wired* and *Fast Company*. Still, you probably shouldn't expect to see it the next time you visit your doctor's office. Before the computer can make real-life clinical recommendations, it must learn to understand and analyze medical information, just as it once learned to ask the right questions on *Jeopardy*. That's where Memorial Sloan-Kettering comes in. The famed cancer institute has signed up to be Watson's tutor, feeding it clinical information extracted from real cases and then teaching it how to make sense of the data. "The process of pulling out two key facts from a *Jeopardy* clue is totally different from pulling out all the relevant information, and its relationships, from a medical case," says Ari Caroline, Sloan-Kettering's director of quantitative analysis and strategic initiatives. "Sometimes there is conflicting information. People phrase things different ways." But Caroline, who approached IBM about the research collaboration, nonetheless predicts that Watson will prove "very valuable"—particularly in a field like cancer treatment, in which the explosion of knowledge is already overwhelming. "If you're looking down the road, there are going to be many more clinical options, many more subtleties around biomarkers . . . There will be nuances not just in interpreting the case but also in treating the case," Caroline says. "You're going to need a tool like Watson because the complexity and scale of information will be such that a typical decision tool couldn't possibly handle it all."

The Cleveland Clinic is also helping to develop Watson, first as a tool for training young physicians and then, possibly, as a tool at the bedside itself. James Young, the executive dean of the Cleveland Clinic medical school, told *The Plain Dealer*, "if we can get Watson to give us information in the healthcare arena like we've seen with more-general sorts of knowledge information, I think it's going to be an extraordinary tool for clinicians and a huge advancement." And WellPoint, the insurance company, has already begun testing Watson as a support tool for nurses who make treatment-approval decisions.

Whether these experiments show real, quantifiable improvements in the quality or efficiency of care remains to be seen. If Watson tells physicians only what they already know, or if they end up ordering many more tests for no good reason, Watson could turn out to be more hindrance than help. But plenty of serious people in the fields of medicine, engineering, and business think Watson will work (IBM says that it could be widely available within a few years). And many of these same people believe that this is only the beginning—that whether or not Watson itself succeeds, it is emblematic of a quantum shift in health care that's just now getting under way.

When we think of breakthroughs in medicine, we conjure up images of new drugs or new surgeries. When we think of changes to the health-care system, byzantine legislation comes to mind. But according to a growing number of observers, the next big thing to hit medical care will be new ways of accumulating, processing, and applying data—revolutionizing medical care the same way Billy Beane and his minions turned baseball into "moneyball." Many of the people who think this way—entrepreneurs from Silicon Valley, young researchers from prestigious health systems and universities, and salespeople of every possible variety—spoke at the conference in Las Vegas, proselytizing to the tens of thousands of physicians and administrators in attendance. They say a range of innovations, from new software to new devices, will transform the way all of us interact with the health-care system—making it easier for us to stay healthy and, when we do get sick, making it easier for medical professionals to treat us. They also imagine the transformation reverberating through the rest of the economy, in ways that may be even more revolutionary.

Health care already represents one-sixth of America's gross domestic product. And that share is growing, placing an ever-larger strain on paychecks, corporate profits, and government resources. Figuring out how to manage this cost growth—how to meet the aging population's medical needs without bankrupting the country—has become the central economic-policy challenge of our time. These technology enthusiasts think they can succeed where generations of politicians, business leaders, and medical professionals have failed.

Specifically, they imagine the application of data as a "disruptive" force, upending health care in the same way it has upended almost every other part of the economy—changing not just how medicine is practiced but who is practicing it. In Silicon Valley and other centers of innovation, investors and engineers talk casually about machines' taking the place of doctors, serving as diagnosticians and even surgeons—doing the same work, with better results, for a lot less money. The idea, they say, is no more fanciful than the notion of self-driving cars, experimental versions of which are already cruising California streets. "A world mostly without doctors (at least average ones) is not only reasonable, but also more likely than not," wrote Vinod Khosla, a venture capitalist and co-founder of Sun Microsystems, in a 2012 TechCrunch article titled "Do We Need Doctors or Algorithms?" He even put a number on his prediction: someday, he said, computers and robots would replace four out of five physicians in the United States.

Statements like that provoke skepticism, derision, and anger—and not only from hidebound doctors who curse every time they have to turn on a computer. Bijan Salehizadeh, a trained physician and a venture capitalist, responded to reports of Khosla's premonition and similar predictions with a tweet: "Getting nauseated reading the anti-doctor rantings of the silicon valley tech crowd." Physicians, after all, do more than process data. They attend at patients' bedsides and counsel families. They grasp nuance and learn to master uncertainty. For their part, the innovators at IBM make a point of presenting Watson as a tool that can help health-care professionals, rather than replace them. Think Dr. McCoy using his tricorder to diagnose a phaser injury on Star Trek, not the droid fitting Luke Skywalker with a robotic hand in *Star Wars*. To most experts, that's a more realistic picture of what medicine will look like, at least for the foreseeable future.

But even if data technology does nothing more than arm health-care professionals with tablet computers that help them make decisions, the effect could still be profound. Harvey Fineberg, the former dean of the Harvard School of Public Health and now the president of the Institute of Medicine, wrote of IT's rising promise last year in *The New England Journal of Medicine,* describing a health-care system that might be transformed by artificial intelligence, robotics, bioinformatics, and other advances. Tools like Watson could enhance the abilities of professionals at every level, from highly specialized surgeons to medical assistants. As a result, physicians wouldn't need to do as much, and each class of professionals beneath them could take on greater responsibility—creating a financially sustainable way to meet the aging population's growing need for more health care.

As an incidental benefit, job opportunities for people with no graduate degree, and in some cases no four-year-college degree, would grow substantially. For the past few decades, as IT has disrupted other industries, from manufacturing to banking, millions of well-paying middle-class jobs—those easily routinized—have vanished. In health care, this disruption could have the opposite effect. It wouldn't be merely a win-win, but a win-win-win. It all sounds far too good to be true—except that a growing number of engineers, investors, and physicians insist that it isn't.

One of these enthusiasts is Daniel Kraft, age 44, whose career trajectory tracks the way medicine itself is evolving. Kraft is a physician with a traditional educational pedigree: an undergraduate degree from Brown and a medical degree from Stanford. He trained in pediatrics and

internal medicine at Harvard-affiliated hospitals in Boston. Then he returned to the West Coast, to Stanford University Hospital, to complete fellowships in hematology and oncology.

But Kraft always had a flair for entrepreneurship and a taste for technology: While in medical school, he started his own online bookstore, selling texts to his classmates at a discount. (He later sold the business, for considerable profit.) At Stanford, Kraft says he used his knowledge of social media to develop a better method for communication among doctors, allowing them to exchange pertinent information while making rounds, for instance, rather than simply texting phone numbers for callbacks. "Here we are at Stanford, heart of Silicon Valley, and all we had were basic SMS text pagers—they could only do phone numbers," Kraft recalls. "So I hacked into a Yahoo Groups thing, so we could send actual text messages through servers. Then it spread to the rest of the hospital."

Thus began Kraft's second, parallel career as an inventor, an entrepreneur, and a professional visionary. He audited classes in bio-design and business, hanging out with computer nerds as much as doctors. Today he holds several patents, including one for the MarrowMiner, a device that allows bone marrow to be harvested faster and less painfully. (Kraft is the chief medical officer for a company that plans to develop it commercially.)

Kraft is also the chairman of the medical track at Singularity University, a think tank and educational institution in Silicon Valley. Initially, Kraft's primary role at Singularity was to offer a few hours of instruction on medicine. But Kraft says he quickly realized that "a lot of people, in gaming, IT, Big Data, devices, virtual reality, psychology—they were all converging on health care, and interested in applying their skills to health care." That led Singularity to establish FutureMed, an annual conference on medical innovation that brings together financiers, physicians, and engineers from around the world. Kraft is the director.

Exponential improvements in the ability of computers to process more and more data, faster and faster, are part of what has drawn this diverse crew to medicine—a field of such complexity that large parts of it have, until recently, stood outside the reach of advanced information technology. But just as significant, Kraft and his fellow travelers say, is the explosion of data available for these tools to manipulate. The Human Genome Project completed its detailed schematic of human DNA in 2003, and for the past several years, companies have provided personal genetic mapping to people with the means to pay for it. Now the price, once prohibitive, is within reach for most people and insurance plans. Researchers have only just begun figuring out how genes translate into most aspects of health, but they already know a great deal about how certain genetic sequences predispose people to conditions like heart disease and breast cancer. Many experts think we will soon enter an era of "personalized" medicine, in which physicians tailor treatments—not just for cancer, but also for conditions like diabetes and heart disease—to an individual patient's genetic idiosyncrasies.

A potentially larger—and, in the short run, more consequential—data explosion involves the collection, transmission, and screening of relatively simple medical data on a much more frequent basis, enabling clinicians to make smarter, quicker decisions about their patients. The catalyst is a device most patients already have: the smartphone. Companies are developing, and in some cases already selling, sensors that attach to phones, to collect all sorts of biological data. The companies Withings and iHealth, for example, already offer blood-pressure cuffs that connect to an iPhone; the phone can then send the data to health-care professionals via e-mail, or in some cases, automatically enter them into online medical records. The Withings device sells for $129; iHealth's for $99. Other firms sell devices that diabetics can use to measure glucose levels. In the U.K., a consortium has been developing a smartphone app paired with a device that will allow users to test themselves for sexually transmitted diseases. (The test will apparently involve urinating onto a chip attached to the phone.)

AliveCor, a San Francisco-based firm, has developed an app and a thin, unobtrusive smartphone attachment that can take electrocardiogram readings. The FDA approved it for use in the U.S. in December. While the device was still in its trial phase, Eric Topol, the chief academic officer at Scripps Health in San Diego and a well-known technology enthusiast, used a prototype of the device to diagnose an incipient heart attack in a passenger on a transcontinental flight from Washington, D.C., to San Diego. The plane made an emergency landing near Cincinnati and the man survived.

As sensors shrink and improve, they will increasingly allow health to be tracked constantly and discreetly—helping people to get over illnesses faster and more reliably—and in the best of cases, to avoid getting sick in the first place. One group of researchers, based at Emory University and Georgia Tech, developed a prototype for one such device called Stealth Vest, which—as the name implies—embeds sensors in a vest that people could wear under their regular clothing. The group designed the vest for teenagers with chronic disease (asthma, diabetes, even sickle-cell anemia) because, by their nature, teenagers are less likely to comply with physician instructions about taking readings or medications. But the same technology can work for everyone. For instance, as Sloan-Kettering's Ari Caroline notes, right now it's hard for oncologists to get the detailed patient feedback they need in order to serve their patients best. "Think about prostate surgery," he says. "You really want to check patients' urinary and sexual function on a regular basis, and you don't get that when they come in once every three or four months to the clinic—they'll just say generally 'good' or 'bad.' The data will only get collected when people are inputting it on a regular basis and it captures their daily lives."

As more and more data are captured, and as computers become better and faster at processing them autonomously, the possibilities keep expanding. One medical-data start-up getting some buzz is a company called Predictive Medical Technologies, based in San Francisco. It is developing a program that sucks in all the data generated in a hospital's intensive-care unit, plugs the information into an algorithm, and then identifies which patients are likely to experience a heart attack or other forms of distress—providing up to 24 hours of warning. A trial is under way at the University of Utah's hospital in Salt Lake City. The eventual goal is to expand the program's capabilities, so that it can monitor conditions throughout the hospital. "You don't just want more data," Kraft says. "You want

actual information in a form you can use. You need to be able to make sense of this stuff. That's what companies like Predictive Medical do."

So how would all these innovations fit together? How would the health-care system be different—and how, from a patient's standpoint, would it feel different—from the one we have today? Imagine you're an adult with a chronic condition like high blood pressure. Today, your contact with the health-care system would be largely episodic: You'd have regular checkups, at which a doctor or maybe a nurse-practitioner would check your blood pressure and ask about recent behavior—diet, exercise, and whatnot. Maybe you'd give an accurate account, maybe you wouldn't. If you started experiencing pain or had some other sign of trouble, you'd make an appointment and come in—but by then, the symptom might well have subsided, making it hard to figure out what was going on.

In the future as the innovators imagine it—"Health 2.0," as some people have started calling it—you would be in constant contact with the health-care system, although you'd hardly be aware of it. The goal would be to keep you healthy—and any time you were in danger of becoming unhealthy, to ensure you received attention right away. You might wear a bracelet that monitors your blood pressure, or a pedometer that logs movement and exercise. You could opt for a monitoring system that makes sure you take your prescribed medication, at the prescribed intervals. All of these devices would transmit information back to your provider of basic medical care, dumping data directly into an electronic medical record.

And the provider wouldn't be one doctor, but rather a team of professionals, available at all hours and heavily armed with technology to guide and assist them as they made decisions. If, say, your blood pressure suddenly spiked, data-processing tools would warn them that you might be in trouble, and some sort of clinician—a nurse, perhaps—would reach out to you immediately, to check on your condition and arrange treatment as necessary. You could reach the team just as easily, with something as simple as a text message or an e-mail. You'd be in touch with them more frequently, most likely, but for much shorter durations—and, for the most part, with less urgency.

Sometimes, of course, office or hospital visits would be necessary, but that experience would be different, too—starting with the hassle of dealing with insurance companies. Watson has a button for submitting treatment proposals to managed-care companies, for near-instant approval, reducing the time and hassle involved in gaining payment authorization. The transformation of the clinical experience could be more profound, although you might not detect it: someone in a white coat or blue scrubs would still examine you, perform tests, prescribe treatment. But that person might have a different background than he'd have today. And as the two of you talked, your exam information would be uploaded and cross-referenced against your medical record (including the data from all those wireless monitors you've been toting around), your DNA, and untold pages of clinical literature.

The evolution toward a more connected system of care has already begun at some large organizations that use team models of care. One such institution is the Group Health Cooperative of Puget Sound, a nonprofit, multi-specialty group practice. Matt Handley, the medical director for quality and informatics, says that about two-thirds of Group Health's patients now use some form of electronic communication, and that these methods account for about half of all "touches" between patients and the group's doctors or nurses. "They set up their own appointments . . . They don't need to call somebody and ask when I'm free," Handley says. "They send messages to doctors; look up lab tests and radiology results; and order refills . . . The fascinating thing is that people of all ages are using it . . . I have people in their 90s who secure-message me."

It's a long way from Group Health to Health 2.0, and Handley is among those who are wary of the hype. Sure, the demos for products like Watson look great. They always do. But can such tools really winnow down information in a way that physicians will find useful? Can they effectively scour new medical literature—some 30,000 articles a month, by Handley's reckoning—and make appropriate use of new evidence? Will they actually improve medicine? "While Watson could sometimes be helpful, it may actually drive up the cost of care," Handley says, by introducing more possible diagnoses for each patient—diagnoses that clinicians will inevitably want to investigate with a bevy of expensive tests. A study in the journal Health Affairs, published in March 2012, found that physicians with instant electronic access to test results tended to order more tests—perhaps because they knew they could see and use the results quickly. It's the same basic principle Handley has identified: if new tools allow providers to process far more information than they do now, providers might respond by trying to gather even more information.

Another reason for skepticism is the widespread lack of good electronic medical records, or EMRs, the foundation on which so many promising innovations rest. Creating EMRs has been a frustratingly slow process, spanning at least the past two decades. And even today the project is a mess: more than 400 separate vendors offer EMRs, and the government is still trying to establish a common language so that they can all "speak" to one another. "Our doctors have state-of-the-art electronic health-record systems," says Brian Ahier, the health-IT evangelist (yes, that is his real title) at the Mid-Columbia Medical Center, in northern Oregon, and a widely read writer on medical innovation. "But for clinical communication" outside the medical center, "they have to print it out, fax it, and then scan" what they get back.

But despite these risks and stumbling blocks, there are reasons to think the next wave of innovations might really stick. One is legislation enacted by the Obama administration. The 2009 Recovery Act—the $800 billion stimulus designed to end the economic crisis—set aside funds for the creation of a uniform standard for electronic medical records. It also made changes to Medicare, so reimbursement to doctors and hospitals now depends partly on whether they adopt EMRs and put them to "meaningful use." The incentives seem to be working: according to a September 2012 survey by the consulting firm CapSite, nearly seven in 10 doctors now use EMRs. The trade publication InformationWeek called this tally a "tipping point."

Under the Affordable Care Act, aka "Obamacare," Medicare will also begin rewarding providers who form integrated organizations, like Group Health Cooperative of Puget Sound, and groups that accept "bundled" payments, so that they are paid based on the number of patients in their care rather than for each service rendered. In theory, this financing scheme should encourage medical practices and hospitals to keep patients healthier over the long term, even if that means spending money up front on technology in order to reduce the frequency of patient visits or procedures. In other words, the new, digital model for health care should eventually become more economically viable.

One sign that medical care is in the midst of a massive transformation, or at least on the cusp of one, is the extraordinary rise in demand for information-technology workers within the health-care sector. All over the country, hospitals are on a hiring binge, desperate for people who can develop and install new information systems—and then manage them or train existing workers to do so. According to one government survey, online advertisements for health-IT jobs tripled from 2009 to 2010. And the growth is likely to continue. The Bureau of Labor Statistics estimates that in this decade, the health-IT workforce will grow by 20 percent. Most experts believe that such growth still won't be nearly enough to fill the demand. But it's the data revolution's ability to change jobs within health care—to alter the daily workflow of medical assistants, nurses, doctors, and care managers—that might have the most far-reaching effects not just on medicine, but also on the economy.

Economists like to say that health care suffers from a phenomenon called "Baumol's disease," or "the Baumol effect," first described half a century ago by the economist William Baumol, in collaboration with a fellow economist named William Bowen. In most occupations, wages rise only when productivity improves. If factory workers get an extra dollar an hour, it's because they can produce extra value, thanks to better training or equipment. Baumol and Bowen observed that certain labor-intensive occupations don't operate by the same principle: job productivity doesn't rise much, but wages go up anyway, because employers need to keep paying workers more in order to stop them from pursuing other lines of work, in other sectors where productivity is rising quickly. That forces the employers to keep raising prices, just to provide the same level of service.

Over time, industries afflicted with Baumol's disease tend to consume a larger and larger proportion of a nation's income, because their cost, relative to everything else, climbs ever upward. The health-care industry has a textbook case of Baumol's disease, and so far, technology hasn't made much of an impact. Just as it still takes five string players to play a Mozart quintet (Baumol's famous example), so it still takes a highly trained surgeon to operate on somebody. "We do now have robots performing surgery, but the robot is under constant supervision of the surgeon during the process," Baumol told a reporter from The New York Times two years ago. "You haven't saved labor. You have done other good things, but it isn't a way of cheapening the process." Likewise, a doctor in a clinic still sees patients individually, listens to their problems, orders tests, makes diagnoses—in the classic economic sense, the process of an office visit is no more efficient than it was 10,30, or 50 years ago.

Now technology could actually change that process, not by making the exam faster but by enabling somebody else to conduct it—or to perform the test, or carry out the procedure. The idea of robots performing surgery or more-routine medical tasks with less supervision is something many experts take seriously—in part because, in the developing world, burgeoning demand for care is already pushing medicine in this direction. As part of an experimental program in Tanzania, rural health workers, many of whom have relatively little medical training, have access to a "decision-support tool" that can help them diagnose and treat illness based on symptoms. And thanks to an initiative called the Maternal Health Reporter, similar caregivers in India can submit patient information to a central data bank, then receive regular reminders about care for pregnant women.

"In Brazil and India, machines are already starting to do primary care, because there's no labor to do it," says Robert Kocher, an internist, a veteran of McKinsey consulting, and a former adviser to the Obama administration. He's now a partner at Venrock, a New York venture-capital firm that invests in emerging technologies, including health-care technology. "They may be better than doctors. Mathematically, they will follow evidence—and they're much more likely to be right." In the United States, Kocher believes, advanced decision-support tools could quickly find a home in so-called minute clinics—the storefront medical offices that drugstores and other companies are setting up in pharmacies and malls. There, the machines could help nonphysician clinicians take care of routine medical needs, like diagnosing strep throat—and could potentially dispense the diagnoses to patients more or less autonomously. Years from now, he says, other machines could end up doing "vascular surgery, fistulas, eye surgery, microsurgery. Machines can actually be more precise than human hands."

Nobody (including Kocher) expects American physicians to turn the keys of their practices over to robots. And nobody would expect American patients accustomed to treatment from live human beings to tolerate such a sudden shift for much of their care, mall-based minute clinics notwithstanding. But because of a unique set of circumstances, the health-care workforce could nonetheless undergo enormous change, without threatening the people already working in it.

Between the aging of the population and the expansion of health-insurance coverage under Obamacare, many more people will seek medical attention in the coming years—whether it's basic primary care or ongoing care for chronic conditions. But we don't have nearly enough primary-care doctors—in practice today or in training—to provide this care. And even if we trained more, we wouldn't have enough money to pay them. With the help of decision-support tools and robotics, health-care professionals at every level would be able to handle more-complicated and more-challenging tasks, helping to shoulder part of the load. And finding enough nurses or technicians or assistants would be a lot easier than finding enough doctors. They don't need as many years to train, and they don't cost as much to pay once their training is finished. According to the Bureau of Labor Statistics, doctors' median annual salary is $166,400, while nurses' is $64,690 and medical assistants' is $28,860.

Health professionals at all levels tend to guard their turf ferociously, lobbying state officials to prevent encroachments from other providers. But the severe shortage of professionals to provide primary care means there should be plenty of work to go around. Already today, there's a push within healthcare-policy circles to more consistently allow providers to "practice at the top of their licenses"—that is, to let the people at each level of training do as much as their training could possibly allow them to do. That would enable higher-wage, more-highly-skilled professionals to focus on work that's truly commensurate with their education. It would also reduce the cost of care. Watson and its ilk could help us take this concept further, by augmenting the capabilities of workers at every skill level. Physicians could lead large teams of mid- and low-level providers, delegating less complicated and more routine tasks. "Having nurses, with the assistance of these artificial-intelligence tools, [do more] frees physicians to perform the higher-level interventions, allowing everyone to practice at the top of their license," Brian Ahier says.

That model actually isn't so different from the collaborative approach that institutions like Group Health have been deploying with such success. "We focus on developing teams—teams of several doctors, physician assistants, nurse-practitioners, and/or nurses," Matt Handley says. "Every day starts with a huddle: the team talks about the day and reviews a couple of topics and cases, figures out who is going to need what, from which provider, and so on."

The providers with less medical training can be more technologically adept, anyway. "The doctor or clinician of course has the high analytic skills, makes the judgment calls, the diagnoses, prescribes medications," says Catherine Dower, an associate director at UC San Francisco's Center for the Health Professions. "But the medical assistants are frequently the ones who can actually use this new technology really well, including tele-health—they can get bio-feeds from patients sitting at home, they can tap insulin and cardiac rates. And then, as this information is fed into a central site, the medical assistant can read and make a decision on which patient should come in and be seen by the doctor, and which one needs some minor modification"—whether that means adjusting medication or scheduling a visit to discuss more-significant changes in treatment or therapy.

For the health-care system as a whole, the efficiencies from the data revolution could amount to substantial savings. One estimate, from the McKinsey Global Institute, suggested that the data revolution could yield onetime heath-care savings of up to $220 billion, followed by a slower rate of growth in health-care costs. Total health-care spending in the U.S. last year was $2.7 trillion, so that would be roughly the equivalent of reducing health-care spending by 7.5 percent up front. That's the best reason to believe that the data revolution will make a difference, even if it never lives up to the hype of its most enthusiastic proponents. The health-care system is so massive, so full of waste, so full of failure, that even a marginal change for the better could save billions of dollars, not to mention quite a few lives.

And, in a small way, it could help us begin to fill the hole that's developed in the middle class. David Autor, an economist at MIT, has noted that for the past generation, technological change in the U.S. has tended to favor highly skilled workers at the expense of those with mid-level skills. Routine clerical functions, for instance, have been automated, contributing to the hollowing-out of the middle class. But in the coming years, health care may prove a large and important exception to that general rule—effectively turning the rule on its head. "Look at physician-assistant positions," Dower says. "They don't require college or a bachelor's degree, just a technical program." And once you're certified, "you come out with a pretty good salary, up in the $75,000-to-$80,000 range." If technological aids allow us to push more care down to people with less training and fewer skills, more middle-class jobs will be created along the way.

"I don't think physicians will be seeing patients as much in the future," says David Lee Scher, a former cardiac electrophysiologist and the president of DLS Healthcare Consulting, which advises health-care organizations and developers of digital health-care technologies. "I think they are transitioning into what I see as super-quality-control officers, overseeing physician assistants, nurses, nurse-practitioners, etc., who are really going to be the ones who see the patients." Scher recognizes the economic logic of this transition, but he's also deeply ambivalent about it, noting that something may be lost—because there are still some things that technology cannot do, and cannot enable humans to do. "Patients appreciate nonphysician providers because they tend to spend more time with them and get more humanistic hand-holding care. However, while I personally have dealt with some excellent mid-level providers, they generally do not manage complex diseases as well as physicians. Technology-assisted algorithms might contribute to narrowing this divide."

Even Watson, which has generated so much positive buzz in medicine and engineering, has its doubters. "Watson would be a potent and clever companion as we made our rounds," wrote Abraham Verghese, a Stanford physician and an author, in *The New York Times.* "But the complaints I hear from patients, family and friends are never about the dearth of technology but about its excesses."

Marty Kohn, from the Watson team, understands such skepticism, and frequently warns enthusiasts not to overpromise what the machine can do. "When people say IT can be

transformative, I get a little anxious," he told me. Partly that's because he thinks technology can't change an industry, or a culture, if the professionals themselves aren't committed to such a transformation—Watson won't change medicine, in other words, if the people who practice medicine don't want it to change. As a physician, Kohn is careful to describe Watson as a "clinical support" tool rather than a "decision making" tool—to emphasize that it's a machine that can help health-care professionals, rather than replace them. "Some technologies are truly transforming health care, providing therapies that never existed before. I don't view IT that way. I view IT as an enabler."

Still, Kohn has reconciled himself to hearing people talk about Watson as if it were a person—he says he's now used to answering the question "Who is Watson?" rather than "What is Watson?" He also likes to tell a story about a speech he gave in Canada, one that, like the Las Vegas presentation, attracted more people than the room could hold. That evening he called his wife, to tell her about the enthusiasm. "That's really great, Marty," he recalls her saying. "Just remember, they were there to meet Watson, not you."

Critical Thinking

1. How far should the automation of medicine go?
2. The computer can retain millions of pieces of information and bring them together in diagnoses. They can outperform humans many times over. Why are they not used much more to date?
3. Predict the future of medicine.

Create Central

www.mhhe.com/createcentral

Internet References

Sociosite
www.topsite.com/goto/sociosite.net
Socioweb
www.topsite.com/goto/socioweb.com
Sociology—Study Sociology Online
http://edu.learnsoc.org
Sociology Web Resources
www.mhhe.com/socscience/sociology/resources/index.htm

JONATHAN COHN is a senior editor at *The New Republic* and the author of *Sick: The Untold Story of America's Health Care Crisis—and the People Who Pay the Price.*

Article   Prepared by: Kurt Finsterbusch, *University of Maryland, College Park*

In Search of the Spiritual

Move over, politics. Americans are looking for personal, ecstatic experiences of God, and, according to our poll, they don't much care what the neighbors are doing.

JERRY ADLER ET AL.

Learning Outcomes

After reading this article, you will be able to:

- Have a clear idea about the state of religion in the United States.
- Notice that Americans not only believe in God in large numbers but believe fairly strongly in the teachings of the Bible.
- Notice that church attendance and other practices remain fairly strong.

The 1960s did not penetrate very deeply into the small towns of the Quaboag Valley of central Massachusetts. Even so, Father Thomas Keating, the abbot of St. Joseph's Abbey, couldn't help noticing the attraction that the exotic religious practices of the East held for many young Roman Catholics. To him, as a Trappist monk, meditation was second nature. He invited the great Zen master Roshi Sasaki to lead retreats at the abbey. And surely, he thought, there must be a precedent within the church for making such simple but powerful spiritual techniques available to laypeople. His Trappist brother Father William Meninger found it in one day in 1974, in a dusty copy of a 14th-century guide to contemplative meditation, "The Cloud of Unknowing." Drawing on that work, as well as the writings of the contemplatives Saint John of the Cross and Saint Teresa of Avila, the two monks began teaching a form of Christian meditation that grew into the worldwide phenomenon known as centering prayer. Twice a day for 20 minutes, practitioners find a quiet place to sit with their eyes closed and surrender their minds to God. In more than a dozen books and in speeches and retreats that have attracted tens of thousands, Keating has spread the word to a world of "hungry people, looking for a deeper relationship with God."

For most of history, that's exactly what most people have been looking for. But only a generation ago it appeared from some vantage points, such as midtown Manhattan, that Americans were on their way to turning their backs on God. In sepulchral black and red, the cover of *Time* magazine dated April 8, 1966—Good Friday—introduced millions of readers to existential anguish with the question *Is God Dead?* If he was,

the likely culprit was science, whose triumph was deemed so complete that "what cannot be known [by scientific methods] seems uninteresting, unreal." Nobody would write such an article now, in an era of round-the-clock televangelism and official presidential displays of Christian piety. Even more remarkable today is the article's obsession with the experience of a handful of the most prestigious Protestant denominations. No one looked for God in the Pentecostal churches of East Los Angeles or among the backwoods Baptists of Arkansas. Muslims earned no notice, nor did American Hindus or Buddhists, except for a passage that raised the alarming prospect of seekers' "desperately" turning to "psychiatry, Zen or drugs."

History records that the vanguard of angst-ridden intellectuals in *Time*, struggling to imagine God as a cloud of gas in the far reaches of the galaxy, never did sweep the nation. What was dying in 1966 was a well-meaning but arid theology born of rationalism: a wavering trumpet call for ethical behavior, a search for meaning in a letter to the editor in favor of civil rights. What would be born in its stead, in a cycle of renewal that has played itself out many times since the Temple of Solomon, was a passion for an immediate, transcendent experience of God. And a uniquely American acceptance of the amazingly diverse paths people have taken to find it. *Newsweek* set out to map this new topography of faith, visiting storefront churches in Brooklyn and mosques in Los Angeles, an environmental Christian activist in West Virginia and a Catholic college in Ohio—talking to Americans of all creeds, and none, about their spiritual journeys. A major poll, commissioned jointly with Beliefnet.com, reveals a breadth of tolerance and curiosity virtually across the religious spectrum. And everywhere we looked, a flowering of spirituality: in the hollering, swooning, foot-stomping services of the new wave of Pentecostals; in Catholic churches where worshipers pass the small hours of the night alone contemplating the eucharist, and among Jews who are seeking God in the mystical thickets of Kabbalah. Also, in the rebirth of Pagan religions that look for God in the wonders of the natural world; in Zen and innumerable other threads of Buddhism, whose followers seek enlightenment through meditation and prayer, and in the efforts of American Muslims to achieve a more God-centered Islam. And, for that matter, at the Church of the Holy Communion, described by the Rev. Gary Jones as "a proper Episcopal church in one of the wealthiest parts of Memphis," where increasingly "personal experience is at the heart of much of what we do." A few years ago Jones added a Sunday-evening service that has evolved into a blend of Celtic evensong with communion. Congregants were invited to make a sign of the cross with holy water. Jones was relieved when this innovation quickly won acceptance. "We thought people would be embarrassed," he says.

Whatever is going on here, it's not an explosion of people going to church. The great public manifestations of religiosity in America today—the megachurches seating 8,000 worshipers at one service, the emergence of evangelical preachers as political power brokers—haven't been reflected in increased attendance at services. Of 1,004 respondents to the *Newsweek/*Beliefnet Poll, 45 percent said they attend worship services weekly, virtually identical to the figure (44 percent) in a Gallup poll cited by *Time* in 1966. Then as now, however, there is probably a fair amount of wishful thinking in those figures; researchers who have done actual head counts in churches think the figure is probably more like 20 percent. There has been a particular falloff in attendance by African-Americans, for whom the church is no longer the only respectable avenue of social advancement, according to Darren Sherkat, a sociologist at Southern Illinois University. The fastest-growing category on surveys that ask people to give their religious affiliation, says Patricia O'Connell Killen of Pacific Lutheran University in Tacoma, Wash., is "none." But "spirituality," the impulse to seek communion with the Divine, is thriving. The *Newsweek/*Beliefnet Poll found that more Americans, especially those younger than 60, described themselves as "spiritual" (79 percent) than "religious" (64 percent). Almost two thirds of Americans say they pray every day, and nearly a third meditate.

These figures tell you more about what Americans care about than a 10,000-foot-high monument to the Ten Commandments. "You can know all about God," says Tony Campolo, a prominent evangelist, "but the question is, do you *know* God? You can have solid theology and be orthodox to the core, but have you *experienced* God in your own life?" In the broadest sense, Campolo says, the Christian believer and the New Age acolyte are on the same mission: "We are looking for transcendence in the midst of the mundane." And what could be more mundane than politics? Seventy-five percent say that a "very important" reason for their faith is to "forge a personal relationship with God"—not fighting political battles.

Today, then, the real spiritual quest is not to put another conservative on the Supreme Court, or to get creation science into the schools. If you experience God directly, your faith is not going to hinge on whether natural selection could have produced the flagellum of a bacterium. If you feel God within you, then the important question is settled; the rest is details.

As diverse as America itself are the ways in which Americans seek spiritual enlightenment. One of the unexpected results of the immigration reform of 1965 was its effect on American religiosity. Even Christian immigrants brought with them unfamiliar practices and beliefs, planting on American soil branches of the True Jesus Church (from China) or the Zairean Kimbangu

Church. Beliefnet, the religious Web site, sends out more than 8 million daily e-mails of spiritual wisdom in various flavors to more than 5 million subscribers. Generic "inspiration" is most popular (2.4 million), followed by the Bible (1.6 million), but there are 460,000 subscribers to the Buddhist thought of the day, 313,000 Torah devotees, 268,000 subscribers to Daily Muslim Wisdom (and 236,000 who get the Spiritual Weight Loss message). Even nature-worshiping Pagans are divided into a mind-boggling panoply of sects, including Wicca, Druidism, Pantheism, Animism, Teutonic Paganism, the God of Spirituality Folk and, in case you can't find one to suit you on that list, Eclectic Paganism.

Along with diversity has come a degree of inclusiveness that would have scandalized an earlier generation. According to the *Newsweek/*Beliefnet Poll, eight in 10 Americans—including 68 percent of evangelicals—believe that more than one faith can be a path to salvation, which is most likely not what they were taught in Sunday school. One out of five respondents said he had switched religions as an adult.

This is not surprising in the United States, which for much of its history was a spiritual hothouse in which Methodism, Mormonism, Adventism, Christian Science, Jehovah's Witnesses and the Nation of Islam all took root and flourished. In America even *atheists* are spiritualists, searching for meaning in parapsychology and near-death experiences. There is a streak in the United States of relying on what Pacific Lutheran's Killen calls "individual visceral experience" to validate religious ideas. American faiths have long been characterized by creativity and individualism. "That's their secret to success," says Alan Wolfe, director of the Boisi Center for Religion and American Public Life at Boston College. "Rather than being about a god who commands you, it's about finding a religion that empowers you."

Empowerment is at the heart of Pentecostalism, which has burgeoned from a single Spirit-touched believer at a Kansas Bible school at the turn of the last century to 30 million adherents in America and more than half a billion worldwide. Marching under the Pentecostal banner is a host of denominations whose names roll off the tongue like a voice from heaven: Church of God, International Church of the Four-square Gospel, International Pentecostal Holiness Church, the Assemblies of God. Among them is a tiny Brooklyn storefront church whose sign grandly proclaims the Cathedral of Deliverance. This is where 43-year-old Ron Cox, who left his mother's large Southern Baptist church in his teens, now lives and works as an assistant to the bishop, Steven Wagnon. He tried Hinduism, but it failed to move him; looked into Buddhism, but lost interest when a Buddhist couldn't tell him the meaning of her chant. But one summer night recently, guided by the voice of God to a Pentecostal revival in full-throated swing, he was transfixed by the sight of worshipers so moved by the Holy Spirit that they were jumping, shouting and falling to the floor in a faint. Soon he, too, was experiencing the ecstasy of the Holy Spirit. Once, it seemed to lift him right out of his body:

"I felt the Spirit come upon me, and it was an overwhelming presence. It was bliss. I thought only 10 or 15 minutes had passed, but three hours had gone by. And I remember just shouting, 'Hallelujah, hallelujah, hallelujah!'"

The bliss Cox felt was mingled with awe—the Holy Spirit was inside his very own body. That helps explain Pentecostalism's historical appeal to the poor and marginalized: rural Southerners, African-Americans and, more recently, Hispanics and other immigrants. It is burgeoning in the developing world. "For people who feel overlooked, it provides a sense that you're a very important person," observes Harvey Cox of the Harvard Divinity School. By the same token, people with social aspirations preferred other churches, but nowadays Pentecostalism—the faith of former attorney general John Ashcroft—has lost its stigma as a religion of the poor. And elements of Pentecostal worship are invading other denominations, a change that coincided with the introduction of arena-style screens in churches, replacing hymnals and freeing up people's hands to clap and wave. Naturally, there is some attenuation as you move up the socioeconomic scale. Babbling in foreign-sounding "tongues" turns into discreet murmurs of affirmation. "An atmosphere that is joyous, ecstatic and emotionally expressive is appearing in all kinds of churches now," says Harvard's Cox, "even if it's not labeled Pentecostal."

Empowerment requires intensity of effort; Americans like the idea of taking responsibility for their own souls. This may be why Buddhism—a religion without a personal god and only a few broad ethical precepts—has made such inroads in the American imagination. "People are looking for transformative experience, not just a new creed or dogma," says Surya Das, a U.S.-born Tibetan lama whose spiritual journey began in 1970, when he was a student from New York's Long Island named Jeffrey Miller. "The Ten Commandments and Sermon on the Mount are already there." In most Buddhist countries, and among immigrants in America, the role of the layperson is to support the monks in their lives of contemplation. But American converts want to do their own contemplating. Stephen Cope, who attended Episcopal divinity school but later trained as a psychotherapist, dropped into a meditation center in Cambridge, Mass., one day and soon found himself spending six hours every Sunday sitting and walking in silent contemplation. Then he added yoga to his routine, which he happily describes as "like gasoline on fire" when it comes to igniting a meditative state. And the great thing is, he still attends his Episcopal church—a perfect example of the new American spirituality, with a thirst for transcendence too powerful to be met by just one religion.

People like that could become panentheists, too—a new term for people who believe in the divinity of the natural universe (like the better-known Pantheists), but also postulate an intelligent being or force behind it. To Bridgette O'Brien, a 32-year-old student in the recently created PhD. program in Religion and Nature at the University of Florida, "the divine is something significant in terms of the energy that pervades the natural world at large." Her worship consists of composting, recycling and daily five-mile runs; she describes herself as "the person that picks the earthworms off the sidewalk after the rain to make sure they don't get stepped on." Those seeking a more structured nature-based religion have many choices, including several branches of Druidism. "I talk to my ancestors, the spirits of nature and other deities on a regular basis," says Isaac Bonewits, a 55-year-old New Yorker who founded one

of the best-known Druid orders. Wicca, the largest Pagan sect, with an elaborate calendar of seasonal holidays and rituals, is popular enough to demand its own military chaplains. Unfortunately from the political standpoint, Wiccans refer to themselves as "witches," although they do not, in fact, worship Satan. This confusion led President Bush, when he was Texas governor, to urge the Army to reconsider allowing Wiccan rites at a military base, with the comment "I don't think witchcraft is a religion."

Unlike Buddhists, Catholics cannot take sole responsibility for their souls; they need the sacraments of the church to be saved. But they, too, have experienced a flowering of spirituality, especially among the "John Paul II Catholics," who were energized by the late pope's call for a new outpouring of the Holy Spirit. Since it arrived in the United States in 1957, the "cursillo" movement has initiated more than a half-million American Catholics into the techniques for seeking a direct communion with God. Cursillo, which means "short course," involves a three-day retreat of silent contemplation and lectures that lean heavily on the spiritual vocabulary of evangelism. Also on the rise is the Adoration of the Eucharist: shifts of silent prayer, sometimes round the clock, before the consecrated host in an otherwise empty church. (You can do the same thing over the Internet; one site says it received 2.5 million hits in a year for its unchanging Webcam image of an altar and a monstrance.) "It's been surprisingly popular," says Robert Kloska, director of campus ministry at Holy Cross College in Indiana. "You wouldn't think in modern society there's such a yearning for silence and mysticism, but there is."

Kloska is less enthusiastic about the other manifestation of spirituality he sees on campus, an affinity for "high-energy, almost charismatic prayer and worship." Catholic Charismatic Renewal, which got its start in 1967 when a Duquesne University group on a weekend retreat felt a visitation by the Holy Spirit, now runs thousands of prayer groups in the United States, where worshipers may speak in tongues or collapse in laughter or tears. "Young people got tired of hearing that once upon a time people experienced God directly," says historian Martin E. Marty of the University of Chicago. "They want it to happen for themselves. They don't want to hear that Joan of Arc had a vision. They want to have a vision." It's a little more problematic when the Holy Spirit visits during a regular mass. Clayton Ebsch, a retired technician, was enthusiastic when a charismatic priest took over Precious Blood Parish in Stephenson, Mich., even after some of his friends left for more traditional parishes. Still, he found that speaking in tongues didn't come naturally. "It was just unfamiliar, speaking gibberish and jibber-jabbering," he says, although he sees one virtue in it: "It humbles you."

The Vatican seems ambivalent about these developments. On the one hand, the church wants to keep the allegiance of adherents who have been deserting to evangelical and Pentecostal churches. Three quarters of Hispanic immigrants to the United States are Catholic, but the figure drops to about half by the third generation in America. On the other hand, the raison d'etre of the church is to mediate between the faithful and God. The future Pope Benedict XVI summed up the Vatican's attitude back in 1983, when he wrote of the relationship between "personal experience and the common faith of the Church." Both are important, he said: "a dogmatic faith unsupported by personal experience remains empty; mere personal experience unrelated to the faith of the Church remains blind." In simpler terms: Let's not get carried away here. Emotions come and go, but the mass endures.

The quest for spiritual union with God is as old as mankind itself, uniting the ancient desert tribes of Mesopotamia with the Christian hermits on their mountaintops with American pop singers at the Kabbalah Centre in Los Angeles, poring over the esoteric wisdom encoded in early Jewish texts. And who can begrudge it to them? Well, David Blumenthal of Emory University's Institute for Jewish Studies, for one. His view of the aspiring scholar Madonna is that "anyone who claims to be a Kabbalist and then sings in public largely in the nude is hardly a Kabbalist." The mystical impulse in Judaism—kept alive for centuries by the tiny, fervent band of Hasidim, but long overshadowed in America by the dominance of the rational, decorous Conservative movement—is reasserting itself. The founding text of Kabbalah, the Zohar, conveys the message that God's power depends on humanity's actions. God needs our worship. "It's the same impulse behind Zen Buddhism, Tibetan masters, Hopi Indians," says Arthur Green, rector of the rabbinical school at Hebrew College in Boston. "The ancient esoteric traditions might have something to teach us about living in this age." Even at Hebrew Union College, a citadel of Reform Judaism, provost Norman Cohen admits that "what the Kabbalah can teach us—how to have a relationship with God—has to be treated seriously."

The Hasidim pray ecstatically; they dance with the Torah; they fast to achieve a higher spiritual state, and they drink wine for the same reason. With their distinctive black frock coats and curly sideburns, they are a visible and growing presence in New York and some other cities. Orthodox Judaism, of which they are a branch, is on the rise among young Jews who trade Friday-night dances and shrimp egg foo yung for a more intense religious experience. Orthodox Rabbi Irving Greenberg calls the phenomenon "Jews by choice," reflecting the reality that Jewish practice is no longer a tribal imperative. In a world in which practically every religion has its own cable-TV channel, to step inside a synagogue becomes an existential choice. "To me, that is the revolution of our time, and I don't mean just Judaism," Greenberg says.

In fact, the same issue is very much on the minds of America's Muslims. Forced to define themselves in the face of an alien—and, in recent years, sometimes hostile—majority, the second generation especially has turned increasingly observant. Unlike their parents, they may attend mosque several times a week and pray five times a day, anywhere they can unroll a prayer mat. It has not been lost on them that the way to fit in in present-day America is to be religious. "When our parents came here in the 1960s or '70s there was a pro-secular culture," explains Yusuf Hussein, 22, who was born in Somalia but came to southern California as a teenager. "For us, being a Muslim is the way to forge our own identity, to move forward, to be modern."

Islam emphasizes the unity of all believers, so American-born Muslims are shedding the cultural accouterments of the many countries from which their parents came, or the political freight of African-American converts. They are intent on forging a purer and more spiritual religion. "It's easier being Muslim and African-American than just being African," says Imam Saadiq Saafir, 60, whose journey took him from Christianity to the Nation of Islam and then to orthodox Sunni Islam. Muslims pray to God without the intervention of a priest or a religious hierarchy; he is never farther away than the Qur'an, which is the direct and unmediated word of Allah. "There are many ways to be spiritual," says Megan Wyatt, a blond Ohioan who converted to Islam three years ago. "People find it in yoga. For me, becoming a Muslim gave me the ultimate connection to God."

So, a generation after the question was posed, we can certainly answer that God seems very much alive in the hearts of those who seek him. We have come a long way, it would appear, from that dark year when the young Catholic philosopher Michael Novak was quoted in *Time*, saying, "If, occasionally, I raise my heart in prayer, it is to no God I can see, or hear, or feel." To make the point, we gave Novak, who is now 72 and among the most distinguished theologians in America, the chance to correct the record on his youthful despair. And he replied that God is as far away as he's ever been. Religious revivals are always exuberant and filled with spirit, he says, but the true measure of faith is in adversity and despair, when God doesn't show up in every blade of grass or storefront church. "That's when the true nature of belief comes out," he says. "Joy is appropriate to the beginnings of your faith. But sooner or later somebody will get cancer, or your best friends will betray you. That's when you will be tested."

So let us say together: *Hallelujah! Praise the Lord! Sh'ma Yisrael. Allahu Akbar. Om.* And store up the light against the darkness.

Critical Thinking

1. Can you explain why Americans are religious (compared to other developed countries)?
2. What is the significance that non-Christian religions are also doing well in America, even those that are looked down on by the majority?
3. What future would you predict for religion in America?

Create Central

www.mhhe.com/createcentral

Internet References

Sociosite
www.topsite.com/goto/sociosite.net
Socioweb
www.topsite.com/goto/socioweb.com
Sociology—Study Sociology Online
http://edu.learnsoc.org
Sociology Web Resources
www.mhhe.com/socscience/sociology/resources/index.htm

With Anne Underwood; Ben Whitford; Juliet Chung; Vanessa Juarez; Dan Berrett and Lorraine Ali.

Unit 6

UNIT

Prepared by: Kurt Finsterbusch, *University of Maryland, College Park*

Social Change and the Future

Fascination with the future is an enduring theme in literature, art, poetry, and religion. Human beings are anxious to know if tomorrow will be different from today, and in what ways it might differ. Coping with change has become a top priority in the lives of many. One result of change is stress. When the future is uncertain and the individual appears to have little control over what happens, stress can be a serious problem. On the other hand, stress can have positive effects on people's lives if they can perceive changes as challenges and opportunities.

Article   Prepared by: Kurt Finsterbusch, *University of Maryland, College Park*

The New Population Bomb
The Four Megatrends That Will Change the World

JACK A. GOLDSTONE

Learning Outcomes

After reading this article, you will be able to:

- Consider that population changes are the foundation for many predictions about the economy and the society.

- Understand that rapid population growth in developing countries and slow or no growth in developed countries rapidly changes the "map" of the world for many other issues.

- Critically examine Goldstone's thesis that the current population dynamics could collapse many governing structures.

Forty-two years ago, the biologist Paul Ehrlich warned in The Population Bomb that mass starvation would strike in the 1970s and 1980s, with the world's population growth outpacing the production of food and other critical resources. Thanks to innovations and efforts such as the "green revolution" in farming and the widespread adoption of family planning, Ehrlich's worst fears did not come to pass. In fact, since the 1970s, global economic output has increased and fertility has fallen dramatically, especially in developing countries.

The United Nations Population Division now projects that global population growth will nearly halt by 2050. By that date, the world's population will have stabilized at 9.15 billion people, according to the "medium growth" variant of the UN's authoritative population database World Population Prospects: The 2008 Revision. (Today's global population is 6.83 billion.) Barring a cataclysmic climate crisis or a complete failure to recover from the current economic malaise, global economic output is expected to increase by two to three percent per year, meaning that global income will increase far more than population over the next four decades.

But twenty-first-century international security will depend less on how many people inhabit the world than on how the global population is composed and distributed: where populations are declining and where they are growing, which countries are relatively older and which are more youthful, and how demographics will influence population movements across regions.

These elements are not well recognized or widely understood. A recent article in *The Economist,* for example, cheered the decline in global fertility without noting other vital demographic developments. Indeed, the same UN data cited by *The Economist* reveal four historic shifts that will fundamentally alter the world's population over the next four decades: the relative demographic weight of the world's developed countries will drop by nearly 25 percent, shifting economic power to the developing nations; the developed countries' labor forces will substantially age and decline, constraining economic growth in the developed world and raising the demand for immigrant workers; most of the world's expected population growth will increasingly be concentrated in today's poorest, youngest, and most heavily Muslim countries, which have a dangerous lack of quality education, capital, and employment opportunities; and, for the first time in history, most of the world's population will become urbanized, with the largest urban centers being in the world's poorest countries, where policing, sanitation, and health care are often scarce. Taken together, these trends will pose challenges every bit as alarming as those noted by Ehrlich. Coping with them will require nothing less than a major reconsideration of the world's basic global governance structures.

Europe's Reversal of Fortunes

At the beginning of the eighteenth century, approximately 20 percent of the world's inhabitants lived in Europe (including Russia). Then, with the Industrial Revolution, Europe's population boomed, and streams of European emigrants set off for the Americas. By the eve of World War I, Europe's population had more than quadrupled. In 1913, Europe had more people than China, and the proportion of the world's population living in Europe and the former European colonies of North America had risen to over 33 percent. But this trend reversed after World War I, as basic health care and sanitation began to spread to poorer countries. In Asia, Africa, and Latin America, people began to live longer, and birthrates remained high or fell only slowly. By 2003, the combined populations of Europe, the United States, and Canada accounted for just 17 percent of the global population. In 2050, this figure is expected to be just 12 percent—far less than it was in 1700. (These projections, moreover, might even understate the reality because they reflect the "medium growth" projection of the UN forecasts, which assumes that the fertility rates of developing countries will decline while those of developed countries will increase. In fact, many developed countries show no evidence of increasing fertility rates.) The West's relative decline is even more dramatic if one also considers changes in income. The Industrial Revolution made Europeans not only more numerous than they had been but also considerably richer per capita than others worldwide. According to the economic historian Angus Maddison, Europe, the United States, and Canada together produced about 32 percent of the world's GDP at the beginning of the nineteenth century. By 1950, that proportion had increased to a remarkable 68 percent of the world's total output (adjusted to reflect purchasing power parity).

This trend, too, is headed for a sharp reversal. The proportion of global GDP produced by Europe, the United States, and Canada fell from 68 percent in 1950 to 47 percent in 2003 and will decline even more steeply in the future. If the growth rate of per capita income (again, adjusted for purchasing power parity) between 2003 and 2050 remains as it was between 1973 and 2003—averaging 1.68 percent annually in Europe, the United States, and Canada and 2.47 percent annually in the rest of the world—then the combined GDP of Europe, the United States, and Canada will roughly double by 2050, whereas the GDP of the rest of the world will grow by a factor of five. The portion of global GDP produced by Europe, the United States, and Canada in 2050 will then be less than 30 percent—smaller than it was in 1820.

These figures also imply that an overwhelming proportion of the world's GDP growth between 2003 and 2050—nearly 80 percent—will occur outside of Europe, the United States, and Canada. By the middle of this century, the global middle class—those capable of purchasing durable consumer products, such as cars, appliances, and electronics—will increasingly be found in what is now considered the developing world. The World Bank has predicted that by 2030 the number of middle-class people in the developing world will be 1.2 billion—a rise of 200 percent since 2005. This means that the developing world's middle class alone will be larger than the total populations of Europe, Japan, and the United States combined. From now on, therefore, the main driver of global economic expansion will be the economic growth of newly industrialized countries, such as Brazil, China, India, Indonesia, Mexico, and Turkey.

Aging Pains

Part of the reason developed countries will be less economically dynamic in the coming decades is that their populations will become substantially older. The European countries, Canada, the United States, Japan, South Korea, and even China are aging at unprecedented rates. Today, the proportion of people aged 60 or older in China and South Korea is 12–15 percent. It is 15–22 percent in the European Union, Canada, and the United States and 30 percent in Japan. With baby boomers aging and life expectancy increasing, these numbers will increase dramatically. In 2050, approximately 30 percent of Americans, Canadians, Chinese, and Europeans will be over 60, as will more than 40 percent of Japanese and South Koreans.

Over the next decades, therefore, these countries will have increasingly large proportions of retirees and increasingly small proportions of workers. As workers born during the baby boom of 1945–65 are retiring, they are not being replaced by a new cohort of citizens of prime working age (15–59 years old).

Industrialized countries are experiencing a drop in their working-age populations that is even more severe than the overall slowdown in their population growth. South Korea represents the most extreme example. Even as its total population is projected to decline by almost 9 percent by 2050 (from 48.3 million to 44.1 million), the population of working-age South Koreans is expected to drop by 36 percent (from 32.9 million to 21.1 million), and the number of South Koreans aged 60 and older will increase by almost 150 percent (from 7.3 million to 18 million). By 2050, in other words, the entire working-age population will barely exceed the 60-and-older population. Although South Korea's case is extreme, it represents an increasingly common fate for developed countries. Europe is expected to lose 24 percent of its prime working-age population (about 120 million workers) by 2050, and its 60-and-older population is expected to increase by 47 percent. In the United States, where higher fertility and more immigration are expected than in Europe, the working-age population will grow by 15 percent over the next four decades—a steep decline from its growth of 62 percent between 1950 and 2010. And by 2050, the United States' 60-and-older population is expected to double.

All this will have a dramatic impact on economic growth, health care, and military strength in the developed world. The forces that fueled economic growth in industrialized countries during the second half of the twentieth century—increased productivity due to better education, the movement of women into the labor force, and innovations in technology—will all likely weaken in the coming decades. College enrollment boomed after World War II, a trend that is not likely to recur in the twenty-first century; the extensive movement of women into the labor force also was a one-time social change; and the technological change of the time resulted from innovators who created new products and leading-edge consumers who were willing to try them out—two groups that are thinning out as the industrialized world's population ages.

Overall economic growth will also be hampered by a decline in the number of new consumers and new households. When developed countries' labor forces were growing by 0.5–1.0 percent per year, as they did until 2005, even annual increases in real output per worker of just 1.7 percent meant that annual economic growth totaled 2.2–2.7 percent per year. But with the labor forces of many developed countries (such as Germany, Hungary, Japan, Russia, and the Baltic states) now shrinking by 0.2 percent per year and those of other countries (including Austria, the Czech Republic, Denmark, Greece, and Italy) growing by less than 0.2 percent per year, the same 1.7 percent increase in real output per worker yields only 1.5–1.9 percent annual overall growth. Moreover, developed countries will be lucky to keep productivity growth at even that level; in many developed countries, productivity is more likely to decline as the population ages.

A further strain on industrialized economies will be rising medical costs: as populations age, they will demand more health care for longer periods of time. Public pension schemes for aging populations are already being reformed in various industrialized countries—often prompting heated debate. In theory, at least, pensions might be kept solvent by increasing the retirement age, raising taxes modestly, and phasing out benefits for the wealthy. Regardless, the number of 80- and 90-year-olds—who are unlikely to work and highly likely to require nursing-home and other expensive care—will rise dramatically. And even if 60- and 70-year-olds remain active and employed, they will require procedures and medications—hip replacements, kidney transplants, blood-pressure treatments—to sustain their health in old age.

All this means that just as aging developed countries will have proportionally fewer workers, innovators, and consumerist young households, a large portion of those countries' remaining economic growth will have to be diverted to pay for the medical bills and pensions of their growing elderly populations. Basic services, meanwhile, will be increasingly costly because fewer young workers will be available for strenuous and labor-intensive jobs. Unfortunately, policymakers seldom reckon with these potentially disruptive effects of otherwise welcome developments, such as higher life expectancy.

Youth and Islam in the Developing World

Even as the industrialized countries of Europe, North America, and Northeast Asia will experience unprecedented aging this century, fast-growing countries in Africa, Latin America, the Middle East, and Southeast Asia will have exceptionally youthful populations. Today, roughly nine out of ten children under the age of 15 live in developing countries. And these are the countries that will continue to have the world's highest birthrates. Indeed, over 70 percent of the world's population growth between now and 2050 will occur in 24 countries, all of which are classified by the World Bank as low income or lower-middle income, with an average per capita income of under $3,855 in 2008.

Many developing countries have few ways of providing employment to their young, fast-growing populations. Would-be laborers, therefore, will be increasingly attracted to the labor markets of the aging developed countries of Europe, North America, and Northeast Asia. Youthful immigrants from nearby regions with high unemployment—Central America, North Africa, and Southeast Asia, for example—will be drawn to those vital entry-level and manual-labor jobs that sustain advanced economies: janitors, nursing-home aides, bus drivers, plumbers, security guards, farm workers, and the like. Current levels of immigration from developing to developed countries are paltry compared to those that the forces of supply and demand might soon create across the world.

These forces will act strongly on the Muslim world, where many economically weak countries will continue to experience dramatic population growth in the decades ahead. In 1950, Bangladesh, Egypt, Indonesia, Nigeria, Pakistan, and Turkey had a combined population of 242 million. By 2009, those six countries were the world's most populous Muslim-majority countries and had a combined population of 886 million. Their populations are continuing to grow and indeed are expected to increase by 475 million between now and 2050—during which time, by comparison, the six most populous developed countries are projected to gain only 44 million inhabitants. Worldwide, of the 48 fastest-growing countries today—those with annual population growth of two percent or more—28 are majority Muslim or have Muslim minorities of 33 percent or more.

It is therefore imperative to improve relations between Muslim and Western societies. This will be difficult given that many Muslims live in poor communities vulnerable to radical appeals and many see the West as antagonistic and militaristic. In the 2009 Pew Global Attitudes Project survey, for example, whereas 69 percent of those Indonesians and Nigerians surveyed reported viewing the United States favorably, just 18 percent of those polled in Egypt, Jordan, Pakistan, and Turkey (all U.S. allies) did. And in 2006, when the Pew survey last asked detailed questions about Muslim-Western relations, more than half of the respondents in Muslim countries characterized those relations as bad and blamed the West for this state of affairs.

But improving relations is all the more important because of the growing demographic weight of poor Muslim countries and the attendant increase in Muslim immigration, especially to Europe from North Africa and the Middle East. (To be sure, forecasts that Muslims will soon dominate Europe are outlandish: Muslims compose just three to ten percent of the population in the major European countries today, and this proportion will at most double by midcentury.) Strategists worldwide must consider that the world's young are becoming concentrated in those countries least prepared to educate and employ them, including some Muslim states. Any resulting poverty, social tension, or ideological radicalization could have disruptive effects in many corners of the world. But this need not be the case; the healthy immigration of workers to the developed world and the movement of capital to the developing world, among other things, could lead to better results.

Urban Sprawl

Exacerbating twenty-first-century risks will be the fact that the world is urbanizing to an unprecedented degree. The year 2010 will likely be the first time in history that a majority of the world's people live in cities rather than in the countryside. Whereas less than 30 percent of the world's population was urban in 1950, according to UN projections, more than 70 percent will be by 2050.

Lower-income countries in Asia and Africa are urbanizing especially rapidly, as agriculture becomes less labor intensive and as employment opportunities shift to the industrial and service sectors. Already, most of the world's urban agglomerations—Mumbai (population 20.1 million), Mexico City (19.5 million), New Delhi (17 million), Shanghai (15.8 million), Calcutta (15.6 million), Karachi (13.1 million), Cairo (12.5 million), Manila (11.7 million), Lagos (10.6 million), Jakarta (9.7 million)—are found in low-income countries. Many of these countries have multiple cities with over one million residents each: Pakistan has eight, Mexico 12, and China more than 100. The UN projects that the urbanized proportion of sub-Saharan Africa will nearly double between 2005 and 2050, from 35 percent (300 million people) to over 67 percent (1 billion). China, which is roughly 40 percent urbanized today, is expected to be 73 percent urbanized by 2050; India, which is less than 30 percent urbanized today, is expected to be 55 percent urbanized by 2050. Overall, the world's urban population is expected to grow by 3 billion people by 2050.

This urbanization may prove destabilizing. Developing countries that urbanize in the twenty-first century will have far lower per capita incomes than did many industrial countries when they first urbanized. The United States, for example, did not reach 65 percent urbanization until 1950, when per capita income was nearly $13,000 (in 2005 dollars). By contrast, Nigeria, Pakistan, and the Philippines, which are approaching similar levels of urbanization, currently have per capita incomes of just $1,800–$4,000 (in 2005 dollars).

According to the research of Richard Cincotta and other political demographers, countries with younger populations are especially prone to civil unrest and are less able to create or sustain democratic institutions. And the more heavily urbanized, the more such countries are likely to experience Dickensian poverty and anarchic violence. In good times, a thriving economy might keep urban residents employed and governments flush with sufficient resources to meet their needs. More often, however, sprawling and impoverished cities are vulnerable to crime lords, gangs, and petty rebellions. Thus, the rapid urbanization of the developing world in the decades ahead might bring, in exaggerated form, problems similar to those that urbanization brought to nineteenth-century Europe. Back then, cyclical employment, inadequate policing, and limited sanitation and education often spawned widespread labor strife, periodic violence, and sometimes—as in the 1820s, the 1830s, and 1848—even revolutions.

International terrorism might also originate in fast-urbanizing developing countries (even more than it already does). With their neighborhood networks, access to the Internet and digital communications technology, and concentration of valuable targets, sprawling cities offer excellent opportunities for recruiting, maintaining, and hiding terrorist networks.

Defusing the Bomb

Averting this century's potential dangers will require sweeping measures. Three major global efforts defused the population bomb of Ehrlich's day: a commitment by governments and nongovernmental organizations to control reproduction rates; agricultural advances, such as the green revolution and the spread of new technology; and a vast increase in international trade, which globalized markets and thus allowed developing countries to export foodstuffs in exchange for seeds, fertilizers, and machinery, which in turn helped them boost production. But today's population bomb is the product less of absolute growth in the world's population than of changes in its age and distribution. Policymakers must therefore adapt today's global governance institutions to the new realities of the aging of the industrialized world, the concentration of the world's economic and population growth in developing countries, and the increase in international immigration.

During the Cold War, Western strategists divided the world into a "First World," of democratic industrialized countries; a "Second World," of communist industrialized countries; and a "Third World," of developing countries. These strategists focused chiefly on deterring or managing conflict between the First and the Second Worlds and on launching proxy wars and diplomatic initiatives to attract Third World countries into the First World's camp. Since the end of the Cold War, strategists have largely abandoned this three-group division and have tended to believe either that the United States, as the sole superpower, would maintain a Pax Americana or that the world would become multipolar, with the United States, Europe, and China playing major roles.

Unfortunately, because they ignore current global demographic trends, these views will be obsolete within a few decades. A better approach would be to consider a different three-world order, with a new First World of the aging industrialized nations of North America, Europe, and Asia's Pacific Rim (including Japan, Singapore, South Korea, and Taiwan, as well as China after 2030, by which point the one-child policy will have produced significant aging); a Second World comprising fast-growing and economically dynamic countries with a healthy mix of young and old inhabitants (such as Brazil, Iran, Mexico, Thailand, Turkey, and Vietnam, as well as China until 2030); and a Third World of fast-growing, very young, and increasingly urbanized countries with poorer economies and often weak governments. To cope with the instability that will likely arise from the new Third World's urbanization, economic strife, lawlessness, and potential terrorist activity, the aging industrialized nations of the new First World must build effective alliances with the growing powers of the new Second World and together reach out to Third World nations. Second World powers will be pivotal in the twenty-first century not just because they will drive economic growth and consume technologies and other products engineered in the First World; they will also be central to international security and cooperation. The realities of religion, culture, and geographic proximity mean that any peaceful and productive engagement by the First World of Third World countries will have to include the open cooperation of Second World countries.

Strategists, therefore, must fundamentally reconsider the structure of various current global institutions. The G-8, for example, will likely become obsolete as a body for making global economic policy. The G-20 is already becoming increasingly important, and this is less a short-term consequence of the ongoing global financial crisis than the beginning of the necessary recognition that Brazil, China, India, Indonesia, Mexico,

Turkey, and others are becoming global economic powers. International institutions will not retain their legitimacy if they exclude the world's fastest-growing and most economically dynamic countries. It is essential, therefore, despite European concerns about the potential effects on immigration, to take steps such as admitting Turkey into the European Union. This would add youth and economic dynamism to the EU—and would prove that Muslims are welcome to join Europeans as equals in shaping a free and prosperous future. On the other hand, excluding Turkey from the EU could lead to hostility not only on the part of Turkish citizens, who are expected to number 100 million by 2050, but also on the part of Muslim populations worldwide.

NATO must also adapt. The alliance today is composed almost entirely of countries with aging, shrinking populations and relatively slow-growing economies. It is oriented toward the Northern Hemisphere and holds on to a Cold War structure that cannot adequately respond to contemporary threats. The young and increasingly populous countries of Africa, the Middle East, Central Asia, and South Asia could mobilize insurgents much more easily than NATO could mobilize the troops it would need if it were called on to stabilize those countries. Long-standing NATO members should, therefore—although it would require atypical creativity and flexibility—consider the logistical and demographic advantages of inviting into the alliance countries such as Brazil and Morocco, rather than countries such as Albania. That this seems far-fetched does not minimize the imperative that First World countries begin including large and strategic Second and Third World powers in formal international alliances.

The case of Afghanistan—a country whose population is growing fast and where NATO is currently engaged—illustrates the importance of building effective global institutions. Today, there are 28 million Afghans; by 2025, there will be 45 million; and by 2050, there will be close to 75 million. As nearly 20 million additional Afghans are born over the next 15 years, NATO will have an opportunity to help Afghanistan become reasonably stable, self-governing, and prosperous. If NATO's efforts fail and the Afghans judge that NATO intervention harmed their interests, tens of millions of young Afghans will become more hostile to the West. But if they come to think that NATO's involvement benefited their society, the West will have tens of millions of new friends. The example might then motivate the approximately one billion other young Muslims growing up in low-income countries over the next four decades to look more kindly on relations between their countries and the countries of the industrialized West.

Creative Reforms at Home

The aging industrialized countries can also take various steps at home to promote stability in light of the coming demographic trends. First, they should encourage families to have more children. France and Sweden have had success providing child care, generous leave time, and financial allowances to families with young children. Yet there is no consensus among policymakers—and certainly not among demographers—about what policies best encourage fertility.

More important than unproven tactics for increasing family size is immigration. Correctly managed, population movement can benefit developed and developing countries alike. Given the dangers of young, underemployed, and unstable populations in developing countries, immigration to developed countries can provide economic opportunities for the ambitious and serve as a safety valve for all. Countries that embrace immigrants, such as the United States, gain economically by having willing laborers and greater entrepreneurial spirit. And countries with high levels of emigration (but not so much that they experience so-called brain drains) also benefit because emigrants often send remittances home or return to their native countries with valuable education and work experience.

One somewhat daring approach to immigration would be to encourage a reverse flow of older immigrants from developed to developing countries. If older residents of developed countries took their retirements along the southern coast of the Mediterranean or in Latin America or Africa, it would greatly reduce the strain on their home countries' public entitlement systems. The developing countries involved, meanwhile, would benefit because caring for the elderly and providing retirement and leisure services is highly labor intensive. Relocating a portion of these activities to developing countries would provide employment and valuable training to the young, growing populations of the Second and Third Worlds.

This would require developing residential and medical facilities of First World quality in Second and Third World countries. Yet even this difficult task would be preferable to the status quo, by which low wages and poor facilities lead to a steady drain of medical and nursing talent from developing to developed countries. Many residents of developed countries who desire cheaper medical procedures already practice medical tourism today, with India, Singapore, and Thailand being the most common destinations. (For example, the international consulting firm Deloitte estimated that 750,000 Americans traveled abroad for care in 2008.)

Never since 1800 has a majority of the world's economic growth occurred outside of Europe, the United States, and Canada. Never have so many people in those regions been over 60 years old. And never have low-income countries' populations been so young and so urbanized. But such will be the world's demography in the twenty-first century. The strategic and economic policies of the twentieth century are obsolete, and it is time to find new ones.

Reference

Goldstone, Jack A. "The new population bomb: the four megatrends that will change the world." *Foreign Affairs* 89.1 (2010): 31. *General OneFile*. Web. 23 Jan. 2010. http://0-find.galegroup .com.www.consuls.org/gps/start.do?proId=IPS& userGroupName=a30wc.

Critical Thinking

1. How will aging populations be taken care of?
2. Why does Goldstone call the current demographics a population bomb?
3. What kind of changes are called for by these population issues?

Create Central

www.mhhe.com/createcentral

Internet References

Sociosite
www.topsite.com/goto/sociosite.net

Socioweb
www.topsite.com/goto/socioweb.com

Sociology—Study Sociology Online
http://edu.learnsoc.org

Sociology Web Resources
www.mhhe.com/socscience/sociology/resources/index.htm

Goldstone, Jack A. From *Foreign Affairs*, vol. 89, no. 1, January/February 2010, pp. 31–43. Copyright © 2010 by Council on Foreign Relations, Inc. Reprinted by permission of Foreign Affairs. www.ForeignAffairs.org

Article   Prepared by: Kurt Finsterbusch, *University of Maryland, College Park*

Full Planet, Empty Plates

Food is the new oil. Land is the new gold.

LESTER R. BROWN

Learning Outcomes

After reading this article, you will be able to:

- Critique Brown's thesis that the world is facing a growing food crisis.

- Review the arguments for environmental limits and subsequent food production limits. Review the arguments against environmental limits.

- Assess the potential for technology to take care of the food problem while taking into account the failure of technology to noticeably increase food production in the past two decades.

Problems in a Hot and Hungry World

In the early spring of 2012, U.S. farmers were on their way to planting some 96 million acres in corn, the most in 75 years. A warm early spring got the crop off to a great start. Analysts were predicting the largest corn harvest on record.

The corn plant is as sensitive as it is productive. Thirsty and fast-growing, it is vulnerable to both extreme heat and drought. At elevated temperatures, the corn plant, which is normally so productive, goes into thermal shock. As spring turned into summer, the thermometer began to rise across the Corn Belt. In the St. Louis, Missouri area, the southern Corn Belt, the temperature climbed to a record 105 degrees Fahrenheit or higher 11 days in a row. The corn crop failed.

Over a span of weeks, we saw how the more extreme weather events that come with climate change can affect food security.

The United States is the leading producer and exporter of corn, the world's feed grain. At home, corn accounts for four-fifths of the U.S. grain harvest. Internationally, the U.S. corn crop exceeds China's rice and wheat harvests combined. Among the big three grains—corn, wheat, and rice—corn is now the leader, with production well above that of wheat and nearly double that of rice.

The U.S. Great Drought of 2012 has raised corn prices to the highest level in history. The world price of food, which has already doubled over the last decade, is slated to climb higher, ushering in a new wave of food unrest. This year's corn crop shortfall will accelerate the transition from the era of abundance and surpluses to an era of chronic scarcity. As food prices climb, the worldwide competition for control of land and water resources is intensifying.

In this new world, access to food is replacing access to oil as an overriding concern of governments. Food is the new oil, land is the new gold. Welcome to the new geopolitics of food.

For Americans who spend only 9 percent of their income on food, the doubling of food prices is not a big deal. But for those who spend 50–70 percent of their income on food, it is a serious matter. There is little latitude for them to offset the price rise simply by spending more. They must eat less.

A recent survey by Save the Children shows that 24 percent of families in India now have foodless days. For Nigeria, the comparable figure is 27 percent. For Peru, it is 14 percent. In a hungry world, hunger often has a child's face. Millions of children are dangerously hungry, some too weak to walk to school. Many are physically and mentally stunted.

Even as hunger spreads, farmers are facing new challenges on both sides of the food equation. On the demand side, there have been two sources of demand growth. The oldest of these is population growth. Each year the world adds nearly 80 million people. Tonight there will be 219,000 people at the dinner table who were not there last night, many with empty plates. Tomorrow night, the next night, and on.

The second source of growing demand for grain is consumers moving up the food chain. As incomes rise, people eat more grain-intensive livestock and poultry products. Today, with incomes rising fast in emerging economies, there are at least 3 billion people moving up the food chain. The largest single concentration of these new meat eaters is in China, which now consumes twice as much meat as the United States.

Now there is a third source of demand for grain: the automobile. In 2011, the United States harvested nearly 400 million tons of grain. Of this, 127 million tons (32 percent) went to ethanol distilleries to fuel cars.

This growing demand for grain has boosted the annual increase in world grain consumption from 20 million tons a year a decade ago to 45 million tons a year today.

On the supply side, farmers continue to wrestle with the age-old threat of soil erosion. Some 30 percent of the world's cropland is losing productive topsoil far faster than nature can replace it. Two huge new dust bowls are forming, one in North-western China and the other in Central Africa.

Beyond the loss of topsoil, three new challenges are emerging on the production front. One, aquifers are being depleted and irrigation wells are starting to go dry in 18 countries that together contain half the world's people. Two, in some of the more agriculturally advanced countries, rice and wheat yields per acre, which have been rising steadily for several decades, are beginning to plateau. And three, the Earth's temperature is rising, threatening to disrupt world agriculture in ways that can only be described as scary.

Among the countries where water tables are falling and aquifers are being depleted are the big three grain producers—China, India, and the United States. In India 175 million people are being fed with grain produced by overpumping. The comparable number for China is 130 million. In the United States, the irrigated area is shrinking in leading farm states with rapid population growth such as California and Texas as aquifers are depleted and irrigation water is diverted to cities.

After several decades of rising grain yields, some of the more agriculturally advanced countries are hitting limits that were not widely anticipated. Rice yields in Japan, a pioneer in raising yields, have not increased for 17 years. In both Japan and South Korea, yields have plateaued at just under 5 tons per hectare. (1 hectare = 2.47 acres.) China's rice yields are now closely approaching those of Japan and may also soon plateau.

A similar situation exists with wheat yields. In France, Germany, and the United Kingdom—the three leading wheat producers in Western Europe—there has been no rise for more than a decade. Other countries will soon be hitting their limits for grain yields.

The newest challenge confronting farmers is global warming. The massive burning of fossil fuels is increasing the level of carbon dioxide in the atmosphere, raising the Earth's temperature and disrupting climate. Historically when there was an extreme weather event—an intense heat wave or a drought—things would likely be back to normal by the next harvest. Now with the climate in flux, there is no "norm" to return to.

For each 1-degree-Celsius rise in temperature above the optimum during the growing season farmers can expect at least a 10-percent decline in grain yields. A study of the effect of temperature on corn and soybean yields in the United States found that a 1-degree-Celsius rise in temperature reduced yields 17 percent. If the world continues with business as usual, failing to address the climate issue, the Earth's temperature during this century could easily rise by 6 degrees Celsius (11 degrees Fahrenheit).

The effect of high temperature on food production is on full display in the United States where the summer drought and heat that covered much of the country, including most of the Corn Belt, will reduce the U.S. corn harvest by 30 percent or more.

As food supplies tighten, the geopolitics of food is fast overshadowing the geopolitics of oil. The first signs of trouble came in 2007, when world grain production fell behind demand.

Grain and soybean prices started to climb, doubling by mid-2008. In response, many exporting countries tried to curb rising domestic food prices by restricting exports. Among them were Russia and Argentina, two leading wheat exporters. Viet Nam, the world's number two rice exporter, banned exports entirely in the early months of 2008.

With key suppliers restricting or banning exports, importing countries panicked. Fearing they might not be able to buy needed grain from the market, some of the more affluent countries, led by Saudi Arabia, China, and South Korea, then took the unusual step of buying or leasing land long term in other countries on which to grow food for themselves. These land acquisitions have since grown rapidly in number. Most of them are in Africa. Among the principal destinations for land hunters are Ethiopia, Sudan, and South Sudan, each of them countries that cannot feed the people who live there; millions of people are being sustained with food donations from the U.N. World Food Program.

As of mid-2012, hundreds of land acquisition deals had been negotiated or were under negotiation, some of them exceeding a million acres. A 2011 World Bank analysis of these "land grabs" reported that at least 140 million acres were involved—an area that exceeds the cropland devoted to corn and wheat combined in the United States. This onslaught of land acquisitions has become a land rush as governments, agribusiness firms, and private investors seek control of land wherever they can find it. Such acquisitions also typically involve water rights, meaning that land grabs potentially affect downstream countries as well.

For instance, any water extracted from the upper Nile River basin to irrigate newly planted crops in Ethiopia, Sudan, or South Sudan will now not reach Egypt, upending the delicate water politics of the Nile by adding new countries that Egypt must compete with for water. Egypt already has to import a great deal of grain.

The potential for conflict is high. Many of the land deals have been made in secret, and much of the time the land involved was already being farmed by villagers when it was sold or leased. Often those already farming the land were neither consulted nor even informed of the new arrangements. And because there typically are no formal land titles in many developing-country villages, the farmers who lost their land have had little support for bringing their cases to court.

Time is running out. The world may be much closer to an unmanageable food shortage—replete with soaring food prices, spreading food unrest, and ultimately political instability—than most people realize.

Solutions ~ Saving Civilization is not a Spectator Sport

On the demand side of the food equation, there are four pressing needs—to stabilize world population, eradicate poverty, reduce excessive meat consumption, and reverse biofuels policies that encourage the use of food, land, or water that could otherwise be used to feed people. We need to press forward on all four fronts at the same time.

The first two goals are closely related. Indeed, stabilizing population depends on eliminating poverty. Even a cursory look at population growth rates shows that the countries where population size has stabilized are virtually all high-income countries. On the other side of the coin, nearly all countries with high population growth rates are on the low end of the global economic ladder.

Shifting to smaller families has many benefits. For one, there will be fewer people at the dinner table. It comes as no surprise that a disproportionate share of malnutrition is found in larger families.

At the other end of the food spectrum, a large segment of the world's people are consuming animal products at a level that is unhealthy and contributing to obesity and cardiovascular disease. The good news is that when the affluent consume less meat, milk, and eggs, it improves their health. When meat consumption falls in the United States, as it recently has, this frees up grain for direct consumption. Moving down the food chain also lessens pressure on the Earth's land and water resources. In short, it is a win-win-win situation.

Another initiative, one that can quickly lower food prices, is the cancellation of biofuel mandates. There is no social justification for the massive conversion of food into fuel for cars. With plug-in hybrids and all-electric cars coming to market that can run on local wind-generated electricity at a gasoline-equivalent cost of 80¢ per gallon, why keep burning costly fuel at four times the price?

On the supply side of the food equation, we face several challenges, including stabilizing climate, raising water productivity, and conserving soil. Stabilizing climate is not easy, but it can be done if we act quickly. It will take a huge cut in carbon emissions, some 80 percent within a decade, to give us a chance of avoiding the worst consequences of climate change. This means a wholesale restructuring of the world energy economy.

The easiest way to do this is to restructure the tax system. The market has many strengths, but it also has some dangerous weaknesses. It readily captures the direct costs of mining coal and delivering it to power plants. But the market does not incorporate the indirect costs of fossil fuels, such as the costs to society of global warming. Sir Nicholas Stern, former chief economist at the World Bank, noted that climate change was the product of a massive market failure.

The goal of restructuring taxes is to lower income taxes and raise carbon taxes so that the cost of climate change and other indirect costs of fossil fuel use are incorporated in market prices. If we can get the market to tell the truth, the transition from coal and oil to wind, solar, and geothermal energy will move very fast. If we remove the massive subsidies to the fossil fuel industry, we will move even faster.

Although this energy transition may seem farfetched, it is moving ahead, and at an exciting pace in some countries. For example, four states in northern Germany now get at least 46 percent of their electricity from wind. For Denmark, the figure is 26 percent. In the United States, both Iowa and South Dakota now get one fifth of their electricity from wind farms. Solar power in Europe can now satisfy the electricity needs of some 15 million households. Kenya now gets one fifth of its electricity from geothermal energy. And Indonesia is shooting for 9,500 megawatts of geothermal generating capacity by 2025, which would meet 56 percent of current electricity needs.

In addition to the carbon tax, we need to reduce dependence on the automobile by upgrading public transportation worldwide to European standards. The world has already proved that passenger rail systems can be electric. As we shift from traditional oil-powered engines to plug-in hybrids and all-electric cars, we can substitute electricity from renewable sources for oil. In the meantime, as the U.S. automobile fleet, which peaked in 2008, shrinks, U.S. gasoline use will continue the decline of recent years. This decline, in the country that consumes more gasoline than the next 16 countries combined, is a welcome new trend.

Along with stabilizing climate, another key component to avoiding a breakdown in the food system is to raise water productivity. This begins with agriculture, simply because 70 percent of all water use goes to irrigation. The least efficient irrigation technologies are flood and furrow irrigation. Sprinkler irrigation, using the center-pivot systems that are widely seen in the crop circles in the western U.S. Great Plains, and drip irrigation are far more efficient. The advantage of drip irrigation is that it applies water very slowly at a rate that the plants can use, losing little to evaporation. It simultaneously raises yields and reduces water use.

Another option is to encourage the use of more water-efficient crops, such as wheat, instead of rice. China banned rice production in the Beijing region. Moving down the food chain also saves water.

Although urban water use is relatively small compared with that used for irrigation, cities too can save water. Some cities now are beginning to recycle much if not most of the water they use. Singapore, whose freshwater supplies are severely restricted by geography, relies on a graduated water tax—the more water you use, the more you pay per gallon—and an extensive water recycling program to meet the needs of its 5 million residents.

The key to raising water use efficiency is price policy. Because water is routinely underpriced, especially that used for irrigation, it is used wastefully. Pricing water to encourage conservation could lead to huge gains in water use efficiency, in effect expanding the supply that could in turn be used to expand the irrigated area.

The third big supply-side challenge after stabilizing climate and raising water productivity is controlling soil erosion. With topsoil blowing away at a record rate and two huge dust bowls forming in Asia and Africa, stabilizing soils will take a heavy investment in conservation measures. Perhaps the best example of a large-scale effort to reduce soil erosion came in the 1930s, after a combination of overplowing and land mismanagement created a dust bowl that threatened to turn the U.S. Great Plains into a vast desert.

In response to this traumatic experience, the United States introduced revolutionary changes in agricultural practices, including returning highly erodible land to grass, terracing, and planting tree shelterbelts.

Another valuable tool in the soil conservation tool kit is no-till farming. Instead of the traditional practice of plowing land and discing or harrowing it to prepare the seedbed, and then using a mechanical cultivator to control weeds in row crops, farmers simply drill seeds directly through crop residues into undisturbed soil, controlling weeds with herbicides when necessary. In addition to reducing erosion, this practice retains water, raises soil organic matter content, and greatly reduces energy use for tillage.

In the United States, the no-till area went from 7 million hectares in 1990 to 26 million hectares (67 million acres) in 2007. Now widely used in the production of corn and soybeans, no-till agriculture has spread rapidly in the western hemisphere, covering 26 million hectares each in Brazil and Argentina and 13 million hectares in Canada. Australia, with 17 million hectares, rounds out the five leading no-till countries.

These initiatives do not constitute a menu from which to pick and choose. We need to take all these actions simultaneously. They reinforce each other. We will not likely be able to stabilize population unless we eradicate poverty. We will not likely be able to restore the earth's natural systems without stabilizing population and stabilizing climate. Nor can we eradicate poverty without reversing the decline of the earth's natural systems.

Achieving all these goals to reduce demand and increase supply requires that we redefine security. We have inherited a definition of security from the last century, a century dominated by two world wars and a cold war, that is almost exclusively military in focus. When the term national security comes up in Washington, people automatically think of expanded military budgets and more-advanced weapon systems. But armed aggression is no longer the principal threat to our future. The overriding threats in this century are climate change, population growth, spreading water shortages, rising food prices, and politically failing states.

It is no longer possible to separate food security and security more broadly defined. It is time to redefine security not just in an intellectual sense but also in a fiscal sense. We have the resources we need to fill the family planning gap, to eradicate poverty, and to raise water productivity, but these measures require a reallocation of our fiscal resources to respond to the new security threats.

Beyond this, diverting a big chunk of the largely obsolete military budget into incentives to invest in rooftop solar panels, wind farms, geothermal power plants, and more energy-efficient lighting and household appliances would accelerate the energy transition. The incentives needed to jump-start this massive energy restructuring are large, but not beyond our reach. We can justify this expense simply by considering the potentially unbearable costs of continuing with business as usual.

We have to mobilize quickly. Time is our scarcest resource. Success depends on moving at wartime speed. It means, for example, transforming the world energy economy at a pace reminiscent of the restructuring of the U.S. industrial economy in 1942 following the Japanese surprise attack on Pearl Harbor on December 7, 1941.

On January 6, 1942, a month after the attack, Franklin D. Roosevelt outlined arms production goals in his State of the Union address to the U.S. Congress and the American people. He said the United States was going to produce 45,000 tanks, 60,000 planes, and thousands of ships. Given that the country was still in a depression-mode economy, people wondered how this could be done. It required a fundamental reordering of priorities and some bold moves. The key to the 1942 industrial restructuring was the government's ban on the sale of cars that forced the auto industry into arms manufacturing. The ban lasted from early 1942 until the end of 1944. Every one of President Roosevelt's arms production goals was exceeded.

If the United States could totally transform its industrial economy in a matter of months in 1942, then certainly it can lead the world in restructuring the energy economy, stabilizing population, and rebuilding world grain stocks. The stakes now are even higher than they were in 1942. The challenge then was to save the democratic way of life, which was threatened by the fast-expanding empires of Nazi Germany and Imperial Japan. Today the challenge is to save civilization itself.

Scientists and many other concerned individuals have long sensed that the world economy had moved onto an environmentally unsustainable path. This has been evident to anyone who tracks trends such as deforestation, soil erosion, aquifer depletion, collapsing fisheries, and the increase in carbon dioxide in the atmosphere. What was not so clear was exactly where this unsustainable path would lead. It now seems that the most imminent effect will be tightening supplies of food. Food is the weak link in our modern civilization—just as it was for the Sumerians, Mayans, and many other civilizations that have come and gone. They could not separate their fate from that of their food supply. Nor can we.

The challenge now is to move our early twenty-first-century civilization onto a sustainable path. Every one of us needs to be involved. This is not just a matter of adjusting lifestyles by changing light bulbs or recycling newspapers, important though those actions are. Environmentalists have talked for decades about saving the planet, but now the challenge is to save civilization itself. This is about restructuring the world energy economy and doing it before climate change spirals out of control and before food shortages overwhelm our political system. And this means becoming politically active, working to reach the goals outlined above.

We all need to select an issue and go to work on it. Find some friends who share your concern and get to work. The overriding priority is redefining security and reallocating fiscal resources accordingly. If your major concern is population growth, join one of the internationally oriented groups and lobby to fill the family planning gap. If your overriding concern is climate change, join the effort to close coal-fired power plants. We can prevent a breakdown of the food system, but it will require a huge political effort undertaken on many fronts and with a fierce sense of urgency.

We all have a stake in the future of civilization. Many of us have children. Some of us have grandchildren. We know what we have to do. It is up to you and me to do it. Saving civilization is not a spectator sport.

Critical Thinking

1. Why will there not be another green revolution to take care of the growing world food problem?

2. What trends have slowed down or reversed and worsened the food problem as a result?

3. Discuss the environmental aspects (land, soil loss, water scarcity, weather extremes, yield limits, etc.) of the food problem.

Create Central

www.mhhe.com/createcentral

Internet References

Sociosite
www.topsite.com/goto/sociosite.net

Socioweb
www.topsite.com/goto/socioweb.com

Sociology—Study Sociology Online
http://edu.learnsoc.org

Sociology Web Resources
www.mhhe.com/socscience/sociology/resources/index.htm

The Washington Post has called **LESTER R. BROWN** "one of the world's most influential thinkers." He started his career as a farmer, growing tomatoes in New Jersey with his brother. After earning a degree in Agricultural Science from Rutgers University, he spent six months in rural India, an experience that changed his life and career. Brown founded the WorldWatch Institute and then the Earth Policy Institute, where he now serves as President. The purpose of the Earth Policy Institute is to provide a vision of an environmentally sustainable economy, a roadmap of how to get from here to there—as well as an ongoing assessment of progress. Brown has authored many books. His most recent is *Full Planet, Empty Plates: The New Geopolitics of Food Scarcity*. It is available online at www.earth-policy.org/books/fpep and at booksellers. Supporting data, endnotes, and additional resources are available for free on the website.

Brown, Lester R. From *Population Press*, December 13, 2012, pp. 14–19. Copyright © 2012 by Lester R. Brown. Used with permission of Earth Policy Institute.

Article   Prepared by: Kurt Finsterbusch, *University of Maryland, College Park*

The World Will Be More Crowded—With Old People

PHILLIP LONGMAN

Learning Outcomes

After reading this article, you will be able to:

- Try to give an even-handed analysis of the birth-dearth issue. Some predict doomsday. Others shrug off the problem. What do you think?

- Another approach is to stimulate births in developed countries. Identify appropriate policies along this line.

- Discuss the political obstacles to any rational proposal.

Actually, the children aren't our future. Demography is not destiny, as is sometimes claimed. The human race could be wiped out by a plague or an asteroid, or transformed by some new technology. But no matter what, today's patterns of fertility, migration, and mortality fundamentally determine how much society will or can change for many generations to come.

And what demography tells us is this: The human population will continue to grow, though in a very different way from in the past. The United Nations' most recent "mid-range" projection calls for an increase to 8 billion people by 2025 and to 10.1 billion by century's end.

Until quite recently, such population growth always came primarily from increases in the numbers of young people. Between 1950 and 1990, for example, increases in the number of people under 30 accounted for more than half of the growth of the world's population, while only 12 percent came from increases in the ranks of those over 60.

But in the future it will be the exact opposite. The U.N. now projects that over the next 40 years, more than half (58 percent) of the world's population growth will come from increases in the number of people over 60, while only 6 percent will come from people under 30. Indeed, the U.N. projects that by 2025, the population of children under 5, already in steep decline in most developed countries, will be falling globally—and that's even after assuming a substantial rebound in birth rates in the developing world. A gray tsunami will be sweeping the planet.

Which countries will be aging most rapidly in 2025? They won't be in Europe, where birth rates fell comparatively gradually and now show some signs of ticking up. Instead, they'll be places like Iran and Mexico, which experienced youth bulges that were followed quickly by a collapse in birth rates. In just 35 years, both Iran and Mexico will have a larger percentage of their populations over 60 than France does today. Other places with birth rates now below replacement levels include not just old Europe but also developing countries such as Brazil, Chile, China, Lebanon, Tunisia, South Korea, and Vietnam.

Because of the phenomenon of hyper-aging in the developing world, another great variable is already changing as well: migration. In Mexico, for example, the population of children age 4 and under was 434,000 less in 2010 than it was in 1996. The result? The demographic momentum that fueled huge flows of Mexican migration to the United States has waned, and will wane much more in the future. Already, the net flow of illegal Mexican immigration northward has slowed to a trickle. With fewer children to support and not yet burdened by a huge surge of elders, the Mexican economy is doing much better than in the past, giving people less reason to leave. By 2025, young people on both sides of the border may struggle to understand why their parents' generation built this huge fence.

Despite these trends, most people conclude from their day-to-day lives that overpopulation is a serious problem. One reason is that more than half the world's population is crowded into urban areas. The high cost of raising children in megacities is a prime reason that global birth rates continue to fall, yet urbanization also makes the larger trend toward depopulation difficult for most to grasp. If the downward trend in birth rates doesn't moderate and stabilize as the U.N. assumes it will, the world as a whole could be losing population as soon as mid-century. And yet few people will likely see that turning point coming, so long as humans continue to pack into urban areas and increase their consumption of just about everything.

Another related megatrend is the rapid change in the size, structure, and nature of the family. In many countries, such as Germany, Japan, Russia, and South Korea, the one-child family is now becoming the norm. This trend creates a society in which not only do most people have no siblings, but also no aunts, uncles, cousins, nieces, or nephews. Many will lack children of their own as well. Today about one in five people in advanced Western countries, including the United States, remains childless. Huge portions of the world's population will thus have no biological relatives except their parents.

And even where children continue to be born, they are being raised under radically different circumstances, as country after country has seen divorce and out-of-wedlock births surge and the percentage of children living with both of their married parents drop sharply. So not only is the quantity of children in the world poised to shrink rapidly, but with current trends, a near majority of them will be raised in ways that are today strongly associated with negative life outcomes.

Are there signs of any of these trends reversing before 2025? Only a few. The percentage of the world's population raised in religious households is bound to rise, if only because adherents to fundamentalism, whether Christians, Jews, or Muslims, tend to have substantially more children than their secular counterparts. And there are certainly many ways—from increased automation and delayed retirement to health-care reform to the provision of baby bonuses—for societies to at least partially adjust to the tidal shift in global demographics.

But don't count on it. To make such sweeping changes would require a widespread understanding of the century's great paradox: The planet may be bursting, but most of this new population is made up of people who have already been born. So get ready for a planet that's a whole lot more crowded—with old people.

Critical Thinking

1. Longman has been calling attention to the birth-dearth issue for 25 years. Is it the looming crisis that he thinks it is?

2. What are the options available to deal with the problem?

3. Our focus should be on the elderly. Since they live much longer than the previous generation, they may have to be treated differently. Should their retirement age increase? Could their resource use be constrained dramatically? Will their voluntary actions be sufficient?

Create Central

www.mhhe.com/createcentral

Internet References

Sociosite
www.topsite.com/goto/sociosite.net

Socioweb
www.topsite.com/goto/socioweb.com

Sociology—Study Sociology Online
http://edu.learnsoc.org

Sociology Web Resources
www.mhhe.com/socscience/sociology/resources/index.htm

PHILLIP LONGMAN, a fellow at the New America Foundation, is author of *The Empty Cradle: Why Falling Birthrates Threaten World Prosperity and What to Do About It.*

Longman, Phillip. Reprinted in entirety by McGraw-Hill with permission from *Foreign Policy*, September/October 2011. www.foreignpolicy.com. © 2011 Washingtonpost. Newsweek Interactive, LLC.

Article   Prepared by: Kurt Finsterbusch, *University of Maryland, College Park*

The Economic Effects of Granting Legal Status and Citizenship to Undocumented Immigrants

ROBERT LYNCH AND PATRICK OAKFORD

Learning Outcomes

After reading this article, you will be able to:

- Lay out the argument that granting legal status and citizenship to undocumented immigrants would be economically beneficial to America.

- Report on what groups might not benefit from the extension of citizenship to undocumented immigrants.

- Review the argument that legal status provides much better opportunities, and therefore, greater pay and productivity that advances the economy.

The movement toward comprehensive immigration reform has accelerated significantly in recent months. A bipartisan "Gang of 8" in the Senate—a group of four Democratic senators and four Republican senators—released a framework for immigration reform on January 28, and the next day President Barack Obama gave a speech launching White House efforts to push for immigration reform. Both proposals contained strong language regarding the need to provide legal status for the 11 million undocumented immigrants living in the country, as well as a road map to full citizenship.

Some lawmakers, however, do not want to extend legal status—let alone citizenship—to the unauthorized. Others have expressed interest in stopping just short of providing full citizenship for the 11 million undocumented immigrants, instead calling for a so-called middle-ground option—to leave undocumented immigrants in a permanent subcitizen status. To be sure, the debate over immigration reform has important legal, moral, social, and political dimensions. Providing or denying legal status or citizenship to the undocumented has implications for getting immigrants in compliance with the law, affects whether or not immigrant families can stay in their country of choice, and determines whether they have the opportunity to become full and equal members of American society.

But legal status and citizenship are also about the economic health of the nation as a whole. As our study demonstrates, legal status and a road map to citizenship for the unauthorized will bring about significant economic gains in terms of growth, earnings, tax revenues, and jobs—all of which will not occur in the absence of immigration reform or with reform that creates a permanent sub-citizen class of residents. We also show that the timing of reform matters: The sooner we provide legal status and citizenship, the greater the economic benefits are for the nation.

The logic behind these economic gains is straightforward. As discussed below, legal status and citizenship enable undocumented immigrants to produce and earn significantly more than they do when they are on the economic sidelines. The resulting productivity and wage gains ripple through the economy because immigrants are not just workers—they are also consumers and taxpayers. They will spend their increased earnings on the purchase of food, clothing, housing, cars, and computers. That spending, in turn, will stimulate demand in the economy for more products and services, which creates jobs and expands the economy.

This paper analyzes the 10-year economic impact of immigration reform under three scenarios. The first scenario assumes that legal status and citizenship are both accorded to the undocumented in 2013. The second scenario assumes that the unauthorized are provided legal status in 2013 and are able to earn citizenship five years thereafter. The third scenario assumes that the unauthorized are granted legal status starting in 2013 but that they are not provided a means to earn citizenship—at least within the 10-year timeframe of our analysis.

Under the first scenario—in which undocumented immigrants are granted legal status and citizenship in 2013—U.S. gross domestic product, or GDP, would grow by an additional $1.4 trillion cumulatively over the 10 years between 2013 and 2022. What's more, Americans would earn an additional $791 billion in personal income over the same time period—and the economy would create, on average, an additional 203,000 jobs per year. Within five years of the reform, unauthorized immigrants would be earning 25.1 percent more than they currently do and $659 billion more from 2013 to 2022. This means that they would also be contributing significantly more in federal, state, and local taxes. Over 10 years, that additional tax revenue would sum to $184 billion—$116 billion to the federal government and $68 billion to state and local governments.

Under the second scenario—in which undocumented immigrants are granted legal status in 2013 and citizenship five years thereafter—the 10-year cumulative increase in U.S. GDP would be $1.1 trillion, and the annual increases in the incomes of Americans would sum to $618 billion. On average over the 10 years, this immigration reform would create 159,000 jobs per year. Given the delay in acquiring citizenship relative to the first scenario, it would take 10 years instead of five for the incomes of the unauthorized to increase 25.1 percent. Over the 10-year period, they would earn $515 billion more and pay an additional $144 billion in taxes—$91 billion to the federal government and $53 billion to state and local governments.

Finally, under the third scenario—in which undocumented immigrants are granted legal status starting in 2013 but are not eligible for citizenship within 10 years—the cumulative gain in U.S. GDP between 2013 and 2022 would still be a significant— but comparatively more modest—$832 billion. The annual increases in the incomes of Americans would sum to $470 billion over the 10-year period, and the economy would add an average of 121,000 more jobs per year. The income of the unauthorized would be 15.1 percent higher within five years. Because of their increased earnings, undocumented immigrants would pay an additional $109 billion in taxes over the 10-year period—$69 billion to the federal government and $40 billion to state and local governments.

These immigration reform scenarios illustrate that unauthorized immigrants are currently earning far less than their potential, paying much less in taxes, and contributing significantly less to the U.S. economy than they potentially could. They also make clear that Americans stand to gain more from an immigration reform policy of legalization and citizenship than they do from one of legalization alone—or from no reform at all. Finally, the magnitude of potential economic gains depends significantly on how quickly reforms are implemented. The sooner that legal status and citizenship are granted to the unauthorized, the greater the gains will be for the U.S. economy.

Analyzing the Economic Effects of Legal Status and Citizenship

Numerous studies and government data sets have shown that positive economic outcomes are highly correlated with legal status and citizenship. Large and detailed government datasets—such as the U.S. Census Bureau's American Community Survey and Current Population Survey—have documented, for example, that U.S. citizens have average incomes that are 40 percent greater or more than the average incomes of noncitizen immigrants, both those here legally and the unauthorized.

Within the immigrant community, economic outcomes also vary by legal status. A study done by George Borjas and Marta Tienda found that prior to 1986 Mexican immigrant men legally

in the United States earned 6 percent more than unauthorized Mexican male immigrants. Research suggests that undocumented immigrants are further "underground" today than they were in 1986—and that they experience an even wider wage gap. Katherine Donato and Blake Sisk, for example, found that between 2003 and 2009, the average hourly wage of Mexican immigrants legally in the United States was 28.3 percent greater than it was for undocumented Mexican immigrants.

In addition, a U.S. Department of Labor study—based on a carefully constructed and large longitudinal survey of the nearly 3 million unauthorized immigrants who were granted legal status and given a road map to citizenship under the Immigration Reform and Control Act of 1986—found that these previously undocumented immigrants experienced a 15.1 percent increase in their average inflation-adjusted wages within five years of gaining legal status. Studies have also reported that citizenship provides an added economic boost above and beyond the gains from legalization. Manuel Pastor and Justin Scoggins, for instance, found that even when controlling for a range of factors such as educational attainment and national origin, naturalized immigrants earned 11 percent more than legal noncitizens.

There are several reasons why legalization and citizenship both raise the incomes of immigrants and improve economic outcomes. Providing a road map to citizenship to undocumented immigrants gives them legal protections that raise their wages. It also promotes investment in the education and training of immigrants that eventually pays off in the form of higher wages and output; grants access to a broader range of higher-paying jobs; encourages labor mobility which increases the returns on the labor skills of immigrants by improving the efficiency of the labor market such that the skillsets of immigrants more closely match the jobs that they perform; and makes it more possible for immigrants to start businesses and create jobs. Each of these reasons is explained in more detail below.

Legal Protections

Legalization allows the newly authorized to invoke the numerous employment rights that they previously could not benefit from—but were in most cases entitled to—due to their constant fear of being deported. Providing unauthorized workers with legal status increases their bargaining power relative to their employers, which in turn lowers the likelihood of worker exploitation and suppressed wages. This means that newly legal immigrants will be better equipped to contest an unlawful termination of employment, to negotiate for fair compensation or a promotion, and to file a complaint if they believe they are being mistreated or abused. Citizenship provides even greater protections than legalization. Citizens, for example, cannot be deported, while immigrants who are legal residents are still subject to deportation under certain circumstances.

Investment in Education and Training

Legal status and a road map to citizenship both provide a guarantee of long-term membership in American society and cause noncitizen immigrants to invest in their English language skills and in other forms of education and training that raise their productivity. Research shows that legal status and a road map to citizenship both create the opportunity and incentive for workers to invest in their labor-market skills at a greater rate than they otherwise would: Nearly 45 percent of the wage increases experienced by newly legalized immigrants is due to upgrades in their human capital. Similarly, a Department of Labor study of newly legalized immigrants found that they had significantly improved their English language skills and educational attainment within five years of gaining legal status and a road map to citizenship.

Access to Better Jobs

Undocumented immigrants are not legally living in the country, nor are they legally permitted to work here. Expensive federal- and state-level employer sanctions on the hiring of undocumented workers further restrict their access to fairly compensated and legal work opportunities because employers are reluctant to hire immigrants. If they do hire immigrants, they may use the threat of these sanctions to justify paying immigrants lower wages than they are due.

Legal noncitizen immigrants also suffer from restricted job access due to lack of citizenship. Many jobs—including many public-sector jobs, as well as high-paying private-sector jobs—are either available only to citizens or require security clearances that noncitizens cannot obtain. In addition, employers often prefer citizens to noncitizens—a form of discrimination that is sometimes permissible under U.S. labor laws. Even where it is unlawful to discriminate, some employers may hire citizens over noncitizens for a variety of reasons, including:

- To ensure that they are not violating the law by mistakenly hiring undocumented immigrants
- Because they may believe that citizens are better employees than noncitizens
- Because they would prefer to hire a co-national rather than a noncitizen

Labor Mobility and Increasing Returns

Legalization, investment in education and training, and access to better jobs leads to greater returns on the labor skills and education of undocumented immigrants. The undocumented also experience increasing returns from the improved labor-market mobility that follows legalization. Prior to legalization, unauthorized immigrants are subject to deportation if they are apprehended and, therefore—regardless of their skills—they tend to pursue employment in low-paying occupations, such as farming, child care, and cleaning services, where their legal status is less likely to be discovered. Thus, unauthorized workers do not receive the same market returns on their skills that comparable but legal workers receive. Prior to legalization, a high school diploma does not result in a statistically significant wage premium over those without this education. After legalization, however, "having a high school diploma or education beyond high school" results in an 11 percent wage premium. In other words, the returns on the labor skills of the legalized improve in part because workers move to sectors where their skills and education are both valued and relevant to the work being conducted. Hence, legalization and citizenship improve

the efficiency of the labor market by ensuring that people are working in fields where their skillsets and training are being used to the fullest extent.

Fostering Entrepreneurship

Legal status and citizenship facilitate noncitizen-immigrant entrepreneurship by providing access to licenses, permits, insurance, and credit to start businesses and create jobs. Despite the legal obstacles to entrepreneurship that noncitizens currently face, the U.S. economy benefits significantly from immigrant innovators. Immigrants—both legal and unauthorized—are more likely to own a business and start a new business than are nonimmigrants. Immigration reform that untethers the creative potential of immigrant entrepreneurs therefore promotes economic growth, higher incomes, and more job opportunities.

Comparing the Undocumented to Naturalized Citizens

In this study, we reach similar findings on the positive earnings impacts of legalization and citizenship on immigrants. We extend the analysis to report the effect that they have on U.S. tax receipts and the overall U.S. economy. Specifically, we analyze what happens to U.S. GDP, personal income, jobs, tax revenues, and the earnings of the 11 million unauthorized immigrants under the three immigration scenarios described above.

A good place to start examining the effect of the undocumented following a road map to citizenship is to compare them to a group that has already followed a similar map: those immigrants who are currently naturalized citizens. In doing such an analysis, we cannot simply assume that the current undocumented population would earn and contribute as much as the present class of naturalized-immigrant citizens has should they obtain the same status. The immigrants who have already become citizens are not necessarily the same in other economically relevant ways—they may, for example, differ in their educational attainment and age.

We deal with this possibility by using a regression analysis that controls for these factors to estimate the economic impact that legal status and citizenship have on the nation and its unauthorized immigrant population. As a first step, we provide an estimate of the income effect of providing citizenship to all noncitizen immigrants, including both those here legally and the unauthorized. We then disaggregate this estimate to calculate the income effect of providing legal status and citizenship to unauthorized immigrants only.

The Income Effect of Citizenship for all Immigrants

In our analysis, we estimate that the income premium of citizenship for all immigrants—both documented and undocumented—by comparing the earnings of naturalized and noncitizen immigrant populations while statistically controlling for observable differences other than citizenship that may affect income-level differences between the two groups. We control

The Economic Effects of Granting Legal Status and Citizenship to Undocumented Immigrants by Robert Lynch and Patrick Oakford

205

for education level; work experience; age; year of arrival in the United States; race/ethnicity; gender differences; country of origin; state of residency; rural versus urban residence; and marital status of naturalized and noncitizen immigrant populations to estimate the effect that citizenship has on earnings. We do so because these factors are likely to be responsible for differences in the earnings of naturalized immigrants and noncitizen immigrants—differences that would remain even if all noncitizens acquired citizenship. We know, for example, that noncitizen immigrants are younger, less educated, and less advanced in their careers than naturalized citizens—differences that would continue to affect the relative earnings of both groups after acquisition of citizenship.

We find that citizenship is associated with a statistically significant boost in the incomes of immigrants—an average of 16 percent (17.1 percent for women and 14.5 percent for men) in 2011. Of course, there is no policy being contemplated today whereby all noncitizens would become citizens. And since our regression analysis mixes already-documented legal noncitizens with undocumented noncitizens, it does not measure the effect of a policy change aimed only at the undocumented. But it does give a good indication of the impact over time of moving people from being unauthorized to legal noncitizens to naturalized citizens—the details of which we disaggregate in the next section of this paper.

Our finding that the income effect of citizenship is positive and significant is consistent with the results of other studies. We provide more details on the findings of these other studies in the appendix.

The Economic Effect of Citizenship on Unauthorized Immigrants: Income Gains from Legalization and Citizenship

If we made the assumption that the income effect of legalization and citizenship combined for the unauthorized is the same as the income effect of citizenship that we estimated for the entire noncitizen immigrant population, then we would conclude that the unauthorized would experience an average increase in income of 16 percent from legalization and citizenship. This estimate, however, understates the true income effect for the unauthorized population because it aggregates the relatively smaller income gains that legal noncitizens get from citizenship alone with the relatively larger income gains that the unauthorized get from legalization and citizenship. In addition, our regression estimate further understates the income effect of citizenship for the unauthorized because the unauthorized are undercounted in the dataset.

Citizenship for the unauthorized provides two clearly distinct but interconnected benefits that significantly impact their earnings and must be taken into account: legal standing and citizenship. We know from the largest and best study of the income effect of legalization—the 1996 U.S. Department of Labor study that analyzed the earnings of the nearly 3 million unauthorized immigrants who were granted legal status and given a road map to citizenship under the Immigration Reform and Control Act of 1986—that the average hourly wage of the newly legalized (but not yet citizen) population increased by 15.1 percent five years after legalization.

Unfortunately, the Department of Labor study did not continue to measure the wage increases that the newly legalized population gained after they acquired citizenship. An additional income effect from citizenship would have occurred on top of the 15.1 percent income increase that followed legalization, which implies that undocumented immigrants would have gained more than a 15.1 percent increase in their earnings from acquiring both legal status and the other benefits of citizenship. For a review of studies that have shown the additional income effect of citizenship, see the appendix.

Nonetheless, with an appropriate adjustment to account for the undercount of unauthorized immigrants, we can use our regression results, the Department of Labor's 1996 study, and a set of reasonable assumptions to estimate the likely full income effect of citizenship for the unauthorized, taking into account both the legalization effect and the further increase in earnings due to the acquisition of citizenship. We can then illustrate the GDP, earnings, job growth, and tax-revenue implications of our estimate for three forms of immigration reform that could start in 2013.

To estimate the effect of citizenship on the earnings of unauthorized immigrants, we decompose the income effect of citizenship that we estimated for all noncitizens—16 percent—into two components: one to estimate the percentage gain in income that the unauthorized experience as a consequence of attaining legal status and the other to estimate the percentage gain in income that they obtain from becoming naturalized citizens. We then add these components and adjust for the undercount of the unauthorized in the dataset to arrive at a likely estimate of the full income effect of citizenship for unauthorized immigrants.

For the first component, we assume that the unauthorized would gain the same 15.1 percent increase in income that unauthorized immigrants experienced from 1986 to 1992 when they obtained legal status, as measured by the Department of Labor. This 15.1 percent increase in wages over five years was due to the immediate impact on earnings of the acquisition of legal status and the subsequent effects on earnings of the acquisition of more education, further mastery of English, access to a broader range of jobs, and other factors that legalization encouraged and made possible.

For the second component, we hold constant the total citizenship effect—16 percent—and then calculate the effect of moving from legal status to citizenship, weighting the effect to reflect the distribution of legal and unauthorized noncitizen immigrants in our sample and the average incomes of the two groups. Our estimate of the second component suggests that previously unauthorized and newly legalized immigrants would experience an additional 10 percent gain in income if they acquired citizenship.

Taking into account both components, our most likely estimate of the full effect of granting legal status and citizenship to unauthorized immigrants is an income gain of 25.1 percent. Of this boost in income, about three-fifths comes from legalization and about two-fifths is attributable to transitioning from legal status to citizenship.

10-year Projections of the Economic Gains from Immigration Reform

In each of the three scenarios we have almost certainly understated the amount of additional taxes that will be paid by undocumented immigrant workers because the tax estimates include only taxes from the increased earnings of the previously undocumented. While it has been widely documented that unauthorized workers are contributing billions of dollars in federal, state, and local taxes each year, the Congressional Budget Office estimates that between 30 percent and 50 percent of the undocumented population fails to declare their income. To the extent that some of these immigrants—who are working in the underground economy—are not reporting their incomes for fear of being discovered and deported, however, legal status and citizenship is likely to push them into the legal economy, where they will be declaring their income and paying billions of dollars in taxes in addition to the amounts that we have calculated above. The reporting of this income, however, may increase business deductions for labor compensation, offsetting part of the tax gain. In addition, some currently unauthorized immigrants who have income taxes withheld may—upon attaining legal status—file returns and claim refunds or deductions and exemptions that will offset some of the tax revenue gained from the higher reporting of income.

Applying our 25.1 percent citizenship effect on the income of the undocumented, we project the economic gains from immigration reform under three scenarios. The first and most politically unlikely scenario—but one that is nonetheless useful for comparison purposes—assumes that legal status and citizenship are both conferred on the undocumented in 2013. The second scenario assumes that the unauthorized are provided legal status in 2013 and citizenship five years thereafter. The third scenario assumes that the unauthorized are granted legal status starting in 2013 but that they are not given a road map to citizenship.

Under the first scenario—both legal status and citizenship in 2013—U.S. GDP would grow by an additional $1.4 trillion cumulatively, and the personal income of Americans would grow an additional $791 billion over the 10 years between 2013 and 2022.30 Over the same time period, there would be an average of 203,000 more jobs per year.

Unauthorized immigrants would also be better off. Within five years they would be earning 25.1 percent more annually. As a consequence, over the full 10-year period, the formerly unauthorized would earn an additional $659 billion and pay at least $184 billion more in federal, state, and local taxes—$116 billion more to the federal government and $68 billion more to state and local governments.

Under the second scenario—legal status in 2013 followed by citizenship five years thereafter—the 10-year cumulative increase

in the economy of the United States would be $1.1 trillion, and the annual increases in the incomes of Americans would sum to $618 billion. Over the 10 years, this immigration reform would create an average of 159,000 jobs per year. Given the delay in acquiring citizenship relative to the first scenario, it would take 10 years instead of five years for the incomes of the unauthorized to increase 25.1 percent. Over the 10-year period, they would earn $515 billion more and pay an additional $144 billion in taxes—$91 billion to the federal government and $53 billion to state and local governments.

Finally, under the third scenario—legal status only starting in 2013—the cumulative gain in U.S. GDP between 2013 and 2022 would be a more modest $832 billion. The annual increases in the incomes of residents of the United States would sum to $470 billion over the 10 years, and the economy would have an average of 121,000 more jobs per year. The income of the unauthorized would be 15.1 percent higher within five years. Over the 10-year period, they would earn $392 billion more and pay an additional $109 billion in taxes—$69 billion to the federal government and $40 billion to state and local governments.

Conclusion

The positive economic impacts on the nation and on undocumented immigrants of granting them legal status and a road map to citizenship are likely to be very large. The nation as a whole would benefit from a sizable increase in GDP and income and a modest increase in jobs. The earnings of unauthorized immigrants would rise significantly, and the taxes they would pay would increase dramatically. Given that the full benefits would phase in over a number of years, the sooner we grant legal status and provide a road map to citizenship to unauthorized immigrants, the sooner Americans will be able to reap these benefits. It is also clear that legalization and a road map to citizenship bestow greater gains on the American people and the U.S. economy than legalization alone.

Critical Thinking

1. If economic analysis favors legal status for immigrants, what arguments are there against it?

2. In many ways immigrants from south of the border have many of the traits that are advocated for citizens, such as religion and family life. It seems like they would fit right in with American culture. What is your view?

3. Should America have a pro-immigration policy?

Create Central

www.mhhe.com/createcentral

Internet References

Sociosite
   www.topsite.com/goto/sociosite.net

Socioweb
www.topsite.com/goto/socioweb.com

Sociology—Study Sociology Online
http://edu.learnsoc.org

Sociology Web Resources
www.mhhe.com/socscience/sociology/resources/index.htm

ROBERT G. LYNCH is the Everett E. Nuttle professor and chair of the Department of Economics at Washington College. His areas of specialization include public policy, public finance, international economics, economic development, and comparative economics. He is the author of several papers and books that have analyzed the effectiveness of government economic policies in promoting economic development and creating jobs. He holds a bachelor's degree in economics from Georgetown University and a master's degree and doctorate in economics from the State University of New York at Stony Brook. PATRICK OAKFORD is a Research Assistant at the Center for American Progress. His research focuses on the economics of immigration policy, labor migration, and the intersection of immigration and employment laws. Patrick received the award for best dissertation in the field of migration studies in 2012 and his work has appeared in The New York Times, National Journal, and The Hill. He holds a master of science degree in migration studies from the University of Oxford and a bachelor's degree in industrial and labor relations from Cornell University.

Lynch, Robert and Oakford, Patrick. Report from *Center for American Progress*, March 20, 2013. Copyright © 2013 by Center for American Progress. Reprinted by permission. www.americanprogress.org

Article

Prepared by: Kurt Finsterbusch, *University of Maryland, College Park*

Can a Collapse of Global Civilization Be Avoided?

Paul R. Ehrlich and Anne H. Ehrlich

Learning Outcomes

After reading this article, you will be able to:

- Evaluate the Ehrlichs' thesis about addressing environmental problems immediately or face the possibility of the collapse of global civilization.

- Give your assessment of how to deal with the problem of Americans overusing the environment.

- Lay out the steps that should be taken to make America sustainable.

1. Introduction

Virtually every past civilization has eventually undergone collapse, a loss of socio-political-economic complexity usually accompanied by a dramatic decline in population size. Some, such as those of Egypt and China, have recovered from collapses at various stages; others, such as that of Easter Island or the Classic Maya, were apparently permanent. All those previous collapses were local or regional; elsewhere, other societies and civilizations persisted unaffected. Sometimes, as in the Tigris and Euphrates valleys, new civilizations rose in succession. In many, if not most, cases, overexploitation of the environment was one proximate or an ultimate cause.

But today, for the first time, humanity's global civilization—the worldwide, increasingly interconnected, highly technological society in which we all are to one degree or another, embedded—is threatened with collapse by an array of environmental problems. Humankind finds itself engaged in what Prince Charles described as 'an act of suicide on a grand scale', facing what the UK's Chief Scientific Advisor John Beddington called a 'perfect storm' of environmental problems. The most serious of these problems show signs of rapidly escalating severity, especially climate disruption. But other elements could potentially also contribute to a collapse: an accelerating extinction of animal and plant populations and species, which could lead to a loss of ecosystem services essential for human survival; land degradation and land-use change; a pole-to-pole spread of toxic compounds; ocean acidification and eutrophication (dead zones); worsening of some aspects of the epidemiological environment (factors that make human populations susceptible to infectious diseases); depletion of increasingly scarce resources, including especially groundwater, which is being overexploited in many key agricultural areas; and resource wars. These are not separate problems; rather they interact in two gigantic complex adaptive systems: the biosphere system and the human socio-economic system. The negative manifestations of these interactions are often referred to as 'the human predicament', and determining how to prevent it from generating a global collapse is perhaps the foremost challenge confronting humanity.

The human predicament is driven by overpopulation, over-consumption of natural resources and the use of unnecessarily environmentally damaging technologies and socio-economic-political arrangements to service Homo sapiens' aggregate consumption. How far the human population size now is above the planet's long-term carrying capacity is suggested (conservatively) by ecological footprint analysis. It shows that to support today's population of seven billion sustainably (i.e. with business as usual, including current technologies and standards of living) would require roughly half an additional planet; to do so, if all citizens of Earth consumed resources at the US level would take four to five more Earths. Adding the projected 2.5 billion more people by 2050 would make the human assault on civilization's life-support systems disproportionately worse, because almost everywhere people face systems with nonlinear responses, in which environmental damage increases at a rate that becomes faster with each additional person. Of course, the claim is often made that humanity will expand Earth's carrying capacity dramatically with technological innovation, but it is widely recognized that technologies can both add and subtract from carrying capacity. The plough evidently first expanded it and now appears to be reducing it. Overall, careful analysis of the prospects does not provide much confidence that technology will save us or that gross domestic product can be disengaged from resource use.

2. Do Current trends Portend a Collapse?

What is the likelihood of this set of interconnected predicaments leading to a global collapse in this century? There have been many definitions and much discussion of past 'collapses', but a future global collapse does not require a careful definition. It could be triggered by anything from a 'small' nuclear war, whose ecological effects could quickly end civilization, to a more gradual breakdown because famines, epidemics and resource shortages cause a disintegration of central control within nations, in concert with disruptions of trade and conflicts over increasingly scarce necessities. In either case, regardless of survivors or replacement societies, the world familiar to anyone reading this study and the well-being of the vast majority of people would disappear.

How likely is such a collapse to occur? No civilization can avoid collapse if it fails to feed its population. The world's success so far, and the prospective ability to feed future generations at least as well, has been under relatively intensive discussion for half a century. Agriculture made civilization possible, and over the last 80 years or so, an industrial agricultural revolution has created a technology-dependent global food system. That system, humanity's single biggest industry, has generated miracles of food production. But it has also created serious long-run vulnerabilities, especially in its dependence on stable climates, crop monocultures, industrially produced fertilizers and pesticides, petroleum, antibiotic feed supplements and rapid, efficient transportation.

Despite those food production miracles, today at least two billion people are hungry or poorly nourished. The Food and Agriculture Organization estimates that increasing food production by some 70 per cent would be required to feed a 35 per cent bigger and still growing human population adequately by 2050. What are the prospects that H. sapiens can produce and distribute sufficient food? To do so, it probably will be necessary to accomplish many or all of the following tasks: severely limit climate disruption; restrict expansion of land area for agriculture (to preserve ecosystem services); raise yields where possible; put much more effort into soil conservation; increase efficiency in the use of fertilizers, water and energy; become more vegetarian; grow more food for people (not fuel for vehicles); reduce food wastage; stop degradation of the oceans and better regulate aquaculture; significantly increase investment in sustainable agricultural and aquacultural research; and move increasing equity and feeding everyone to the very top of the policy agenda.

Most of these long-recommended tasks require changes in human behaviour thus far elusive. The problem of food wastage and the need for more and better agricultural research have been discussed for decades. So have 'technology will save us' schemes such as building 'nuclear agro-industrial complexes', where energy would be so cheap that it could support a new kind of desert agriculture in 'food factories', where crops would be grown on desalinated water and precisely machine fertilized. Unhappily, sufficiently cheap energy has never been produced by nuclear power to enable large-scale agriculture to move in that direction. Nor has agriculture moved towards feeding people protein extracted from leaves or bacteria grown on petroleum. None of these schemes has even resulted in a coordinated development effort. Meanwhile, growing numbers of newly well-off people have increased demand for meat, thereby raising global demand for feed grains.

Perhaps even more critical, climate disruption may pose insurmountable biophysical barriers to increasing crop yields. Indeed, if humanity is very unlucky with the climate, there may be reductions in yields of major crops, although near-term this may be unlikely to affect harvests globally. Nonetheless, rising temperatures already seem to be slowing previous trends of increasing yields of basic grains, and unless greenhouse gas emissions are dramatically reduced, dangerous anthropogenic climate change could ravage agriculture. Also, in addition to falling yields from many oceanic fish stocks because of widespread overfishing, warming and acidification of the oceans threaten the protein supply of some of the most nutritionally vulnerable people, especially those who cannot afford to purchase farmed fish.

Unfortunately, the agricultural system has complex connections with all the chief drivers of environmental deterioration. Agriculture itself is a major emitter of greenhouse gases and thus is an important cause of climate disruption as well as being exceptionally vulnerable to its consequences. More than a millennium of change in temperature and precipitation patterns is apparently now entrained, with the prospect of increasingly severe storms, droughts, heat waves and floods, all of which seem already evident and all of which threaten agricultural production.

Land is an essential resource for farming, and one facing multiple threats. In addition to the serious and widespread problems of soil degradation, sea-level rise (the most certain consequence of global warming) will take important areas out of production either by inundating them (a 1 m rise would flood 17.5% of Bangladesh), exposing them to more frequent storm surges, or salinizing coastal aquifers essential for irrigation water. Another important problem for the food system is the loss of prime farmland to urbanization, a trend that seems certain to accelerate as population growth steadily erodes the per capita supply of farmland.

The critical importance of substantially boosting the inadequate current action on the demographic problem can be seen in the time required to change the trajectory of population growth humanely and sensibly. We know from such things as the World War II mobilizations that many consumption patterns can be altered dramatically within a year, given appropriate incentives. If food shortages became acute, then a rapid reaction would ensue as hunger became much more widespread. Food prices would rise, and diets would temporarily change (e.g. the number of meals consumed per day or amount of meat consumed) to compensate the shortage.

Over the long term, however, expanding the global food supply and distributing it more equitably would be a slow and difficult process. Even though a major famine might well provoke investment in long-needed improvements in food production and distribution, they would take time to plan, test and implement.

Furthermore, agriculture is a leading cause of losses of biodiversity and thus of the critical ecosystem services supplied to agriculture itself (e.g. pollination, pest control, soil fertility, climate stability) and other human enterprises. Farming is also a principal source of global toxification, as has been clear since the days of Carson, exposing the human population to myriad subtle poisons. These pose further potential risks to food production.

3. What Needs to be done to Avoid a Collapse?

The threat from climate disruption to food production alone means that humanity's entire system for mobilizing energy needs to be rapidly transformed. Warming must be held well below a potential 58C rise in global average temperature, a level that could well bring down civilization. The best estimate today may be that, failing rapid concerted action, the world is already committed to a 2.48C increase in global average temperature. This is significantly above the 28C estimated a decade ago by climate scientists to be a 'safe' limit, but now considered by some analysts to be too dangerous, a credible assessment, given the effects seen already before reaching a one degree rise. There is evidence, moreover, that present models underestimate future temperature increase by overestimating the extent that growth of vegetation can serve as a carbon sink and underestimating positive feedbacks.

Many complexities plague the estimation of the precise threats of anthropogenic climate disruption, ranging from heat deaths and spread of tropical diseases to sea-level rise, crop failures and violent storms. One key to avoiding a global collapse, and thus an area requiring great effort and caution is avoiding climate-related mass famines. Our agricultural system evolved in a geological period of relatively constant and benign climate and was well attuned to twentieth-century conditions. That alone is cause for substantial concern as the planet's climates rapidly shift to new, less predictable regimes. It is essential to slow that process. That means dramatically transforming much of the existing energy mobilization infrastructure and changing human behaviour to make the energy system much more efficient. This is possible; indeed, sensible plans for doing it have been put forward, and some progress has been made. The central challenge, of course, is to phase out more than half of the global use of fossil fuels by 2050 in order to forestall the worst impacts of climate disruption, a challenge the latest International Energy Agency edition of World Energy Outlook makes look more severe. This highlights another dilemma. Fossil fuels are now essential to agriculture for fertilizer and pesticide manufacture, operation of farm machinery, irrigation (often wasteful), livestock husbandry, crop drying, food storage, transportation and distribution. Thus, the phase-out will need to include at least partial substitution of non-fossil fuels in these functions, and do so without greatly increasing food prices.

Unfortunately, essential steps such as curbing global emissions to peak by 2020 and reducing them to half of present levels by 2050 are extremely problematic economically and politically. Fossil fuel companies would have to leave most of their proven reserves in the ground, thus destroying much of the industry's economic value. Because the ethics of some businesses include knowingly continuing lethal but profitable activities, it is hardly surprising that interests with large financial stakes in fossil fuel burning have launched a gigantic and largely successful disinformation campaign in the USA to confuse people about climate disruption and block attempts to deal with it.

One recurrent theme in analyses of the food problem is the need for closing 'yield gaps'. That means raising yields in less productive systems to those typical of industrial agriculture. But climatic conditions may change sufficiently that those industrial high yields can themselves no longer be sustained. Thus, reducing the chances of a collapse calls for placing much more effort into genetic and ecological research related to agriculture and adopting already known environmental-friendly techniques, even though that may require trading off immediate corporate profits for social benefits or long-term sustainability.

Rationalizing energy mobilization alone may not be enough to be enough to maintain agricultural production, let alone allow its great expansion. Human water-handling infrastructure will have to be re-engineered for flexibility to bring water to crops in an environment of constantly changing precipitation patterns. This is critical, for although today only about 15 per cent of agricultural land is irrigated, it provides some 40 per cent of the grain crop yield. It seems likely that farming areas now rain-fed may someday need to be irrigated, whereas irrigation could become superfluous elsewhere, and both could change more or less continually. For this and many other reasons, the global food system will need to quickly evolve an unprecedented flexibility, never before even contemplated.

One factor making the challenges more severe is the major participation in the global system of giant nations whose populations have not previously enjoyed the fossil energy abundance that brought Western countries and Japan to positions of affluence. Now they are poised to repeat the West's energy 'success', and on an even greater scale. India alone, which recently suffered a gigantic blackout affecting 300 million people, is planning to bring 455 new coal plants on line. Worldwide more than 1200 plants with a total installed capacity of 1.4 million megawatts are planned, much of that in China, where electricity demand is expected to skyrocket. The resultant surge in greenhouse gases will interact with the increasing diversion of grain to livestock, stimulated by the desire for more meat in the diets of Indians, Chinese and others in a growing global middle class.

4. Dealing with Problems Beyond Food Supply

Another possible threat to the continuation of civilization is global toxification. Adverse symptoms of exposure to synthetic chemicals are making some scientists increasingly nervous about effects on the human population. Should a global threat materialize, however, no planned mitigating responses (analogous to the ecologically and politically risky 'geoengineering' projects often proposed to ameliorate climate disruption) are waiting in the wings ready for deployment.

Much the same can be said about aspects of the epidemiological environment and the prospect of epidemics being enhanced by rapid population growth in immune-weakened societies, increased contact with animal reservoirs, high speed transport and the misuse of antibiotics. Nobel laureate Joshua Lederberg had great concern for the epidemic problem, famously stating, 'The survival of the human species is not a preordained evolutionary program'. Some precautionary steps that should be considered include forbidding the use of antibiotics as growth stimulators for livestock, building emergency stocks of key vaccines and drugs (such as Tamiflu), improving disease surveillance, expanding mothballed emergency medical facilities, preparing institutions for imposing quarantines and, of course, moving as rapidly as possible to humanely reduce the human population size. It has become increasingly clear that security has many dimensions beyond military security and that breaches of environmental security could risk the end of global civilization.

But much uncertainty about the human ability to avoid a collapse still hinges on military security, especially whether some elements of the human predicament might trigger a nuclear war. Recent research indicates that even a regional scale nuclear conflict, as is quite possible between India and Pakistan, could lead to a global collapse through widespread climatic consequences. Triggers to conflict beyond political and religious strife easily could include cross-border epidemics, a need to gain access to food supplies and farmland, and competition over other resources, especially agricultural water and (if the world does not come to its energy senses) oil. Finding ways to eliminate nuclear weapons and other instruments of mass destruction must move even higher on civilization's agenda, because nuclear war would be the quickest and surest route to a collapse.

In thinking about the probability of collapse, one must obviously consider the social disruptions associated with elements of the predicament. Perhaps at the top of the list should be that of environmental refugees. Recent predictions are that environmental refugees could number 50 million by 2020. Severe droughts, floods, famines and epidemics could greatly swell that number. If current 'official' predictions of sea-level rise are low (as many believe they are), coastal inundations alone could generate massive human movements; a 1 m rise would directly affect some 100 million people, whereas a 6 m rise would displace more than 400 million. Developing a more comprehensive system of international governance with institutions planning to ameliorate the impacts of such catastrophes would be a major way to reduce the odds of collapse.

5. The Role of Science

The scientific community has repeatedly warned humanity in the past of its peril, and the earlier warnings about the risks of population expansion and the 'limits to growth' have increasingly been shown to be on the right track. The warnings continue. Yet many scientists still tend to treat population growth as an exogenous variable, when it should be considered an endogenous one—indeed, a central factor. Too many studies

asking 'how can we possibly feed 9.6 billion people by 2050?' should also be asking 'how can we humanely lower birth rates far enough to reduce that number to 8.6?' To our minds, the fundamental cure, reducing the scale of the human enterprise (including the size of the population) to keep its aggregate consumption within the carrying capacity of Earth, is obvious but too much neglected or denied. There are great social and psychological barriers in growth manic cultures to even considering it. This is especially true because of the 'endarkenment'—a rapidly growing movement towards religious orthodoxies that reject enlightenment values such as freedom of thought, democracy, separation of church and state, and basing beliefs and actions on empirical evidence. They are manifest in dangerous trends such as climate denial, failure to act on the loss of biodiversity and opposition to condoms (for AIDS control) as well as other forms of contraception. If ever there was a time for evidence-based (as opposed to faith-based) risk reduction strategies, it is now.

How can scientists do more to reduce the odds of a collapse? Both natural and social scientists should put more effort into finding the best ways of accomplishing the necessary re-modelling of energy and water infrastructure. They should develop better ways of evaluating and regulating the use of synthetic chemicals, a problem that might abate somewhat as availability of their fossil fuel sources fades (even though only about 5% of oil production flows into petrochemical production). The protection of Earth's remaining biodiversity (especially the crucial diversity of populations) must take centre stage for both scientific specialists and, through appropriate education, the public. Scientists must continually call attention to the need to improve the human epidemiological environment, and for control and eventual elimination of nuclear, chemical and biological weapons. Above all, they should expand efforts to understand the mechanisms through which cooperation evolves, because avoiding collapse will require unusual levels of international cooperation.

Is it too late for the global scientific community to collect itself and start to deal with the nexus of the two complex adaptive systems and then help generate the necessary actions to move towards sustainability? There are certainly many small scale science-based efforts, often local, that can provide hope if scaled up. For example, environmental non-govenmental organizations and others are continually struggling to halt the destruction of elements of biodiversity (and thus, in some cases, of vital ecosystem services), often with success. In the face of the building extinction crisis, they may be preserving nuclei from which Earth's biota and humanity's ecosystem services, might eventually be regenerated. And some positive efforts are scaling up. China now has some 25 per cent of its land in ecosystem function conservation areas designed to protect both natural capital and human well-being. The Natural Capital Project is helping improve the management of these areas. This is good news, but in our view, many too few scientists are involved in the efforts needed, especially in re-orienting at least part of their research towards mitigating the predicament and then bringing their results to the policy front.

6. The Need for Rapid Social/Political Change

Until very recently, our ancestors had no reason to respond genetically or culturally to long-term issues. If the global climate were changing rapidly for Australopithecus or even ancient Romans, then they were not causing it and could do nothing about it. The forces of genetic and cultural selection were not creating brains or institutions capable of looking generations ahead; there would have been no selection pressures in that direction. Indeed, quite the opposite, selection probably favoured mechanisms to keep perception of the environmental background steady so that rapid changes (e.g. leopard approaching) would be obvious. But now slow changes in that background are the most lethal threats. Societies have a long history of mobilizing efforts, making sacrifices and changes, to defeat an enemy at the gates, or even just to compete more successfully with a rival. But there is not much evidence of societies mobilizing and making sacrifices to meet gradually worsening conditions that threaten real disaster for future generations. Yet that is exactly the sort of mobilization that we believe is required to avoid a collapse.

Perhaps the biggest challenge in avoiding collapse is convincing people, especially politicians and economists, to break this ancient mould and alter their behaviour relative to the basic population-consumption drivers of environmental deterioration. We know that simply informing people of the scientific consensus on a serious problem does not ordinarily produce rapid changes in institutional or individual behaviour. That was amply demonstrated in the case of cigarettes, air pollution and other environmental problems and is now being demonstrated in the obesity epidemic as well as climate disruption.

Obvious parallels exist regarding reproduction and overconsumption, which are especially visible in what amounts to a cultural addiction to continued economic growth among the already well-off. One might think that the mathematics of compound interest would have convinced everyone long ago that growth of an industrialized economy at 3.5 per cent annually cannot long continue. Unfortunately, most 'educated' people are immersed in a culture that does not recognize that, in the real world, a short history (a few centuries) of exponential growth does not imply a long future of such growth.

Besides focusing their research on ways to avoid collapse, there is a need for natural scientists to collaborate with social scientists, especially those who study the dynamics of social movements. Such collaborations could develop ways to stimulate a significant increase in popular support for decisive and immediate action on the predicament. Unfortunately, awareness among scientists that humanity is in deep trouble has not been accompanied by popular awareness and pressure to counter the political and economic influences implicated in the current crisis. Without significant pressure from the public demanding action, we fear there is little chance of changing course fast enough to forestall disaster.

The needed pressure, however, might be generated by a popular movement based in academia and civil society to help guide humanity towards developing a new multiple intelligence, 'foresight intelligence' to provide the long-term analysis and planning that markets cannot supply. Foresight intelligence could not only systematically look ahead but also guide cultural changes towards desirable outcomes such as increased socio-economic resilience. Helping develop such a movement and foresight intelligence are major challenges facing scientists today, a cutting edge for research that must slice fast if the chances of averting a collapse are to be improved.

If foresight intelligence became established, many more scientists and policy planners (and society) might, for example, understand the demographic contributions to the predicament, stop treating population growth as a 'given' and consider the nutritional, health and social benefits of humanely ending growth well below nine billion and starting a slow decline. This would be a monumental task, considering the momentum of population growth. Monumental, but not impossible if the political will could be generated globally to give full rights, education and opportunities to women, and provide all sexually active human beings with modern contraception and backup abortion. The degree to which those steps would reduce fertility rates is controversial, but they are a likely win-win for societies.

Obviously, especially with the growing endarkenment, there are huge cultural and institutional barriers to establishing such policies in some parts of the world. After all, there is not a single nation where women are truly treated as equal to men. Despite that, the population driver should not be ignored simply because limiting overconsumption can, at least in theory, be achieved more rapidly. The difficulties of changing demographic trajectories mean that the problem should have been addressed sooner, rather than later. That halting population growth inevitably leads to changes in age structure is no excuse for bemoaning drops in fertility rates, as is common in European government circles. Reduction of population size in those over-consuming nations is a very positive trend, and sensible planning can deal with the problems of population aging.

While rapid policy change to head off collapse is essential, fundamental institutional change to keep things on track is necessary as well. This is especially true of educational systems, which today fail to inform most people of how the world works and thus perpetuate a vast culture gap. The academic challenge is especially great for economists, who could help set the background for avoiding collapse by designing steady-state economic systems, and along the way destroying fables such as 'growth can continue forever if it's in service industries', or 'technological innovation will save us'. Issues such as the importance of comparative advantage under current global circumstances, the development of new models that better reflect the irrational behaviour of individuals and groups, reduction of the worship of 'free' markets that infests the discipline, and tasks such as making information more symmetrical, moving towards sustainability and enhancing equity (including redistribution) all require re-examination. In that re-examination, they would be following the lead of distinguished economists in dealing with the real world of biophysical constraints and human well-being.

At the global level, the loose network of agreements that now tie countries together, developed in a relatively recent stage of cultural evolution since modern nation states appeared, is utterly inadequate to grapple with the human predicament. Strengthening global environmental governance and addressing the related problem of avoiding failed statehood are tasks humanity has so far refused to tackle comprehensively even as cultural evolution in technology has rendered the present international system (as it has educational systems) obsolete. Serious global environmental problems can only be solved and a collapse avoided with an unprecedented level of international cooperation. Regardless of one's estimate of civilization's potential longevity, the time to start restructuring the international system is right now. If people do not do that, nature will restructure civilization for us.

Similarly, widely based cultural change is required to reduce humanely both population size and overconsumption by the rich. Both go against cultural norms, and, as long feared, the overconsumption norm has understandably been adopted by the increasingly rich subpopulations of developing nations, notably India and China. One can be thrilled by the numbers of people raised from poverty while being apprehensive about the enormous and possibly lethal environmental and social costs that may eventually result. The industrial revolution set civilization on the road to collapse, spurring population growth, which contributed slightly more than overconsumption to environmental degradation. Now population combined with affluence growth may finish the job.

Needless to say, dealing with economic and racial inequities will be critically important in getting large numbers of people from culturally diverse groups to focus their minds on solving the human predicament, something globalization should help. These tasks will be pursued, along with an emphasis on developing 'foresight intelligence', by the nascent Millennium Alliance for Humanity and the Biosphere (the MAHB; http://mahb.stanford.edu). One of its central goals is to try to accelerate change towards sustainability. Since simply giving the scientific facts to the public will not do it, among other things, this means finding frames and narratives to convince the public of the need to make changes.

We know that societies can evolve fundamentally and unexpectedly, as was dramatically demonstrated by the collapse of communist regimes in Europe in 1989. Rather than tinkering around the edges and making feeble or empty gestures towards one or another of the interdependent problems we face, we need a powerful and comprehensive approach. In addressing climate change, for instance, developing nations need to be convinced that they (along with the rest of the world) cannot afford (and do not need) to delay action while they 'catch up' in development. Indeed, development on the old model is counterproductive; they have a great opportunity to pioneer new approaches and technologies. All nations need to stop waiting for others to act and be willing to do everything they can to mitigate emissions and hasten the energy transition, regardless of what others are doing.

With climate and many other global environmental problems, polycentric solutions may be more readily found than global ones. Complex, multi-level systems may be better able to cope with complex, multi-level problems, and institutional change is required at many levels in many polities. What scientists understand about cultural evolution suggests that, while improbable, it may be possible to move cultures in such directions. Whether solutions will be global or polycentric, international negotiations will be needed, existing international agencies that deal with them will need strengthening, and new institutions will need to be formed.

7. Conclusions

Do we think global society can avoid a collapse in this century? The answer is yes, because modern society has shown some capacity to deal with long-term threats, at least if they are obvious or continuously brought to attention (think of the risks of nuclear conflict). Humanity has the assets to get the job done, but the odds of avoiding collapse seem small because the risks are clearly not obvious to most people and the classic signs of impending collapse, especially diminishing returns to complexity, are everywhere. One central psychological barrier to taking dramatic action is the distribution of costs and benefits through time: the costs up front, the benefits accruing largely to unknown people in the future. But whether we or more optimistic observers are correct, our own ethical values compel us to think the benefits to those future generations are worth struggling for, to increase at least slightly the chances of avoiding a dissolution of today's global civilization as we know it.

We are especially grateful to Joan Diamond, Executive Director of the MAHB, for her ideas on foresight intelligence, and to the Beijer Institute of Ecological Economics for two decades of provocative discussions on topics related to this paper. This paper has benefited from comments from Ken Arrow, Scott Barrett, Andy Beattie, Dan Blumstein, Corey Bradshaw, Greg Bratman, Paul Brest, Jim Brown, Bob Brulle, Gretchen Daily, Lisa Daniel, Timothy Daniel, Partha Dasgupta, Nadia Diamond-Smith, Tom Dietz, Anantha Duraiappah, Riley Dunlap, Walter Falcon, Marc Feldman, Rachelle Gould, Larry Goulder, John Harte, Mel Harte, Ursula Heise, Tad Homer-Dixon, Bob Horn, Danny Karp, Don Kennedy, Michael Klare, Simon Levin, Jack Liu, David Lobell, Doug McAdam, Chase Mendenhall, Hal Mooney, Fathali Moghaddam, Dennis Pirages, Graham Pyke, Gene Rosa, Lee Ross, Jose Sarukhan, Kirk Smith, Sarah Soule, Chris Turnbull and Wren Wirth. Two of the best and most thorough anonymous reviewers we have ever encountered helped us improve the manuscript. The work was supported by Peter and Helen Bing and the Mertz Gilmore Foundation.

Critical Thinking

1. What is your assessment of the state of the planet?

2. What specifically are the most worrisome environmental problems?

3. The Ehrlichs wonder whether the collapse of global civilization can be avoided. Do they have convincing data supporting this conclusion?

Create Central

www.mhhe.com/createcentral

Internet References

Sociosite

www.topsite.com/goto/sociosite.net

Socioweb

www.topsite.com/goto/socioweb.com

Sociology—Study Sociology Online

http://edu.learnsoc.org

Sociology Web Resources

www.mhhe.com/socscience/sociology/resources/index.htm

PAUL EHRLICH is a Professor of Biology and President of the Center for Conservation Biology at Stanford University, and Adjunct Professor at the University of Technology, Sydney. His research interests are in the ecology and evolution of natural populations of butterflies, reef fishes, birds and human beings. ANNE EHRLICH is a Senior Research Scientist in Biology at Stanford and focuses her research on policy issues related to the environment

Article   Prepared by: Kurt Finsterbusch, *University of Maryland, College Park*

A Radical Approach to the Climate Crisis

CHRISTIAN PARENTI

Learning Outcomes

After reading this article, you will be able to:

- Consider a wide range of options for dealing with global warming.
- Develop a political economy theory that you use, like Parenti does, to judge the likelihood of implementing mitigations and adaptations to global warming.
- Judge the case Parenti makes for the necessity of a radical approach to global warming.

Several strands of green thinking maintain that capitalism is incapable of a sustainable relationship with non-human nature because, as an economic system, capitalism has a growth imperative while the earth is finite. One finds versions of this argument in the literature of eco-socialism, deep ecology, eco-anarchism, and even among many mainstream greens who, though typically declining to actually name the economic system, are fixated on the dangers of "growth."

All this may be true. Capitalism, a system in which privately owned firms must continuously out-produce and out-sell their competitors, may be incapable of accommodating itself to the limits of the natural world. However, that is not the same question as whether capitalism can solve the more immediate climate crisis.

Because of its magnitude, the climate crisis can appear as the sum total of all environmental problems—deforestation, overfishing, freshwater depletion, soil erosion, loss of biodiversity, chemical contamination. But halting greenhouse gas emissions is a much more specific problem, the most pressing subset of the larger apocalyptic panorama.

And the very bad news is, time has run out. As I write this, news arrives of an ice-free arctic summer by 2050. Scientists once assumed that would not happen for hundreds of years.

Dealing with climate change by first achieving radical social transformation—be it a socialist or anarchist or deep-ecological/neo-primitive revolution, or a nostalgia-based *localista* conversion back to a mythical small-town capitalism—would be a

very long and drawn-out, maybe even multigenerational, struggle. It would be marked by years of mass education and organizing of a scale and intensity not seen in most core capitalist states since the 1960s or even the 1930s.

Nor is there any guarantee that the new system would not also degrade the soil, lay waste to the forests, despoil bodies of water, and find itself still addicted to coal and oil. Look at the history of "actually existing socialism" before its collapse in 1991. To put it mildly, the economy was not at peace with nature. Or consider the vexing complexities facing the left social democracies of Latin America. Bolivia, and Ecuador, states run by socialists who are beholden to very powerful, autonomous grassroots movements, are still very dependent on petroleum revenue.

A more radical approach to the crisis of climate change begins not with a long-term vision of an alternate society but with an honest engagement with the very compressed timeframe that current climate science implies. In the age of climate change, these are the real parameters of politics.

Hard Facts

The scientific consensus, expressed in peer-reviewed and professionally vetted and published scientific literature, runs as follows: For the last 650,000 years atmospheric levels of CO_2—the primary heat-trapping gas—have hovered at around 280 parts per million (ppm). At no point in the preindustrial era did CO_2 concentrations go above 300 ppm. By 1959, they had reached 316 ppm and are now over 400 ppm. And the rate of emissions is accelerating. Since 2000, the world has pumped almost 100 billion tons of carbon into the atmosphere—about a quarter of all CO_2 emissions since 1750. At current rates, CO_2 levels will double by mid-century.

Climate scientists believe that any increase in average global temperatures beyond 2 degrees Celsius above preindustrial levels will lead to dangerous climate change, causing large-scale desertification, crop failure, inundation of coastal cities, mass migration to higher and cooler ground, widespread extinctions of flora and fauna, proliferating disease, and possible social collapse. Furthermore, scientists now understand that the earth's climate system has not evolved in a smooth linear fashion. Paleoclimatology has uncovered evidence of sudden shifts in the earth's climate regimes. Ice ages have stopped and started not in a matter of centuries, but decades. Sea levels (which are actually uneven across the globe) have risen and fallen more rapidly than was once believed.

Throughout the climate system, there exist dangerous positive-feedback loops and tipping points. A positive-feedback loop is a dynamic in which effects compound, accelerate, or amplify the original cause. Tipping points in the climate system reflect the fact that causes can build up while effects lag. Then, when the effects kick in, they do so all at once, causing the relatively sudden shift from one climate regime to another.

Thus, the UN's Intergovernmental Panel on Climate Change says rich countries like the United States must cut emissions 25 percent to 40 percent below 1990 levels by 2020—only seven years away—and thereafter make precipitous cuts to 90 percent below 1990 levels by 2050. This would require global targets of 10 percent reductions in emissions per annum, starting now. Those sorts of emissions reductions have only occurred during economic depressions. Russia's near total economic collapse in the early 1990s saw a 37 percent decrease in CO_2 emissions from 1990 to 1995, under conditions that nobody wants to experience.

The political implications of all this are mind-bending. As daunting as it may sound, it means that it is *this society* and *these institutions* that must cut emissions. That means, in the short-term, realistic climate politics are reformist politics, even if they are conceived of as part of a longer-term anti-capitalist project of totally economic re-organization.

Dreaming the Rational

Of course, successful reformism often involves radical means and revolutionary demands. What other sort of political pressure would force the transnational ruling classes to see the scientific truth of the situation? But let us assume for a second that political elites faced enough pressure to force them to act. What would be the rational first steps to stave off climate chaos?

The watchwords of the climate discussion are *mitigation* and *adaptation*—that is, we must mitigate the causes of climate change while adapting to its effects. Mitigation means drastically cutting our production of CO_2 and other greenhouse gases, such as methane and chlorofluorocarbons, that prevent the sun's heat from radiating back out to space.

Mitigation means moving toward clean energy sources, such as wind, solar, geothermal, and tidal kinetic power. It means closing coal-fired power plants, weaning our economy off fossil fuels, building a smart electrical grid, and making massive investments in carbon-capture and -sequestration technologies. (That last bit of techno-intervention would have to be used not as a justification to keep burning coal, as is its current function, but to strip out atmospheric CO_2 rapidly and get back to 350 ppm and away from the dangerous tipping points.)

Adaptation, on the other hand, means preparing to live with the effects of climatic changes, some of which are already underway and some of which are inevitable. Adaptation is both a technical and a political challenge.

Technical adaptation means transforming our relationship to non-human nature as nature transforms. Examples include building seawalls around vulnerable coastal cities, giving land back to mangroves and everglades so they can act to break tidal surges during giant storms, opening wildlife migration corridors so species can move away from the equator as the climate warms, and developing sustainable forms of agriculture that can function on an industrial scale even as weather patterns gyrate wildly.

Political adaptation, on the other hand, means transforming social relations: devising new ways to contain, avoid, and deescalate the violence that climate change is fueling and will continue to fuel. That will require progressive economic redistribution and more sustainable forms of development. It will also require a new diplomacy of peace building.

Unfortunately, another type of political adaptation is already under way—that of the armed lifeboat. This adaptation responds to climate change by arming, excluding, forgetting, repressing, policing, and killing. The question then becomes how to conceive of adaptation and mitigation as a project of *radical* reform—reforms that achieve qualitative change in the balance of power between the classes.

The core problem in the international effort to cut emissions is fundamentally the intransigence of the United States: it failed to ratify the Kyoto Protocol and has played an obstructionist role at subsequent negotiations. Domestically, progress has been just as frustratingly slow. We have no carbon tax, nor any program of robust investment in clean technology. Even the minimal production tax credit for clean energy generated by solar, wind, and hydro power has not been locked in as a long-term commitment. This creates uncertainty about prices, and, as a result, private investment in clean tech is stalling.

China, on the other hand, though now the world's second-largest economy and largest greenhouse gas polluter, is moving ahead with a fast-growing clean-tech industry—that is to say, with mitigation. The Chinese wind sector has grown steadily since 2001. "According to new statistics from the China Electricity Council," reported American Progress senior fellow Joseph Romm, "China's wind power production actually increased more than coal power production for the first time ever in 2012." This growth is the result, in part, of robust government support: China has invested $200.8 billion in stimulus funding for clean tech. Estimates of U.S. stimulus funding for clean technology range from $50 to $80 billion.

The European Union is also moving forward to create a €1 trillion regional supergrid. Germany and Portugal in particular are moving aggressively to expand their already quite large clean-tech sectors. Action in the core industrial economies is essential because only they have the infrastructure that can propel the clean-tech revolution and transform the world economy.

A De Facto Carbon Tax

Environmental economists tend to agree that the single most important thing the United States could do to accelerate the shift to clean energy would be to impose a carbon tax. Despite our political sclerosis and fossil fuel fundamentalism, the means to do that already exist.

First and foremost, there is the Environmental Protection Agency, which could achieve significant and immediate emissions reductions using nothing more than existing laws and current technologies. According to Kassie Siegel at the Center for Biological Diversity, "The Clean Air Act can achieve everything we need: a 40 percent reduction of greenhouse gas emissions over 1990 levels by 2020."

Government procurement is one of the hidden tools of American capitalism's "shadow socialism."

Rather boring in tone and dense with legalistic detail, the ongoing fight over EPA rulemaking is probably the most important environmental battle in a generation. Since 2007, thanks to the pressure and lawsuits of green activists, the EPA has had enormous—but under-utilized—power. That was the year when the Supreme Court ruled, in *Massachusetts v. Environmental Protection Agency,* that the agency should determine whether greenhouse gases threaten human health. In December 2010, the EPA published a science-based "endangerment finding," which found that CO_2 and five other greenhouse gases are, in fact, dangerous to human life because they cause global warming.

Once the EPA issues an endangerment finding, it is legally bound to promulgate regulations to address the problem. The first of these post–*Massachusetts v. EPA* "tailoring rules" were for "mobile sources." Between 2011 and 2012, regulations for cars and for trucks went into effect. Then the EPA set strict limits for new power plants in 2012. But other major sources of greenhouse gas pollution—like existing electric power plants (which pump out roughly 40 percent of the nation's total GHG emissions), oil refineries, cement plants, steel mills, and shipping—have yet to be properly regulated pursuant to *Massachusetts v. EPA.*

If the EPA were to use the Clean Air Act—and do so "with extreme prejudice"—it could impose a de facto carbon tax. Industries would still be free to burn dirty fossil fuels, but they would have to use very expensive, and in some cases nonexistent, new technology to meet emission standards. Or they would have to pay very steep and mounting fines for their emissions. Such penalties could reach thousands of dollars per day, per violation. Thus, a de facto carbon tax. Then cheap fossil fuel energy would become expensive, driving investment toward carbon-neutral forms of clean energy like wind and solar. For extra measure we could end fossil fuel subsidies. Before long, it would be more profitable to invest in clean energy sources than dangerous and filthy ones.

Big Green Buy and U. S. "Shadow Socialism"

According to clean-tech experts, innovation is now less important than rapid, large-scale implementation. In other words,

developing a clean-energy economy is not about new gadgets but about new policies. Most of the energy technologies we need already exist. You know what they are: wind farms, concentrated solar power plants, geothermal and tidal power, all feeding an efficient smart grid that, in turn, powers electric vehicles and radically more energy-efficient buildings.

But leading clean technologies remain slightly more expensive than the old dirty-tech alternatives. This "price gap" is holding back the mass application of clean technology. The simple fact is that capitalist economies will not switch to clean energy until it is cheaper than fossil fuel. The fastest way to close the price gap is to build large clean-tech markets that allow for economies of scale. But what is the fastest way to build those markets? More research grants? More tax credits? More clumsy pilot programs?

No. The fastest, simplest way to do it is to reorient government procurement away from fossil fuel energy and toward clean energy and technology—to use the government's vast spending power to create a market for green energy. Elsewhere, I have called this the Big Green Buy. Consider this: federal, state, and local government constitute more than 38 percent of our GDP. In more concrete terms, Uncle Sam owns or leases more than 430,000 buildings (mostly large office buildings) and 650,000 vehicles. (Add state and local government activity, and all those numbers grow by about a third again.) The federal government is the world's largest consumer of energy and vehicles, and the nation's largest greenhouse gas emitter.

Government procurement is one of the hidden tools of American capitalism's "shadow socialism." By shadow socialism I refer to the massively important but often overlooked role of government planning, investment, subsidy, procurement, and ownership in the economic development of American capitalism. A detailed account of that history is offered in Michael Lind's book *Land of Promise.* From railroads, to telecommunications, and aviation and all the attendant sub-industries of these sectors, government has provided the capital and conditions for fledging industries to grow large. For example, government didn't just fund the invention of the microprocessor; it was also the first major consumer of the device. Throughout the 1950s, more than half of IBM's revenue came from government contracts. Along with money, these contracts provided a guaranteed market and stability for IBM and its suppliers, and thus attracted private investment—all of which helped create the modern computer industry.

Now consider the scale of the problem: our asphalt transportation arteries are clogged with 250 million gasoline-powered vehicles sucking down an annual $200 to $300 billion worth of fuel from more than 121,000 filling stations. Add to that the cost of heating and cooling buildings, jet travel, shipping, powering industry, and the energy-gobbling servers and mainframes that are the Internet, and the U.S. energy economy reaches a spectacular annual tab of 1.2 trillion dollars.

A redirection of government purchasing would create massive markets for clean power, electric vehicles, and efficient buildings, as well as for more sustainably produced furniture, paper, cleaning supplies, uniforms, food, and services. If government bought green, it would drive down marketplace prices sufficiently that the momentum toward green tech would become self-reinforcing and spread to the private sector.

Executive Order 13514, which Obama signed in 2009, directed all federal agencies to

> increase energy efficiency; measure, report, and reduce their greenhouse gas emissions from direct and indirect activities; conserve and protect water resources through efficiency, reuse, and storm water management; eliminate waste, recycle, and prevent pollution; leverage agency acquisitions to foster markets for sustainable technologies and environmentally preferable materials, products, and services; design, construct, maintain, and operate high performance sustainable buildings in sustainable locations.

The executive order also stipulates that federal agencies immediately start purchasing 95 percent through green-certified programs and achieve a 28 percent greenhouse gas reduction by 2020. But it has not been robustly implemented.

Government has tremendous latitude to leverage green procurement because it requires no new taxes, programs, or spending, nor is it hostage to the holy grail of sixty votes in the Senate. It is simply a matter of changing how the government buys its energy, vehicles, and services. Yes, in many cases clean tech costs more up front, but in most cases, savings arrive soon afterward. And government—because of its size—is a market mover that can leverage money-saving deals if it wishes to.

Protest and the "Relative Autonomy" of the State

Why would the capitalist state move to euthanize the fossil fuel industry, that most powerful fraction of the capitalist class? Or put another way, how can the state regain some of its "relative autonomy" from capital? History indicates that massive, crisis-producing protest is one of the most common reasons a modern state will act against the interests of specific entrenched elites and for the "general interest" of society. When the crisis of protest is bad enough, entrenched elites are forced to take a loss as the state imposes ameliorative action for the greater good of society.

Clearly, we need to build a well-organized, broadly supported, yet tactically and strategically radical movement to demand proper climate policy. For such a movement to be effective it must use myriad tactics, from lawsuits and lobbying to direct action such as tree-sits, road blockades, and occupations aimed at the infrastructure of the fossil fuel industry. Only by disrupting the working of the political and economic system as a whole can we forge a consensus that ending the fossil fuel sector is essential. (The work of Francis Fox Piven and Richard Cloward is, in my opinion, still among the best in tracing the dynamic of this process of rebellion and reform.)

At question, then, is not just the state's capacity to evolve, but the capacity of the American people to organize and mobilize on a massive scale. Far be it from me to say exactly how such movements could or should be built, other than the way they always have been: by trial and error and with good leadership. Movement building is a mass and organic process.

The Rebellion of Nature

Along with protest, a more organic source of crisis is already underway and may also help scare political elites into confronting big carbon. Climate change is a "rebellion of nature," by which I mean the disruption caused by ecological breakdown. The history of environmental regulation in the West is, in many ways, the story of protest and advocacy combining with the rebellion of nature at the local (urban) scale. Together, they have forced rudimentary regulation in the name of health and sanitation.

By the 1830s, America's industrial cities had become perfect incubators of epidemic disease, particularly cholera and yellow fever. Like climate change today, these diseases hit the poor hardest, but they also sickened and killed the wealthy. Class privilege offered some protection, but it was not a guarantee of safety. And so it was that middle-class "goo-goos" and "mug-wumps" began a series of reforms that contained and eventually defeated the urban epidemics.

First, garbage-eating hogs were banned from city streets, then public sanitation programs of refuse collection began, sewers were built, safe public water provided, and housing codes were developed and enforced. Eventually, the epidemics of cholera stopped. Soon other infectious diseases, such as pulmonary tuberculosis, typhus, and typhoid, were largely eliminated. At the scale of the urban, capitalist society solved an environmental crisis through planning and public investment.

Climate change is a problem of an entirely different order of magnitude, but these past solutions to smaller environmental crises offer lessons. Ultimately, solving the climate crisis—like the nineteenth-century victory over urban squalor and epidemic contagions—will require a re-legitimation of the state's role in the economy.

The modern story of local air pollution offers another example of the "rebellion of nature." As Jim McNeil outlines in *Something New Under The Sun,* smog inundations in industrial cities of the United States and Europe used to kill many people. In 1879–1880 smog killed 3,000 Londoners, and in Glasgow a 1909 inversion—where cold air filled with smoke from burning coal was trapped near the ground—killed 1,063. As late as 1952, a pattern of cold and still air killed 4,000 people in London, according to McNeil, and even more according to others. By 1956, the Britons had passed a clean air act that drove coal out of the major cities. In the United States there was a similar process. In 1953, smog in New York killed between 170 and 260 people, and as late as 1966 a smog inversion killed 169 New Yorkers. All of this helped generate pressure for the Clean Air Act of 1970.

Today, a similar process is underway in China. Local air quality is so bad that it is forcing changes to Chinese energy policy. A major World Bank study has estimated that "the combined health and non-health cost of outdoor air and water pollution for China's economy comes to around $US 100 billion a year (or about 5.8% of the country's GDP)." People across China are protesting pollution. Foreign executives are turning down positions in Beijing because of the toxic atmospheric stew that western visitors have taken to calling "airpocalypse." The film director Chen Kaige, who won the Palme d'Or for his 1993 film *Farewell*

My Concubine, told the world he couldn't think or make films because of the Chinese capital's appallingly bad air.

These local pressures are a large part of what is driving Chinese investment in renewable energy. Last year China added more energy capacity from wind than from the coal sector.

Capitalism vs. Nature?

Some of the first thinkers to note a conflict between capitalism and non-human nature were Karl Marx and Friedrich Engels. They came to their ecology through examining the local problem of relations between town and country—expressed simultaneously as urban pollution and rural soil depletion. In exploring this question they relied on the pioneering work of soil chemist Justus von Liebig. And from this small-scale problem, they developed the idea of capitalism creating a rift in the metabolism of natural processes.

Here is how Marx explained the dilemma:

> Capitalist production collects the population together in great centers, and causes the urban population to achieve an ever-growing preponderance. This has two results. On the one hand it concentrates the historical motive force of society; on the other hand, it disturbs the metabolic interaction between man and the earth, i.e., it prevents the return to the soil of its constituent elements consumed by man in the form of food and clothing; hence it hinders the operation of the eternal natural condition for the lasting fertility of the soil. . . . All progress in capitalist agriculture is a progress in the art, not only of robbing the worker, but of robbing the soil.

And as with "soil robbing," so too concentrations of atmospheric CO_2: the natural systems are out of sync; their elements are being rearranged and redistributed, ending up as garbage and pollution.

It may well be true that capitalism is incapable of accommodating itself to the limits of the natural world. But that is not the same question as whether or not capitalism can solve the climate crisis. Climate mitigation and adaptation are merely an effort to buy time to address the other larger set of problems that is the whole ecological crisis.

This is both a pessimistic and an optimistic view. Although capitalism has not overcome the fundamental conflict between its infinite growth potential and the finite parameters of the planet's pollution sinks, it has, in the past, addressed *specific* environmental crises.

Anyone who thinks the existing economic system must be totally transformed before we can deal with the impending climate crisis is delusional or in willful denial of the very clear findings of climate science. If the climate system unravels, all bets are off. The many progressive visions born of the Enlightenment will be swallowed and forgotten by the rising seas or smashed to pieces by the wrathful storms of climate chaos.

Critical Thinking

1. Assuming humans caused global warming, what do you think should be done to reduce it?

2. How can we adapt to global warming?

3. Why does Parenti think that moderate approaches to mitigation and adaptation will not work? Do you agree?

Create Central

www.mhhe.com/createcentral

Internet References

Sociosite
    www.topsite.com/goto/sociosite.net
Socioweb
    www.topsite.com/goto/socioweb.com
Sociology—Study Sociology Online
    http://edu.learnsoc.org
Sociology Web Resources
    www.mhhe.com/socscience/sociology/resources/index.htm

CHRISTIAN PARENTI is a professor of sustainable development at the School for International Training, Graduate Institute. He is a contributing editor to the *Nation* and the author of four books, the most recent being *Tropic of Chaos: Climate Change and the New Geography of Violence* (Nation Books, July 2011).

Parenti, Christian. From *Dissent*, Summer 2013, pp. 51–57. Copyright © 2013 by Foundation for Study of Independent Ideas, Inc. Reprinted by permission of University of Pennsylvania Press. www.dissentmagazine.org

Article   Prepared by: Kurt Finsterbusch, *University of Maryland, College Park*

A Thousand Years Young

An "anti-aging activist" identifies the medical and biochemical advances that could eventually eliminate all the wear and tear that our bodies and minds suffer as we grow old. Those who undergo continuous repair treatments could live for millennia, remain healthy throughout, and never fear dying of old age.

AUBREY DE GREY

Learning Outcomes

After reading this article, you will be able to:

- Understand that Aubrey de Grey's approach to life extension is to constantly rejuvenate the body as it deteriorates.

- Assuming that de Grey is right, consider how people would change their lifestyles.

- Understand the many specific treatments that would together greatly extend life.

L et me first say very explicitly: I don't work on longevity. I work on health. People are going to live longer as a result of the therapies I will describe, but extended longevity is a side effect—a consequence of keeping people healthy. There is no way in hell that we are going to keep people alive for a long time in a frail state. People will live longer only if we succeed in keeping them healthy longer.

The problem of aging is unequivocally humanity's worst medical problem. Roughly 100,000 people worldwide die every day of it, and there's an awful lot of suffering that happens before you die. But I feel that the defeat of aging in the foreseeable future is a realistic proposition. We will have medicine that will get aging under control to the same level that we now have most infectious diseases under control.

This article will describe what aging is, what regenerative medicine is, and what the various alternative approaches are to combat aging and postpone the ill health of old age. I'll then go into the details of the approach that I feel we need to take and what my expectations are for the future.

Regenerative medicine is any medical intervention that seeks to restore some part of the body—or the whole body—to how it was before it suffered some kind of damage. It could be damage that happened as the result of an acute injury, such as spinal cord damage. But it could also be damage that accumulated as a chronic condition over a long period of time.

Aging is a side effect of being alive in the first place. *Metabolism* is the word that biologists use to encompass all the aspects of being alive—all the molecular and cellular and systemic processes that keep us going from one day to the next and from one year to the next.

Ongoing lifelong side effects of metabolism—i.e., *damages*—are created throughout life. For whatever reason, damage is not repaired when it occurs. So damage accumulates. For a long time, the amount of damage is tolerable, and the metabolism just carries on. But eventually, damage becomes sufficiently extensive that it gets in the way of metabolism. Then metabolism doesn't work so well, and *pathologies*—all the things that go wrong late in life, all the aspects of age-related ill health—emerge and progress.

Geriatrics versus Gerontology

Traditionally, there have been two themes within the study of aging that aim to actually do something about this process. One is the *geriatrics* approach, which encompasses pretty much everything that we have today in terms of medical treatments for the elderly.

The geriatrics approach is all about the pathology. It focuses on old people in whom the pathologies are already emerging, and strives to slow down their progression so that it takes longer for those pathologies to reach a life-threatening stage.

The *gerontology* approach, on the other hand, says that prevention is better than cure. This approach assumes that it will be more effective to dive in at an earlier point in the chain of events and clean up metabolism so that it creates these various types of damage at a slower rate than it naturally would. The effect would be to postpone the age at which damage reaches the level of abundance that is pathogenic.

The two approaches both sound pretty promising, but they're really not. The problem with the geriatrics approach is that aging is awfully chaotic, miserable, and complicated. There are many things that go wrong with people as they get older, and they tend to happen at much the same time. These problems interact, exacerbating each other, and damage accumulates. Even later in life, as damage continues to accumulate, the pathologies of old age become progressively more and more difficult to combat.

The geriatric approach is thus intervening too late in the chain of events. It's better than nothing, but it's not much better than nothing.

So that leaves us with the gerontology approach. Unfortunately, the gerontology approach has its own problem: Metabolism is complicated. What we know about how metabolism works is completely dwarfed by the utterly astronomical amount that we *don't* know about how metabolism works. We have no prospect whatsoever of being able to interfere in this process in a way that does not simply do more harm than good.

A Maintenance Approach

There are some Volkswagen Bugs that are 50 years old or more and still running. And the reason is because those VW Bugs have been extraordinarily well maintained. If you maintain your car only as well as the law requires, then it will only last 15 years or so. But if you do a lot more, then you can do a lot better. Maintenance works.

Now what does that tell us about the human body? Well, quite a lot, because the human body is a machine. It's a really complicated machine, but it's still a machine. So there is a third way of combating aging by postponing age-related ill health. This is the *maintenance* approach. We go in and periodically repair the damage that metabolism creates, so as to prevent that damage from accumulating and reaching the level that causes the pathology of old age to emerge and to progress.

Maintenance is a much more promising approach than either geriatrics or gerontology. First, the maintenance approach is preemptive, so it doesn't have this problem of this downward spiral of the geriatrics approach.

Second, the maintenance approach avoids the problem of the gerontology approach because it does not attempt to intervene with metabolism; we merely fix up the consequences. In other words, we let metabolism create these various types of damage at the rate that it naturally does, and then repair the damages before they cause pathology. We can get away with not understanding very much at all about how metabolism creates damage. We just have to characterize the damage itself and figure out ways to repair it.

That's pretty good news, but it gets better. It also turns out that damage is simpler than its causes or its consequences. All the phenomena that qualify as damage can be classified into one of seven major categories:

- Junk inside cells.
- Junk outside cells.
- Too few cells.
- Too many cells.
- Chromosome mutations.
- Mitochondria mutations.
- Protein cross-links.

By "junk inside cells," I am referring to the molecular byproducts of normal biologic processes that are created in the cell and that the cell, for whatever reason, does not have the machinery to break down or to excrete. Those byproducts simply accumulate, and eventually the cell doesn't work so well. That turns out to be the main cause of cardiovascular disease and of macular degeneration.

"Junk outside cells" means things like senile plaques in Alzheimer's disease. This creates the same molecular damage, but in this case it is in the spaces between cells.

"Too few cells" simply means cells are dying and not being automatically replaced by the division of other cells. This is the cause of Parkinson's disease, the particular part of the brain in which neurons happen to die more rapidly than in most parts of the brain and they're not replaced. When there are too few of them, that part of the brain doesn't work so well.

But here's the really good news. We actually have a pretty good idea how to fix all of these types of damage. Here is the same list of types of damage, and on the right is the set of approaches that I feel are very promising for fixing them:

Damage	Treatment
Junk inside cells	transgenic microbial hydolases
Junk outside cells	Phagocytosis by immune stimulation
Too few cells (cell loss)	cell therapy
Too many cells (death-resistant cells)	suicide genes and immune stimulation
Chromosome mutations	telomerase/ALT gene deletion plus periodic stem-cell reseeding
Mitochondria mutations	allotopic expression of 13 proteins
Protein cross-links	AGE-breaking molecules and enzymes

Stem-cell therapy replaces those cells that the body cannot replace on its own. That includes joint degeneration and muscular-skeletal problems. For example, arthritis ultimately comes from the degeneration of the collagen and other extracellular material in the joints, which happens as a result of insufficient regeneration of that tissue.

The SENS Foundation: Doing Something About Aging

I'm the chief officer of a 501(c)3 public charity based in California. The mission of the SENS Foundation is to develop, promote, and enable widespread access to regenerative medicine as solutions to the disabilities and diseases of aging.

Is there any competition in this work? Are other people trying other things? The short answer is, Not really. There are other people, of course, looking at ways to postpone aging and age-related ill health. But regenerative medicine is really the only game in town when we're talking about serious postponement of age-related ill health. And the SENS Foundation really is the hub of that concept.

We are a charity, so if you are a billionaire, please see me! But of course it's not just money we need. We need people's time and expertise. If you're a biologist, work on relevant things. Write to us and ask us for advice about what to work on, because we need more manpower in this area. If you're a conference organizer, have me to speak. If you're a journalist, come and interview me. It's all about getting the word out.

—*Aubrey de Grey*

Details: The SENS Foundation, www.sens.org; e-mail foundation@sens.org.

For some other medical conditions, such as Alzheimer's, we need to restore the functions of those cells that are already there by getting rid of the garbage accumulating outside them. Toward that purpose, there are phase-three clinical trials for the elimination of senile plaques in the brains of Alzheimer's patients. This is a technology using vaccination that we at the SENS Foundation are extending to the elimination of other types of extracellular garbage.

In fact, we now have an enormous amount of detail about how we're going to reverse each of the seven categories of age-related damage, so that's why I feel that my estimates of how long it's going to take to get there are likely to be borne out accurately.

Case in Point: Cleaning the Cellular Garbage

I'm going to talk about one example: the garbage that accumulates inside cells. I'm going to explain what *transgenic microbial hydrolases* are.

White blood cells, called macrophages, sweep along a healthy adult's artery walls to clean up miscellaneous detritus, typically lipo protein particles that were transporting cholesterol around the body from one place to another and that got stuck in the artery wall. Macrophages are very good at coping with cholesterol, but they are not so good at coping with certain derivatives of cholesterol, such as oxysterols. These contaminants end up poisoning macrophages. The macrophages become unable even to cope with native cholesterol, and then they themselves break down, lodging in the artery walls. This is the beginning of an atherosclerotic plaque. The results are cardiovascular disease, heart attacks, or strokes. In the eye, this phenomenon causes macular degeneration.

To combat this problem, we might adapt bioremediation technology from environmental decontamination. The technology that is used to break down pollutants in the environment could be adapted for biomedical purposes, breaking down the body's contaminants.

If we could apply this bioremediation process to our own cells, we could combat the initial process that turns young people into old people in the first place. A very simple idea. The question is, does it work? Bioremediation for getting rid of pollutants works really well: It's a thriving commercial discipline.

There are a number of oxidized derivatives of cholesterol, but the nastiest in abundance and toxicity is 7-ketocholesterol—public enemy number one in atherosclerosis. We have tried "feeding" it to many different strains of bacteria. Most of them can't do anything with it, but we've found two strains of bacteria that gorge themselves on it. After only 10 days, the material is completely gone.

The next step is to figure out how these bacteria are able to do this from a genetic basis. From there, we could try to turn 7-ketocholesterol back into native cholesterol. But there are other steps that we can use—remember that I said we're looking to avoid the problem of things neither being broken down nor excreted. There are modifications that we can make to compounds that are toxic that simply promote their excretion rather than promoting their degradation.

So that's all pretty good news. But don't get me wrong. This is really hard. This is a very ambitious, long-term. project. The processes we hope to develop must work in vivo. What we are seeking is a truly definitive, complete cure for cardiovascular disease and for other pathologies caused by the accumulation of molecular garbage inside cells.

Escape Velocity: From Longevity To Immortality?

I do not claim that any of the work I've just described is going to be a "cure" for aging. I claim, rather, that it's got a good chance of adding 30 years of extra healthy life to people's lives. I call that *robust human rejuvenation*. And 30 years is better than nothing, but it sure does not equate to defeating aging completely. So what's the rest of my story?

The rest of the story is that it's not something that's going to work just on people who haven't been conceived yet. It's stuff that is going to work on people who are already middle-aged or older when the therapies arrive.

This is fundamentally what it all comes down to. The maintenance approach is so cool because repairing damage buys time.

At age zero, people start off with not much damage. Time goes on, they age, damage accumulates, reserve is depleted, and eventually, they get down to a certain point—the frailty threshold—and that's when pathologies start to happen. Then they're not long for this world.

Now take someone who is in middle age. You have therapies that are pretty good, but not perfect, at fixing the damage. They can be rejuvenated, but not all the way. These therapies do not reduce the rate at which damage is created. Aging happens at the normal rate.

Then we reapply the same therapies again and again. But consider that the interval between the first and second applications of these therapies to some particular individual may be 15 to 20 years. That's a long time in biomedical technology, and it means that the person is going to get new and improved therapies that will not only fix the types of damage that they could fix 15 years previously, but also fix some types of damage that they could not fix 15 years previously.

So after the second rejuvenation, our hero is not only more thoroughly rejuvenated than he would be if he'd gotten the old therapies, but he's actually more rejuvenated than he was when he got the old therapies, even though at that point he was chronologically younger. Now we see this phenomenon where we don't hit diminishing returns on additional therapies. People over the long term will be getting progressively younger as they're getting chronologically older. They'll remain far away from reaching the frailty threshold, however long that they live. They will only be subjected to the risks of death and ill health that affect young adults. They never become more susceptible to ill health simply as a result of having been born a long time ago.

There's some minimum rate at which we have to improve the comprehensiveness of these therapies in order for the general trend in increased life span to be upwards rather than downwards. And that minimum rate is what I call *longevity escape velocity*. It's the rate at which these rejuvenation therapies need to be improved in terms of comprehensiveness following that first step—the first-generation therapies that give robust human regeneration—in order to stay one step ahead of the problem and to outpace the accumulation of damage that they cannot yet repair.

So is it realistic? Are we likely actually to reach longevity escape velocity and to maintain it? We are. Consider powered flight as an illustrated example: There are very big differences between fundamental breakthroughs and incremental refinements of those breakthroughs. Fundamental breakthroughs are very hard to predict. Mostly people think they're not going to happen right up until they already have happened.

Incremental refinements, meanwhile, are very much more predictable. Leonardo da Vinci probably thought he was only a couple of decades away from getting off the ground. He was wrong. But once the Wright brothers got there, progress was ridiculously rapid. It only took 24 years for someone to fly solo across the Atlantic (that was Lindbergh), 22 more years until the first commercial jet liner, and 20 more years until the first supersonic airlines.

Can we actually give more direct evidence that we are likely to achieve longevity escape velocity? I believe that we can.

An Age-Busting Virtuous Cycle

A few years ago I worked with others on a computer simulation of the aging process to see what the impact would be of these interventions coming in at a realistic schedule. We started by imagining a population of adults who were all born in 1999. Everyone is alive at age zero and almost everyone survives until age 50 or 60, at which point they start dropping like flies; hardly anyone gets beyond 100.

Next, we imagined another population whose intrinsic risk of death at any given age is the same as for the first, but who are receiving these therapies. But they only start receiving them when they are already 80 years old. That population's survival rate will actually mostly coincide with the first population's survival rate, because obviously half the population or so is dead by age 80 and those who are still living are already in a reasonably bad way.

But what if population number two started getting these therapies 10 years earlier, when they're only 70? Initially, the same story is the case—there is not a lot of benefit. But gradually, the therapies get the upper hand. They start to impose genuine rejuvenation on these people so that they become biologically younger and less likely to die. Some of them reach 150, by which time they have very little chance of dying of *any* age-related cause. Eventually, there is exactly no such risk.

And if they're 60 years old when the therapies begin? Then almost half of them will get to that point. So we calculated, group by group.

Here's the real kicker: I was ludicrously over-pessimistic in the parameters that I chose for this simulation. I said that we would assume that the therapy would only be doubled in their efficacy every 42 years. Now, 42 years: That's the difference between Lindbergh's *Spirit of St. Louis* and the *Concorde!* But even then, we unambiguously see longevity escape velocity.

So it's inescapable. If and when we do succeed in developing these rejuvenation therapies that give us those first couple of decades more of health and the postponement of age-related ill health, then we will have done the hard part. The sky is the limit after that.

Here is what it means. At the moment, the world record for life span is 122. We won't be getting anyone who is 150 until such time as we do develop these technologies that give us robust human rejuvenation. But we will have done the hard part, so people not much younger than that will be able to escape aging indefinitely, living even to age 1,000.

A thousand is not pulled out of the air. It's simply the average age—plus or minus a factor of two—that people would live to if we already didn't have aging, if the only risks of death were the same risks that currently afflict young adults in the Western world today.

Should we be developing these therapies? We are ignorant about the circumstances within which humanity of the future will be deciding whether to use these technologies or not. It could actually be a no-brainer that they will want to use them. And if we have prevented them from using them by not developing them in time, then future generations won't be very happy. So it seems to me that we have a clear moral obligation to develop these technologies so as to give humanity of the future the choice. And the sooner, the better.

Critical Thinking

1. Would you like to live 1,000 years? Aubrey de Grey says that the technology will be developed to make that happen for you or your grandchildren.

2. What would be the impacts on social life and society if healthy life extended for hundreds of years?

3. Why is de Grey's message largely ignored by the media?

Create Central

www.mhhe.com/createcentral

Internet References

Sociosite
  www.topsite.com/goto/sociosite.net
Socioweb
  www.topsite.com/goto/socioweb.com
Sociology—Study Sociology Online
  http://edu.learnsoc.org
Sociology Web Resources
  www.mhhe.com/socscience/sociology/resources/index.htm

Aubrey de Grey is a biomedical gerontologist and chief science officer of the SENS Foundation (www.sens.org). He is the author (with Michael Rae) of *Ending Aging* (St. Martin's Press, 2007) and editor-in-chief of the journal *Rejuvenation Research*. This article draws from his presentation at WorldFuture 2011 in Vancouver.

Article   Prepared by: Kurt Finsterbusch, *University of Maryland, College Park*

Engineering the Future of Food

JOSH SCHONWALD

Learning Outcomes

After reading this article, you will be able to:

- Identify the arguments for and against using genetically modified organisms (GMOs) to greatly improve and extend life.
- Evaluate Schonwald's argument that "Tomorrow's genetically modified food and farmed fish will be . . . far healthier than much of what we eat today."
- Evaluate the arguments against GMOs.

Tomorrow's genetically modified food and farmed fish will be more sustainable and far healthier than much of what we eat today—if we can overcome our fears and embrace it. Here's how one foodie learned to stop worrying and love "frankenfood."

The Plant Transformation Facility at the University of California, Davis, has been the scene of more than 15,000 "transgenic events," which is the term molecular biologists use when they blast DNA from one life form into another. In room 192 of Robbins Hall, a brick building not far from the student union, thousands of microscopic plantlets grow in Petri dishes bathed in pink and fluorescent blue light.

Here, molecular biologists can mix what were previously sexually incompatible species together using a gas-pump-like tool called the Helium Particle Delivery System. Using bullets (literally) made out of gold, they fire genes from one species into another in a bombardment chamber. The Davis lab has given birth to grapes spiked with jellyfish, tomatoes spiked with carp, transgenic squash, transgenic carrots, transgenic tomatoes.

Another important site in genetic engineering history, an innocuous office building about a ten-minute drive from Robbins Hall, is the birthplace of the most audacious plant in the history of high-tech plants. Among biotech people and anti-biotech people, this plant, a tomato, needs no introduction. The so-called Flavr Savr was supposed to be the game changer—longer shelf life, better yield, better taste. Calgene, the company that created the Flavr Savr, claimed it could bring "backyard flavor" to the supermarket tomato.

Achieving "backyard flavor" in an industrial-scale, California-grown tomato has long been one of the holy grails of the $4 billion-plus tomato industry. During the pre-tomato launch

hype-a-thon, the president of Calgene claimed that genetic engineering could not only bring us the tomato of our childhood dreams, but also remake the taste of the tomato, tailored to our every desire: "Eventually we're going to design acidic tomatoes for the New Jersey palate and sweet tomatoes for the Chicago palate."

The Flavr Savr turned out to be the Edsel of the produce world, a spectacular failure not just for Calgene, but for the whole biotech industry. This purportedly longer-shelf-life tomato became the lightning rod for much of the anti-genetically modified organism (GMO) movement. People learned about other transgenic crops—a potato with a chicken gene, tobacco with a firefly gene, and, perhaps most notoriously, a tomato with an Arctic flounder gene, which provided an image for a Greenpeace anti-GMO campaign. Nongovernmental organizations cried foul. Consumers were alarmed. It was an op-ed about the Flavr Savr where the term Frankenfood first appeared. As for the tomato's taste, most reports said that, far from achieving backyard flavor, it was not that great.

By 1997, supermarkets stopped stocking the bioengineered tomato. The Flavr Savr was a financial disaster for Calgene.

But that was almost fifteen years ago.

One fall day, across campus from the Helium Particle Delivery System, I went to visit Kent Bradford, the director of UC Davis's Seed Biotechnology Center and presumably among the best-positioned people at Davis to answer my burning question: Whatever happened after the Flavr Savr?

The Culinary Potential of Frankenfood

Genetic engineering obviously didn't stop with the Flavr Savr debacle; the use of GMOs has exploded. Many genetically engineered foods can be found throughout our food supply. Genetically modified soybeans and canola dominate the market, which means that most processed food—everything from your spaghetti to your Snickers bar—has GM ingredients. More than 90% of American cotton and 80% of corn crops come from GM seed. All of these crops, though, are what are called "commodity crops." They're not what you pick up at your local greengrocer. They're industrial crops, secondary ingredients. Not what interested me.

What I wanted to know is what was happening with the quest to achieve "backyard flavor"? And what I couldn't get out of my head was this claim that tomatoes could be engineered for precise tastes—"acidic tomatoes for the New Jersey palate and sweet tomatoes for the Chicago palate."

What was going on? Did they just stop working on "sweet tomatoes for the Chicago palate"? Wouldn't the Flavr Savr creators be intent on redemption, going back to the bench to try again? Or did everything just stop?

Strangely, Bradford, a plant geneticist who has been at UC Davis since the early 1980s, shared my curiosity about the post-Flavr Savr world—he just had a different way of explaining it.

"Yes. Where are all these output traits?" he said. (Input traits are breederspeak for what's so often critical to agriculture—disease resistance, insect resistance, adaptability to particular environments. An output trait is breeder parlance for what I was looking for—traits that improve taste and texture, traits that could change the dining experience of the future.)

Bradford had observed that, almost twenty years after the biotech revolution began, there were few signs of any "Second Generation" crops. The First Generation was the commodity crops: soybean, maize, cotton, canola, sugar beets. Most expected that, after the first wave of crops proved their worth, the next wave would be more consumer focused—better tomatoes, tastier lettuce. But biotech specialty crops (that's the crop scientist term for produce) hadn't appeared. In fact, a GMO specialty crop hadn't been commercialized since 1998. Even Bradford, a longtime biotech believer, considered, "Maybe the genes weren't working?"

A few years ago, Bradford and his collaborator Jamie Miller set out to find out "what was going on" with bioengineered specialty crops. They surveyed the leading plant science journals and tracked GM crop field trials—all subject to government regulation—from 2003 to 2008. Searching for citations related to specialty crops, they found that research not only had never stopped but was thriving.

"There was research on 46 different species," says Bradford. "More than 300 traits were being tested." A lot of it was on input traits (disease, weed resistance), but breeders had also experimented with output traits. "It was happening at the research level, but it just didn't move to the next step. It just stopped there."

There was an obvious explanation, Bradford says, sighing. "It was regulatory."

Post Flavr Savr, in response to growing consumer concerns about transgenic breeding, a regulatory process was created that treated genetically modified foods differently from conventionally bred crops. If you have iceberg lettuce, using classic plant-breeding techniques (crossing, back-crossing), the assumption is that the resulting lettuce is safe. There's no requirement for pretesting. You just introduce the product into the market. But with GMOs, Bradford says, the attitude was that "it's guilty until proven innocent."

A genetically engineered crop must pass review by the U.S. Department of Agriculture, the Environmental Protection Agency, and the Food and Drug Administration before it is commercialized. The cost could range from $50,000 to tens of millions of dollars to win regulatory approval. For every "transgenic event," the genetic engineer must show exactly what genes went into the plant and how they function, and then prove how the plant makeup has been altered. That research is costly. So is plant storage. Once a transgenic creation is spawned at the Plant Transformation Facility, it is whisked to the UC Davis Controlled Environment Facility, where it will stay in a tightly secured warehouse. Or it will be airmailed to some other place, where it'll live out its life in another intensely biosecure environment.

The process is costly and time-consuming, which partly explains why biotech crop development is largely in the hands of the agribusiness giants—the Monsantos, Syngentas, and Bayer Crop Sciences of the world—who have the resources to undertake the process. With such high approval costs, big companies have favored commodity crops with market potential for hundreds of millions of dollars in sales, not tens of millions.

We talked about the reasons for what Bradford calls "the bottleneck" for the biotech specialty crops. It was NGOs such as Greenpeace and the Union of Concerned Scientists that were the bogeymen, in his view. Big Organic, a $20 billion industry, had a vested interested in stopping GMOs. Back in 2000, when the USDA was developing the National Organic Program standards, the first draft did not prohibit genetically modified foods, but then activists launched an anti-GMO campaign, flooding the USDA with a tidal wave of letters—275,026, to be exact. The USDA then determined that genetically modified organisms would not be included under the standard for organic produce. Being deemed un-kosher in the organic world is a hard stigma to overcome.

The anti-GMO movement hasn't lost momentum; the Non-GMO Project has become the fastest-growing food eco-label in North America, with sales eclipsing $1 billion in 2011. As for Europe: After a 12-year moratorium on GMO crops, the European Union greenlighted a GMO potato—but not for human consumption. It would be used to produce higher levels of starch, which is helpful for industries like paper manufacturing. In short, the European market is still overwhelmingly closed for genetically modified foodstuffs.

What If the World Embraced Agricultural Biotechnology?

According to the World Health Organization, 250 million children worldwide, mostly in the developing world, have diets lacking in vitamin A. Between 250,000 and 500,000 of these children go blind every year. Yet, there is a crop, developed more than 13 years ago, that is fortified with vitamin A compounds. If children unable to get vitamin A from other protein sources simply eat this crop, they will not go blind and die. It is named "golden rice" because of its yellowish hue, and every health organization in the world has declared it to be safe to eat.

But golden rice was not bred through traditional means; it was bred in a lab. So golden rice is, by its opponents' definition, Frankenfood, and therefore, like many other GMO crops, it's been ferociously opposed.

Now let's say that golden rice does get approved (as some predict it will in 2013), and let's say it saves millions of children from starvation and blindness in Asia. Or let's say bioengineered crops slow down the creation of algal dead zones in the Gulf of Mexico. Or a low-fat, anti-cancer potato becomes a smash hit at McDonald's. Consumer worries about GMOs evaporate, becoming as anachronistic as fears of microwave ovens causing cancer. The regulatory barriers are gone; transgenic plants are treated the same as any other. The Monsanto juggernaut is over; small, boutique companies and open-source plant breeders in the comfort of a Brooklyn loft have a chance to contribute to the vegetable economy. Then what happens?

- Food will look different. There will almost surely be more varieties. Austrian heirloom lettuce varieties like Forellenschluss and heirloom tomatoes like the Brandywines and Cherokee Purples could become readily available. So many vegetables today aren't commercially viable because of disease vulnerabilities or production inefficiencies. But in a genetically engineered future, all the flaws that make them ill-suited for commercialization become mere speed bumps.

"You could have disease immunity almost immediately," says Bradford. "And it would be very easy to take care of these other variables. Instead of taking a decade to ready a crop for commercialization, it will take a matter of months."

It's possible that colors would change. You could find pink lettuce and blue arugula—maybe with a green orange slice for St. Patrick's Day. Color becomes malleable because it's often a single trait.

- Food will taste different. It is also likely, some geneticists say, that in 2035 some lettuces won't taste anything like lettuce. The notion of tomatoes with customized flavor was a reckless ambition in the 1990s when the Flavr Savr debuted; modifying taste is among the most challenging tasks for plant geneticists. You can silence a gene in the potato genome, tuning down the bitterness or acidic quality, but it's still a fractional impact on taste.

Taste is complex. A tomato, for instance, has between five and twenty compounds that influence flavor. Changing flavor requires not one gene, but packages of genes, and the genes must be placed precisely. Then there is texture, inextricably linked to flavor. Modifying taste eludes technologists today, but in the next ten years, that could change, as bio-engineers will be able to choose from a genetic cassette—stacks of genes that together confer desired traits. With a few mouse clicks, geneticists say, they could choose from a range of flavors, textures, and colors.

"Think of it like Photoshop," says C. S. Prakash, director of the Center for Plant Biotechnology Research at Tuskegee University. "At some point that won't be a far-fetched metaphor." It will be technologically possible, therefore, to create a Caesar salad without the Caesar dressing; the flavor of the Caesar could be bred into the lettuce.

Textures would also be far easier to change. You could bite into an apple that has the consistency of a banana. In a biotech-friendly future, fruits and vegetables would merely be another frontier for adventurous and often mind-bending culinary pioneers.

- We'll see produce that doesn't spoil. In a biotech future, the sell-by dates will be different; instead of rushing to eat your lettuce in a week, looseleaf lettuce could languish, unsealed, for a month or more. One of the

huge problems in the produce industry is perishability, with close to one-third of all fresh fruits and vegetables produced lost to overripening or damage during shipment. But bioengineers are already making progress in changing the post-harvest behavior of plants. By having an enzyme shut off, an apple has been modified so that it won't turn brown after it is sliced, and a banana has been engineered to ripen more slowly.

Although small organic farmers are often the most hostile to technologized solutions and may be the least likely group to adopt high-tech crops, it's possible that GMOs could change the farmers' markets in places like Chicago or Buffalo.

"In New York and Illinois, it's pretty hard to grow a lot of crops because they're going to freeze," explains Dennis Miller, a food scientist at Cornell University. "But you could engineer in frost tolerance. You could extend the growing season and bring in more exotic crops into new regions. I don't know if we'll be growing bananas in upstate New York, but it would expand the options for locally grown fruits and vegetables."

How Frankenfood Will Improve Health

Most breeders expect that the biggest change for consumers would be something that's already familiar to any Whole Foods shopper. We already have calcium-fortified orange juice and herbal tea enhanced with antioxidants, but in an agbiotech-friendly world, the produce section would likely be overflowing with health enhancements. Orange potatoes enhanced with beta-carotene, calcium-enhanced carrots, and crops with enhanced antioxidants are already in the pipeline. By the 2030s, vegetables and fruits will be vitamin, nutrient, and beneficial-gene-delivery vehicles.

To illustrate how this would play out, Prakash points to the work of Cynthia Kenyon, a University of California-San Francisco molecular biologist, who extended the life span of a ground worm by six times by changing a gene called "def 2."

While this is in the realm of basic science, Prakash also suggests that, if something like a "fountain of youth" gene is found to benefit humans, it could be bred into vegetables. By combining genetics and plant science, a whole new realm of products would likely appear.

Some geneticists envision a future in which crop development would become a highly collaborative process: Nutritionists, geneticists, physicians, chefs, and marketers would work to develop new fruits and vegetables aimed at various consumer wants.

Another Kind of Foodie Hero

A scientist in a white lab coat doesn't conjure the same feelings as a micro-farmer in a straw hat. Growing fish in a warehouse isn't quite as stirring as pulling them out of a choppy Alaskan sea. A meat-spawning bioreactor doesn't have the same allure as a dew-covered Virginia pasture.

But it's time to broaden the foodie pantheon.

Let's continue to celebrate our heirloom-fava-bean growers and our grass-fed-goat herders. Let's carefully scrutinize the claims of nutritional science and keep a wary eye on new technologies, especially those with panacea-like claims from multinational corporations with monopolistic aims and a history of DDT and Agent Orange production. But let's not be so black-and-white; let's not be reflexively and categorically opposed to any and all technological solutions. Savoring the slowest food and foraging for wild asparagus shouldn't be viewed as at odds with championing lab-engineered vitamin A-enhanced rice that could save children from blindness.

Pairing a locally grown, seasonal mesclun mix from an organic micro-farm with cobia, a saltwater fish grown in an industrial-sized warehouse, is not an incompatible, ethically confused choice.

I make this point because of the rising tide of food-specific neo-Luddism in America. While well intentioned and often beneficial in its impact, this foodie fundamentalism is unfortunately often associated with a dangerous antiscientism. If we're going to meet the enormous challenges of feeding the world's still-growing population, we are going to need all the ingenuity we can bring to bear.

My modest hope: Let's keep an open mind. Let's consider even the fringy, sometimes yucky, maybe kooky ideas. Let's not miss opportunities to build a long-term sustainable future for our planet.

"The process is costly and time consuming, which partly explains why biotech crop development is largely in the hands of the agribusiness giants."

"With a few mouse clicks, geneticists say, they could choose from a range of flavors, textures, and colors."

Critical Thinking

1. What do you think about using GMOs to greatly improve the taste in foods?
2. Should the golden rice story prove the case for the need for GMOs?
3. What are the myriad of potential benefits of GMOs according to Schonwald?

Create Central

www.mhhe.com/createcentral

Internet References

Sociosite
www.topsite.com/goto/sociosite.net
Socioweb
www.topsite.com/goto/socioweb.com
Sociology—Study Sociology Online
http://edu.learnsoc.org
Sociology Web Resources
www.mhhe.com/socscience/sociology/resources/index.htm

Article   Prepared by: Kurt Finsterbusch, *University of Maryland, College Park*

How Innovation Could Save the Planet

Ideas may be our greatest natural resource, says a computer scientist and futurist. He argues that the world's most critical challenges—including population growth, peak oil, climate change, and limits to growth—could be met by encouraging innovation.

RAMEZ NAAM

Learning Outcomes

After reading this article, you will be able to:

- Understand both the benefits and the costs of long-term economic progress.

- Evaluate Ramez Naam's thesis that "Innovation Could Save the Planet."

- Notice the many specific ideas and innovations that could address the major problems.

The Best of Times: Unprecedented Prosperity

There are many ways in which we are living in the most wonderful age ever. We can imagine we are heading toward a sort of science-fiction Utopia, where we are incredibly rich and incredibly prosperous, and the planet is healthy. But there are other reasons to fear that we're headed toward a dystopia of sorts.

On the positive side, life expectancy has been rising for the last 150 years, and faster since the early part of the twentieth century in the developing world than it has in the rich world. Along with that has come a massive reduction in poverty. The most fundamental empowerer of humans—education—has also soared, not just in the rich world, but throughout the world.

Another great empowerer of humanity is connectivity: Access to information and access to communication both have soared. The number of mobile phones on the planet was effectively zero in the early 1990s, and now it's in excess of 4 billion. More than three-quarters of humanity, in the span of one generation, have gotten access to connectivity that, as my friend Peter Diamandis likes to say, is greater than any president before 1995 had. A reasonably well-off person in India or in Nigeria has better access to information than Ronald Reagan did during most of his career.

With increased connectivity has come an increase in democracy. As people have gotten richer, more educated, more able to access information, and more able to communicate, they have

demanded more control over the places where they live. The fraction of nations that are functional democracies is at an all-time high in this world—more than double what it was in the 1970s, with the collapse of the Soviet Union.

Economically, the world is a more equal place than it has been in decades. In the West, and especially in the United States, we hear a lot about growing inequality, but on a global scale, the opposite is true. As billions are rising out of poverty around the world, the global middle classes are catching up with the global rich.

In many ways, this is the age of the greatest human prosperity, freedom, and potential that has ever been on the face of this planet. But in other ways, we are facing some of the largest risks ever.

The Worst of Times: The Greatest Risks

At its peak, the ancient Mayan city of Tikal was a metropolis, a city of 200,000 people inside of a civilization of about 20 million people. Now, if you walk around any Mayan city, you see mounds of dirt. That's because these structures were all abandoned by about the mid-900s AD. We know now what happened: The Mayan civilization grew too large. It overpopulated. To feed themselves, they had to convert forest into farmland. They chopped down all of the forest. That, in turn, led to soil erosion. It also worsened drought, because trees, among other things, trap moisture and create a precipitation cycle.

When that happened, and was met by some normal (not human-caused) climate change, the Mayans found they didn't have enough food. They exhausted their primary energy supply, which is food. That in turn led to more violence in their society and ultimately to a complete collapse.

The greatest energy source for human civilization today is fossil fuels. Among those, none is more important than oil. In 1956, M. King Hubbert looked at production in individual oil fields and predicted that the United States would see the peak of its oil production in 1970 or so, and then drop. His prediction largely came true: Oil production went up but did peak in the 1970s, then plummeted.

Oil production has recently gone up in the United States a little bit, but it's still just barely more than half of what it was in its peak in the 1970s.

Hubbert also predicted that the global oil market would peak in about 2000, and for a long time he looked very foolish. But it now has basically plateaued. Since 2004, oil production has increased by about 4%, whereas in the 1950s it rose by about 4% every three months.

We haven't hit a peak; oil production around the world is still rising a little bit. It's certainly not declining, but we do appear to be near a plateau; supply is definitely rising more slowly than demand. Though there's plenty of oil in the ground, the oil that remains is in smaller fields, further from shore, under lower pressure, and harder to pump out.

Water is another resource that is incredibly precious to us. The predominant way in which we use water is through the food that we eat: 70% of the freshwater that humanity uses goes into agriculture.

The Ogallala Aquifer, the giant body of freshwater under the surface of the Earth in the Great Plains of the United States, is fossil water left from the melting and the retreat of glaciers in the end of the last Ice Age, 12,000-14,000 years ago. Its refill time is somewhere between 5,000 and 10,000 years from normal rainfall. Since 1960, we've drained between a third and a half of the water in this body, depending on what estimate you look at. In some areas, the water table is dropping about three feet per year.

If this was a surface lake in the United States or Canada, and people saw that happening, they'd stop it. But because it's out of sight, it's just considered a resource that we can tap. And indeed, in the north Texas area, wells are starting to fail already, and farms are being abandoned in some cases, because they can't get to the water that they once did.

Perhaps the largest risk of all is climate change. We've increased the temperature of the planet by about 2°F in the last 130 years, and that rate is accelerating. This is primarily because of the carbon dioxide we've put into the atmosphere, along with methane and nitrous oxide. CO_2 levels, now at over 390 parts per million, are the highest they've been in about 15 million years. Ice cores go back at least a million years, and we know that they're the highest they've been in that time. Historically, when CO_2 levels are high, temperature is also high. But also, historically, in the lifetime of our species, we've actually never existed as human beings while CO_2 levels have been this high.

For example, glaciers such as the Bear and Pedersen in Alaska have disappeared just since 1920. As these glaciers melt, they produce water that goes into the seas and helps to raise sea levels. Over the next century, the seas are expected to rise about 3 to 6 feet. Most of that actually will not be melting glaciers; it's thermal expansion: As the ocean gets warmer, it gets a little bit bigger.

But 3 to 6 feet over a century doesn't sound like that big a deal to us, so we think of that as a distant problem. The reality is that there's a more severe problem with climate change: its impact on the weather and on agriculture.

In 2003, Europe went through its worst heat wave since 1540. Ukraine lost 75% of its wheat crop. In 2009, China had a once-in-a-century level drought; in 2010 they had another once-in-a-century level drought. That's twice. Wells that had given water continuously since the fifteenth century ran dry. When those rains returned, when the water that was soaked up by the atmosphere came back down, it came down on Pakistan, and half of Pakistan was under water in the floods of 2010. An area larger than Germany was under water.

Warmer air carries more water. Every degree Celsius that you increase the temperature value of air, it carries 7% more water. But it doesn't carry that water uniformly. It can suck water away from one place and then deliver it in a deluge in another place. So both the droughts are up and flooding is up simultaneously, as precipitation becomes more lumpy and more concentrated.

In Russia's 2010 heat wave, 55,000 people died, 11,000 of them in Moscow alone. In 2011, the United States had the driest 10-month period ever in the American South, and Texas saw its worst wildfires ever. And 2012 was the worst drought in the United States since the Dust Bowl—the corn crop shrank by 20%.

So that's the big risk the world faces: that radical weather will change how we grow food, which is still our most important energy source—even more important than fossil fuels.

A number of people in the environmentalist movement are saying that we have to just stop growing. For instance, in his book Peak Everything: Waking Up to the Century of Declines, Richard Heinberg of the Post-Carbon Institute says that the Earth is full. Get used to it, and get ready for a world where you live with less wealth, and where your children live with less wealth, than any before.

I don't think this idea of stopping growth is realistic, because there are a top billion people who live pretty well and there are another 6 billion who don't and are hungry for it. We see demand rising for everything—water, food, energy—and that demand is rising not in the United States or Europe or Canada or Australia. It's rising in the developing world. This is the area that will create all of the increased demand for physical resources.

Even if we could, by some chance, say That's enough, sorry, we're not going to let you use these resources, which is doubtful, it wouldn't be just, because the West got rich by using those natural resources. So we need to find a different way.

Ideas as a Resource Expander, Resource Preserver, and Waste Reducer

The best-selling environmental book of all time, Limits to Growth, was based on computer modeling. It was a simple model with only about eight variables of what would happen in the world. It showed that economic growth, more wealth, would inevitably lead to more pollution and more consumption of finite resources, which would in turn take us beyond the limits and lead ultimately to collapse.

While it's been widely reported recently that its predictions are coming true, that's actually not the case. If you look at the vast majority of the numbers that the researchers predict in this model, they're not coming true.

Why did they get these things wrong? The most important thing that the forecasters did was underestimate the power of new ideas to expand resources, or to expand wealth while using fewer resources. Ideas have done tremendous things for us. Let's start with food.

In *The Population Bomb* (1968), Paul Ehrlich predicted that food supply could not support the population, just as Malthus did. But what's happened is that we've doubled population since 1960, and we've nearly tripled the food supply in total. We've increased by 30%–40% the food supply per person since the 1960s.

Let's look at this on a very long time scale. How many people can you feed with an acre of land? Before the advent of agriculture, an acre of land could feed less than a thousandth of a person. Today it's about three people, on average, who can be fed by one acre of land. Pre-agriculture, it took 3,000 acres for one person to stay alive through hunting and gathering. With agriculture, that footprint has shrunk from 3,000 acres to one-third of one acre. That's not because there's any more sunlight, which is ultimately what food is; it's because we've changed the productivity of the resource by innovation in farming—and then thousands of innovations on top of that to increase it even more.

In fact, the reason we have the forests that we have on the planet is because we were able to handle a doubling of the population since 1960 without increasing farmland by more than about 10%. If we had to have doubled our farmland, we would have chopped down all the remaining forests on the planet.

Ideas can reduce resource use. I can give you many other examples. In the United States, the amount of energy used on farms per calorie grown has actually dropped by about half since the 1970s. That's in part because we now only use about a tenth of the energy to create synthetic nitrogen fertilizer, which is an important input.

The amount of food that you can grow per drop of water has roughly doubled since the 1980s. In wheat, it's actually more than tripled since 1960. The amount of water that we use in the United States per person has dropped by about a third since the 1970s, after rising for decades. As agriculture has gotten more efficient, we're using less water per person. So, again, ideas can reduce resource use.

Ideas can also find substitutes for scarce resources. We're at risk of running out of many things, right? Well, let's think about some things that have happened in the past.

The sperm whale was almost hunted into extinction. Sperm whales were, in the mid-1800s, the best source of illumination. Sperm whale oil—spermaceti—was the premier source of lighting. It burned without smoke, giving a clear, steady light, and the demand for it led to huge hunting of the sperm whales. In a period of about 30 years, we killed off about a third of the sperm whales on the planet.

That led to a phenomenon of "peak sperm-whale oil": The number of sperm whales that the fleet could bring in dropped over time as the sperm whales became more scarce and more afraid of human hunters. Demand rose as supply dropped, and

the prices skyrocketed. So it looked a little bit like the situation with oil now.

That was solved not by the discovery of more sperm whales, nor by giving up on this thing of lighting. Rather, Abraham Gesner, a Canadian, discovered this thing called kerosene. He found that, if he took coal, heated it up, captured the fumes, and distilled them, he could create this fluid that burned very clear. And he could create it in quantities thousands of times greater than the sperm whales ever could have given up.

We have no information suggesting that Gesner was an environmentalist or that he cared about sperm whales at all. He was motivated by scientific curiosity and by the huge business opportunity of going after this lighting market. What he did was dramatically lower the cost of lighting while saving the sperm whales from extinction.

One more thing that ideas can do is transform waste into value. In places like Germany and Japan, people are mining landfills. Japan estimates that its landfills alone contain 10-year supplies of gold and rare-earth minerals for the world market. Alcoa estimates that the world's landfills contain a 15-year supply of aluminum. So there's tremendous value.

When we throw things away, they're not destroyed. If we "consume" things like aluminum, we're not really consuming it, we're rearranging it. We're changing where it's located. And in some cases, the concentration of these resources in our landfills is actually higher than it was in our mines. What it takes is energy and technology to get that resource back out and put it back into circulation.

Ideas for Stretching the Limits

So ideas can reduce resource use, can find substitutes for scarce resources, and can transform waste into value. In that context, what are the limits to growth?

Is there a population limit? Yes, there certainly is, but it doesn't look like we're going to hit that. Projections right now are that, by the middle of this century, world population will peak between 9 billion and 10 billion, and then start to decline. In fact, we'll be talking much more about the graying of civilization, and perhaps underpopulation—too-low birthrates on a current trend.

What about physical resources? Are there limits to physical resource use on this planet? Absolutely. It really is a finite planet. But where are those limits?

To illustrate, let's start with energy. This is the most important resource that we use, in many ways. But when we consider all the fossil fuels that humanity uses today—all the oil, coal, natural gas, and so on—it pales in comparison to a much larger resource, all around us, which is the amount of energy coming in from our Sun every day.

The amount of energy from sunlight that strikes the top of the atmosphere is about 10,000 times as much as the energy that we use from fossil fuels on a daily basis. Ten seconds of sunlight hitting the Earth is as much energy as humanity uses in an entire day; one hour of sunlight hitting the Earth provides as much energy to the planet as a whole as humanity uses from all sources combined in one year.

This is an incredibly abundant resource. It manifests in many ways. It heats the atmosphere differentially, creating winds that we can capture for wind power. It evaporates water, which leads to precipitation elsewhere, which turns into things like rivers and waterfalls, which we can capture as hydropower.

But by far the largest fraction of it—more than half—is photons hitting the surface of the Earth. Those are so abundant that, with one-third of 1% of the Earth's land area, using current technology of about 14%-efficient solar cells, we could capture enough electricity to power all of current human needs.

The problem is not the abundance of the energy; the problem is cost. Our technology is primitive. Our technology for building solar cells is similar to our technology for manufacturing computer chips. They're built on silicon wafers in clean rooms at high temperatures, and so they're very, very expensive.

But innovation has been dropping that cost tremendously. Over the last 30 years, we've gone from a watt of solar power costing $20 to about $1. That's a factor of 20. We roughly drop the cost of solar by one-half every decade, more or less. That means that, in the sunniest parts of the world today, solar is now basically at parity in cost, without subsidies, with coal and natural gas. Over the next 12-15 years, that will spread to most of the planet. That's incredibly good news for us.

Of course, we don't just use energy while the Sun is shining. We use energy at night to power our cities; we use energy in things like vehicles that have to move and that have high energy densities. Both of these need storage, and today's storage is actually a bigger challenge than capturing energy. But there's reason to believe that we can tackle the storage problem, as well.

For example, consider lithium ion batteries—the batteries that are in your laptop, your cell phone, and so on. The demand to have longer-lasting devices drove tremendous innovations in these batteries in the 1990s and the early part of the 2000s. Between 1991 and 2005, the cost of storage in lithium ion batteries dropped by about a factor of nine, and the density of storage—how much energy you can store in an ounce of battery—increased by a little over double in that time. If we do that again, we would be at the point where grid-scale storage is affordable and we can store that energy overnight. Our electric vehicles have ranges similar to the range you can get in a gasoline-powered vehicle.

This is a tall order. This represents perhaps tens of billions of dollars in R&D, but it is something that is possible and for which there is precedent.

Another approach being taken is turning energy into fuel. When you use a fuel such as gasoline, it's not really an energy source. It's an energy carrier, an energy storage system, if you will. You can store a lot of energy in a very small amount.

Today, two pioneers in genome sequencing—Craig Venter and George Church—both have founded companies to create next-generation biofuels. What they're both leveraging is that gene-sequencing cost is the fastest quantitative area of progress on the planet.

What they're trying to do is engineer microorganisms that consume CO_2, sunlight, and sugar and actually excrete fuel as a byproduct. If we could do this, maybe just 1% of the Earth's surface—or a thirtieth of what we use for agriculture—could provide all the liquid fuels that we need. We would conveniently grow algae on saltwater and waste water, so biofuel production wouldn't compete for freshwater. And the possible yields are vast if we can get there.

If we can crack energy, we can crack everything else:

- Water. Water is life. We live in a water world, but only about a tenth of a percent of the water in the world is freshwater that's accessible to us in some way. Ninety-seven percent of the world's water is in the oceans and is salty. It used to be that desalination meant boiling water and then catching the steam and letting it condense.

Between the times of the ancient Greeks and 1960, desalination technology didn't really change. But then, it did. People started to create membranes modeled on what cells do, which is allow some things through but not others. They used plastics to force water through and get only the fresh and not the salty. As a result, the amount of energy it takes to desalinate a liter of water has dropped by about a factor of nine in that time. Now, in the world's largest desalination plants, the price of desalinated water is about a tenth of a cent per gallon. The technology has gotten to the point where it is starting to become a realistic option as an alternative to using up scarce freshwater resources.

- Food. Can we grow enough food? Between now and 2050, we have to increase food yield by about 70%. Is that possible? I think it is. In industrialized nations, food yields are already twice what they are in the world as a whole. That's because we have irrigation, tractors, better pesticides, and so on. Given such energy and wealth, we already know that we can grow enough food to feed the planet.

Another option that's probably cheaper would be to leverage some things that nature's already produced. What most people don't know is that the yield of corn per acre and in calories is about 70% higher than the yield of wheat. Corn is a C 4 photosynthesis crop: It uses a different way of turning sunlight and CO_2 into sugars that evolved only 30 million years ago. Now, scientists around the world are working on taking these C 4 genes from crops like corn and transplanting them into wheat and rice, which could right away increase the yield of those staple grains by more than 50%.

Physical limits do exist, but they are extremely distant. We cannot grow exponentially in our physical resource use forever, but that point is still at least centuries in the future. It's something we have to address eventually, but it's not a problem that's pressing right now.

- Wealth. One thing that people don't appreciate very much is that wealth has been decoupling from physical resource use on this planet. Energy use per capita is going up, CO_2 emissions per capita have been going up a little bit, but they are both widely outstripped by the amount of wealth that we're creating. That's because we can be more efficient in everything—using less energy per unit of food grown, and so on.

This again might sound extremely counterintuitive, but let me give you one concrete example of how that happens. Compare the ENIAC—which in the 1940s was the first digital computer ever created—to an iPhone. An iPhone is billions of times smaller, uses billions of times less energy, and has billions of times more computing power than ENIAC. If you tried to create an iPhone using ENIAC technology, it would be a cube a mile on the side, and it would use more electricity than the state of California. And it wouldn't have access to the Internet, because you'd have to invent that, as well.

This is what I mean when I say ideas are the ultimate resource. The difference between an ENIAC and an iPhone is that the iPhone is embodied knowledge that allows you to do more with less resources. That phenomenon is not limited to high tech. It's everywhere around us.

So ideas are the ultimate resource. They're the only resource that accumulates over time. Our store of knowledge is actually larger than in the past, as opposed to all physical resources.

Challenges Ahead for Innovation

Today we are seeing a race between our rate of consumption and our rate of innovation, and there are multiple challenges. One challenge is the Darwinian process, survival of the fittest. In areas like green tech, there will be hundreds and even thousands of companies founded, and 99% of them will go under. That is how innovation happens.

The other problem is scale. Just as an example, one of the world's largest solar arrays is at Nellis Air Force Base in California, and we would need about 10 million of these in order to meet the world's electricity needs. We have the land, we have the solar energy coming in, but there's a lot of industrial production that has to happen before we get to that point.

Innovation is incredibly powerful, but the pace of innovation compared to the pace of consumption is very important. One thing we can do to increase the pace of innovation is to address the biggest challenge, which is market failure.

In 1967, you could stick your hand into the Cuyahoga River, in Ohio, and come up covered in muck and oil. At that time, the river was lined with businesses and factories, and for them the river was a free resource. It was cheaper to pump their waste into the river than it was to pay for disposal at some other sort of facility. The river was a commons that anybody could use or abuse, and the waste they were producing was an externality. To that business or factory, there was no cost to pumping waste into this river. But to the people who depended upon the river, there was a high cost overall.

That's what I mean by a market externality and a market failure, because this was an important resource to all of us. But no one owned it, no one bought or sold it, and so it was treated badly in a way that things with a price are not.

That ultimately culminated when, in June 1969, a railway car passing on a bridge threw a spark; the spark hit a slick of oil a mile long on the river, and the river burst into flames. The story made the cover of Time magazine. In many ways, the environmental movement was born of this event as much as it was of Rachel Carson's Silent Spring. In the following three years, the United States created the Environmental Protection Agency and passed the Clean Water and Clean Air acts.

Almost every environmental problem on the planet is an issue of the commons, whether it's chopping down forests that no one owns, draining lakes that no one owns, using up fish in the ocean that no one owns, or polluting the atmosphere because no one owns it, or heating up the planet. They're all issues of the commons. They're all issues where there is no cost to an individual entity to deplete something and no cost to overconsume something, but there is a greater cost that's externalized and pushed on everybody else who shares this.

Now let's come back again to what Limits to Growth said, which was that economic growth always led to more pollution and more consumption, put us beyond limits, and ends with collapse. So if that's the case, all those things we just talked about should be getting worse. But as the condition of the Cuyahoga River today illustrates, that is not the case.

GDP in the United States is three times what it was when the Cuyahoga River caught on fire, so shouldn't it be more polluted? It's not. Instead, it's the cleanest it's been in decades. That's not because we stopped growth. It's because we made intelligent choices about managing that commons.

Another example: In the 1970s, we discovered that the ozone layer was thinning to such an extent that it literally could drive the extinction of all land species on Earth. But it's actually getting better. It's turned a corner, it's improving ahead of schedule, and it's on track to being the healthiest it's been in a century. That's because we've reduced the emissions of CFCs, which destroy ozone; we've dropped the amount of them that we emit into the atmosphere basically to zero. And yet industry has not ground to a halt because of this, either. Economic growth has not faltered.

And one last example: Acid rain—which is primarily produced by sulfur dioxide emitted by coal-burning power plants—is mostly gone as an issue. Emissions of sulfur dioxide are down by about a factor of two. That's in part because we created a strategy called cap and trade: It capped the amount of SO_2 that you could emit, then allowed you to swap and buy emission credits from others to find the optimal way to do that.

The cost, interestingly enough, has always been lower than projected. In each of these cases, industry has said, This will end things. Ronald Reagan's chief of staff said the economy would grind to a halt, and the EPA would come in with lower cost estimates. But the EPA has always been wrong: The EPA cost estimate has always been too high.

Analysis of all of these efforts in the past shows that reducing emissions is always cheaper than you expect, but cleaning up the mess afterwards is always more expensive than you'd guess.

Today, the biggest commons issue is that of climate change, with the CO_2 and other greenhouse gases that we're pumping into the atmosphere. A logical thing to do would be to put a price on these. If you pollute, if you're pumping CO_2 into the atmosphere and it's warming the planet, so you're causing harm to other people in a very diffuse way. Therefore, you should be paying in proportion to that harm you're doing to offset it.

But if we do that, won't that have a massive impact on the economy? This all relates to energy, which drives a huge fraction of the economy. Manufacturing depends on it. Transport depends on it. So wouldn't it be a huge problem if we were to actually put a price on these carbon emissions?

Well, there has been innovative thinking about that, as well. One thing that economists have always told us is that, if you're going to tax, tax the bad, not the good. Whatever it is that you tax, you will get less of it. So tax the bad, not the good.

The model that would be the ideal for putting a price on pollution is what we call a revenue-neutral model. Revenue-neutral carbon tax, revenue-neutral cap and trade. Let's model it as a tax: Today, a country makes a certain amount of revenue for its government in income tax, let's say. If you want to tax pollution, the way to do this without impacting the economy is to increase your pollution tax in the same manner that you decrease the income tax. The government then is capturing the same amount of money from the economy as a whole, so there's no economic slowdown as a result of this.

This has a positive effect on the environment because it tips the scales of price. Now, if you're shopping for energy, and you're looking at solar versus coal or natural gas, the carbon price has increased the price of coal and natural gas to you, but not the cost of solar. It shifts customer behavior from one to the other while having no net impact on the economy, and probably a net benefit on the economy in the long run as more investment in green energy drives the price down.

Toward a Wealthier, Cleaner Future

The number-one thing I want you to take away is that pollution and overconsumption are not inevitable outcomes of growth. While tripling the wealth of North America, for instance, we've gone from an ozone layer that was rapidly deteriorating to one that is bouncing back.

The fundamental issue is not one of limits to growth; it's one of the policy we choose, and it's one of how we structure our economy to value all the things we depend upon and not just those things that are owned privately.

What can we do, each of us? Four things:

First is to communicate. These issues are divisive, but we know that beliefs and attitudes on issues like this spread word of mouth. They spread person to person, from person you trust to person you trust. So talk about it. Many of us have friends or colleagues or family on the other side of these issues, but talk about it. You're better able to persuade them than anyone else is.

Second is to participate. By that I mean politically. Local governments, state and province governments, and national governments are responsive when they hear from their constituents about these issues. It changes their attitudes. Because so few constituents actually make a call to the office of their legislator, or write a letter, a few can make a very large impact.

Third is to innovate. These problems aren't solved yet. We don't have the technologies for these problems today. The trend lines look very good, but the next 10 years of those trend lines demand lots of bright people, lots of bright ideas, and lots of R&D. So if you're thinking about a career change, or if you know any young people trying to figure out what their career is now, these are careers that (A) will be very important to us in the future and (B) will probably be quite lucrative for them.

Last is to keep hope, because we have faced problems like this before and we have conquered them every time. The future isn't written in stone—it could go good or bad—but I'm very optimistic. I know we have the ability to do it, and I think we will. Ultimately, ideas are our most important natural resource.

Critical Thinking

1. Do the facts seem to support an optimistic future or a pessimistic future?
2. What is the potential of new ideas and new technologies?
3. Technologies have brought great benefits and considerable problems. Can technologies and new ideas now solve those problems?

Create Central

www.mhhe.com/createcentral

Internet References

Sociosite
www.topsite.com/goto/sociosite.net
Socioweb
www.topsite.com/goto/socioweb.com
Sociology—Study Sociology Online
http://edu.learnsoc.org/
Sociology Web Resources
www.mhhe.com/socscience/sociology/resources/index.htm

RAMEZ NAAM is a computer scientist and author. He is a former Microsoft executive and current fellow of the Institute for Ethics and Emerging Technologies.

Naam, Ramez. Originally published in the March/April 2013 issue of *The Futurist*. Copyright © 2013 by World Future Society, Bethesda, MD. Used with permission. www.wfs.org

Article   Prepared by: Kurt Finsterbusch, *University of Maryland, College Park*

The Year in Hate and Extremism, 2010

Mark Potok

Learning Outcomes

After reading this article, you will be able to:

- Consider the role of hate groups in the prospects of terrorism.

- Evaluate the role of the media in stimulating the rise of hate and extremist groups.

- Ascertain the beliefs that are held by many of the hate groups.

For the second year in a row, the radical right in America expanded explosively in 2010, driven by resentment over the changing racial demographics of the country, frustration over the government's handling of the economy, and the mainstreaming of conspiracy theories and other demonizing propaganda aimed at various minorities. For many on the radical right, anger is focusing on President Obama, who is seen as embodying everything that's wrong with the country.

Hate groups topped 1,000 for the first time since the Southern Poverty Law Center began counting such groups in the 1980s. Anti-immigrant vigilante groups, despite having some of the political wind taken out of their sails by the adoption of hard-line anti-immigration laws around the country, continued to rise slowly. But by far the most dramatic growth came in the antigovernment "Patriot" movement—conspiracy-minded organizations that see the federal government as their primary enemy—which gained more than 300 new groups, a jump of over 60%.

Taken together, these three strands of the radical right—the hatemongers, the nativists and the antigovernment zealots—increased from 1,753 groups in 2009 to 2,145 in 2010, a 22% rise. That followed a 2008–2009 increase of 40%.

What may be most remarkable is that this growth of right-wing extremism came even as politicians around the country, blown by gusts from the Tea Parties and other conservative formations, tacked hard to the right, co-opting many of the issues important to extremists. Last April, for instance, Arizona Gov. Jan Brewer signed S.B. 1070, the harshest anti-immigrant law in memory, setting off a tsunami of proposals for similar laws across the country. Continuing growth of the radical right could be curtailed as a result of this shift, especially since Republicans, many of them highly conservative, recaptured the U.S. House last fall.

But despite those historic Republican gains, the early signs suggest that even as the more mainstream political right strengthens, the radical right has remained highly energized. In an 11-day period this January, a neo-Nazi was arrested headed for the Arizona border with a dozen homemade grenades; a terrorist bomb attack on a Martin Luther King Jr. Day parade in Spokane, Wash., was averted after police dismantled a sophisticated anti-personnel weapon; and a man who officials said had a long history of antigovernment activities was arrested outside a packed mosque in Dearborn, Mich., and charged with possessing explosives with unlawful intent. That's in addition, the same month, to the shooting of U.S. Rep. Gabrielle Giffords in Arizona, an attack that left six dead and may have had a political dimension.

It's also clear that other kinds of radical activity are on the rise. Since the murder last May 20 of two West Memphis, Ark., police officers by two members of the so-called "sovereign citizens" movement, police from around the country have contacted the Southern Poverty Law Center (SPLC) to report what one detective in Kentucky described as a "dramatic increase" in sovereign activity. Sovereign citizens, who, like militias, are part of the larger Patriot movement, believe that the federal government has no right to tax or regulate them and, as a result, often come into conflict with police and tax authorities.

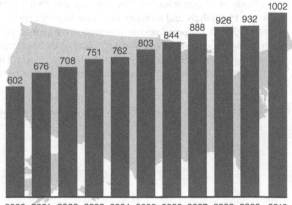

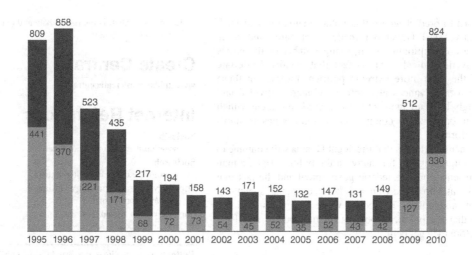

Another sign of their increased activity came early this year, when the Treasury Department, in a report assessing what the IRS faces in 2011, said its biggest challenge will be the "attacks and threats against IRS employees and facilities [that] have risen steadily in recent years."

Extremist ideas have not been limited to the radical right; already this year, state legislators have offered up a raft of proposals influenced by such ideas. In Arizona, the author of the S.B. 1070 law—a man who just became Senate president on the basis of his harshly nativist rhetoric—proposed a law this January that would allow his state to refuse to obey any federal law or regulation it cared to. In Virginia, a state legislator wants to pass a law aimed at creating an alternative currency "in the event of the destruction of the Federal Reserve System's currency"—a longstanding fear of right-wing extremists. And in Montana, a state senator is working to pass a statute called the "Sheriffs First Act" that would require federal law enforcement to ask local sheriffs' permission to act in their counties or face jail. All three laws are almost certainly unconstitutional, legal experts say, and they all originate in ideas that first came from ideologues of the radical right.

There also are new attempts by nativist forces to roll back birthright citizenship, which makes all children born in the U.S. citizens. Such laws have been introduced this year in Congress, and a coalition of state legislators is promising to do the same in their states. And then there's Oklahoma, where 70% of voters last November approved a measure to forbid judges to consider Islamic law in the state's courtrooms—a completely groundless fear, but one pushed nonetheless by Islamophobes. Since then, lawmakers have promised to pass similar laws in Arizona, Florida, Louisiana, South Carolina, Tennessee and Utah.

After the Giffords assassination attempt, a kind of national dialogue began about the political vitriol that increasingly passes for "mainstream" political debate. But it didn't seem to get very far. Four days after the shooting, a campaign called the Civility Project—a two-year effort led by an evangelical conservative tied to top Republicans—said it was shutting down because of a lack of interest and furious opposition. "The worst

E-mails I received about the Civility Project were from conservatives with just unbelievable language about communists and some words I wouldn't use in this phone call," director Mark DeMoss told *The New York Times*. This political divide has become so sharp that everything is black and white, and too many conservatives can see no redeeming value in any opponent.

A *Washington Post*/ABC News poll this January captured the atmosphere well. It found that 82% of Americans saw their country's political discourse as "negative." Even more remarkably, the poll determined that 49% thought that negative tone could or already had encouraged political violence.

Last year's rise in hate groups was the latest in a trend stretching all the way back to the year 2000, when the SPLC counted 602 such groups. Since then, they have risen steadily, mainly on the basis of exploiting the issue of undocumented immigration from Mexico and Central America. Last year, the number of hate groups rose to 1,002 from 932, a 7.5% increase over the previous year and a 66% rise since 2000.

At the same time, what the SPLC defines as "nativist extremist" groups—organizations that go beyond mere advocacy of restrictive immigration policy to actually confront or harass suspected immigrants or their employers—rose slightly, despite the fact that most of their key issues had been taken up by mainstream politicians. There were 319 such groups in 2010, up 3% from 309 in 2009.

But like the year before, it was the antigovernment Patriot groups that grew most dramatically, at least partly on the basis of furious rhetoric from the right aimed at the nation's first black president—a man who has come to represent to at least some Americans ongoing changes in the racial makeup of the country. The Patriot groups, which had risen and fallen once before during the militia movement of the 1990s, first came roaring back in 2009, when they rose 244% to 512 from 149 a year earlier. In 2010, they rose again sharply, adding 312 new groups to reach 824, a 61% increase. The highest prior count of Patriot groups came in 1996, when the SPLC found 858 (see chart).

It's hard to predict where this volatile situation will lead. Conservatives last November made great gains and some of them are championing a surprising number of the issues pushed by the radical right—a fact that could help deflate some of the even more extreme political forces. But those GOP electoral advances also left the Congress divided and increasingly lined up against the Democratic president, which is likely to paralyze the country on such key issues as immigration reform.

What seems certain is that President Obama will continue to serve as a lightning rod for many on the political right, a man who represents both the federal government and the fact that the racial make-up of the United States is changing, something that upsets a significant number of white Americans. And that suggests that the polarized politics of this country could get worse before they get better.

Critical Thinking

1. Why have hate groups substantially increased since 2000?
2. Why have patriot and militia groups increased radically since 2008?

3. To what extent is the rise of hate and extremism due to the Obama presidency?

Create Central

www.mhhe.com/createcentral

Internet References

Sociosite
www.topsite.com/goto/sociosite.net

Socioweb
www.topsite.com/goto/socioweb.com

Sociology—Study Sociology Online
http://edu.learnsoc.org

Sociology Web Resources
www.mhhe.com/socscience/sociology/resources/index.htm

Editor's note:—Since the article was published, authorities have changed their view of an incident in Dearborn, Mich., that is mentioned. Initially, it was believed that the Michigan suspect was planning an attack based on hatred of Muslims. In fact, it turns out that Roger Stockham is an American convert to Sunni Islam, and reportedly was angry at the mosque in question because it was Shi'ite.

Article
Prepared by: Kurt Finsterbusch, *University of Maryland, College Park*

War in the Fifth Domain

Are the Mouse and Keyboard the New Weapons of Conflict?

THE ECONOMIST

Learning Outcomes

After reading this article, you will be able to:

- Contemplate the ramifications of cyberwar.

- Understand that the United States must develop horrific cyberwar capabilities just to protect ourselves from cyber threats.

- Understand the amount of cyber espionage that is going on right now.

A t the height of the cold war, in June 1982, an American early-warning satellite detected a large blast in Siberia. A missile being fired? A nuclear test? It was, it seems, an explosion on a Soviet gas pipeline. The cause was a malfunction in the computer-control system that Soviet spies had stolen from a firm in Canada. They did not know that the CIA had tampered with the software so that it would "go haywire, after a decent interval, to reset pump speeds and valve settings to produce pressures far beyond those acceptable to pipeline joints and welds," according to the memoirs of Thomas Reed, a former air force secretary. The result, he said, "was the most monumental non-nuclear explosion and fire ever seen from space."

This was one of the earliest demonstrations of the power of a "logic bomb". Three decades later, with more and more vital computer systems linked up to the internet, could enemies use logic bombs to, say, turn off the electricity from the other side of the world? Could terrorists or hackers cause financial chaos by tampering with Wall Street's computerised trading systems? And given that computer chips and software are produced globally, could a foreign power infect high-tech military equipment with computer bugs? "It scares me to death," says one senior military source. "The destructive potential is so great."

After land, sea, air and space, warfare has entered the fifth domain: cyberspace. President Barack Obama has declared America's digital infrastructure to be a "strategic national asset" and appointed Howard Schmidt, the former head of security at Microsoft, as his cyber-security tsar. In May, the Pentagon set up its new Cyber Command (Cybercom) headed by General Keith Alexander, director of the National Security Agency (NSA). His mandate is to conduct "full-spectrum" operations—to defend American military networks and attack other countries' systems. Precisely how, and by what rules, is secret.

Britain, too, has set up a cyber-security policy outfit, and an "operations centre" based in GCHQ, the British equivalent of the NSA. China talks of "winning informationised wars by the mid-21st century". Many other countries are organising for cyberwar, among them Russia, Israel and North Korea. Iran boasts of having the world's second-largest cyber-army.

What will cyberwar look like? In a new book, Richard Clarke, a former White House staffer in charge of counterterrorism and cyber-security, envisages a catastrophic breakdown within 15 minutes. Computer bugs bring down military e-mail systems; oil refineries and pipelines explode; air-traffic-control systems collapse; freight and metro trains derail; financial data are scrambled; the electrical grid goes down in the eastern United States; orbiting satellites spin out of control. Society soon breaks down as food becomes scarce and money runs out. Worst of all, the identity of the attacker may remain a mystery.

In the view of Mike McConnell, a former spy chief, the effects of full-blown cyberwar are much like a nuclear attack. Cyberwar has already started, he says, "and we are losing it." Not so, retorts Mr Schmidt. There is no cyberwar. Bruce Schneier, an IT industry security guru, accuses securocrats like Mr Clarke of scaremongering. Cyberspace will certainly be part of any future war, he says, but an apocalyptic attack on America is both difficult to achieve technically ("movie-script stuff") and implausible except in the context of a real war, in which case the perpetrator is likely to be obvious.

For the top brass, computer technology is both a blessing and a curse. Bombs are guided by GPS satellites; drones are piloted remotely from across the world; fighter planes and warships are now huge data-processing centres; even the ordinary foot-soldier is being wired up. Yet growing connectivity over an insecure internet multiplies the avenues for e-attack; and growing dependence on computers increases the harm they can cause.

By breaking up data and sending it over multiple routes, the internet can survive the loss of large parts of the network. Yet some of the global digital infrastructure is more fragile. More than nine-tenths of internet traffic travels through undersea fibre-optic cables, and these are dangerously bunched up in a few choke-points, for instance around New York, the Red Sea or the Luzon Strait in the Philippines. Internet traffic is directed by just 13 clusters of potentially vulnerable domain-name servers. Other dangers are coming: weakly governed swathes of Africa are being connected up to fibre-optic cables, potentially creating new havens for cyber-criminals. And the spread of mobile internet will bring new means of attack.

The internet was designed for convenience and reliability, not security. Yet in wiring together the globe, it has merged the garden and the wilderness. No passport is required in cyberspace. And although police are constrained by national borders, criminals roam freely. Enemy states are no longer on the other side of the ocean, but just behind the firewall. The ill-intentioned can mask their identity and location, impersonate others and con their way into the buildings that hold the digitised wealth of the electronic age: money, personal data and intellectual property.

Mr Obama has quoted a figure of $1 trillion lost last year to cybercrime—a bigger underworld than the drugs trade, though such figures are disputed. Banks and other companies do not like to admit how much data they lose. In 2008 alone, Verizon, a telecoms company, recorded the loss of 285m personal-data records, including credit-card and bank-account details, in investigations conducted for clients.

About nine-tenths of the 140 billion e-mails sent daily are spam; of these about 16% contain moneymaking scams, including "phishing" attacks that seek to dupe recipients into giving out passwords or bank details, according to Symantec, a security-software vendor. The amount of information now available online about individuals makes it ever easier to attack a computer by crafting a personalised e-mail that is more likely to be trusted and opened. This is known as "spear-phishing".

The ostentatious hackers and virus-writers who once wrecked computers for fun are all but gone, replaced by criminal gangs seeking to harvest data. "Hacking used to be about making noise. Now it's about staying silent," says Greg Day of McAfee, a vendor of IT security products. Hackers have become wholesale providers of malware—viruses, worms and Trojans that infect computers—for others to use. Websites are now the favoured means of spreading malware, partly because the unwary are directed to them through spam or links posted on social-networking sites. And poorly designed websites often provide a window into valuable databases.

Malware is typically used to steal passwords and other data, or to open a "back door" to a computer so that it can be taken over by outsiders. Such "zombie" machines can be linked up to thousands, if not millions, of others around the world to create a "botnet". Estimates for the number of infected machines range up to 100m. Botnets are used to send spam, spread malware or launch distributed denial-of-service (DDoS) attacks, which seek to bring down a targeted computer by overloading it with countless bogus requests.

The Spy Who Spammed Me

Criminals usually look for easy prey. But states can combine the criminal hacker's tricks, such as spear-phishing, with the intelligence apparatus to reconnoitre a target, the computing power to break codes and passwords, and the patience to probe a system until it finds a weakness—usually a fallible human being. Steven Chabinsky, a senior FBI official responsible for cyber-security, recently said that "given enough time, motivation and funding, a determined adversary will always—always—be able to penetrate a targeted system."

Traditional human spies risk arrest or execution by trying to smuggle out copies of documents. But those in the cyberworld face no such risks. "A spy might once have been able to take out a few books' worth of material," says one senior American military source, "Now they take the whole library. And if you restock the shelves, they will steal it again."

China, in particular, is accused of wholesale espionage, attacking the computers of major Western defence contractors and reputedly taking classified details of the F-35 fighter, the mainstay of future American air power. At the end of 2009, it appears to have targeted Google and more than a score of other IT companies. Experts at a cyber-test-range built in Maryland by Lockheed Martin, a defence contractor (which denies losing the F-35 data), say "advanced persistent threats" are hard to fend off amid the countless minor probing of its networks. Sometimes attackers try to slip information out slowly, hidden in ordinary internet traffic. At other times they have tried to break in by leaving infected memory-sticks in the car park, hoping somebody would plug them into the network. Even unclassified e-mails can contain a wealth of useful information about projects under development.

"Cyber-espionage is the biggest intelligence disaster since the loss of the nuclear secrets [in the late 1940s]," says Jim Lewis of the Centre for Strategic and International Studies, a think-tank in Washington, DC. Spying probably presents the most immediate danger to the West: the loss of high-tech know-how that could erode its economic lead or, if it ever came to a shooting war, blunt its military edge.

Western spooks think China deploys the most assiduous, and most shameless, cyberspies, but Russian ones are probably more skilled and subtle. Top of the league, say the spooks, are still America's NSA and Britain's GCHQ, which may explain why Western countries have until recently been reluctant to complain too loudly about computer snooping.

The next step after penetrating networks to steal data is to disrupt or manipulate them. If military targeting information could be attacked, for example, ballistic missiles would be useless. Those who play war games speak of being able to "change the red and blue dots": make friendly (blue) forces appear to be the enemy (red), and vice versa.

General Alexander says the Pentagon and NSA started co-operating on cyberwarfare in late 2008 after "a serious intrusion into our classified networks". Mr Lewis says this refers to the penetration of Central Command, which oversees the wars in Iraq and Afghanistan, through an infected thumb-drive. It took a week to winkle out the intruder. Nobody knows what, if any, damage was caused. But the thought of an enemy lurking in battle-fighting systems alarms the top brass.

That said, an attacker might prefer to go after unclassified military logistics supply systems, or even the civilian infrastructure. A loss of confidence in financial data and electronic transfers could cause economic upheaval. An even bigger worry is an attack on the power grid. Power companies tend not to keep many spares of expensive generator parts, which can take months to replace. Emergency diesel generators cannot make up for the loss of the grid, and cannot operate indefinitely. Without electricity and other critical services, communications systems and cash-dispensers cease to work. A loss of power lasting just a few days, reckon some, starts to cause a cascade of economic damage.

Experts disagree about the vulnerability of systems that run industrial plants, known as supervisory control and data acquisition (SCADA). But more and more of these are being connected to the internet, raising the risk of remote attack. "Smart" grids, which relay information about energy use to the utilities, are promoted as ways of reducing energy waste. But they also increase security worries about both crime (eg, allowing bills to be falsified) and exposing SCADA networks to attack.

General Alexander has spoken of "hints that some penetrations are targeting systems for remote sabotage". But precisely what is happening is unclear: are outsiders probing SCADA systems only for reconnaissance, or to open "back doors" for future use? One senior American military source said that if any country were found to be planting logic bombs on the grid, it would provoke the equivalent of the Cuban missile crisis.

Estonia, Georgia and WWI

Important thinking about the tactical and legal concepts of cyber-warfare is taking place in a former Soviet barracks in Estonia, now home to NATO's "centre of excellence" for cyber-defence. It was established in response to what has become known as "Web War 1", a concerted denial-of-service attack on Estonian government, media and bank web servers that was precipitated by the decision to move a Soviet-era war memorial in central Tallinn in 2007. This was more a cyber-riot than a war, but it forced Estonia more or less to cut itself off from the internet.

Similar attacks during Russia's war with Georgia the next year looked more ominous, because they seemed to be coordinated with the advance of Russian military columns. Government and media websites went down and telephone lines were jammed, crippling Georgia's ability to present its case abroad. President Mikheil Saakashvili's website had to be moved to an American server better able to fight off the attack. Estonian experts were dispatched to Georgia to help out.

Many assume that both these attacks were instigated by the Kremlin. But investigations traced them only to Russian "hacktivists" and criminal botnets; many of the attacking computers were in Western countries. There are wider issues: did the cyber-attack on Estonia, a member of NATO, count as an armed attack, and should the alliance have defended it? And did Estonia's assistance to Georgia, which is not in NATO, risk drawing Estonia into the war, and NATO along with it?

Such questions permeate discussions of NATO's new "strategic concept", to be adopted later this year. A panel of experts headed by Madeleine Albright, a former American secretary of state, reported in May that cyber-attacks are among the three most likely threats to the alliance. The next significant attack, it said, "may well come down a fibre-optic cable" and may be serious enough to merit a response under the mutual-defence provisions of Article 5.

During his confirmation hearing, senators sent General Alexander several questions. Would he have "significant" offensive cyber-weapons? Might these encourage others to follow suit? How sure would he need to be about the identity of an attacker to "fire back"? Answers to these were restricted to a classified supplement. In public, the general said that the president would be the judge of what constituted cyberwar; if America responded with force in cyberspace it would be in keeping with the rules of war and the "principles of military necessity, discrimination, and proportionality".

General Alexander's seven-month confirmation process is a sign of the qualms senators felt at the merging of military and espionage functions, the militarisation of cyberspace and the fear that it may undermine Americans' right to privacy. Cyber-command will protect only the military ".mil" domain. The government domain, ".gov", and the corporate infrastructure, ".com" will be the responsibility respectively of the Department of Homeland Security and private companies, with support from Cybercom.

One senior military official says General Alexander's priority will be to improve the defences of military networks. Another bigwig casts some doubt on cyber-offence. "It's hard to do it at a specific time," he says. "If a cyber-attack is used as a military weapon, you want a predictable time and effect. If you are using it for espionage it does not matter; you can wait." He implies that cyber-weapons would be used mainly as an adjunct to conventional operations in a narrow theatre.

The Chinese may be thinking the same way. A report on China's cyber-warfare doctrine, written for the congressionally mandated US-China Economic and Security Review Commission, envisages China using cyber-weapons not to defeat America, but to disrupt and slow down its forces long enough for China to seize Taiwan without having to fight a shooting war.

Apocalypse or Asymmetry?

Deterrence in cyber-warfare is more uncertain than, say, in nuclear strategy: there is no mutually assured destruction, the dividing line between criminality and war is blurred and identifying attacking computers, let alone the fingers on the keyboards, is difficult. Retaliation need not be confined to cyberspace; the one system that is certainly not linked to the public internet is America's nuclear firing chain. Still, the more likely use of cyber-weapons is probably not to bring about electronic apocalypse, but as tools of limited warfare.

Cyber-weapons are most effective in the hands of big states. But because they are cheap, they may be most useful to the comparatively weak. They may well suit terrorists. Fortunately, perhaps, the likes of al-Qaeda have mostly used the internet for propaganda and communication. It may be that jihadists lack the ability to, say, induce a refinery to blow itself up. Or it may be that they prefer the gory theatre of suicide-bombings to the anonymity of computer sabotage—for now.

Critical Thinking

1. How dangerous is cyber war?
2. With most things run by computer, think of all the settings that could be changed to cause specific or astronomical damages.
3. What would life be like if almost all computers and chips were destroyed?

Create Central

www.mhhe.com/createcentral

Internet References

Sociosite
www.topsite.com/goto/sociosite.net

Socioweb
www.topsite.com/goto/socioweb.com

Sociology—Study Sociology Online
http://edu.learnsoc.org

Sociology Web Resources
www.mhhe.com/socscience/sociology/resources/index.htm

Article   Prepared by: Kurt Finsterbusch, *University of Maryland, College Park*

A New End, a New Beginning
Prepare for Life as We Don't Know It

JOHN L. PETERSEN

Learning Outcomes

After reading this article, you will be able to:

- Understand the problems and systems failures that will require a major transformation to very different systems.

- Evaluate the capacity of our government to deal with today's problems.

- Explain why governments fail.

Predicting the future is a fool's errand. It is fraught with so much complexity and uncertainty that the best one can do with integrity is to array potential alternatives—scenarios—across the horizon, and then try to think about what might be done if one of those alternative worlds materializes.

> **"The End Is Near" has always been doomsayers' favorite slogan, but is it now finally true? The trends suggest the end of an era may indeed be near, as growing complexity and proliferating crises threaten to obliterate "life as we know it." The time is now to prepare for the life we don't yet know.**

Scenario planning has certainly been an effective discipline, helping many organizations to imagine potentialities that probably otherwise wouldn't have shown up in their field of view. But as I facilitate organizations going through these exercises, the little, nagging voice in the back of my head is not asking, "What is the array of possible futures?" Rather, it is always wondering, "What is the future really going to be?" We want concreteness. We want predictions.

I think that no one knows for sure what the future will bring, but after some time of being in the "future business," one begins to be able to discriminate between what is substantive and structural and what is largely speculative. For me, at least, some things have an intuitive sense of being real and important,

and the rest of the possibilities lack just enough gravitas that I know they're only "ideas." That intuitive sense is supported when it becomes possible to triangulate from a number of independent sources that all point to the same conclusion.

People always ask me after my talks, "With all of these converging trends, what is 2012 really going to look like?" It happened again in a recent radio interview. Mostly I hedge and dance a bit and say that I don't know for sure, but I believe there will be a new world, and a new human will come out of all of the current turmoil. The notion of cooperation will shape the way people see themselves and the rest of the world, and there will be new institutions and functions, etc. Pretty general stuff.

But, over a year ago, the notion that all of this big change could spell a substantial reconfiguration of the familiar country that I have lived in all of my life began to gel in a way that moved that notion beyond being just a possibility—a wild card—into the realm of plausibility. I now have come to believe that such a transformation is likely and will happen—soon.

Ideas like this are so big and disruptive that it is really quite hard to get to the place where we take them seriously. For most of us, our lives are evolutionary—punctuated, perhaps with trauma now and then, but mostly populated by events that are familiar, even if they don't always make personal sense. The concept that everything might change is so foreign to any experience that most of us have ever had that, even if we say the words and talk about the possibility, we really don't internalize what this might mean.

Certain other thinkers jumped to the natural conclusion quite some time ago. Dmitry Orlov, for example, first started to build a theory of superpower collapse that included the United States in 1995. Only in the last few years has he been talking publicly about his ideas and the ultimate direction of U.S. trends.

James Howard Kunstler, a wonderfully entertaining and provocative writer, was very clear about the systemic and structural nature of the larger problem in his 2006 book, *The Long Emergency*. He clearly sees the demise of America coming this way. His always interesting blog is a weekly assessment of where we're going wrong.

My colleague David Martin outlined the financial dominoes that were going to fall in a talk at The Arlington Institute in July 2006. Implicit in his treatise is the collapse of the U.S. and global financial systems, but again, it's one thing to hear such views and quite another to really believe them.

After I listened to such people and pondered what they said, I began telling my friends that I thought we were seeing the beginning of the end of the United States as we've known it. I didn't think they really believed it, at least initially, but recently we have seen Singapore, for instance, reportedly making major leadership changes in its government investment company to reposition the nation away from the United States and the U.S. dollar.

> **Huge, extraordinary, global trends . . . are converging to precipitate a historic big transition event.**

Indicators of Big Change Ahead

There are numerous indicators that suggest the big change is coming:

- **Multiple trends are converging.** Huge, extraordinary, global trends, any number of which would be enough to derail our present way of life, are converging to precipitate a historic big transition event. A partial list would include:
  - The global financial system is collapsing. During the next few months, it appears that wave after wave of blows will strike the system, raising the very real possibility that it will experience large-scale failure sometime before the end of the year.
  - We have reached the beginning of the end of petroleum. Global production has been flat for the last three years. Senior oil company executives are now saying that they will not be able to pump more. Supply will likely begin to decrease significantly after we move across the peak. Prices will increase again if the demand holds up. This is important because our present way of life is built upon petroleum.
  - The global climate system is changing—some say it is getting much warmer, others now suggest a mini ice age within the next decade. In any case, increased irregularities in local climates will probably result, with attendant problems in agriculture, natural disasters, and economies.
  - The cost of food is increasing rapidly as a result of global shortages not seen in 40 or 50 years. This could be exacerbated by increasing energy costs and climate changes. Lester R. Brown of the Earth Policy Institute believes that food shortages may bring down civilizations.
  - The effects of larger solar eruptions hitting the earth through tears in the magnetosphere surrounding our planet will likely disrupt global communications, weather, perhaps satellites, and even organic life over the next three to four years.
- **Problems are much larger than government.** Peak oil, climate change, and the financial meltdown all have the potential to significantly overwhelm the capabilities of

government to respond to them. If bureaucracies can't deal with the aftermath of a natural disaster like Katrina, something ten or more times that damaging would leave most people fending for themselves. If these extraordinary, disruptive events end up being concurrent, then the whole system will be at risk.

- **The problems are structural.** They're systemic. Some of these issues, especially the financial, oil, and food problems, are also a product of how we live, our priorities, and our paradigms. We are creating the problems because of our values and principles. Without extraordinary, fundamental changes in the way we see ourselves and the world, we will keep getting what we are getting.
- **Leaders think the old system can be "rebooted."** Almost everyone in leadership positions in the Obama administration and in other countries wants to make the old system well again. Jim Kunstler has said it well:

Among the questions that disturb the sleep of many casual observers is how come Mr. O doesn't get that the conventional process of economic growth—based, as it was, on industrial expansion via revolving credit in a cheap-energy-resource era—is over, and why does he keep invoking it at the podium? Dear Mr. President, you are presiding over an epochal contraction, not a pause in the growth epic. Your assignment is to manage that contraction in a way that does not lead to world war, civil disorder or both. Among other things, contraction means that all the activities of everyday life need to be downscaled including standards of living, ranges of commerce, and levels of governance.

"Consumerism" is dead. Revolving credit is dead—at least at the scale that became normal the last thirty years. The wealth of several future generations has already been spent and there is no equity left there to refinance.

The above indicators of change suggest the reasons behind the following.

- **We're not dealing with the structural issues.** All of the biggest efforts are attempts to reinflate the financial bubble and to keep the mortally wounded institutions alive. The knee-jerk reactions come from the same people who helped to design and feed the present system. These people are also deluded—they think (or act like) they know what they are doing. They don't realize that . . .
- **The situation is so complex that no one really understands it.** The Global Business Network's Peter Schwartz, reporting on a conversation with the *Financial Times*'s Martin Wolf, said that Wolf's key point was that the nature and scale of the credit crisis is so novel that it's not clear we know what we're doing when we try to stop it. He is deeply worried. Steve Roach of Morgan Stanley said at the World Economic Forum annual meeting at Davos that he agreed with Wolf: We are in uncharted waters. Nassim Nicholas Taleb, author of *The Black Swan: Impact of the Highly Improbable* (Random

House, 2007), says the financial system is so complex that it is impossible for anyone to understand it, and because of that complexity it is inevitable that it will exhibit significant, unanticipated behaviors (his Black Swans) that career across the planet.

- **The issues are global.** Economies are contracting around the world, with a huge rise in unemployment. Japan's exports are falling, and factories are closing in China, which means that products aren't being shipped.

- **The system is fundamentally out of balance.** Common sense is largely absent from many big, sweeping U.S. government edicts. The Transportation Security Administration, for example, wants to make pilots produce background checks on members of their family (and their business associates) in order to legally give them rides in noncommercial, private airplanes. The Agriculture Department wants all small farmers to put GPS/RFID tags on all of their animals so that chickens, cows, horses, and goats can be tracked, on a day-to-day basis, by the government. And most of the U.S. federal budget goes to the military and military-related agencies. This kind of growth, of course, is what brought down the Soviet Union.

Why Government Fails to Respond to Challenge

If the natural solutions to these massive issues include innovation, foresight, adaptability, sustainability, and resilience, it is unlikely that a thinking American could be found who would suggest that the source for these capabilities would be our government. Those who are in charge have no new ideas about how this all should work. They're also slow, and this situation needs fast, agile responses. There is an additional problem. Even if it did have good ideas, the government wouldn't be able to effectively implement them because:

- **It suffers from too much inertia, and too many lawyers and lobbyists.** There is a huge, well-funded effort in place to maintain the status quo or to shift the future to benefit one group at the expense of others. It would be impossible within the present system to initiate dramatic change when the threat was still on the horizon. Every group or organization that might be negatively affected would fight in Congress and the courts to keep themselves alive, regardless of what was at stake for the larger community. Only when the crisis was about to crash down on everyone—when adequate time and resources for effective response were nonexistent—might everyone pull together for the common good.

- **Potential solutions take too long to implement.** These issues are so gigantic that confronting and redirecting them takes a long time. One study, for example, suggested that a national crash program to find alternatives for oil would need to have been started 20 years before the peak, in order that there will be no

significant disruption of the underlying systems. We do not operate with either that foresight or that resolve.

- **Supply chains are long and thin.** Globalism and just-in-time production have produced supply chains in most areas of commerce that are very long—often to the other side of the earth—and very fragile. There are many places between there and here where something can go wrong. If and when that happens, necessities will not be available. In those situations, people resort to unconventional and/or antisocial behavior.

- **Six hundred trillion dollars in derivatives is a house of cards.** Looming over the whole financial situation is an almost unfathomable quantity of financial instruments—derivatives—which are essentially casino bets with no underlying value supporting the transaction. Warren Buffett calls them "financial weapons of mass destruction," and they could bring the whole system down. Derivatives only work if there is confidence in the system—you believe the casino will really pay your winnings. If other things in the environment erode that confidence, there is the real possibility that things will rapidly fall to pieces.

- **Cooperation is unlikely; protectionism will prevail.** Instead of countries cooperating with each other to deal with these big transnational problems, we're seeing a pulling back to protect each country's perceived short-term interests, regardless of what the implications might be in the longer term. At the same time, we're all connected to each other in very complicated ways, so if any substantial pieces of the system don't work, it will affect all of the other ones.

- **History says it's time.** Perhaps what is most compelling to me is that history strongly suggests that the time is right for an upset—they always happen about now in the historical cycles. Big punctuations in the equilibrium of evolution have produced extraordinary, fundamental reorganizations to life on this planet on a regular, accelerating basis from the beginning of time as we know it. We make progress as a species when we are forced in one way or another to evolve into seeing ourselves and the world in new ways. Necessity is the mother of invention—or should be!

So, it doesn't look to me like we're going to be able to do what might be needed to maintain the present system. It is likely that we're at one of those extraordinary moments in history when each of us gets the opportunity to play an important role in not only transitioning to a new world, but also designing it.

What to Do in the Face of Unprecedented Change

Two specific actions come to mind that should help individuals and institutions prepare for this change.

1. **Plan for the transition.** Start to think now about how you're going to provide for yourself and those who are important to you in a time when many things don't

work the way they always have in the past. There are many websites and books on this subject, but the key concept is cooperation. You can't do this alone. Start to work together with like-minded individuals to sustain yourself, regardless of whether your concerns are food, water, shelter, transportation, or finances.

2. **Start thinking about the new world.** Now is the time to begin contemplating the design of the new world. Governments should be doing this. Companies should start skunk works. Big international organizations should put it on their agendas.

Here's the catch. This might not happen. The "system" might not collapse. Personally, I think that if there is any one person that has the potential to at least soften this transition it is Barack Obama. As I've suggested, he will have his hands full just trying to get the underlying people and institutions to think differently and act fast enough, but if anyone has the chance to pull it off, he would be the one. Already, he's getting the government to move faster and in more substantive ways than any of his predecessors. It may be, by the way, that he will be the best person to wind down the old system and develop a new one. It's all of the other folks running the government that I'd be concerned about—the ones who continue to see the world as it used to be.

There are any number of reasons why this scenario might not manifest itself, not least of which is that there will be many thousands, if not millions, of people who will be working very hard to assure that the system doesn't come apart (but then, they may be doing the wrong things).

It seems to me, therefore, that flexibility and permeability (allowing new ideas to get through) are of critical importance here. Remember the first law of Discordianism: "Convictions cause convicts." Whatever you believe imprisons you.

So, stay loose. The winners need to transcend, not try to work their way through all of this. Concentrate on building the new world. Don't get emotionally involved in the daily reports of the current global erosion.

Additional Resources

America's Defense Meltdown: Pentagon Reform for President Obama and the New Congress, edited by Winslow Wheeler (Stanford Security Studies, 2009). In sharp contrast to the political apparatchiks protesting that more money is needed to reverse the shrinking, aging, and declining readiness of the Army, Navy, and Air Force, few seem to understand that budget increases are a primary cause of the problems, a symptom clearly described in this new book.

"Asymmetric Collateral Damage: Basel II, the Mortgage House of Cards, and the Coming Economic Crisis," a talk by David Martin, CEO of M.CAM, for The Arlington Institute (July 12, 2006), www.arlingtoninstitute.org/dr-david-e-martin.

Crash Course, a "concise video seminar on how our economy, energy systems, and environment interact, and how they will impact the future," at www.chrismartenson.com.

Reinventing Collapse by Dmitry Orlov (New Society, 2008).

A Vision for 2012: Planning for Extraordinary Change by John L. Petersen (Fulcrum Publishing, 2008).

"Why Obama's 'Rescue' Misses the Mark and the Coming Financial Collapse Just Got Worse" by David Martin of M.CAM (February 15, 2009), http://invertedalchemy.blogspot.com/.

Critical Thinking

1. Do you agree with Petersen's thesis that "Problems are larger than government"?
2. What course of action would you propose in the situation that Petersen describes?
3. Can you refute the thesis of the demise of America?

Create Central

www.mhhe.com/createcentral

Internet References

Sociosite
www.topsite.com/goto/sociosite.net

Socioweb
www.topsite.com/goto/socioweb.com

Sociology—Study Sociology Online
http://edu.learnsoc.org

Sociology Web Resources
www.mhhe.com/socscience/sociology/resources/index.htm

JOHN L. PETERSEN is president of The Arlington Institute, a nonprofit, future-oriented think tank. Among his books are WFS bestsellers *The Road to 2015* (1994), *Out of the Blue* (1997), and *A Vision for 2012* (2008). His address is The Arlington Institute, P.O. Box 86, Berkeley Springs, West Virginia 25411. E-mail johnp@arlingtoninstitute.org. PETERSEN also discussed these ideas in a chapter of the World Future Society's 2009 conference volume, *Innovation and Creativity in a Complex World,* which may be ordered from www.wfs.org/wfsbooks.htm.

Originally published in the September/October 2009, issue of *The Futurist.* Copyright © 2009 by World Future Society, 7910 Woodmont Avenue, Suite 450, Bethesda, MD 20814; phone: 301/656-8274. Used with permission. www.wfs.org

Article   Prepared by: Kurt Finsterbusch, *University of Maryland, College Park*

A User's Guide to the Century

JEFFREY D. SACHS

Learning Outcomes

After reading this article, you will be able to:

- Understand the major trends and institutional arrangements that will shape the future.

- Consider "the promise of shared prosperity . . . and also the risk of global conflict" and the forces moving in each direction.

- Evaluate Jeffrey Sachs' thesis that "Old models of statecraft and economics won't suffice."

The "new world order" of the twenty-first century holds the promise of shared prosperity . . . and also the risk of global conflict. This is the paradox of our time. The scale of human society—in population, level of economic production and resource use, and global reach of production networks—gives rise to enormous hopes and equally momentous challenges. Old models of statecraft and economics won't suffice. Solutions to our generation's challenges will require an unprecedented degree of global cooperation, though the need for such cooperation is still poorly perceived and highly contested by political elites and intellectuals in the United States and elsewhere.

Our world is characterized by three dominant patterns: rapid technological diffusion, which creates strong tendencies toward technological and economic convergence among major regions of the world; extensive environmental threats resulting from the unprecedented scale of global economic activity and population; and vast current inequalities of income and power, both between and within countries, resulting from highly diverse patterns of demography, regional endowments of natural resources, and vulnerabilities to natural and societal disruptions. These characteristics hold the possibilities of rapid and equalizing economic growth, but also of regional and global instability and conflict.

The era of modern economic growth is two centuries old. For the first one hundred years, this was a strong *divergence* in economic growth, meaning a widening gap in production and income between the richest regions and the rest of the world. The dramatic divergence of per capita output, industrial production and living standards during the nineteenth century between the North Atlantic (that is, Western Europe and the United States) and the rest of the world was accentuated by several factors. The combination of first-mover industrialization, access to extensive coal deposits, early development of market-based institutions, military dominance resulting from vast industrial power, and then colonial dominance over Africa and Asia all contributed to a century of *economic divergence,* in which the North Atlantic greatly expanded its technological lead (and also military advantage) vis-à-vis the rest of the world. The apogee of "Western" relative dominance was roughly the year 1910. Until the start of World War I, this economic and technological dominance was nearly overpowering.

The period 1910–1950 marked a transition from global economic divergence to economic convergence. Most importantly, of course, was Europe's self-inflicted disaster of two world wars and an intervening Great Depression, which dramatically weakened Europe and proved to be the downfall of the continent's vast overseas empires. Below the surface, longer-term forces of convergence were also stirring. These deeper forces included the global spread of literacy, Western science, the modern technologies of transport and communications, and the political ideas of self-determination and economic development as core national objectives.

Since 1950, we have entered into an era of global convergence, in which much of the non-Western world is gradually catching up, technologically, economically, geopolitically and militarily. The North Atlantic is losing its uniquely dominant position in the world economy. The technological and economic catching-up, most notable of course in Asia, is facilitated by several factors—the spread of national sovereignty following European colonialism; vastly improved transport and communications technologies; the spread of infectious-disease control, mass literacy and public education; the dissemination of global scientific and engineering knowledge; and the broad adoption of a valid "catch-up model" of economic development based on technology imports within a mixed public-private system. The system was modeled heavily on the state-led market development of Japan, the only non-Western country to succeed in achieving modern industrialization during the nineteenth century. Japan's economic development following the Meiji Restoration in 1868 can indeed be viewed as the invention of "catch-up growth."

The modern age of convergence, begun with Japan's rapid rebuilding after World War II, was extended in the 1950s and 1960s by the rise of Korea, Taiwan, Hong Kong and Singapore, all built on an export-led growth model using U.S. and Japanese technologies and institutions. Convergent economic growth then spread through Southeast Asia (notably Indonesia, Malaysia and Thailand) in the 1970s and 1980s, again supported by Japanese and U.S. technologies, and Japanese aid and development concepts. The convergence patterns were greatly expanded with the initiation of rapid market-based growth in China after 1978 (which imitated strategies in East and Southeast Asia) and then India in the 1980s (and especially after market-based reforms initiated in 1991). In the early twenty-first century, both Brazil and Mexico are similarly experiencing rapid technological catch-up.

In economic terms, the share of global income in the North Atlantic is now declining quickly as the emerging economies of Asia, the Middle East and Latin America grow rapidly. This is, of course, especially true when output and income are measured in purchasing-power-adjusted terms, thereby adding weight to the share of the emerging economies. By 2050, Asia will be home to more than half of global production, up from around 20 percent as of 1970. In geopolitical terms, the unipolar world of the North Atlantic is over. China, India, Brazil and other regional powers now fundamentally constrain the actions of the United States and Western Europe. This shift to multipolarity in geopolitics is bound to accelerate in the coming decades.

Modern economic growth did not end humans' dependence on their physical environment, contrary to the false impressions sometimes given by modern urban life. Our food still comes from farms, not from supermarkets and bakeries. Our crops still demand land and water, not simply microwaves and gas grills. Our industrial prowess has been built mainly on fossil fuels (first coal, then oil and natural gas), not merely on cleverness and efficiency. Our food production demands enormous inputs of energy and water, not only high-yield seeds. The bottom line is that the growth of the world economy has meant a roughly commensurate growth in human impacts on the physical world, not an escape from such impacts. These anthropogenic impacts are now so significant, and indeed threatening to the sustainable well-being of humans and other species, that Nobel Laureate Paul Crutzen (a codiscoverer of the human-induced loss of stratospheric ozone) has termed our age the Anthropocene, meaning the geological epoch when human activity dominates or deranges the earth's major biogeophysical fluxes (including the carbon, nitrogen and water cycles, among others).

The world economy is now characterized by 6.7 billion people—roughly ten times more than in 1750—producing output at a rate of roughly $10,000 per person per year in purchasing-power-adjusted prices. The resulting $67 trillion annual output (in approximate terms, as precision here should not be pretended) is at least one hundredfold larger than at the start of the industrial era. The human extent of natural-resource use is unprecedented—indeed utterly unrecognizable—in historical perspective, and is now dangerous to long-term well-being. While the typical economist's lighthearted gloss is that Malthusian resource pessimism was utterly and fully debunked generations ago—overcome by human ingenuity and technical know-how—it is more correct to say that the unprecedented level of global human output has been achieved not by overcoming resource constraints, but by an unprecedented appropriation of the earth's natural resources.

In fact, the current rate of resource use, if technologies remain constant, is literally unsustainable. Current fossil-fuel use would lead to the imminent peak of oil and gas production within years or decades, and of conventional coal deposits within decades or a century or two. We would see dangerous human impacts on the global climate system, and hence regional climates in all parts of the world, through greenhouse-gas emissions. The appropriation of up to half of the earth's photosynthetic potential, at the cost of other species, would occur. There would be massive deforestation and land degradation as a result of the increasing spatial range and the intensification of farming and pasture use; massive appropriation of freshwater resources, through depletion of fossil aquifers, diversion of rivers, melting of glaciers, drainage of wetlands, destruction of mangroves and estuaries, and other processes. And, an introduction of invasive species, pests and pathogens through a variety of human-induced changes.

The mistaken belief that we've overcome "similar" resource constraints in the past is no proof that global society will do it again, or at least do it successfully without massive economic and social upheavals, especially in view of the fact that our earlier "solutions" were rarely based on resource-saving technologies. Indeed, most earlier "solutions" to resource constraints typically involved new ways to "mine" the natural environment, not to conserve it. This time around, human societies will have to shift from resource-using technologies to resource-saving technologies. Some of the needed technologies are already known but often not widely used, while others will still have to be developed, demonstrated and diffused on a global scale.

Human pressures on the earth's ecological systems are bound to increase markedly in the years ahead. The global economy has been growing between 3 and 5 percent per year, meaning the economy will take fourteen to twenty-three years to double. Thus, the intense environmental and resource pressures now occurring will increase markedly and in short order. The catch-up growth of the largest emerging markets—Brazil, China and India, with around 40 percent of the world's population—is based squarely on the adoption and diffusion of resource-intensive technologies, such as coal-fired power plants and standard internal-combustion-engine vehicles.

The age of convergence offers the realistic possibility of ending extreme poverty and narrowing the vast inequalities within and between countries. The catching-up of China and India, for example, is rapidly reducing the national poverty rates in both countries. Other regions will also experience rapid declines in poverty rates. Yet the actual record of poverty reduction and trends in inequality leave major gaps in success. There are many parts of the planet where the numbers, and sometimes even proportions, of people in extreme poverty are rising rather than falling. Even more generally, the gaps between the rich and poor within nations seem to be widening markedly in most parts of the world.

Significant regions of the world—including sub-Saharan Africa, Central Asia, and parts of the Andean and Central American highlands—have experienced increasing poverty during the past generation. These places left behind by global economic growth tend to display some common infirmities. For example: long distances from major global trade routes, land-locked populations, heavy burdens of tropical diseases, great vulnerabilities to natural hazards (such as earthquakes, tropical storms and the like), lack of nonbiomass energy resources, lack of low-cost access to irrigation, difficult topography (e.g., high elevations and steep slopes), widespread illiteracy and a rapid growth of population due to consistently high fertility rates.

These conditions tend to perpetuate extreme poverty, and often lead to a vicious circle in which poverty contributes to further environmental degradation, persistence of high fertility rates, and social conflicts and violence, which in turn perpetuate or intensify the extreme poverty. These vicious circles (or "poverty traps") can be broken, but to succeed often requires external financial and technological assistance. Assistance like building infrastructure raises productivity and thereby controls the interlocking problems of transport costs, disease, illiteracy, vulnerability to hazards and high fertility. Without the external assistance, a continuing downward spiral becomes much more likely. The adverse consequences can then include war, the spread of epidemic diseases, displaced populations and mass illegal migration. On top of this can be the spread of illicit activities (drug trafficking, smuggling, kidnapping and piracy) and continued serious environmental degradation with large-scale poaching, land degradation and rampant deforestation, to name a few.

The global forces of demographic change, economic convergence and global production systems are also apparently contributing to rising inequalities within societies. Technological advances favor educated workers and leave uneducated workers behind. The entry of China and India into the global trading and production system, similarly, has pushed down the relative wages of unskilled workers in all parts of the world. Geography has played a key role, favoring those regions and parts of countries which are most easily incorporated into global production systems and which are well endowed with energy, fertile land, water and climate conducive to food production. Rapid population growth in rural and poverty-stricken regions (sub-Saharan Africa) has dramatically lowered well-being in these places. In general, urban dwellers have done better than rural dwellers in the past twenty years in almost all parts of the world.

Even relatively homogeneous societies are facing major challenges of social stability as a result of massive changes in demographic patterns and economic trends across ethnic, linguistic and religious communities. By 2050, roughly half of the U.S. population will be "white, non-Hispanic," down from around 80 percent as of 1950. This trend reflects both the differential fertility rates across different subpopulations as well as the continued rapid in-migration of Hispanics into the United States. Such large demographic changes can potentially create major fissures in society, especially when there have been long histories of intercommunal strife and suspicion.

The new world order is therefore crisis prone. The existence of rapidly emerging regional powers, including Brazil, China and India, can potentially give rise to conflicts with the United States and Europe.

The combination of rapid technological diffusion and therefore convergent economic growth, coupled with the natural-resource constraints of the Anthropocene, could trigger regional-scale or global-scale tensions and conflicts. China's rapid economic growth could turn into a strenuous, even hot, competition with the United States over increasingly scarce hydrocarbons in the Middle East, Africa and Central Asia. Conflicts over water flow in major and already-contested watersheds (among India, Bangladesh and Pakistan; China and Southeast Asia; Turkey, Israel, Iraq and Jordan; the countries of the Nile basin; and many others) could erupt into regional conflicts. Disagreements over management of the global commons—including ocean fisheries, greenhouse gases, the Arctic's newly accessible resources, species extinctions and much more—could also be grounds for conflict.

The continuation of extreme poverty, and the adverse spillovers from laggard regions, could trigger mass violence. Local conflicts can draw in major powers, which then threaten expanded wars—as in Afghanistan, Somalia and Sudan. When poverty is combined with rapid population growth and major environmental shocks (such as prolonged droughts in the Sahel and the Horn of Africa) there is a distinct likelihood of mass population movements, such as large-scale illegal migrations of populations escaping hunger and destitution. Such movements in the past have contributed to local violence, as in South Africa of late, and even to war, as in Darfur.

These intersecting challenges of our crowded world, multi-polarity, unprecedented demographic and environmental stresses, and the growing inequalities both within and between countries, can trigger spirals of conflict and instability—disease, migration, state failure and more—and yet are generally overlooked by the broad public and even by many, if not most, foreign-policy analysts. The instability of the Horn of Africa, the Middle East and Central Asia has been viewed wrongly by many in the U.S. public and foreign-policy community mainly as the battleground over Islamic extremism and fundamentalism, with little reflection on the fact that the extremism and fundamentalism is often secondary to illiteracy, youth unemployment, poverty, indignation, economic hopelessness and hunger, rather than religion per se. The swath of "Islamic" extremist violence across the African Sahel, Horn of Africa, and into the Middle East and Central Asia lies in the world's major dryland region, characterized by massive demographic, environmental and economic crises.

The security institutions—such as ministries of defense—of the major powers are trained to see these crises through a military lens, and to look for military responses, rather than see the underlying demographic, environmental and economic drivers—and the corresponding developmental options to address them. Genuine global security in the next quarter century will depend on the ability of governments to understand the true interconnected nature of these crises, and to master the scientific and technological knowledge needed to find solutions.

In the United States, I propose a new Department for International Sustainable Development, which would oversee U.S. foreign assistance and initiatives related to sustainable development in low-income countries, including water, food production, disease control and climate-change adaptation and mitigation.

I propose five major guideposts for a more-functional foreign policy in the coming years. First, we will need, on a global scale, to develop and diffuse new sustainable technologies so that the global economy can continue to support broad-based economic growth. If we remain stuck with our current technologies, the world will face a zero-sum struggle for increasingly scarce resources across competing regions. The new sustainable technologies will not arise from market forces alone. All major technological advances, such as the introduction of large-scale solar or nuclear power, will require massive public-sector investments (in basic science, demonstration projects, diffusion of proven technologies and regulatory framework) alongside the R&D of private markets. These public investments will be global-scale, internationally cooperative efforts.

Free-market ideologues who are convinced that technologies emerge from market forces alone should think again. They might compare the successful government-led promotion of nuclear power in France with the failure of the private-sector-led nuclear-power industry in the United States, which failed because of a collapse in U.S. public confidence in the safety of the technology. Similarly, they can examine the highly successful public-private partnerships linking the public-sector National Institutes of Health with the private-sector pharmaceutical industry, or the public-sector investments that underpinned the start-up of computer and Internet technologies.

Second, we will need to address the still-rapid rise of the world's population, heavily centered in the world's poorest countries. Sub-Saharan Africa is on a trajectory that will expand its population from around 800 million to 1.8 billion by 2050, according to the medium-fertility forecast of the United Nations Population Division. Yet that extent of population increase, an added 1 billion people, resulting from Africa's very high fertility rates, would actually be a grave threat to Africa's economy, political stability and environment, and would inevitably spill over adversely into the rest of the world. Rapid and voluntary fertility reduction in Africa is possible, if girls can be encouraged to stay in school through the secondary level; if family planning and contraception are made widely available; if child mortality is reduced (giving confidence to parents to reduce fertility rates); and if women are economically empowered.

Third, the world will need to address critical failings in the management of the global commons, most importantly, by restricting greenhouse-gas emissions, protecting the oceans and biodiversity, and managing transnational water resources sustainably at the regional level. Of course several global treaties have committed the world's nations to do just this, but these treaties have yet to be implemented. Three treaties of overriding importance are the UN Framework Convention on Climate Change, the UN Convention on Biological Diversity and the UN Convention to Combat Desertification. If these treaties are honored, the global commons can be sustainably managed.

Fourth, we will need to take seriously the risks of impoverished "failed states," to themselves, to their neighborhoods and to the world. The poorest and least-stable countries are rife with risks to peace and avoidable human tragedies like the 10 million children each year who die tragically and unnecessarily before their fifth birthday, largely the result of extreme poverty. Darfur, the Horn of Africa, Yemen, Afghanistan, Pakistan, Sri Lanka and elsewhere are places trapped in vicious cycles of extreme violence and poverty. These poverty-conflict traps can be broken, most importantly if the donors of the G-8, the oil-rich states in the Middle East, and the new donors in Latin America and Asia will pool their efforts to ensure the success of the Millennium Development Goals in today's impoverished and fragile regions.

Fifth, and finally, we require a new analytical framework for addressing our generation's challenges, and a new governmental machinery to apply that framework. Traditional problems of statecraft—the balance of power, alliances, arms control and credible deterrence—certainly will continue to play a role, but we need to move beyond these traditional concepts to face the challenges of sustainable development ahead. Will our era be a time of wondrous advances, based on our unprecedented scientific and technological know-how, or will we succumb to a nightmare of spreading violence and conflict? We face world-shaping choices. Our global challenges are unique to our generation, in scale and character. Vision, leadership and global cooperation will be our most important resources for ensuring our future well-being.

Critical Thinking

1. Given the conditions that Sachs identifies ("These intersecting challenges of our crowded world, multipolarity, unprecedented demographic and environmental stresses, and the growing inequalities both within and between countries, can trigger spirals of conflict and instability-disease, migration, state failure and more") how should the world proceed?

2. Why is abolishing poverty necessary to a peaceful and well functioning world?

3. Sachs views extraordinary cooperation as necessary for solving the world's problems. Cooperation within and between nations is at a very low level. How can the world succeed?

Create Central

www.mhhe.com/createcentral

Internet References

Sociosite
www.topsite.com/goto/sociosite.net

Socioweb
www.topsite.com/goto/socioweb.com

Sociology—Study Sociology Online
http://edu.learnsoc.org

Sociology Web Resources
www.mhhe.com/socscience/sociology/resources/index.htm

Jeffrey D. Sachs is the director of the Earth Institute at Columbia University and author of *Common Wealth: Economics for a Crowded Planet* (Penguin, 2008).

Article   Prepared by: Kurt Finsterbusch, *University of Maryland, College Park*

Making Modernity Work:
The Reconciliation
of Capitalism and Democracy

GIDEON ROSE

Learning Outcomes

After reading this article, you will be able to:

- Understand how democracy and capitalism often opposed each other but survived together for more than 150 years.

- Identify the flaws as well as the benefits of capitalism and of democracy.

- Consider how national democracies can articulate effectively with global capitalism.

W e are living, so we are told, through an ideological crisis. The United States is trapped in political deadlock and dysfunction, Europe is broke and breaking, authoritarian China is on the rise. Protesters take to the streets across the advanced industrial democracies; the high and mighty meet in Davos to search for "new models" as sober commentators ponder who and what will shape the future.

In historical perspective, however, the true narrative of the era is actually the reverse—not ideological upheaval but stability. Today's troubles are real enough, but they relate more to policies than to principles. The major battles about how to structure modern politics and economics were fought in the first half of the last century, and they ended with the emergence of the most successful system the world has ever seen.

Nine decades ago, the political scientist Harold Laski noted that with "the mass of men" having come to political power, the challenge of modern democratic government was providing enough "solid benefit" to ordinary citizens "to make its preservation a matter of urgency to themselves." A generation and a half later, with the creation of the postwar order of mutually supporting liberal democracies with mixed economies, that challenge was being met, and as a result, more people in more places have lived longer, richer, freer lives than ever before. In ideological terms, at least, all the rest is commentary.

The Birth of the Modern

In the premodern era, political, economic, and social life was governed by a dense web of interlocking relationships inherited from the past and sanctified by religion. Limited personal freedom and material benefits existed alongside a mostly unquestioned social solidarity. Traditional local orders began to erode with the rise of capitalism in the eighteenth and nineteenth centuries, as the increasing prevalence and dominance of market relationships broke down existing hierarchies. The shift produced economic and social dynamism, an increase in material benefits and personal freedoms, and a decrease in communal feeling. As this process continued, the first modern political ideology, classical liberalism, emerged to celebrate and justify it.

Liberalism stressed the importance of the rule of law, limited government, and free commercial transactions. It highlighted the manifold rewards of moving to a world dominated by markets rather than traditional communities, a shift the economic historian Karl Polanyi would call "the great transformation." But along with the gains came losses as well—of a sense of place, of social and psychological stability, of traditional bulwarks against life's vicissitudes.

Left to itself, capitalism produced longterm aggregate benefits along with great volatility and inequality. This combination resulted in what Polanyi called a "double movement," a progressive expansion of both market society and reactions against it. By the late nineteenth and early twentieth centuries, therefore, liberalism was being challenged by reactionary nationalism and cosmopolitan socialism, with both the right and the left promising, in their own ways, relief from the turmoil and angst of modern life.

The catastrophic destruction of the Great War and the economic nightmare of the Great Depression brought the contradictions of modernity to a head, seemingly revealing the bankruptcy of the liberal order and the need for some other, better path. As democratic republics dithered and stumbled during the 1920s and 1930s, fascist and communist regimes seized control of their own destinies and appeared to offer compelling alternative models of modern political, economic, and social organization.

Over time, however, the problems with all these approaches became clear. Having discarded liberalism's insistence on personal and political freedom, both fascism and communism quickly descended into organized barbarism. The vision of the future they offered, as George Orwell noted, was "a boot stamping on a human face-forever." Yet classical liberalism also proved unpalatable, since it contained no rationale for activist government and thus had no answer to an economic crisis that left vast swaths of society destitute and despairing.

Fascism flamed out in a second, even more destructive world war. Communism lost its appeal as its tyrannical nature revealed itself, then ultimately collapsed under its own weight as its nonmarket economic system could not generate sustained growth. And liberalism's central principle of laissez faire was abandoned in the depths of the Depression.

What eventually emerged victorious from the wreckage was a hybrid system that combined political liberalism with a mixed economy. As the political scientist Sheri Berman has observed, "The postwar order represented something historically unusual: capitalism remained, but it was capitalism of a very different type from that which had existed before the war—one tempered and limited by the power of the democratic state and often made subservient to the goals of social stability and solidarity, rather than the other way around." Berman calls the mixture "social democracy." Other scholars use other terms: Jan-Werner Müller prefers "Christian Democracy," John Ruggie suggests "embedded liberalism," Karl Dietrich Bracher talks of "democratic liberalism." Francis Fukuyama wrote of "the end of History"; Daniel Bell and Seymour Martin Lipset saw it as "the end of ideology." All refer to essentially the same thing. As Bell put it in 1960:

Few serious minds believe any longer that one can set down "blueprints" and through "social engineering" bring about a new utopia of social harmony. At the same time, the older "counter-beliefs" have lost their intellectual force as well. Few "classic" liberals insist that the State should play no role in the economy, and few serious conservatives, at least in England and on the Continent, believe that the Welfare State is "the road to serfdom." In the Western world, therefore, there is today a rough consensus among intellectuals on political issues: the acceptance of a Welfare State; the desirability of decentralized power; a system of mixed economy and of political pluralism.

Reflecting the hangover of the interwar ideological binge, the system stressed not transcendence but compromise. It offered neither salvation nor utopia, only a framework within which citizens could pursue their personal betterment. It has never been as satisfying as the religions, sacred or secular, it replaced. And it remains a work in progress, requiring tinkering and modification as conditions and attitudes change. Yet its success has been manifest—and reflecting that, its basic framework has remained remarkably intact.

The Once and Future Order

The central question of modernity has been how to reconcile capitalism and mass democracy, and since the postwar order came up with a good answer, it has managed to weather all subsequent challenges. The upheavals of the late 1960s seemed poised to disrupt it. But despite what activists at the time thought, they had little to offer in terms of politics or economics, and so their lasting impact was on social life instead. This had the ironic effect of stabilizing the system rather than overturning it, helping it live up to its full potential by bringing previously subordinated or disenfranchised groups inside the castle walls. The neoliberal revolutionaries of the 1980s also had little luck, never managing to turn the clock back all that far.

All potential alternatives in the developing world, meanwhile, have proved to be either dead ends or temporary detours from the beaten path. The much-ballyhooed "rise of the rest" has involved not the discrediting of the postwar order of Western political economy but its reinforcement: the countries that have risen have done so by embracing global capitalism while keeping some of its destabilizing attributes in check, and have liberalized their polities and societies along the way (and will founder unless they continue to do so).

Although the structure still stands, however, it has seen better days. Poor management of public spending and fiscal policy has resulted in unsustainable levels of debt across the advanced industrial world, even as mature economies have found it difficult to generate dynamic growth and full employment in an ever more globalized environment. Lax regulation and oversight allowed reckless and predatory financial practices to drive leading economies to the brink of collapse. Economic inequality has increased as social mobility has declined. And a loss of broad-based social solidarity on both sides of the Atlantic has eroded public support for the active remedies needed to address these and other problems.

Renovating the structure will be a slow and difficult project, the cost and duration of which remain unclear, as do the contractors involved. Still, at root, this is not an ideological issue. The question is not what to do but how to do it—how, under twenty-first-century conditions, to rise to the challenge Laski described, making the modern political economy provide enough solid benefit to the mass of men that they see its continuation as a matter of urgency to themselves.

Critical Thinking

1. Do you think that "the combination of capitalism and democracy is one of the greatest human achievements and must be preserved"?

2. What changes in capitalism and democracy are needed at this time?

3. What features of the current American political system undermine or reduce democracy?

Create Central

www.mhhe.com/createcentral

Internet References

Sociosite
www.topsite.com/goto/sociosite.net
Socioweb
www.topsite.com/goto/socioweb.com

Sociology—Study Sociology Online
http://edu.learnsoc.org
Sociology Web Resources
www.mhhe.com/socscience/sociology/resources/index.htm

GIDEON ROSE is editor of *Foreign Affairs,* and is a former National Security Council official.

Article   Prepared by: Kurt Finsterbusch, *University of Maryland, College Park*

The Future of the Liberal World Order

Internationalism after America

G. JOHN IKENBERRY

Learning Outcomes

After reading this article, you will be able to:

- Understand that although China, India, Brazil, and other non western states have increasing international prominence and may not be liberal, they will support the international liberal regime from which they have benefitted enormously.

- Consider whether the principles undergirding the passing world order will also undergird the coming world order.

- Understand the basis for current and future international conflicts.

There is no longer any question: wealth and power are moving from the North and the West to the East and the South, and the old order dominated by the United States and Europe is giving way to one increasingly shared with non-Western rising states. But if the great wheel of power is turning, what kind of global political order will emerge in the aftermath?

Some anxious observers argue that the world will not just look less American—it will also look less liberal. Not only is the United States' preeminence passing away, they say, but so, too, is the open and rule-based international order that the country has championed since the 1940s. In this view, newly powerful states are beginning to advance their own ideas and agendas for global order, and a weakened United States will find it harder to defend the old system. The hallmarks of liberal internationalism—openness and rule-based relations enshrined in institutions such as the United Nations and norms such as multilateralism—could give way to a more contested and fragmented system of blocs, spheres of influence, mercantilist networks, and regional rivalries.

The fact that today's rising states are mostly large non-Western developing countries gives force to this narrative. The old liberal international order was designed and built in the West. Brazil, China, India, and other fast-emerging states have a different set of cultural, political, and economic experiences, and they see the world through their anti-imperial and anticolonial pasts. Still grappling with basic problems of development, they do not share the concerns of the advanced capitalist societies. The recent global economic slowdown has also bolstered this narrative of liberal international decline. Beginning in the United States, the crisis has tarnished the American model of liberal capitalism and raised new doubts about the ability of the United States to act as the global economic leader.

For all these reasons, many observers have concluded that world politics is experiencing not just a changing of the guard but also a transition in the ideas and principles that underlie the global order. The journalist Gideon Rachman, for example, says that a cluster of liberal internationalist ideas—such as faith in democratization, confidence in free markets, and the acceptability of U.S. military power—are all being called into question. According to this worldview, the future of international order will be shaped above all by China, which will use its growing power and wealth to push world politics in an illiberal direction. Pointing out that China and other non-Western states have weathered the recent financial crisis better than their Western counterparts, pessimists argue that an authoritarian capitalist alternative to Western neoliberal ideas has already emerged. According to the scholar Stefan Halper, emerging-market states "are learning to combine market economics with traditional autocratic or semiautocratic politics in a process that signals an intellectual rejection of the Western economic model."

But this panicked narrative misses a deeper reality: although the United States' position in the global system is changing, the liberal international order is alive and well. The struggle over international order today is not about fundamental principles. China and other emerging great powers do not want to contest the basic rules and principles of the liberal international order; they wish to gain more authority and leadership within it.

Indeed, today's power transition represents not the defeat of the liberal order but its ultimate ascendance. Brazil, China, and India have all become more prosperous and capable by operating inside the existing international order—benefiting from its rules, practices, and institutions, including the World Trade Organization (WTO) and the newly organized G-20. Their economic success and growing influence are tied to the liberal internationalist organization of world politics, and they have deep interests in preserving that system.

In the meantime, alternatives to an open and rule-based order have yet to crystallize. Even though the last decade has brought remarkable upheavals in the global system—the emergence of new powers, bitter disputes among Western allies over the United States' unipolar ambitions, and a global financial crisis and recession—the liberal international order has no competitors. On the contrary, the rise of non-Western powers and the growth of economic and security interdependence are creating new constituencies for it.

To be sure, as wealth and power become less concentrated in the United States' hands, the country will be less able to shape world politics. But the underlying foundations of the liberal international order will survive and thrive. Indeed, now may be the best time for the United States and its democratic partners to update the liberal order for a new era, ensuring that it continues to provide the benefits of security and prosperity that it has provided since the middle of the twentieth century.

The Liberal Ascendancy

China and the other emerging powers do not face simply an American-led order or a Western system. They face a broader international order that is the product of centuries of struggle and innovation. It is highly developed, expansive, integrated, institutionalized, and deeply rooted in the societies and economies of both advanced capitalist states and developing states. And over the last half century, this order has been unusually capable of assimilating rising powers and reconciling political and cultural diversity.

Today's international order is the product of two order-building projects that began centuries ago. One is the creation and expansion of the modern state system, a project dating back to the Peace of Westphalia in 1648. In the years since then, the project has promulgated rules and principles associated with state sovereignty and norms of great-power conduct. The other project is the construction of the liberal order, which over the last two centuries was led by the United Kingdom and the United States and which in the twentieth century was aided by the rise of liberal democratic states. The two projects have worked together. The Westphalian project has focused on solving the "realist" problems of creating stable and cooperative interstate relations under conditions of anarchy, and the liberal-order-building project has been possible only when relations between the great powers have been stabilized. The "problems of Hobbes," that is, anarchy and power insecurities, have had to be solved in order to take advantage of the "opportunities of Locke," that is, the construction of open and rule-based relations.

At the heart of the Westphalian project is the notion of state sovereignty and great-power relations. The original principles of the Westphalian system—sovereignty, territorial integrity, and nonintervention—reflected an emerging consensus that states were the rightful political units for the establishment of legitimate rule. Founded in western Europe, the Westphalian system has expanded outward to encompass the entire globe. New norms and principles—such as self-determination and mutual recognition among sovereign states—have evolved within it, further reinforcing the primacy of states and state authority. Under the banners of sovereignty and self-determination, political movements for decolonization and independence were set in motion in the non-Western developing world, coming to fruition in the decades after World War II. Westphalian norms have been violated and ignored, but they have, nonetheless, been the most salient and agreed-on parts of the international order.

A succession of postwar settlements—Vienna in 1815, Versailles in 1919, Yalta and Potsdam in 1945, and the U.S., Soviet, and European negotiations that ended the Cold War and reunified Germany in the early 1990s—allowed the great powers to update the principles and practices of their relations. Through war and settlement, the great powers learned how to operate within a multipolar balance-of-power system. Over time, the order has remained a decentralized system in which major states compete and balance against one another. But it has also evolved. The great powers have developed principles and practices of restraint and accommodation that have served their interests. The Congress of Vienna in 1815, where post-Napoleonic France was returned to the great-power club and a congress system was established to manage conflicts, and the UN Security Council today, which has provided a site for great-power consultations, are emblematic of these efforts to create rules and mechanisms that reinforce restraint and accommodation.

The project of constructing a liberal order built on this evolving system of Westphalian relations. In the nineteenth century, liberal internationalism was manifest in the United Kingdom's championing of free trade and the freedom of the seas, but it was limited and coexisted with imperialism and colonialism. In the twentieth century, the United States advanced the liberal order in several phases. After World War I, President Woodrow Wilson and other liberals pushed for an international order organized around a global collective-security body, the League of Nations, in which states would act together to uphold a system of territorial peace. Open trade, national self-determination, and a belief in progressive global change also undergirded the Wilsonian worldview—a "one world" vision of nation-states that would trade and interact in a multilateral system of laws. But in the interwar period of closed economic systems and imperial blocs, this experiment in liberal order collapsed.

After World War II, President Franklin Roosevelt's administration tried to construct a liberal order again, embracing a vision of an open trading system and a global organization in which the great powers would cooperate to keep the peace—the United Nations. Drawing lessons from Wilson's failure and incorporating ideas from the New Deal, American architects of the postwar order also advanced more ambitious ideas about economic and political cooperation, which were embodied in the Bretton Woods institutions. This vision was originally global in spirit and scope, but it evolved into a more American-led and Western-centered system as a result of the weakness of postwar Europe and rising tensions with the Soviet Union. As the Cold War unfolded, the United States took command of the system, adopting new commitments and functional roles in both security and economics. Its own economic and political system became, in effect, the central component of the larger liberal hegemonic order.

Another development of liberal internationalism was quietly launched after World War II, although it took root more slowly and competed with aspects of the Westphalian system. This was the elaboration of the universal rights of man, enshrined in the UN and its Universal Declaration of Human Rights. A steady stream of conventions and treaties followed that together constitute an extraordinary vision of rights, individuals, sovereignty, and global order. In the decades since the end of the Cold War, notions of "the responsibility to protect" have given the international community legal rights and obligations to intervene in the affairs of sovereign states.

Seen in this light, the modern international order is not really American or Western—even if, for historical reasons, it initially appeared that way. It is something much wider. In the decades after World War II, the United States stepped forward as the hegemonic leader, taking on the privileges and responsibilities of organizing and running the system. It presided over a far-flung international order organized around multilateral institutions, alliances, special relationships, and client states—a hierarchical order with liberal characteristics.

Today's international order is not really American or Western—even if it initially appeared that way.

But now, as this hegemonic organization of the liberal international order starts to change, the hierarchical aspects are fading while the liberal aspects persist. So even as China and other rising states try to contest U.S. leadership—and there is indeed a struggle over the rights, privileges, and responsibilities of the leading states within the system—the deeper international order remains intact. Rising powers are finding incentives and opportunities to engage and integrate into this order, doing so to advance their own interests. For these states, the road to modernity runs through—not away from—the existing international order.

Joining the Club

The liberal international order is not just a collection of liberal democratic states but an international mutual-aid society—a sort of global political club that provides members with tools for economic and political advancement. Participants in the order gain trading opportunities, dispute-resolution mechanisms, frameworks for collective action, regulatory agreements, allied security guarantees, and resources in times of crisis. And just as there are a variety of reasons why rising states will embrace the liberal international order, there are powerful obstacles to opponents who would seek to overturn it.

To begin with, rising states have deep interests in an open and rule-based system. Openness gives them access to other societies—for trade, investment, and knowledge sharing. Without the unrestricted investment from the United States and Europe of the past several decades, for instance, China and the other rising states would be on a much slower developmental path. As these

countries grow, they will encounter protectionist and discriminatory reactions from slower-growing countries threatened with the loss of jobs and markets. As a result, the rising states will find the rules and institutions that uphold nondiscrimination and equal access to be critical. The World Trade Organization—the most formal and developed institution of the liberal international order—enshrines these rules and norms, and rising states have been eager to join the WTO and gain the rights and protections it affords. China is already deeply enmeshed in the global trading system, with a remarkable 40 percent of its GNP composed of exports—25 percent of which go to the United States.

China could be drawn further into the liberal order through its desire to have the yuan become an international currency rivaling the U.S. dollar. Aside from conferring prestige, this feat could also stabilize China's exchange rate and grant Chinese leaders autonomy in setting macroeconomic policy. But if China wants to make the yuan a global currency, it will need to loosen its currency controls and strengthen its domestic financial rules and institutions. As Barry Eichengreen and other economic historians have noted, the U.S. dollar assumed its international role after World War II not only because the U.S. economy was large but also because the United States had highly developed financial markets and domestic institutions—economic and political—that were stable, open, and grounded in the rule of law. China will feel pressures to establish these same institutional preconditions if it wants the benefits of a global currency.

Internationalist-oriented elites in Brazil, China, India, and elsewhere are growing in influence within their societies, creating an expanding global constituency for an open and rule-based international order. These elites were not party to the grand bargains that lay behind the founding of the liberal order in the early postwar decades, and they are seeking to renegotiate their countries' positions within the system. But they are nonetheless embracing the rules and institutions of the old order. They want the protections and rights that come from the international order's Westphalian defense of sovereignty. They care about great-power authority. They want the protections and rights relating to trade and investment. And they want to use the rules and institutions of liberal internationalism as platforms to project their influence and acquire legitimacy at home and abroad. The UN Security Council, the G-20, the governing bodies of the Bretton Woods institutions—these are all stages on which rising non-Western states can acquire great-power authority and exercise global leadership.

No Other Order

Meanwhile, there is no competing global organizing logic to liberal internationalism. An alternative, illiberal order—a "Beijing model"—would presumably be organized around exclusive blocs, spheres of influence, and mercantilist networks. It would be less open and rule-based, and it would be dominated by an array of state-to-state ties. But on a global scale, such a system would not advance the interests of any of the major states, including China. The Beijing model only works when one or a few states opportunistically exploit an open system of markets. But if everyone does, it is no longer an open system but a fragmented, mercantilist, and protectionist complex—and everyone suffers.

It is possible that China could nonetheless move in this direction. This is a future in which China is not a full-blown illiberal hegemon that reorganizes the global rules and institutions. It is simply a spoiler. It attempts to operate both inside and outside the liberal international order. In this case, China would be successful enough with its authoritarian model of development to resist the pressures to liberalize and democratize. But if the rest of the world does not gravitate toward this model, China will find itself subjected to pressure to play by the rules. This dynamic was on display in February 2011, when Brazilian President Dilma Rousseff joined U.S. Treasury Secretary Timothy Geithner in expressing concern over China's currency policy. China can free-ride on the liberal international order, but it will pay the costs of doing so—and it will still not be able to impose its illiberal vision on the world.

Democracy and the rule of law are still the hallmarks of modernity and the global standard for legitimate governance.

In the background, meanwhile, democracy and the rule of law are still the hallmarks of modernity and the global standard for legitimate governance. Although it is true that the spread of democracy has stalled in recent years and that authoritarian China has performed well in the recent economic crisis, there is little evidence that authoritarian states can become truly advanced societies without moving in a liberal democratic direction. The legitimacy of one-party rule within China rests more on the state's ability to deliver economic growth and full employment than on authoritarian—let alone communist—political principles. Kishore Mahbubani, a Singaporean intellectual who has championed China's rise, admits that "China cannot succeed in its goal of becoming a modern developed society until it can take the leap and allow the Chinese people to choose their own rulers." No one knows how far or fast democratic reforms will unfold in China, but a growing middle class, business elites, and human rights groups will exert pressure for them. The Chinese government certainly appears to worry about the long-term preservation of one-party rule, and in the wake of the ongoing revolts against Arab authoritarian regimes, it has tried harder to prevent student gatherings and control foreign journalists.

Outside China, democracy has become a near-universal ideal. As the economist Amartya Sen has noted, "While democracy is not yet universally practiced, nor indeed universally accepted, in the general climate of world opinion democratic governance has achieved the status of being taken to be generally right." All the leading institutions of the global system enshrine democracy as the proper and just form of governance—and no competing political ideals even lurk on the sidelines.

The recent global economic downturn was the first great postwar economic upheaval that emerged from the United States, raising doubts about an American-led world economy and Washington's particular brand of economics. The doctrines of neoliberalism and market fundamentalism have been discredited, particularly among the emerging economies. But liberal internationalism is not the same as neoliberalism or market fundamentalism. The liberal internationalism that the United States articulated in the 1940s entailed a more holistic set of ideas about markets, openness, and social stability. It was an attempt to construct an open world economy and reconcile it with social welfare and employment stability. Sustained domestic support for openness, postwar leaders knew, would be possible only if countries also established social protections and regulations that safeguarded economic stability.

Indeed, the notions of national security and economic security emerged together in the 1940s, reflecting New Deal and World War II thinking about how liberal democracies would be rendered safe and stable. The Atlantic Charter, announced by Roosevelt and Winston Churchill in 1941, and the Bretton Woods agreements of 1944 were early efforts to articulate a vision of economic openness and social stability. The United States would do well to try to reach back and rearticulate this view. The world is not rejecting openness and markets; it is asking for a more expansive notion of stability and economic security.

Reason for Reassurance

Rising powers will discover another reason to embrace the existing global rules and institutions: doing so will reassure their neighbors as they grow more powerful. A stronger China will make neighboring states potentially less secure, especially if it acts aggressively and exhibits revisionist ambitions. Since this will trigger a balancing backlash, Beijing has incentives to signal restraint. It will find ways to do so by participating in various regional and global institutions. If China hopes to convince its neighbors that it has embarked on a "peaceful rise," it will need to become more integrated into the international order.

China has already experienced a taste of such a backlash. Last year, its military made a series of provocative moves—including naval exercises—in the South China Sea, actions taken to support the government's claims to sovereign rights over contested islands and waters. Many of the countries disputing China's claims joined with the United States at the Regional Forum of the Association of Southeast Asian Nations (ASEAN) in July to reject Chinese bullying and reaffirm open access to Asia's waters and respect for international law. In September, a Chinese fishing trawler operating near islands administered by Japan in the East China Sea rammed into two Japanese coast guard ships. After Japanese authorities detained the trawler's crew, China responded with what one Japanese journalist described as a "diplomatic 'shock and awe' campaign," suspending ministerial-level contacts, demanding an apology, detaining several Japanese workers in China, and instituting a de facto ban on exports of rare-earth minerals to Japan. These actions—seen as manifestations of a more bellicose and aggressive foreign policy—pushed ASEAN, Japan, and South Korea perceptibly closer to the United States.

As China's economic and military power grow, its neighbors will only become more worried about Chinese aggressiveness, and so Beijing will have reason to allay their fears. Of course, it might be that some elites in China are not interested in practicing restraint. But to the extent that China is interested in doing so, it will find itself needing to signal peaceful intentions—redoubling its participation in existing institutions, such as the ASEAN Regional Forum and the East Asia Summit, or working with the other great powers in the region to build new ones. This is, of course, precisely what the United States did in the decades after World War II. The country operated within layers of regional and global economic, political, and security institutions and constructed new ones—thereby making itself more predictable and approachable and reducing the incentives for other states to undermine it by building countervailing coalitions.

More generally, given the emerging problems of the twenty-first century, there will be growing incentives among all the great powers to embrace an open, rule-based international system. In a world of rising economic and security interdependence, the costs of not following multilateral rules and not forging cooperative ties go up. As the global economic system becomes more interdependent, all states—even large, powerful ones—will find it harder to ensure prosperity on their own.

Growing interdependence in the realm of security is also creating a demand for multilateral rules and institutions. Both the established and the rising great powers are threatened less by mass armies marching across borders than by transnational dangers, such as terrorism, climate change, and pandemic disease. What goes on in one country—radicalism, carbon emissions, or public health failures—can increasingly harm another country.

Intensifying economic and security interdependence are giving the United States and other powerful countries reason to seek new and more extensive forms of multilateral cooperation. Even now, as the United States engages China and other rising states, the agenda includes expanded cooperation in areas such as clean energy, environmental protection, nonproliferation, and global economic governance. The old and rising powers may disagree on how exactly this cooperation should proceed, but they all have reasons to avoid a breakdown in the multilateral order itself. So they will increasingly experiment with new and more extensive forms of liberal internationalism.

Time for Renewal

Pronouncements of American decline miss the real transformation under way today. What is occurring is not American decline but a dynamic process in which other states are catching up and growing more connected. In an open and rule-based international order, this is what happens. If the architects of the postwar liberal order were alive to see today's system, they would think that their vision had succeeded beyond their wildest dreams. Markets and democracy have spread. Societies outside the West are trading and growing. The United States has more alliance partners today than it did during the Cold War. Rival hegemonic states with revisionist and illiberal agendas have been pushed off the global stage.

It is difficult to read these world-historical developments as a story of American decline and liberal unraveling.

Paradoxically, the challenges facing the liberal world order now are artifacts of its success.

In a way, however, the liberal international order has sown the seeds of its own discontent, since, paradoxically, the challenges facing it now—the rise of non-Western states and new transnational threats—are artifacts of its success. But the solutions to these problems—integrating rising powers and tackling problems cooperatively—will lead the order's old guardians and new stakeholders to an agenda of renewal. The coming divide in world politics will not be between the United States (and the West) and the non-Western rising states. Rather, the struggle will be between those who want to renew and expand today's system of multilateral governance arrangements and those who want to move to a less cooperative order built on spheres of influence. These fault lines do not map onto geography, nor do they split the West and the non-West. There are passionate champions of the UN, the WTO, and a rule-based international order in Asia, and there are isolationist, protectionist, and anti-internationalist factions in the West.

The liberal international order has succeeded over the decades because its rules and institutions have not just enshrined open trade and free markets but also provided tools for governments to manage economic and security interdependence. The agenda for the renewal of the liberal international order should be driven by this same imperative: to reinforce the capacities of national governments to govern and achieve their economic and security goals.

As the hegemonic organization of the liberal international order slowly gives way, more states will have authority and status. But this will still be a world that the United States wants to inhabit. A wider array of states will share the burdens of global economic and political governance, and with its worldwide system of alliances, the United States will remain at the center of the global system. Rising states do not just grow more powerful on the global stage; they grow more powerful within their regions, and this creates its own set of worries and insecurities—which is why states will continue to look to Washington for security and partnership. In this new age of international order, the United States will not be able to rule. But it can still lead.

Critical Thinking

1. Will the open and rule-based liberal world order continue or decline as China, India, Brazil, and other non western states that are less democratic become more prominent?

2. As the hierarchy of world nations changes, will the ideas and principles that underlie the global order also change? Should they change?

3. Will territorial boundaries and the principle of nonintervention hold up as the global order changes?

Create Central

www.mhhe.com/createcentral

Internet References

Sociosite
www.topsite.com/goto/sociosite.net

Socioweb
www.topsite.com/goto/socioweb.com

Sociology—Study Sociology Online
http://edu.learnsoc.org

Sociology Web Resources
www.mhhe.com/socscience/sociology/resources/index.htm

G. JOHN IKENBERRY is Albert G. Milbank Professor of Politics and International Affairs at Princeton University and the author of *Liberal Leviathan: The Origins, Crisis, and Transformation of the American World Order* (Princeton University Press, 2011), from which this essay is adapted.